The World *of* Music

HUGO D. MARPLE

Professor of Music
Texas Tech University

Allyn *and* Bacon, *Inc.* • Boston

TO MY FATHER
who helped many
to know and love music

Library of Congress Cataloging in Publication Data

Marple, Hugo Dixon, 1920-
    The world of music.

    Includes bibliographies.
    1. Music—Analysis, appreciation. I. Title.
MT6.M2785W7   780'.15   73-80935

Printed in the United States of America.

Contents

Contents

Contents

Preface

This book is written especially for young people. Today, more than ever before, they wish to understand why music is a Fine Art, why it speaks to man sometimes better than words, and why it expresses feelings so intimately and accurately.

Classes which probe these questions often are titled "Learning to Listen," "Appreciation of Music," or "Introduction to Music Literature." This book will assist in all of these areas: one will learn better how to listen and hear what music says, he will appreciate the art of music to a greater extent, and he will be introduced to the literature of music and the breadth of sound experiences it can provide.

Largely nontechnical, this book will suffice for the person who has had little or no previous exposure to music, or for someone who, having participated in musical experiences in public schools with no intent of being a professional, desires to renew his interest in music and gain additional information concerning this art.

The material is presented in a nonhistorical, nonchronological manner. Such a disposition outlines a development from simple to complex forms, melodies, harmonic structures, and aesthetic possibilities. Beginning with folk music, it assists the student in realizing a continual extension in the range of expression in this art.

During the first chapters, texts (words) aid the student in understanding the intent of the composer, sensing music's adjuvant role, and comprehending style and form. In later chapters, perceiving the role of music for the dance aids the student in understanding music which relies mainly upon form for its organization, development of phrase for its complexity, and extension of melodic ideas for its length.

History and chronology are not the basis for the organization of the book. Although present, it is the study of styles and forms which is emphasized so that the young person may begin to understand why music sounds as it does, why it expresses what it does, and why the composer is considered an artist as a result of this expressive ability.

Biography is not a major factor either, and yet an attempt is made to have the student see the composer as a real person confronted by mundane problems, who was once young, who loved, who was often depressed by external situations and social conditions, and yet who expressed through his music the feelings of the times in which he lived.

So that you may continually note changes of style within a given form, each chapter contains compositions from more than one period. This continual juxtaposition permits you to hear and compare music from various eras throughout the extent of the course.

Every attempt has been made to include music which will appeal to young people, particularly the person who purports to have a limited background. But quality music of many types is the goal. No chapter contains all the music which might be profitable for a young person to hear; consequently, choices have been made by considering how well a composition exemplifies a form, a period, or expresses musical ideas which have contemporary significance or relationships. From these examples it is hoped that the student will proceed on his own to investigate, to listen, and to build his own repertoire of musical understandings as well as a library of books, tapes, and records.

Music will probably change considerably during the next several decades. The student who reads this text will be prepared to use this foundation in the future, and should be prepared to begin to understand any changes which may develop. To approach the new with perspective, with an open mind, and with some ability to evaluate, denotes an intelligent approach to the art.

Hugo D. Marple

Introduction

To be of maximum usefulness, a book designed for introductory classes in music literature should be flexible and adjust easily to a number of situations. At the same time it should assist the aims of the teacher and be attractive to the student.

INDIVIDUAL REQUIREMENTS

Each school and teacher demand some different consideration from a book. Mechanical factors such as the length of the course and the number of class days per week affect the learning potential. In addition, some schools have listening laboratories available for students, while others do not, thus extending or limiting the amount of material which may be covered.

    a. *The Two-Semester Course.* A book of twenty-seven chapters fits well into the thirty weeks of a two-semester course. Ample material will be found in each chapter to supply the teacher with discussion and musical examples.

    Because the book divides itself easily into two parts, students who enter a course in the second semester will not be placed at a disadvantage. The organization of the material enables the new student to move through the later chapters as easily as the person who has been in the course longer. Little or no review should be needed.

    b. *The One-Semester Course.* This material was used for a one-semester course for a number of years. The instructor in this situation has three options:

    1. *Omit some of the chapters.* This would depend upon the instructor, his understanding of the needs of the students, his goals for the course, and his

desire to emphasize certain aspects. (It is possible for this book to be used as adjunct reading in choral or instrumental literature classes.)

2. *Omit some of the material from each chapter.* Since ample material will be found in each chapter, some of the examples could be omitted. This in no way would rob from the effectiveness of the procedure, since the sequence would not be harmed by certain omissions.

3. *Assign some of the material for out-of-class reading or listening.* Some of the material in the text could be read prior to the discussion of items in the class period. If a listening lab were available, or if students were required to purchase a number of cassette tapes or recordings, many of the examples could be heard out of class, so that class time could be reserved for discussion and playing of the most important items.

All three methods have been used with considerable success.

BACKGROUND OF THE TEACHER

A course is taught from the perspective of the teacher, taking into consideration the goals as he conceives them. Thus, some items may be emphasized while others are given less stress. Such variances will not put any student at a disadvantage later in the course. This book adapts comfortably to faculties of a great many backgrounds and interests. During its ten years of development and trial, it has been used by applied teachers, theorists, musicologists, music education teachers, and ensemble directors. Since the emphasis is not upon history or chronology, teachers easily appreciate the variety of values in its organization and quickly sense the students' growth in musical understandings.

BACKGROUND OF THE STUDENT

Most important of all, this volume considers the student, what he brings to such a course, and what he expects to gain.

a. *Popular music is an important part of the study.* Almost all young people know and have an affinity with popular music. Indeed, some of them honestly believe this to be *their* music, while they disown the so-called "art music" as belonging to another group of individuals. The student soon comes to understand that music from and for the people forms the basis of all of our music. This is explained at the beginning of the book through the use of folk songs and composed folk songs; again, near the center of the book, popular instrumental music is outlined and explained. Not only is this an excellent beginning for a study which wishes to speak to the amateur, but it also attempts to assist the young person in making value judgments concerning the music which he hears regularly. The young person should be a more discerning listener whether he be in the concert hall or tuned to the "First Forty" on his local radio station.

Beginning at this point, the student should then proceed into more sophisticated listening and value judgments.

b. *A developmental approach services most young people.* Although we teach history chronologically, we do not teach mathematics, biology, chemistry, government, or English in this manner. More often the student comprehends the organization in these classes as beginning with a simple concept and advancing toward the more complicated one. Such an approach will assist the young amateur in music. Music teachers have had a tendency to lean too much upon the chronological, so that by the time the student arrives at music which should have current interest for him he has built up a defensive wall against it. A book which begins with the Romantic Period on the premise that this music is most easily accessible for young people, has not adequately sampled the tastes of this group. The recent popularity of contemporary and Baroque music seems to negate such adult preconceptions.

c. *Change is interesting and reflective of all times.* Beginning with simple forms, the student learns to appreciate and understand change as a constant quality and not a recent development. Understanding the evolution of form assists the student in comprehending the nature of music of his own time and the changes which have or will come to it.

DEVELOPMENTAL CHARTS

Throughout the book charts indicate the development of the forms which are being studied. These charts are not in any sense chronological, and no time sequence is intended. Rather, they help the student associate forms with a common root, assist in understanding the relationship of simple forms with those of more complexity, and aid in better understanding interrelationships. For the most part the more complex forms are shown near the bottom of the chart, and the simple forms near the top. However, little significance should be placed upon whether one form is positioned higher on a chart than another. The line relationship is what is paramount. All of the interrelationships are not shown, since the chart is meant to be used by the amateur, and more subtle connections could be confusing. After the completion of the course, the student may wish to rearrange the chart based upon his understanding of these relationships, or he may wish to add lines, forms, or subforms. Any reworking will indicate his own special understanding.

Each chapter of the book opens with such a chart. Those in the earlier portions of the book will contain fewer forms, while almost all forms will be included in the later portions. The charts have been printed so that the form discussed in each particular chapter appears in bold type, while those studied earlier appear in lighter type, enabling the student to recognize the relationship of the new form to those previously studied.

The charts may be used as departure points for initial discussions of the new forms to be studied, to show the relationships to those previously encountered, and to bridge material between chapters.

RECORDING LISTS

The recording list at the end of each chapter can guide student and teacher alike. The student may wish to use the recordings for additional listening during the course or in years to come; the teacher may use them as a reference or as a discography. No list is meant to be complete for any given chapter, and more records are listed than minimally necessary to teach the course.

Most of the recordings listed throughout the book will be found in current Schwann catalogues. Although particular versions of a work may be cited in the lists, other versions of the same composition may be equally valuable. Some older recordings may be listed, and if these specific versions are preferred, record companies, stores, or libraries may be able to furnish them.

Through this book I hope to add to the musical understanding of young people, to encourage them to be more inquisitive in the field of music, and to broaden the horizon of their concept of the art.

ACKNOWLEDGMENTS

Many persons have directly or indirectly assisted with the production of this text, and I am grateful for each contribution.

It would be impossible to single out all persons associated with the Texas Tech library staff who have upon one occasion or another been of assistance, but one should mention particularly James Platz, Elizabeth D. Elle, Paul Mertes-Young, and their associates.

J. Frank Turner, chairman of the department of music of Santa Monica College, and Richard McGowan, department of music literature of Texas Tech, read the manuscript and made helpful suggestions.

Special thanks should be given to Paul Mertes-Young, who assisted in locating and securing the photographs for the text.

PART ONE

Vocal Music

Section A *Music from and for the People*

Chapter 1

Folk and Primitive Music

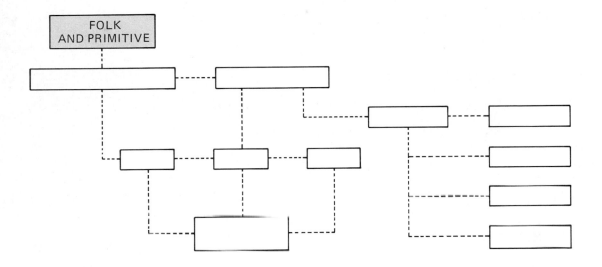

When Joan Baez, Pete Seeger, or the Weavers sing a folk song, they bring a long tradition into focus for the twentieth century; or when your friends in college or those who live down the block begin to strum a guitar, a mandolin, or a banjo and sing a rote-learned love or protest song, they are carrying on this same tradition of individual expression which comes to us from years ago. Folk singers have sung to themselves and to those who would listen for thousands of years, and although the details and exact situations have changed, many general characteristics of folk song remain.

FOLK SONG

Almost every dormitory has an ensemble of balladeers and guitar pickers. Most young people know the subtle distinction between Country Western, Blue Grass, Nashville, and other types of expression which have come to the fore during the last decade. Some even may be familiar with the Child ballads and know their value for the general area of folk music.

Almost everywhere in America these days a renewed interest in folk music, as well as its imitations, has developed. In our regard for the better life, for the ecological, for the simple rather than the complicated, the folk song seems to speak effectively and represent all of these concerns in a manner which other music does not. With a strong tie to their heritage some groups of people in our country still cling to the simple life, the soil, the individual expression of feeling and beauty through hand crafts, painting, and particularly through music of a comparatively simple structure. It is not that these people ignore the TV, the international situation, and the movies. It is just that the folk singer and his songs emphasize a simplicity that seems lost to so many.

Left: Joan Baez (Courtesy of Folklore Productions, Boston); right:
Pete Seeger in concert (Photograph by Frank Moy, Jr.).

In this chapter we will examine the folk song; in the following chapter we will consider music which imitates the folk idiom. Both of these types appeal to a large audience and both are attractive. Sociologically and musically, a study of the two types will be interesting and worthwhile.

GENERAL CHARACTERISTICS

Six characteristics and their various subheadings will assist us in recognizing and understanding the folk song.

Irregular Meters and Rhymes

Although the folk song is strophic, it often has trouble complying with other aspects of the poetic form. *Strophic* indicates that the words are versed and that each verse is sung to the same music. Not only folk songs use this form, but also church hymns, patriotic songs, college songs, and many other songs sung under various circumstances. Since the folk song is often the expression of a person with limited understanding of poetry, the rhyme, meter, and syntax are often slighted or ignored.

The following verse, taken from a folk song which describes how the parents of a young lady locked her up so that she could not see a particular boy friend, shows a lack of skill at rhyme scheme and meters:

> *Once I courted a charming beauty bright,*   10: / ‿ ‿‿ / ‿ /
> *I courted her by day and I courted her by night.*   13: ‿ / ‿ / ‿ / ‿‿ / ‿ / ‿
> *I courted her for love and love I did intend.*   12: ‿ / ‿ / ‿ / ‿ / ‿ / ‿
> *I'm sure she never had any right to complain.*   12: ‿ / ‿ / ‿ / ‿‿ / ‿ /

> **(AAFS—Library of Congress 41 74 B2)**

This song rhymes the first two lines of each verse while the last two lines carry their own rhyme. The second rhyming pair of lines in this first verse places "intend" with "complain." Since this American song offers no translation difficulty, we know the originator considered the meaning to be more important than the rhyme scheme.

In the same verse the meter also loses its regularity with an irregular number of syllables in the lines. The meaning of the song is clear, but the poetic flow indicates an amateur.

Such irregularities come from an attempt to imitate poetry or songs learned from others. Even to a singer who cannot read and write, it becomes obvious that a strophic song has many verses. The term strophic may never be used, but the understanding exists. In order to imitate known songs the folk composer will adopt the strophic idea, will attempt to rhyme, may misplace the meter, may stumble in syntax, but will often compose a song much loved by himself and perhaps by others.

More Attention to Text than to Music

In the preceding example the point has been made that the person who first sang the song, as well as those who repeated it, was more concerned with the song as an expressive medium than as poetry. Since personal expression was important, the song told of something immediate or something witnessed recently. The music was of so little value that often a tune was used from another song, or perhaps two tunes were pushed together in some way. If the singer had a modest or poor voice, perhaps almost no tune would be heard. (Listen particularly to "A Cowboy's Life" as listed further in the chapter.) Thorp's *Songs of the Cowboys*[1] states:

> Cowboy songs were always sung by one person, never by a group. I never did hear a cowboy with a real good voice; if he had one to start with, he always lost it bawling at cattle, or sleeping out in the open, or telling the judge he didn't steal that horse. To the contrary, some of the radio cowboys have beautiful voices.
>
> The cowboy hardly ever knew what tune he was singing his song to; just some old, old tune that he had heard and known as a boy. Very often the old familiar airs were used. The people of Texas didn't know the "Star Spangled Banner," but they all knew some cowboy tunes.

Many of the texts were sung to the same tunes, but as the songs were repeated the tunes became more distinctive; the distinctive songs were often the ones best remembered.

Words from the Common Man

The texts used common language because this expressed best for the singer the emotions and situations described. Furthermore, these were songs for the common man, and he saw no use in special words. Many times the originator considered his song a personal item or of local interest, and the words he chose were suitable for himself or his immediate listeners.

Whether it be the songs of the American cowboy, the Southern mountain folk, or the contemporary city folk singer, if a song and some verses were known, it would be possible to add a few more in the right situation.

> Every cowboy knew a few verses of songs, and if he had a little whiskey in him, or was heading for town with wages in his pocket, he might make up a few. These weren't "cultured" songs. Sometimes the rhymes didn't match well. Often the language was rough and for publication had to be heavily expurgated.[2]

Not only were the words those used everyday, but they also were stereotyped and full of overstatement. For example, the girls in the songs are always beauties; the men are always brave, or very bad; the skin is always fair; the storms, the worst; the rains, the hardest; the sky, the most beautiful; the rose always smells the most beautiful. Overstatements are continual and match the stereotypes. "Old Joe Clark" is typical:

---

[1] *Songs of the Cowboys*, N. Howard Thorp. Clarkson N. Potter, Inc., New York, page 16.
[2] *Ibid.*

Old Joe Clark's a friend of mine,
Tell you the reason why.
Keeps good whiskey round his house,
Good old rock and rye.

Old Joe Clark had a house
Sixteen stories high.
And every story in that house
Was filled with chicken pie.

(AAFS—Library of Congress,
Album 2)

The urge toward creativity existed, but the ability to create an artistic poem never was present. Common words were heard everywhere. Two verses from two more songs will assist this understanding:

The cowboy's life is a dreary old life
All out in the sleet and the snow
When winter time comes he begins to think
Where his summer wages go.

The cowboy's life is a dreary, dreary life
He's driven through heat and cold
I'm almost froze with the water on my clothes
A riding through the heat and the cold.

(AAFS—Library of Congress, Album 28)

There's more pretty girls than one,
There's more pretty girls than one,
Whenever I ramble round
There's more pretty girls than one.
Mama told me last night
She gave me good advice
She told me to stop my rambling round
And marry me a wife.

(AAFS—Library of Congress,
Album 21)

Common Emotions

The folk song usually conveys those common emotions which are universal, hence its wide appeal. The most common subjects are death, love, disappointment, fear, and humor. Death may be of a beloved sweetheart, a kindly mother; or the death of a criminal, the murder of a notorious personage, or the suicide of the hunted. Love songs may include treachery, loss of a loved one through circumstance of a failure to meet, or what a war may cast asunder. Love songs are more common in European folk material than in other geographical regions of the world. Humor may be expressed through a dialogue song, a circumstance described, or even a riddle postulated.

Often the folk song translates emotion into a common or public symbol, so that around the verse or sentiment thousands can rally for a cause. This was precisely the device used by the folk song singers during the sixties when they sang their protest songs against the Vietnam war.

Most of the emotions mentioned above are well-known to most of us through the folk idiom. Humorous songs probably are least well-known. A couple of examples will suffice:

> O says the robin as he run
> Wished I had a bottle of rum
> And a pretty girl a sittin on my knee
> Lord, how happy, I would be.[3]

A riddle song may also be a humorous song. The following contains some Latin phrases, and it is supposed that the song could have come down to us from the time of the English Reformation, when the words of the church were placed in humorous songs to show the disdain for the Latin:

> I had four brothers over the sea.
> Perry merry dictum domini
> They each brought a present unto me.
> Perry merry dictum domini
> Partem quantum perry merry centum
> Perry merry dictum domini.[4]

Text Changes

The usual folk song runs through a series of versions. These changes are not based on whim, but rather upon the uncertainties of oral conveyance which is typical of this material, particularly in its early stages. As the song moves from one locale to another, the words and sometimes the events change to fit the immediate situation; for example, the name of the girl may be changed or the name of the deed itself. Other times the song is not heard correctly, there is forgetting, or a lack of understanding in the context of the situation.

---

[3] *Anglo-American Folksong Style,* Abrahams and Foss. Prentice-Hall, Inc., Englewood Cliffs, N.J., 1968, page 90.

This folk song statement parallels the well-known stanza 12 from the *Rubaiyat of Omar Khayyam* by Edward Fitzgerald:

> A Book of Verses beneath the Bough
> A Jug of Wine, a Loaf of Bread—and Thou
> Beside me singing in the Wilderness.
> Oh, Wilderness were Paradise enow!

[4] *Folklore Keeps the Past Alive,* Arthur Palmer Hudson. University of Georgia Press, Athens, 1962, page 10.

A good example of this comes from *"A Cowboy's Life."*   One version lists a
verse as follows:

> *You are speaking of your farms, you are speaking of your charms*
> *You are speaking of your silver and gold;*
> *But a cowboy's life is a dreary, dreary life*
> *He's driven through the heat and the cold.*

A later version of the same verse contained a new word:

> *You talk about your farms and your chantain charms*
> *Your chantain silver and gold, etc.*

Since a word such as "chantain" was little understood, a substitution was made
to include a word which had more meaning to the average person:

> *You talk of your farms and your Chinaman charms*
> *Your Chinaman's silver and gold.*

(AAFS—Library of Congress, Album 28)

To some this was the nearest word they knew to the sound of the original. To
others it was justifiably *Chinaman*, since these people worked on the railroads
of the west, saving money carefully, and were known by the cowboy as he moved
across the land.   Another folk song and its change can be cited:

> *When I was a little boy, I worked on Market Square*
> *O money I did pocket, but I never did it fair.*
> *I rode upon the lakes and learned to rob and steal,*
> *And when I made a great haul, how happy I did feel!*

Another version has been sung:

> *When I was a young man I lived upon the square,*
> *I never had any pocket change, and I hardly thought it fair;*
> *But out upon the highway I went to rob and steal,*
> *And when I met a peddler, oh, how happy I did feel!*

(AAFS—Library of Congress, 3190-A1)

When this song moved into the west, the cowboys sang it in a slightly different
version, one which fit their locale:

> *Well, when I was a cowboy, I rode out on the line,*
> *I used to pocket money, and didn't dress so very fine,*
> *I rode out on the prairie to learn to rob and steal,*
> *An' when I downed the cowman, How jolly I did feel!*[5]

(AAFS—Library of Congress, 847-A1)

---

[5] *Native American Balladry*, G. Malcolm Laws, Jr.   American Folklore Society, Philadelphia,
1950, page 83.

Melody More Important than Harmony

Words held prime place, the tune carried less significance, but the harmony of these folk songs had almost no importance. Many times the composer of the song might not be capable of providing an accompaniment, but even if he did, it carried little value for the real impact of the song.

Repetition of melody and often repetition of the words assisted in organizing the form. The repetition of the melody indicated to the listener when a new verse had begun. It also assisted the singer in his memory, since he could place the greater part of his attention on the words and very little on the repetitive tune.

In songs where repeated lines or refrains were used, the repetition aided the listener as well as the singer. It enabled the listener to follow the song more easily, since the repeated lines came always at a predictable place and enabled him to fully savor the meaning of the new lines while the repeated lines were sung. Then, too, the repetitions aided the memory of the listener, since he knew there was only a certain amount of new material. Finally, the constant chanting of the repeated line embedded the entire song upon the memory of the listener so that he was less likely to forget it or to consider its impact negligible.

Although a tune might have been commonplace when first sung, through its constant revision it became honed into an interesting and individual melody. The attractiveness of a melody usually is in relation to its uniqueness.

DEFINITION

Having discussed some of the characteristics of folk songs, a definition might assist in distinguishing the genuine article from the commercially manufactured or imitative type.

Song of the Common Man

The folk song, not intended for the educated or the schooled, comes from an amateur singer and presents a personal, simple expression. While some music intends a more intellectual expression for the person whose esthetic thoughts are more schooled, folk music is the intimate expression of the less artistically experienced.

Song of the Community

Although some individual composes the folk song, it is the community which makes the final judgment of its merit and its relevancy. This is not always the village community. In the case of the cowboy, the cowboys themselves make up the community. The collection of men who considered themselves cowboys altered, accepted, and changed their songs until one version became more often sung than another. Some songs were sung and rarely repeated; in such cases the community believed them of little value. Others were retained. For some communities these songs link the past to the present; they bring an important event, emotion, or item constantly to the attention of the individual or the newcomer. If this seems important to the community, the song persists.

Song Based on an Oral Tradition

Folk songs have rarely been written down until they have been sung over and over. Usually they are transmitted from person to person in an informal situation. Such mediums as the recording, the radio, or TV are so recent a means of transmission that they could affect the very nature of the folk song tradition by eliminating the possibility of the changes which have helped the form to evolve. There could be an end to the various versions, to the communal regulation, an end to the forgetting with word substitutions, and to the adaptation to the immediate locale which has molded the songs and aided their refinement.

Songs of Peasant Lore

True folk music is not primitive but comes from a less literate portion of a literate society. It is an expression of feelings and ideas which they believe important and is one method of relating and emphasizing these to each other. The speech accented songs are the more meditative, while the rhythm controlled songs turn to the outer world reflecting social involvement.

A definition: A folk song relays orally to its own community the feelings and ideas of a particular segment of society.

AMERICAN COWBOY SONGS

Because of the advance of civilization and the amalgamation of cultures, it is often difficult to hear folk music in an original form. The Library of Congress records are invaluable in this regard. One of the true folk song areas of our country was the Western Plains and Southwest, where between the 1860s and 1890s about 40,000 cowboys lived and worked, driving about ten million cattle toward the northern markets or rail heads where these cattle were sold for an estimated 250 million dollars.

A trip up the trail made a distinct break in the monotonous life of the big ranches, often situated hundreds of miles from where the conventions of society were observed. The ranch community consisted usually of the boss, the straw boss, the cowboys proper, the horse wrangler, and the cook—often a Negro. These men lived on terms of practical equality. Except in the case of the boss, there was little difference in the amounts paid each for his services. Society, then, was here reduced to its lowest terms. The work of the men, their daily experiences, their thoughts, their interests, were all in common. Such a community had necessarily to turn to itself for entertainment. Songs sprang up naturally, some of them tender and familiar lays of childhood, others original compositions, all genuine, however crude and unpolished. Whatever the most gifted men could produce must bear the criticism of the entire camp, and agree with the ideas of a group of men. In this sense, therefore, any song that came from such a group would be the joint product of a number of them, telling perhaps the story of some stampede they had all fought to turn, some crime in which they all shared equally, some comrade's tragic death which they had all witnessed. The song-making did not cease as the men went up the trail. Indeed the songs were here utilized for very practical ends. Not only were sharp rhythmic yells—sometimes beaten into verse—employed to stir up lagging cattle, but also during the long watches the night guards, as they rode around and round the herd, improvised cattle lullabies which quieted the animals and soothed them to sleep. Some of the best of the so-called "dogie songs" seem to have been created for the purpose of preventing cattle stampedes—such songs coming straight from the heart of the cowboy, speaking familiarly to his herd in the stillness of the night.[6]

We have discussed the texts of some of these songs in the earlier pages of this chapter. Now let us listen to some of the cowboy tunes to consider the musical characteristics.

Music's basic elements are MELODY, RHYTHM, TEMPO, AND FORM. *Melody* is the tune—the relationship of lowness and highness—pitches and their movement in space. *Rhythm* indicates the manner of movement of the melody or accompaniment in time: regular, irregular, drawn out, quick. *Tempo* is the overall speed of the song. *Form* considers the repeats of the melody if any and the manner of these repeats, the manner of organization.

Study Procedures

1. Listen to the cowboy song "A Cowboy's Life" as heard on the Library of Congress Recording of Cowboy Folk Songs (AAFS L-28). What type of singer have you heard? Does he sound authentic? What is the tempo of the song? Is it fast, slow, or modestly fast? Do the syllables move regularly or are they irregular? Does the melody have a narrow pitch range or is it often moving low and then high? Can you ascertain any form? Is it strophic? Or does it continually move into new tunes? If strophic, can you hear any related melodic portions within each verse?
2. Listen to other cowboy songs and try to ascertain the musical characteristics of each.

6 *Cowboy Songs and Other Frontier Ballads*, John A. Lomax. Sturgis and Walton Company, 1916; Macmillan Company, New York, 1938.

Cowboy Songs, Ballads, and Cattle Calls—**Library of Congress**   **AAFS L-28**
   "The Cowboy's Life Is a Very Dreary Life"
   "The Streets of Laredo"
   "The Night Herding Song"
      (Note particularly the statement concerning the origin of this song.)

The Cowboy—His Songs, Ballads, and Brag Talk—**Folkways**   **FH-5723**
   "Little Joe, the Wrangler"
   "The Streets of Laredo"

SOUTHERN MOUNTAIN SONGS

A second prolific area of folk material and one which has continued from early settlers until this century, is located in the Southern Appalachias. These folk have retained the singing tradition that was a part of their forefathers when they first came to this country in the eighteenth and nineteenth centuries. Although they have not lived in seclusion, until recently their singing traditions have not felt the impact of commercial or artistic characteristics. John Jacob Niles, a singer and searcher of folk material, once told me that he had found songs and word usage in the Southern Appalachias which were exactly as they had existed in Elizabethan England. The recent growth of music and recording in Nashville has resulted from the love of singing and the maintenance of certain folk characteristics of the people in that area.

Most of the songs which have come from the early European-Anglo tradition are strophic in nature, with four lines to the stanza. This has meant that the songs have been sung with four phrases to the verse, since in folk material a phrase is almost always equal to a line of poetry. Although some early European songs are still sung, much of the folk material of this area has been composed while families have lived in this country. The tonal arrangement of these songs varies to include major, minor, and pentatonic tonalities, the pentatonic (a five-note scale) has a more elemental approach to musical organization, while minor songs often have a plaintive sound which cannot be found with other pitch systems.

The contour of the melodic lines of these Anglo-American folk songs is usually more varied than much other folk material. The contour of the melody has to do with its highness and lowness and where this highness and lowness may come in the song. It is this contour which makes each song or instrumental composition different. A song may begin on a certain note and repeat the exact same one for the second syllable. However, how it moves from that point will be the distinguishable contour of the melody. When this contour is too similar to another song, it probably will be soon forgotten due to lack of individuality. Thus, the contour enables the listener to remember the song, and this is even more important to a singer.

The combination of phrase and contour gives a song its unique musical character. Many folk songs rely upon a kind of musical tension built up through the first three lines of the song, which is resolved during the last line. Often the first two lines are builders of tension with the second ending in such a way as to create on the part of the listener a desire to continue. This is called the *semi-* or *mid-cadence*. The last two lines are usually designed so as to resolve this tension.

Study Procedures

1. The following collection of Anglo-American Folk Songs will prove interesting and exemplary of the preceding discussion. *Note:* All Library of Congress recordings contain more material than that listed in the subheadings of this chapter. Suggested listening examples are supplied.

    Anglo-American Ballads—**Library of Congress**   **AAFS L-1**
      "Barbara Allen"
      "The Devil's Nine Questions"

    Anglo-American Ballads—**Library of Congress**   **AAFS L-7**

    Anglo-American Songs and Ballads—**Library of Congress**   **AAFS L-12**
      "My Parents Raised Me Tenderly"
      "Froggie Went A-Courtin"
      "The Singing Alphabet"
      "Sweet William"

    Anglo-American Songs and Ballads—**Library of Congress**   **AAFS L-14**
      "Barbara Allen"
      "The Cherry Tree Carol"
      "Old Smoky"
      "Fiddle-I-Fee"

    Anglo-American Songs and Ballads—**Library of Congress**   **AAFS L-21**
      "Sourwood Mountain"
      "Shoo Fly"
      "There's More Pretty Girls Than One"
      "On a Bright and Summer's Morning"
      "Sweet William"
      "The Barnyard"

    Anthology of American Folk Music, Vol. I   **Folkways   FA-2951**
      "The Wagoners Lad"

    Anthology of American Folk Music, Vol. II   **Folkways   FA-2952**
      "Old Dog Blue"

    Ballads of the American Revolution   **Folkways   FA-2152**
      "Bunker Hill"
      "Yankee Doodle"

    Music in America—Society for the Preservation of American Musical Heritage   **MIA-97**
      "A Voyage to Virginia"

Who Built America   **Folkways   FC-7402**
   "Erie Canal"
   "Drill, Ye Tarriers, Drill"

Additional Folk Songs

2. Another folk song group in our American heritage contains the sailor songs of the early nineteenth century. Listen to one or more of these so that later we may compare them to their more modern versions.

   American Sea Songs and Shanties—**Library of Congress**   **LC 1893 LP   AAFS L-27**
                                                             LC 1891 LP   AFS L-26

L-26 A 1	"Haul the Bowline"
L-26 A 3	"The Drunken Sailor"
L-27 A 2	"Blow the Man Down"
L-27 A 3	"Blow the Man Down"
L-27 B 1	"Rio Grande"

3. Additional folk song groupings may contain interest for certain sections of the country or for particular individuals.

   Folk Music from Wisconsin—**Library of Congress**   **AAFS L-55**
   Songs and Ballads of the Anthracite Miners—**Library of Congress**   **AAFS L-16**
   Songs and Ballads of the Assassination of Presidents —
   Library of Congress   AAFS L-29
   Songs of the Michigan Lumberjacks—**Library of Congress**   **AAFS L-56**
   Songs of the Mormons and the West—**Library of Congress**   **AAFS L-30**

4. Folk songs and dances have been recorded from many geographical sections of the world. Of particular interest to the listener usually have been the folk songs of Spain, France, China, Japan, and the Caribbean. Visit your school music library or the public library in your community and find folk material which you believe would be of interest to your class. Before playing these records, explain why you believe them to fit the folk song characteristics and definition.

PRIMITIVE MUSIC

Although this chapter examines folk music most commonly found in our country, a look at primitive music will give us some background for the folk song, provide comparisons, and at the same time permit us to make certain distinctions which may not be clear.

Primitive music distinguishes itself from folk music principally by the nature of the culture from which it comes. Music within a simple culture where there is no direct association with a high culture can be considered primitive. In contrast, folk music comes from a poorly educated group within a highly advanced culture. Some general aspects of primitive music may indicate the roots of music we hear today.

Some place, some time, music began. No one knows exactly how or when. Since man drew rather detailed pictures on the walls of his caves between 30,000 and 15,000 B.C., it is surmised that music must have begun within the same period.

Some have stated that music began when man attempted to imitate animals; others, that man was attempting to express himself in a mating call; that he was attempting to communicate over a longer distance than the speaking voice would permit; that it was a means of facilitating team work or effort; that it was impassioned speech.

Most likely, however, it would seem that music developed when non-linguistic sounds of pitch, stress, and duration were employed for communication much as young children use before they learn to talk.

It seems logical that singing preceded instruments and that the earliest song made use of only one or two pitches. Later, a single intelligible line was sung and repeated over and over for emphasis or esthetic reasons. When two or more lines on one subject were placed together, a simple stanza developed. Later, more than one verse was needed for repeated sections, extensions, or seemingly disparate thoughts held together by mood or a central idea.

Expressive words placed in organized form helped primitive man with his prayer, helped organize his movements, and later became an esthetic expression and a basis for his singing.

Much of the early poetry of primitive man could have been used as a basis for movement. As the body moved, it would have influenced the rhythm of the words used to express an emotion or thought. Little by little as the rhythms were repeated over and over again, they would have taken on interval significance until a song would have resulted. But dance was more important and earlier than song, since many dances exist without music. Many were accompanied by the special sounds of feet, of the mouth, and finally of instruments. Gesture could have been the only movement along with poetry for many years.

Finally, music was added to poetry. Speech became song when it conformed to tone and rhythm. The tone evolved, as we have just stated, from the rhythm of the speech.

After its development, song served numerous purposes: it aided the religious observance, assisted storytelling, abetted the preparation for and sustained the spirit of war; it was tied to work, to the hunt, to the rituals of death, birth, marriage, and to almost every practical event. As Miriam Makeba states in her book on African song,

> In Africa, music has always been more directly related to daily life than in Europe. European children are usually taught songs from fairy tales or from history, whereas the songs of African children more often deal with the familiar and immediate. Whether it is a song about a wayside medicine man, a song to encourage warriors going into battle, a boating song, puberty rite songs, marching songs, cowherding songs, harvest songs, drinking songs, hunting songs, war songs, funeral dirges, ceremonial songs, wedding songs, cradle songs, ritual songs—in every instance music and song are interwoven with African life.[7]

---

[7] *The World of African Song*, Miriam Makeba. Quadrangle Books, Chicago, 1971, page 17.

In early music instruments did not accompany the voice. Later, voices and instruments were used together, but rarely with the same rhythm or melody. This combination of more than one simultaneous melody or rhythm came to be known as *polyphony*.

Sex plays a role in the music of all primitive societies. In some, women are the sole purveyors of music (Japan, or a few American Indian tribes); in others, only the men may sing and use the instruments (some African tribes).

Throughout primitive societies almost all consider that a melody and its words are so interlinked as not to be separated, changed, or substituted. The Eskimo has the simplest of primitive musics, while the people of Africa, the most complicated. This has led some scholars to consider that climate affects the basic nature of music.

Study Procedures

1. The only primitive music native to the United States is that of the American Indian. Musicologists have studied the music of the Indian and noted that various geographic regions and tribes produce music with somewhat different characteristics. For example, the Plains Indians had high voices while the Pueblo sang with a low, growly voice. Eastern tribes used a type of responsorial singing, the Northwest used a small range with complex rhythms, the California Indians used two separate sections in their songs, while the tribes of the Great Basin used paired phrases. The Pueblo Indians almost always descended in line as they sang each phrase.

   Listen to a recording of an Indian song or dance and describe in detail those musical characteristics which you hear. Does the music have a narrow range or a wide range? Are instruments used? If so, are the rhythms complex or simple? Do you hear any repetition in the melody? Does this repetition have any consistency?

   The following are excellent sources of American Indian music:

   Apache—**Library of Congress**   **AAFS L-42**
   Delaware, Cherokee, Choctaw, Creek—**Library of Congress**   **AAFS L-37**
   Navaho—**Library of Congress**   **AAFS L-41**
   Plains: Commanche, Cheyenne, Kiowa, Caddo, Wichita, Pawnee—
   Library of Congress   **AAFS L-39**
   Pueblo: Taos, San Ildefonso, Zuni, Hopi—**Library of Congress**   **AAFS L-43**
   Seneca Songs from Coldspring Longhouse—**Library of Congress**   **AAFS L-17**
   Sioux—**Library of Congress**   **AAFS L-40**
   Songs of the Chippewa—**Library of Congress**   **AAFS L-22**
   Songs from the Iroquois Longhouse—**Library of Congress**   LC-1950 LP   AFS L-6
      Side A, No. 4   "The Tracker's Boasting Chant"
      Side B, No. 3   "The Scalp Dance"
      Side B, No. 5   "The Warrior's Stomp Dance"
   Songs of the Menominee Mandan and Hidatsa—**Library of Congress**   **AAFS L-33**
   Songs of the Pawnee and Northern Ute—**Library of Congress**   **AAFS L-25**
   Songs of the Sioux—**Library of Congress**   **AAFS L-23**
   Songs of the Yuma, Cocopa, and Yaqui—**Library of Congress**   **AAFS L-24**

2. African music came to this country through the blacks and became a part of our culture through the well-known area of jazz. This transition will be discussed in Chapter 15. With our study of primitive music it would be advantageous to examine a few examples of African music.

Listen to a recording of primitive African music and answer the same questions which you answered concerning the music of the American Indian: Does the music have a narrow or wide range? Are instruments used? If so, what do they sound like? Are the rhythms of the instruments complex or simple? Do you hear repetition in the rhythm? In the melody? Does this repetition have any consistency or any form? In addition, decide in your own mind what makes African music different. Can you place these differences into words? How would you compare the two musics? Which of the two do you prefer? Why? Even though both are primitive, which seems the more advanced? Why?

SUGGESTED LISTENING:

Afro-Bahian Religious Songs—**Library of Congress**   AAFS L-13
UNESCO Anthology of African Music
Album BM 30L-2307:   No. 5, "Kalangu Music and Singing"
                     No. 13, "Corn Grinding Song"
Album BM 30L-2309:   No. 8, "Man's Song Accompanied by a Drum"
                     No. 9, "Song of Tuareg Women"
                     No. 15, "Song of Young Girl Accompanied by Handclaps"

Bibliography—Chapter 1

ABRAHAMS, ROGER, and GEORGE FOSS, *Anglo-American Folksong Style.* Englewood Cliffs, N.J.: Prentice-Hall, Inc., 1968.

ANDERSEN, ARTHUR OLAF, *Geography and Rhythm.* Tucson, Ariz.: University of Arizona, 1935.

BOWRA, C. M., *Primitive Song.* Cleveland: World Publishing Co., 1962.

DAMAS, LEON, *African Songs of Love, War, Grief and Abuse.* Ibadan: Mbari Publications, 1961.

ELSON, LOUIS C., *The National Music of America.* Boston: L. C. Page and Co., 1924.

FINKELSTEIN, SYDNEY, *Composer and Nation.* New York: International Publishers, 1960.

HUDSON, ARTHUR PALMER, *Folklore Keeps the Past Alive.* Athens, Ga.: University of Georgia Press, 1962.

LAWS, G. MALCOLM, JR., *Native American Balladry.* Philadelphia: The American Folklore Society, 1950.

LIBRARY OF CONGRESS, *Check-list of Recorded Songs in the English Language in the Archive of American Folk Song.* Washington, D.C.: U.S. Government Printing Office, 1942.

———, *A Selection of Folk Songs, Ballads, Dances, etc.* Washington, D.C.: U.S. Government Printing Office, 1959.

LLOYD, A. L., *Folk Song in England.* New York: International Publishers, 1967.

LOMAX, JOHN, *Cowboy Songs and Other Frontier Ballads.* New York: Sturgis and Walton Co., 1916.

MAKEBA, MIRIAM, *The World of African Song.* Chicago: Quadrangle Books, 1971.

NETTL, BRUNO, *Folk and Traditional Music of the Western Continents.* Englewood Cliffs, N.J.: Prentice-Hall, Inc., 1965.

———, *An Introduction to Folk Music in the United States.* Detroit: Wayne State University Press, 1960.

———, *Music in Primitive Culture.* Cambridge, Mass.: Harvard University Press, 1956.

SACHS, CURT, *The Rise of Music in the Ancient World.* New York: W. W. Norton and Co., Inc., 1943.

SHELTON, ROBERT, *The Face of Folk Music*. New York: Citadel Press, 1968.
THORP, N. HOWARD, *Songs of the Cowboys*. New York: Clarkson N. Potter, Inc., 1966.
WALLASCHEK, RICHARD, *Primitive Music*. New York: Da Capo Press, 1970.

Recordings—Chapter 1

Recordings for this chapter will be found in the text material or with the Study Procedures.

Additional examples of Anglo-American Songs and Ballads, Sea Songs and Chanties, folk songs of nationality or laboring groups, primitive songs of African natives or American Indians would be appropriate.

Chapter 2

Composed Folk Song

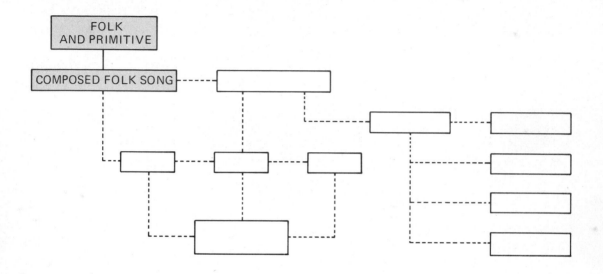

The alterations in folk songs which evolved over a period of time most often adapted them to other situations or geographical locations, focused the vocabulary, or smoothed the meter.

The modifications discussed in this chapter tend to modernize the musical aspects, polish the surface, and in subtle ways make the song more adaptable to a larger listening audience. Such changes include musical arrangements, the addition of professional accompaniments, the use of regular meters, and some word alteration to assist with rhyme, meaning, or style. Original folk materials are usually treated to this kind of refinement.

In addition, another type of folk song exists, one written as a copy of a folk style. This is a polished and arranged composition before it is ever heard. It is possible that most of the folk material with which you are familiar belongs to this latter classification.

ARRANGEMENTS

Many folk tunes have been rearranged by musicians for particular purposes. The arranger recognizes innate beauty within the original, hears the harmonic possibilities, or understands the general appeal of the expressive character of the song. He may rework it into a composition which remains close to the original in text, rhythm, and meter, or he may alter it considerably so that it takes on a new character. With the latter, the melody may be maintained, but the rhythm changed, the tempo different, the harmony more modern, and it may be performed by an entirely different type of musical group than the original.

American folk songs have interested our people for years. Even for those who do not verbalize their interest in music, these songs have contained the raw material of music in such a way as to carry an emotional impact. Thousands of folk songs have been discarded and forgotten. These tunes and verses which have stood the test of time and continued in popularity usually have an interesting melody, an attractive rhythm, and a text which speaks of the human condition in an appealing or sympathetic manner—something with which most of us can empathize. In addition, the melody and the words fit together so as to be expressive while being attractive to the ear.

American Cowboy Songs

Many arrangements of cowboy songs exist. Some of these are for the band, the orchestra, the solo singer, or the choir. Vocal arrangements seem to be more popular, since the texts carry the original color and emotion of the West.

To assist in understanding how folk music changes through arranging, let us reexamine some of the old cowboy tunes. Listen to the original folk song as recorded on the Library of Congress records. Then compare it to a rearranged version.

Study Procedures

1. Two recordings feature the same three cowboy tunes: Library of Congress, and the *Folksongs of the Frontier* by the Roger Wagner Chorale. The Library of Congress versions, as we noted in Chapter 1, were recorded as remembered by old cowboys. The Roger Wagner Chorale recorded rearranged versions of the same tunes. Listen to both versions of at least three of these melodies and compare the musical characteristics. The outlines below will assist you with your listening and attempt to bring into focus several musical understandings. Be sure to complete the blank spaces or answer the questions after listening, then discuss them with your classmates.

    "Night Herding Song": **L-28 and Capitol P-8332**
       Harmony: More complex, smooth, and polished than the original
       Melody: Same as original or more refined? How? In what places?

Form: Strophic—3 verses plus an ending. How many lines to a verse? 5 lines and "Hi-Ho"; each line of poetry becomes a phrase of music. Can you hear each phrase and how the music creates the phrase effect? Which phrase climaxes each verse? How is this accomplished?

Text: Same as original or different?

Rhythm: Mostly even or mostly uneven?

Tempo: Fast, slow, moderate?

Meter: Words of each verse fit the melody. How many unaccented syllables between each accented syllable? Is this regular or irregular?

Rhyme: Good rhyme words, or a misfit?

Dynamics: Does the song become louder or softer or remain about the same?

"Bury Me Not on the Lone Prairie":   **L-49 and Capitol P-8332**

Harmony: Unison voices in first verse
Harmony humming with melody in accordian, second verse
Harmony humming with melody in solo, third verse

Melody: Reorganized tune for the fourth verse. Are other verses same as the original?

Form: Strophic—4 verses. How many phrases to the verse? Are any alike?

Text:

Rhythm:

Tempo:

Meter: What is the scan of the accented and unaccented syllables?

Rhyme:

Dynamics:

"Chisholm Trail":   **L-50 and Capitol P-8332**

Harmony:

Melody:

Form: Strophic—how many verses? How many phrases to verse? Are any phrases alike? Do you hear the refrain?

Text:

Rhythm:

Tempo:

Meter:

Rhyme:

Dynamics:

2. Other folk songs may be found on different recordings, and some will have been recorded previously by the Library of Congress if you wish to compare them with the original. When you listen be sure to review the musical characteristics listed above. They will assist you in hearing more accurately.

a. Arranged Folk Songs: "Black Is the Color," "I've Been Working on the Railroad," "Cindy," "On Top of Old Smokey," "Skip to Mah Lou," "Streets of Laredo," "Blue Tail Fly"—Roger Wagner Chorale   **Capitol P-8324**

b. Arranged Folk Song: "There's More Pretty Girls Than One"—Hank Locklin, **Victor LSP-3588**

c. Arranged Folk Songs: "John Henry," "Down in the Valley," "Bill Bailey"—Chet Atkins   **Victor LSP-2025**

3. Two interesting recordings contain old sailor songs: *Sea Chanties* by the Robert Shaw Chorale, and *Five Sea Chanties* sung by William Warfield. Some of these tunes also are heard on the Library of Congress recordings L-2, L-26, and L-27. Listen to the rearrangements of the sailor songs as heard on either recording and

HEAVING AT THE ANCHOR CAPSTAN
'Oh, an' awaaay, ye rollin' river!' (Anchor Shanty)

Reproduction of page 174, from Shanties from the Seven Seas,
*collected by Stan Hugill (London: Routledge & Kegan
Paul Ltd.; New York: E. P. Dutton & Co., Inc., 1961).*

organize your opinion of the work through the musical characteristics outlined above.

"Shenandoah," one of the most famous sailor songs, stems from a history so mixed that it has been difficult for even authorities to trace it to a reliable root. Nonetheless, the attractive tune has persisted with comparatively few changes. One version describes the Missouri River, the cavalry version tells of Nancy in Kansas City, another uses Shenandoah as an Indian chief with a beautiful daughter (this version is recorded by Wagner), a black version has been used as a sailor song, and finally, the Shenandoah River runs through Virginia slave country. Modern arrangements often mix words from more than one version so that the text becomes difficult to unravel.

Five Sea Chanties, William Warfield   **Columbia ML-2206**
Folk Songs of the New World: "Shenandoah," "Drunken Sailor," Roger Wagner
    Capitol P-8324
Sea Chanties, Robert Shaw   **Victor LSC-2551**

4. Most Negro spirituals have been rearranged for vocal performance. A detailed discussion of the background of the Negro spiritual will be found in Chapter 15. For now listen to some spirituals sung in a recorded version. Then ascertain those characteristics which you could describe as being part of the arrangement. Which characteristics belong to the original folk song?

"Deep River," Robert Shaw Chorale   **Victor LSC-2247**
"He's Got the Whole World in His Hands," Marian Anderson   **Victor LSC-2592**

5. Benjamin Britten, English contemporary composer, has taken several folk songs of the British Isles and made a contemporary arrangement for them. Listen particularly to the accompaniment, for it is here where Britten has placed his emphasis, leaving the melody, rhythm, meter, and form very similar to the originals. After hearing the melody and noting the use of text and rhyme with that of melody, listen carefully to the accompaniment. This is the first independent melodic accompaniment we have heard. Most folk song accompaniments follow the melodic line. This independent type of accompaniment, although not in any way a contemporary idea, does offer an opportunity for you to ascertain if it is possible to hear two musical ideas simultaneously. Why would the composer choose the type of accompaniment for each song? Does the accompaniment add to the mood and the meaning of the text? Do you believe that the accompaniment is performed more artistically than accompaniments for some folk songs?

For the text listed below, note particularly the word usage and folk vocabulary, which illustrates that although the accompaniment has been arranged, little has been altered in the original words.

"Little Sir William"

Easter day was a holiday Of all days in the year,
And all the little fellows went out to play But Sir William was not there.

Mama went to the School wife house And knocked at the ring,
Saying, "Little Sir William, if you are there, Pray let your mother in."

The School wife open'd the door and said: "He is not here today.
He is with the little schoolfellows out on the green Playing some
*   pretty play."*

Mama went to the Boyne water That is so wide and deep,
Saying, "Little Sir William, if you are there, Oh pity your mother's
*   weep."*

"How can I pity your weep, mother, And I so long in pain?
For the little pen knife sticks close to my heart And the School
*   wife hath me slain.*

Go home, go home my mother dear And prepare my winding sheet,
For tomorrow morning before 8 o'clock, You with my body shall meet.

And lay my Prayer Book at my head, And my grammar at my feet,
That all the little school fellows as they pass by May read them for
*   my sake."*

COMPOSED FOLK SONGS

The folk song idiom appeals to many composers because of its directness and simplicity; consequently, they write original compositions imitating this style. These composed folk songs ascribe to the following characteristics:

1. The composer associates with the song. With a folk song, although usually composed by one person, time and uncertainty obscure the creator. With a composed folk song not only is the composer known, but his name remains with the song. In addition, even the first version of the song has been notated, and with the original version known, it is often used. If arrangements are made, they may not be long lasting and are recognized immediately as arrangements.

2. The text is polished, the vocabulary from correct usage, and the meter consistent. The composer writes the texts or uses texts which he finds appropriate. Although not great poetry, the lines rarely contain poor English or incorrect meter unless the composer attempts to imitate a provincial style.

3. The subject matter of the imitated folk song copies the folk song itself—love, lonesomeness, war, old times, fond memories, patriotism, etc.

4. Using attractive melodies which are easily remembered, the tunes do not attempt a wide pitch range or unusual musical ideas. Rather, they emphasize steps or common skips.

5. To be easily comprehended, the simple form concentrates upon the strophic. Some use the chorus or refrain as a balance and for easily remembered repetition.

Songs of Stephen Foster

One universally recognized writer of the composed folk song was Stephen Foster, American, born on the fourth of July in 1826. He composed about 200 songs. Since the minstrel was the most popular entertainment of our country at that time, he wrote for such productions; others were the love ballads of the day. Many have become accepted into the folk song literature of our country. You may know one or more of his songs by title: "Oh! Susanna," "Camptown Races," "Old Folks at Home," "My Old Kentucky Home," "Massa's in the Cold, Cold Ground," "Oh! Lemuel," "Ring the Banjo," "Come Where My Love Lies Dreaming," "The Glendy Burk," "Old Black Joe," "Beautiful Dreamer," "Ah! May the Red Rose Live Always," "If You've Only Got a Moustache," and "Jeanie with the Light Brown Hair." From the titles alone one can ascertain if they are minstrel songs reminiscent of the black and the south, love songs, reunion or parting songs, in memory of a beautiful girl, or nonsense songs. Americans carried many of these with them across the plains into the West, altering their words to fit the immediate situation, be it the war with Mexico or the discovery of gold.

Study Procedures

1. Listen to one or more Stephen Foster songs, noting their musical characteristics such as form, rhythm, the expanse and extent of the melody, the tempo, the meter of the text and music. Discuss with your classmates what is different in each song and what

are the similar musical characteristics. What makes Foster's songs different from the original folk songs we heard of the American cowboy, the American sailor, or the American Negro? (Mormon Tabernacle Choir—**Columbia MS-7149,** or Robert Shaw Chorale—**Victor LSC-2295**).

2. The folk song often takes years to develop. In our country up to the 1930s the folk song singers sang those songs learned through community traditions. When these singers began to record and to sing regularly over radio they soon ran out of material. In addition, recording companies desired material which could be copyrighted. Consequently, large numbers of composed folk songs began to be created. Today, many so-called Nashville performers are singing and writing songs in a composed and imitative folk song style. Listen to one or more of these performers and describe in your own words why these songs belong to the music of this chapter. It is the hope of every performer and composer that his songs outlast his personal performance. What songs of your choice do you believe will last as long as the songs of Stephen Foster? Why do you believe this to be true? Play one song for your class which you believe will stand the test of time, and tell why you believe this. Be sure to discuss the song in terms of musical characteristics which we learned earlier in the chapter, for it is these musical characteristics which assist in longevity. What other aspects of the song might you point to that could assist its popularity during the next twenty years? Do not limit yourself to the following albums, although they could act as a guide in your selection:

Joan Baez, *Best*   **Roulette 8045**
              David's Album   **Vanguard 79308**
Glen Campbell, *Galveston*   **Capitol St-210**
Johnny Cash, *From Sea to Shining Sea*   **Columbia 18-10-0344**
Country Girls Sing Country Songs   **Camden CAS-959**
Bob Dylan, *Greatest Hits*   **Columbia 18-10-0220**
Great Country Stars Sing Their Great Hits   **Capitol 8XT-2739**
Pete Seeger, *Folk Songs and Ballads*   **Stinson S-90**
              Where Have All the Flowers Gone?   **Folkways 31026**
Hank Snow, *The Southern Cannonball*   **Camden CAS-680**
              Favorite Country Hits   **Victor P-8S 1041**

Bibliography—Chapter 2

ABRAHAMS, ROGER, and GEORGE FOSS, *Anglo-American Folksong Style.* Englewood Cliffs, N.J.: Prentice-Hall, Inc., 1968.

BRITTEN, BENJAMIN, *Folksong Arrangements, Volume I, British Isles.* London: Boosey and Hawkes, 1943.

HOWARD, JOHN TASKER, *Stephen Foster, America's Troubadour.* New York: Thomas Y. Crowell Company, 1934.

HUGILL, STAN, *Shanties from the Seven Seas.* New York: E. P. Dutton and Co., Inc., 1961.

JACKSON, GEORGE PULLEN, *White and Negro Spirituals.* New York: J. J. Augustin, 1944.

———, *White Spirituals in the Southern Uplands.* Chapel Hill, N.C.: University of North Carolina Press, 1933.

LAWS, G. MALCOLM, JR., *Native American Balladry.* Philadelphia: American Folklore Society, 1964.

LIBRARY OF CONGRESS, *Folk Music Catalogue.* Washington, D.C.: U.S. Government Printing Office, 1959.

LOMAX, JOHN A., *Cowboy Songs and Other Frontier Ballads.* New York: Macmillan Company, 1938.

Odum, Howard W., and Guy B. Johnson, *The Negro and His Songs.* Hatboro, Pa.: Folklore Associates, Inc., 1964.

Thorp, N. Howard, *Songs of the Cowboys.* New York: Clarkson N. Potter, 1966.

———, *A Treasury of Stephen Foster.* New York: Random House, 1946.

Walters, Raymond, *Stephen Foster.* Princeton, N.J.: Princeton University Press, 1936.

Yoder, Don, *Pennsylvania Spirituals.* Lancaster, Pa.: Pennsylvania Folklife Society, 1961.

Recordings—Chapter 2

American Folk Songs	Library of Congress	AAFS LC-2
		26
		27
		28
		49
		50
Country Girls Sing Country Songs		Camden CAS-959
Deep River	Robert Shaw	Victor LSC-2247
Folk Songs	Benjamin Britten	Victor LSC-2718
Folk Songs of the Frontier	Roger Wagner Chorale	Capitol P-8332
Folk Songs of the New World	Roger Wagner Chorale	Capitol P-8324
The Girls Get Prettier	Hank Lacklin	Victor LSP-3588
He's Got the Whole World in His Hands	Marian Anderson	Victor LM-2592
Hum and Strum with Chet Atkins	Chet Atkins and Chorus	Victor LSP-2025
Old American Songs	William Warfield	Columbia ML-2206
Sea Chanties	Robert Shaw	Victor LSC-2551
The Southern Cannonball	Hank Snow	Camden CAS-680
Susan Reed in Folk Songs	Susan Reed	Columbia ML-4368

Chapter 3

The Composed Song

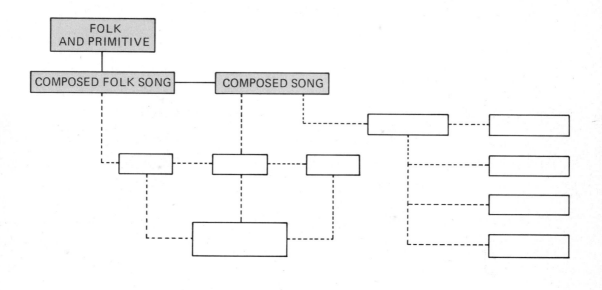

The previous two chapters dealt with song material which was the occasional effort and/or inspiration of an amateur. Wittingly or unwittingly, because of his knowledge of people and their emotions he was able to sing or compose a song which spoke to many persons and in some way became an expression of their own feelings. Chapter 1 placed emphasis upon such songs where the unknown composer intuitively knew people better than he knew music or poetry. Chapter 2 concerned itself with a retention of these same feelings but balanced them with a certain skill in musical expression.

As to be expected, another type of song developed, one which strived for a higher quality than a folk song, which was more carefully written by a schooled musician, but which still contrived for popular appeal through carefully executed music and words written to attract the attention of the people through common sentiments and moods. Showing talent but not genius, such songs often aroused a restricted immediate appeal but attained steady popularity over a long period of years.

"I Love You Truly," by Carrie Jacobs Bond meets all of these criteria. This song, although discussing a common subject, does not read as if it were a folk song. Used for years at weddings, it has appealed to old and young alike and for this reason was chosen as our first example.

I Love You Truly

Words and Music by Carrie Jacobs Bond

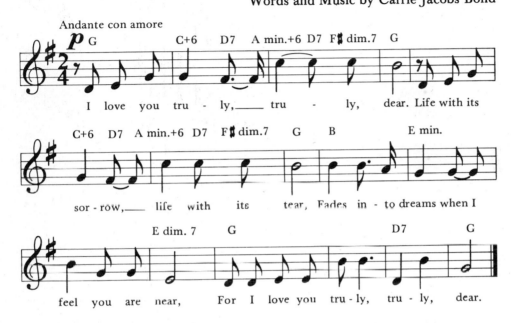

By examining the song carefully, several characteristics become obvious:

1. *Mediocre poetry.* The rhyme scheme, vocabulary, and meter determine immediately that an honest poetic effort exists. The emphasis is upon poignant meaningful phrases attempting artistic expression.

2. *Coordinate music.* a) The tune is built to propel the singer and listener from one portion of the song to the next; b) obviously expressive, the melody emphasizes a certain unity with the words so that with only one hearing the listener senses much of its attractiveness; c) the chordal structure is more complex and adds to the general effect; d) the accompaniment, still meant for the amateur pianist and usually duplicating the melodic line, may be more complex and include changing inner voices, minor dissonances, or countermelodies.

3. *Emotional unity.* The melody not only fits the meter of the text, but the tune attempts to provide an emotional description for the words. To say it another way, the tune rarely could be placed with other words and be as effective.

4. *Deep-seated, less demonstrative emotions and sentiments.* The emphasis is upon recall and memory, the subdued or mellowed sentiment, the speaking of the heart.
5. *A variety of form.* To engender its appeal, music makes use of *form*, which is the manner it repeats or fails to repeat musical characteristics. When a short tune repeats during a composition it becomes easier to remember for the listener and easier to sing for the performer. More importantly, however, repetition subconsciously gives an aesthetic feeling of balance which enhances the effect of the song.

Study Procedures

1. Examine the words and music for "I Love You Truly," and then review the characteristics mentioned above. Can you find each characteristic represented? Are these obviously different from those of a folk song? A composed folk song?
2. Choose other songs that you may have heard sung and compare them to the characteristics listed above.

AN INTRODUCTION TO FORM

As we just stated, form guides the aesthetic effect of the song. This being true, it becomes an important basis for our consideration of all music throughout this book. An introduction to it is most appropriate for the song material in this chapter.

Form denotes the manner of repetition in musical material. It is possible to write a composition wherein the repetitions come often and regularly. Other compositions use little or no repetitions. This molding of the musical material gives each construction its architectural design and enables us to understand its function, but also to appreciate its beauty and artistic nature. When the melody and the form unite carefully, usually an aesthetic product results. The words may or may not be outstanding; the tune may or may not be of high quality; but if this unity exists between melody and form, its appeal will be recognizable, probably general, and the composition will have a considerably longer existence than otherwise.

As in algebra, the terms used in musical form usually are letters which represent portions of the composition. In other words, the letter A could be used for a part of a song. If that same melody and rhythm were repeated, another letter A would be used to indicate this repetition. If the melody and rhythm were to change so that we would hear a new tune, then a different letter would be used, most likely the letter B. One could use letters X and Y, or G and H, or even numbers. Any of these would be appropriate.

Study Procedures

1. Again let us examine "I Love You Truly." Study the music, not trying to read the notes but to understand the contour of the vocal line. Notice that the melody is exactly the same for the second line of poetry as for the first. If we were to represent this melody with a letter, we could say that this song begins AA. Such a statement would indicate that we recognize the melody of the first line is repeated for the second line. The third line of poetry, "Fades into dreams when I feel you are near," does not contain the same melody. This could be given a letter indication of B. The final line of the song also is different, so it would be represented by still another letter. Thus, we could state that the form of the song is represented by the letters AABC.

2. Study the song "In the Gloaming," (p. 32) and consider the form of the song by using the letter representations to indicate differences and samenesses of melodic lines.

   This song uses two-line groupings or eight measures of music as a basic unit. In music such a grouping may be called a *phrase*. The word phrase indicates a pause or a break in the musical flow. In songs, such a break or pause often follows closely the lines of poetry or the text. In this song, the text material could be phrased after the word "darling" or after the word "low." Because of the manner of repetition in the melody we will consider the phrase as breaking at measure eight. There is often disagreement as to the phrasing of musical material, and this difference leads to varying interpretations. By examining this song we notice that it contains four phrases of eight measures each. It is this regularity which brings some of its aesthetic effect to the listener. The form could be described as AABA.

   In this particular composition an additional phrase has been added at the end of the song. It, too, contains eight measures but its melody is different from any in the earlier portions of the song. In reality, it is an ending and its musical name is *coda*. The addition of this coda, not often found in popular songs, adds much to the general character of the composition. This is a device borrowed from more schooled composers, but used effectively in this popular melody.

3. Examine the song "The Rosary" (p. 33) and ascertain the form. Use letter symbols to indicate your understanding.

   Consider the entire composition: does it divide itself into two main parts? three main parts? or four main parts? This example shows an irregularity which contrasts obviously with the regularity of "In the Gloaming." The first main part of this song contains eight measures; the second main part contains seven measures; the third main part contains ten measures; all reflect the irregularity of the line lengths of the original poem. The form letter indicators should reflect these differences. Yet, because each section begins with the same melody the similarities should be evident also. Prime signs are used to indicate differences where similarities predominate. An A and A' mean two phrases have much in common despite minor differences. The overall form of this composition would be AA'A".

   Each of the main sections could be subdivided into phrases, and each phrase should be examined for similarities or differences in the material used throughout the song. Thus the first two lines of poetry are set to the same melodic phrase, while the following two lines use a different tune for each of the lines.

   The following diagram would be appropriate:

Main Sections	A	A'	A"
Phrases	k k m o	k k m p	k k m r

In the Gloaming

Mete Orred

Annie F. Harrison

Andante

In the gloam - ing, O my dar - ling! When the lights are dim and low, And the qui - et shad - ows fall - ing,

with animation

Soft - ly come and soft - ly go. When the winds are sob - bing — faint - ly With a gen - tle, un - known woe,

a tempo

Will you think of me and love me As you did once long a - go? It was best to leave you thus,_____ Best for you and best for me._____

The Rosary

Words by Robert Cameron Rogers

Music by Ethelbert Nevin

By reading again the diagram (p. 31) one would know that there are three main sections to the song which are all similar but which have somewhat different endings. Each main section contains four subsections; each of the first three phrases are alike, while the ending phrase in each main section is different. Such an analysis tells us much about the song and the manner in which the composer has put it together. Just as in any other creative endeavor, be it cooking, dressmaking, or building a house, the manner of "putting it together" is important to the result.

4. Examine "Glow Worm" and consider the form.

Although the melodic line appears somewhat different in the second phrase as compared to the first, it is really the same tune written at a higher pitch. In music,

Glow Worm

Words by Lilla Gayley Robinson   Music by Paul Lincke

this is known as a *sequence*. This means that a tune can be repeated at a different pitch and still be recognized as the same tune. To correctly indicate this in a form outline, use the same prime signs which show small alterations of the melody: AA', etc.

With this in mind, what would be the form of "Glow Worm"?

Most of the songs which we have examined in this chapter are built with a verse and refrain or verse and chorus. The chorus often follows each verse in the singing and usually contains one set of words, while the verse portion often contains several verses of poetry to indicate some progression in the situation described by the song. When any song contains more than one verse to the same music, it is known as *strophic*. Some songs are written so as not to appear strophic even when they are.

Because of minor alterations in the melody these are completely written out, but because of their being only small differences in the repeated portions the strophic principle still applies. These are known as *modified strophic* songs. Which of the songs used in this chapter are strophic, and which are modified strophic?

5. Review each of the songs as they relate to the five characteristics which were discussed in the early portion of the chapter. Can you recognize why all of these songs have been considered favorites with millions of people at various times in the past, and why they are still considered favorites for singing?

Bibliography—Chapter 3

BONI, MARGARET, ed., *Fireside Book of Favorite American Songs*. New York: Simon and Schuster, 1952.

———, *Fireside Book of Love Songs*. New York: Simon and Schuster, 1954.

———, *Songs of the Gilded Age*. New York: Golden Press, 1960.

EMURIAN, ERNEST K., *Living Stories of Favorite Songs*. Boston: W. A. Wilde Company, 1958.

EWEN, DAVID, *Songs of America*. Chicago: Ziff-Davis Publishing Company, 1947.

GELLER, JAMES J., *Famous Songs and Their Stories*. New York: Garden City Publishers, Inc., 1940.

LEVY, LESTER S., *Grace Notes in American History*. Norman, Okla.: University of Oklahoma Press, 1967.

LLOYD, RUTH and NORMAN, eds., *The American Heritage Songbook*. New York: American Heritage Publishing Company, Inc., 1969.

SPAETH, SIGMUND, *A History of Popular Music in America*. New York: Random House, 1948.

YERBURY, GRACE D., *Song in America*. Metuchen, N.J.: The Scarecrow Press, Inc., 1971.

Section B *Simple Music for Religious Service*

Chapter 4 *Chant*

Chapter 5 *The Hymn*

Chapter 6 *The Anthem and the Motet*

Chapter 4

Chant

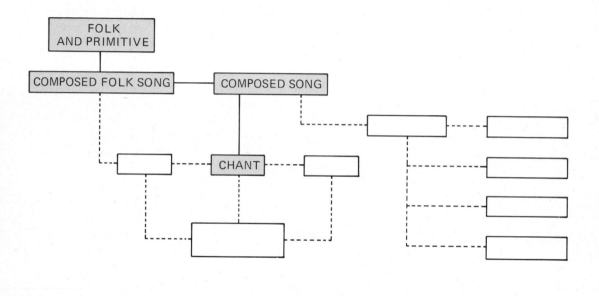

We want a Touchdown!
We want a Touchdown!

When this repeated cry rings through a stadium, a modern chant compels and absorbs the participants with as intense a spellbinding and mesmerizing effect as the ritual of many a former worshiper at the altar or shrine of a favorite god. If you listen carefully to the touchdown chant, a kind of tune evolves with the words, and although never written down, the same tune unfolds no matter whether in California or New Jersey, whether for the junior high school game or for the pros.

The characteristics of this chant are obvious: a few well-known words and repetitions. These words are important to the immediate situation and their constant repetition brings forth a kind of tune or melody built upon the accent of the words, enabling the group to even better articulate its concerns than if they expressed them alone or without the intoning. In addition, the tune and the words carry an emotion which would not be present if the chant had not developed.

These must be the same kind of results that were desired by early singers of chant. Realizing that the effect from group chanters was striking, it was further reasoned that if a single person chanted a song, a prayer, or a psalm, he also could produce an effect not possible with normal reading.

Chant is very old; we have written records of it being used in India as early as the fourth millennium B.C. No doubt it developed much earlier, but like folk song, its history is incomplete.

Because of the melodic limitations of early song and singing, the word chant was often believed to apply to any vocal utterance. However, gradually it became appropriated more consistently to special kinds of activities. The Incas used chant in their worship in the temples; the North American Indian used chant to assist with the supplication for health or the weather; the Hindu had chants for the planting of seeds, for the fertilization of the crop, and for the harvest; the African Negro chanted during his work, his recreation, and religious observance; the Roman chanted special poems with kithara accompaniment; and the Hebrew chanted the psalms in the synagogues. By reviewing these, it would appear that any solicitous supplication seemed to demand chant more than other types of activities. So it is with the modern sports fan, who seems to be praying for, more than demanding a touchdown. Like his ancestor of another time and place, the modern chanter has a notion that the power of the chant, the intoned word, has a greater influence upon the eventual outcome of the situation than the same request from a single voice or from a group not involved with the incantation.

These ideas seem obvious even to the child as he chants, "Billy's got a girl!" and he inherently understands that the intonation will have a more ringing effect than mere spoken words. Like our ancestors, the child often improvises a dance to accompany the chant, thus increasing its emotional impact and offering himself a kind of physical release to the emotion of the moment.

But the sports arena is not the only location for chant in our contemporary world. We, too, have more often consigned it to the religious world and it is here that it has become stylized and has made its greatest musical impact.

To understand the reason for this statement, we must go back in history to a time when the center of civilization was centered around the Mediterranean. The Greeks had ruled this part of the world for years, and although they had developed a type of chant through the song and recitative of the drama, they were less interested in its emotional impact and its beauty.

Although Rome inherited the Grecian arts, music added little to daily life except as an accompaniment to personal routines, never becoming a vital part of Roman affairs or relationships.

Neither was the Roman Empire sympathetic to the peoples it had conquered, many of whom considered music a vital part of life and worship. One such folk were the Hebrews, whose religious life dated back through the populace of the Mesopotamian Valley and through whose religious life music had been a vital part for centuries.

When Constantinople became the seat of power of the empire, the court of the emperors produced a new art, partly religious in sound, definitely solemn and dignified. The churches of the Eastern portion of the empire, including Jerusalem, Alexandria, and Antioch, accepted this music as a model for music of the fast growing Christian church. The first impact of this model was to acknowledge music as a part of the service. This was a major step, since many in the West had concluded that music was entirely too pagan for such inclusion. Secondly, accepting the fact that music could sound solemn, the emphasis was changed to accent the vocal rather than the instrumental. Thirdly, it became obvious that music could be artistic, and so began an attempt to raise the music of the church to an art form.

Generally speaking, the chant of the synagogue had remained about at the level of folk song for many centuries.[1] But with this emphasis from the court of Byzantium a much more formal music developed using the Hebrew Chant and Byzantine and classical Greek standards as a basis.

What evolved was a music especially designed for the church, made up mostly of Hebrew chants of the Psalms with strong Eastern influences. The development was further determined by the exclusion of musical instruments, particularly those normally associated with dances, love making, eating, etc. which included the psalterium (harp), the tuba (straight trumpet), the flute, the drum, and the tibia (double oboe). There was an obvious exclusion of harshness and noisiness.

Church music followed the Hebrew order. For centuries the rites at the Jewish temple had been much more formal and traditional than those at the synagogue. The synagogue had services three times a day as outlined in Daniel (6:10), and partly from this the Christian church organized the services of the hours. The synagogue chant had been responsorial, and in adapting this the Christian church developed chants that were responsorial and antiphonic. For hundreds of years chant had used a limited range, and the Christian church also limited its range. And so developed a unique stylistic music, with obvious characteristics that lent themselves beautifully to the new worship of the church.

But these musical goals culminated slowly. Taking almost five centuries to develop, many styles and regional differences became apparent. About 600 A.D., upon the request of Pope Gregory, the music of the Mass and offices was most carefully organized to bring a methodical and harmonious arrangement to the service of the church.

The organization and systematizing of the music and order of worship took years, and many must have contributed to the process. However, Pope Gregory received the major portion of the credit and Gregorian Chant is the usual name for that music which has served the church for the past 1,300 years. Nor has the music been altered to any great extent.

---

[1] *New Oxford History of Music,* ed. Edgar Wellesz; Vol. I. Oxford University Press, 1951, pages 60–66.

Let us briefly examine this organization.

The services of the church are of two general types: a more formal service for the large congregation, and the less well-known, more intimate devotional services. The former has come to be known as the Mass, although originally it was called the Eucharist because the service is the celebration of the Lord's Supper with reference to His sacrifice upon the Cross. The term "mass" comes from its final phrase, when the celebrating clergy dismisses the congregation with, "Ite missa est."

The second type of service, the offices of the hours, has come to us from two sources: the Christian vigils during the time of repression of the faith, and the synagogue services of the Jewish people.

The music of the Mass is divided into two parts, the Proper and the Ordinary. The Ordinary are those portions that may be performed day after day, while the Proper are those chants that can be sung only for one particular day of the church year.

The Ordinary of the service contains the Kyrie, Gloria, Credo, Sanctus, and Agnus Dei.

The Proper of the service contains the Introit, Gradual, Alleluia, Offertory, and Communion.

These come in order as listed above, but move from Ordinary to Proper throughout the service.

The offices include the Psalms with antiphons, Magnificats, hymns, antiphons to the Virgin Mary, and Responsories. The offices are more often simple music as compared to the Mass, particularly that Mass using the choir.

The style of singing is of three types: syllabic (one note to each syllable of the text), neumatic (two to four notes to one syllable of text), and melismatic (four or more notes per syllable of text). Psalm tones, antiphons, and hymns are most often syllabic. Introits, Communions, and Responsories are more often neumatic in style, while the Gradual, the Alleluia, and the tract are usually melismatic.

With this background in history and style, you should be prepared to hear chant of various types. Most important of all, listen to the flowing style, the syllable rhythm (neumatic, melismatic), and the phrase rhythm, noting the various lengths of phrases and how the music smoothly moves, hesitates, and moves again. When the singing hesitates, the melody usually drops or falls; this is known as a *cadence*. Remember also that the melodies of these chants are not obvious and not easy to remember unless you hear them many times. The melodic character of this music, tuneful but reserved, attractive but never trite, has recommended it to many modern composers as a basis for religious as well as secular works. Consequently, one reason for studying chant is to assist in understanding its use in other forms.

THE BEGINNING OF POLYPHONY

In the first part of this chapter we explored single-line music, or music without harmony. No countersounds or additional musical lines were involved with chant from its inception to about 900 A.D.

This was not particularly the extent of music through this period. Although this is only conjecture, the Middle East may have led the way to polyphonic music through the complexity of their accompaniments and natural vocal experimentation. In the East and the West the drones and consonant chords of instrumental music combined with vocal lines to introduce the idea of more than one simultaneous sound or pitch well before it was accepted formally. The church had made its musical stand and had placed emphasis in the direction of chant, which was single-line music only.

But certain portions of the Christian domain were not particularly interested in the musical style or melodies of chant, and accepted it grudgingly. The northwestern sections of Europe preferred the folk music of their own regions and the more natural, rugged, heavier sounds to the more lyrical, flowing melodies that had come from the East and which were more easily and quickly assimilated by the Mediterranean peoples. When these Northwestern rhythms and harmonies did break into the music of the church, they were introduced in a way so as to continue chant style, including all of the melodies and characteristics of chant.

Because of musical conflict between the North and the Mediterranean world, the center of development for new music in the Western world was France, since here the two ideas met upon middle ground. This earliest of harmonic music was called *organum*. The origin of the word is not clear but it in no way relates to the organ, the musical instrument.

Once adapted, organum was not static during the time of its use, but did affect tremendously the music of the church, even though chant as a monodic form was not lost or completely abandoned. Instead, types of organum evolved using the chant as a basis for its forms and primary melodies.

Early organum (parallel) was strict and permitted a note-for-note relationship in its harmony, employing only certain musical intervals. The sounds were parallel, and their visual reproduction is shown in the diagram below:

It was about 150 years before another obvious advancement took place in harmony. This was known as *free organum,* and this style of music permitted the voices more freedom. These musical sounds would look like the diagram below:

Melismatic organum, a third type which was used almost entirely during the twelfth century, permitted the upper voice considerable movement, but the lower voice was restricted to a few held notes. These few notes were the original chant, and the upper part was a composed musical line.

These three developments in music were important, since they opened the door for polyphony, prepared for the introduction of a musical rhythm, and indirectly led to a more interesting and widely divergent secular music.

During the development of organum, it became evident that the voices were singing more complex music and that with the addition of more than one voice line it was possible to sing together if 1) the voices sang the exact same number of notes, or 2) one part could sing the chant at a very slow pace, while the upper voice sang his independent tune with many notes against one for the lower voice.

Out of this expansion of the musical structure came a system for controlling the various voice or instrumental parts based upon rhythmic formulae. These rules of rhythm were known as *rhythmic modes,* and often a voice part singing in one rhythmic mode would maintain that mode throughout. A kind of rhythmic monotony developed in many instances.

And so the stage had been set for a new development in music in which harmony and rhythm would interact to originate many new forms and new sounds. The people of northwestern Europe would build upon this past to develop heights not then dreamed of.

Study Procedures

1. Listen to a series of short excerpts, including chant through strict organum to a composition by Perotin. Notice that, as the parts become more complex and the rhythm more obvious, the melody is less flowing and often assumes a kind of punctuated style.

2. Listen to the three types of organum, noting changes which were to lead to later styles of music.

Bibliography—Chapter 4

APEL, WILLI, *Gregorian Chant*. Bloomington, Ind.: Indiana University Press, 1958.

BINDER, A. W., *Biblical Chant*. London: Peter Owen Ltd., 1960.

FERGUSON, DONALD N., *A History of Musical Thought*. New York: F. S. Crofts and Co., 1938.

GOLDRON, ROMAIN, *Ancient and Oriental Music*. New York: H. S. Stuttman Co., 1968.

HARMAN, ALEC, *Man and His Music*. Fair Lawn, N.J.: Essential Books, 1958.

LANG, PAUL HENRY, ed., *Music in Western Civilization*. New York: W. W. Norton and Co., Inc., 1941.

POLIN, CLAIRE C. J., *Music of the Ancient Near East*. New York: Vantage Press, Inc., 1954.

REESE, GUSTAVE, *Music in the Middle Ages*. New York: W. W. Norton and Co., Inc., 1968.

SEAY, ALBERT, *Music in the Medieval World*. Englewood Cliffs, N.J.: Prentice-Hall, Inc., 1965.

TANABE, HISAO, *Japanese Music*. Kokusai Bunka Shinkokai, 1959.

WELLESZ, EGON, *Eastern Elements in Western Chant*. New York: Humanities Press, Inc., 1968.

WELLESZ, EGON, ed., *Oxford History of Music*. London: Oxford University Press, 1929–1938.

WERNER, ERIC, *The Sacred Bridge*. New York: Columbia University Press, 1960.

Recordings—Chapter 4

The following records were used in the preparation of this chapter. Other suitable records may be available in the future or may be in school or city libraries from past editions. All would be appropriate listening:

Ambrosian Chants	Chant of 500 to 900 A.D.	VOX DLBX-207
The Azuma Kabuki	Japanese ancient ceremonial chant	Columbia 4925 LP-278
Folk and Primitive Music, Vol. XI	Japanese chant	Columbia SL-214 LP-304
History of Music in Sound, Vols. I, II	Lamaist chanting, Indian rice transplanting song, Jewish music, Islamic call to prayer	RCA LM-6057
Masterpieces of Music Before 1750	Chant, organum, free organum, organum of Perotin	Haydn Society HS-9038
Music of Perotin	Organum	Bach Guild BGS-70656
Notre Dame Organa	Organum	Experiences Anonymous EA-0021
Perotin Organum	Organum	Bach Guild BGS-5045

A Treasury of Early Music	Chant and organum	Haydn Society HSE 7-9100
A Treasury of Gregorian Chant	Gregorian chant	VOX STPL-516.420 516.480 516.470
2000 Years of Music	Greek music, Jewish music, organum	Decca LP-18

Chapter 5

The Hymn

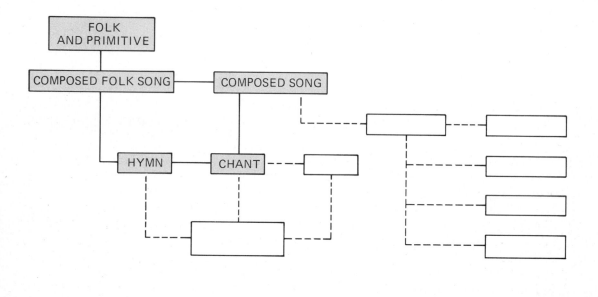

The folk song and chant are forms that originated with the people. The folk song has been retained by the people, but chant has been appropriated by the established church. The hymn is still another musical form to have come from the people, and like the folk song, its dynamism still remains in their jurisdiction.

Just as it began, it is still a religious commentary upon the facets of devotional life. Usually this commentary took the form of a poem or some elaboration of the prayers, psalms, meditations, or stories of the religious situation.

References to hymns have been made in almost every civilization. There have been hymns to most gods, or idols, hymns to the Sun where it was worshiped, and even poetic hymn contests at the games in early Grecian times. But the hymns rooted in the Judaic tradition are the most plentiful, diverse, and musically interesting.

Much like chant, the hymns of early Christendom came from the Hebrews through the Byzantine church. In the East the churches considered hymns a great asset to worship which the Western church never could appreciate. During the time of Christ Hebrew hymns based upon the Psalms were in use, but the

East exerted its own influence not only upon the music but also upon the words, giving them more poetic character.

When Christianity became the religion of the Empire in A.D. 313, the hymns that had long been underground broke forth and spread over the then known world. Christian hymns were much in favor in Milan and the bishop there, St. Ambrose, did much to foster them. The result was easy to remember tunes quite similar to popular songs and thus differing from chant. Usually comprising eight stanzas of four lines each, the melodies contained one note to the syllable.

By the fourth century religious song had developed into two well-known categories, the hymn and psalm, and liturgical singing usually called chant. As the chant became more the prerogative of the choir and the priest, the hymn became more the music of the people.

WORDS OF THE HYMN

As stated, the texts of the earliest Christian hymns were poetic versions of the Psalms or poems of the religious faith. These had originally been in Hebrew, Greek, or Semitic, but with the ascendancy of Latin, the church services were read in Latin and, consequently, the hymns of devotion were written by the faithful in that language. By the fourth century the singing of psalms was responsorial or antiphonal chant, while the hymns were poetic, using a more tuneful, songlike music.

An early example of a poem-hymn entitled "O Splendor of God's Glory Bright" has been translated from the Latin by Robert Bridges, once poet lauriate of England. The original was written about A.D. 360 and is accredited to St. Ambrose.

O Splendor of God's Glory bright,
O thou that bringest light from light,
O light of light, light's living spring,
O Day, all days illumining.[1]

A second such poetic Latin hymn is the well-known Advent song now often used as a Christmas carol, "O Come, O Come Emmanuel."

The third period of hymn writing came at the time of the Protestant Reformation. Luther understood the value of the hymn and its relation to the language of the common man as opposed to the liturgical chant and song of the church. Realizing the hymn to be a musical and worship form of the people, he translated thirty-six hymns from the Latin, revised four German hymns that the people knew, paraphrased six hymns from scripture, and wrote

---

[1] *A Survey of Christian Hymnody,* William Jensen Reynolds. Holt, Rinehart and Winston, Inc., New York, 1963, page 144.

nine hymns himself.   These are the known Luther hymns, the most famous being "Ein feste Burg," which is one of his original compositions (see Chapter 10 for a musical development).   In one respect, it was similar to earlier hymns in that it was a paraphrase of Psalm 46.   Luther's major musical impact came by his placing native language hymns into the formal service.

In most countries where the Protestant faith was to be a major influence during the next two hundred years, Calvin, Knox, and the Wesleys followed in Luther's footsteps, writing hymns for the Protestant church of Switzerland, Scotland, England, and the United States as well as Northern Europe.

THE
VVHOLE
BOOKE OF PSALMES
Faithfully
TRANSLATED *into* ENGLISH
Metre.

Whereunto is prefixed a difcourfe de-
claring not only the lawfullnes, but alfo
the neceffity of the heavenly Ordinance
of finging Scripture Pfalmes in
the Churches of
God.

Coll. III.

*Let the word of God dwell plenteoufly in
you, in all wifdome, teaching and exhort-
ing one another in Pfalmes, Himnes, and
fpirituall Songs, finging to the Lord with
grace in your hearts.*

Iames V.

*If any be afflicted, let him pray, and if
any be merry let him fing pfalmes.*

Imprinted
1640

Reproduction of title page from **The Bay Psalm Book** *(Facsimile
reprint of the First Edition, by the University of Chicago Press).*

Although Calvin was convinced that a hymn in the language of the people should be a part of the service, he differed from Luther in one major concern. Calvin decided that his followers should revert to the letter as well as the spirit of the Old and New Testament in their hymns by singing only the Psalms. Since these Biblical songs were originally in Hebrew and translated into Latin, neither of which he wished to use, Calvin sought poets to vulgarize them. Although some of the results were quite attractive, most of them in the hands of lesser talents became clumsy and often humorous.

Calvin's musical influence spread throughout Europe and to the young America, where the psalm-singing colonists prompted the publication of the famous *Bay Psalm Book*. This first published and printed book in North America went through over one hundred editions.

Two famous European psalters of that period were the Sternhold and Hopkins and the Ainsworth. The first few lines of Psalm 23 from these famous psalters are given below so that a comparison can be made.

Sternhold and Hopkins

My shepherd is the living Lord
Nothing therfore I need,
In pastures fair near pleasant streams,
He setteth me to feed.

Ainsworth

Jehovah feedeth me, I shall not lack;
In grassy folds He down dooth make me lye;
He gently leads me quiet water by.
He dooth return my soul; for His name sake
In paths of justice leads me quietly.

Bay

The Lord to mee a shepheard is,
Want therefore shall not I:
He in the folks of tender grasse,
Doth cause me down to lie.

To waters calm mee gently leads,
Restore my soule doth hee:
He doth in paths of righteousness
For his name's sake leade mee.

The fourth period of hymn writing came in the early 1700s, when Isaac Watts introduced a new type of hymn to the English-speaking churches. His poems were rigidly metrical, but their main difference lay in his emphasizing the experiences, feelings, and thoughts of Christians. One of his most famous hymns, still heard regularly in Christian churches throughout the world, is based upon Psalm 90 and is often sung at a time of national sorrow or rejoicing. It has been the second national anthem of England.

O God, our help in ages past
Our hope for years to come,
Our shelter from the stormy blast,
And our eternal home.

His famous Christmas hymn "Joy to the World" is still used, as well as "When I Survey the Wondrous Cross," written for communion and based upon Galatians 6:14.

When I survey the wondrous cross
Where the young Prince of Glory died,
My richest gain I count but loss,
And pour contempt on all my pride.

Watts was the first English hymn writer to capture the true Reformation feelings of the people in his verse because he spoke of the theology of the New Testament without losing the strength and meaning of the Jewish past. He wrote his verse in three meters: common, long, and short (see page 53), because he had been trained in classical forms, but these limits never seemed a hindrance. Watts also had a knack with words which attracted the attention of the singer or reader from the first line of the hymn. Being a minister he wrote hymns that interpreted the Bible and, consequently, accompanied well the sermons of ministers from that day to this.

One of the great hymn writers of Europe and America was Charles Wesley, brother of the founder of the Methodist church. The Wesley hymns also were involved with the personal feelings of the Christian and the Christian life. Many of his hymns were echoed throughout the great revivals of America and Europe during the later 1700s and are still sung today.

Included in his efforts are such well-known hymns as "Christ the Lord is Risen Today," "Hark the Herald Angels Sing," and "Christ, Whose Glory Fills the Skies." Compare the two verses below to those of former writers of hymns. These hymns derive their titles from the first line of each verse.

Jesus, Lover of my soul,
Let me to thy bosom fly,
While the nearer waters roll,
While the tempest still is high;
Hide me, O my Savior Hide,
Till the storm of life is past;
Safe into the haven guide,
O receive my soul at last!

Love divine, all loves excelling,
Joy of heaven, to earth come down,
Fix in us thy humble dwelling,
All thy faithful mercies crown;
Jesus, thou art all compassion,
Pure unbounded love thou art;
Visit us with thy salvation,
Enter every trembling heart.

These hymns are longer versed, but Wesley also used more and different meters than previous writers. One hears an evangelical emphasis in these lines not present in other verses. Wesley wrote of a personal experience of salvation that appealed to the new convert in England and in the frontier areas of America.

With the Wesley emphasis on evangelism, an entire new world of hymn writing came upon the scene. Literally thousands of writers of hymns wrote songs of personal experience and are still writing them. Some have gained the acceptance of the majority of churchgoers; others have the satisfaction of being termed popular favorites with Christians and non-Christians because of the catchiness of the words or tune.   Because of their failure to meet the standards of quality in poetry or music or both, gospel songs rely heavily upon an emotional emphasis that is immediately obvious, with an evangelistic emphasis that pervades the light texts which lack lyrical beauty.   Many of these gospel songs came from our campground meetings and still are sung at revival meetings even today. Recently recording sales of this kind of religious music have skyrocketed.

To discuss adequately all of the writers of hymns would require a multi-volumed work.   Instead, this brief summary has been an overview and has listed only two or three hymn writers.   For additional information, the reader is directed to the bibliography at the end of the chapter.

MUSIC FOR THE HYMN

Music and the words of hymns have never been monogamous.   Because of the common meter of the words many tunes fit more than one set of words and are so used.   Texts for hymns were written with little thought of a specific tune, or only with the hope that some craftsman would compose one at a later time.

The earliest hymn tunes were *monophonic,* or single lines of sound. Even though a number of persons might be singing together only one line of music was sung.   Although in that regard similar to chant, the tunes were more obviously melodic and more appealing.   Early tunes had various melodic and rhythmic characteristics, depending upon whether they were Byzantine or Western European.

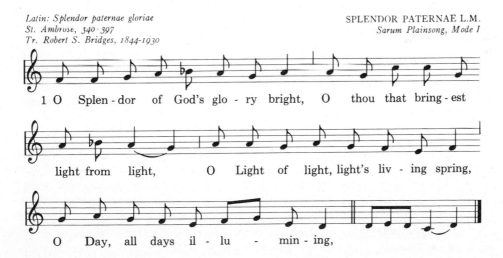

O Splendor of God's Glory Bright

Latin: *Splendor paternae gloriae*
St. Ambrose, 340-397
Tr. Robert S. Bridges, 1844-1930

SPLENDOR PATERNAE L.M.
Sarum Plainsong, Mode I

1 O Splen-dor of God's glo-ry bright, O thou that bring-est
light from light, O Light of light, light's liv-ing spring,
O Day, all days il-lu - min-ing,

From *A Survey of Christian Hymnody,* William Jensen Reynolds. Holt, Rinehart and Winston, Inc., New York, 1963, page 144.

It would have been technically possible to use a Byzantine tune with a Latin poem by St. Ambrose if one wished, since the words were carefully scanned so as to fit a number of possible tunes or even liturgical chants.

From the tenth century through the later fifteenth, it is possible that some vocal or instrumental harmony was used with hymns but this would not be of major importance, since hymn singing has always placed its primary emphasis upon the tune and much less upon the harmony. Most likely instrumental accompaniments were used in homes and at small gatherings outside the church, as this was the custom of the people in secular music. The kind of accompaniment would have made little difference to the singing or meaning of the hymn.

A modern writing of the Ambrosian hymn used earlier in this chapter (page 51) will give an idea of the simplicity of the melodic line and its monophonic character.

The second period of hymn music came at the time of the Reformation. Notation had progressed so that music could profitably be printed and hymn books could be circulated to the congregation. The texts and music were rarely paired so that in some books the tunes were printed together at the back of the book, while the verses appeared together at the front. Other editions placed a verse and a tune on opposite pages but not with any intention that the two necessarily should be sung together.

Luther's intent that the congregation sing hymns within the formal service became a reality so strong that the power of the hymn book spread to the home and to the school as well as the church. The German hymn, known as the *chorale* (over 100,000 were written during this period), became the basis not only for the expressions of faith, but also for numerous musical forms of a much more refined and intricate texture. Some of these we shall study throughout this book.

When Calvin restricted hymn texts to the Psalms he inadvertently restricted the music as well, so that the singers of the Psalms used tunes which were more closely aligned to chant than the German chorale, the latter leading to a later adoption of accompaniments and part singing. In addition, the rhythm of the Calvin psalms was more regular and less experimental. Consequently, the Reformation, but more obviously the German chorale, opened the door for more important musical compositions, gave the people greater interest in congregational singing in the service, and prepared the way for the accompaniment to become a major part of the hymn and vocal texture.

The third period of hymn music runs from the early 1700s to the present day. During this time the four-part hymn became prominent, with considerable emphasis placed on the contrapuntal texture of each line. Since early in the eighteenth century, hymn books have carried at least one verse of the words of each hymn bracketed within the music. Unconsciously, this has associated the hymn with a particular tune, but it has been merely a case of printing what the singer had known for some time: that the tune for one hymn seemed to modulate more naturally to the words of some verses than others.

The Wesley hymn placed greater emphasis on evangelism and personal feeling in relation to the gospel. But the unity of sentiment and music secured the popularity of his writings. His tunes were more interesting vocally, more involved with the Romantic period in sentiment and sound, made greater use of the variety of meter and rhythms available, and captured the essence of the camp meeting and revival meeting without cheapening his lyrics or melodies.

The music of the gospel song is often of a less devotional nature. Following more closely the popular song of the day, it is more introspective and less likely to praise, adore, or thank. Since popular tunes have been used for hymns for years, it becomes difficult to fault the practice. However, one point should be made: hymn tunes that survive any period of time are distillations of popular melodies, and not the popular dance or folk tunes themselves. Consequently, the emphasis seen today in the gospel song as it imitates the Broadway show tunes, the rock song, or the pseudo folk–Negro-spiritual idioms, will not produce hymns that will last longer than the current pop tune. Rather, the synthesis of these styles will produce hymns that will speak to the congregations in new ways. This synthesis has not been achieved by any writers to date, although contemporary hymn writers hope they will be able to capture it.

INFORMATION CONCERNING HYMNS

Hymn books customarily give complete data for each hymn and tune.

The name at the top left is that of the author of the text; the name at the top right is the composer of the tune if that is known. If not, the source of the tune is usually given, and often the approximate date.

Each tune is named so that a person can refer to the name of the melody without using the first line of any text. Tunes often differ from one text to another.

The meter of each hymn is usually given at the top center of the page, although some publications will vary the location of these numerals. The numerals give the syllables of each line of poetry in the hymn and the number of lines to the verse. The letter D after the numbers signifies a *doubled verse.* The letters CM represent *common meter,* or a verse of 8 6 8 6; SM represents *short meter* and a verse of 6 6 8 6; LM signifies *long meter,* with each line containing eight syllables, thus, 8 8 8 8. The rhyme scheme is usually indicated with small letters such as a b a b, showing that lines one and three are rhymed and lines two and four; a verse could be rhymed in the style of a b c b, so that only two lines would rhyme, the second and the fourth.

Examine the hymn below and ascertain if you can find all of the information just discussed:

A Mighty Fortress Is Our God

Based on Psalm 46
Martin Luther, 1483-1546
Tr. Frederick H. Hedge, 1805-1890

EIN' FESTE BURG 8.7.8.7.6.6.6.6.7.
Melody by Martin Luther, 1483-1546

1 A might-y for-tress is our God, A bul-wark nev-er fail-ing;
2 Did we in our own strength con-fide, Our striv-ing would be los-ing,
3 And though this world, with dev-ils filled, Should threat-en to un-do us,
4 That word a-bove all earth-ly powers, No thanks to them, a-bid-eth;

Our help-er he a-mid the flood Of mor-tal ills pre-vail-ing.
Were not the right man on our side, The man of God's own choos-ing.
We will not fear, for God hath willed His truth to tri-umph through us.
The Spir-it and the gifts are ours Through him who with us sid-eth.

For still our an-cient foe Doth seek to work us woe; His craft and power are
Dost ask who that may be? Christ Je-sus, it is he; Lord Sab-a-oth his
The prince of dark-ness grim, We trem-ble not for him; His rage we can en-
Let goods and kin-dred go, This mor-tal life al-so; The bod-y they may

great, And armed with cru-el hate, On earth is not his e-qual.
name, From age to age the same, And he must win the bat-tle.
dure, For lo, his doom is sure: One lit-tle word shall fell him.
kill; God's truth a-bid-eth still, His king-dom is for-ev-er. A-men.

SOURCE OF TEXT: Klug's *Gesangbuch*, Wittenberg, 1529. SOURCE OF TRANSLATION: W. H. Furness's *Gems of German Verse*, Philadelphia, 1853; and later the same year in Hedge and Huntington's *Hymns for the Church of Christ*, Boston. SOURCE OF TUNE: Klug's *Gesangbuch*, Wittenberg, 1529.

From *A Survey of Christian Hymnody*, William Jensen Reynolds. Holt, Rinehart and Winston, Inc., New York, 1963, page 156.

Music was ubiquitous in the lonely cabins of the frontier (Courtesy of The Bettmann Archive, Inc., New York).

Hymnals provide indices for each of these kinds of information: Index of Authors, Translators, Sources; Index of Composers, Sources, Arrangers; Metrical Index (this lists all the tunes by meter, enabling tune interchange); Index of Tunes, and Index of First Lines.

Study Procedures

1. Howard Hanson has written a *Cherubic Hymn* for orchestra and chorus. This work uses a Byzantine text. Compare the text to other hymn texts in this chapter, and decide why the composition was so named.
2. Benjamin Britten has written a composition entitled *Hymn to the Virgin*. Why is this a hymn? What style of hymn writing does it favor? How is it similar to the Hanson composition? How is it different?
3. Compare a Byzantine or Hebrew hymn, a Luther hymn, and a Wesley hymn. In your own words, describe the musical differences.
4. Lukas Foss and Charles Ives have both written "Psalms." How do these compare to hymns? Could they carry the name of hymn? Why?

Bibliography—Chapter 5

Bailey, Albert Edward, *The Gospel in Hymns.* New York: Charles Scribner and Sons, 1950.
Benson, Louis F., *The English Hymn.* Richmond, Va.: John Knox Press, 1962.
Ferguson, Donald N., *A History of Musical Thought.* New York: F. S. Crofts and Co., 1938.

HUGHES, DOM ANSELM, ed., *New Oxford History of Music, Vol. II.* New York: Oxford University Press, 1954.

LANG, PAUL HENRY, ed., *Music in Western Civilization.* New York: W. W. Norton and Co., Inc., 1941.

REESE, GUSTAVE, *Music in the Middle Ages.* New York: W. W. Norton and Co., Inc., 1968.

REYNOLDS, WILLIAM JENSEN, *A Survey of Christian Hymnody.* New York: Holt, Rinehart and Winston, Inc., 1963.

SACHS, CURT, *The Rise of Music in the Ancient World.* New York: W. W. Norton and Co., Inc., 1943.

SCHOLES, PERCY, *The Puritans and Music.* London: Oxford University Press, 1934.

WELLESZ, EGON, *A History of Byzantine Music and Hymnography.* London: Oxford University Press, 1961.

Recordings—Chapter 5

A Mighty Fortress	Mormon Tabernacle Choir	Columbia MS-6162
A Mighty Fortress	Robert Shaw Chorale	Victor LSC-2199
Arias, Anthems, Chorales of American Musicians		Columbia ML-5427
Beverly Shea		Camden CAL-653
Britten: *Hymn to the Virgin*		Oiseau 60037
Buddhist Hymns and Chants		Folkways 4449
Byzantine Hymns		World Series S9102
Coptic Music		Folkways 8960
Faith of Our Fathers	Mormon Tabernacle Choir	Harvest 11370
Foss: *Psalms*		CRI S-123
Hanson: *Psalms*		Mercury 90429
Ives: *Psalms*		Columbia MS-7321
Lift Up Your Heads		Odeon CSD-3627
Lutheran Hour Hymns		Word 9003 9006 9023
Methodist Hymns		Pye CCL-40002
O for a Thousand Tongues to Sing		Wicks 832 WO-782
Onward Christian Soldiers	Mormon Tabernacle Choir	Harvest 11272
St. John Divine Hymns		Word 9009
Songs of Christian and Hebrew Faiths	Robert Shaw Chorale	Victor LSC-2760

Chapter 6

The Anthem and the Motet

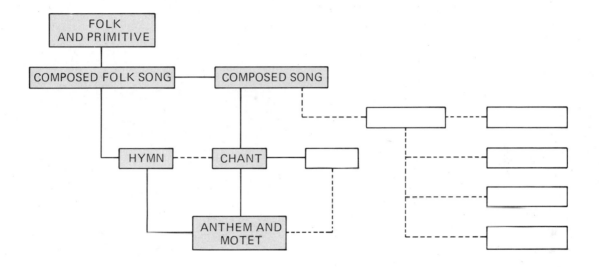

The anthem is a simple vocal form resulting directly from the consequences of the Reformation in England. This form did not develop directly from the people but grew as a response to the needs of the church at a time when changes were being made.

The anthem, then, is a religious form in music that is simple in structure and in musical content. Its purpose is not too different from the hymn, the praise of God, but it has almost always been the sole responsibility of the choir or a special group of singers or performers. The word comes from ant-hymn, which is a combination and contraction of antiphon and hymn. The antiphon was a versicle, a chant sung before and after psalms, while the hymn denoted a praise application to a more common base of participation and understanding.

Although the Reformation in England had been begun by Henry VIII, there were those about the throne who were determined not to let Henry's death deter them from fulfilling the intent of what the Reformation could mean. About six months after the coronation of the ten-year-old King Edward VI, a Royal Committee visited the principal churches in England making suggestions as to the conduct of the services.

Some of their statements requested that no more than two candles be lit at Mass, that bells be rung only before the service, that Latin processions be changed to English, that robes of the clerics be discontinued, and (amazing enough) that the cathedral musicians be no longer required to tonsure their hair (shave the head).[1] Apparently musicians and hair have been associated for many years.

At one Cathedral, the Visiting Committee was most specific concerning music:

> The choir shall from henceforth sing or say no anthems of our Lady or other Saints, but only of our Lord, and them not in Latin; but choosing out the best and most sounding to Christian religion they shall turn the same into English, setting thereunto a plain and distinct note for every syllable one: they shall sing them and none other.

Although at first the concern was for a translation, this need not have troubled the church long, for many musicians rose to the challenge and supplied both anthems and services that did fit the English language well.

Even though the anthem seems to be a direct descendent from the motet,[2] from the first there were obvious differences and these differences stem from the Royal Injunction, so that anthems were rhythmically more obvious, containing more emphasis upon harmony, and syllabic with shorter phrases.

THE RENAISSANCE

The anthem developed in the latter part of the Renaissance period (1450–1600). Because it grew from this period, the new form could not help but take on some of the characteristics of its time. These stylistic qualities included more depth of expression in text and music, better balance of parts and form, development of artistic standards, clarity of lines, and greater pleasantness within the sound. Earlier attempts at harmony had often been uneven, irregular, and unbalanced, with the use of some intervals only as a technical rather than an expressive device.

Within the period of the Renaissance the harmonic structure of musical compositions more and more took on the qualities listed above, so that many of the compositions from this period do not sound antique but as if they had been composed only a few years ago. Consequently, much of the music of this period is still sung in the churches, high schools, and colleges with a considerable amount of interest.

---

[1] *Music and the Reformation in England, 1549–1660*, Peter Le Huray. Oxford University Press, 1967, page 8.
[2] A choral composition, most prominent in the Middle Ages and Renaissance, usually unaccompanied, with a Latin text and intended to be sung at Vespers, one of the offices.

THE VERSE ANTHEM

Although the anthem originated during the reign of Henry VIII, it was abandoned during the Cromwell period. However, during the Restoration it made
a re-entry with greater pomp and emphasis because Charles II, recently influenced
by the music of the French court, was interested in church music that offered
greater variety in form and musical sound. Weinandt and Young report the
remarks of a Thomas Tudway concerning the new King:

> His Majesty who was a brisk, & Airy Prince, comeing to the Crown in the
> Flow'r & vigour of his Age, was soon, if I may so say, tyr'd with the Grave and
> Solemn way, And Order'd the Composers of this Chappell to add Symphonys
> &c with Instruments to their Anthems . . . .[3]

But the instrumental musicians were not of the same training in churchly
matters as the customs had so diligently prescribed for the choir boys and men.
In the same text we find a humorous incident related as a result of bringing
town musicians into the gallery to play the anthems:

> On one occasion, through some misunderstanding with the vicar, the bands-
> men, although present in church, refused to play, and the vicar, who was be-
> tween eighty and ninety years of age, asked from the pulpit, "Are you going
> to play or not?" To which Pennicott answered for himself and the bands-
> men, "No!" The parson rejoined, "Well, then, I'm not going to preach," and
> forthwith came down out of the pulpit in a rage. Later, after the service was
> over and the parson walked down the village street, the band came out with
> their instruments and gave him "horn-fair" or "rough music" to the vicarage.
> On another occasion, the same band went out on strike. As they would not
> play at the service of the church, the vicar called upon all the inns in the
> village, and was successful in "freezing the taps"—that is, the landlords agreed
> not to serve any of the band with liquor. The bandsmen retorted by white-
> washing the vicar's windows from top to bottom of the house during the
> night.[4]

Despite these local problems, many of the anthems composed during the
formative period used an instrumental accompaniment, and to lend vocal variety
some of the text was sung by a soloist, preceding or alternating with a choral
section. In some of the earliest of verse anthems the choral parts merely repeated some of the text which the soloist had just sung.

One of the finest examples of a verse anthem is by Orlando Gibbons, a
composer of high stature whose name we shall hear again in connection with the
madrigal. His verse anthem entitled *This Is the Record of John* was composed
in 1623.

---

[3] *The Anthem in England and America*, Elwyn A. Wienandt and Robert H. Young. Free
Press, New York, 1970, page 45.
[4] *Ibid.*, page 129.

This Is the Record of John

In this verse anthem the tenor sings three solos interspersed with a choral statement by the choir. Each time the choir sings some of the same words just sung by the soloist.

The tenor solos followed by the choral portions give a balance through variety; the very nature of the words almost insists that they be sung with expressiveness; note also that the pleasant chordal sounds establish a different effect than chant. Adapted from the music of the French court, the style of accompaniment is typical of this Restoration period.

The text for this anthem is given so that you may follow the singing more easily and comprehend its form:

SOLOIST: This is the record of John, when the Jews sent the Priests and Levites from Jerusalem to ask him: Who art thou? And he confessed and denied not, and said plainly: I am not the Christ.

CHOIR: And he confessed and denied not, and said plainly: I am not the Christ.

SOLOIST: And they asked him: Who art thou then? Art thou Elias? And he said: I am not. Art thou the prophet? And he answered: No.

CHOIR: And they asked him: Who art thou then? Art thou Elias? And he said: I am not. Art thou the prophet? And he answered: No.

SOLOIST: Then said they unto him: Who art thou that we may give an answer unto them that sent us? What sayest thou of thyself? And he said: I am the voice of him that crieth in the wilderness: make straight the way of the Lord.

CHOIR: And he said: I am the voice of him that crieth in the wilderness: make straight the way of the Lord.

Study Procedures

1. As you listen, note that the first response and second solo are shorter than the other two, thus giving a kind of balance that we will notice in larger forms at a later time in musical history.
2. Compare this to Handel's treatment of some of these lines in the oratorio *Messiah* (Tenor Solo 2).

THE FULL ANTHEM

Exhibiting a greater continuity from the motet, the full anthem was also prominent during the formative days. As the title explains, this was a selection for the entire choir with no change in texture throughout. So that you may compare the full anthem with the verse anthem, listen to another Gibbons anthem entitled *O Lord, Increase My Faith.*

O Lord, Increase My Faith

This text gives the impression that it could have been part of the liturgy of the church, and yet we know that anthems were almost always included in the service without becoming a part of the liturgy. Like the earlier motet, this anthem is unaccompanied and would give a variety to the service through its choral style that would not be found in the singing of chant, the singing of hymns, or the reading of the prayers or scripture. This follows closely the concept that music should be syllabic and not highly melismatic.

> O, Lord, increase my faith, strengthen me and confirm me in Thy true faith; endue me with wisdom, charity, and patience, in all my adversity, sweet Jesus, say Amen.

Study Procedures

1. Compare the musical qualities found in the two anthems by Gibbons. Which of the two do you prefer? Why? State your reasons in musical terms.
2. The anthem is an outgrowth of the Flemish motet. Prepare a report on the motet of the sixteenth century showing its relationship to the anthem.

THE ACCENT ON THE ANTHEM

As the eighteenth century approached less emphasis was placed upon the service in the Chapel Royal and similar cathedrals throughout England. Anthems were written during the next hundred or more years for the parish church and the volunteer musician who was not as skillful as those of the cathedral churches. Poor material was not necessarily the result. Although poor and dull anthems were written, material of quality was also available. It did mean that the organ was almost always the accompaniment, since instrumental accompaniments were rarely possible; since soloists were not as accomplished, more emphasis was placed upon the choral sound; and lastly, that the melodies were simple so that material could be more quickly and easily read.

The surest method of writing assimilatory choral music was to use a known hymn as a basis for the words and melody. This type of anthem grew in popularity throughout England, Protestant Europe, and the United States.

TWO HYMN ANTHEMS

The two hymn anthems chosen for study are from early American history. The first is written by a colonial composer, Daniel Read. Born in November 1757, he was Connecticut's most famous musician during his lifetime. Although there are only six of his anthems extant (these six were published seventeen times before 1800), he is best known for his collections of psalms, hymns, and anthems, for he was a publisher and bookbinder as well as an operator of a general store.

This anthem was written to the hymn text of "While Shepherds Watched Their Flocks by Night," and is a type of fuguing tune.[5] The second hymn-anthem is based on the chorale "O Sacred Head Now Wounded." Chorale is a German word for hymn, and members of religious faiths who are tied closely with the German language often use that term instead of hymn.

This hymn text has been ascribed to St. Bernard of Clairvaux, who lived 1091–1153. The most famous tune for this hymn was composed by Hassler about 1600, but the best-known arrangement is attributed to J. S. Bach, used by him in his *St. Matthew Passion*. Despite the credentialed background of this hymn it is doubtful if Herbst knew of Bach's use, since Bach's music was not well-known outside of a particular part of Germany until the middle 1800s.

Johannes Herbst, composer of this hymn-anthem, came to America in 1786 to serve as minister of a Moravian church in Lancaster, Pennsylvania. Being of German heritage, this chorale would have been well-known to him as a young man. The Moravians were knowledgeable musicians and their churches reflected this in many ways. Most obvious in this example are the quality of the vocal writing, the variety in the instrumental interludes, and the method of handling repeats. The words of this hymn are the same as those found in many hymn books today.

> *O Sacred Head, now wounded*
> *   With grief and shame weighed down,*
> *Now scornfully surrounded*
> *   With thorns, Thine only crown;*
> *O Sacred Head, what glory,*
> *   What bliss, till now was Thine!*
> *Yet though despised and gory,*
> *   I joy to call Thee mine.*

Study Procedures

1. Which of the two American anthems discussed in the text do you believe is of a higher musical quality? Upon what do you base your judgment?
2. Listen to other early American anthems by Billings, Antes, Michael, or Leinbach. Do these have similarities to the Read and Herbst? What would be those similarities as you hear them?

---

[5] During the latter half of the eighteenth century, William Billings, America's first professional musician, composed in what he called a "fuguing style" and has been remembered for it. Other musicians, either hearing of the style or having heard some of Billings's compositions, often copied the effect which requires the voices to make quick repeated entrances singing short phrases.

3. Compare these early American anthems with those by Gibbons. How would you describe the differences?

THE NINETEENTH AND TWENTIETH CENTURIES

The verse anthem, full anthem, and hymn-anthem served the churches well no matter what the time or period. Although many were increasingly evangelistic, most of the anthems followed the same characteristics of the original ones: mostly syllabic, easily moving melodies that were for the most part quickly learned and sung, and modestly moving parts in the harmony. Dependent upon the occasion, instrumental accompaniments were added when the composer believed the situation warranted it.

Although evangelism and the romantic period brought more poor quality anthems into the churches than before, some composers were able to blend the two concepts and produce anthems of high quality.

At the time that Charles Wood composed "Hail, Gladdening Light," he was more influenced by the motet and the higher forms of poetry as a result of the Oxford Movement than by the gospel song. This anthem is a three-part form, just as the verses indicate. Notice the tone painting, which is a musical coloration imitating the color impressions of the words. The chantlike sounds that appear in the first verse on the words "Holiest of Holies" contrast the bright, brilliant sounds in the choir on the first three words of the anthem. In the second verse the music is much more quiet and subdued, equating the text. The third verse of the poem has music that repeats from the first verse, with some alterations during the last two lines in order to bring the composition to a brilliant close.

Hail, gladdening light, of His pure glory poured,
Who is th' Immortal Father,
Heavenly, Blest, Holiest of Holies,
Jesu Christ, our Lord.

Now we are come to the sun's hour of rest,
The lights of evening round us shine,
We hymn the Father, Son and Holy Spirit Divine.

Worthiest art Thou at all times to be sung
With undefiled-tongue
Son of our God, Giver of life alone,
Therefore in all the world
Thy glories, Lord, they own.

Creation, Prologue (Ussachevsky)

Motets have had too varied and complex a history to be covered fully in this text. Suffice it to say that not all of them were of a religious nature or focused on the Christian religion. Consequently, contemporary composers have a wide background upon which to build when writing for a twentieth century choral ensemble.

This contemporary work features four choirs and an accompaniment of electronically recorded sounds. The text is taken from two sources, neither of which is sung in English, but both concern themselves with the creation of the world as described by two divergent sources.

The oldest record of the creation, the *Enuma Elish*, dates from the writing of the Assyrians about the eighteenth century B.C. Written in a Babylonian dialect known as Akkadian, the title comes from the first two words of the text, "When above." Some of the early lines are used as a basis for the Ussachevsky composition.

When above the heaven had not yet been named,
And below the earth had not yet been called by a name;
When Apsu primeval, their begetter,
Mummu, and Tiamat, she who gave birth to them all,
Still mingled their waters together,
And no pasture land had been formed and not even a reed marsh
    was to be seen;
When none of the other gods had been brought into being,
When they had not yet been called by their names,
And their destinies had not yet been fixed,
At that time were the gods created with them.[6]

This epic poem relates the story of the divine parents, Apsu and Tiamat, who lived alone in the world with their only son, Mummu. Apsu was the primeval sweet-water ocean, and Tiamat the salt water ocean, while Mummu was the mist rising from the two and hovering over them. These three mingled as one and contained the elements from which, later, the universe was made.

The second early (A.D. 10) non-Christian record of the creation used in the composition comes from the beginning lines of the *Metamorphoses* of Ovid, the well-known Roman poet. One initial paragraph comes from a free translation of the famous poem by Frank Justus Miller:

Before the sea was, and the lands, and the sky that hangs over all, the face of Nature showed alike in her whole round, which state have men called chaos; a rough, unordered mass of things, nothing at all save lifeless bulk and warring seeds of ill-matched elements heaped in one. No sun as yet shone forth upon the world, nor did the waxing moon renew her slender horns; not yet did the earth hang poised by her own weight in the circumambient air, nor had the ocean stretched her arms along the far reaches of the lands. And, though there was both land and sea and air, no one could tread that land, or

---

[6] *The Babylonian Genesis*, Alexander Heidel. The University of Chicago Press, Chicago, 1951, page 18.

swim that sea; and the air was dark. No form of things remained the same; all objects were at odds, for within one body cold things strove with hot, and moist with dry, soft things with hard, things having weight with weightless things.[7]

Four choirs antiphonally (in alternation) use parts of the above texts to portray a musical interpretation of the creation.

Study Procedures

1. Why would a composer choose to use antiphonal choirs for such a composition? Why would electronic sounds make an appropriate accompaniment?
2. Find a brief definition of motet which you believe would be appropriate for this contemporary composition. How does it differ in general characteristics from an early motet of the Renaissance period? How is it similar?

THE CAROL ANTHEM

The *carol* is a name given a devotional song of joyful character for a special day or occasion. Since carols are often sung at Christmas in the church along with hymns, it is only natural that these would be used as the basis for some anthems. "Hilariter" is a contemporary Easter anthem based on a carol, and because it is such a special day in the celebration of the church, history suggests that an instrumental accompaniment be used.

The wording of the text is somewhat old-fashioned; in keeping with this, the music at times reacquaints us with the extended antiphonic use of the alleluia, and some older sounds of chant and harmony as if we had left the period of organum only a century ago.

The form of the anthem is AABA with obvious contrasts in the center section.

The whole bright world rejoices now, Hilariter;
The birds do sing on every bough, Alleluia.

Then shout beneath the racing skies, Hilariter;
To him who rose that we might rise, Alleluia.

And all you living things make praise, Hilariter;
He guideth you on all your ways, Alleluia.

He Father, Son, and Holy Ghost, Hilariter!
Our God most high, our joy and boast, Alleluia.

---

[7] *Metamorphoses*, Ovid, tr. by Frank Justus Miller. G. P. Putnam's Sons, New York, 1916, page 3.

Thousands of anthems have been written, many by some of the greatest composers. The church was most fortunate that at the time of the inception of the anthem writers such as Byrd, Tye, Morley, Gibbon, Locke, and other quality composers deigned to guide and establish a norm. But though great composers have contributed some literature to this form, in all fairness it should be stated that most of the anthems have been written by lesser composers, and in many instances the anthem has "made" the composer.

The anthem takes on added significance when one realizes that this simple form supplies much of the musical literature for high school and college choirs.

Study Procedures

1. Listen to other anthems of the twentieth century by Shaw, Dickinsen, Willan, or Vaughan Williams. How do these compare to the Wood? Select one which you prefer and state why.
2. Listen to a Renaissance motet by Josquin, Lasso, A. Gabrieli, Palestrina, Morales, or Byrd, and compare its musical characteristics to one of the anthems.

THE NATIONAL ANTHEM

A patriotic national anthem probably is better known than many religious anthems. But the question arises whether the term anthem is the appropriate term for a national song.

There is considerable human pride in both country and religion. In times of strife and national concern, whether it be war, great elation, or mourning of a dead hero, the feeling of devotion to the nation is not unlike the devotion, reverence, and pride that one feels for his God, church, or religion.

Considering that a national anthem is sung by all the people and not by a special group, that most national anthems are verselike or strophic, that they are not elongated, and that they have a style which is people-centered, it would seem more appropriate to call these songs national hymns.

Paul Nettl, in his book *National Anthems,* states that the hymnlike character of national songs belonged much more to nations of some fifty years ago or earlier, while the newer nations have chosen songs of a more military or marchlike character. This being the case, perhaps even the term hymn is not fitting for some patriotic songs.

Study Procedure

Listen to national anthems of Great Britain, Canada, the United States, and France. Notice the hymn qualities in each. Which is most hymnlike? Why?

Bibliography—Chapter 6

DANIEL, RALPH T., *The Anthem in New England Before 1800*. Evanston, Ill.: North-western University Press, 1966.

DICKINSON, EDWARD, *Music in the History of the Western Church*. New York: Haskell House Publishers, Ltd., 1969.

ETHERINGTON, CHARLES L., *Protestant Worship Music*. New York: Holt, Rinehart and Winston, 1965.

HEIDEL, ALEXANDER, *The Babylonian Genesis*. Chicago: University of Chicago Press, 1951.

LE HURAY, PETER, *Music and the Reformation in England, 1549–1660*. New York: Oxford University Press, 1967.

MILLER, FRANK JUSTUS, tr., *The Metamorphoses of Ovid*. New York: G. P. Putnam's Sons, 1929.

NETTL, PAUL, *National Anthems*. New York: Storm Publishers, 1952.

STEVENSON, ROBERT, *Protestant Church Music in America*. New York: W. W. Norton and Co., Inc., 1966.

WIENANDT, ELWYN A., *Choral Music of the Church*. New York: The Free Press, 1966.

WIENANDT, ELWYN A., and ROBERT H. YOUNG, *The Anthem in England and America*. New York: The Free Press, 1970.

Recordings—Chapter 6

Antes	*Go, Congregation, Go*	Col ML-5427
Billings	*Easter Anthem*	Vic LM-1201
Byrd	*Christ Rising Again*	Vic LM-136
Dickinsen	*The Shepherds' Story*	Par CS-7003
Richard Dirksen	*Hilariter*	Wicks 832 WO 782
Farrant	*A Call to Remembrance*	Par CS-7002
Gibbons	*O Lord, Increase My Faith*	Allegro 3038
	The Eyes of All Wait Upon Thee	" "
	Almighty and Everlasting God	" "
	O God, the King of Glory	" "
	This Is the Record of John	" "
Handel	*Coronation Anthem*	Cap. G-7141
	Great Shepherd of a Loyal Flock	Wicks SHC-42366
Herbst	*O Sacred Head Now Wounded*	Col ML-5427
Leinbach	*Hosanna*	" " "
Leisring	*Let All Ye Sons and Daughters Sing*	Par CS-7002
	Lift Up Your Heads	Vic LM-136
Michael	*Hearken! Stay Close to Jesus*	Col ML-5427
Peter	*It Is a Precious Thing*	" " "
Praetorius	*Behold, Thou Hast Made My Days*	Vic LM-6029
	Wie schön leuchtet der Morgenstern	" " "
Daniel Read	*While Shepherds Watched Their Flocks*	Decca DL-710073
Martin Shaw	*Fanfare for Christmas Day*	Par CS-7003
Stennet	*'Tis Finished*	Vic LM-1201
Tallis	*Hear the Voice and Prayer of Thy Servant*	Haydn Society 7-9101

Vaughan Williams	*Lord, Thou Hast Been Our Refuge*	Key No. 14
Weelkes	*Hosanna to the Son of David*	Angel 35381
Willan	*The Three Kings*	Par CS-7003
Wood	*Hail, Gladdening Light*	Angel 35381

Section C *Emphasis Upon Artistic Expression*

Chapter 7

The Art Song

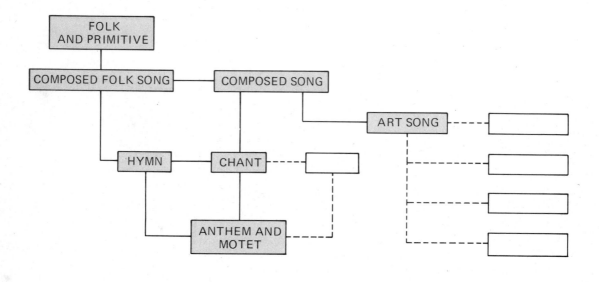

As stated in the first three chapters, song sprang up with every civilization and has persisted through the ages with each nationality, ethnic group, or geographic region adding or protecting distinctive aspects. As song matured a certain quantity gradually became somewhat more sophisticated and refined.

About the beginning of the nineteenth century a quality of song developed that was of such a high level that it became known as *art song*. Its unique characteristics are to be discussed shortly.

Musical events had so evolved that the art song was almost inevitable. Some contributing factors were the beginning of the Romantic period, the invention of the piano, Viennese life, the youth of Franz Schubert, the past history of the song, and the romantic poets. Without evaluating them qualitatively, let us examine each in turn.

THE HISTORY OF THE SONG

Song had reached a high level during the latter part of the 1700s. Many composers had written for the voice, particularly in connection with the church, the salon, or the stage. Most notably Mozart, Beethoven, Haydn, and Handel had written meritorious songs; but for the most part their greatest vocal efforts serviced larger forms and simple songs did not receive major emphasis, so that only rarely were they outstanding. Gradually, song had pushed itself up through the musical world from a mundane emotional outlet or an uncouth piece of entertainment to a point where major composers had been attracted to it, but not as an individual art form. One last step remained to be taken.

INVENTION OF THE PIANO

A new keyboard instrument had been invented by Cristofori about 1720 and given the name of pianoforte (more precisely, gravicembalo col piano e forte), which called attention to the ability of this instrument to play both soft and loud. This quality had been an impossibility with its predecessor, the harpsichord. Beethoven had written for the piano and his sonatas indicate his demands for the new instrument and its ability to play nuances from loud to soft. However, it remained for Schubert to bring to the song this same ability, wherein the piano added obviously to the artistic effect. In the early 1800s Erard improved Cristofori's original key mechanism, enabling the performer to repeat the same pitch at a rapid rate. This improvement was of artistic benefit to Schubert and his concept of the accompaniment for the art song.

LIFE IN VIENNA

Vienna had been a cultural center for many years; in fact, it had become known as the center of the world of music. During the latter part of the eighteenth century cultural life reached a new high. Sir William Henry Hadow, editor of the *Oxford History of Music,* has stated that if asked to name the three greatest artistic periods of history, he would cite, first, Periclean Athens, next, Elizabethan England, and third, the Vienna of the second half of the eighteenth century and the first quarter of the nineteenth. It was during this celebrated time that Schubert entered into the musical life of Vienna, the era that knew of Beethoven's last string quartets, his mighty *Missa solemnis,* his *Ninth Symphony;* it knew also of Weber's *Der Freischütz* and *Euryanthe,* as well as Rossini's *L'Italiana in Algeri;* Shakespeare was played regularly in one or more of the theaters, while others constantly played new and older repertoire; light music was a constant entertainment in the music halls, salons, homes, restaurants, and cafes. As one observer noted, during the afternoons and evenings it was an almost impossible task to find a chair at a table in any restaurant in the city; people seemed to have so much money that social life was constant. In a world such as this the song was almost always evident, and there was a most fertile ground for a new type of vocal artistry.

THE ROMANTIC PERIOD

Being dissatisfied with the established methods and approaches to literary forms, the shallow content, and superficial meanings, the young literary figures of the late 1700s instigated a relook at the Middle Ages with its accent upon knights, maidenhood in flower, and great deeds to be done, with all their religious and romantic implications. Here was the idealism of youth stating that the contemporary world had too many complications that could not be remedied by the single person; consequently, a look at the past would ignite within his soul a realization that would make the present more meaningful. This was a romantic way of perceiving life, and the term was adopted by the literary people of the time to signify their longing for something nonexistent, whether it be the good life, ideal love, or union with nature.

Nonetheless, Romanticism did not mean the end of Classical concepts, since the former incorporated some of the ideas of Classicism along with another school of thought from that time: *Sturm und Drang* (Storm and Stress). Romanticism, being the most individualistic, explored the subconscious and unconscious. With a broad appeal to the intellectual as well as the unsophisticated, Romanticism made an impression that has yet not been forgotten.

In the field of music composers turned to the obvious expression of their personal emotions or inner desires, hoping that such expression would awaken similar feelings within the listener. In order to express themselves more freely, forms that had been established during the Classical period were stretched, reappropriated, or even disregarded. Another method of exerting this expression was through a description of nature, with many lesser musicians attempting a direct imitation of it. Because of the emphasis on the longing for that which did not exist, much of the music was melancholy, but through this melancholy came a release or a satisfaction that brought enjoyment. Music was so successful at describing these longings and at the same time sharpening the imagination of the emotions, that it was referred to as the true Romantic art.

Some of the more obvious characteristics of the Romantic period were:

1. An emphasis on emotion or expression of the inner self.
2. Less attention to convention or form, although form was not completely forgotten.
3. A longing for the nonexistent.
4. An examination of personal thought and feeling.
5. An attention to nature.

6. A satisfaction through the melancholy.
7. An attempt to have art bring satisfaction to every level of perception.

THE ROMANTIC POET

Januslike, Goethe stands surveying the Classical and Romantic periods. Although considered the outstanding figure of the first, he was truly the inspiration for much literature and poetry of the latter. Not only was Goethe an indirect contributor to literature of the Romantic period, but many artists and professionals found within his work an inspiration which brought into existence a number of ideas which were significant for the times. It has been said that song will follow if poetry will lead. Poetry did lead by presenting a large body of high quality works from a number of poets who were honored or respected. Music rose to the occasion.

THE YOUNG SCHUBERT

Schubert, being born in a suburb of Vienna in 1797, saw the city at its peak of intellectual and artistic creativity. It was soon to be the center of political discussions that postdated the Napoleonic Wars. Musically, its influence was greatly enriching for a person with talent, and so it attracted many musicians of

A Schubert evening with his friends (Archives of the Austrian National Library).

diverse types.   The Romantic movement in literature was at its height, and poetic expression by young artists throughout Germany was the norm.   Looking back, it seems Schubert was elected to amalgamate these forces, bringing Romantic ideals, poetic understanding, and sympathy to create the art song.   Joining other young artists in renouncing old forms and procedures, Schubert placed an emphasis upon the song that had not been there before, so that serious composers thereafter could not but consider his ideals and standards.   The song was always a popular vehicle of the people, but in addition, it was now to develop an artistic side which would express the highest emotions of man in an artistic manner, conveying across the ages those never-to-be-forgotten feelings of one generation to another.

THE ART SONG

Song had been artistic for many years, but Schubert was the first to see those possibilities which in the end created the art song.   The characteristics that Romantic composers realized may be listed in seven categories:

1. The accompaniment describes, assists, and furthers the meaning of the text.   Schubert, and other art song composers to follow him, placed considerable emphasis on the accompaniment and its ability to portray the meaning of the song along with the text and the voice.   Consequently, Schubert's accompaniments were more descriptive than those used by earlier composers.   As you listen to the following art songs, listen particularly to the accompaniment and how it attempts to capture the mood and meaning of the words.   Do not mistake this as literally trying to paint a musical picture, since this can become cute, clever, humorous at the wrong time, or even cheap.   Rather, the intent is beyond the immediate.   The composer finds those particular sounds which will arouse for any number of listeners the specific meaning that the words may have.   Consequently, the music must not paint a specific picture but merely suggest that which will bring a determinative meaning to a large number of people.

2. The melodic line must add to the meaning of the words.   Not only must the vocal line of the art song be attractive, but also the emotional impact of this melodic line should enhance the words.   A composer attempts to balance the melody with the text so that neither overshadows the other.   A clever or attractive tune quickly whistled or hummed may be of shallow content or call too much attention to itself.   Most art songs have an appeal that leads to the listener's satisfaction, but rarely from one hearing; usually, repeated hearings bring its balance of beauty into emotional perspective.

3. The text usually has a quality of its own.   Many art songs use a text which was famous before being used by the composer.   In fact, some of the verses were written by outstanding poets of the day, and in some cases the poet's reputation exceeded that of the composer.   For example, when Schubert set Goethe's words for "The Erlking," the latter was unimpressed, for he believed

that his poetry was in no way enhanced by the music. At that time Goethe's poem was the more popular, but history has altered this. In a few instances the text is of modest quality; more often the text has commended itself to the composer because he sees within it an opportunity to forge an artistic item based on the quality of the poetry.

4. The form of the music must fit the emotional effect conveyed by the text. Most folk songs or songs of a modest quality are strophic. Although some art songs are strophic ("Who Is Sylvia?" for example), frequently the form is more complex. When through-composed, no repeats of the music exist, although some melodic fragments could be repeated to unify the composition. Uppermost is the desire of the composer to express the text in a meaningful manner. To do this he may choose any form which his artistic sensitivity believes to best express the emotion and meaning of the text. The decision by the composer on this point often will determine the final quality of the composition.

5. A balance must be achieved between poetry, accompaniment, and singing. The vocal line, being the main conveyor of the text, should not be so outstanding or placed in such a position that the accompaniment cannot add its function; nor should the text be hidden so that the meaning cannot come through to the listener. In some folk songs the melody is of little importance while the text is so overemphasized that it remains only a "good" song no matter how artistically performed.

6. The song must be superior vocal music. The vocal interpreter cannot make the most of a song unless the composer has been attentive to details of vowel and consonant placement, the flow of the text, and the length of phrases in connection with breathing. In an art song these three items must be carefully attended to, so that the singer may have an opportunity to interpret it in a manner befitting the composition. This brings us to the last point.

7. The art song is almost always sung in the native language, although there are occasional translations. Consequently, on some art song records you will find the same artist singing in German, French, Hebrew, Swedish, and English. The reason should be obvious: the composer wished to maintain the exact subtle meanings of the original poem, the poetic word flow, the nuances of the language of the poet, and it was these that he set to music and tried to balance with the music of the vocal line and accompaniment. The art song is such a delicate work of art that usually a translation disturbs this balance, so that an artistic work no longer exists. It may be a good song, but the artistry is missing.

FIVE SCHUBERT ART SONGS

As just discussed, strophic form is most often used in the simple song, yet it is occasionally used by art song composers. Two attractive songs in this form are discussed below.

It was rare for Schubert to use anything other than a text by a German poet. However, a friend of his had translated a Shakespearean poem into German, and since Shakespeare was a favorite of the playgoing public of Vienna at the time it is not unusual that Schubert would have considered this love poem attractive.

The tune moves easily and simply until near the end of each verse, when two large leaps in the voice, one upward, the other downward, focus the intensity. As the voice reaches its highest point, the piano plays similar leaps at a very low pitch. Together these bring a climax to each verse.

The text for each art song is given. Do not read only the English, and do not only read the poems. A suggested procedure is to listen to the song following the original text. On a second hearing, follow the original and simultaneously read the translated text. In this manner you will be able to capture some of the nuances of text and music as well as the meaning.

(William Shakespeare, 1564–1616)

"An Silvia"	"To Silvia"
Was ist Silvia, saget an,	*Who is Silvia? What is she,*
Das sie die weite Flur preist?	*That all our swains commend her?*
Schön und zart seh ich sie nahn,	*Hold, fair, and wise is she,*
Auf Himmelsgunst und Spur weist,	*The heavens such grace did lend her,*
Dass ihr alles untertan.	*That she might admired be.*
Ist sie schön und gut dazu?	*Is she kind as she is fair?*
Reiz lebt wie milde Kindheit;	*For beauty lives with kindness;*
Ihrem Aug eilt Amor zu,	*Love doth to her eyes repair,*
Dort heilt er seine Blindheit,	*To help him of his blindness;*
Und verweilt in süsser Ruh.	*And, being help'd, inhabits there.*
Darum Silvia, tön, O Sang,	*Then to Silvia, let us sing,*
Der holden Silvia Ehren;	*That Silvia is excelling;*
Jeden Reiz besiegt sie lang,	*She excels each mortal thing*
Den Erde kann gewähren:	*Upon the dull earth dwelling.*
Kränze ihr und Seitendklang.	*To her let us garlands bring.*

The text for a second strophic song was written by Franz von Schober, the poet, a young contemporary of Schubert's. This little tune has the voice skipping downward in what would appear to be awkward intervals; however, these intervals fit the text so well that they appear to enhance it and thus become attractive. The climax of each verse arrives when the voice climbs gradually to the highest note of the song.

(Franz Schober, 1798–1883)

"An die Musik"	"To Music"
Du holde Kunst, in wie viel grauen Stunden,	*O lovely art, in those many bleak hours*
Wo mich des Lebens wilder Kreis um strickt,	*When life's concerns surround me,*
Hast du mein Herz zu warmer Lieb' entzünden,	*You have brought love to my heart*
Hast mich in eine bess're Welt entrückt.	*Or opened vistas of other worlds.*

Oft hat ein Seufzer, deiner Harf entflossen,
Ein süsser heiliger Akkord von dir,
Den Himmel bess'rer Zeiten mir erschlossen'
Du holde Kunst, ich danke dir dafür.

Often a sigh from your harp
Or a heavenly sound from you
Has unlocked new feelings or good times,
O lovely Art, I thank you.

"Gretchen at the Spinning Wheel," Schubert's first successful song, written in 1814 when he was 17, comes from the works of a most famous poet of the time, Goethe, who had taken the old German Faust fable and made of it a poetic masterpiece.

This composition not only has a spinning type of accompaniment but it also is built so that one almost believes that the form is repetitious; yet Schubert always leads us in another direction. Short phrases do repeat, but like Margaret in the song, her mind not on her spinning, Schubert leads the melodies in other directions also. The true unity of the piece is in the accompaniment figure which runs continuously through the song except for one break just beyond the midpoint. This break in the figure carries relief bringing a momentary contrast.

(Johann Goethe, 1749–1832)

"Gretchen am Spinnrade"

Meine Ruh ist hin,
Mein Herz ist schwer;
Ich finde sie nimmer
Und nimmermehr.

Wo ich ihn nicht hab',
Ist mir das Grab,
Die ganze Welt
Ist mir vergällt.

Mein armer Kopf
Ist mir verrückt,
Mein armer Sinn
Ist mir zerstückt.

Meine Ruh ist hin,
Mein Herz ist schwer;
Ich finde sie nimmer
Und nimmermehr.

Nach im nur schau' ich
Zum Fenster hinaus,
Nach ihm nur geh' ich
Aus dem Haus.

Sein hoher Gang,
Sein' edle Gestalt,
Seines Mundes Lächeln,
Seiner Augen Gewalt,

"Margaret at the Spinning Wheel"

My soul is troubled,
My heart is heavy,
I shall not find happiness
Ever again.

Unless he is mine
Life is worthless,
The whole world
Is bitter for me.

My poor head
Seems confused,
All thought
Is fragmented.

My soul is troubled,
My heart is heavy,
I shall not find happiness
Ever again.

I stand at the window
Just to see him,
I go from the house
To wait for him.

His manly walk,
His noble figure,
The smile on his mouth,
His pleasant eyes,

Und seiner Rede
Zauberfluss,
Sein Händedruck,
Und ach, sein Kuss!

His speech
Flows magically,
The touch of his hand,
And O, his kiss!

Meine Ruh ist hin,
Mein Herz ist schwer;
Ich finde sie nimmer
Und nimmermehr.

My soul is troubled,
My heart is heavy,
I shall not find happiness
Ever again.

Mein Busen drängt
Sich nach ihm hin;
Ach, dürft' ich fassen
Und halten ihn

I yearn
For him alone.
Ah, If I could
But hold him close

Und küssen ihn,
So wie ich wollt',
An seinen Küssen
Vergehen sollt!

And kiss him
As I wish,
And as we kiss,
Know it is forever.

Meine Ruh ist hin,
Mein Herz ist schwer.

My soul is troubled,
My heart is heavy.

"In Springtime" is a slightly more complex form. Schubert uses two main thematic ideas, but keeps changing them as needed to fit the text. The form of the song (A B A' B a B ending) is given additional variety by the number of times Schubert moves the tonal center. Although this is an obvious characteristic of the Romantic period and of the art song in particular, in this song the tonal center changes five times within the first phrase, which must be a type of record for any composer of that time. For the listener the most obvious change occurs as the main theme enters for the third time; here the song obviously moves into the minor.

(Ernst Schulze, 1789–1817)

"Im Frühling"

Still sitz ich an der Hügels Hang,
    Der Himmel ist so klar,
Das Lüftchen spielt im grünen Thal,
Wo ich beim ersten Frühlingstrahl
    Einst, ach! so glücklich war.

Wo ich an ihrer Seite ging
    So traulich und so nah,
Und tief im dunkeln Felsenquell
Den schönen Himmel blau und hell
    Und sie im Himmel sah.

Sieh, wie der bunte Frühling schon
    Aus Knosp und Blüthe blickt!
Nicht alle Blüthen sind mir gleich,
Am liebsten pflückt' ich von dem Zweig
    Von welchem sie gepflückt.

"In Spring"

Quietly I sit on the sloping hill,
    The sky so clear;
A gentle breeze plays in the green valley
Where I, during earlier springtimes,
    Had been so happy.

It was there I walked beside her
    So intimate and so near,
And deep within the dark, rocky spring
Was reflected the beautiful bright, blue sky
    And her image in heaven.

See, how the colorful spring already
    Appears with buds and blooms!
Not all blossoms seem alike to me;
I like best to pick from those branches
    From which she picked.

Denn Alles ist wie damals noch,
  Die Blumen, das Gefild,
Die Sonne scheint nicht minder hell,
Nicht minder freundlich schwimmt in Quell
  Das blaue Himmelsbild.

Es wandeln nur sich Will' und Wahn,
  Es wechseln Lust und Streit;
Vorüber flieht der Liebe Glück,
Und nur die Liebe bleibt zurück-
  Die Lieb' und, ach! das Leid.

O wär ich doch ein Vöglein nur
  Dort an dem Wiesenhang,
Dann blieb' ich auf den Zweigen hier
Und sang ein süsses Lied von ihr
  Den ganzen Sommer lang.

For all seems as before—
  The flowers, the meadows,
The sun shines just as brightly;
The blue reflections of the sky
  Swim no less clearly in the spring.

One's desires and dreams change,
  And pleasures become anguish;
The happiness of love disappears
And only the love remains,
  The love, and yes, the grief.

O! If I were a bird
  There on the meadow.
I would remain on these branches
And sing a sweet song of her
  The whole summer long.

Our discussion of Schubert would not be complete without his most famous art song, "Erlkönig" ("The Erlking"). The words by Goethe tell the story of a father carrying his sick child in his arms on horseback. The fevered child sees the Erlking, and as every German child knows, if the King of the Elves touches him, he will die.

Schubert was challenged in this poem not only by the movement of the horse, but by the mood and voice of three characters, the father, the son, and the Erlking. Notice how the Erlking pleads his case near the beginning but becomes demanding near the end of the song; also, the child becomes more concerned as the journey continues. Schubert uses a running figure in the bass with two falling concluding tones to portray the ominous spirit of the text. This figure reoccurs throughout.

Almost an instant success for the 17-year-old Schubert, this song has been sung in thousands of concerts throughout the world by singers of many nationalities. It is through-composed.

(Johann Goethe, 1749–1832)

"Der Erlkönig"

Wer reitet so spät durch Nacht und Wind?
Es ist der Vater mit seinem Kind;
er hat den Knaben wohl in dem Arm,
er fasst ihn sicher, er hält ihn warm.

"Mein Sohn, was birgst du so bang dein
  Gesicht?"
"Siehst, Vater, du den Erlkönig nicht?
den Erlenkönig mit Kron' und Schweif?"
"Mein Sohn, es ist ein Nebelstreif."

"Du liebes Kind, komm, geh' mit mir!
gar schöne Spiele spiel' ich mit dir;
manch' bunte Blumen sind an dem Strand,
meine Mutter hat manch' gülden Gewand."

"The Erlking"

Who rides so late through night and wind?
It is the father with his child.
He holds the boy within his arm,
He clasps him tight, he keeps him warm.

"My son, why hide your face in fear?"

"See, father, the Erlking's near.
The Erlking with crown and wand."
"Dear son, 'tis but a misty cloud."

"Ah, sweet child, come with me!
Such pleasant games I'll play with thee!
Such pleasant flowers bloom in the field,
My mother has many a robe of gold."

"Mein Vater, mein Vater, und hörest du nicht
was Erlenkönig mir leise verspricht?"
"Sei ruhig, bleibe ruhig, mein Kind;
in dürren Blättern säuselt der Wind."

"Willst, feiner Knabe, du mit mir geh'n?
meine Töchter sollen dich warten schön;
meine Töchter führen den nächtlichen Reih'n
und wiegen und tanzen und singen dich ein."

"Mein Vater, mein Vater, und siehst du nicht
    dort
Erlkönigs Töchter am düstern Ort?"
"Mein Sohn, mein Sohn, ich seh' es genau.
es scheinen die alten Weiden so grau."

"Ich liebe dich, mich reizt deine schöne Gestalt;
und bist du nicht willig, so brauch' ich Gewalt."
"Mein Vater, mein Vater, jetzt fasst er mich an!
Erlkönig hat mir ein Leids gethan!"

Dem Vater grauset's, er reitet geschwind
er hält in Armen das ächzende Kind,
erreicht den Hof mit Müh' und Noth:
in seinen Armen das Kind war todt!

"Oh father, father, do you not hear
What the Erlking whispers in my ear?"
"Be still, my child, be calm;
'Tis but the withered leaves in the wind."

"My lovely boy, wilt go with me?
My daughters fair shall wait on thee,
My daughters nightly revels keep,
They'll sing and dance and rock thee to sleep."

"Oh father, father, see you not

The Erlking's daughters in yon dark spot?"
"My son, my son, the thing you see
Is only the old gray willow tree."

"I love thee, thy form enflames my sense;
And art thou not willing, I'll take thee hence!"
"Oh father, father, he grasps my arm,
The Erlking has done me harm!"

The father shudders, he speeds ahead,
He clasps to his bosom the sobbing child,
He reaches home with pain and dread:
In his arms the child lay dead!

Erlkönig.
Goethe.

(Orig. G moll.)

Op. 1.

Schnell. ♩ = 152.

1 From Vol. I (Peters No. 20B) of *Schubert Songs*.   Reprinted by permission of the publisher, C. F. Peters Corporation, New York, N.Y.

Wer rei _ tet so spät   durch Nacht und

Wind?   Es ist   der Va _ ter mit sei _ nem

Kind;   er hat den Kna _ ben wohl in dem Arm,   er

faßt   ihn si_cher, er hält ihn warm.

Mein Sohn, was birgst du so bang dein Ge_sicht?

dir,   manch bun _ _ te Blu _ men sind an   dem

Strand;   meine Mut _ ter hat manch gül _ _ den Ge_wand." „Mein

Va _ ter,mein Va_ter, und hö_rest du nicht,   was Er_len_kö_nig mir lei _ se ver_

spricht?_   Sei   ru_hig,   bleibe ruhig,mein Kind;   in dürren

Blättern säuselt der Wind.   „Willst, fei _ ner Kna_be, du mit mir gehn?meine

Study Procedures

1. Choose one of the Schubert songs and discuss the balance which was achieved between poetry, accompaniment, and the vocal line.
2. Probably you are most familiar with the strophic song form. Which of the through-composed songs did you prefer? Why do you suppose this was true? Are you aware of the through-composed nature of the song? Did this seem out of place for you?
3. How does the accompaniment describe? Is this a detailed description or is it subtle?
4. If you were a composer of art songs, what contemporary poem would you wish to set to music? Do you believe the poem expressive of your feelings at least in part? Generally speaking, what kind of accompaniment would you believe appropriate for your poem?

ANOTHER GERMAN ART SONG COMPOSER

Born thirteen years after Schubert, Robert Schumann turned to the art song the year of his marriage, 1840, when he suddenly discovered the beauty and unity of poetry and music. Almost all of his songwriting took place in that year. As a younger man, Schumann had been involved with practicing and composing for the piano and writing as a critic for his own art and music magazine.

Schumann believed that the piano should not only develop an appropriate mood for the singer and text but that it should be a partner in the musical process as well. Consequently, the piano takes on an increased importance which is witnessed by more and longer piano interludes and postludes.

Because we will study a Schumann song cycle later, the selected art songs are all relatively short.

THREE SCHUMANN ART SONGS

"Widmung" ("Dedication") is a declaration of love, and the short piano introduction sets the lilting mood which runs through the first portion of the song.
When the words declare that "you are refreshing, you are peace," the music quiets
noticeably, the tonal center of the music changes, while the voice line moves
at a seemingly slower pace.   The song ends with a restatement of the first part
in text and melody.   To create an appropriate ending, the voice jumps upward
just before the final notes.

(Friedrich Rückert, 1788–1866)

"Widmung"	"Dedication"
Du meine Seele, du mein Herz,	*You are my Soul, you are my heart,*
Du meine Wonne, du mein Schmerz,	*You are my delight, you are my grief.*
Du meine Welt, in der ich lebe,	*You are the world in which I live,*
Mein Himmel du, darein ich schwebe,	*My heaven in which I exist.*
O du mein Grab, in das hinab	*O, you are the consolation*
Ich ewig meinen Kummer gab!	*For my every depression.*
Du bist die Ruh, du bist der Frieden,	*You are refreshing, you are peace,*
Du bist der Himmel mir beschieden.	*You were sent to me from heaven.*
Dass du mich liebst, macht mich mir wert,	*Since you love me, I respect myself,*
Dein Blick hat mich vor mir verklärt,	*Your glance exhilarates me,*
Du hebst mich liebend über mich,	*Your love lifts me up.*
Mein guter Geist, mein bessres Ich!	*You are my inner strength, my better self.*
Du meine Seele, du mein Herz,	*You are my Soul, you are my heart,*
Du meine Wonne, du mein Schmerz,	*You are my delight, you are my grief.*
Du meine Welt, in der ich lebe,	*You are the world in which I live,*
Mein Himmel du, darein ich schwebe,	*My heaven in which I exist.*
Mein guter Geist, mein bessres Ich!	*You are my inner strength, my better self.*

The poem "Der Nussbaum" ("The Nut Tree") is made up of couplets, and
two melodies comprise each couplet to create a sustained mood.   Schumann
treats these couplets almost identically, with the piano contributing almost as
much as the voice.   To add variety, the fourth couplet has a change of melody
and then a return, in which both melodies are used.   This is the story of a young
girl who dreams of love and marriage, and this song captures the mood of her
dreaming.   One author called this a miracle of monotony.   A A A B A B Ending.

(Julius Mosen, 1803–1867)

"Der Nussbaum"	"The Nut Tree"
Es grünet ein Nussbaum vor dem Haus,	*A nut tree greens before the house,*
duftig, luftig breitet er blättrig die Aeste aus.	*fragrant, it spreads its leaves.*
Viel liebliche Blüten stehen d'ran;	*Many beautiful blossoms outline its edge*
linde Winde konnen, sie herzlich zu umfah'n	*and gentle breezes carress them lovingly.*

Es flüstern je zwei, zu zwei gepaart,	*They whisper, two by two, in pairs,*
neigend, beugend zierlich zum Kusse die Häuptchen zart	*bending, bowing their heads to kiss.*
Sie flüstern von einem Mägdelein, das dächte die Nächte und Tage lang	*They whisper of a maiden, who dreams both day and night, but not of riches;*
wusste ach!, Selber nicht was.	
Sie flüstern-Wer mage verstehn so gar leise Weis?	*They whisper—to those who understand so soft a song,*
Flüstern von Bräutgam und nächstem Jahr,	*whisper of a bridegroom and next year;*
Das Mägdlein horchet, es rauscht im Baum;	*The maiden listens, the tree rustles;*
Sehnend, wähnend sinkt es lächelnd in Schlaf und Traum.	*dreaming, she smilingly drops to sleep.*

The next love song is as contemporary as any shy girl or any girl whose true beauty might be hidden. Yet, when the correct lover comes to her and places her in the proper light she blooms and glows and sparkles and love is within her.

The music is through-composed, containing a rhythmic unity instead of a melodic one. A few chords introduce the voice and then almost immediately the beautiful low bass line of the piano. The second verse of the text is accompanied at a higher level than the other verses, and follows the voice line into the third stanza, rising and falling, matching the contour of the voice.

(Heinrich Heine, 1797–1856)

"Die Lotosblume"	"The Lotus Flower"
Die Lotosblume ängstigt	*The lotus blossom fears*
sich vor der Sonne Pracht,	*the intensity of the sun,*
Und mit gesenktem Haupte	*And with lowered head*
erwartet sie träumend die Nacht.	*waits, dreaming of the night.*
Der Mond, der ist ihr Buhle,	*The moon, who is her lover,*
er weckt sie mit seinem Licht,	*calls her with his light*
Und ihm entschleiert sie freundlich	*And to him she willingly unveils*
ihr frommes Blumengesicht.	*her quiet, glowing face.*
Sie blüht und glüht und leuchtet,	*She blossoms, glows, and sparkles*
und starret stumm in die Höh'	*and, looking up quietly,*
Sie duftet und weinet und zittert	*Sighs, trembles, and sheds a tear*
vor Liebe und Liebesweh,	*for the beauty of love,*
vor Liebe und Liebesweh.	*for the beauty of love.*

Study Procedures

1. Compare any one Schumann art song with one by Schubert. Discuss musical or artistic characteristics.
2. The form for "Der Nussbaum" is almost strophic, while the other songs are more obviously through-composed. Why would Schumann choose to repeat his melody so often in this song? Would you have done the same? If not, why?

A FRENCH ART SONG

Any form so meaningful, emotional, and expressive could not be retained by one period, the Romantic. Rather, it has permeated the musical scene from its inception until the present. As the art song became an accepted form in all of Europe and even beyond, the musical style changed with the composer and the time of writing, some nationalistic tendencies became evident, but the original art song characteristics persisted. If space permitted we could study the works of French, Italian, and Russian composers with benefit.

Debussy, one of the great composers of France, lived at the turn of the twentieth century and wrote a number of art songs in the impressionistic style. His work is a high point in twentieth century French art song. "Noel des Enfants" protests the cruelties to children during the First World War. This Christmas children's prayer to Santa Claus requests revenge and love, but at the same time expresses bewilderment.

The agitated piano accompaniment, typifying a feeling of high emotion, is reminiscent of that used by Schubert in many of his songs. But these are not the melodic or the harmonic lines of Schubert. Although the music begins with a simplistic tune, the melodic line becomes more complex as the emotion increases. Melodies A and B seem almost too attractive for this kind of song, but these pentatonic melodies, a favorite of impressionistic Debussy, are ideal to express a reminiscence of childhood.

The AB AC D AB E form of the small composition provides an interesting childlike repetition which brings a simplicity to the work.

This was Debussy's last composition. He completed the song the night before entering the hospital for a cancer operation. After the operation he was so ill from radium treatments that he was unable to compose.

(Claude Debussy, 1862–1918)

"Noel des Enfants"	"Prayer to Santa"
Nous n'avons plus de maisons! *Les ennemis ont tout pris,* *jusqu'à notre petit lit!*	*We're homeless!* *The enemy took everything,* *even to our little bed!*
Ils ont brûlé l'école et notre maître aussi.	*They burned up the school and our schoolmaster too.*
Ils ont brûlé l'église et monsieur Jésus-Christ	*They burned up the church and monsieur Jesus Christ*
Et le vieux pauvre qui n'a pas pu s'en aller!	*and the poor old beggarman who was unable to get away!*
Nous n'avons plus de maisons. *Les ennemis ont tout pris,* *jusqu'à notre petit lit!* *Bien sûr! papa est à la guerre,* *pauvre maman est morte!* *avant d'avoir vu tout ça.* *Qu'est ce que l'on va faire?*	*We're homeless.* *The enemy took everything,* *even to our little bed!* *To be sure, papa is away at the war,* *poor mama died* *before she could see all that.* *What are we going to do?*

Noël! petit Noël! n'allez pas chez eux,
n'allez plus jamais chez eux,
Punissez-les!

Vengez les enfants de France!
Les petits Belges, les petits Serbes,
et les petits Polonais aussi!
Si nous en oublions, pardonnez-nous.
Noël! Noël! surtout, pas de joujoux,
Tâchez de nous redonner le pain quotidien.

Nous n'avons plus de maisons!
Les ennemis ont tout pris,
jusqu'à notre petit lit!
Ils ont brûlé l'école et notre maître aussi.

Ils ont brûlé l'église et monsieur Jésus-Christ

Et le vieux pauvre qui n'a pas pu s'en aller!

Noël! écoutez-nous, nous n'avons plus de petits
   sabots:
Mais donnez la victoire aux enfants de France!

Noël! petit Noël! do not go to their homes,
never go to their homes again,
punish them!

Avenge the children of France!
The little Belgians, the little Serbs
and the little Poles too!
If we forget about them, forgive us.
Noël! Noël! Above all, no toys,
try to give us back our daily bread.

We're homeless!
The enemy took everything,
even to our little bed!
They burned up the school and our school-
   master too.
They burned up the church and monsieur
   Jesus Christ
and the poor old beggarman who was unable
   to get away!
Noël! listen to us, we go barefoot now:

but give the victory to the children of France![2]

AN AMERICAN ART SONG

In the United States art songs were composed almost as early as in some of the countries of Europe. Part of the reason for this, of course, was that many of America's first composers of merit were trained in Europe before coming home to work and teach.

One of the more contemporary composers, at least by sound and concept, was Charles Ives, who published over 100 songs. One of these concerns the death of a cowboy, "Charlie Rutlage." The first and last stanzas of this song repeat the music, but in other stanzas Ives has asked that the voice and the piano perform in a most unorthodox fashion: the voice rises in pitch and as the tension mounts turns more to a semisinging style, while the accompaniment becomes wilder and finally uses the fist on the keys.

Ives was attempting two ideas with this song. Maintaining the original intent of the art song, he also wanted to synthesize the flavor of the American cowboy. He is most successful at this with his rhythmic introduction and the vocal line. Here we see an artist not imitating a cowboy tune or even inventing one, but using his talents to synthesize the flavor of many cowboy tunes and styles of singing. Ives's second goal was to use a semisinging style to bring a kind of emotional impact to the listener that could not have been accomplished in any other way. Compare the manner of treating the end of the fourth verse with the ending of "Der Erlkönig" by Schubert.

---

[2] Reproduction autorisée par les Editions DURAND & Cie, Editeurs-propriétaires PARIS.

(Anon)

"Charlie Rutlage"

Another good cowpuncher has gone to meet his fate.
I hope he'll find a resting place within the golden gate.
Another place is vacant on the ranch of the XIT
Twill be hard to find another that is liked as well as he.

The first that died was Kid White, a man both tough and brave.
While Charlie Rutlage makes the third to be sent to his grave;
Caused by a cowhorse falling while running after stock.
It was on the spring round-up, a place where death men mock.

He went forward one morning on a circle through the hills.
He was gay and full of glee, and free from earthly ills;
But when it came to finish up the work on which he went,
Nothing came back from him, his time on earth was spent.

Twas as he rode the round-up, an XIT turned back to the herd.
Poor Charlie shoved him in again, his cutting horse he spurred.
Another turned! at that moment his horse the creature spied
And turned and fell with him; beneath, poor Charlie died.

His relations in Texas his face never more will see,
But I hope he'll meet his parents, will meet them face to face,
And that they will grasp him by the right hand at the shining throne
*   of grace.*

Study Procedures

1. The Debussy piece is evidently a war protest song. What is different here than some of the war protest songs you have heard over the past few years? Why would Debussy's song be considered an art song, and some of the recent songs merely ballads or folk songs? Think back over the characteristics we studied through earlier chapters of the text.
2. Note the folk song character of the poem chosen by Ives; note the irregular poetic rhythm. What makes this an art song and not a folk song?

A CONTEMPORARY ADAPTATION

Sequenza III by Luciano Berio bases its vocal utterance upon the poem written below. However, it is not sung as a poem, but rather, a series of vowel sounds, words, or word clusters become the ingredients for the vocal line. The sounds explore the human singing voice and because of their arrangement take on the effect of a song for the listener.

Give me a few words   *to build a house*
for a woman to sing   *before night comes.*[3]
a truth allowing us

---

[3] By courtesy and permission of Vox Productions, Inc.

Study Procedures

1. After listening to this composition enumerate those characteristics which it has in common with the art songs studied earlier in the chapter.
2. What in the Ives song is similar to the musical characteristics in the Berio? By listening to both of them could you know that Berio is an outgrowth of the period which produced the Ives?
3. Can you grasp the artistic nature of this composition? Could you explore your own voice in a similar fashion? If so, would it be a personal expression of your artistic nature?

THE SONG CYCLE

Any number of art songs connected or related in some manner are known as a *song cycle*. The group may relate a sequence of ideas and consequently be somewhat narrative in purpose. Other cycles may be connected by a common origin or give a series of thoughts concerning a single item stressing the meditative. The latter often presents differing approaches to the same idea with little or no sequence and no immediately evident connection unless explained. The former gives an obvious progression of events so that the listener may follow them more easily.

Numerous song cycles have been written during the past almost 200 years. The cycle re-emphasizes the importance of the song and song forms. Through this form the song reached a length and posture that equaled other larger forms used by musicians for choral and instrumental works.

Frauenliebe und Leben (Schumann)

A Woman's Love and Life was a series of poems written by Adalbert Chamisso (1781–1838), a well-known poet of the Romantic period. Schumann chose this series of poems to show the emotions of a woman as she first sees a man she could love, her meeting, her engagement, her wedding, and other events in her life. It is a series of songs strictly from the female point of view, and unabashedly romantic.

When first listening to the cycle some may prefer not to listen to all the songs at one sitting. If so, choose two or three that might attract you and note the qualities of each. The texts are given in both German and English and the form of each section is listed, so that you may more clearly comprehend the music as it makes its statements and returns.

Suggested Listening Sequence: 4, (2–3), (5–7), (1–8), 6

Frauenliebe und Leben   A Woman's Love and Life

I (Strophic)

"Seit ich ihn gesehen"   "Since I First Saw Him"

Seit ich ihn gesehen,   Since I first saw Him
Glaub' ich blind zu sein,   I believe myself blind,
Wo ich hin nur blicke,   Wherever I look
Seh' ich ihn allein;   I see only him—
Wie im wachen Traume   Awake or in a dream,
Schwebt sein Bild mir vor,   His image haunts me,
Taucht aus tiefsten Dunkel   Crashing brightly from on high
Heller nur empor.   Into my dark life.

Sonst ist licht-und farblos   Everywhere is light, but dull
Alles um mich her,   All about me here.
Nach der Schwestern Spiele   I desire no longer
Nicht begehr' ich mehr,   To join my sister's play,
Möchte lieber weinen   I would rather weep
Still im Kämmerlein;   Alone in my room;
Seit ich ihn gesehen,   Since I first saw him
Glaub' ich blind zu sein.   I am not myself.

II (A A B A' C C' A")

"Er, der Herrlichste von Allen"   "He, Most Beloved of Men"

Er, der Herrlichste von Allen,   He, most beloved of men,
Wie so milde, wie so gut!   So gentle as well as good,
Holde Lippen, klares Auge,   Attractive lips, clear eyes,
Heller Sinn und fester Mut.   Alert mind and strong spirit.

So wie dort in blauer Tiefe   Like a star in the deep, blue sky
Hell und herrlich jener Stern,   Shining brightly with splendor,
Also er an meinem Himmel   So he shines in my heaven:
Hell und herrlich, hehr und fern.   Bright, magnificent, sublime from afar.

Wandle, wandle deine Bahnen,   Wander, wander on your path,
Nur betrachten deinen Schein,   Concerned solely with your light;
Nur in Demut ihn betrachten,   Only in humility can one consider
Selig nur und traurig sein!   His happiness and his sorrow.

Höre nicht mein stilles Beten,   Heed not my quiet prayers
Deinem Glücke nur geweiht;   Which concern your fate
Darfst mich, niedre Magd, nicht kennen,   From a lowly maid unacquainted
Hoher Stern der Herrlichkeit!   With the highest star of mankind.

Nur die Würdigste von Allen   Only the worthiest of all
Darf beglücken deine Wahl,   Could be your choice,
Und ich will die Höhe segnen   And I will bless her
Viele tausendmal!   A thousand times over.

Will mich freuen dann und weinen,   Then I shall weep despite my joy,
Selig, selig bin ich dann;   Happy, happy though I be for you,
Sollte mir das Herz auch brechen,   My heart shall be broken.
Brich, o Herz! Was liegt daran?   Break, O heart! What then for you?

93

Er, der Herrlichste von Allen,
Wie so milde, wie so gut!
Holde Lippen, klares Auge,
Heller Sinn und fester Mut.

He, most beloved of men,
So gentle as well as good,
Attractive lips, clear eyes,
Alert mind and strong spirit.

III (A B A A Ending)

"Ich kann's nicht fassen, nicht glauben"

"I Cannot Really Believe It"

Ich kann's nicht fassen, nicht glauben
Es hat ein Traum mich berückt;
Wie hätt' er doch unter Allen
Mich Arme erhöht und beglückt?

I cannot really believe it,
It seems to be a dream;
Why has he chosen me
Above all others?

Mir war's, er habe gesprochen:
'Ich bin auf ewig dein!'
Mir war's—ich träume noch immer,
Es kann ja nimmer so sein!

He said to me:
"I will be yours forever."
I am still dreaming;
No, it can never be!

O lass im Traume mich sterben,
Geweiget an seiner Brust,
Den seligen Tod mich schlürfen
In Tränen unendlicher Lust.

O let me die in this dream
Ever close to him,
Then blessed death
Would be unending pleasure.

Ich kann's nicht fassen, nicht glauben,
Es hat ein Traum mich berückt;
Wie hätt' er doch unter Allen
Mich Arme erhöht und beglückt?

I cannot really believe it,
It seems to be a dream;
Why has he chosen me
Above all others?

IV (A B A C A)

"Du Ring an meinem Finger"

"O Ring on My Finger"

Du Ring an meinem Finger,
Mein goldenes Ringelein,
Ich drücke dich fromm an die Lippen,
Dich fromm an das Herze mein.

O ring on my finger,
My little ring of gold,
I press you to my lips
And then gently to my heart.

Ich hatt' ihn ausgeträumet,
Der Kindheit friedlich schönen Traum,
Ich fand allein mich verloren
Im öden, unendlichen Raum.

I had given up dreaming
The beautiful dreams of childhood—
All life seemed barren,
A deserted, unending room.

Du Ring an meinem Finger,
Da hast du mich erst belehrt,
Hast meinem Blick erschlossen
Des Lebens unendlichen, tiefen Wert.

O ring on my finger,
You have first taught me
How my view of life has changed
To an unending life of joy.

Ich will ihm dienen, ihm leben,
Ihm angehören ganz,
Hin selber mich geben, und finden
Verklärt mich in seinem Glanz.

I will serve him, love him,
Belong to him entirely,
Give myself to him, and find
A new life within his.

Du Ring an meinem Finger,
Mein goldenes Ringelein,
Ich drücke dich fromm an die Lippen,
Dich fromm an das Herze mein.

O ring on my finger,
My little ring of gold,
I press you to my lips
And then gently to my heart.

V (A A' A B A")

"Helft mir, ihr Schwestern"

Helft mir, ihr Schwestern,
Freundlich mich schmücken,
Dient der Glücklichen heute, mir,
Windet geschäftig
Mir um die Stirne
Noch der blühenden Myrte Zier!

Als ich befriedigt,
Freudigen Herzens,
Sonst dem Geliebten im Arme lag,
Immer noch rief er,
Sehnsucht im Herzen,
Ungeduldig den heutigen Tag.

Helft mir, ihr Schwestern,
Helft mir verscheuchen
Eine törichte Bangigkeit,
Dass ich mit klarem
Aug' ihn empfange,
Ihn, die Quelle der Freudigkeit.

Bist, mein Geliebter,
Du mir erschienen,
Gibst du mir, Sonne, deinen Schein,
Lass mich in Andacht,
Lass mich in Demut,
Lass mich verneigen dem Herren mein!

Streuet ihm, Schwestern,
Streuet ihm Blumen,
Bringet ihm Knospende Rosen dar.
Aber euch Schwestern
Grüss' ich mit Wehmut,
Freudig scheidend aus eurer Schaar!

"Help Me, My Sisters"

Help me, my sisters,
Kindly adorn me;
Serve the happy one today:
Quickly wind
The blooming myrtle
Round my forehead.

Many times
With joyous hearts,
While embraced arm in arm,
He spoke
Of the longing in his heart,
Impatient of this day's coming.

Help me, my sisters,
Help me to put away
A foolish anxiety,
Then with open heart
I will receive him—
The fountain of my joy.

Since, my love,
You first appeared to me,
You are my sun, my light.
Let me in devotion,
Let me in humility
Bow to my Lord.

Sisters, strew for him,
Strew for him flowers;
Bring rosebuds for him.
But, my sisters, I say
Goodbye with a bit of sorrow,
Knowing I must leave you.

VI (A A B A)

"Süsser Freund, du blickest"

Süsser Freund, du blickest
Mich verwundert an,
Kannst es nicht begreifen,
Wie ich weinen kann;
Lass der feuchten Perlen
Ungewohnte Zier
Freudig hell erzittern
In dem Auge mir.

Wie so bang mein Busen.
Wie so wonnevoll,
Wüsst' ich nur mit Worten,
Wie ich's sagen soll;
Komm und birg dein Antlitz

"Sweet Friend, You Look"

Sweet friend, you look
At me in surprise,
Can you not understand
How I can weep?
These unaccustomed pearls
Are bright tears in my eyes
Indicating deep joy
For me.

How anxious I feel—
My heart bursts with yearning;
I have too few words
To express my true feeling.
Come and place your head

Hier an meiner Brust,	Here on my breast
Will ins Ohr dir flüstern	While I whisper in your ear
Alle meine Lust.	Of my delight.
Weisst du nun die Tränen,	Can you not guess
Die ich weinen kann,	Why I am weeping?
Sollst du nicht sie sehen,	Should you not perceive it,
Du geliebter Mann?	My beloved husband?
Bleib' an meinem Herzen,	Stay against my heart,
Fühle dessen Schlag,	Feeling the beat;
Dass ich fest und fester	Hold me close, closer,
Nur dich drücken mag!	Closer still!
Hier an meinem Bette	Here by my bed
Hat die Wiege Raum,	Place the cradle
Wo sie still verberge	Which will soon hold
Meinen holden Traum;	My fondest dreams.
Kommen wird der Morgen,	Come that morning
Wo der Traum erwacht,	When the dream is reality,
Und daraus dein Bildnis	Your image
Mir entgegen lacht!	Will smile back at me.

VII (A A' A A")

"An meinem Herzen, an meiner Brust"	"Embrace Me, Hug Me"
An meinem Herzen, an meiner Brust	Embrace me, hug me;
Du meine Wonne, du meine Lust.	You are my delight, my pleasure;
Das Glück ist die Liebe, die Lieb' ist das Glück,	Happiness is love, love is happiness;
Ich hab's gesagt, und nehm's nicht zurück.	I said it, and won't retract it.
Hab' überschwenglich mich geschätzt,	Before I was happy
Bin überglücklich aber jetzt;	But now overjoyed,
Nur die da säugt, nur die da liebt	She loves best who
Das Kind, dem sie die Nahrung gibt.	Nurses her child upon her breast.
Nur eine Mutter weiss allein,	Only a mother knows truly
Was lieben heisst und glücklich sein.	What love and happiness is.
O wie bedaur' ich doch den Mann,	O how I pity a man
Der Mutterglück nicht fühlen kann.	Who cannot know this joy.
Du lieber, lieber Engel du,	O darling, darling Angel,
Du schauest mich an und lächelst dazu!	You look at me and laugh;
An meinem Herzen, an meiner Brust,	O my darling on my breast,
Du meine Wonne, du meine Lust!	My pleasure, my delight.

VIII   (Through-Composed, Piano Ending from I)

"Nun hast du mir den ersten Schmerz getan"	"Now You Have Grieved Me for the First Time"
Nun hast du mir den ersten Schmerz getan,	Now you have grieved me for the first time—
Der aber traf:	Now there is sadness.
Du schläfst, du harter unbarmherz'ger Mann,	You sleep, you strong, unmerciful man,
Den Todesschlaf.	The sleep of death.

Es blicket die Verlassne vor sich hin,
  Die Welt ist leer;
Geliebet hab' ich und gelebt, ich bin
  Nicht lebend mehr.

Ich zieh' mich in mein Innres still zurück,
  Der Schleier fällt;
Da hab' ich dich und mein verlornes Glück,
  Du meine Welt!

I gaze about forsaken,
  The world is empty;
I had love and I lived,
  But I live no more.

I close my memories about me,
  The veil falls;
Within I have myself, and the lost happiness
  Of our world!

IX. Epilogue
"Dream of Those Days"

Dream of those days
Now far away,
Granddaughter of mine,
Sweet child,
Listen, before this weary one
Is wrapped in shroud,
Listen to my blessing
While you are young.

You see grey hair
Thin and faded,
I was once, as you,
Young and full of life.
I loved, as you love,
As you, was also a bride.
But you too will grow old
And become grey.

Time passes,
Walking continually;
So, constantly preserve
Your inner treasures.
I have once said,
And it is true,
Happiness is love,
Love is happiness.

When I placed my husband
In his grave
I kept my love
True in my heart.
My heart was broken
But my courage continued strong,
And the ashes of old age
Are preserved by the hallowed fire.

Listen, before the weary one
Is wrapped in shroud,
Listen while you are young
To my blessing;
If the heart breaks
Hold fast your courage,
Then the pain of love
Will be your utmost good.

This epilogue to Chamisso's cycle of poems was not set by Schumann.

Hermit Songs (Barber)

This cycle of songs is by Samuel Barber, a contemporary American. He has chosen a series of poems written during the eighth to thirteenth centuries by Irish monks. As they copied manuscripts in their cells, they wrote personal thoughts on the margins of their books.

No forms for the songs are given in the hope that you will be able to work these out with your classmates.

Suggested Listening Sequence: 4, 7, 8, 1, 2, 9, 10, 6, 5, 3.

Samuel Barber (Courtesy of G. Schirmer, Inc., New York).

Study Procedures

1. What differences do you notice between the art song and the song cycle? Is it only a difference of length?
2. Compare the different musical styles of the two song cycles in our text. How would you best describe the music of Schumann? How would this compare to the music of Barber? Which style of music do you prefer? State your reasons in musical terms.
3. Choose one song from each cycle which you believe best exemplifies the spirit and the musical qualities of the entire cycle. Why do you believe this to be true?
4. *Circles,* a contemporary vocal expression by Luciano Berio with poetry by e. e. cummings, uses a group of three poems. The singer sings each poem in order and then reverses the order, so that Poem A is heard both first and last, poem B is heard second and fourth, with poem C heard but once. Because of the treatment of the vocal lines and the arrangement of the poetic expression, it is difficult to understand the texts unless you have the words before you. They may be found in *Collected Poems,* e. e. cummings (Harcourt, Brace, and World, Inc., New York, 1923, 1963).

Poem A: No. 25 stinging gold swarms upon the spires
Poem B: No. 76 riverly is a flower
Poem C: No. 221 n(o)w the how

Listen to this composition and explain why you believe it to be an art song, and how this composition fits our definition of a song cycle.

Visage (Berio)

Contemporary composers consider electronic music a widening of the sound spectrum and a widening of the emotional impact which music can provide to the listener.

Visage is a collection of sounds, some electronic, some a vocal expression. The electronic sounds act as an accompaniment to the vocal sounds. The vocal sounds are almost entirely meaningless, although at times the interpretation of these nonsense syllables is so lifelike as to suggest a foreign language. Occasionally the Italian word "parole" (word) is heard but this is the only actual word used. The accompaniment coordinates well and assists in establishing a mood for the vocal expressions, adding greatly to the overall effect.

Although not a song cycle in the historical sense, this is a collection of five vocal expressions forming one composition. There is no obvious break between the sections, although a few seconds of silence separates them.

1. Struggle: effort of making a speaking sound
2. Romantic or poetic expression
3. Catastrophe and fantasy
4. Anger, fright, fear
5. Revenant or wraith (apparition)

Study Procedures

1. Describe in your own words why this composition is similar to a song cycle. What does it have in common with the two cycles studied earlier in the chapter?
2. Give the sections new titles; the ones I have chosen are not those of the composer. How would you describe the various sections?

Bibliography—Chapter 7

FIEDLER, H. G., *The Oxford Book of German Verse*. London: Oxford University Press, 1915.

GOETHE, JOHANN, *Faust*. London: Oxford University Press, 1963.

MILLER, PHILIP L., *The Ring of Words*. New York: Doubleday and Co., 1966.

PLANTINGA, LEON B., *Schumann as Critic*. New Haven, Conn.: Yale University Press, 1967.

PORTER, ERNEST G., *Schubert's Song Technique*. London: Dennis Dobson, 1961.

THOMAS, R. HINTON, *Poetry and Song in the German Baroque*. London: Oxford University Press, 1963.

Recordings—Chapter 7

	American Art Songs		Duke DWR-6417
Barber	*Hermit Songs*	Price	Columbia ML-4988
Berio	*Circles*	Berberian	Mainstream MS-5005

PART 1   Vocal Music

Berio	*Sequenza III*		Candide CE-31027
Berio	*Visage*	Berberian	Candide CE-31027
Debussy	*Noel des Enfants*	De Los Angeles	Angel S-3640
Schubert	*Art Songs*		Angel 35022
Schubert	*Art Songs*		Vanguard VSD-2086
Schubert-Schumann	*Art Songs*		London OS-25757
Schumann	*Art Songs*		DGG 138655
Schumann	*Art Songs*		London LL-940
Schumann	*Frauenliebe und Leben*		Victor LM-2275

Chapter 8

The Madrigal

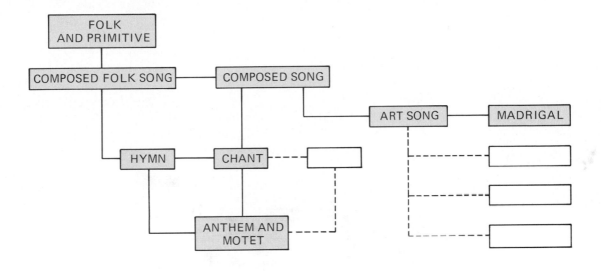

Every year hundreds of young people in high schools and colleges enjoy the singing of madrigals and rediscover the same pleasure experienced by sixteenth century singers. Their stimulation and satisfaction comes from the singing of a modestly difficult part song, interesting in rhythm, semi-independent of other voices or singers, with a text well suited to the music.

This part song may contain from four to eight vocal lines, with the usual number being five. With the singing group a bit larger than a quartet, the part writing may be more complex and the tonal colors more interesting. In performance, whether today or originally, one or two persons to the part or line provides a more independent musical situation than most choral music.

Originating in Italy about 1300, the madrigal went through two phases of development. The early form, very little connected to the ones most often sung these days, consisted of a series of rigidly controlled and skillfully organized three-line verses whose main concern was the contemplation of nature. During the Renaissance in the sixteenth century the term was again used for poetic verse by Italian poets for a type of short lyric poem with irregular form. Although the verses varied from six to sixteen, the musicians usually appropriated only two or three for their songs. The lines contained seven to eleven syllables and spoke of love more often than other subjects. These poems set to music by composers of the period became known as madrigals also, and the style and form was adopted by the English as their major secular music of the Elizabethan period.

We shall limit our discussion to the English madrigal, since it is most often heard and by understanding it one indirectly learns something of the Italian Renaissance madrigal as well.

BACKGROUND OF THE ENGLISH MADRIGAL

The England of the late 1500s, having just revelled in the defeat of the Spanish Armada and enjoying a period of economic expansion, sought to improve its general artistic position as well. Since Italy was considered the center for the arts of the then known world, England took note of the madrigal and its development by Flemish and Italian composers, working with Italian poets in an attempt to bring a new style of refinement and expression both to poetry and music. Similarly motivated, English poets and musicians, but particularly the musicians, adopted the madrigal as a form to assist their goal.

Specifically, the English madrigal was sometimes transplantation and translation of appropriate poems and music from Italy. Since the meters of the languages were different, a direct translation was not possible, but rather adaptation. Many of the tunes were arrangements of the rhythmic style and melodic intentions of the Italians without being exact copies. Other madrigals were completely English. For the most part, although there were exceptions, modest poems of a serious intent were set to music for a less serious purpose.

The madrigal was house music. There were no public concerts at the time, so if music was to be heard it was either in church, at the home, or in the taverns. The taverns had their own type of secular music; the new English church (as we noted in Chapter 5) had requested the musicians of the time to concern themselves with music appropriate to the new service. Many of these same composers were also interested in secular music, and the madrigal was a most interesting and productive form.

Consistent with the times, men who were considered educated should be concerned with and somewhat schooled in the arts. Many could write a modest poem, read music, and play acceptably on the lute. In addition they were able to sing. For the sake of the madrigal reading music became most important, since at that time choral music was written with only one vocal line available to a person, and so he was not able to observe other musical lines as he read his own.

Henry Peacham, writing in *The Compleat Gentleman* in 1622, stated that one of the qualifications of a gentleman was "to be able to sing your part sure, at first sight, withall to play the same upon your Violl or the exercise of your lute."[1]   It apparently was a custom in better homes of the time for the mistress of the house to pass out the part books after the evening meal and for those present to take part in the singing of madrigals and part songs.   Those who were unable to participate were considered of poor education.   From this background comes the custom today of madrigal singers sitting about a table often decorated with candles or other props, and singing part songs.

The point of this description is to bring to the fore the conditions under which these songs were performed, but also to underline that the madrigal was a popular song of the time and had a strong following.   There are some authorities who believe that since the poetry was light and rather repetitious in intent, the madrigal soon became, like so many popular songs, an item from which popular taste turned.   As we noted in an earlier chapter, 1600 witnessed an introduction of homophonic music and consequently the solo song would have been more ardently pursued, considering the madrigal a type of outdated form.

DEFINING THE FORM

But if the poetry of the madrigal was not England's best (the authors of many of the poems are unknown; Shakespeare was not set once, while Edmund Spenser was set only five times[2]), the music represents the most noted composers at the time.   Gibbons and Byrd, who were well-known as writers of anthems and masses for the church, wrote madrigals but were not prolific writers in this form. It has been surmised that Byrd, although proving his ability with an occasional song in this form, cared little for this kind of easy and frivolous material.

Following the Italians, madrigal was a general term embracing three obvious types of song material.   The verse and music of highest quality and most subtle meanings was termed the madrigal.   Those of lesser quality and usually with poems of a prescribed type were known as *canzonets*, while those of little quality and usually with a refrain of nonsense syllables were called *ballet* (pronounced as if written *ballot*).   In Thomas Morley's book *A Plaine and Easie Introduction to Practicall Musicke* (1597), he discusses the three types:

---

1 *The English Madrigal*, Edmund H. Fellowes.   Oxford University Press, London, 1935, page 19.
2 Burney, a famous English music historian of the day, wrote: "Indeed, in more than twenty sets, published between the year 1588 and 1624, during a period of near forty years, including almost four hundred and fifty madrigals and songs in parts, it would be difficult to find any one, of which the words can be perused with pleasure.   The sonnets of Spenser and Shakespeare, many of which are worthy of their authors, were indeed not published till about the end of the six-

---

The Elizabethan Madrigal, Joseph Kerman.   American Musicological Society, Galaxy Music Corporation, New York, page 2.

The light musicke hath beene of late more deepely dived into, so that there is no vanitie which in it hath not been followed to the ful: but the best kind of it is termed Madrigal, a word for the etymologie of which I can give no reason: yet use sheweth that it is a kind of musicke made upon songs and sonnets, such as Petrarcha and manie Poets of our time have excelled in. The second degree of gravitie in this light musicke is given to Canzonets, that is little short songs which is in the composition of the Musicke a counterfet of the Madrigal. There be also another kind, of Ballets, commonly called Fa las, a slight kind of musick it is, and I take it devised to be danced to voices.

The poetry will give some clue as to the appeal of the madrigal with the people of the time, and will also assist in guiding us to understand the form:

This sweet and merry month of May,
*   While Nature wantons in her prime,*
And birds do sing, and beasts do play
*   For pleasure of the joyful time,*
I choose the first for hollyday,
*   And greet Eliza with a rhyme:*
O beauteous Queen of second Troy
*   Take well in worth a simple toy.*[3]

Now is the month of maying
When merry lads are playing
Fa la la la la la la la.

Each with his bonny lass
Upon the greeny grass.
Fa la la la la la la la.

The Spring, clad all in gladness,
Doth laugh at Winter's sadness
Fa la la la la la la la.

And to the bagpipe's sound
The nymphs tread out their ground
Fa la la la la la la la.

Fie then! why sit we musing
Youth's sweet delight refusing?
Fa la la la la la la la.

Say, dainty nymphs, and speak,
Shall we play barley-break?
Fa la la la la la la la.

"This sweet and merry month of may," attributed to Thomas Watson, an English poet interested in the madrigal, was used by William Byrd for a tribute to the Queen and was one of his few madrigals. "Maying" is anonymous

---

teenth century; but afterwards, it is wonderful that none of them were set by our best musical composers."

[3] In the lines on the left the reference to Eliza means Queen Elisabeth, then Queen of England and the pride of the British. This was the famous Elizabethan period, when toasting the Queen was not only symbolic of a most patriotic gesture but a poetic nicety as well. Under the supervision of Thomas Morley, a madrigal writer of the time and truly the father and instigator of madrigals in England, seventeen composers in 1603 had written a musical tribute to Queen Elizabeth entitled *The Triumphs of Oriana*, in which each of the composers contributed an appropriate vocal selection. This madrigal by Byrd was not part of the set, but he would have been under obvious pressure to produce such a tribute, and this piece was published separately.

and was used by Morley for a ballet which comes from a kind of song for a dance, with the music composed by Morley in a dancelike rhythm. The "fa las" assist the character of the piece but more importantly, since the poem had no refrain line for the musician to use, nonsense syllables were added to assure the proper ballet form. Some composers chose "no no" and others "lirum, lirum" for the refrain.

Although not consistent, poems for the ballets tend to have a seven-point line, as shown by this one.

Let us examine two other poems:

Thule, the period of Cosmography,
  Doth vaunt of Hecla, whose sulphureous fire
Doth melt the frozen clime and thaw the sky;
  Trinacrian Aetna's flames ascend not higher.
These things seem wondrous, yet more wondrous I
Whose heart with fear doth freeze, with love doth fry.

The Andalusian merchant, that returns
Laden with cochineal and China dishes,
Reports in Spain how strangely Fogo burns
  Amidst an ocean full of flying fishes.
These things seem wondrous, yet more wondrous I
Whose heart with fear doth freeze, with love doth fry.

Flora gave me fairest flowers
None so fair in Flora's treasure.
  These I placed on Phyllis' bowers
She was pleased, and she my pleasure.
Smiling meadows seem to say:
Come, ye wantons, here to play.

Both of these poems discuss love, yet the differences in structure, use of language, meter, and style are evident immediately. "Thule" was set as a madrigal, while "Flora" represents the canzonet, light in textual quality, and usually of six lines with an a b a b c c rhyme scheme. It contains the kind of cleverness often found in the lyrics of this period, which often deludes the reader and listener in its true intent.

A still more introspectively complex type of poem was used as a madrigal. This poem by Sir Walter Raleigh is reminiscent of two others which are also quoted:

What is our life? a play of passion.
  Our mirth the music of division.
Our mothers' wombs the tiring-houses be,
  Where we are dressed for this short comedy.
Heaven the judicious sharp spectator is,

That sits and marks still who doth act amiss.
Our graves that hide us from the searching sun
  Are like drawn curtains when the play is done.
Thus march we, playing, to our latest rest,
  Only we die in earnest, that's no jest.

Raleigh

Happy, O happy he, who not affecting
  The endless toils attending worldly cares,
With mind reposed, all discontents rejecting,
  In silent peace his way to heaven prepares,
Deeming his life a scene, the world a stage
Whereon man acts his weary pilgrimage.

Anonymous

All the world's a stage,
And all the men and women merely players.
  They have their exits and their entrances,
And one man in his time plays many parts,
  His acts being seven ages.

William Shakespeare
As You Like It, **Act II, scene vii**

By comparing the poetry it becomes possible to assume the relationship of the music the composer might use. The ballets would be lightest and least intricate, the canzonets would be modestly so, while those termed madrigals would contain certain degrees of sophistication. Perhaps you have already assumed that the Sir Walter Raleigh poem would inspire complex vocal lines.

MUSICAL CHARACTERISTICS

The words *homophonic* and *contrapuntal* give us some indication of the method used by musicians of the period to increase the musical complexity of the songs. Homophonic indicates that the singers use the same words at the same time, moving with the same rhythm. This is the usual structure of a part song such as "My Country 'Tis of Thee" or the "Fight Song" of your school. Counterpoint permits the composer to use the voices in different rhythms simultaneously, but more importantly, to introduce each voice at a different time with the same tune. This becomes a complex song somewhat related to a round.

In the following examples notice two things: how the voices sing particular words and phrases at different times, and how far ahead or behind some may be when the word is sung. Also notice that the voices sing at a different time as they enter, thus making the text more difficult to understand and the music more complex. In fact, this was the complaint of one of Pepys in his diary in 1667:

> Singing with many voices is not singing but a sort of instrumental music, the sense of the words being lost by not being heard, and especially as they set them with fugues of words, one after another.[4]

This kind of problem confronts us in listening to some madrigals, particularly those in contrapuntal style; the more complex the verse, the more complex the music. As we stated earlier, this is singers' music and not meant to be listened to in concert. Consequently, the singer knows what he is singing, often hears the same text being used by others moments before he himself sings it and moments afterward, and in this realization comes a musical appreciation that can never be fully understood by the listener.

Our best suggestion is to take the text and follow carefully, trying to hear the musical meaning first in one voice and then in another. Several hearings may be needed to acquire the type of aural attention one must use for this music. Nor is this the only form of music where this type of device will be used. Contrapuntal music began earlier than the madrigal and continued through to later forms; consequently, beginning with these verses will assist with other forms where the contrapuntal lines are not so closely knit.

In order to assist you with this kind of understanding and hearing, let us begin with only the text placed in the same order as in one of the madrigals we shall hear later:

---

[4] *The Elizabethan Madrigal, op. cit.,* page 11.

"Fusca, in Thy Starry Eyes" (Tomkins)

1	Fus ca	in thy star–ry eyes
2	Fus — ca	in thy star-ry eyes
3	Fus– ca In thy star ——— ry	eyes in
4	Fus ca	in thy star–ry eyes
5	Fus ca	in thy star-ry eyes

1	thine eyes Love in black still mourning dies	
2	in thy star–ry eyes	Love in black still
3	thy star–ry eyes Love in black still mourning dies	Love in black still
4	Love in black still mourning dies	Love in black still
5	in thy star–ry eyes	Love in black still

1	still mourn– ing dies still mourn– ing dies
2	mourning dies still mourn ing dies still mourn– ing dies
3	mourning dies still mourn– ing dies still mourn– ing dies
4	mourning dies still mourning dies still mourn–ing dies
5	mourning dics still mourn– ing dies

1	
2	Fa la la Fa la la la la la la la la la la la la
3	Fa la la la la Fa la la la la la Fa la la la la la la la la Fa la la la
4	Fa la la la la la Fa la la la la la Fa la la la la la la Fa
5	

Study Procedures

1. Listen to this portion of this ballet several times, so that you may acquaint yourself with the interplay between the voices. You may need to follow one voice per hearing until you have listened three or four times. Then gradually you will come to hear several voices moving and entering simultaneously.
2. Another example, using different kinds of entrances and counterwords, will prove interesting and helpful:

"Sister, Awake" (Bateson)

1		Sis –ter, a– wake, close not	your	eyes, The day her light,	the
2	Sister, awake, close not your eyes, close not		your eyes	The day her light dis–clos
3				The day her light dis–clos
4				
5				

1	day her light dis clos ——— es, and the bright morn	ing	doth
2	es the day her light dis clos– es	and the bright morn	ing
3	es her light dis clos —— es, and the bright morn	ing	and
4	The day her light dis clos — es	And the	bright
5			

1	a— rise, and the bright morn–ing doth a–rise, doth a–rise.
2	doth a–rise, doth a– rise. Out of her bed
3	the bright morn ing doth a – rise, doth a–rise. Out of her bed
4	morn ing doth a rise, doth a– rise.
5	

1	Out of her bed of Ros–es out of her bed of Ros– es See
2	of Ros–es Out of her bed of Ros–es, her bed of Ros– es See
3	of Ros–es out of her bed of Ros – es See
4	Out of her bed of Ros–es her bed of Ros——— es See
5	See, See

3. It now seems appropriate to look at the music for these two madrigals. Do not consider it necessary to read the music, but rather, try to ascertain the direction of movement for the different vocal lines and the similarity of this movement between the voice parts. In "Sister, Awake" note the resemblance of the entrance between voice two and voice one, and again between voice three and voice four. Your eye will note many similarities of direction, and in listening your eye will guide you to still others.

FUSCA, IN THY STARRY EYES.

To Mr. *Phinees Fletcher.*

la la,   Fa   la la la   la la la la

p
Fa   la la la la,   Fa   la la la la la,   Fa   la la la la la la la la,

p
Fa   la la la la,   Fa   la la la la la,   Fa   la   la   la

Fa la la la
la   la la la   la_____   la la la   la   la,

Fa   la   la la la   la la   la la,

la   la la,   Fa la   la,

mf
Fa   la la la la   la,

mf

111

CANTUS.

Thou hast lov -

QUINTUS.

-mong so ma - ny slain, so ma - ny slain, Thou hast

- so ma - ny slain, so ma - ny slain, Thou hast lov - ed

ma - ny slain, so ma - ny slain, so ma - ny slain,

ma - ny slain, so ma - ny slain, so ma - ny slain, Thou hast lov - ed

- ed none a - gain, hast lov - ed none a - gain, Fa la la

lov - ed none a - gain, lov-ed none a - gain, Fa

none, hast lov - ed none a - gain, Fa la

Fa la la, Fa

none a - gain, hast lov - ed none, hast lov - ed none a - gain,

la   la,   Fa   la la,   Fa   la   la,   Fa   la la,   Fa

la   la la   la,   Fa   la   la   la,   Fa   la,

la,   Fa   la   la,   Fa___

la la, Fa la la   la la,   Fa la la, Fa la la la la

Fa   la la, Fa la la, Fa la   la

cresc.

la la, Fa la   la   la la   la,

cresc.

Fa   la la, Fa la la, Fa la   la   la la   la

cresc.

—   la la la,   Fa   la la la,   Fa   la la, Fa

cresc.

la, Fa   la   la,   Fa   la la la la   la,

cresc.

la, Fa   la,   Fa   la la, Fa la la, Fa la   la

cresc.

SISTER, AWAKE.

-ing doth _____ a - rise, and the bright morn-ing doth a - rise, doth a -

the bright morn - ing doth a - rise, doth _____ a -

-ing, and the bright morn - ing doth a - rise, doth a -

And the bright morn - ing doth _____ a - rise, doth a -

-rise. Out of her bed of

-rise. Out of her bed of Ros - es, Out of her

-rise. Out of her bed of Ros - es,

-rise. Out of her bed of Ros - es,

Ros - es, out of her bed of Ros - es: See,

bed of Ros - es, her bed of Ros - es: See,

out of her bed of ____ Ros - es: See,

her bed of Ros - es: See,

See, see,

see the clear Sun, the world's bright Eye, the world's bright Eye, in at our

see the clear Sun, the world's bright Eye, the world's bright Eye,

see, see,___ the clear Sun, the___ world's, the world's bright Eye,

see, ____ the clear Sun, ____ the world's bright Eye, in at our

see, the clear Sun, the world's bright Eye,

-ing. Lo how he blush - eth to e-spy us I - dle

-ing. Lo how he blush-eth to e - spy us I - dle

-ing. Lo how he blush - eth to e - spy us I - dle

-ing. Lo how he blush - eth to e - spy, to e-spy

-ing. Lo how he blush - eth to e - spy us I - dle

wench - es sleep - ing, _____ us

wench - es sleep - ing, us I - dle wench - es sleep -

wench - es sleep - ing, us I - dle wench - es

us I - dle wench - es sleep - ing, us I - dle

wench - es sleep - ing, us I - dle wench - es sleep - -

Idle wench-es sleep-ing. There-fore a-wake, make haste I ___

___ ing. There-fore a-wake, make haste I ___

sleep ___ ing. There-fore a-wake, make haste I

wench-es sleep ___ ing. There-fore a-wake, make haste I

___ ing. There-fore a-wake, make haste I

say, and let us with-out stay - ing, all in our gowns of

say, and let us with-out ___ stay-ing, ___

say, and let us with-out stay - ing, all in our gowns of

say, and let us with-out stay - ing, all in our gowns of

say, and let us with-out stay - ing,

122

TWO ADDITIONAL PROCEDURES

Madrigal writers often used two additional compositional techniques in their writing. One was known as *chromaticism,* and the other as *tone painting.* Neither originated with the madrigal but came from an earlier period. In tone painting the composer attempts to bring a descriptive sound to the word similar to what the word might indicate in its meaning. For example, the word "up" is often followed by tones that move upward. This is also true of heaven, sky, clouds, or other similar words. The word "run" would mean that the music would move faster. When this is handled poorly a humorous situation results; treated professionally, it may be most effective.

In the John Wilbye madrigal "Fly Not So Swift, My Dear," one can notice tone painting on the following words: "fly," "dying," "crying," "kill," "nimble dancing," and "downs." Although in good taste, the effect built into the music on these words is most obvious to the amateur listener.

Chromaticism is more difficult to define, since it is more obvious by sight than by hearing. However, in the Wilbye madrigal "Oft Have I Vowed" it may be obvious. This device makes use of altered half steps in the music that, although in harmony with other parts, are not the pitches most common for that voice, and could be considered extraneous material inserted to give the effect of weaving downward or climbing carefully upward. In this particular composition the male voices particularly may be heard descending in a chromatic pattern near the end of the composition.

A CONTEMPORARY ADAPTATION

The characteristics of the madrigal are sometimes used in more modern vocal literature without fulfilling the exact requirements of the form. "Leiyla and the Poet," although not a madrigal in the historical sense, makes use of some of the devices of the madrigal in an interesting way. Using some electronic sounds, the composer, Halim El-Dabh of Egypt, employs conventional instruments and voices with tape manipulation technic and speed transpositions.

In the later period (1600–1620) of its development in Italy and England the madrigal became more soloistic, and at times a simple accompaniment was used. These features have become a part of this contemporary composition.

Listen to this composition carefully and you will hear a simple A B A form with an introduction and a coda. The following diagram will assist you in your understanding:

Introduction
   Electronic sound (whistlelike in character)
   Polyphonic entrance of voices

Main Section
   A: Soloist and polyphonic voice (repetitive sound of Leiyla)
   B: Increase in 1) importance of accompaniment
                   2) intensity
   A: Return of soloist and polyphonic voice
Coda
   Same as introduction

Finally, it should be pointed out that all the poets, musicians, and lovers did not take too seriously all that was written and sung in these madrigals. Some of the songs and poems are humorous over and above being gay, while some are down to earth even though others are philosophical. Two short poems will suffice as examples:

I go before, my darling,
Follow thou to the bower
In the close alley
There we will together,
Sweetly kiss each other
And like two wantons dally.

Music some think no music is
Unless she sing of clip and kiss
And bring to wanton tunes "fie fie"
Or "ti ha," "ta ha" or "I'll cry."
But let such rhymes no more disgrace
Music sprung of heavenly race.

Study Procedures

1. Listen to other madrigals than those studied in the text. Can you hear the difference between the ballet, the canzonet, and the madrigal? Why do we today consider all of these madrigals?
2. Most high schools and colleges have madrigal groups. Request one of these groups to sing for your class. Can you hear the contrapuntal nature of the music? Does this detract from your understanding of the words? Does it enhance the musical quality of the composition as compared to homophonic structures?

Bibliography—Chapter 8

BROWN, DAVID, *Thomas Weelkes.* New York: Frederick A. Praeger, 1969.

COX, F. A., *English Madrigals in the Time of Shakespeare.* London: J. M. Dent and Co., 1899.

EINSTEIN, ALFRED, *The Italian Madrigal.* Princeton, N.J.: Princeton University Press, 1949.

FELLOWES, EDMUND H., *The English Madrigal.* London: Oxford University Press, 1935.

———, *The English Madrigal Composers.* London: Oxford University Press, 1958.

———, *English Madrigal Verse, 1588–1632.* London: Oxford University Press, 1929.

———, *William Byrd.* London: Oxford University Press, 1936.

KERMAN, JOSEPH, *The Elizabethan Madrigal.* New York: Galaxy Music Corp., 1962.

PATTISON, BRUCE, *Music and Poetry of the English Renaissance.* London: Methuen and Co. Ltd., 1970.

ROWLAND, DANIEL B., *Mannerism, Style and Mood.* New Haven, Conn.: Yale University Press, 1964.

STEVENS, DENIS, *Thomas Tomkins.* New York: Dover Publications, 1967.

Recordings—Chapter 8

"Flora Gave Me Fairest Flowers" (Wilbye)	Westminster WMS-1006
"Fusca, in Thy Starry Eyes" (Tomkins)	Westminster WMS-1006
"Happy, O Happy He" (Wilbye)	Westminster WMS-1006
"I Go Before, My Darling" (Morley)	Westminster WMS-1006
"Now Is the Month of Maying" (Morley)	Westminster WMS-1006
"Sister, Awake" (Bateson)	Columbia ML-4517
"This Sweet and Merry Month of May" (Byrd)	Decca DL-79406
"Thule, the Period of Cosmography" (Weelkes)	Westminster WMS-1006
"What Is Our Life?"	Columbia ML-4517

Many other madrigals and recordings would prove beneficial as additional material and references for this chapter.

Additional Suggestion for Listening

Cuatro Madrigales Amatorios   (Rodrigo)   (Angel 35937)

Why would the composer call these madrigals?

What obvious differences exist between these songs and others studied earlier?

The Spanish madrigal existed during the Renaissance. Was it similar to the English madrigal?

Section D *Vocal Music of Larger Forms*

Chapter 9

The Mass

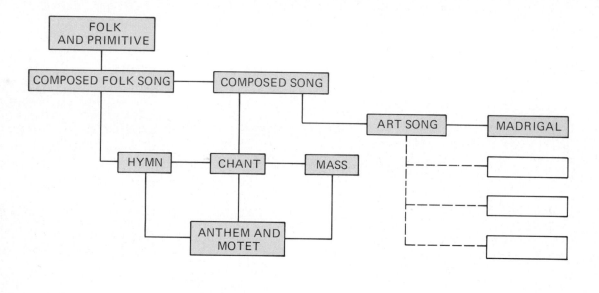

The mass is an old but still amazingly active form. There are several reasons for this.

1. The form is perpetuated by the Christian Church. Although most persons usually associate the word "mass" with the Roman Catholic service, its evolution from such a broad geographic area and long historic period commands an interest generally as well as specifically. The Greek Orthodox church service and the Russian Orthodox service were derived from the same stem, since these churches were formed as a result of the Great Schism of 1054. Consequently, persons from the East moving to other areas of the globe during migrations were quick to see this similarity and retain the mass as a universal method of worship. For several years immediately after the Reformation in Europe and England, the Protestant church used the mass in Latin, gradually moving parts of the service to the native language of the people. Today the Protestant church still makes use of the format of the mass in many inconspicuous ways, although some minor denominations would be hesitant to admit these relationships. Even Jewish service music has certain common roots with Grego-

rian chant, which was the musical element of the early mass. Consequently, large numbers of people have been continuously affected by the service of the mass.

2. The texts are universal in appeal, and consequently speak to people even beyond their formal religious and liturgical concerns. Although for years the mass was sung in Latin, the texts for many of the ordinary sections of the mass were well-known and sung by the people in and out of church. One or two sections came from the Greek, indicating their early life, since as you recall, Greek was the language in which the early Christian wrote. Reading the texts of the ordinary sections of the mass will underline these universal characteristics.

Kyrie

Kyrie eleison	*Lord, have mercy*
Christe eleison	*Christ, have mercy*
Kyrie eleison	*Lord, have mercy*

Gloria

Gloria in excelsis Deo	*Glory to God on high.*
Et in terra pax hominibus bonae voluntatis.	*And on earth peace to men of good will.*
Laudamus te. Benedicimus te.	*We praise Thee. We bless Thee.*
Adoramus te. Glorificamus te.	*We worship Thee. We glorify Thee.*
Gratias -agimus tibi propter magnam gloriam tuam.	*We give thanks to Thee for Thy great glory*
Domine Deus, Rex caelestis,	*O Lord God, heavenly King,*
Deus Pater omnipotens.	*God the Father Almighty.*
Domine Fili unigenite Jesu Christe.	*O Lord, the only begotten Son, Jesus Christ.*
Domine Deus, Agnus Dei, Filius Patris.	*O Lord God, Lamb of God, Son of the Father.*
Qui tollis peccata mundi, miserere nobis.	*That takest away the sins of the world, have mercy on us.*
Qui tollis peccata mundi, suscipe deprecationem nostram.	*Thou that takest away the sins of the world, receive our prayer.*
Qui sedes ad dexteram Patris, miserere nobis.	*Thou that sittest at the right hand of the Father, have mercy on us.*
Quoniam tu solus sanctus.	*For Thou only art holy;*
Tu solus Dominus.	*Thou only art the Lord;*
Tu solus altissimus, Jesu Christe.	*Thou only, O Jesus Christ,*
Cum Sancto Spiritu, in gloria Dei Patris. Amen.	*With the Holy Ghost, art most high in the glory of God the Father. Amen.*

Credo

Credo in unum Deum, Patrem omnipotentem, factorem caeli et terrae visibilium omnium et invisibilium.	*I believe in one God, the Father Almighty, maker of heaven and earth, and of all things visible and invisible.*
Et in unum Dominum Jesum Christum	*And in one Lord Jesus Christ,*
Filium Dei unigenitum.	*the only begotten Son of God,*
Et ex Patre natum ante omnia saecula.	*born of the Father before all ages.*
Deum de Deo, lumen de lumine,	*God of God, light of light,*
Deum verum de Deo vero.	*true God of true God*
Genitum, non factum	*begotten, not made,*
consubstantialem Patri:	*consubstantial with the Father,*
per quem omnia facta sunt.	*by whom all things were made.*
Qui propter nos homines,	*Who for us men*

et propter nostram salutem descendit de caelis.
Et incarnatus est de Spiritu Sancto
ex Maria Virgine: ET HOMO FACTUS EST.
Crucifixus etiam pro nobis sub Pontio Pilato:
Passus, et sepultus est.
Et resurrexit tertia die,
secundum Scripturas. Et ascendit in caelum:
sedet ad dexteram Patris.
Et iterum venturus est cum gloria
judicare vivos et mortuos:
cujus regni non erit finis.
Et in Spiritum Sanctum Dominum
et vivificantem: qui ex Patre
Filioque procedit.
Qui cum Patre, et Filio simul adoratur et
    conglorificatur:
qui locutus est per Prophetas.
Et unam sanctam catholicam et apostolicam
    Ecclesiam.
Confiteor unum baptisma in remissionem
    peccatorum
Et exspecto resurrectionem mortuorum.
Et vitam venturi saeculi. Amen.

and for our salvation, came down from heaven
and was incarnate by the Holy Ghost
of the Virgin Mary, AND WAS MADE MAN.
He was crucified also for us, suffered under
    Pontius Pilate,
died, and was buried.
And the third day He rose again
according to the Scriptures, and ascended into
    heaven.
He sitteth at the right hand of the Father,
and He shall come again with glory
to judge the living and the dead,
of whose kingdom there shall be no end.
And I believe in the Holy Spirit of God
The Lord and giver of Life, who cometh from
    the Father
And the Son
who together with the Father and Son is adored
    and glorified,
who spoke by the prophets.
And in one holy Catholic and Apostolic church.
I confess one baptism for the remission of sins,
And I look for the resurrection of the dead,
And the life of the world to come. Amen.

Sanctus-Benedictus

Sanctus, Sanctus, Sanctus
Dominus Deus Sabaoth.
Pleni sunt caeli et terra gloria tua.
Hosanna in excelsis.

Holy, Holy, Holy,
Lord God of Hosts.
Heaven and earth are full of Thy glory.
Hosanna in the highest.

Benedictus qui venit in nomine Domini.

Blessed is he that cometh in the name of the
    Lord.

Hosanna in excelsis.

Hosanna in the highest.

Agnus Dei

Agnus Dei, qui tollis peccata mundi, miserere
    nobis.
Agnus Dei, qui tollis peccata mundi, miserere
    nobis.

Lamb of God, that takest away the sins of the
    world, have mercy on us.
Lamb of God, that takest away the sins of the
    world, have mercy on us.

Agnus Dei, qui tollis peccata mundi, dona
    nobis pacem.

Lamb of God, that takest away the sins of the
    world, grant us peace.

3. The forms for the sections of the ordinary are appealing to a musician because of their potential. When examining the texts one notices immediately differences in their length as well as their meters. This variety instigated a tendency toward certain forms. For example, the Kyrie is usually an ABA form or an ABC form. The Gloria and Credo are more apt to be through-composed, although the texts may be arranged in sections inviting a more specific form. The Agnus Dei is obviously an AAB form, although it could be used as an ABA or AAA. These generalizations, although common, still leave composers innumerable possibilities, which make for the attractive element.

4. Portions of the mass used for every celebration of the service, which could mean every day of the year, are known as the ordinary. The sung portions of the ordinary invite musical treatment because of the regularity of performance. It was these portions, first sung by the congregation, that attracted the attention of those interested in creating a musical expression for the service, and it is still these same portions that attract the creative artist today.

5. The texts lend themselves to numerous musical styles. Although biblical, the words are not limited to one situation or meaning. Any history of the mass gives almost an equally interesting general history of music. Early periods of music have produced masses that were monodic in nature; some of the earliest polyphonic music centered around the mass; while the large, lush sounds of the Romantic period are well reflected in certain mass compositions. No style of music seems inappropriate to these texts.

6. The mass invites differences in concept of creativity. Some persons look upon the mass as a personal, almost intimate type of devotion, and musical settings have been made which stress that aspect of the music and form. Other masses have been written that consider the mass as a group celebration, with appropriate magnificence of display, ceremonial considerations, and musical settings. Many masses fit the complete gamut between these two extremes. Because of these possibilities, the form attracts the artist to express himself personally.

Since the first musical setting of the ordinary in about A.D. 1000, these factors have led to the writing of an extraordinary number of masses. The form seems much alive because today there are lay and religious persons who wish to make the mass more meaningful to the people. Consequently, this medium is being used by contemporary musicians to express their spiritual concerns, yet using stylistic expressions that speak of the contemporary experience and the present situation.

Two such masses warrant our attention. These are not outstanding musical compositions, but they illustrate attempts to express this form with music common to the twentieth century. The first mass is a musical setting in a folk style that has been popular and appealing in the early 1970s, while the second is a jazz mass which speaks of a different type of modernity.

Folk Song Mass (Ray Repp)

This musical setting of the ordinary in an imitative folk style uses a guitar and a string bass as accompaniment. The voices are a group of males singing for the most part in unison, but occasionally in two parts. The harmony in the folk-pop style of the 1960s at times promotes the illusion of being an imitation of medieval organum.

Kyrie: AAA BBB AAA. Simple and direct; rhythmic, but more in the style of modified chant.

Gloria: Through-composed, although some small phrases do repeat. A solo chanter is used for the first phrase, which indicates a relationship to liturgical masses. Quite rhythmic after the first line, a ritard and Amen are used to alter the rhythm near the end. This section moves mostly by step, similar in melodic content to the Kyrie.

Sanctus: A A B A. Again reminiscent of the Gloria and Kyrie, but not as joyful as the Gloria.

Lord's Prayer: Through-composed. This is the Catholic Church version of the prayer, omitting the usual last line. The folk idiom becomes obvious when the musical phrases do not fit the phrasing of the words. This melody is different from that used in other sections, being more tuneful.

Agnus Dei: A A' A. The same melody as the Kyrie.

This mass, meant for congregational singing, intends that the people again will participate in the celebration by means of the ordinary of the service as they did originally. The melodies are simple; most of the mass is in unison, and when parts do exist they are brief and obvious. The emphasis is upon the words, the contemporary rhythm, and the folklike sound throughout. Occasionally a sound in the melody and the music reminds one of chant, but the guitar accompaniment quickly dispels this.

Jazz Mass (Joe Masters)

This setting of the ordinary of the mass uses two styles almost simultaneously: sophisticated jazz, and the Broadway show tune. Unlike the Repp version, this is meant for listening, and as such joins those musical mass settings that have been frequent over the last five or six hundred years. The singers, a small group of mixed voices using the pop singing style, are accompanied by a club group or jazz ensemble, with the piano being the most aurally prominent instrument because of its constant intimacy with the voices.

Kyrie: A [A] B A [A] ([A] = women with melody). A stepwise instrumental introduction which is reminiscent of chant, but in an obvious jazz style. Male versus female voices in a simulated antiphonal effect.

Gloria: Four obvious sections. In the liturgical fashion, one voice chants the first phrase, while the chorus completes the verse of scripture in a show-tune chordal style. The first phrase is in direct contrast to the second section, which is fast and joyful; a piano interlude introduces a meditative slow section beginning with the words "O Lord, the Only Begotten Son." This is similar to the first section in feeling, but soon turns to a quick, syncopated section to end the Gloria.

Credo: A B interlude B' A extended for ending. The Credo begins and ends in an interesting adaptation of a congregational response; the phrase "One God" is repeated a number of times. The second section, in show tune style, uses the vocal solo, a feature of the mass setting since the seventeenth century, when the solo voice was used more extensively in opera as well as religious music.

Although not common in chanted masses, it is a common contrast in musical settings. The choral third section uses textual painting, particularly through the phrases referring to Pontius Pilate and the trial of Christ. The B section in repeat is again a solo, while the responsing work by the chorus returns to restate the original phraseology of the Credo in an obviously more spirited style than the solo portions.

Sanctus: A B A Coda. The first section makes use of some interesting scale-like passages for chorus. In the second section the drummer picks up the rhythm of the singers and uses it as a basis for his improvisation. The first section returns and is extended into the coda, where the piano uses the same scale passages of the singers as a basis for his improvisation. This is a fast and lively section.

Agnus Dei: A A' A''. The first line is given to a soloist; the second line is sung by the chorus, while the soloist sings an obbligato. The third line is similar but with more obvious harmony.

There are two additional sections to the mass: the *Benedictus* and the *Lord's Prayer.* Dating from the eighteenth century, it has been common for composers to break the Sanctus into two parts, giving the Benedictus a separate setting. The Lord's Prayer, being known so well by the people, occasionally is included with the ordinary of the mass.

By hearing these two contemporary works, the mass is introduced as an old form, but one still adaptable to two obviously different styles. Each composer hopes to use his contemporary style to show the meaningfulness of the form to the immediate situation, and these examples illustrate this. Composers for generations have attempted to explain life in their times through the mass.

Although these two examples are meaningful in light of the popular musical attempts of the day, probably neither will be considered of musical value in a few years. Those musical compositions which stand the test of time and are of value in interpreting a given century or period to later people are those examples of the highest quality art of the time represented. This is not because only high quality art is kept by man, but upon surveying the past man sees within art objects of high quality the general characteristics of the period, while lesser works reveal them so poorly or so indirectly as to become difficult to understand as examples.

The study of other masses, not only of historical interest, will also attest to the consistency of the form despite a diversity of style.

TWO SPANISH MASSES

Mass in Honor of the Blessed Virgin Mary (Anonymous, XIV Century)

During the study of music in Western civilization it is often forgotten that Spain was once a major country in commerce, literature, and the arts. The court of

Ferdinand and Isabella, sponsor of Columbus, is given meager consideration, since the rumor that the Queen sold her jewels to finance the voyage would indicate provincialism and poverty.   However, the Spanish had a rich development in the arts.   Their sea and commerce traffic with other centers, especially Italy, not only kept them informed, but aided them in leading other countries in art forms.   In fact, theirs was the first court to have a completely native art supplied by native artists.   *The Mass of the Virgin* is from an earlier time, but nonetheless imposing.   The melodies for this particular work came from England, but the treatment is typically Spanish.   Eleanor, Queen of Spain c. 1150 to 1175 and the daughter of Henry II of England, was known to have taken musicians with her to the Spanish court.   This was the beginning link with musical England and Flanders.

Study Procedures

1. This is a troped mass.   The word "trope" means that additional texts were inserted after or between the original biblical words, many times explaining or focusing the general text to a more specific situation.   This is true here.
    Compare the formality of the Kyrie to the less formal musical sounds of the other portions of the mass.
2. A sequence substitutes for two sections in this mass.   A *sequence* is an ending melody at one time sung without words after the last word of the Psalm.   Later, texts were added to this music, and finally the melody was separated from the original section of the mass altogether.
    In the Sequence the text is in rhymed Latin couplets followed by the choral response of "Ave Maria."   Consider the regularity of the tune of the couplets and the Ave Marias.
3. Contrast the smooth flow of the chant in the Sanctus and Agnus as compared to the rhythmic sections of the tropes.
4. Consider the attractiveness of the small percussion instruments and their addition to the mass.

Misa Criolla (Ariel Ramirez)

This contemporary mass, sung in Spanish, makes use of Argentinian rhythms and melodic traditions.   Another contemporary composer uses the mass form to bring added meaning and expression to the folk medium, and vice versa.

Study Procedures

1. Note the interesting use of chorus and soloist, obviously not in the Western tradition.
2. This is basically a gay and happy mass; why would the only solemn music come with the Agnus Dei?
3. The fluidity of the sung Spanish contrasts to the usual Latin, with much of a line of

the text being articulated quickly, while a particular vowel might be elongated beyond other portions of the line. Do we do this in English?

4. Describe the interesting method of using the instruments as accompaniment.

5. Each section of the mass is built upon a different rhythm from the secular world. Could you sing or imitate them? The Credo rhythm is the most complicated. Would you agree this is appropriate?

6. Although the choral singing is interesting and a vital part of the mass, it is not difficult to execute, and could be used by a congregation in connection with a choir. Why do we not know this music?

7. Describe the interesting manner of using the harpsichord, an old and recently revived instrument. Why would it be included in the accompaniment?

TWO OUTSTANDING MASSES

Mass for Five Voices (Byrd)

This is one of three masses by the great English composer, William Byrd. In the chapter on the madrigal we discussed one of his lighter compositions, but this mass better represents his work. A Catholic, working and living under a Protestant Queen, Byrd wrote his masses in honor of the Catholic Church even though they could have been sung in the newer service of the Church of England. The Renaissance period throughout Europe is noted for its beauty in a cappella choral music, and this composition is a particular example.

Study Procedures

1 The smoothness of line, the blending of voices, the emphasis upon purity of sound with little coloration exemplify the Renaissance. What other composition is similar in these qualities?

2. The work is not repetitious in melody, and yet does it maintain a similarity of sound, harmony, and texture? Is this essential for the style?

3. Listen particularly for the entrances of the voices. Do you hear each voice that begins the given theme usually in imitation of the leader?

Mass in G (Schubert)

In the chapter on the art song Schubert's vocal style was introduced. In this composition we note certain similarities in his approach to choral music. Written during his youth when he was about eighteen, this work was composed almost the same year as "Der Erlkönig." Although a good example in the Romantic style, this mass does not request a large orchestra or a huge chorus to complement an unusually large compositional frame, which was characteristic of many later works from the period.

Study Procedures

1. Compare the role of the soloists and how they function in regard to the text and in comparison with the chorus.
2. The Kyrie, Sanctus, and Credo are comparably short for the amount of text, while the Benedictus and Agnus Dei are disproportionately longer. What would be the aesthetic reasons for Schubert preferring this organizational balance?
3. Listen for the manner in which Schubert handles the text so that words in earlier sections are seldom repeated, and yet they carry interesting accents, cadence points, and melodic movement.

SPECIAL MASSES

Votive Mass—said at the request of a priest. This mass has no special music.

Nuptial Mass—said at the time of marriage. This mass often contains music, but no specific music has been composed for it. Often the service contains special music beforehand, this usually being nonliturgical but with religious implications. In some Protestant churches it has been customary for the music of the wedding ceremony to be chosen by the bridal couple. In some informal churches this music could become quite simplistic, secular, or raucous. Recently some of the more formal Protestant denominations have placed limits upon the type and style of music allowable for a wedding in the sanctuary.

Requiem Mass—said at the time of burial or on All Souls Day. The liturgy has inspired some of the great composers to use this form. Music for a requiem mass has often been commissioned by the wealthy, resulting in large, ornate compositions. Most notable of these are the Mozart, Verdi, and Berlioz Requiems.

Our study will limit itself to the more often performed and simple Fauré *Requiem*.

Requiem (Fauré)

The music for the requiem or the service of the dead may be traced to the catacombs of Rome. Here the Christians of early times hid from the persecutions, worshiped their God by saying the service as they knew it, and singing hymns of praise; here also they buried their dead. From the words and pictures carved in the rock near the burials one comes to understand something of their attitude toward death. The persecutions often were so continuous and brutal that death was looked upon as a welcome change from earthly existence; believers could look forward to an afterlife of joy and peace. It was the word "peace," along with "rest" and "joy," that was found most often in the inscriptions on the walls of the catacombs. Death was not to be feared, but welcomed, and those left living were praying for peace, joy, and rest for the dead as they left this earthly life.

*Gabriel Fauré at the age of 18, wearing the uniform of the pupils of
the Niedermeyer School (From the collection of Marie-Louise
Boellmann; Courtesy of French Cultural Services,
New York).*

Many poems were written which described the desire of those left behind for the
dead one to pray and intercede for them in heaven.

The songs and hymns that were sung, consequently, must have been anything but remorseful. This was not a particularly sad occasion, but one of joy
leading to peace. The early worship of the service of the dead carried none of
the fear and sadness that crept into the service during later years.

Some of the great Requiems in existence today stress the concept of fear,
penalty, or concern for retribution, always reminding the listener of the eternal
hell that awaits the sinful. Fauré, on the other hand, turned more toward the
original Christian concept and included almost entirely only those texts that point
toward the glory of God, the unity of the soul with God through death, and the
positive approach that can come from faith as a Christian.

Five musical characteristics become obvious as we listen to the music:

1. Although no plainchant is used in the composition, the work seems to give
   the impression of chant. This is due partly to the calmness of the writing,
   the simplicity of the melodic lines, and the syllabic style.

2. Unlike most music of the late nineteenth century, this composition contains an unusually large number of repeated notes. The parts as well as the melodies move so often in a line on the same pitch, and yet the manner of the accompaniment gives the listener the impression that this is not happening or is not monotonous.

3. Fauré was most skillful in using what is technically known as *modal implications* in his compositions. Although this is an old manner of organizing pitches predating scales, a modern setting bridges the old to the new.

4. The accompaniment, organ and orchestra, is simple. Since Fauré had a limited knowledge of orchestration, some authorities believe his friends must have sketched in the parts. The violins, woodwinds, and brasses play sparingly, while the tone color of the major portion of the work is achieved with the lower, deeper, and richer sounds. In the voice parts the writing is also simple, but the harmonies balance with the unison portions to give an effective beauty.

5. Although Fauré uses the solo voice on three occasions in the *Requiem*, it in no way seems to be a vocal exercise; in many ways it does not seem to break the texture or offer the usual obvious contrast to the musical structure.

The text for the Fauré *Requiem* follows. Compare this to the text for the general mass. In certain cases it could be helpful if one did not listen to the composition in its exact order the first time. Some students have benefited from a different order. One suggestion might be: Libera Me, Sanctus, Offertorium, Introit and Kyrie, Pie Jesu, In Paradisum, Agnus Dei.

Introit

Requiem aeternam dona eis Domine:	*Grant them rest Eternal, O Lord:*
et lux perpetua luceat eis.	*And Let eternal light shine upon them.*
Te decet hymnus Deus in Sion	*A Hymn of praise is owed to you, O God, In Zion*
et tibi reddetur votum in Jerusalem:	*And vows will be offered to you in Jerusalem.*
exaudi orationem meam,	*Hear my plea, O Lord,*
ad te omnis caro veniet.	*And to you all flesh will come.*

Kyrie

Kyrie eleison.	*Lord, have mercy.*
Christe eleison.	*Christ, have mercy.*

Offertorium

Domine Jesu Christe, Rex gloriae	*O Lord, Jesus Christ, King of Glory,*
libera animas defunctorum	*Free the souls of the dead*
de poenis inferni, et de profundo lacu:	*From punishments in hell and from the infernal pit.*
de ore leonis ne absorbeat eas Tartarus;	*Deliver them from the lion's mouth lest Tartarus swallow them up,*
ne cadant in obscurum.	*Lest they be cast into darkness.*

Hostias et preces tibi Domine	We offer you, O lord, sacrifices and prayers of praise.
laudis offerimus: tu suscipe pro animabus illis, quarum hodie memoriam facimus:	Receive them in behalf of those spirits Who, today, we remember.
fac eas, Domine, de morte transire ad vitam.	Make them, O Lord, cross over from death to life,
Quam olim Abrahae promisisti et semini ejus.	Which once you promised to Abraham and his descendants.

Sanctus

Sanctus, Sanctus, Sanctus Dominus Deus Sabaoth.	Holy, Holy, Holy, Lord God of Hosts,
Pleni sunt caeli et terra gloria tua. Hosanna in excelsis.	Heaven and Earth are filled with your glory, Hosanna in the highest.

Pie Jesu

Pie Jesu Domine, dona eis requiem, sempiternam requiem.	Holy Lord Jesus, give them rest, eternal rest.

Agnus Dei

Agnus Dei, qui tollis peccata mundi:	Lamb of God, who takes away the sins of the world,
dona eis requiem.	Give them rest.
Agnus Dei, qui tollis peccata mundi:	Lamb of God, who takes away the sins of the world,
dona eis requiem.	Give them rest.
Agnus Dei, qui tollis peccata mundi:	Lamb of God, who takes away the sins of the world,
dona eis requiem sempiternam.	Give them everlasting rest.

Response: Libera Me

This section is not part of the Mass, but follows it on such occasions. It has often been used by composers as part of their requiems.

Libera me, Domine, de morte aeterna, in die illa tremenda: Quando caeli movendi sunt et terra: Dum veneris judicare saeculum per ignem. Tremens factus sum ego, et timeo, dum discussio venerit, atque ventura ira.	Free me, O Lord, from eternal death On that formidable day When the heavens and earth will be shaken As you will come to judge the world by fire. I am fearful and trembling until judgment and wrath shall come.
Dies illa, dies irae, calamitatis et miseriae, dies magna et amara valde. Requiem aeternam dona eis Domine: et lux perpetua luceat eis.	O day, O that day, O day of wrath, of calamity and misery, That great and very bitter day. Give them eternal rest, O Lord, And let everlasting light shine upon them.

In Paradisum

This section also is not part of the Mass, but is sung as the coffin is being carried from the church. Note the optimistic faith which is part of this text.

In paradisum deducant angeli	*May the angels escort you into Paradise,*
in tuo adventu suscipant te martyres	*May the martyrs receive you at your arrival*
et per ducante in civitatem sanctam Jerusalem;	*And guide you through into the Holy City, Jerusalem.*
Chorus angelorum te suscipiat	*May a choir of angels receive you,*
et cum Lazaro quondam paupere aeternam habeas requiem.	*And with Lazarus, once poor, May you have everlasting rest.*

Additional Listening

After this introduction to the mass, other compositions may prove interesting. Many well-known masses and requiems are available from any music library. One additional contemporary work should be mentioned: the *War Requiem* of Benjamin Britten. Although not an easy work at first hearing, the composition proves interesting in format, since it combines war poems by an English World War I poet with the requiem service in Latin, performed by a mixed choir, boys' choir, soloists, and orchestra.

Bibliography—Chapter 9

AMIOT, FRANÇOIS, *History of the Mass.* New York: Hawthorn Books, 1959.

BUSSARD, PAUL, *The Meaning of the Mass.* Washington, D.C.: Catholic University of America Press, 1942.

PENNINGTON, KENNETH D., *A Historical and Stylistic Study of the Melodies of Gabriel Fauré.* Ann Arbor, Mich.: University Microfilms, Inc., 1961.

PERCIVAL, ALLEN, *History of Music.* London: Universities Press, Ltd., 1967.

ROBERTSON, ALEC, *Requiem, Music of Mourning and Consolation.* New York: Frederick A. Praeger, Inc., 1968.

SACHS, CURT, *Our Musical Heritage.* Englewood Cliffs, N.J.: Prentice-Hall, Inc., 1955.

ULRICH, HOMER, and PAUL PISK, *A History of Music and Musical Style.* New York: Harcourt, Brace and World, Inc., 1963.

VUILLERMOZ, EMILE, *Gabriel Fauré.* Philadelphia: Chilton Book Company, 1969.

WIENANDT, ELWYN A., *Choral Music of the Church.* New York: Free Press, 1965.

Recordings—Chapter 9

Byrd	*Mass for Five Voices*	Choir of King's College	Argo ZRG-5226
Fauré	*Requiem*	Roger Wagner Chorale	Capitol P-8241

Masters	*Jazz Mass*	Joe Masters	Columbia CS-9398
Ramirez	*Misa Criolla*		Philips PCC-619
Repp	*Mass for Young Americans*	Ray Repp	F.E.L. 022
Schubert	*Mass in G*	Robert Shaw Chorale	Victor LM-1784
Spanish Medieval Music	*Mass of the Virgin*	New York Pro Musica	Decca DL-79416

Chapter 10

The Cantata

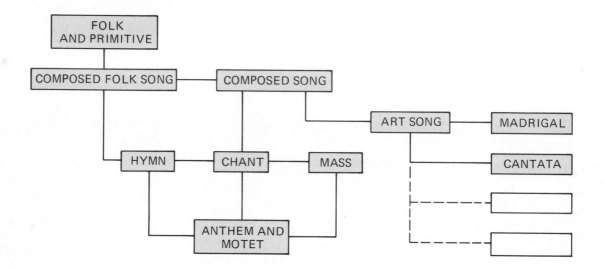

There are times when a composer wishes to express an idea in a more generous or comprehensive manner. This means the composition can be longer and at the same time more complex. Several ways are open for him to bring length and complexity to a composition and still retain artistic characteristics.

THE LARGER FORM

What might be the reason for wishing something to be more extensive? That question relates to one which asks why a person would wish to add a second verse to a song. He might wish to tell more than could be told in one verse. As we noted in the art song, if a second verse of a poem were used the music might not be the same as for the first verse. The composer might choose to write new music. In other words, there could be more to say, and the composer might wish to say it differently than something immediately before. As we have worked with form through preceding chapters, this term has come to mean the way a melody is treated, and the use of new melodies in contrast.   Similar ideas remain valid in larger forms.

a. If a composer wishes to make a composition longer he could repeat the melody exactly as we heard it before.   If this were a short melody then the repetition would make it a bit longer, but not much.   If the melody were long and involved, then the repetition would add considerably to the length.

b. Another method open to the composer repeats the melody but alters it so that it takes on new interest for the listener.   In fact, the alteration could be so subtle that the listener might not be aware of it until he has heard the composition more than one time.   In contrast, the alteration could be so complex that the listener might not even be aware that he hears the same melodic idea, and consequently believes it to be something new.

c. Still another method open to the composer takes a little fragment of the original tune and expands it until it becomes an important second tune by itself.   This may be likened to a cook who cuts out cookies or biscuits from a large piece of dough.   When finished he makes from the many little scraps a tart or some completely different pastry pleasing to the eye and the taste.

d. The most obvious method is to write new material that will make the composition longer.

In larger choral or instrumental works, all of these ideas are used, depending upon the wishes of the composer, his artistic talent, and his understanding of what might seem artistically appropriate at a given moment.   In the same set of circumstances, a second composer might choose a different solution and create a composition which would be equally effective.

A DEFINITION

The cantata uses three expressive musical ideas.   To some extent all of these have been discussed in a preceding chapter, but because of their relationship to the cantata a review is appropriate.   As a first definition, a *cantata* is a musical form of some size making use of three musical means of expression: the aria, the recitative, and the chorus.

Aria[1] is merely a professional name for song.   We have heard many songs

---

[1] For those interested in contemporary music, a parenthetical insertion at this point might prove interesting.   John Cage has written a composition entitled *Aria with Fontana Mix,* performed by soprano with electronic tape.   This aria is a study of what the voice can do; it covers a mixture of styles and a variety of languages.   Accompanying the voice, instead of the usual piano or ensemble, is an electronic tape made of sounds distorted by electronic means. This is a personal type of singing, as if we were listening to a solitary person vocalizing her thoughts in a "stream of consciousness" style.

Study Procedures

1. What is similar to an aria in this composition?   Why would a composer give it such a title?
2. Wherein do the artistic features lie?
3. Separate the voice from the accompaniment.   Which seems more songlike?   Why?   Could either part stand alone and remain expressive?

since the beginning of the course. Some have been simple. If they are obviously folk songs they will never be called arias; but if they are of an artistic nature, they could be. Usually an aria is an artistic expression implying a major emphasis upon the music rather than the words, although the words are not insignificant. Thus, arias have a musical form other than strophic. Through continuity, such a song could have a relation to other pieces of music. We will discuss the aria in more detail in Chapter 11.

Recitative means that the singer is using a speechlike approach to a text. Usually it will not sound like the chant of a religious service, but the style is not dissimilar, since it emphasizes the character and rhythm of the words. The singer often will follow the accents of the words and their meaning in the little melodic phrases which are used. The bare accompaniment, usually a few chords here and there, places additional emphasis upon the singer and the text. Although melodic, in that it does not remain on one pitch, it often is not tuneful. The rhythm of the words is more often followed than a musical rhythm. Usually the recitative precedes an aria, or is interjected between two other more lyrical parts.

A *chorus* is, as it implies, a choral selection. Composers prescribe a chorus to function in several ways even in the same composition. At one point the chorus may be used for emphasis to repeat an emotion which has been expressed earlier; or it could be used as an observer, helping the audience understand what has happened or what is taking place; it might elaborate upon an idea; or bring a musical climax to a section of the work. In any of these uses the larger vocal forces use one or more musical devices: straight choral singing, contrapuntal singing, antiphonal singing with accompaniment, or antiphonal singing with smaller or larger vocal groups. Not all of these will be used in every composition, and the composer must decide which will best service his intent.

To recapitulate: the cantata is a musical form of considerable length making use of three musical means of expression for the purpose of emphasizing a single idea.

We now have added a most important phrase to the definition. The cantata, in the strictest sense, is not involved with a plot or story. Rather, it develops a single idea for the benefit of the listener. It is expressive, contemplative, and personal. In these three ways it differs obviously from other large vocal forms.

The cantata is *chamber music,* meaning that it was intended for a small audience. In this sense, at least, it is intended to be intimate and personal. For this same reason it adapted itself well to the church or a religious service, where the emphasis could be upon the smaller audience as compared to the concert hall, but also where the emphasis could be upon the contemplative. Because of its expressive emphasis the musical means are more apt to be mainly the aria and recitative, rather than the chorus; it uses smaller ensembles for accompaniment rather than the large orchestra. Some cantatas are written for one solo voice with or without a final chorus. Others make use of four solo voices, and these could then become the chorus when they all sing together. The exact combinations of personnel and forms are details which are left up to the composer.

An example of Baroque architecture: Vaux-le-Vicomte (Courtesy of French Cultural Services, New York).

THE BACH SACRED CANTATA

Two reasons exist for studying the Bach sacred cantata: first, although a large number of secular cantatas have been written over the years, it has been in the sacred area that the cantata has made the greatest impact and it is here that this form has its largest following. Secondly, Johann Sebastian Bach, one of the great composers of all times, exemplifies well the Baroque period, and his sacred music has been admired and extolled for generations. His output in cantatas alone numbers almost 300, and although these do not all have the same form, they do fit well into the categories and definitions which we have outlined above.

Ein feste Burg (Bach)

In looking at Bach's *Cantata No. 80* several general points come to our attention:
    a. The cantata carries a familiar title: "A Mighty Fortress Is Our God." This is one of the great hymns of the Christian Church, the battle cry of the Reformation, and now accepted by Protestant and Catholic churches alike as

a great statement of faith. If not familiar before, you will remember this tune from Chapter 5.

b. The cantata is composed of eight sections. As we originally stated, one method of extending a work is to divide it into several sections, each of which could be different in some way and yet deal with the subject at hand. Bach has done this with considerable variety and yet definite continuity.

c. The use of the three musical constructs is well exemplified throughout this composition. Bach uses the chorus three times, recitative twice, and arias four times.

d. Four solo voices are used in this work: soprano, alto, tenor, and bass. No accommodation has been made for instrumental interludes, since the emphasis here is upon the hymn text and the meaning of the words.

In many of his church services Bach used instruments as an accompaniment for the choir either as he chose or as they were available. Reformation Sunday in Germany at the time of Bach would have been celebrated with considerable flair, and it would follow that a larger orchestra would be available and deemed more desirable than for regular services. Consequently, the accompaniment, using two trumpets, timpani, two oboes, and strings, is larger than for many other cantatas. Even so, one can readily realize this is not a large group and in no way should be considered as such.

When Bach cantatas are sung these days in churches the accompaniment is often small; when performed in a concert hall, the accompaniment may be larger, since the orchestra is available and the dramatic effect is thereby enhanced. During such occasions less emphasis is placed on the personal, intimate, and devotional impact of the music.

Study of the Composition

The sections of the cantata will be studied in an order other than as written. This is only a study procedure. After the study is complete, you should listen to it in its correct order so as to acquire the effect intended by the composer.

VIII—Chorale

The composition ends with this section. It is a straightforward singing of the chorale melody known from the hymn. The harmonization is by Bach, and could be different from the one sung in some churches. Since most recordings of this work are in the original German, a translation of the words will be given.

The Word of God will firm abide
Against Our foes assailing
For He will battle on our side,
An ally never failing.

That Word above all earthly powers
No thanks to them abideth;
The Spirit and the gifts are Ours
Through Him who with us sideth;

Tho' they take from me here
All that I hold dear
I will not complain,
Their vantage will be vain,
God's might is all-prevailing.

Let good and kindred go,
This mortal life also;
The body they may kill:
God's truth abideth still,
His kingdom is for ever.

Although both verses are translations of Martin Luther's original, the text at the right may seem more familiar, since it is found in a number of hymnals.

V—Chorus

The fifth section is also for the chorus, and makes use of the third verse of the hymn text. In order to give variety to the music, however, Bach has written the melody and accompaniment in a different rhythm so that the music has a lilt or gallop as it moves along. Technically speaking, he has changed this from the usual 4/4 signature to 6/8.

The accompaniment begins the tune playing the first phrase, and then moves away from it to play agitated scalelike passages or repetitious portions that seem to have nothing to do with the melody. In fact, they are musical configurations which have been used by Bach to provide an accompaniment to the chorus, and this accompaniment is more dancelike than religious. This is an excellent example of Bach's tone painting wherein the busyness of the accompaniment portrays the powers of evil which try to batter the faithful. Musically this is well done, since the entire accompaniment seems completely oblivious of the main theme of the chorus. Eight different times throughout this section the orchestra begins the hymn tune, only to move from it after the first phrase as if to detract our attention from the main concern, or to draw the faithful from their duties. In other words, we have warring (competing) parties which Bach has provided purposely, with the orchestra furnishing the competition to the chorus, whose main task is to sing the tune in unison. Bach chose unison in this section for two reasons: to have the chorus singing parts while the orchestra is battling with such a complicated accompaniment would have diluted the contrasting effect; also, the composer wrote symbolically of the unified posture Christians should have if they are to work against evil in the world. The text is printed below, again in two versions:

Though fiends appear on every hand
All eager to devour us,
We need not fear; we can withstand
And baffle all their power.
The Arch-Fiend of all,
Shall not us appall,
His might is laid low,
He cannot strike a blow
One word from God will fell him.

And though this world, with devils filled
Should threaten to undo us;
We will not fear, for God hath willed
His truth to triumph through us:
The prince of darkness grim,
We tremble not for him;
His rage we can endure,
For lo! his doom is sure,
One little word shall fell him.

IV—Soprano Aria

As the title implies this is a solo for the soprano. Because it is an aria it should be songlike, placing considerable emphasis upon the music as compared to the text.

The words do not come from the hymn text. Rather, they are poetic adaptations of the meaning of the hymn. Only the flavor of the hymn is retained.

As mentioned earlier, one method of lengthening a composition is to repeat some of the melody. This is done in this aria. The following text indicates the repeats; this will assist you in understanding the musical repeats as well.

Come dwell within my heart
Come dwell within my heart
Lord Jesus, my desire
Lord Jesus, my desire.

Bid evil all depart
Bid evil all depart
And let Thine image
Ever shine within me.

Out, vile and horrible Sin
Out, vile and horrible Sin
Out, Out, Out, Out, Out, Out, Out,
Out, vile and horrible Sin
Out, vile and horrible Sin.

Come dwell within my heart
Come dwell within my heart
Lord Jesus, my desire
Lord Jesus, my desire
Lord Jesus, my desire.

A	A'	B	A
x x y extended	x' x' y' extended	through-composed	x x y extended

The complete aria, then, makes use of an A A' B A form with the subsections as illustrated.

VI—Tenor Recitative

Musically this section is quite short, but the text is lengthy. Usually the recitative covers many more words than an aria, since the style is conducive to a declamatory statement. Near the end of the recitative the music becomes more tuneful where the words declare that "salvation now is sure."

So take thy stand with Jesus' blood-bespattered banner,
O soul of mine,
And trust thee ever in His power divine!
Yea, He will lend his might to gain for thee thy crown in glory.
Go joyous forth to Fight!
If thou but hear God's Word and do as He command thee,
No foe, however mighty, can withstand thee.
Salvation now is sure.
Salvation now is sure.

III—Bass Recitative and Arioso

In many ways this section is similar to section VI. With a few guides you should be able to lead yourself through this short number so that you are able to hear the items listed. As in section VI, the first portion is a recitative. When the last line is realized, a more tuneful section begins; this is known as an *arioso,* meaning a style midway between a recitative and an aria. In the arioso, the melody repeats itself three times; the third time it is a deviation of the first two, since an ending is imminent. Again, the words are not taken directly from the hymn, but rather, expand upon the mood of the hymn text.

Thou child of God, consider what complete devotion
*   the Savior showed for you in His supreme atonement,*
Whereby He rose triumphant over Satan's Horde
*   and human sin and error and all things base.*
Let not, then in your being, the Evil One have any place.
Let not your sins convert the Heaven there within you, into a desert!
Repent now of your guilt in tears,
*   that Christ the Lord to you be fast united;*
*   that Christ the Lord to you be fast united;*
*   that Christ the Lord to you be fast united.*

VII—Duetto

This duet for the alto and the tenor could be called an aria for two if so desired. The voice melody is played first by the oboe da caccia, a rather rare instrument of the alto range, and the violins. Much of the vocal line is in counterpoint. Listen carefully and ascertain if you are able to hear how the different voices enter no matter whether they be instrumental or human. The melody is an elaborate treatment of fragments of the middle of the hymn tune. This might be difficult to hear, but with more than one playing, some of the familiarity will be evident. The form is shown below:

A		A'		B	C	A
x y	extended and contrapuntal	x y'	extended and contrapuntal	z z z	chromatic	instrumental only

II—Aria for Bass and Soprano Choir

This section differs from others in at least one way: the bass sings alone against the soprano section of the choir. The sopranos are singing the second verse of the hymn, and although the original tune is evident, in some places it becomes more florid than the hymn tune. This adds some variety for the listener, and also gives the unanimity needed for a long composition.

The melody of the bass voice is related to the accompaniment. As we found in section V, the florid accompaniment in the orchestra and continuo reminds us of the war between right and wrong. The bass, who performs almost continuously, and consequently at the same time as the soprano section, sings something entirely different both as to text and to music. His text is a statement to those who would be faithful, almost as if it were an admonition or a cheer encouraging them to continue the fight. The music for the bass aria resembles the orchestral part more than the hymn tune sung by the sopranos. The implication is that the sopranos need the encouragement from the bass, since he sings from a vantage point within or near the forces of evil and his encouragement for good almost equals those forces. The hearing of these contrasting parts should not be difficult, since the melodic lines vary greatly and the voice ranges are so obvious.

Standing alone are we undone,
The Fiend would soon enslave us;
But for us fights a mighty One
Whom God has sent to save us.
Ask ye, who this be?
Christ Jesus is He,
Lord God of Sabaoth,
There is no other God;
He can and will uphold us.

Did we in our own strength confide,
Our striving would be losing;
Were not the right man on our side,
The man of God's own choosing:
Dost ask who that may be?
Christ Jesus, it is He;
Lord Sabaoth his Name,
From age to age the same,
And He must win the battle.

Bass Aria
Every soul by God created,
Has by Christ been liberated.
They who Jesus' standard bear,
To His service dedicated,
All will in His victory share.

Since the hymn words are longer than the poem sung by the bass, the latter is repeated, sometimes in parts and at other times completely.

I—Chorus

This chorus is not an easy one to understand, and yet the melody of the hymn tune pervades the music constantly. Several factors account for this difficulty.

a. The section is long. After you have heard it several times you will not consider this an overly long treatment. In reality Bach uses the hymn tune in almost a direct manner. The length comes from the extension of each line of the melody.

b. The section is contrapuntal. Each voice begins the tune as we know it, and then continues with a variation of the tune as other voices sing the melody. This type of contrapuntal writing is often difficult to hear but not so difficult to see. For that reason the score for the first section has been included. If you do not read music, nevertheless, consider that the score can be of use to you. Look at the printed page to gain more from the hearing. Particularly is this true, since the score is marked to indicate the lines of the hymn.

c. The words of the hymn do not occur simultaneously, since the music is contrapuntal, and hearing becomes more complex when the words of vocal materials do not come exactly together. This is not a new technique. Many compositions have used this musical device throughout the years. Today, it is used in popular songs and commercials.

d. You are probably not as familiar with this melody as the churchgoers were when this cantata was originally performed. They were as familiar with this melody as we are with "The Star Spangled Banner." Consequently, it was not difficult for them to grasp the significance of the complexity of this kind of writing. In addition, it added a dimension of importance to the tune when a composer treated a melody in this manner. This chorus is the first verse of the hymn, which would be the most familiar to people just as many first verses are more familiar to us.

A stronghold sure is God our Lord	1. *A mighty fortress is our God*
Whose strength will never fail us;	2. *A bulwark never failing;*
He keeps us free from all the horde	3. *Our helper he amid the flood*
Of troubles that assail us.	4. *Of mortal ills prevailing;*
Our ever evil foe	5. *For still our ancient foe*
Would fain work us woe;	6. *Doth seek to work us woe;*
With might and deep guile	7. *His craft and power are great,*
He plans his projects vile	8. *And, armed with cruel hate,*
On earth there's not one like him.	9. *On earth is not his equal.*

The constantly contrapuntal lines add additional music after the statement of the melody in order to continue the harmony. Follow the numbers of the lines of the text, and you will be able to see how the parts follow one another and how each part sings a portion of the original tune while other voices sing composed harmony.

Ein feste Burg ist unser Gott

Johann Sebastian Bach
1685–1750

From Eulenburg Score Edition No. 1003, Ernst Eulenburg Ltd., London-Zürich. Used by permission.

Rejoice in the Lamb (Britten)

This Britten cantata offers four contrasting items to the Bach:

1. It is a short musical work of sixteen minutes.
2. It is contemporary, having been written in 1943 for the fiftieth anniversary of St. Matthew's Church in Northampton, England.
3. The musical styles are contrasting.
4. Bach based his cantata upon a famous hymn; Britten chose words by a famous English poet.

Some items are in agreement:

1. Both were written for the service of the church.
2. Both employ soloists.
3. Both works use the standard concepts of expression for the cantata: aria, recitative, and chorus.
4. Both are for the glory of God and affirm that faith to the listener.

Text

The text for the Britten cantata is taken from a long collection of religious statements by the English poet, Christopher Smart. This is typical of Britten, since he has chosen literary works by comparatively unknown but quality writers as the basis for many of his compositions. These writers usually come from a period much earlier than Britten himself, and yet as treated by the composer the words take on a contemporary feeling and sound.

Christopher Smart was born into the laboring class. Because of his obvious talent and the friendship of his family with many well-known persons, he was able to be well educated. He studied Latin and Greek, but upon turning to poetry won the famous Seatonian Prize five of the first six years it was offered. His excesses in drinking and spending resulted in his being committed to prison and later to a hospital for the insane. While an inmate of the hospital he wrote the poem *Jubilate Agno,* from which this cantata is taken.

As originally written, the text of the poem consisted of phrases beginning with the word "Let" found on the left pages, while lines beginning with the word "For" were found on the right pages. Smart had intended for these to be used antiphonally, reminiscent of early church days, and particularly of the church during the Renaissance. It is indeed surprising that Britten did not take advantage of this so that the listener could hear the original intent of the words.

Although the poem was written for responsive reading, it likewise was written to be meaningful to the person reading down the pages, as if he were reading the usual book. Some of the lines which follow will exemplify this. The "Let" portions were filled with little-known references to Biblical, Greek, and Roman characters, minutiae, and symbolism, while the "For" portions were contemporary reactions to these ideas. Within these contrasts the rareness of the poem became evident, and because of these, when published, the book only led to additional accusations by writers and laymen that Smart was truly insane.

He also took to prophecy with many lines devoted to what he believed would take place.

> For I prophecy that the King will have grace to put the crown
>   upon the altar.
> For I prophecy that the name of King of England will be given to
>   Christ alone.
> For I prophecy that men will live to a much greater age, this ripens apace
>   God be praised.
> For I prophecy that they will grow taller and stronger.
> For I prophecy that all Englishmen will wear their beards again.[2]

The cantata is in ten parts, all short. A reading through of the words will assist you before hearing it with music. As you read remember the main purpose is to assist the reader in recognizing that "The earth is the Lord's, and the fullness thereof." Benjamin Britten and Christopher Smart wanted us to recognize that all creatures of the earth do praise the Lord in their own way, and that we as humans must be continually aware of the many ways we should praise Him. The original title, *Jubilate Agno*, assists us with the meaning of the poem. Let us acknowledge praise, let us recognize praise, let us understand praise, let us allow praise, are all meanings encompassed within the Latin title.

I—Chorus

*Rejoice in God, O ye Tongues; give the glory to the Lord, and the
    Lamb.
Nations and languages, and every Creature, in which is the breath of
    Life.
Let man and beast appear before him and magnify his name together.*

II—Chorus

*Let Nimrod, the mighty hunter, bind a Leopard to the altar, and
    consecrate his spear to the Lord.
Let Ishmael dedicate a Tyger, and give praise for the liberty in which
    the Lord has let him at large.
Let Balaam appear with an Ass, and bless the Lord his people and
    his creatures for a reward eternal.
Let Daniel come forth with a Lion, and praise God with all his might
    through faith in Christ Jesus.
Let Ithamar minister with a Chamois, and bless the name of Him,
    which cloatheth the naked.
Let Jakim with the Satyr bless God in the dance.
Let David bless with the Bear—The beginning of victory to the Lord—
    to the Lord the perfection of excellence.*

---

2 *Jubilate Agno*, Christopher Smart, edited by W. H. Bond. Rupert Hart-Davis, London; Harvard University Press, Cambridge, Mass., 1954, pages 133 and 139.

III—Chorus

Hallelujah from the heart of God, and from the hand of the artist inimitable, and from the echo of the heavenly harp in sweetness magnifical and mighty.

IV—Soprano Solo

For I will consider my Cat Jeoffry.
For he is the servant of the Living God, duly and daily serving him.
For at the first glance of the glory of God in the East he worships in his way.
For this is done by wreathing his body seven times round with elegant quickness.
For he knows that God is his Savior.
For God has blessed him in a variety of his movements.
For there is nothing sweeter than his peace when at rest.
For I am possessed of a cat, surpassing in beauty, from whom I take occasion to bless Almighty God.

V—Alto Solo

For the Mouse is a creature of great personal valour.
For–this is a true case–Cat takes female mouse–male mouse will not depart, but stands threat'ning and daring.
. . . If you will let her go, I will engage you, as prodigious a creature as you are.
For the Mouse is a creature of great personal valour.
For the Mouse is of an hospitable disposition.

VI—Tenor Solo

For the flowers are great blessings.
For the flowers have their angels even the words of God's Creation.
For the flower glorifies God and the root parries the adversary.
For there is a language of flowers.
For flowers are peculiarly the poetry of Christ.

VII—Chorus

For I am under the same accusation with my Savior–
For they said, he is beside himself.
For the officers of the peace are at variance with me, and the watchman smites me with his staff.
For Silly fellow! Silly fellow! is against me and belongeth neither to me nor to my family.
For I am in twelve Hardships, but he that was born of a virgin shall deliver me out of all.

VIII—Bass Solo (Recitative)

For H is a spirit and therefore he is God.
For K is king and therefore he is God.
For L is Love and therefore he is God.
For M is musick and therefore he is God.

IX—Chorus

For the instruments are by their rhimes.
For the Shawn rhimes are lawn fawn moon boon and the like.
For the Harp rhimes are sing ring string and the like.

For the Cymbal rhimes are bell well toll soul and the like.
For the Flute rhimes are tooth youth suit mute and the like.
For the Bassoon rhimes are pass class and the like.
For the Dulcimer rhimes are grace place beat heat and the like.
For the Clarinet rhimes are clean seen and the like.
For the Trumpet rhimes are sound bound soar more and the like.
For the Trumpet of God is a blessed intelligence and so are all the
*   instruments in HEAVEN.*
For GOD the father Almighty plays upon the HARP of stupendous
*   magnitude and melody.*
For at that time malignity ceases and the devils themselves are at
*   peace.*
For this time is perceptible to man by a remarkable stillness and
*   serenity of soul.*

X—Chorus

Hallelujah from the heart of God, and from the hand of the artist
*   inimitable, and from the echo and the heavenly harp in sweetness*
*   magnifical and mighty.*

The Music

Britten's musical ideas for this cantata are built around two main themes. The first is a one-pitch, multirhythm incantation, which he uses from time to time throughout the work. Because of its constant use the second becomes the more important: an upward scale passage of five notes beginning on the tonic and progressing upward. The rhythm and pitch of this scale change throughout the work, and at times the scale is extended briefly to give the section some variety. After the variety is achieved he returns to the simple original version.

Both of these ideas are unusually simple. One wants to suggest that the simplicity is reminiscent of the simplicity of the words. This would be unfair, though, since many of the themes from accepted masterworks are simple melodic ideas. Rather, it would be more to the point to suggest that the simplicity of the music only enhances the words so they may shine through to the listener.

Unusual from the standpoint of organization of a cantata are the first three sections, which are all for chorus. This would not be feasible were it not a short work. The listener could assume these three sections were one. Three solos follow, which again show the original approach Britten uses in the organization of this cantata. After a chorus, the bass sings his recitative, and the work ends with two choruses. The major emphasis is upon the chorus, probably dictated in part by the dedication of this work to the choir and the minister.

I—Chorus

This short section is practically all on one note, bringing to mind the earlier plainchant. In some ways this section acts as an introduction or fanfare. The straight singing of the voices contrasts sharply to the dissonant accompaniment. Only as we approach the ending of the section do the voices move upward, taking a traditional chant ending.

II—Chorus

In contrast to the slow introduction, the second section is rapid. In addition, the time signatures have been altered enough and the ones chosen rare enough so the listener hears constant rhythm imbalances. When the words discuss the dance, Britten chooses to use a melismatic approach to the words. The scale passages in this section neatly balance the repetitious pitches, combining the two main melodic ideas.

III—Chorus

Again the mood changes as the choir sings the "hallelujahs" in a slow tempo but with quiet joy. The scale theme is most prominent here.

IV—Soprano Solo

Most of this section makes use of the scale theme. The ornate solo part parallels the accompaniment. The form of the aria, dictated by the words, is one of almost constant repetition with small variations to add variety.

Introduction   A A' A' ending   A' A''   Coda (same as Introduction)

V—Alto Solo

The rather repetitious accompaniment contrasts with the smoother vocal line and the faster tempo of the previous aria.

A   B   A

The middle section differs from the two A sections mostly through interval and key changes, bringing out the character of the words which point to the unique bravery of the mouse.

VI—Tenor Solo

Again, here is a simple solo as to form and simple as to accompaniment. The repetitious accompaniment figures help give the flowing effect which the words suggest. The slow tempo of this section gives variety and underlines the intent of the composer to establish a scheme of alternating tempos.

A A A extended   B B′ A′   A extended
_____

VII—Chorus

This section borrows its effect from the first chorus, wherein much of the music moves along on one pitch. When it does vary the part writing is simple and often in unison. When the text speaks of hardships, Britten uses a contrapuntal device and a minor scale to assist the tone painting. The brief contrapuntal effect, more simple than those used by Bach, could escape the listener.

VIII—Bass Recitative

The use of letter text at this point of the composition is not as meaningful as Christopher Smart's entire sequence, in which he enumerated various implied meanings for each letter of the alphabet. The last line of the recitative acts as an introduction to the next chorus. This is typical recitative style.

IX—Chorus

Again in this section, the text belongs to that portion of the poem in which Smart was writing merely to wear away the days and to keep his mental capacities sharp. He used words and phrases in other than usual ways and with often insignificant cross-references. On the other hand, the words make a singable text which speaks poetically of music and imply the effect music may bring to praise. The music condenses the scale theme, which means that the composer uses some of the notes of the scale and omits others. For the first time in the cantata an antiphonal effect is used as voices answer one another with rhyming words. It is in this chorus that Britten skips about the text, putting together certain lines and phrases which Smart had not combined in this manner. This is the last section of fast tempo and leads directly to the final chorus.

X—Chorus

An exact repeat of the "Hallelujah" used as section III, this obvious little three-part form makes a fitting ending to the entire cantata.

A B A
_____

Study Procedure

The two cantatas studied are good examples of two style periods in the history of music. As you listen to music you should constantly be aware of differences in sound and, even though you are not a musician, you should attempt to explain in your own words why the music sounds as it does. This skill can be developed only after some practice, so you should answer this question with almost everything you hear. Rethink how each of the cantatas sounded to you and in what ways they were different. Your teacher will assist you.

Carmina Burana (Orff)

A contemporary cantata undoubtedly of interest to university students was composed by Carl Orff in 1937 but not performed in the United States until 1954. Despite the use of a large orchestra, three soloists, chorus, and a boys' choir, the form and means of expression stipulate a cantata.

This is a collection of songs based upon poems by thirteenth century university students, vagabonds, poets, and wandering minstrels, which discuss drinking, gambling, singing, and making love. What could be more interesting for college students to write about or study?

The Text

Interestingly enough, the words chosen by Orff for his cantata were found in 1803 in an old Bavarian monastery in the Alps not far from Munich. Because the monastery had been operated by the Benedictine order, it was known as the Benediktbeuern: the first part of the word referring to the order, and the latter part to the village of Beuren where the monastery is located. This village name is part of the title of the cantata. The first word of the title means "songs."

An introduction precedes the three parts of the cantata. This choral prelude discusses the Fortune of the World by lamenting that "we should mourn together, for fate crushes the brave." Part One is dedicated to spring, the second to songs of the tavern (drinking and gambling), and the third to love.

We will concern ourselves only with the third section, or that dealing with love. Though most persons are interested in love, this section warrants study because of the dramatic music and its organization. It is hoped that you will become interested in hearing more of this cantata.

Remember as you read through the text that this translation from popular Latin or peasant French and German has been somewhat altered from the sometimes obscene language which the students preferred to express their moods.

Orff has written several compositions involving older texts. He has been asked the reason for this and replied, "Even though I have used old material, fairy tales and legends, I do not feel them as old, but rather as valid. The timely element disappears, and only the spiritual power remains. My entire interest is in the expression of spiritual realities. I write to convey a spiritual attitude." His choice of words should not be confused with the religious, since he means those ideas having to do with feelings which are common to all.

The text for the third portion of the cantata follows. The twenty-fifth section is a repeat of the first section, which Orff uses as both introduction and closing.

15—Soprano Solo and Boys' Chorus

The God of Love flies everywhere and is seized by desire.
Young men and young women are rightly joined together.
  If a girl lacks a man
  she misses all delight;
  darkest night is at the
  bottom of her heart:
This is bitterest fate.

16—Baritone Solo

Day and night and all the world are opposed to me,
  and the sound of maidens' voices makes me weep.
Alas, I am filled with sighing and fear.
Thy lively face makes me weep a thousand tears
  because thy heart is made of ice.
Thy single kiss would bring me back to life.

17—Soprano Solo

There stood a maid in a red tunic;
When it was touched the tunic rustled. Eia!

There stood a girl, like a rose;
Her face was radiant, her mouth bloomed. Eia!

18—Baritone Solo and Chorus

My heart is filled with sighing.
I am longing for thy beauty.
My misery is great.
  Manda liet, manda liet,
  My sweetheart does not come.
May the Gods look with favor on my desire
To undo the bonds of her virginity.
  Manda liet, manda liet,
  My sweetheart does not come.

19—Soli (3 Tenors, Baritone, 2 Basses)

When a boy and a maiden are alone together,
  happy is their union.
Their passions mount, and modesty disappears.
An ineffable pleasure pours through
  their limbs, their arms, their lips.

20—Double Chorus

Come, come, do not let me die.
Hyrca, hyrca, nazaza, trillirivos.
Pretty is thy face,
  the look of thine eyes,
  the braids of thy hair;
O how beautiful thou art!

Redder than the rose,
  whiter than the lily,
  more beautiful than all the rest;
  always I shall glory in thee.

21—Soprano Solo

I am suspended between love and chastity,
  but I choose what is before me
  and take upon myself the sweet yoke.

22—Soli (Soprano and Baritone, Chorus, and Boys' Chorus)

Pleasant is the season, O maidens;
  now rejoice, ye lads.
Oh, Oh, Oh, with love I bloom for a maiden,
  my new, new love, of which I perish.
Yielding gratifies me;
Refusing makes me grieve.
Oh, Oh, Oh, with love I bloom for a maiden,
  my new, new love, of which I perish.

In winter man's desires are passive;
  the breath of spring makes him lascivious.
Oh, Oh, Oh, with love I bloom for a maiden,
  my new, new love, of which I perish.

My maidenhood excites me,
  but my innocence keeps me apart.
Oh, Oh, Oh, with love I bloom for a maiden,
  my new, new love, of which I perish.

Come, my mistress, come with joy,
  come, my beauty, for I die.
Oh, Oh, Oh, with love I bloom for a maiden,
  my new, new love, of which I perish.

23—Soprano Solo

Sweetest boy, I give my all to you!

24—Chorus

Hail to thee, most beautiful, most precious gem,
  hail, pride of virgins, most glorious virgin.
Hail, light of the world,
  hail, rose of the world.
Blanziflor and Helena, Venus generosa!

25—Chorus

O Fortune, variable as the moon,
  always dost thou wax and wane.
Detestable life, first dost thou mistreat us,
  and then, whimsically, thou heedest our desires.
As the sun melts the ice, so dost thou dissolve
  both poverty and power.
Monstrous and empty fate,
  thou, turning wheel, art mean,
  voicing good health at thy will.

Veiled in obscurity,
Thou dost attack me also.
To thy cruel pleasure I bare my back.
Thou dost threaten my emotion and weakness with tortures.
At this hour, therefore, let us
*   pluck the strings without delay.*
Let us mourn together,
*   for fate crushes the brave.*[3]

The Music

The third portion of this cantata consists of eleven sections. Of these, five involve the chorus, five are for soloists, and the boys' choir is heard during the first and eighth sections.

Some general observations concerning Orff's style should be helpful before listening. For the most part the sections will sound similar to the music of folk songs with simple harmonies and accompaniments, and melodies which one can whistle. This work, not intellectually complex, will be easily understood with only a few hearings.

In this composition we hear contemporary music of a different type than Barber's *Hermit Songs,* Ramirez's *Mass,* or Britten's cantata, all of which we have now studied. This music is a kind of revolt in two directions. First, it speaks against the Romantic period and its complexities, sweet harmonies, and chromatic chordal movements. At the same time, it speaks against contemporary music which is dissonant, often unharmonic, with apparently little feeling for the tune and the heart. The attention of the listener is drawn to the text and its general effect with the music, rather than to intricate harmony or counterpoint. One hears the driving rhythm of the music and its simple melodies, the simplicity being reminiscent of folk tunes or plainsong. At times the orchestra is used as a percussion instrument; at other times, as if it were an organ sustaining chords made up of interesting pitches and timbres. Changes are often and obvious, with much of the melody in short repetitive phrases.

Study Procedures

1. A detailed analysis of this cantata is not intended, since it is hoped that you will be able to make some musical observations for yourself. Consider the following items as you listen:
   a. Are you hearing a chorus, aria, or recitative?
   b. Some of the sections are strophic. Can you find these?
   c. Some sections are rhapsodic and distort the rhythmic and tonal structure.
   d. Some sections maintain almost the same dynamic level throughout; other sections constantly and obviously vary the dynamics.

---

[3] Copyright © 1937 by B. Schott's Sohne. Used by permission.

e. One section uses antiphonal effects. Do you hear this?

f. Most of the sections have accompaniments which are almost identical to the voice parts. Other sections use the orchestra as a featured performer.

g. Obvious contrasts exist between staccato style and lyric style.

h. Much of the singing moves by step, resulting in a simple style for voices.

i. Because many of the sections in this work are short, you should be able to consider the form, listening for the repeats and melodic changes.

2. Differences in style exist between the two contemporary composers and the representative works which we have heard. Describe these differences in your own words.

3. Differences exist between the style of the Baroque period as exemplified by Bach and contemporary styles. How would you describe these differences?

4. If you were a composer and wished to write a cantata what topics would you choose? As to the text, what might be the basis for your writing?

5. What differences exist between a song cycle and a cantata?

REVIEW

This chapter has introduced a larger vocal form known as the *cantata,* which came into existence shortly after 1600. Along with other forms of that time it placed emphasis upon melodic elements with simple accompaniments. We have explored the recitative, aria, and chorus, and at the same time introduced the religious and secular cantata. Two of the cantatas studied were from the contemporary period, one based upon folksong like melodies, while the other, although simple in structure, sounded much more complex. The Bach cantata represented the Baroque period of artistic endeavor with its ecstasy, intricacies, and contrapuntal organizations. Although one of the important musical forms of the Baroque period, the cantata has been effective in later periods, down to the present day.

Review the preceding nine chapters by writing review paragraphs similar to the one you have just read for this chapter.

Bibliography—Chapter 10

BUKOFZER, MANFRED, *Music in the Baroque Era.* New York: W. W. Norton and Co., Inc., 1947.

HANNAM, WILLIAM S., *Notes on the Church Cantatas of J. S. Bach.* London: Oxford University Press, 1928.

SCHWEITZER, ALBERT, *J. S. Bach.* New York: Dover Publications, Inc., 1966.

TERRY, CHARLES SANFORD, *Joh. Seb. Bach Cantata Texts.* London: The Holland Press, 1964.

Recordings—Chapter 10

Bach, J. S.	*Ein feste Burg (Cantata No. 80)*	Amsterdam Phil.	Vanguard S-219
Britten	*Rejoice in the Lamb*	Shaw Chorale	RCA LSC-2759
Orff	*Carmina Burana*	Boston Symphony	RCA LSC-3161

Chapter 11

The Oratorio

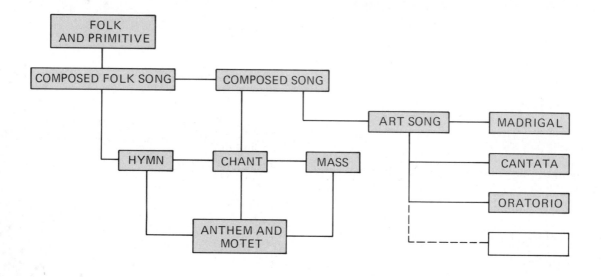

Imagine if you will a musical composition longer than the cantata, making use of the same organizational ideas but with an emphasis upon the narrative; this form is the *oratorio*. Originally the definitive aspects were not so obvious, but time has destined for this form a specific position between the meditative religious cantata and the secular staged opera.

CHARACTERISTICS

As we know the oratorio today, the characteristics are distinct:

1. Events may unfold sequentially as in a play, or as dramatic, contemplative related material. Both of these may occur in the same oratorio at different times. We will study one of each type, but in all of these works events transpire on a large scene.

2. Characters assist in relating the story, and the accompaniment and singing aid the listener in understanding the personalities and events that

circumscribe them at a given time. As in some plays, one performer may take more than one role, although not simultaneously. Since an oratorio is usually sung in concert style, the characters (soloists) are seated near the front of the stage, but no action or stage movement is involved.

3. An emphasis is placed upon the chorus, which plays several roles; in this respect it is similar to the chorus of the Greek drama. At times the chorus could be a narrator, or the general populace involved in the action; it could describe events in such a way as to partially substitute for scenery, lighting, or stage effects; or, it could comment upon the action, advising the listener as to what has happened, what is in progress, or what might happen. At times the commentary could be judgmental or philosophical. Each role for the chorus affects the type of vocal writing the composer chooses and the musical effects he places at its disposal. Many times the action moves back and forth from the soloists to the chorus, so that without the chorus the development and continuity would be incomplete.

4. The oratorio form uses the aria, recitative, and chorus. Since the oratorio grew out of musical developments at the early portion of the seventeenth century, the aria and recitative were preferred methods of conveying mood and description. For the vocalist these forms are still valid. As we found with the cantata, a later development produced the arioso, which is used in oratorios as well.

5. Rapid dialogue is not a part of the oratorio. In this respect it is unlike a play. Rarely do the characters speak back and forth, but usually the dialogue is more drawn out, with emphasis upon the quality of the statement rather than upon dialogue or repartee.

6. Staging, scenery, and costumes are usually absent. During the early days of the oratorio staging and costumes were a common part of the presentation. However, as the form developed, and as it turned more toward the religious statement, staging and costumes were eliminated. The development of oratorio is contemporary with that of opera, and although there have been times when oratorio took on some of the attributes of opera, the form, if it were to be a valid one, had to find an independent role. The presentation of oratorio within the church and in the concert hall delineated its unique possibilities and limitations more clearly.

7. The implied action of the narrative challenges the mind through the word. The earliest oratorios were religious poems which presented a dialogue between God and the Soul or Heaven and Hell. These were costumed, and modest actions were a part of the presentation. However, in later years the action was conveyed solely through the words; this gave a greater scope of possibility to the composer, permitting him to move the scene quickly from one locale to another, and from one time to another, painting with broad strokes through the life of his characters. The mind of the listener can create within itself the necessary locale for the action, and in this way the story becomes more meaningful than if imposed by the limitation of built props on a stage.

8. Many oratorios enlist the services of a narrator, who as storyteller, keeps the various portions of the composition in focus. He may join with the chorus in this function, or he may take over this function from the chorus, permitting them other tasks. Most often his role, although important, makes use only of the recitative, since this is more suited to description. The narrator is most prominent in the *Passion*, a particular type of oratorio which limits itself to the events of the final week in the life of Christ. Passions are and have been most prominent in the Germanic tradition, and were presented during Holy Week to bring to the people a dramatic statement of those days.

9. The oratorio is usually religious. Although secular oratorios are possible, and some have been written, the form is predominately biblical in content.

Although originating with the Italians during the latter part of the sixteenth century as a part of popular religious services, and continuing through the German religious traditions of the seventeenth century, it was the English people in the eighteenth century who accepted the form and promoted its development.

HANDEL AND THE ORATORIO

George Frederick Handel was German-born and early trained in German opera as an accompanying violinist and harpsichordist. At the age of twenty he wrote and produced his first opera, and a year later went to Italy to study as well as to compose and produce his own works. While in Italy he also wrote two oratorios, which are mentionable mainly because of his later interest in the form. Although a German during his early life, he became an English citizen at the age of forty-two, partly because he was enjoying life in England, and partly because a former German only recently had become King George I of England.

At first Handel had gone to England to present one of his operas. His considerable success led to a return trip, but other operas were only modestly received and he did not attain the favor with the English public or within musical circles for which he had hoped. Several reasons help to explain this, none of which are personal, but relate more to the British and the times in which Handel found himself:

1. Opera was considered an Italian form of music and entertainment. Although England borrowed freely from the Italians at an earlier time (consider the madrigal that we discussed in Chapter 8), during the eighteenth century a nationalistic spirit developed more strongly against Italian opera in London, particularly when producers imported singers and castrati to present performances in a time-honored formula. Most of the operas were in the Italian style, sung in Italian and using Italian themes and stories, while the British were turning gradually toward a more local art form. *The Beggar's Opera*, being an English ballade presentation, signaled the ending of Italian opera in England during that century.

2. The use of castrati concerned the English people. Most of the Italian style operas used castrati for some of the roles, and this alteration of the male physique disturbed the moral sensitivity of the English people considerably more than the Italians, who still used these singers into the nineteenth century. Since castrati were synonymous with Italian style opera then presented throughout Europe, any resultant censorship tended at the same time to limit the overall presentation.

3. The opera appeared more and more artificial to the English. The plots and the manner of presentation, including a continuous use of set pieces, bothered the English, who were more realistically minded than Baroque opera would admit. In other words, the training of composers in the Italian style tended to negate the flexibility sought by the practical minded English. Perhaps the situation in the United States today is not completely unlike this.

4. Opera was considered an affront to English Protestantism. Since Italian opera was imported from Rome, the seat of the Catholic church, religious conservatists of that time associated the aforementioned problems with Catholicism, and relegated opera to the snobbish entertainment of the aristocracy. Since the middle class was growing in economic and political status, this attitude only assisted the demise of Italian opera in England.

Handel had produced approximately thirty-five operas, most of them in England, when he decided after considerable personal introspection to abandon that form in favor of oratorio. Before this decision was made, and during the time of his work on operas, he had already written several oratorios, none of which had been received with great acclaim. However, he correctly read his talents and the inclinations of the British audiences, for through his oratorios he was destined to become a famous composer known worldwide not only in his own time but throughout posterity.

The oratorio sung in English was most attractive to the people of England, since many of the problems mentioned earlier were eliminated. In addition, the oratorio appealed to the religious sensitivity of the people. Although the time of the Puritans had passed, within the lower classes there existed a strong feeling for the Bible and the religious. Even though considered entertainment on a folk theme by many, the great dramatic narratives of the Old Testament offered pictures of suffering and victory that were personal as well as nationalistic in implication. Although the Bible speaks of Jewish history, the English associated themselves and their country closely with the lessons of the Old Testament, and the suffering and victories of the Jewish monarchs and prophets sounded so familiar to the British as to arouse a personal affinity. Making use of these feelings was one basis for Handel's success.

Another portion of success came from Handel's ability to employ the chorus with prominent passages in such a way that the choral tradition in England was enhanced. This same tradition for singing of religious material was one factor in the success of Wesley in his appeal to the common man outside the traditional English church.

The aria, borrowed from the Italian opera but sung in English, offered an opportunity to produce beauty through song material that was appealing; the recitative carried the narrative in a manner that was understood by commoner and aristocracy alike. But the choruses thrilled the audiences in a manner that was never possible in opera, since there the chorus had played only a small role if any at all.

Paradoxically, Handel wrote one oratorio that was almost entirely choral, and this did not please the English nearly so much as the mixture of soloists and chorus wherein the soloists could assist in the portrayal of characters, thus satisfying their love of the dramatic.

There were other nonmusical reasons for the success of the oratorio at that time. During Lent there was a restriction upon opera as well as other drama presentations, and Handel capitalized upon the British desire for dramatic entertainment while the theaters were closed. For a number of years he presented a series of his oratorios, other types of semireligious music, and his own organ concertos with himself at the keyboard.

Blind during the last eight years of his life, he continued to accompany his oratorio presentations at the organ. In 1759 the *Messiah* was the final presentation of his Lenten series one week before Good Friday. He died the following Saturday, the day before Easter, at the age of 74, and was buried at Westminster Abbey among kings and notables.

THE BAROQUE PERIOD

Before studying the music of Handel, let us examine a few general characteristics of the period in which he lived and relate these to music generally, so that we may better understand him in relation to his time.

Originally the word "baroque" meant grotesque or irregular in shape, and was applied to art forms of 1600 to 1750 because they appeared to be of an unusual nature compared to those of the preceding Renaissance. (Review the general characteristics of the Renaissance in Chapter 6.) However, in the perspective of time historians have realized this to be a legitimate era of its own with artistic characteristics that mirror well the period and its people, during which time there arose a number of musical forms still valid today.

Some of the characteristics conspicuous in the Handel oratorio should be described:

1. This is the period of the *thorough bass* technique. In this style accompaniments usually included a keyboard instrument playing chordal backgrounds to the melody while the bass line of the keyboard also was played by a low sounding instrument, usually the cello, but at times the bassoon, the bass viol, or the trombone. On the written page of music the bass line would be written along with chord symbols, so that the accompanist would read the chords and improvise appropriately for the melodic line. This tended to emphasize

the outer melodic and bass lines. In the oratorio we will hear this thorough bass technique in some recitatives, when the harpsichord provides the chordal background while the cellos of the orchestra double the bass line. In the arias the harpsichord will provide an appropriate figured accompaniment, and once again the bass line will be duplicated by the lower strings. It is this combination of doubling a bass line plus improvising at the keyboard that is characteristic of the period and that gives the meaning of the term.

2. Contrasting effects were important to the musical structure. In the oratorio this becomes evident in the contrast of solo versus chorus, which is the texture of one voice as compared to many. Although not so evident in a recording, this also produced the contrast of loud and soft which became most evident within a concert hall. Either loud or soft was the accepted dynamic level, partly because the instruments of that time were usually not able to provide as great a range of dynamics as we now enjoy.

3. The accompanied vocal solo, particularly the recitative, was a new musical idea during the Baroque period, yet the textured polyphony of the Renaissance was not abandoned. In the oratorio the melodic lines of the recitatives are in direct contrast to the accompaniments. Some accompaniments are semimelodic, while others are only punctuating chords. This latter type is known as *recitativo secco* or *dry recitative*.

4. Polyphonic styles are still a part of the chordal texture, but an increasing emphasis is placed upon homophonic sounds. Homophony defines a chordal structure, usually where all voices follow the same rhythm simultaneously, including a unified statement of the text. Although it often becomes difficult to fully comprehend the interweaving lines of a Bach cantata, the polyphonic lines in *Messiah* will be more readily understood since they are often less complex, they are not as long, and you will be hearing this type of texture with more experience.

5. The Baroque considered this life problematic, or attacked it with vitality; renounced its conflicts, or embraced it with intense vigor; but at all times placed appropriate emphasis upon the future. Also, this was the era of longing and self-denial mixed with high spirits, vigor, and ecstacy. Consequently, for some the Bible offered abundant hope and salvation through faith; for most the Bible poetically described personal yearning, submission of self, and gave examples of heroic figures who were not always winners, but whose abundant vigor could be contemplated if not emulated. These attitudes were reflected in the biblical texts chosen for oratorios, thus assuring their popularity. It also explains why Old Testament figures were more popular than New Testament ones.

6. This was the period of the rise of monody. Combine this with the feelings expressed above, and the musical result is sad or tender recitatives followed by melodies that abound in an outward demonstration of feeling for a situation or concern. This emotional expression led naturally to a reinstitution of tone-painting, and Handel uses this musical device constantly. It also re-

sulted in florid vocal lines which not only are expressive of the implied condition, but tend to accent the word so that it carries added weight or meaning to the listener.   The Baroque period is known for its extravagantly twisted lines, curving ornamentations, and theatrical effects, and hearing musical evidences of these things only indicates to what extent Handel was a man of his time.

Messiah—The Text

We study *Messiah* because this is the most famous oratorio in existence, having been sung in almost every major language in the world, and still sung each Easter and Christmas throughout Christendom in small churches, large cathedrals, and concert halls.   Millions of people have sung its magnificent choruses as well as heard its message of hope and faith.

The work is divided into three parts, reminding us of Handel's earlier opera writing.   Our study will concentrate on the more performed first section, often referred to as the Christmas Section.   This portion deals with the prophecy and the birth of Christ; the second section deals with the ministry of Christ, His death, and resurrection; the final section stresses the reward of eternal life for the faithful.

Although the first section is more often heard and performed, many times other portions of the work are inserted into the Christmas portion.   The most

Left: Fishamble-Street Musick Hall in Dublin, scene of the first performance of Handel's oratorio Messiah, *conducted by the composer in 1742; right: the same scene as it appears today (Courtesy of Irish Tourist Board; Bord Failte Photo).*

notable example is the "Hallelujah Chorus," which was placed by Handel at the end of the second portion glorifying the Resurrection.   Since each conductor probably has a favorite solo or chorus which he believes should always be included in performances, other numbers may be reordered and included.   Since the work is minimally sequential, this is easily accomplished.

Time permitting, listen to and study additional selections from the work. Your teacher will be able to guide you in making choices which will be interesting and musically valuable.

1. Overture

2. Recitative–Tenor

Comfort ye, comfort ye My people, saith your God; speak ye comfortably to Jerusalem; and cry unto her, that her warfare is accomplished, that her iniquity is pardoned.

The voice of him that crieth in the wilderness; Prepare ye the way of the Lord: make straight in the desert a highway for our God.

3. Aria–Tenor

Every valley shall be exalted, and every mountain and hill made low, the crooked straight and the rough places plain.

4. Chorus

And the glory of the Lord shall be revealed, and all flesh shall see it together; for the mouth of the Lord hath spoken it.

5. Recitative–Bass

Thus saith the Lord of Hosts: Yet once a little while and I will shake the heavens and the earth, the sea and the dry land; and I will shake all nations; and the desire of all nations shall come.

The Lord, whom ye seek, shall suddenly come to His temple, even the messenger of the covenant, whom ye delight in; behold He shall come, saith the Lord of Hosts.

6. Aria–Bass

But who may abide the day of His coming? and who shall stand when He appeareth? For He is like a refiner's fire.

7. Chorus

And He shall purify the sons of Levi, that they may offer unto the Lord an offering in righteousness.

8. Recitative–Alto

Behold! A Virgin shall conceive and bear a Son, and shall call His name Emmanuel, God with us.

9. Aria–Alto and Chorus

O thou that tellest good tidings to Zion, get thee up into the high mountain: O thou that tellest good tidings to Jerusalem, lift up thy voice with strength; lift it up, be not afraid; say unto the cities of Judah, Behold your God!

Arise, shine, for thy light is come; and the glory of the Lord is risen upon thee.

10. Recitative–Bass

For, behold, darkness shall cover the earth, and gross darkness the people; but the Lord shall arise upon thee, and His glory shall be seen upon thee, and the Gentiles shall come to thy light, and kings to the brightness of thy rising.

11. Aria–Bass

The people that walked in darkness have seen a great light; and they that dwell in the land of the shadow of death, upon them hath the light shined.

12. Chorus

For unto us a Child is born, unto us a Son is given, and the government shall be upon His shoulder; and His name shall be called Wonderful, Counsellor, The Mighty God, The Everlasting Father, The Prince of Peace.

13. Pastoral Symphony–Orchestra

14. Recitative–Soprano

There were shepherds abiding in the field, keeping watch over their flocks by night.

15. Recitative–Soprano

And lo! the angel of the Lord came upon them, and the glory of the Lord shone 'round about them, and they were sore afraid.

16. Recitative–Soprano

And the angel said unto them, Fear not; for behold I bring you good tidings of great joy, which shall be to all people; for unto you is born this day in the City of David, a Savior, which is Christ the Lord.

17. Recitative–Soprano

And suddenly there was with the angel a multitude of the heavenly hosts, praising God, and saying:

18. Chorus

Glory to God in the highest, and peace on earth, goodwill towards men.

19. Aria–Soprano

Rejoice greatly, O daughter of Zion! Shout, O daughter of Jerusalem! behold, thy King cometh unto thee!

He is the righteous Savior, and He shall speak peace unto the heathen.

20. Recitative–Alto

Then shall the eyes of the blind be opened and the ears of the deaf unstopped; then shall the lame man leap as a hart, and the tongue of the dumb shall sing.

21. Aria–Alto

He shall feed His flock like a shepherd: and He shall gather the lambs with His arm, and carry them in His bosom, and gently lead those that are with young.

22. Aria–Soprano

Come unto Him, all ye that labour and are heavy laden, and He will give you rest. Take His yoke upon you, and learn of Him, for He is meek and lowly of heart, and ye shall find rest unto your souls.

23. Chorus

His yoke is easy and His burthen is light.

44. Chorus

Hallelujah: for the Lord God Omnipotent reigneth.
   The kingdom of this world is become the kingdom of our Lord, and of His Christ; and He shall reign for ever and ever.
   King of Kings, and Lord of Lords.
   Hallelujah!

The accompaniment is for a comparatively small orchestra of strings, a few woodwinds, and occasionally a brass section with percussion. Four soloists and the chorus proclaim the text.

1. A slow introduction is played loudly the first time but softly when repeated. The second part of the overture is fugal, meaning that the sections of the orchestra do not enter together, and although they begin with the same melody they may alter it later in order to maintain the harmonic fabric. The first violins begin, followed by the second violins, and then the lower strings. The imitative phrases are often sequential and short. There is a slow ending phrase.

2. A steady rhythm accompanies the tenor, and each line of text is repeated to provide emphasis and form. The recitative is in two parts, the first being more arioso, while the second part, a recitative with an occasional punctuating chord over a bass line, is referred to as recitativo secco.

3. This introductory aria contains florid or melismatic sections as heard on the word "exalted" as it climbs to a high pitch. There is tone painting on

the word "crooked," while the word "low" is obviously lower than other portions of the line. The word "plain" is sung in sequence. The entire verse is repeated with melodic variations, and the orchestra repeats its introduction at the end.

4. With the first entrance in the alto voices, the fugal statements begin while melismatic lines are sung in accompanying parts. Imitation abounds but there are homophonic portions for the climaxes. A ritard assists the ending.

5. A punctuating orchestra contrasts the melismatic line of the bass voice.

6. This aria is in two sections: the first, melodic and smooth; the second section, fast with florid scale passages. The word "appeareth" comes in a sequential line which is the reverse direction of the tenor sequential line in the first aria. Each section is repeated, with the first being shortened and the second altered to provide an appropriate ending.

7. The following chorus borrows the melismatic lines from the preceding bass aria and sings these on the word "purify." Again Handel prefers fugal entrances that lead toward homophonic sections for climaxes.

8. Only harpsichord, cellos, and string bass participate in what is known as a continuo accompaniment.

9. The violins of the orchestra are used antiphonally with and as an obbligato to the voice, creating an interesting contrast in melodic line and pitch color. This aria returns to the beginning but the repeat is altered to include the phrase "the glory of the Lord is risen upon thee," with the word "glory" given obvious emphasis through a florid line. Bursting into the aria, the chorus sings the same text and melody, mostly homophonically, contributing a sparkling climax to the solo. The orchestra plays an extended ending which is a repeat of an interlude from the solo portion.

10. The orchestra plays a steady repeating figure independent of the vocal line, giving an obvious pulsating emphasis accompaniment of the bass recitative.

11. This unique aria contains little harmony in the accompaniment, offering an obvious contrast to the fugal lines and block chordal style of the choruses as well as the accompaniment of other solos. When used, harmony occurs only during a few climax points and interludes. This is a simple melodic line repeated four times to produce a double section with some variation in the line for contrast.

12. Again the chorus follows the formula of fugal entrances and melismatic accompanying lines, becoming less contrapuntal toward the dramatic descriptive declamations of "Wonderful, Counsellor," . . . which we hear four times. Also heard four times is the opening phrase, and with each new statement the following imitative entrances are closer together until finally the texture is almost homophonic.

13. Using strings only, this simple but effective interlude acts as a prelude to the shepherds' story. This mood-setter acts as a divider between the prophecy and the birth. It uses ABA form.

14, 15, 16, 17. These four recitatives for soprano quickly describe the birth of Christ as told to the shepherds. The first and third are slow paced, with the third being obviously meditative. The second and fourth are quick, with an agitated string accompaniment. The fourth part directs us into the chorus of angels.

18. This chorus begins with only the high voices of the choir. Although occasionally fugal, it is mostly homophonic and surprisingly short and simple, fading away into the night before we have time to fully comprehend what has been sung. Did Handel feel a need for a short chorus, or did he wish to give the impression that the shepherds heard the angels only briefly?

19. Here is another aria in da capo form, which returns to the beginning after a contrasting section; it uses ABA form. The center portion is obviously more meditative, slower and less florid. Notice the dancing string parts and the jubilant melody in the A section, classifying it as one of the more immediately attractive melodic lines.

20. This is a simple recitative, straightforward, with minimal accompaniment.

21, 22. This is a two-part solo for alto and soprano, although originally written for soprano only. Strophic in nature, the second section extends to achieve an ending.

23. This chorus, amazingly simple considering that it ends the first part, also acts as a continuing force toward the more somber second part. Occasionally fugal in style, it states its text in an easy to understand manner that gives the impression of lightness befitting the word "easy."

44. This chorus is the most famous one in existing choir literature. It has been reported that when originally sung the audience was so entranced and thrilled that it arose from its seats, and this custom has continued to this day. It is in the grand triumphant march style so dear to the hearts of the British and upon which Handel was able to capitalize. Beginning with a burst on the word "Hallelujah" in homophonic style, it reverses the formula which Handel had established and which any audience might expect; consequently, the fugal phrases come later. In two obvious sections, the additional extended ending section permits the sopranos to climb higher and higher with mounting tension on the phrase "King of Kings and Lord of Lords." The outstanding use of the melody and the rhythm of the word "hallelujah" has captured the ears and hearts of millions.

Elijah (Mendelssohn)

A little over one hundred years after *Messiah* (*Messiah,* 1742—*Elijah,* 1846) another German composer visiting in England produced what has been considered by many as the greatest oratorio of the nineteenth century, *Elijah* by Mendelssohn. Unlike Handel, who was fifty-seven at the time of *Messiah,* Mendelssohn was thirty-five when he wrote his famous oratorio, and had written only one before (*St. Paul*), which also had been received with great success in

England. Handel had paved the way for later oratorio successes, because his works had been sung with increasing interest after his death, even prompting the organization of oratorio societies. Other composers had written in this form, some with modest success, but none had reached the pinnacle that was reserved for Handel and Mendelssohn.

Having been a frequent visitor in England, Mendelssohn knew its people. He had first made a visit when twenty to assist with the conducting of his *Symphony in C minor.* On his ninth visit he presented *Elijah,* having conducted his previously written *St. Paul* on a visit in 1837. Each visit to England brought celebrations and parties until he became fatigued, but he nonetheless wrote constantly of his desire not to forego any moment of it. After his *Elijah* performance he was regarded with such esteem that he was invited to Buckingham Palace, where he played the piano while Queen Victoria turned pages and Prince Albert, her husband, sang (he was most interested in music). When finished, the Queen inquired if Mendelssohn had any request and he asked if he might tour the palace nursery. This was a most obvious request by a young father of five children to a young mother of nine. Whereupon the nursery was visited and the conversation revolved about diapers, formulas, and growth patterns. Such an historical footnote shows the common ground with which Mendelssohn was received by his hosts during his visits.

Felix Mendelssohn-Bartholdy at the age of 20 (Copyright Staatsbibliothek Berlin).

A letter to Mendelssohn's brother gives us considerable insight into the reception of his music:

Birmingham, August 26, 1846

My dear brother,

From the very first you took so kind an interest in my "Elijah," and thus inspired me with so much energy and courage for its completion, that I must write to tell you of its first performance yesterday. No work of mine ever went so admirably the first time of execution, or was received with such enthusiasm, by both the musicians and the audience, as this oratorio. It was quite evident at the first rehearsal in London, that they liked it, and liked to sing and to play it; but I own I was far from anticipating that it would acquire such fresh vigor and impetus at the performance. Had you only been there! During the whole two hours and a half that it lasted, the large hall, with its two thousand people, and the large orchestra, were all so fully intent on the one object in question, that not the slightest sound was to be heard among the whole audience, so that I could sway at pleasure the enormous orchestra and choir, and also the organ accompaniments. How often I thought of you during the time! More especially, however, when the "sound of abundance of rain" came, and when they sang and played the final chorus with furor, and when, after the close of the first part, we were obliged to repeat the whole movement. Not less than four choruses and four airs were encored, and not one single mistake occurred in the whole of the first part; there were some afterwards in the second part but even these were but trifling. A young English tenor sang the last air with such wonderful sweetness, that I was obliged to collect all my energies not to be affected, and to continue beating time steadily. As I said before, had you only been there! But tomorrow I set off on my journey home. We can no longer say, as Goethe did, that the horses' heads are turned homewards but I always have the same feeling on the first day of my journey home. I hope to see you in Berlin in October, when I shall bring my score with me, either to have it performed, or at all events to play it over to you, and Fanny and Rebecca; but I think probably the former (or rather both). Farewell, my dear Brother; if this be dull, pray forgive it. I have been repeatedly interrupted, and in fact it should only contain that I thank you for having taken such part in my "Elijah," and having assisted me with it. Your

Felix[1]

Again a composer turned to the Old Testament for his drama, and again England was the seat of the success. Arias, recitatives, and choruses make up the body of the work; however, this composition is more dramatic and the progression of events more obvious. The interplay between characters speaks of the action so decidedly that on certain occasions the oratorio has been presented in a staged version.

Mendelssohn was successful with the layman and professional alike because of his mastery of melody, his knowledge of orchestration, and his ability

---

1 Letters of Felix Mendelssohn Bartholdy, edited by Paul and Carl Mendelssohn. Leypoldt and Holt, New York, 1868, page 363.

to combine the dramatic with the accepted forms from the seventeenth century. The work makes its strongest appeal through the choruses, although several of the solos have been favorites for years and sung repeatedly. The scenes are concise and to the point; in fact, one might not be able to follow the action of the work if he were not aware of the events in the life of Elijah the prophet as related in the Bible. But Mendelssohn knew or had faith that the English audiences were knowledgeable.

Mendelssohn had preferred that his characters appear as live persons and not as if they were merely retelling the story. He made this request to his librettist, Pastor Schubring, who assisted with the text. However, much credit goes also to William Bartholomew, a friend and collaborator of many years who had translated a number of Mendelssohn's songs and earlier works into English. His was a particularly difficult task, since Schubring and Mendelssohn had used the old Luther Bible for the original German text. Bartholomew knew that if the work were to have any appeal it must be sung in what sounded like the King James version, since this was well-known and considered to be the English Bible; in addition, the accents within the line were most important, both for the singers and for the musical effect. To make the task still more difficult, Mendelssohn had delayed giving the first draft to Bartholomew until late in May for the August performance.

Elijah—The Text

This large work is too long for a complete study; consequently, we will concentrate upon two portions of the oratorio, both of which come in the first section. The first portion includes the curse and the ensuing drought during which the Lord provides for Elijah. The second portion for our study is the famous Mount Carmel scene between Elijah and the prophets of Baal.

1. Recitative–Elijah

As God the Lord of Israel liveth, before whom I stand, there shall not be dew nor rain these years, but according to my word.

2. Overture–Orchestra

3. Chorus–The People

Help, Lord! Wilt Thou quite destroy us?
The harvest now is over, the summer days are gone, and yet no power cometh to help us! Will then the Lord be no more God in Zion?

4. Recitative Chorus–The People

The deeps afford no water; and the rivers are exhausted! The suckling's tongue now cleaveth for thirst to his mouth; the infant children ask for bread, and there is no one breaketh it to feed them!

5. Duet and Chorus–The People

Lord! bow Thine ear to our prayer! Zion spreadeth her hands for aid; and there is neither help nor comfort.

6. Recitative–Obadiah

Ye people, rend your hearts, and not your garments, for your transgressions the Prophet Elijah hath sealed the heavens through the word of God. I therefore say to ye, forsake your idols, return to God; for He is slow to anger, and merciful, and kind and gracious, and repenteth Him of the evil.

7. Aria–Obadiah

If with all your hearts ye truly seek Me, ye shall ever surely find Me. Thus saith our God.

Oh! that I knew where I might find Him, that I might even come before His presence.

8. Chorus–The People

Yet doth the Lord see it not; He mocketh at us; His curse hath fallen down upon us; His wrath will pursue us, till He destroy us!

For He, the Lord our God, He is a jealous God; and He visiteth all the father's sin on the children to the third and the fourth generation of them that hate Him. His mercies on thousands fall—fall on all them that love Him, and keep His commandments.

9. Recitative–An Angel

Elijah! get thee hence; Elijah! depart and turn thee eastward: thither hide thee by Cherith's brook. There shalt thou drink its waters; and the Lord thy God hath commanded the ravens to feed thee there: so do according unto His word.

10. Recitative–An Angel

Now Cherith's brook is dried up, Elijah, arise and depart, and get thee to Zarepath; thither abide: for the Lord hath commanded a widow woman there to sustain thee. And the barrel of meal shall not waste, neither shall the cruse of oil fail, until the day that the Lord sendeth rain upon the earth.

22. Recitative–Elijah

As God the Lord of Sabaoth liveth, before whom I stand, three years this day fulfilled, I will show myself unto Ahab; and the Lord will then send rain again upon the earth.

23. Recitative–Ahab

Art thou Elijah? art thou he that troubleth Israel!

24. Chorus

Thou art Elijah, thou, he that troubleth Israel!

25. Recitative–Elijah

I never troubled Israel's peace: it is thou, Ahab, and all thy father's house. Ye have forsaken God's commands; and thou hast followed Baalim!

Now send and gather to me the whole of Israel unto Mount Carmel; there summon the prophets of Baal, and also the prophets of the groves, who are feasted at Jezebel's table. Then we shall see whose God is the Lord.

26. Chorus

And then we shall see whose God is God the Lord.

27. Recitative–Elijah

Rise then, ye priests of Baal: select and slay a bullock, and put no fire under it: uplift your voices, and call the god ye worship; and I then will call on the Lord Jehovah: and the God who by fire shall answer, let him be God.

28. Chorus

Yea, and the God who by fire shall answer, let him be God.

29. Recitative–Elijah

Call first upon your god: your numbers are many; I, even I, only remain, one prophet of the Lord! Invoke your forest-gods and mountain-deities.

30. Double Chorus–Priests of Baal

Baal, we cry to thee; hear and answer us! Heed the sacrifice we offer! Baal, O hear us and answer us!

Hear us, Baal! Hear, mighty god! Baal, O answer us! Baal, let thy flames fall and extirpate the foe! Baal, O hear us!

31. Recitative–Elijah

Call him louder, for he is a god! He talketh; or he is pursuing; or he is on a journey; or peradventure, he sleepeth; so awaken him: call him louder.

32. Chorus–Priests of Baal

Hear our cry, O Baal! now arise! wherefore slumber?

33. Recitative–Elijah

Call him louder! he heareth not. With knives and lancets cut yourselves after your manner; leap upon the altar ye have made; call him, and prophesy. Not a voice will answer you; none will listen, none heed you.

34. Chorus–Priests of Baal

Baal! Hear and answer, Baal! Mark how the scorner derideth us! Hear and answer!

35. Recitative and Aria–Elijah

Draw near, all ye people: come to me!
Lord God of Abraham, Isaac, and Israel! this day let it be known that Thou art God; and that I am Thy Servant! O show to all this people that I have done these things according to Thy word! O hear me, Lord, and answer me; and show this people that Thou art Lord God: and let their hearts again be turned!

36. Quartet–Angels

Cast thy burden upon the Lord, and He shall sustain thee. He never will suffer the righteous to fall: He is at thy right hand.
Thy mercy, Lord, is great; and far above the heavens. Let none be made ashamed that wait upon Thee.

37. Recitative–Elijah

O Thou, who makest Thine angels spirits; Thou, whose ministers are flaming fires, let them now descend!

38. Chorus–The People

The fire descends from Heaven; the flames consume His offering. Before Him upon your faces fall!
The Lord is God: O Israel, hear! Our God is one Lord: and we will have no other gods before the Lord!

Elijah—The Music

Although the format belongs to the Baroque, the music for this oratorio represents the Romantic period. A synthesis of the latter will be found in Chapter 7, but you will notice immediately several differences from a Baroque composition. The vocal lines are much less florid, almost no tone painting, no harpsichord, a fuller orchestra throughout but particularly in the recitatives, a more obvious role for the orchestra, and a greater emphasis upon the recitative.

1. Ominous brasses introduce the first recitative and return again near its end. A most effective use of unaccompanied singing is heard briefly.

2. The overture occupies a most unusual position, after the first recitative. However, this abruptly brings the attention of the audience to the curse and then to the mood of the overture as it sets the stage for the remainder of the work. Continuing with the ominous mood of the recitative by beginning in the low strings with its fugal entrances, the strings lead into a rushing section which is predictive of coming events. Note the effective use of timpani and brass as punctuators while the music builds to the entrance of the chorus.

3. A strong homophonic cry precedes a quieter, somewhat fugal descriptive section. A change of rhythm and accompanimental texture introduces a prayer followed by a restatement of the early theme. A quiet ending leads into the recitative.

4. This unusual choral recitative features each section of the chorus singing one of the lines. This gives the interesting effect of a large group singing of their individual concerns.

5. A chantlike choral obbligato accompanies a melodic duet representing the plea of the people versus the more specific statements of individuals. The form is AB with an extended ending.

6. This secco recitativo blooms on the word "God" to a more melodic statement.

7. This lovely melody has been a favorite with tenors since the first performance, and one hears it occasionally in recital and often at church services. The form is AA′ BB′ A″.

8. Reintroducing anxiety into the performance, this chorus begins with a change of tempo as well as a step toward the dramatic. Mainly homophonic, the second section is choralelike and prayerful. Resisting the suggestion of Schubring, who thought that old German chorales should be a part of the composition, Mendelssohn included original choralelike sections several times throughout the work. In this instance the chorus becomes more dramatic near the end of the number. This chorus is in two sections with an extended ending.

9–10. Both of these recitatives exhibit a smooth orchestral background, quite different from the harpsichord and continuo often used by Handel. At times the vocal line becomes quite melodic.

22. The brasses again introduce a recitative in order to reinstate the mood of the beginning and to bring this recitative into symmetry with the curse. Beginning and ending with an arioso, the middle section is secco.

23. Tension mounts quickly in the orchestra, which introduces the voice of King Ahab. His melodic line is similar to the one used by the chorus as they restate his accusation.

24. This brief chorus is like a spontaneous cry and the rhythm is developed in such a manner as to give the impression of a recitative.

25. Beginning with the preceding chorus, we have a continuing dialogue between Elijah and the people: short and long choruses interspersed with recitatives by Elijah. The recitatives are varied in color and melodic line, depending upon the mood of the text and the type of declamation needed by Elijah to produce an emotional effect upon his listeners.

26. The chorus melodically imitates Elijah's last line but expands upon it by extending its harmonic possibilities and its emotions.

28. Again the chorus imitates Elijah's last line melodically but with a dramatic ending.

30. This double chorus features the men versus the women in simple antiphonal singing, with most melodic lines in repetition. Echo effects are introduced in the second section near the end in two main sections; the form is AB.

31. This antagonistic statement by Elijah is only meant to tease and plague the people.

32. Fast articulated brass introduce this short chorus.

33. Quick changes between major and minor assist in portraying the mood established by Elijah as he sways the people.

34. Each of the choruses pleading to Baal has increased in tension. Part of this tension is created by the orchestral accompaniment, part by the melodic lines and the voice writing for the chorus, part from the repetitious phrases pitting men against the women, and in this final chorus from the silent portions that come near its end.

35. Here is one of the excellent melodies of the oratorio and perhaps the melodic high point of this portion of the work. The statement of the text fits excellently with the melody and the prayerful mood that fittingly needs to be projected after the raucous Baal choruses.

36. A mixed quartet sings this famous interlude and the orchestra intercedes occasionally to assist with the mood. The orchestral ending is taken from the preceding Elijah aria. The four lines of text, interpreted as four lines of singing, are similar to a hymn or chorale. The form is AABC.

37. Beginning prayerfully, this recitative finishes with an emotional cry that prays for consideration. The increase of tension is enhanced by a vocal line which uses a fanfare figure.

38. This chorus contains two parts. The first, probably the most florid writing that we have heard, is meant to portray the fire descending and lighting the altar. The second portion is choralelike and prayerlike in its statement.

Belshazzar's Feast (William Walton)

Born in 1902, William Walton is a composer of the twentieth century. Although his music is not any longer a part of the avant garde, he writes in a style that definitely belongs to this time. His oratorio *Belshazzar's Feast* is a direct descendant of the two previously studied though greatly different. Some differences will be quickly perceived. Only a baritone soloist participates. In Part I he sings with choral accompaniment; in Part II he is the narrator as he describes the city of Babylon in a long unaccompanied recitative. In true English tradition, the chorus is the main focus in this work, singing almost the entire short oratorio. The orchestra assumes the second most important role, and during Part II it is augmented by two brass choirs adding to the brilliance and lustre.

The Text

Only Part II will receive our particular attention. Other portions of the work are equally interesting, and if possible should be heard.

Part I of the oratorio, mostly based upon Psalm 81, recounts the sorrow of the people of Israel at the time of their Babylonian captivity. They tell of their remorse and inabilities, even finding it difficult to sing when requested by their captors. The section ends with the prophecy that the great city of Babylon will be overthrown and "shall be found no more at all."

Here is the text for Part II:

A. Recitative

Babylon was a great city,
Her merchandise was of gold and silver,
Of precious stones, of pearls, of fine linen,
Of purple, silk, and scarlet,
All manner vessels of ivory,
All manner vessels of most precious wood,
Of brass, iron, and marble,
Cinnamon, odors, and ointments,
Of frankincense, wine, and oil,
Fine flour, wheat and beasts.
Sheep, horses, chariots, slaves;
And the souls of men.

B. Chorus

In Babylon, Belshazzar the King
Made a great feast,
Made a feast to a thousand of his lords
And drank wine before the thousand.

Belshazzar, whiles he tasted the wine,
Commanded us to bring the gold and silver
*   vessels,*
Yea! the golden vessels, which his father
*   Nebuchadnezzar,*
Had taken out of the temple that was in
*   Jerusalem.*

He commanded us to bring the golden vessels
Of the temple of the house of God.
That the King, his Princes, his wives
And his concubines might drink therein.

Then the King commanded us:
Bring ye the cornet, flute, sackbut, psaltery
And all kinds of music: they drank wine again
From the sacred vessels.

And then saith the King:

C. Solo

Praise ye, The God of Gold!

D. Chorus

Praise ye, The God of Gold
Praise ye, The God of Silver
Praise ye, The God of Iron
Praise ye, The God of Stone
Praise ye, The God of Wood
Praise ye, The God of Brass
Praise ye the Gods.

E. Chorus

Thus in Babylon, the mighty city,
Belshazzar the King, made a great feast
Made a feast to a thousand of his lords,
And drank wine before the thousand.
Belshazzar, whiles he tasted the wine
Commanded us to bring the gold and silver
*   vessels*
That the King, his Princes, his wives
And his concubines might drink therein.

F. Chorus

After they had praised their strange gods,
The idols and the devils,
False gods that can neither see nor hear,
Called they for the timbrel and the pleasant
*   harp*
To extol the glory of the King.
Then they pledged the King before the people,
Crying: Thou, O King, are King of Kings.
O King, live for ever, live for ever.[2]

The Music

A. This recitative is unaccompanied and the vocal lines for the baritone are organized so that they give the effect of a street caller selling his wares. The drama increases noticeably on the last line, "And the souls of men."

---

[2] Text selected and arranged from Biblical sources by Osbert Sitwell. Reprinted by permission of Oxford University Press.

B. The next chorus not only describes the feast of Belshazzar but establishes the moral situation around which the fall of the city was centered. Belshazzar, wishing to celebrate most splendidly, and to demonstrate his universality, power, and subjugation of conquered peoples, called for the sacred vessels that had been used solely for the worship of God by the people of Israel. This was the ultimate act of disregard for their God. For the most part this is a straightforward statement of the text, although certain words such as "wives," "concubines," "cornet," and "music" receive special coloration in the choral writing or the orchestration. The choral writing is typical of Walton in his twentieth century style, but at the same time it is descriptive of the emotion of the celebration at which we are a witness and a participant. The chorus plays two roles in this section. First, it describes the event. Secondly, it takes the part of the Jewish people as we hear the text state: "He commanded us to bring the golden vessels of the temple of the house of God."

C. The chorus introduces the words of the king, and the baritone solo sings but one line. This has been written into the text to give a textural change for the listener, but more importantly, to dramatize the command of Belshazzar for those at his feast to sing praises to the commercial substances that were the daily idols of the people of the city.

D. Section D is an outstanding chorus partly because it is a modern version of tone painting, and since the text calls for praises to the various gods it enables the composer to use orchestral colors to the fullest. Listen carefully to the accompaniment as this section is being sung, noting that specific percussion instruments assist with the coloring of certain lines of the text as sung by the chorus. The triangle aids with the word "silver," the gong, cymbals, and bells with "iron," the xylophone and the woodblock with "wood," and the cymbal and drum with "stone." In addition, the two brass choirs assist in this section to add size of sound and breadth of dynamics to the praise sections. Walton shows us the British inclination for a good march to accompany ceremonial pomp. If you listen carefully you will hear some of the same coloration devices and orchestration technics that he uses in his *Coronation March,* which we will hear in Chapter 16. You will recall that we spoke of the acceptance by the people of the "Hallelujah Chorus" partly because it carried implications of a march of pomp in emotion and coloration. The same may be said of this portion of Walton's oratorio.

E. After so brilliant a section, it becomes necessary to offer some change to the listener. The tempo is quickly increased during a brief orchestral interlude and a moment of silence follows. Before the pledge to the king, Walton reintroduces a portion of the description of the feast, and at the same time reiterates the major concern of the banquet, the misuse of the temple vessels.

F. This section increases in intensity, with the musical climax coming on the last line in the text. Since the coloration of the choir and orchestra was so well displayed during section D, the final portion of Part II is sung with mounting emotion and vocal brilliance, but without repetition. The orchestra concludes the section with a brief but brilliant ending.

Textwise, Part III is the climax of the oratorio. Belshazzar sees unexplainable writing on the wall and hears of his own destruction as well as that of his country. He is slain that night and the prophecy of the Israelites is complete. The final sections of the work are devoted to the praise of God with a final verse, "Then sing aloud to God our strength, Make a joyful noise unto the God of Jacob. For Babylon the Great is fallen, Alleluia!"

A most dramatic portion of the story has been omitted in this oratorio. The text, taken from the Old Testament book of Daniel, makes no mention of Daniel, even though it is he who translates the writing on the wall. The story as sung is complete, but for those who know the role of Daniel in the series of events, his presence lurks behind the first fatal prophecy and the ominous banquet scene. Walton wished to place the emphasis upon the banquet and not upon Daniel, and this in turn made it possible to feature the chorus and the brilliance of the singing rather than the drama. The writing on the wall and its meaning is sung by the baritone soloist, yet the lines are given little musical emphasis.

Study Procedures

1. Compare the differences that you hear in the three oratorios now studied.
2. How would you describe the differences in vocal lines in the three works?
3. How would you describe the choral writing in *Belshazzar's Feast?*

Additional Listening

Listen to *Joseph and the Amazing Technicolor Dreamcoat,* by Webber and Rice.

The composer has termed this a cantata. By the definitions used in this chapter, would you agree? Why, or why not?

Describe the musical content of the work in relation to the three oratorios heard previously.

What is the role of the narrator in *Joseph?* Of the chorus? Are these usages traditional?

Describe the various styles of music used throughout the work. Did you hear the Lawrence Welk imitation? Which selection sounded as if it were a takeoff of a Broadway tune? Could you name others?

THE PASSION

A special type of oratorio, the passion, has many of the characteristics of the former but is specifically concerned with the final days in the life of Christ. This dramatic narrative began its long history in the church, where it was first enacted by priests singing plainsong; later it was almost completely choral motets; in Germany, chorales by the congregation were inserted to add participation on the part of the people; and finally, the form, influenced by opera, was taken from the church into the concert hall as an artistic concert work. Most of the musical characteristics are similar to the oratorio because it uses arias, recitatives, and choruses, makes use of a narrator (often called Evangelist), uses the text of the Bible from one of the Gospels, and relates the narrative in sequential fashion. Partly because of the interest of the Protestant churches, and partly because of the success and high quality of the passions of Schütz and Bach, this form has been particularly successful in German musical history.

Beginning with the earliest presentations, Christ had been traditionally a low voice, that of the narrator a high male voice. In the passions of Bach the narrator became a countertenor (male alto) or a tenor with a particularly high voice range. In the earliest passions the crowd was represented by one person, usually of high voice, and this part was sung with greater speed as compared to Christ or the narrator. In later versions, however, the people were represented by a chorus.

Today those passions that are considered of highest quality usually come from the German church tradition, including two by J. S. Bach. In style these are not too unlike cantatas, since they include solos which are often poetic interpretations of the scripture, recitatives by the narrator which carry the events of the story, and chorale choruses which can be sung by the congregation; if sung by a choir, variations of the well-known chorale tunes could be included.

A CONTEMPORARY PASSION

For our limited study we will focus our attention upon a contemporary passion. Although important musically, the Bach works are in many ways similar to the cantatas we have already studied. An introduction to recent style seems appropriate in order to give as much exposure to the contemporary spectrum of musical sound as possible. For comparison purposes, listening to a portion of Bach's *St. Matthew Passion* would be advisable.

Passion According to St. Luke (Penderecki)

Krzysztof Penderecki wrote his passion in 1966 in a unique contemporary style. In most respects it is quite advanced in its musical materials. As the title indicates, the work is taken from one of the Gospels. However, the composer has followed a custom of an earlier time by placing between the scenes of the passion itself certain passages from the Psalms and sections of the Roman Missal. Most of the latter are hymns or poems of a meditative nature concerning the passion. The psalms are a carefully chosen group of verses which, in the context of the passion, take on a new meaning and relate unbelievably well to the main events of Holy Week. They too are treated as meditative verses placed carefully with the narrative of Luke.

At first hearing, the unique vocal and instrumental sounds could lead the listener into concluding this work has little or no relation to the historical passion. Upon more careful observation, however, the composition appears in a direct line from the old German passions with their inserted chorales. Not the congregation but the choir sings the meditative psalms and poems, while the musical texture is contemporary and unique.

Penderecki writes music of the mind and the psychology of the persons involved. Not descriptive music that adorns the exterior scene, rather it attempts to portray the inner feelings, the tensions and emotions, the fears and meditative thoughts of the main characters of the passion. Consequently, the choir and orchestra are expected to participate in a new manner; while the intent of the soloists remains the same, they sing vocal lines which are quite different from those of past periods.

Although the orchestra makes use of many of the standard instruments, the writing for them is often not by section as much as singly or in unusual combinations, so as to permit the listener to hear some of their particular qualities. Pretaped sounds are added to the orchestra. The voices of the choir participate as the crowd, but also as narrator. When they fulfill the latter role, they often become involved in the emotion of the text and read their lines to enhance the drama of the moment.

The meditations of the work are usually in a slow tempo, so that the rhythm of the words or music is all but indistinguishable. In contrast the scenes are quite rhythmic, not in a metric sense, but as of one effect following another.

The Text

For the present we will concentrate upon only the latter portion of Part I, which begins as Christ is seized in the Garden and taken to the high priest's house. This section ends with the trial before Pilate with the crowd calling for Christ to be crucified. The sung text is in Latin, and was chosen by the composer partly because of its singing qualities and vowel possibilities. Again, the sung text appears at the left of the page, with a line-for-line translation at the right.

A. Choir (Meditation)
Jerusalem, Jerusalem,
convertere ad Dominum, Deum Tuum.

Jerusalem, Jerusalem
turn to the Lord, Your God.   (Roman Breviary)

B. Choir (Meditation)
ut quid, Domine, recessisti longe,
despicis in opportunitatibus
in tribulatione, Domine?

Why does thou stand afar off, O Lord?
Why dost thou hide thyself
in times of trouble, O Lord?   (Psalm 10)

194

C. Choir, Soloists, Narrator

Comprehendentes autem eum,	*Then they seized him and led him away,*
duxerunt ad domum principis sacerdotum:	*bringing him into the high priest's house.*
Petrus vero sequebatur a longe.	*Peter followed at a distance.*
Quem cum vidisset ancilla	*Then a maid,*
quaedam sedentem ad lumen,	*seeing Peter as he sat in the light*
et eum fuisset intuita, dixit:	*and gazing at him, said,*
"Et hic cum illo erat."	*"This man also was with him."*
"Mulier, non novi illum."	*"Woman, I do not know him."*
Et post pusillum alius videns eum, dixit:	*And a little later someone else saw and said,*
"Et tu de illis es."	*"You are also one of them."*
"O homo, non sum."	*"Man, I am not."*
Et intervallo facto quasi horae unius,	*And after an interval of about an hour*
alius quidam affirmabat, dicens:	*still another insisted, saying,*
"Vere et hic cum illo erat;	*"Certainly this man also was with him;*
nam et Galilaeus est."	*for he is a Galilean."*
"Homo, nescio quid dicis."	*"Man, I do not know what you are saying."*
Et continuo adhus illo loquente	*And immediately, while he was speaking,*
cantavit gallus.	*the cock crowed.*
Et conversus Dominus respexit Petrum.	*And the Lord turned and looked at Peter.*
Recordatus est Petrus verbi Domini.	*And Peter remembered the word of the Lord.*
Et egressus foras flevit amare.	*And he went out and wept bitterly.*

D. Chorus (Meditation)

Judica me, Deus,	*Vindicate me, O God,*
et discerne causam meam.	*and defend my cause. (Psalm 43)*

E. Choir, Soloist, Narrator

et viri, qui tenebant illum,	*Now the men who were holding Jesus*
illudebant ei, caedentes:	*mocked him, and beat him;*
et velaverunt eum, et percutiebant faciem eius,	*They also blindfolded him and reviled him,*
et interrogabant eum, dicentes:	*and asked him,*
"Prophetiza, quis est, qui te percusset?	*"Prophesy! Who is it that struck you?*
Tu ergo es Filius Dei?"	*Are you the Son of God, then?"*
"Vos dicitis, quia ego sum."	*"You say that I am."*

F. Female Soloist

Jerusalem, Jerusalem,	*Jerusalem, Jerusalem*
convertere ad Dominum, Deum Tuum.	*turn to the Lord, your God. (Roman Breviary)*

G. Choir (Meditation)

Miserere mei, Deus,	*Be gracious to me, O God,*
quoniam conculcavit me homo:	*for men trample upon me;*
tota die impugnans tribulavit me.	*all day long foemen oppress me. (Psalm 56)*

H. Choir, Soloists, Narrator

Et surgens omnis multitudo eorum,	*Then the whole company of them arose,*
duxerunt illum ad Pilatum.	*and brought him before Pilate.*
Coeperunt autem accusare illum, dicentes:	*And they began to accuse him, saying,*
"Hunc invenimus subvertentem gentem nostram,	*"We have found this man perverting our nation,*
et prohibentem tributa dare Caesari,	*and forbidding us to give tribute to Caesar,*
et dicentem se Christum regem esse."	*and saying that he himself is Christ a King."*

"Tu es Rex Judaeorum?"
"Tu dicis."
"Nihil invenio causea in hoc homine."
Et remisit eum ad Herodem.
Herodes autem interrogabat illum multis sermonibus:
at opse nihil illi respondebat.
Sprevit autem illum Herodes
indutum veste alba
et remisit ad Pilatum.
Pilatus autem convocatis
principibus sacerdotum, dixit ad illos:
"Ecce nihil dignum morte
actum est ei.
Emendatum ergo illum dimittam."
"Tolle hunc,
et dimitte nobis Barabbam."
Iterum autem Pilatus locutus est ad illos,
volens dimittere Jesum.
At illi succlamabant, dicentes:
"Crucifige, crucifige illum."
"Quid enim mali fecit iste?
Nullam causam mortis invenio in eo."
"Crucifige, crucifige illum."

"Are you King of the Jews?"
"You have said so."
"I find no crime in this man."
And he sent him to Herod.
Herod questioned him at some length;
but he made no answer.
Herod mocked him;
then arraying him in gorgeous apparel,
he sent him back to Pilate.
Pilate then called together
the chief priests and said to them,
"Behold, nothing deserving death
has been done by him;
I will therefore chastise him and release him."
"Away with this man,
and release to us Barabbas."
Pilate addressed them once more,
desiring to release Jesus;
but they shouted out,
"Crucify him, crucify him!"
"What evil has he done?
I have found in him no crime deserving death."
"Crucify, crucify him!"

The Music

A. Beginning with bells and unison singing, the chantlike melody moves slowly in the male voices and low instruments. This section is almost entirely in unison and on almost one pitch. Only occasionally is there a change and yet no monotony because of the interesting antiphonal effects of the three choirs and the timing of their entrances.

B. Again in a chantlike melodic line, the women's voices begin. When polyphony is used it echoes early writing. Again the emotional effect comes from the entrances of the voices. The last word is in four-part writing that sounds suddenly refreshing although it is disarmingly simple.

C. As an introduction, bells and electronic sounds are used. The chorus becomes the narrator with irregular entrances and moblike statements. Suddenly, the babbling is stabbed by a female solo voice accusing Peter, with the most effective orchestration a part of the emotional situation. Again the chorus plays the mob and accuses Peter. The narrator ends the section with his descriptive lines.

D. A low solo voice is heard, and although melodic, the pace and the accompaniment seem to give the impression of a neutralizing element. The text and melody are repeated but with a new low-pitched accompaniment.

E. Greatly agitated, the high strings introduce this section. The tremolo continues into the low strings, and finally the orchestra completes the stage setting with amazing sounds including electronic effects. The chorus enters and then answers the orchestra in nonsense syllables. The narrator sets the scene, the choir responds with a taunt, and the baritone sings the famous line of Christ: "You say that I am."

F. This is the same text as A, this time sung by a solo soprano using a new melody with contorted leaps. The ending is exactly as in A.

G. Beginning in chant style, the male chorus precedes the women's voices. Elongated dissonant sounds assist with the effect of this meditative poem and the slow pace adjusts to the implied meanings in the words. The men enter on a unison beneath a long-held dissonance in the female voices. Almost no rhythm is evident. This is a true motet in contemporary style.

H. Combining electronic music with special effects in the orchestra, the dissonance increases and finally subsides to a unison preceding the entrance of the choir on a neutral syllable. The narrator, speaking by the choir, and solo voices continue the drama. The choir again reads the lines in so irregular a rhythm that it becomes difficult to hear the words, but the effect is magnetic. "Crucify him" is sung three times by the choir to end Part I.

Study Procedures

1. Using the examples outlined in this chapter, compare the passion to the regular oratorio. Be sure to include a statement on form, text, style, and history.
2. After working through this chapter trace the development of the recitative, the style of arias, and the role of the chorus in the oratorio and passion.
3. Considering only the style of the music and not the form or text, how would you describe the differences between the Walton and the Penderecki?
4. Using the Penderecki as a guide for your statement and considering it in relation to other compositions in this chapter, what would you predict about the style of music in the year 2000?
5. If you were to compose a contemporary oratorio, what narrative or text would you use and why?
6. Listen to *Jesus Christ Superstar*. Compare it to the Penderecki in overall effect. Where does it violate oratorio form? Where does it lose its consistency of style? Where is it most effective? Why?

Bibliography—Chapter 11

DANNREUTHER, EDWARD, ed., *Oxford History of Music:* Vol. VI, "The Romantic Period." London: Oxford University Press, 1932.

FERGUSON, DONALD N., *A History of Musical Thought.* New York: Appleton-Century-Crofts, Inc., 1959.

FULLER-MAITLAND, J. A., ed., *Oxford History of Music:* Vol. IV, "The Age of Bach and Handel." London: Oxford University Press, 1931.

LANG, PAUL HENRY, *George Frederic Handel.* New York: W. W. Norton and Company, Inc., 1966.

————, *Music in Western Civilization.* New York: W. W. Norton and Company, Inc., 1941.

MELLERS, WILFRID, *Romanticism and the 20th Century.* Bristol, England: Burleigh Press, 1957.

SELDON-GOTH, G., ed., *Felix Mendelssohn Letters.* New York: Pantheon Books, Inc., 1945.

WERNER, ERIC, *Mendelssohn.* New York: Free Press of Glencoe, 1963.

YOUNG, PERCY M., *The Choral Tradition.* New York: W. W. Norton and Company, Inc., 1962.

Recordings—Chapter 11

Handel	*Messiah*	Boult, London	London A-4403
Mendelssohn	*Elijah*	Sargent, Liverpool	Angel C-3558
Penderecki	*Passion According to St. Luke*	Cologne Radio	Victor VICS-6015
Walton	*Belshazzar's Feast*	Ormandy, Philadelphia	Columbia ML-5667

Additional Suggestions for Listening

Honegger	*Jeanne d'Arc au Bûcher*	Ormandy, Philadelphia	Columbia SL-178
	King David	Honegger	Westminster WAL-204
Webber	*Jesus Christ Superstar*	Original Cast	Decca DXA-7206
	Joseph and the Amazing Technicolor Dreamcoat	Joseph Consortium	Scepter SPS-588X

Chapter 12

Opera

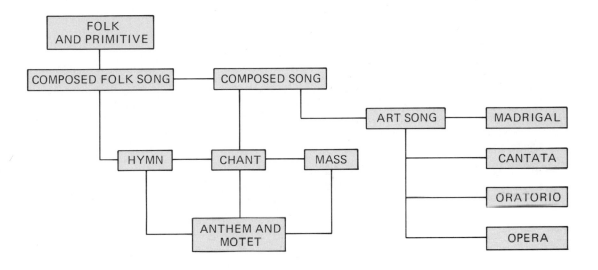

As we have already seen, the dramatic element in music has frequently been prominent. As soon as words were put to music more drama was present or implied. Following this reasoning, the folk song overshadows the folk tune; the through-composed art song relates the emotion of an idea or event more realistically than the strophic; the cantata and the oratorio relate more closely to the theatrical than any of the previously studied forms. Opera takes one additional step, and this step is a large one, becoming a play with music; yet it is quite different from a play. These differences should be examined so that the form will be understood and not dismissed prematurely.

Opera is a complex art form usually including music, drama, costuming, poetry, acting, and dance. It must combine most or all of these into one production with a certain skill and balance which become unmanageable without a master hand.

Since its earliest beginnings in the early 1600s, opera has had a heterogeneous following. When one combines the several arts mentioned above, the attraction may be multiple for many or singular for a few. Some are attracted by the music, some by the drama, and some by the personalities and abilities of the prima donnas. Still others are attracted by the mere spectacle and the number of artists involved to produce it.

Much opera has been written that appeals mainly to the light and frivolous; others have featured the drama of tragedy; a number of them are spectacles including almost a hundred persons on the stage, while fewer feature one or two singers. If successful, each work has been planned to give a dramatic impact, and the method and emphasis follows the intent of the composer.

Related to a Play

Even though an opera contains music and singing, there are several ways in which it is similar to a play:

1. A story is told through action on the stage. In the cantata and oratorio a major device could be the meditative sections which guided the listener to think upon a given subject or idea. Although the soliloquy is possible in drama and in opera, dialogue is used to develop the plot, with the characters moving on and off stage in a planned manner to give a lifelike impression of a dramatic event. The story is begun, the characters interact, the plot becomes obvious while the characters move to resolve the concern or conflict. The method of solution determines the type of drama and opera.

2. Scenery is used to bring vividness to the telling of the story. A play may have most impressive sets; or, plays are sometimes staged which call for little or no scenery. Most directors, however, try to employ some kind of set that will relay to the observer a lifelike impression of the locale of the play. In opera, the same is true. Most of the major operas are staged with a great emphasis upon scenery, so that in some of the larger and more respected opera houses the sets are 30 or so feet high and the stage is so deep that it enables one to build sets which resemble large outdoor scenes or huge indoor rooms of large estates or castles. Often the sets for opera are themselves considered works of art, since they add greatly to the overall effect. You may recall that "Oscars" and "Tonys" are awarded yearly for the best set design in a movie or a play on Broadway. In opera, valued sets retained by the designing company may be rented throughout the world. It is not uncommon for a set to be shipped from Rome, Paris, or London to Chicago, San Francisco, or New York for a production, and in some cases a set built and designed in the late nineteenth century may still be circulating or may be stored until reinstituted for a given performance or series of performances.

3. Costumes are used to assist the characters with their roles. Just as in a play, the costumes assist greatly in the development of a character, particularly if his is a supporting role. In plays where scenery is only suggestive, much emphasis is still placed upon appropriate costumes. Even in a play about a period of time only five or ten years ago, costume details will be meticulously researched and adhered to. Movies place considerable emphasis upon costumes,

particularly those involving any time era except the present. All of these statements are equally true in opera. Since many operas come from an earlier period or are placed in a time period other than the present, costumes become a major concern. They give the audience an insight into the period as well as the particular person involved, and incidentally assist us in identifying the various persons on stage. This becomes particularly important in opera, since the medium of singing is often so foreign to the listener that he cannot rely upon voice color alone to aid character identification. The large auditoriums where operas are usually presented, blur discernment of the unique features of the face and carriage.

4. Lighting is used to assist with the staging. In a play lighting can be an important factor in the plot. The set may be an ordinary living room and the time could be the middle of the day. Nonetheless, the lighting gives a feeling of mood and highlights the characters at different places on the stage as they speak particular lines, or it can accent certain portions of the scenery. More obvious are the special effects that call for evening scenes, night scenes, or partially dark rooms or other places. Again, all of these statements are true of opera, becoming all the more important if the performance is given in a large stage area where the rear of the stage may need special lighting so that perspective may be enhanced. In some musicals a spotlight follows the characters around the stage as they sing or speak their lines. This is not usually done in opera, where the lighting of special characters is much more subtle and professional.

Differences from a Play

On the other hand, opera is quite different from a play. These points need to be emphasized:

1. The characters sing what they have to relate rather than speak lines. Often this disturbs the person who has little experience with opera, since it seems so unnatural. Although it is not the usual method of conveying our thoughts to our friends or family, yet it is not as foreign as one might conclude. An uninhibited child will often sing of his feelings, and even occasionally sing his conversation to a friend. This habit does not persist, since he mimics his elders who are only speaking. Even an adult might sing if he is not aware of the presence of another person; this is particularly true at a time of ease, great joy, or pleasant surroundings. The old cliché of singing in the shower is not inaccurate, since the person is alone and feeling the stimulation of the water. Paddling alone in a canoe on an open lake often leads to humming or singing a soft, smooth song. It is not too unusual at such times for a human being to begin to sing. Opera only extends these feelings to a constant routine.

Remember that opera is an art form, and art never duplicates life; exact duplications fail to be art. Just as the folk song singer believes that the love or sorrow he feels can best be stated in song, so in opera songs should be considered an obvious outgrowth of the artistic in man.

2. Singing tends to portray the emotions and inner feelings as well as the meaning of the words being sung. Growing naturally from the previous point, just as the spoken words of the individual do not remain at the same intensity or the same pitch level, so in singing. The type of singing heard in opera gives us an indication of the emotion of the singer. Consequently, love songs are mellow or often bravura as the lover declares himself; the anger of the moment can produce fiery vocal lines. This tends to bring us back to art, since the strophic song portrays these feelings less well than the art song.

In opera the musical line assists us with an understanding of inner feelings even though the text might indicate otherwise. In the case of the play, the manner of speaking a line, or perhaps a look while the line is being said, will betray one's inner feelings. Opera also makes use of these devices, but the musician has built the inner feelings into the various sounds, not always having to rely upon the inflection of the voice or the look on the face.

3. Accompaniment is frequently used to complement the vocal line and add color and emotion to the work. In drama it has often been customary to add background or occasional music to assist with the emotions of the moment. Shakespeare on occasion had his characters sing, particularly in the comedies. In an opera the music is continuous, and so the composer relies upon the accompaniment for assistance. Many times the orchestra sets the mood through the overture; or, an orchestral interlude will assist with a change of mood or indicate that which has not been sung. For example, in some operas the orchestra plays a particular theme each time a certain character is about to enter the stage, or even more complex, each time the character is mentioned on stage or even thought of. An opera is almost always accompanied by an orchestra, unless it be a simple and modest production. The colorations possible in the orchestra add greatly to the subtle meanings of the drama.

4. A chorus is often used to add color, variety, a lifelike situation, or as in the oratorio or cantata, to give a point of view or comment. The contrast between the soloists and the chorus makes a most pleasant change of musical texture. On stage the chorus may take part in the action of a scene, so that in a large opera one may find up to a hundred persons moving about on stage as part of a banquet scene, a mob at a coronation, or a party given by one of the characters. When all of these persons appear in appropriate dress, the scene becomes colorful and most plausible. In some of the earlier operas the chorus may be required to comment concerning a situation, and they are then less mobile. In later operas, however, a chorus is rarely introduced unless it can be a realistic and believable part of the action. In the opera *Carmen*, a group of children are a part of the first act. This is most plausible, since they enter following a group of soldiers who change the guard in the town square. On such an occasion children would be expected to be present to see the maneuvers and to copy the action. In *Madama Butterfly* the chorus is present only in the first act, being a part of the wedding party; this is a most logical time for a group of girls to gather to sing their good wishes to the bride, who was their partner and friend.

5. Action often stops to permit the singers to share with the audience their thoughts as characters. Although at times this is not unlike the soliloquies of plays, in an opera these delays in the action are more frequent, and they often occur in ensemble scenes as well as in solo scenes. In fact, they may come just at the moment when the audience expects the action to advance most rapidly. When the composer wishes to focus attention on a particular character or emotion, the time is apropos for an aria.

Arias tend to delay the action, so usually they are followed by recitatives which restore the action with obvious haste. Occasionally the pace of the action may confuse the careless listener. Particularly is this true in the latter stages of a comedy, where actions proceed rapidly toward the happy ending.

In more recent operas emphasis is placed upon the recitative, and arias often occur further apart. In earlier times, the audience often came to the theater for the purpose of hearing the voices of the singers, the beautiful or artistic work they could perform, and the use the composer could make of the voice or the music. In this case the aria was the center of attention. More recently composers have placed more emphasis upon the action, and less upon the beauty of the vocal line.

6. Many times several characters sing simultaneously with different words, to convey to the listener the various emotions of the moment. This kind of musical activity is most confusing to the novice. Not only does the action stop for an aria, but suddenly several performers are singing together so that the listener cannot understand the text. The main purpose here is the effect that this kind of participation produces. Sometimes the composer will introduce the lines so that each person will sing alone at first, and then all will sing together. The emotion is then more important than the words themselves. Also, the combining of voices in such a manner gives the desired textural change, as well as the musical opportunity to combine the voices in a kind of fugal composition.

Several other points could be mentioned briefly. Because of the great variety of arts involved, opera is an expensive form to produce and needs the assistance of magnanimous financing. Sometimes this means unusually high admission prices, so that a relatively few people get to enjoy the production. A donor may be needed to produce a given work. Recently, wealthy families or commercial firms have assisted with a new production or a new design for an older opera. In earlier times a prince or a member of the royal family may have been a patron of the arts. In many countries, governments support the arts and assist with opera as a worthy undertaking. Although this is not done to any extent in the United States, it is often the case in Europe, where opera houses are partially supported from public funds. Because of these complexities, opera is often considered a "snob" art. This opinion has grown, and in the United States a concerted effort needs to be made to dispel it.

As has been inferred earlier, opera makes use of the aria, recitative, and chorus. In addition a ballet or dance group may assist. The tradition of dancing in opera comes from France, and although its history is much too complex and detailed for our study, the inclusion of ballet in opera is no more out of place than in some movies you may have seen. Usually the dancing is in the style of the period in which the opera was written, and this in itself is an artistic insight into the manner of life of the people.

As we noted in discussing cantata and oratorio, word painting was an interesting musical device that often assisted with the emotional effect of a piece. This is also true in opera, although it is used less here, since the action, scenery, and other factors take care of so much of it.

Particularly in modern operas, word rhythm is most important to the flow of the musical lines. For this reason, there are those who believe that one should sing an opera in the original language of its writing. In Europe this practice is little followed, consequently it is rare to find an opera in Paris that is not sung in French, or an opera in Rome not sung in Italian. In the United States we claim to be more artistic, but in reality this is a holdover from the days when opera was presented mainly for those able to understand a foreign language and to appreciate an opera written by a European composer. Thus when an Italian opera was presented, the Italian-speaking people would flock to the performance, and likewise with operas from other countries.

Today few people in this country understand the native tongues of our forefathers, yet the tradition lingers on the premise that it is more artistic. Although the artistic argument may contain merit for some situations and perhaps some operas, yet most lines in almost all operas could be stated equally well in a number of languages. In our country universities are not timid about presenting their operas in English, which accounts largely for the success of their presentations on campus.

In the introduction to his book on opera Charles Hamm states:

> A tradition has been built up in this country that opera is the most difficult, intellectual, esoteric of all art forms, one which can be enjoyed or appreciated only after a rigorous period of apprenticeship. . . . The way one learns to "enjoy" an opera, for instance, is to study it enough to learn who the major characters are and what their relationships are to one another. . . . A German or Italian or Russian, by contrast, goes to the opera house with the expectation that the opera he is to see that evening will make itself understandable to him.[1]

And well he might, because it will be sung in his native tongue, while in our country the original language of the composition will be used, so that if a person does not at least read the plot before entering the theatre he could miss all of the dramatic meaning and implications.

Contrapuntal writing may be used in operas, although most of the writing is less complex than that for instrumental compositions or for the more developed choral compositions. Since the emphasis is upon the drama, a bit more simple music is needed to carry the impact of the plot.

---

1 *Opera,* Charles Hamm. Allyn and Bacon, Inc., Boston, 1966, page vii.

This brings into focus one of the controversial points of opera: the importance of the action and the drama versus the importance of the music. Conflicting viewpoints exist for almost every presentation; one version will emphasize the drama of the plot, while another may present the music as paramount to the action. If a happy medium cannot be found the production may appear dull because the action is lifeless and often unreal; if the action is primary, often the singers complain that they are moving about the stage with little breath or energy remaining to sing their best lines or arias. This kind of debate may go much deeper into the philosophical meaning of the work and the intent of the composer.

Although of interest, the history of opera is much too detailed for this book. There are many fine books for those who may wish them, since the form has attracted writers since its early days. Of all those forms we have studied to date, none have been chronicled so carefully as opera. Not unlike the movies or TV, opera fans have become devoted to both the form and the performers.

Where a country has enjoyed a rich drama, opera has been less strong. But where drama has not been particularly commanding, opera has risen to fill the gap. At the present time we are witnessing a strength in drama in this country and perhaps throughout Western civilization. Thus new operas are not being written to the same extent as in the eighteenth and nineteenth centuries.

Madama Butterfly (Puccini)

For over 250 years Japan had been closed off as a nation except for two visits a year from Dutch merchants. In 1853 President Franklin Pierce sent Commodore Perry into the harbor of Tokyo to request trading rights. In the years that followed Japan became more outward-looking, even to the point of attempting land acquisition in Manchuria. Such aggressive acts brought her into war with Russia in 1904.

During these fifty years of growth and expansion, the United States traded regularly with Japan, and at home interest in ideas and items from the Orient increased. It was not unusual, then, that a play should capitalize upon such interest. Based on a story by John Long, a Philadelphia lawyer who also had a keen interest in literature, David Belasco, a prominent dramatist and theater man, wrote and produced a one-act play entitled *Madame Butterfly* which was an immediate success in New York; so much so, in fact, that a month later he opened the play in London. In the house at opening night was Giacomo Puccini, a well-known and popular opera composer of the time. He happened to be in London seeking a libretto for an opera and attended the theater. Although he did not understand English, the play was immediately meaningful to him and its possibilities attractive. Although delayed somewhat in the writing by an automobile accident, Puccini presented *Butterfly* in 1904 to a completely unsympathetic audience.

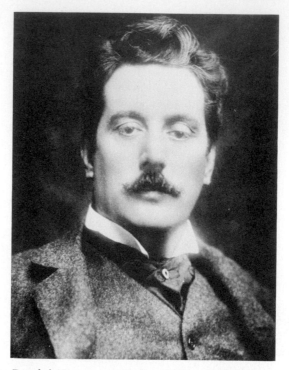

Giacomo Puccini (Courtesy of Italian Cultural Institute, New York).

After some revision, Puccini again presented the work with a different cast in a different city. This time the work was received more positively. Other performances were soon given around the world, including one in South America conducted by Toscanini. Almost immediately four performances were given in New York in English, and then finally one in New York in Italian, with Farrar singing the part of Butterfly and Caruso singing Pinkerton.

Two of Puccini's letters give us some indications of his feelings about performances in America:

To his sister Nitteti

Paris
November 14, 1906

Dear Nitteti,

Elvira is here with me and will write to you. We speak of you so often, and I should like to write to you, but I never find the time.

Do not believe that I am so very well. I have some very bad days. My accursed diabetes gives me a great deal of trouble.

We shall be ready for the performance in the beginning of December. How it bores me to stay here so long! I should like to be at Torre or Chiatri, in solitude and peace.

Butterfly continues her triumphal career: Washington, Baltimore, Boston, and yesterday, New York—always in English. In January I am going to New York for Manon, Butterfly, Tosca, and then Butterfly in Italian at another theater, the great Metropolitan.

But first I shall return to Italy if only for a few days. I have to come, besides, for clothes. I must get a fur-lined coat because it is very cold in New York.[2]

To Tito Ricordi

New York
February 18, 1907

Dear Tito,

Butterfly went very well as far as the Press and public were concerned, but not so as to please me. It was a performance without poetry. Farrar is not too satisfactory. She sings out of tune, forces her voice, and it does not carry well in the large space of the theater. I had to struggle to obtain two full dress rehearsals, including the final. Nobody knew anything. Dufrich had not taken the trouble to study the mise en scene, because the composer was there. Vigna did his very well, but whenever I left the field there were disasters.

However, it went well, on the whole, and the Press is unanimous in its praise. This is the first day that I have been able to write after six days of influenza which m'a tue. I am sailing on the 26th in the Kronprinz. I wanted to go to Niagara but now I have neither the desire nor the time to go.[3]

The reception of these performances and several others around the world assured its success. It has become one of the most popular operas of all time and still attracts professional companies, amateur community efforts, and university presentations. This is true partly because the music depicts so carefully the emotions felt by so many. In addition, the story becomes ever renewed with soldiers and sailors stationed in foreign countries or as we witness insincere love within ourselves or our acquaintances. Young people are continually reliving the burdens of the plot.

The Play

It is unusual for an opera to be based upon an American play. Since the play is comparatively short, it will be worthwhile to read the original material from which the opera came. This has several advantages. Since the opera is usually recorded in Italian, a study of the play will give you an accessible introduction

---

2 From the book *Letters of Giacomo Puccini,* mainly connected with the composition and production of his operas. Edited by Giuseppe Adami. Translated by Ena Makin. Copyright, 1931, by J. B. Lippincott Company, page 162. Reprinted, as abridged, by permission of the publishers.
3 *Ibid.,* page 168.

Scene from Act I of a production of Puccini's opera Madama Butterfly,
*performed at the Dallas Civic Opera in 1970; shown are
Renata Scotto and Bruno Prevedi (Photograph by
Andy Hanson, Dallas, Texas).*

to the plot.   More important, it will enable you to compare the two art forms,
the play and the opera.   Notice how the librettist has elaborated upon certain
scenes to provide the composer with material for vocal development.   For
example, an entire first act has been added, including new characters and a
chorus.   Occasionally a line from the play is used, but usually the dialogue differs
so as to better fit the demands of opera.

MADAME BUTTERFLY[4]

*The play takes place in Japan in Madame Butterfly's little house at the foot of
Higashi Hill, facing the harbor.   Everything in the room is Japanese save the American
locks and bolts on the doors and windows and an American flag fastened to a tobacco
jar.   Cherry blossoms are abloom outside, and inside.   A sword rack, a shrine on which
lie a sword and a pair of men's slippers, a chest of drawers on top of which is a tray
containing two red poppies, rouge, powder and hair ornaments, a stand for the tobacco*

---

4 From the book *Six Plays by David Belasco*.   Published by Little, Brown, and Company, Boston,
1928, pages 13–32.

jar and tea, are the only pieces of furniture in the room.   As the curtain rises, Madame Butterfly is spraying the growing flowers with a small watering pot.   She snips off two little bunches, lays them on a plate of rice which she sets reverently on the shrine, then kneels, putting her hands on the floor, her forehead on them.

MADAME BUTTERFLY:	Oh, Shaka! Hail! Hail! Also perceive! Look down! I have brought a sacrifice of flowers and new rice. Also, I am quite clean. I am shivering with cleanness. Therefore grant that Lef-ten-ant B. F. Pik-ker-ton may come back soon. *(She rises, claps her hands, comes down to a floor cushion, and sits, fanning herself.)*
SUZUKI:	*(Entering with a low bow).* Madame Butterfly's wish?
MADAME BUTTERFLY:	Suzuki, inform me, if it please you, how much more nearer beggary we are to-day than yesterday?
SUZUKI:	Aye. *(She takes some coins from a small box in her sleeve, and lays them in three piles on her palm, touching them as she speaks.)* Rin, yen, sen. . . .
MADAME BUTTERFLY:	*(Reprovingly).* Suzuki, how many time I tellin' you—no one shall speak anythin' but those Unite' State' languages in these Lef-ten-ant Pik-ker-ton's house? *(She pronounces his name with much difficulty.)* Once more—an' I put you outside shoji! . . . That's one thin' aeverbody got recomlec' account it's 'Merican house—his wife, his maid.
SUZUKI:	*(Mouthing to herself, making no sound, counting on her fingers).* Two dollar. *(She drops the money into the box, giving it to Madame Butterfly.)*
MADAME BUTTERFLY:	O, how we waste my husban's be-autiful moaneys! Tha's shame! Mos' gone.
SUZUKI:	This moaney hav' kept us two year. . . . Wha's happen to us now, if he don' come back?
MADAME BUTTERFLY:	*(Scoffing, putting the money in her sleeve).* O, if he don' come back! . . . Course he come back! He's gone so long accoun' he's got business in those his large country. If he's not come back to his house, why he sign Japanese lease for nine hundred and ninety-nine year for me to live? Why he put 'Merican lock to bolt it door, to shut it window? Answer me those question.
SUZUKI:	*(Doubtfully).* I dunno.
MADAME BUTTERFLY:	Of course you dunno! You don' know whichaever. Wael I goin' tell you: to keep out those which are out, and in, those which are in. Tha's me. *(She rises, goes to the window and looks out.)*
SUZUKI:	But he don't writin' no ledder.
MADAME BUTTERFLY:	'Merican men don' naever write ledder—no time.
SUZUKI:	*(Cynically).* Aye . . . I don' naever know 'Merica navy man with Japanese wive come back.
MADAME BUTTERFLY:	*(Impassively, her eyes narrowing).* Speak concerning marriage once more, you die! *(She fans herself. Suzuki salaams and backs quickly toward the door. Madame Butterfly claps her hands and Suzuki pauses.)* Don' come back! Lef-ten-ant B. F. Pik-ker-ton don' come back! Ha! Me! I know w'en he

comes back—he told me. W'en he goin' 'way, he say in tha's doors: "Madame Butterfly, I have had ver' nice times with my Japanese sweets heart, so now I goin' back to my own country and here's moaney—an' don' worry 'bout me—I come back w'en 'Robins nes' again!' " Ha-ha! Tha's w'en he come back—w'en robins nes' again.

(She sways her head triumphantly from side to side, fanning herself.)

SUZUKI: *(Not impressed).*   Yaes, I didn't like ways he said it—like those . . .

(She imitates a flippant gesture of farewell.)

MADAME BUTTERFLY: *(Laughing).*   Aha, tha's 'Merican way sayin' good-bye to girl. Yaes, he come back w'en robins nes' again. Shu'h! Shu'h! *(She claps her hands with delight. Suzuki, with a look of unbelief, starts to go.)* Sa-ey! Why no "shu'h" on you face for? Such a fools! *(Looking towards the window.)* O look! Suzuki—a robins. The firs' these Spring! Go, see if he's stay for nes'.

SUZUKI: *(Looking).*   It *is* a robins, O Cho-Cho-San!

MADAME BUTTERFLY: *(Running to the window).*   O! O!

SUZUKI: But he's fly away.

MADAME BUTTERFLY: O! How they are slow this year! Sa-ey, see if you don' fin' one tha's more in-dus-trial an' domestics.

SUZUKI: *(Looking out).*   There are none yet.

MADAME BUTTERFLY: But soon they nes' now. Suzuki, w'en we see that ship comin' in—sa-ey—then we goin' put flowers aevery where, an' if it's night, we goin' hang up mos' one thousan' lanterns—eh-ha?

SUZUKI: No got moaney for thousan'.

MADAME BUTTERFLY: Wael, twenty, mebby; an' sa-ey, w'en we see him comin' quick up path—*(imitates)* so—so—so—*(lifts her kimono and strides in a masculine fashion)* to look for liddle wive—me—me jus' goin' hide behind shoji *(making two holes with her wet finger in the low paper shoji and peeking through)* an' watch an' make believe me gone 'way; leave liddle note—sayin': "Goon-bye, sayonara, Butterfly." . . . Now he come in. . . . *(Hides.)* Ah! An' then he get angry! An' he say all kinds of 'Merican languages—debbils—hells! But before he get too angry, me run out an' flew aroun' his neck! *(She illustrates with Suzuki, who is carried away and embraces her with fervor.)* Sa-ey! *You* no flew roun' his neck—jus' me. *(They laugh in each other's arms.)* Then he'll sit down an' sing tha's liddle 'Merican song—O, how he'll laugh. . . . *(She sings as though not understanding a word of it.)*

"I call her the belle of Japan—of Japan,
 Her name it is O Cho-Cho-San, Cho-Cho-San!
 Such tenderness lies in her soft almond eyes,
 I tell you, she's just 'ichi ban.' "

(Laughs.) Then I'll dance like w'en I was Geisha girl.

(She dances as Sharpless, the American consul, appears in the doorway, followed by the Nakodo.)

NAKODO: This is the house, your Excellency.

SHARPLESS: *(Removing his clogs outside).*   You may wait.

(Nakodo bows and Sharpless enters.)

I beg pardon. . . .
(Madame Butterfly, still dancing, begins the song again.
Sharpless goes to the door and knocks to attract her attention.)

MADAME BUTTERFLY: Ah!
(Suzuki, bowing low, leaves the room.)

SHARPLESS: This is Madame Cho-Cho-San?

MADAME BUTTERFLY: No, I am Mrs. Lef-ten-ant B. F. Pik-ker-ton.

SHARPLESS: I see. . . . Pardon my interruption. . . . I am Mr. Sharpless, the American consul.

MADAME BUTTERFLY: *(Once more salaaming to the ground, drawing in her breath between her teeth to express pleasure).* O, your honorable excellency, goon night—no, not night yaet: aexcuse me, I'm liddle raddle',—I mean goon mornin', goon evenin'. Welcome to 'Merican house, mos' welcome to 'Merican girl! *(Pointing to herself. They both bow.)* Be seat. *(Sharpless sits on a cushion on the floor, and Madame Butterfly sits at a little distance. There is a slight pause.)* How are those health? You sleepin' good? How are that honorable ancestors —are they well? And those parens'? That grandmother—how are she?

SHARPLESS: Thanks. They're all doing well, I hope.

MADAME BUTTERFLY: *(She claps her hands; Suzuki enters and puts the little stand between them and leaves the room).* Accep' pipe, your Excellency. O, I forgettin'—I have still of those large American cigarette.
(Madame Butterfly gestures towards Pinkerton's tobacco jar decorated with the flag of his country.)

SHARPLESS: *(Accepting a cigarette while she fills her pipe).* Thanks. I'm on a little visit of inquiry, Madame Butterfly,—your name, I believe, in our language. Lieutenant Pinkerton wrote to me to find out—

MADAME BUTTERFLY: *(Almost breathless).* Ah, you have hear from him? He is well?

SHARPLESS: O, he's all right.

MADAME BUTTERFLY: *(Relieved).* Ah! Tha's mak' me mos' bes' happy female woman in Japan—mebby in that whole worl'—w'at you thing?

SHARPLESS: Ha—ha! *(Puffing at the cigarette.)* Sawdust. Pinkerton must have left these!

MADAME BUTTERFLY: O! I so glad you came. . . . I goin' as' you a liddle question.

SHARPLESS: Well?

MADAME BUTTERFLY: You know 'bout birds in those your country?

SHARPLESS: Something.

MADAME BUTTERFLY: Tha's what I thing—you know aeverything. Tha's why your country sen' you here.

SHARPLESS: You flatter me.

MADAME BUTTERFLY: O, no, you got big head.

SHARPLESS: Pinkerton again—I can hear him!

MADAME BUTTERFLY: O, aexcuse me: I forgettin' my manners. I got liddle more raddle. *(She offers him her pipe which he gravely touches, returning it. She touches it again, then puts it down.)* Now, what you know 'bout jus' robins?

SHARPLESS: What?

MADAME BUTTERFLY: 'Bout when do they nes' again? Me, I thing it mus' be mor'

SHARPLESS:	early in Japan as in America, accoun' they nestin' here now. O, at the same time, I fancy.
MADAME BUTTERFLY:	*(Disappointed).* Yaes? . . . then they's nestin' there. *(Then taking hope again.)* Sa-ey, I tell you—perhaps some time sooner, some time later, jus' how they feel like.
SHARPLESS:	Possibly. Why do you ask?
MADAME BUTTERFLY:	Because Lef-ten-ant B. F. Pik-ker-ton say he will come back to me w'en the robins nes' again.
SHARPLESS:	*(To himself).* Poor devil! One of his infernal jokes.
MADAME BUTTERFLY:	*(Clapping her hands).* Me, I thing it's time. . . . I've wait so long. *(Suzuki enters with a tea-pot. Madame Butterfly gives Sharpless a cup of tea.)*
NAKODO:	*(Appearing at the door).* Tea, most illustrious?
MADAME BUTTERFLY:	Ah! Enter, Nakodo. Your presence lights up my entire house. *(She gives him a cup. Accepting it, he goes up to a cushion and sits.)* Tha's bad man. W'en my husban's gone 'way, he try for get me marry again.
NAKODO:	The rich Yamadori. Madame Cho-Cho-San is very poor.
MADAME BUTTERFLY:	*(Bowing politely).* O, liddle ol' frien'; those are my business.
NAKODO:	Rejected advice makes the heart sad.
MADAME BUTTERFLY:	We-el, if those heart hurt you so much, you better not arrive here no more.
SHARPLESS:	Madame Butterfly; may I ask—er—where are your people?
NAKODO:	They have outcasted her!
MADAME BUTTERFLY:	Sa-ey, tha's foanny! My people make me marry when I don' want; now I am marry, they don' want. Before I marry Lef-ten-ant B. F. Pik-ker-ton, my honorable Father—*(she bows low—Nakodo bows—Sharpless bows)* die—he's officer. These are his sword . . . *(pointing to an inscription)* 'tis written. . . . *(She holds out the sword that the inscription may be read.)*
NAKODO:	*(Reading).* "To die with honor, when one can no longer live with honor." *(He bows, then turns and bows towards the shrine and goes back to his cushion where he sits.)*
MADAME BUTTERFLY:	He's kill' himself accoun' he soldier of Emperor an' defeat in battle. Then we get—O—ver' poor. Me? I go dance liddle. Also I thing if some rich man wish me, I gettin' marry for while, accoun' my grandmother, *(she bows respectfully—Nakodo bows—Sharpless politely nods)* don' got no food, no obi. Then ol' Nakodo, he say a *(Nakodo picks up his cushion and moves down to join in the conversation)* man's jus' as' him for nice wive for three monse. Nakodo tell him he don' know none more nizer as me.
NAKODO:	*(Salaaming).* Nizer as you.
MADAME BUTTERFLY:	*(Salaaming).* Nizer as me.
SHARPLESS:	*(Looking from one to the other).* Couldn't be nicer! . . . *(He salaams profoundly—then all salaam.)*
MADAME BUTTERFLY:	Then Nakodo say—
NAKODO:	I say—I don' lig him account he 'Merica—jin.
MADAME BUTTERFLY:	He also remark with me that he is barbarian an' beas'. But aeveryone say: "Yaes, take him—take him beas'—he's got

moaneys." So I say for jus' liddle while, perhaps I can stan'. So Nakodo bring him. . . .

NAKODO: . . . For look-at meeting.

MADAME BUTTERFLY: *(Laughing).* Me? Well, I thing that day Lef-ten-ant B. F. Pik-ker-ton is jus' a god! Gold button—lace on his unicorn. At firs', I frightened—he hol' my hans' so close—like—*(she illustrates by giving both hands to Sharpless)* and kizz. Japanese girl no lig' kizz; but when Lef-ten-ant B. F. Pik-ker-ton kizz me, I like ver' much. . . . What's use lie? It's not inside of me. *(Noticing that her hands are still in Sharpless'.)* O, I beg your honorable pardon. *(She tucks her hands in her sleeves.)* So we's gettin' marry and then his ship order away an' me—I am jus' waitin'—sometimes cryin', sometimes watchin', but always waitin'.

NAKODO: *(In the doorway—bowing with servility).* My client, the prosperous Yamadori, approaches for the third time to-day.

MADAME BUTTERFLY: Now I have my liddle joke again. You watch, he comes all time to make smash with me.

SHARPLESS: Pinkerton's slang.

(Yamadori enters, attended by two servants. Sharpless rises and bows ceremoniously. Madame Butterfly does not rise, but bends her head and fans herself coquettishly. The two servants squat.)

YAMADORI: Mr. Sharpless: always a pleasure to meet you here or in New York.

SHARPLESS: Thanks, Mr. Yamadori.

MADAME BUTTERFLY: *(Coquettishly).* You have somethin' nize say to me again to-day?

YAMADORI: Perseverance shall be the religion of my life until the capricious Butterfly deigns to believe me.

MADAME BUTTERFLY: You goin' tell me 'gain you kill yourself I don' make kizz with you?

YAMADORI: *(Very much embarrassed—looking at consul).* O!

MADAME BUTTERFLY: You can speak—consul know—I been tellin' him 'bout your liddle foolishness.

YAMADORI: Such treatment, Mr. Sharpless, is one of the penalties we incur when madly in love with a charming woman.

MADAME BUTTERFLY: Tha's ver' nize. Ha-ha!

(Winks behind her fan at Sharpless.)

SHARPLESS: Heavens! Pinkerton's very wink.

(Madame Butterfly gives a cup of tea to Yamadori who drinks it and rolls a cigarette.)

YAMADORI: *(To Sharpless).* I am in Japan for two months—a pleasure trip. Do you blame me?

(Pointing to Madame Butterfly.)

MADAME BUTTERFLY: Aevery time he come home, get 'nother woman: must have mor'en eight now.

YAMADORI: But I *married* them all. . . .

MADAME BUTTERFLY: O *he!* He jus' marry whenaever he thing 'bout it.

YAMADORI: You shall be different. I will bury *you* with my ancestors. *(To Sharpless.)* I offered her a thousand servants.

NAKODO: *(Stunned).* Thousan'!

MADAME BUTTERFLY:	Ha! *(Fans.)*
YAMADORI:	And a palace to live in.
	(The Nakodo is overcome by such generosity.)
MADAME BUTTERFLY:	He!
YAMADORI:	Everything her heart can wish.
MADAME BUTTERFLY:	Ha! Ha!
YAMADORI:	Is that not enough? *(She shakes her head.)* Then in the presence of this statesman of integrity, I will give you a solemn writing. *(Sharpless gives him a quizzical glance.)* Is *that* enough?
MADAME BUTTERFLY:	Wha's good of that to married womans? *(Pointing to herself.)*
YAMADORI:	According to the laws of Japan, when a woman is deserted, she is divorced. *(Madame Butterfly stops fanning herself and listens.)* Though I have travelled much abroad, I know the laws of my own country.
MADAME BUTTERFLY:	An' I know laws of my *husban's* country.
YAMADORI:	*(To Sharpless).* She still fancies herself married to the young officer. If your Excellency would explain. . . .
MADAME BUTTERFLY:	*(To Sharpless).* Sa-ey, when some one gettin' married in America, don' he stay marry?
SHARPLESS:	Usually—yes.
MADAME BUTTERFLY:	Well, tha's all right. I'm marry to Lef-ten-ant B. F. Pik-ker-ton.
YAMADORI:	Yes, but a Japanese marriage!
SHARPLESS:	Matrimony is a serious thing in America, not a temporary affair as it often is here.
MADAME BUTTERFLY:	Yaes, an' you can't like 'Merican mans. Japanese got too many wive, eh?
SHARPLESS:	*(Laughing).* We are not allowed more than one at a time.
MADAME BUTTERFLY:	Yaes, an' you can't divorce wive like here, by sayin': "walk it back to parent"—eh?
SHARPLESS:	O, no.
MADAME BUTTERFLY:	Tha's right, aexactly. When I as' Lef-ten-ant B. F. Pik-ker-ton, he explain those law to me of gettin' divorce in those Unite' State'. He say no one can get aexcept he stan' up before Judge 2—3—4—7—year. Ver' tiresome. Firs' the man he got tell those Judge all he know 'bout womans; then womans, she got tell; then some lawyer quarrel with those Judge; the Judge get jury an' as' wha' they thing—an' if they don' know, they'll all get put in jails. Tha's all right! *(Folds hands.)*
YAMADORI:	Your friend has told her everything she wanted him to tell her.
MADAME BUTTERFLY:	*(Who has paid no attention).* Tha's ver' nize, too, that 'Merican God.
SHARPLESS:	I beg your pardon?
MADAME BUTTERFLY:	Once times, Lef-ten-ant B. F. Pik-ker-ton—
YAMADORI:	*(Aside to Sharpless).* Pinkerton again!
MADAME BUTTERFLY:	He's in great troubles, an' he said "God he'p me"; an' sunshine *came right out*—and God he did! Tha's ver' quick—Japanese gods take more time. Aeverything quick in America. Ha—me—sometime I thing I pray large American God to get him back soon; but no use,—he don' know me where *I* live. *(Attracted by a sound.)* Wha's that? . . . You hear?

SHARPLESS:	No. *(Madame Butterfly runs to the window and listens; then takes up the glasses while Sharpless speaks in a low voice to Yamadori.)* Lieutenant Pinkerton's ship was due yesterday. His young wife from America is waiting here to meet him. *(At the word "wife," Yamadori smiles—takes his fan from his sleeve and fans himself. The Nakodo, who is listening, is struck by an idea and departs in such haste that he tumbles over one of Yamadori's attendants who jabbers at him.)* I'm devilish sorry for that girl.
YAMADORI:	Then tell her the truth.
MADAME BUTTERFLY:	Aexcuse me; but I always hearin' soun' like ship gun—ha—ha—tha's naturels.
YAMADORI:	*(Preparing to go).* Good morning, Mr. Sharpless. *(Shaking hands. Turning to Madame Butterfly.)* I leave you to-day. To-morrow the gods may prompt you to listen to me! *(He bows.)*
MADAME BUTTERFLY:	*(Bowing).* Mebby. *(Yamadori and attendants go off, bowing. She turns to Sharpless.)* Mebby not. Sa-ey, somehow couldn't you let that Lef-ten-ant B. F. Pik-ker-ton know they's other all crazy 'bout me?
SHARPLESS:	Madame Butterfly, sit down. *(While she, struck by his solemn manner, looks at him and obeys, he removes the tea-pot and sits on the stand, to the astonishment of Madame Butterfly.)* I am going to read you part of a letter I have received from Pinkerton. *(He takes a letter from his pocket.)*
MADAME BUTTERFLY:	O, jus' let me look at those ledder! *(She slips it under her kimono on her heart and with an indrawn breath, hands it back.)* Now read quick, you mos' bes' nice man in all the whole worl'.
SHARPLESS:	*(Reads).* "Find out about that little Jap girl. What has become of her? It might be awkward now. If little Butterfly still remembers me, perhaps you can help me out and make her understand. Let her down gently. You won't believe it, but for two weeks after I sailed, I was dotty in love with her." *(Sharpless is amazed to see Madame Butterfly convulsed with silent joy.)*
MADAME BUTTERFLY:	Oh, all the gods how it was sweet!
SHARPLESS:	Why really—
MADAME BUTTERFLY:	Tha's what I'm afraid: that he loave' me so much he's goin' desert his country an' get in trouble with American eagle—what you thing? Oh, it's more bedder I wait than those!
SHARPLESS:	*(Folding the letter).* No use—you can't understand. Madame Butterfly, suppose this waiting should never end; what would become of you?
MADAME BUTTERFLY:	Me? I could dance, mebby, or—die?
SHARPLESS:	Don't be foolish. I advise you to consider the rich Yamadori's offer.
MADAME BUTTERFLY:	*(Astonished).* You say those? You, 'Merican consul?—when you know that me, I am marry?
SHARPLESS:	You heard Yamadori: it is not binding.
MADAME BUTTERFLY:	Yamadori lies!

SHARPLESS:	His offer is an unusual opportunity for a girl who—for any Japanese girl in your circumstances.
MADAME BUTTERFLY:	(Enraged—she claps her hands). Suzuki! The excellent gentleman—(bowing sarcastically) who have done us the honor to call—he wish to go hurriedly. His shoes—hasten them! (Suzuki, who has entered carrying a jar, gets Sharpless' clogs and gives them to him—then passes off with her jar.)
SHARPLESS:	(Holding the clogs awkwardly). I'm really very sorry.
MADAME BUTTERFLY:	No, no, don' be angery. But jus' now you tol' me—O, gods! You mean— (Looks at him pitifully.) I not Lef-ten-ant B. F. Pik-ker-ton's wive—Me?
SHARPLESS:	Hardly.
MADAME BUTTERFLY:	O, I— (She sways slightly. Sharpless goes to her assistance, but she recovers and fans herself.) Tha's all right. I got liddle heart illness. I can't . . . I can't someways give up thingin' he'll come back to me. You thing tha's all over? All finish? (Dropping her fan. Sharpless nods assent.) Oh, no! Loave don' forget some thin's or wha's use of loave? (She claps her hands—beckoning off.) Loave's got remember . . . (pointing) some thin's!

(A child enters.)

SHARPLESS:	A child. . . . Pinkerton's? . . .
MADAME BUTTERFLY:	(Showing a picture of Pinkerton's). Look! Look! (Holding it up beside the child's face.) Tha's jus' his face, same hair, same blue eye. . . .
SHARPLESS:	Does Lieutenant Pinkerton know?
MADAME BUTTERFLY:	No, he come after he goe. (Looking at the child with pride.) You thing fath-er naever comes back—tha's what you thing? He do! You write him ledder; tell him 'bout one bes' mos' nize bebby aever seen. . . . Ha—ha! I bed all moaneys he goin' come mos' one million mile for see those chil'. Surely this is tie—bebby. Sa-ey, you didn' mean what you said 'bout me not bein' marry? You make liddle joke? (Moved, Sharpless nods his head in assent, to the great relief of Madame Butterfly.) Ha! (She lays the baby's hand in Sharpless'.) Shake hand consul 'Merican way.
SHARPLESS:	(Shaking hands with the child.) Hm . . . hm . . . what's your name?
MADAME BUTTERFLY:	Trouble. Japanese bebby always change it name. I was thinkin' some day w'en he come back, change it to Joy.
SHARPLESS:	Yes . . . yes . . . I'll let him know. (Glad to escape, he takes an abrupt departure.)
SUZUKI:	(In the distance, wailing). Ay . . . ay . . . ay . . .
MADAME BUTTERFLY:	Tha's wail . . .
SUZUKI:	(Nearer). O, Cho-Cho-San! (Madame Butterfly goes to the door to meet Suzuki.) Cho-Cho-San!
MADAME BUTTERFLY:	Speak!
SUZUKI:	We are shamed through the town. The Nakodo—
NAKODO:	(Appearing). I but said the child—(he points to the baby, whom Madame Butterfly instinctively shelters in her arms) was a badge of shame to his father. In his country, there are homes for such unfortunates and they never rise above the

stigma of their class. They are shunned and cursed from birth.

MADAME BUTTERFLY:	*(Who has listened stolidly—now with a savage cry, pushing him away from her until he loses his balance and falls to the floor.)* You lie!
NAKODO:	*(On the floor).* But Yamadori—
MADAME BUTTERFLY:	*(Touching her father's sword).* Lies! Lies! Lies! Say again, I kill! Go . . . *(The Nakodo goes quickly.)* Bebby, he lies . . . Yaes, it's lie. . . . When your fath-er knows now they speak, he will take us 'way from bad people to his own country. I am finish here. *(Taking the American flag from the tobacco jar and giving it to the child.)* Tha's your country—your flag. Now wave like fath-er say w'en excite—wave like "hell!" *(Waves the child's hand.)* Ha'rh! Ha'rh! *(A ship's gun is heard.)* Ah! *(Madame Butterfly and Suzuki start for the balcony. Madame Butterfly runs back for the child as the gun is heard again; then returning to the shoji, looks through the glasses.)* Look! Look! Warship! Wait . . . can't see name. . . .
SUZUKI:	Let me—
MADAME BUTTERFLY:	No! Ah! Name is "Con-nec-ti-cut"! His ship! He's come back! He's come back! *(Laughing, she embraces Suzuki—then sinks to the floor.)* He's come back! Those robins nes' again an' we didn' know! O, bebby, bebby—your fath er come back! Your fath-er's come back! O! O! *(Shaking a bough of cherry blossoms, which fall on them both.)* This is the bes' nize momen' since you was borned. Now your name's Joy! Suzuki: the Moon Goddess sent that bebby straight from Bridge of Heaven to make me courage to wait so long.
SUZUKI:	Ah, ship's in. . . .
MADAME BUTTERFLY:	*(Rising in great excitement).* Hoarry, Suzuki, his room. *(Suzuki pulls out a screen to form a little room.)* We mus' hoarry—*(picking flowers from the pots and decorating the room)* like we got eagle's wings an' thousan' feets. His cigarettes. *(Setting the jar in the room.)* His slipper. *(Suzuki gets them from the shrine.)* His chair, Suzuki—hustle! *(Suzuki hastens off. Madame Butterfly shakes a cushion and drops it on the floor.)* His bed. *(Suzuki enters with a steamer chair, which she places upside down.)* Now his room fixed! *(Suzuki closes the shoji. Madame Butterfly adjusts the chair and sets the lanterns about the room.)* Bring me my wides' obi, kanzashi for my hair, poppies—mus' look ver' pretty!
SUZUKI:	Rest is bes' beauty. He not come yet. Sleep liddle firs'. . . .
MADAME BUTTERFLY:	No, no time *(Taking up a small mirror and looking critically at herself).* He mus' see me look mos' pretty ever. You thing I change since he went away—not so beauty? *(Suzuki is silent.)* W'at? . . . I am! *(Brandishing the mirror.)* Say so!
SUZUKI:	Perhaps you rest liddle, once more you get so pretty again.
MADAME BUTTERFLY:	*Again?* . . .
SUZUKI:	Trouble, tha's make change. . . .
MADAME BUTTERFLY:	Moach change. *(Still looking in the glass.)* No, I am no more pretty—an' he come soon. *(On her knees in front of Suzuki —resting her forehead on the maid's feet.)* Ah, Suzuki, be kin'

with me—make me pretty . . . don' say you can't—you moas'. An' to-morrow, the gods will. Ah, yes! You can—you can— you got to! Bring powder, comb, rouge, henna, fix it hair like on wedding day. *(Suzuki brings the toilet articles and they sit on the floor. Suzuki puts the poppies and pins in Madame Butterfly's hair, and she, in turn, dresses the baby, enveloping him in an obi, so wide that it almost covers the child.)* Now, bebby, when you cry, he'll sing you those liddle 'Merican song he sing me when I cry—song all 'Merican sing for bebby. *(Sitting with the baby in front of her, swaying it by the arms, she sings.)*

> "Rog'—a—bye, bebby,
>   Off in Japan,
> You jus' a picture,
>   Off of a fan."

(Suzuki has found it very difficult to finish the toilet, but at last she accomplishes it. Madame Butterfly lifts the baby up, gives it a doll, then touches it with rouge and adds a final dash of rouge to her own face.) Now for watch for pa-pa!
(Putting the flag in the child's hand, she takes it up to the window and makes three holes in the shoji, one low down for the baby. As the three look through the shoji, they form the picture she has already described.)

(During the vigil, the night comes on. Suzuki lights the floor lamps, the stars come out, the dawn breaks, the floor lights flicker out one by one, the birds begin to sing, and the day discovers Suzuki and the baby fast asleep on the floor; but Madame Butterfly is awake, still watching, her face white and strained. She reaches out her hands and rouses Suzuki.)

SUZUKI: *(Starting to her feet, surprised and looking about the room).* He no come?

MADAME BUTTERFLY: No. . . .

SUZUKI: *(Pityingly).* Oh! . . .

MADAME BUTTERFLY: *(With an imperious gesture).* No "Oh"! He will come. . . . Bring fresh flowers. *(She collects the lanterns as Suzuki brings in fresh flowers. Madame Butterfly tears up the roses and throws their leaves in Pinkerton's room. Then pointing to the upper part of the house.)* Now I watch from liddle look out place. *(She picks up the child whose doll drops from its hand.)* Have mos' bes' nize breakfas' ready w'en he come.
(She leaves the room and Suzuki goes to prepare the breakfast.)
(The stage is empty. Very faintly a strain of "I call her the Belle of Japan" is heard. Madame Butterfly is singing that she may not weep. A pause. Some one knocks on the door. Lieutenant Pinkerton's voice calls outside the shoji.)

LIEUTENANT PINKERTON: Madame Butterfly? Madame Butterfly? *(Coming into the room, he looks about.)* Butterfly?

SHARPLESS: *(Following him).* They've seen the ship—these decorations were not here when I called.

MADAME BUTTERFLY: *(Singing to hush the baby).*
> "Rog'—a—bye, bebby,
>   Off in Japan,"

(Lieutenant Pinkerton listens to the song coming from above.)
> "You jus' a picture,
> Off of a fan."

LIEUTENANT PINKERTON: She is watching the ship. *(Noticing the screened-off part of the room.)* My room . . . just as it used to look . . . my chair. *(Picking up the doll which the child has dropped.)* Poor kid! Poor little devil! . . . Sharpless, I thought when I left this house, the few tears, sobs, little polite regrets, would be over as I crossed the threshold. I started to come back for a minute, but I said to myself: "Don't do it; by this time she's ringing your gold pieces to make sure they're good." You know that class of Japanese girl and—

SHARPLESS: *(Seeing Nakodo who is at the shoji).* Look here: I have something to settle with you! *(Nakodo comes in cautiously.)* Why did you seek out my friend's wife at the pier?

LIEUTENANT PINKERTON: Why did you tell her that story—the child and all? Answer me?

NAKODO: *(To Sharpless).* Your Excellency, I but thought if trouble came between the two women, he would surely break with Cho-Cho-San, and then she would be glad to marry the rich Yamadori and I get big fee. *(Exit.)*

SHARPLESS: You'll never get it. *(To Pinkerton.)* She'll starve first.

LIEUTENANT PINKERTON: Sharpless, thank God, that's one thing I can do—money. *(He takes out an envelope containing some money.)*

SHARPLESS: What did your wife say, Pinkerton?

LIEUTENANT PINKERTON: Well, it was rather rough on her, only married four months. Sharpless, my Kate's an angel,—she offered to take the child . . . made me promise I'd speak of it to Butterfly.

MADAME BUTTERFLY: *(Calling from above).* Suzuki?

SHARPLESS: She's coming.
(Pinkerton instinctively draws behind the screen.)

MADAME BUTTERFLY: *(Coming down the stairs with the sleeping baby on her back, calling).* Suzuki? Come for bebby. *(Kissing the child.)* Nize liddle eye, pick out of blue sky, all shut up.

LIEUTENANT PINKERTON: *(Aside to Sharpless, his eyes fixed on the mother and child).* I can't face it! I'm going. Give her the money.

SUZUKI: *(Entering, and seeing Pinkerton as he passes out of the door).* Ah!
(Sharpless gives her a warning gesture.)

MADAME BUTTERFLY: *(Seeing Suzuki's astonished face).* Wha'—? *(She puts the baby in Suzuki's arms. Suzuki goes out quickly. Madame Butterfly sees the Consul.)* You! Oh! *(Joyously.)* You seen him?

SHARPLESS: Yes.

MADAME BUTTERFLY: An' you tole him?

SHARPLESS: Well . . .

MADAME BUTTERFLY: But you tole him . . . of bebby?

SHARPLESS: Yes.

MADAME BUTTERFLY: *(Wiping her dry lips).* Yaes . . . tha's right. Tha's what I—as' you do . . . an'—an' what he *say?*

SHARPLESS: Well . . . *(Taking out the envelope, and giving her the money which she takes without looking at it.)* He said—er—he was crazy to see you and—*(aside)* What the devil can I say! *(To* *her.)* You know he can't leave the ship just yet. *(Pointing to the package in her hand.)* That is in remembrance of the past. He wishes you to be always happy, to have the best of luck; he hopes to see you soon—and—*(The lies die out on his lips.)*

MADAME BUTTERFLY: *(Bending and kissing his hand).* All—all the gods in the heavens bless you!
(Overcome, she staggers. Sharpless catches her, puts her into the chair—she leans against him—her face upraised, her eyes closed.)

(Kate, entering hurriedly.)

KATE: Has Lieutenant Pinkerton gone? Has my husband been here?
(Madame Butterfly hears and opens her eyes.)

SHARPLESS: For God's sake— *(He looks at Madame Butterfly whose eyes are fixed on his with a look of despair.)* Come, we can over-take him.

KATE: *(In a lower voice).* Did he speak to her of the—

SHARPLESS: No.

KATE: Then I will ask. *(For the first time seeing Madame Butterfly.)* Is this— *(Sharpless nods and goes. There is a short pause, while the two women look at each other; then Madame Butterfly, still seated, slowly bows her head.)* Why, you poor little thing . . . who in the world could blame you or . . . call you responsible . . . you pretty little plaything.
(Takes Madame Butterfly in her arms.)

MADAME BUTTERFLY: *(Softly).* No—playthin' . . . I am Mrs. Lef-ten-ant B. F.—No—no—now I am, only—Cho-Cho-San, but no playthin'. . . . *(She rises, then impassively.)* How long you been marry?

KATE: Four months. . . .

MADAME BUTTERFLY: *(Counting on her fingers).* Oh . . . four.

KATE: Won't you let me do something for the child? Where is he? *(Madame Butterfly gestures toward the next room. Kate, seeing the child.)* Ah! The dear little thing! May I—

MADAME BUTTERFLY: No! Can look . . . no can touch. . . .

KATE: Let us think first of the child. For his own good . . . let me take him home to my country. . . . I will do all I would do for my own.

MADAME BUTTERFLY: *(Showing no emotion).* He not know then—me—his mother?

KATE: It is hard, very hard, I know; but would it not be better?

MADAME BUTTERFLY: *(Taking the money-box from her sleeve, and giving the coins to Kate.)* Tha's his . . . two dollar. All tha's lef' of his moaneys. . . . I shall need no more. . . . *(She hands Kate the envelope which Sharpless has just given.)* I lig if you also say I sawry—no—no—no—glad—*glad!* I wish him that same happiness lig he wish for me . . . an' tell him . . . I shall be happy . . . mebby. Thang him . . . Mister B. F. Pik-ker-ton for also that kindness he have been unto me . . . an' permit me to thang *you,* augustness, for that same. . . . You—you mos' bes' lucky girl in these whole worl'. . . . Goon-night—
(She stands stolidly with her eyes closed.)

KATE: *(Wiping her eyes).* But the child?

MADAME BUTTERFLY: Come back fifteen minute. . . . *(With closed eyes, she bows politely.)* Sayonara. *(Kate reluctantly goes.)* God he'p me, but no sun kin shine. *(Suzuki, who has listened, sinks at Madame Butterfly's feet.)* Don' cry, Suzuki, liddle maiden . . . accoun' I dizappoint, a liddle dizappoint'—don' cry. . . . *(Running her hand over Suzuki's head—as she kneels.)* Tha's short while ago you as' me res'—sleep. . . . *(Wearily.)* Well— go way an' I will res' now. . . . I *wish* res'—sleep . . . long sleep . . . an' when you see me again, I pray you look whether I be not beautiful again . . . as a bride.

SUZUKI: *(Understandingly, sobbing).* No—no—no.

MADAME BUTTERFLY: So that I suffer no more—goon bye, liddle maiden. *(Suzuki does not go. Madame Butterfly claps her hands, and sobbing, Suzuki leaves the room. Madame Butterfly bolts the shoji and the door, lights fresh incense before the shrine, takes down her father's sword and reads the inscription:)* "To die with honor . . . when one can no longer live with honor." . . . *(She draws her finger across the blade, to test the sharpness of the sword, then picks up the hand glass, puts on more rouge, rearranges the poppies in her hair, bows to the shrine, and is about to press the blade of the sword against her neck, when the door is opened and the child is pushed into the room by Suzuki, who keeps out of sight. Madame Butterfly drops the sword and takes the baby in her arms. A knocking is heard but she pays no heed. She sets the child on a mat, puts the American flag in its hand, and, picking up the sword, goes behind the screen that the child may not see what she is about to do. A short pause—the sword is heard to drop. Madame Butterfly reappears, her face deathly—a scarf about her neck to conceal the wound. Suzuki opens the door, sees the face of her mistress—backs out of the room in horror. Madame Butterfly drops to her knees as she reaches the child, and clasps it to her. A hand is thrust through the shoji and the bolt is drawn.)*
(Kate enters quickly, urging the reluctant Pinkerton to follow her.)

LIEUTENANT PINKERTON: *(Discerning what she has done).* Oh! Cho-Cho-San!
(He draws her to him with the baby pressed to her heart. She waves the child's hand which holds the flag—saying faintly:)

MADAME BUTTERFLY: Too bad those robins didn' nes' again. *(She dies.)*

The Music

Puccini was already a successful composer when he wrote *Butterfly*. He had received experience with previous dramatic works, so he knew what would be satisfactory musical drama and had an instinctive sense as to what appeals to an audience. From his letters we know the libretto was examined minutely, and small details added much to the effect for which he was striving. His writers often vowed that they would not work with him again because he would insist on changes and new versions to take care of details that he believed important. Two additional letters illustrate these points:

To Giulio Ricordi (Puccini's publisher)

Torre del Lago
May 3, 1902

My dear Signor Giulio,

About Butterfly you are right a thousand times; the flower scene must be more flowery. However, the duet could begin in stanzas with Suzuki outside and then continue in the way which you suggest, to the greater interest, both scenic and musical, of the piece.

It is a good idea to garland the child with flowers!

I shall write to Giacosa to keep him awake.

I am working (and glad of it) at Act I, and am getting on well.

I have composed the passage for the entry of Butterfly, and am pleased with it.[5]

To Giulio Ricordi

Torre del Lago

My dear Signor Giulio,

I have had a visit today from Mme Ohyama, wife of the Japanese Ambassador. She told me a great many interesting things and sang some native songs to me. She has promised to send me some native Japanese music. I sketched the story of the libretto for her, and she liked it, especially as just such a story as Butterfly's is known to her as having happened in real life.

She does not approve of the name Yamadori, on the ground that it is feminine and otherwise not appropriate; because in Japan they are accustomed in their plays to use names which suggest, or are suitable to, the various types and characters. The uncle's name of Yaxonpide is wrong too. Similarly the names Sarundapiko, Isaghi, Sganami, etc., are all wrong. Mme Ohyama is at Wiareggio, where I shall go to see her and take notes of what she sings to me.

She is very intelligent and, although plain, is attractive.[6]

Study Procedures

1. Because of the length of *Butterfly* our study will concentrate upon the final act. Hopefully, you will wish to hear other portions of the opera after this introduction. Notice the following items, to help you understand its effect:
   a. The manner in which the drama builds from beginning to end.
   b. How effectively Puccini makes use of the characters even though some of them are on stage comparatively little.
   c. The focus of the opera upon a woman from a woman's point of view; do you believe that Puccini overemphasized his sympathy for women?
   d. The feeling of balance in the work even though the two women are on stage for most of the performance.
   e. The length of the second act, with only one major emotion sustained: the anticipation of Butterfly and our empathy with her.

---

5 *Letters of Giacomo Puccini, op. cit.,* page 145.
6 *Ibid.,* page 146.

    f. Although the orchestra plays an oriental theme occasionally, the effect throughout is one of Italian Romantic expression.

    g. The singing lines, not only in the arias but also in the recitatives, which sing with more melody than we have witnessed before.

    h. How cleverly Puccini has included portions of "The Star Spangled Banner" whenever the two Americans sing of their country or their way of life.

    i. The music shifts from light and gay, to meditative, to emotional and tense, with Puccini recognizing that even a tragedy cannot provide tragic music continually. The balance gives maximum effect.

    j. In the original story Butterfly is convinced to return to the life of a dancing girl. Considering your ideas of Japanese youth and the dramatic effect, which ending seems more realistic?

2. Read the play, then listen to Act III of the opera. You may wish to follow the score.
3. Listen to other portions of the opera. A libretto will assist you.

Act III, Music

In the play the period of silence denoting the night watch was considered an artistic touch. Puccini had written the original opera in two acts with an interlude, also to signify the passing of night. In his revised version this music serves as an introduction to Act III; at the same time he describes the passing night with the emotions of the waiting hours, while constantly hinting of the coming tragedy. The music from the love duet of the first act reminds us vividly of Butterfly's feelings. When the curtain parts we hear the sailors working on the docks at the break of morning. This happy Oriental melody reminds us of the world beyond the tensions of one household.

After morning greetings, Butterfly sings a simple but beautiful lullaby to her son. Notice the final upward note indicative of the buoyant feelings of Butterfly in her ecstacy.

Pinkerton's love theme is heard as he enters. The dialogue moves easily until Kate is seen. At this point the intensity heightens toward the trio in which each sings of his concerns: Sharpless, trying to persuade and soothe; Suzuki, lamenting her mistress's position; Pinkerton, suddenly realizing the impact of his inconsiderateness.

Butterfly enters, and upon finding Kate the vocal line and the orchestra depict completely her bewilderment and then her grief.

Two short statements by Butterfly are exquisite: in the first, she wishes Kate well; in the second, she agrees to give up her son.

The final aria by Butterfly weeps in the orchestra as well as in the voice.

The orchestra ends the opera in almost a unison phrase, Oriental in sound, which is the same melody heard in Act II when Butterfly relates her dream.[7]

---

[7] Copyright © 1905 by G. Ricordi & Company, copyright renewed. Used with permission.

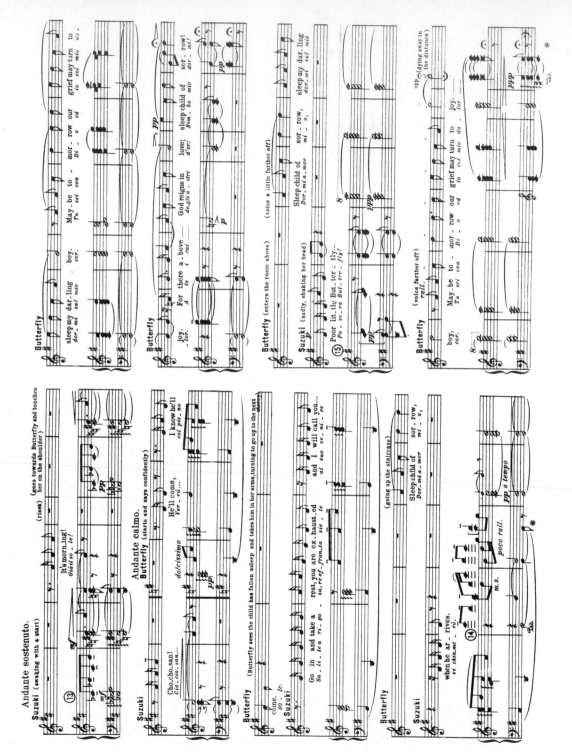

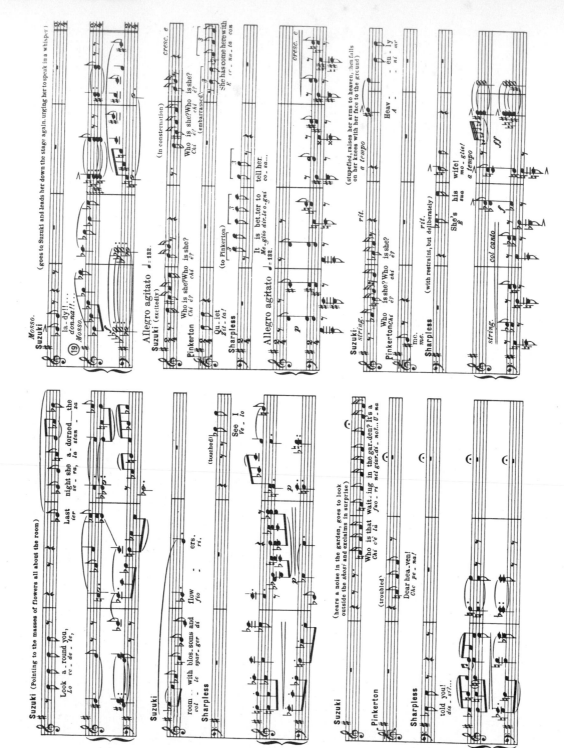

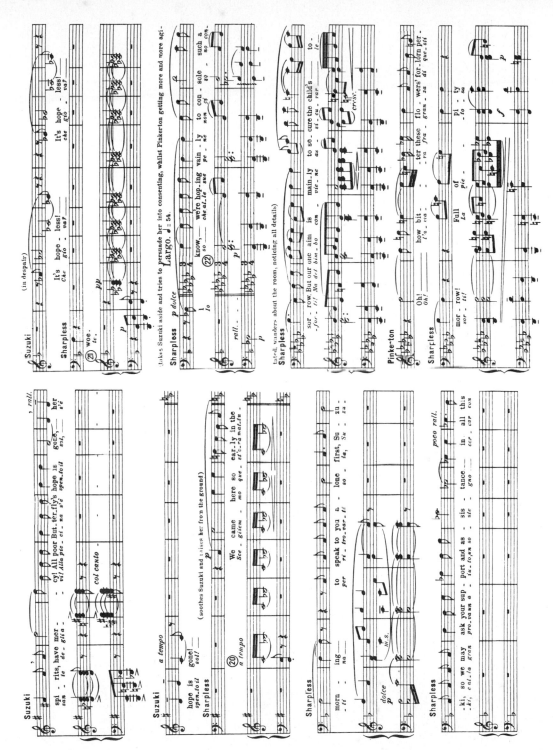

Suzuki
Pinkerton
Sharpless
All of her hopes and dreams shat-tered! All of her
A - ni-me san-te de - già a - vi!... Al pic
go - ing, for ev - er count-ing the stea-dy flow
sa li e no - ve ra - ti n'hai gior-ni e l'o
zu - ki and bring her in here, Su - zu - ki, go bring her in -
par la con quel - la pi - a, suv - vi - a, con-du - ci-la
(Sharpless pushes her into the garden to join Mrs Pinkerton)
rit.
sun-shine, all joy is gone!
-ci - na s'è spen-to il sol!
(overcome by emotion and unable to restrain his tears, approaches Sharpless and says to him resolutely)
ing of days and hours!
re, i gior-ni e l'o - re!
I can not bear to
Non pos-so ri-ma
-side, go bring her in - side. Go and talk to her!
qui, con-du - ci-la qui. Vien, Su - zu - ki, vien!
p celando
(going away)
How to tell her!
Oh! me tri-sta!
stay. Sharpless, I cannot re-main here. Re-member how I
-ner: Sharpless, v'a-spet-to per vi - a... Non ve l'a - ve - ro
Allegro agitato.
Pinkerton (giving Sharpless some money)
See to her needs, pro-vide some re-sourc - es... How cru - el
Da - te - le vo - i qual-che soc - cor - so... mi strug - ge
warned you?
det - to.
23
Allegro agitato:
my re-morse is, how cru - el my re-morse is.
dal ri - mor - so, mi strug - ge dal ri - mor - so.
rall.
Remem - ber what I told you? Then I fore-saw it clear-ly: "Re -
l'el dis - si? vi ri - cor - da? quan - do la man vi die - de: "ba -
24
- mem - ber, she loves sincere - ly!", My pro - phe - cy came true! Deaf to friend-ly
- da - te! El - la ci cre - de," e fui pro - fe - ta al - lor! Sor - da ai con -

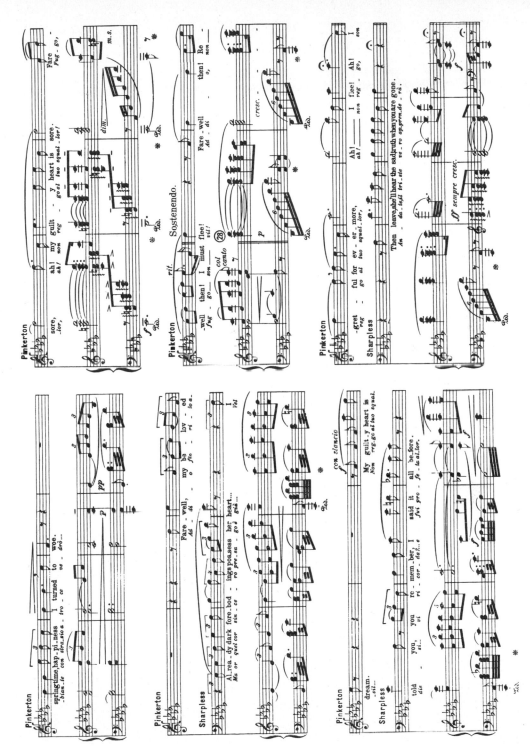

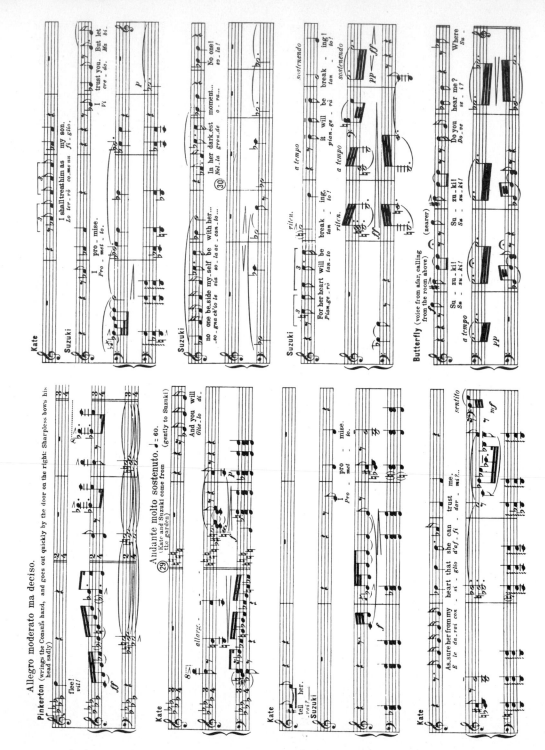

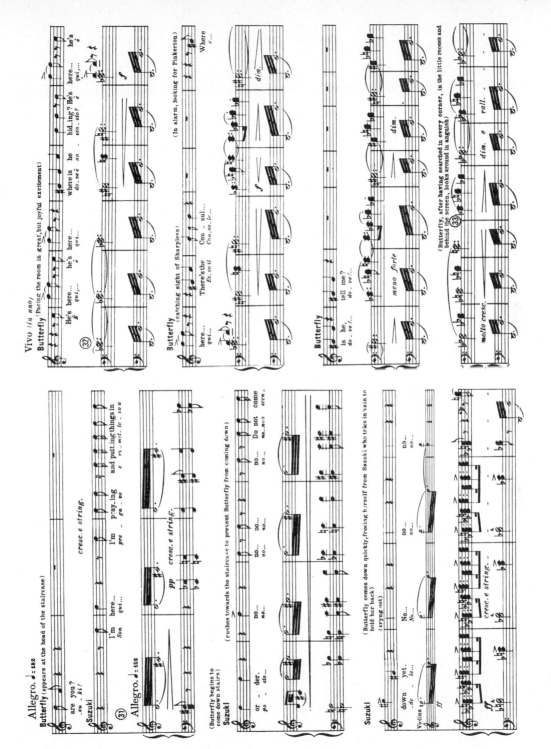

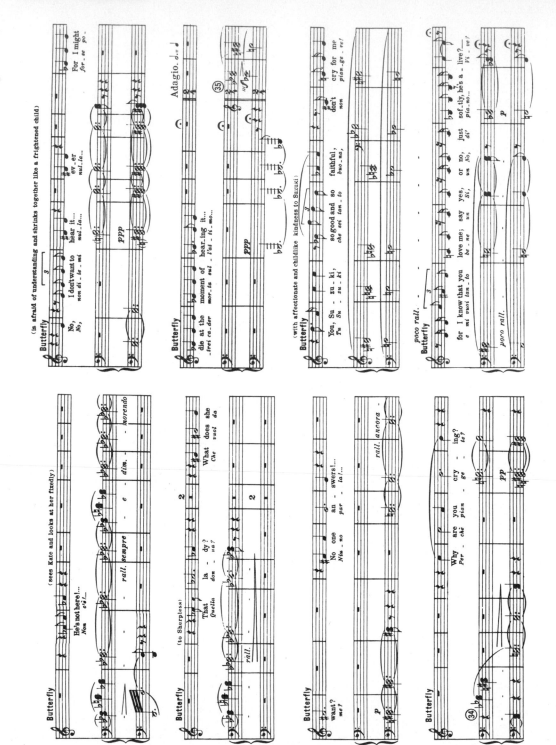

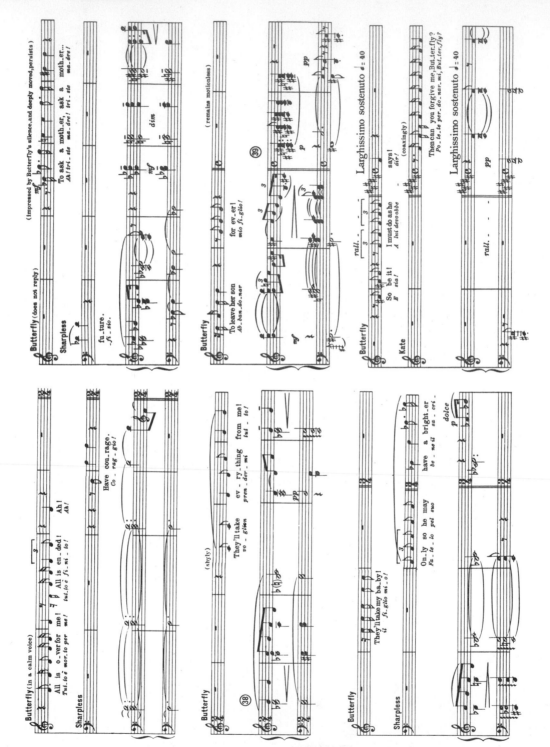

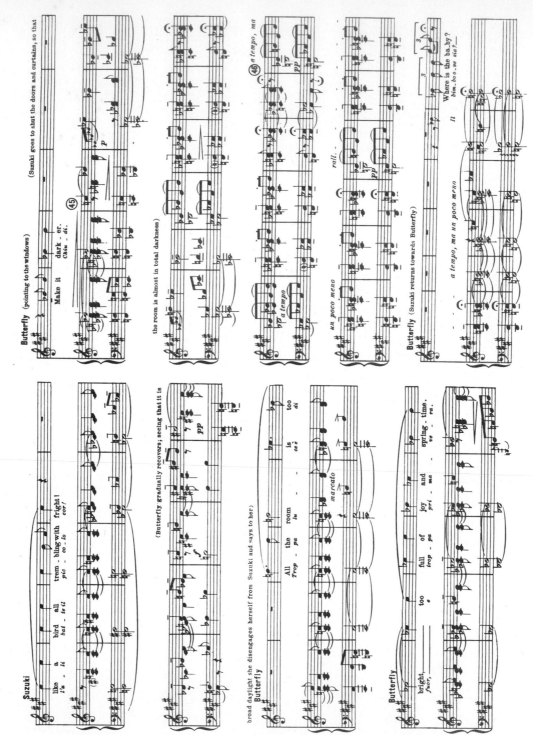

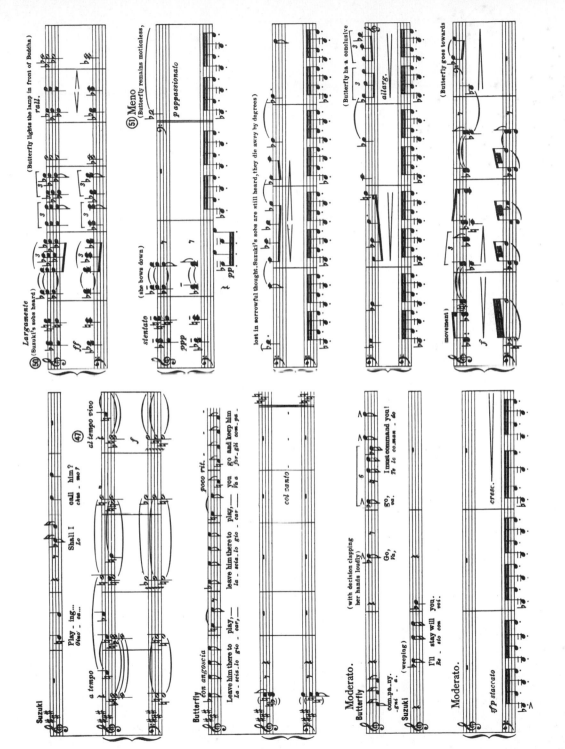

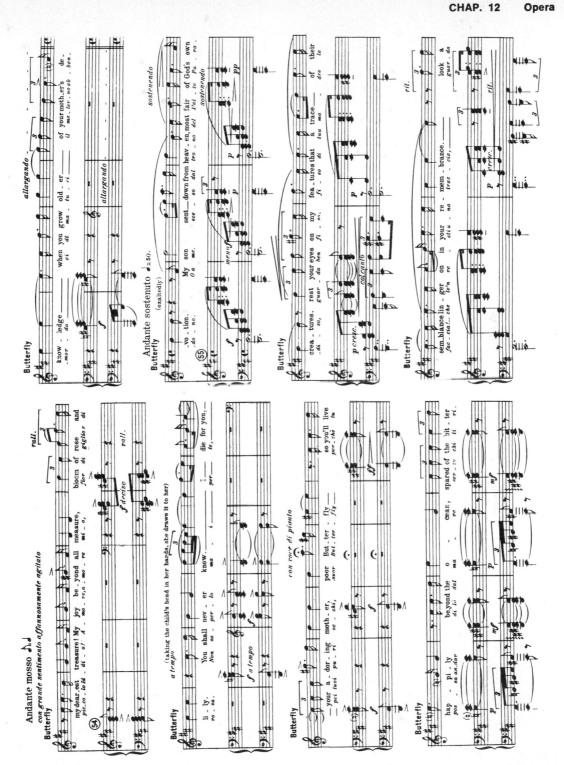

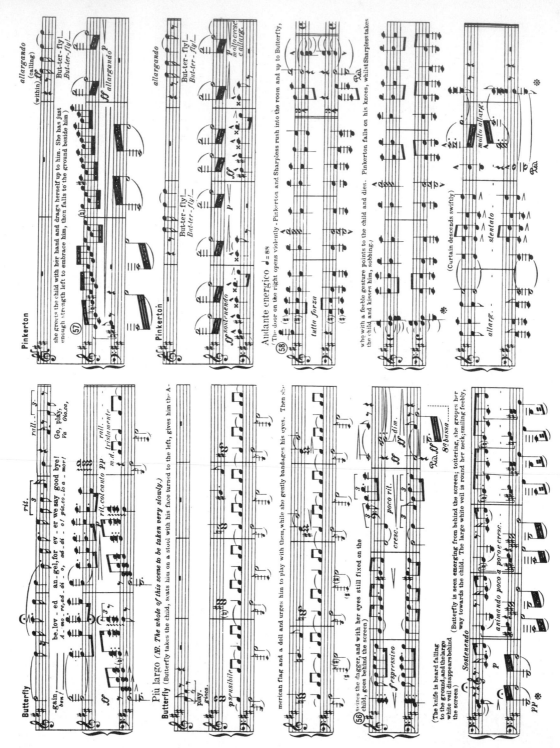

The Marriage of Figaro (Mozart)

Rarely does any one man have the high esteem, the personal vicissitudes, the political favor, the imprisonment, the wealth, the poverty, the political daring, and the artistic temperament of Caron de Beaumarchais.   His life was so inconsistent, so filled with opposing considerations, that a novel which related it accurately would be unbelieved.   Although loyal to the French monarch, he favored freedom for all men and in order to demonstrate his strong feelings in this direction personally paid for arms for 25,000 men in the Revolutionary Army of the United States.   Before Lafayette had assisted the colonies, before other European countries had come to our aid, before Franklin had visited the French court, Beaumarchais spoke to the French king in our behalf and had given of his own money for weapons and ammunition that enabled Americans to win the decisive battle of Saratoga.

His political and personal intrigues, interesting or discouraging as they were, only seemed to assist him in understanding his time, the feelings of the people, and in portraying them in his plays, two of which enjoy enduring fame

Pierre Augustin Caron de Beaumarchais, author of The Barber of Seville *(1775) and* The Marriage of Figaro *(1784); portrait by Nattier (1732–1799) (Courtesy of French Cultural Services, New York).*

as the libretti of famous operas. With memorable music they have continued to please audiences all over the world by reflecting the age and the society during which and for which they were written. Part of their success came from the personal life of Beaumarchais himself, who lived his problems in the public eye; another part was created by King Louis XVI of France, who, after reading *Figaro,* stated that the play should never be given in public because of its forwardness and its affrontery in describing the commoner and in its equal disrespect for royalty. Some have called this comedy the beginning of the French Revolution, and yet if you read the play you wonder how such an innocent domestic comedy could earn such a unique and tremendous reputation.

Combining sexual implications, seduction, and a political message, Beaumarchais was sure to capture the interest of the public. Even now the play reads well and could sustain its place in the theater. The lines are cleverly made, and the slapstick comedy of the fourth act, where kisses and blows are intended for one person but find rest on another, is equal to anything found in present-day movies or TV. Just as today, a show banned in one city becomes a hit in another, so with *Figaro:* being banned for almost five years, when finally permitted it created a social stir. The following quote (April 27, 1784) gives us some idea of the scene:

> All Paris from the earliest morning thronged the doorways of the Theater Francais, ladies of the highest rank dining in the dressing-rooms of the actresses in order to be sure of their places. The guards were overwhelmed, the doors broken in, the railings gave way before the pressure of the crowds, and when the curtain rose upon the scene, the finest collection of talent the Theater Francais ever possessed was there with but one thought to bring out the best of the comedy, flashing with wit, carrying one away in its movement and audacity which, if it shocked some of the boxes, enflamed and electrified the pit.[8]

Mozart and *Figaro*

The success of the play immediately attracted Mozart and he asked Da Ponte for a libretto. This was soon forthcoming, and by comparing the play and the opera one can see that the dialogue could be adapted quickly into a fitting instrument for the aria and chorus. Mozart's opera had a number of modestly successful performances beginning May 1, 1786, but has become even more famous down through the years. Because of the restrictions placed upon such a politically oriented script, Da Ponte, with Mozart's agreement, eliminated some of the strong speeches which denounced royalty. Even so, the opera still makes royalty the inferiors of the servants, when both Suzanne and Figaro not only advise the mistress and master as to what actions to follow, but at the same time wrap

---

8 *The Barber of Seville* and *The Marriage of Figaro,* Beaumarchais, translated with Introduction by John Wood. Penguin Books, Baltimore, 1964, page 23.

them about their fingers in their cleverness. Taking a popular play, and a strong one at that, and turning it into an opera could result in an overshadowing of the music. Not so with a master such as Mozart; it is because of his strong music that the play is so well-known. He combined the strength of emotion of his German background with the musical style of the Italian comic opera, to produce a masterpiece.

Study Procedures

1. Read the play in its original form; it is available in paperback as footnoted above.
2. Listen at least to the first act and consider the musical qualities of the work.
   a. The arias are singable in a kind of way that could easily appeal to numerous persons. If you hear them two or three times in succession you will most likely find yourself whistling or humming them. Mozart could produce a most pleasant tune without in any way bordering on the trite.
   b. The recitatives are truly like spoken dialogue in their speed. This is obviously different from the recitatives we heard in *Butterfly* or in the oratorios.
   c. The recitatives are accompanied by the harpsichord, which was the style of the time, and yet the orchestra enters for the arias so easily and quickly that one rarely misses the orchestral color elsewhere.
   d. The lightness of the music causes it to sparkle along with the wit of the text. Mozart is known for his brightness of musical contours and orchestration, and this opera is a beautiful example of these qualities.
   e. When Mozart requires a duet the interchange of line is so facile and seems so natural that we are not aware that a special kind of operatic form is taking place. For example, the first duet of Figaro and Suzanne, each with his mind on his own problem, seems so realistic a situation that we are hardly aware of an operatic duet being sung.
   f. The choruses are bright and light, so that one believes in their presence rather than in a conspired entrance to alter the stage composition.

Unfortunately, the opera is not recorded in English, although it sings well in English translation and enables one to appreciate the unity of words and music so much more. Good translations and original texts are usually supplied with all record albums. Most university presentations of *Figaro* are in English, and these productions enable audiences to join in the fun, and at the same time to obtain a fascinating picture of eighteenth century France and prerevolutionary manners and sentiments.

Wozzeck (Berg)

In 1824, in the city of Leipzig, Johann Christopher Woyzeck was hanged for murdering his mistress, Frau Woost. This was the first hanging in that city within thirty years, creating considerable concern because the people were not completely sure that Woyzeck had been responsible for his actions. He had come to trial and because there was some reason to believe that he was not mentally secure, an investigation was ordered by the court. A Dr. Clarus was asked to examine the guilty party and ascertain if he had been rational at the time of the killing. After a studied investigation the doctor reported that Woyzeck was sane and should be executed. As the day of execution approached some doubt as to the sanity of the convicted man still persisted, and so the court asked Dr. Clarus to proceed with a further study. Again the doctor returned the same verdict, and Woyzeck was hanged. Even after his death large numbers of people discussed the case with uncertainty. This was not because Woyzeck had many friends, for he was a poor, unskilled person with little respect in his community. For years he had been involved with Frau Woost, and admitted openly to have loved her. In fact, she was the only person who had expressed interest in him and the only person with whom he had been friendly. To complicate the case, Frau Woost was known to have an interest in soldiers and to Woyzeck's consternation often became involved with younger men. This disturbed Woyzeck so greatly that he confessed to hearing voices and that a force outside himself insisted that he "stab, stab." After his death the case was re-opened, bringing considerable restudy, whereupon Woyzeck was found to be insane and not responsible for his actions.

This famous case was discussed widely in lay and professional journals of the time. A scientific researcher by the name of Georg Büchner wrote this series of events into a play which he left unfinished at his death at the age of 23, but which has been considered far in advance of its time and has influenced many later playwrights. It is this same play which is the basis for the opera *Wozzeck* by Alban Berg (1925).

Büchner had been withdrawn and sarcastic as a young child who thought that most of school was dull. His father, a physician, had encouraged him to be a scientific researcher, for both of them could see the great future ahead for research in the sciences. As a college student he had become a revolutionary, but after one brief brush with the police he realized that the poor did not wish to be freed from their yoke, and so he turned to individual study and writing. At the age of twenty he was awarded an honorary doctorate and a position at the University of Zurich because of his discoveries concerning the nervous system of fishes. During the three years of his work at the University he taught by day and wrote plays, poems, and stories at night. One of these plays was *Woyzeck*.

In this play Büchner's philosophy was expressed most openly. The poor are the victims of the socially elite, but all men are victims of nature and society. No man has any determination; that which appears to be self-determination is a lie, and all of history is fatalistic. He wrote in a letter, "The individual is only scum on the wave, greatness a pure accident; to master it is impossible, but to recognize it is the highest [insight]."

In his play he took many of the incidents of real life and used them to express his ideas. His passive hero becomes the victim of a sequence of events within his own life and the persons about him, none of whom mean him direct harm, but all of whom eventually lead to his destruction.

The play is unusual in several respects. The characters do not speak to each other in dialogue so much as in a series of monologues, each of which tells us something about the general scene in which one finds himself, something about his character, and most importantly, about his pondering of life and its complexities. In order to accomplish this, Büchner has given the play twenty-four or twenty-five scenes (depending upon the editor and the version read), each of which are surprisingly brief, but each sentence reveals some pertinent psychological point concerning the character and the play. Since this has all been discussed at great length by critics of literature, you might find it interesting to read some of the commentary.

Berg and *Wozzeck*

Unquestionably, Berg wished to retain the overall mood and effect of the play, for he adopted its structure, placing his opera into fifteen scenes, omitting nine. Using an original and inaccurate edition, he mistakenly misspelled the hero's name; consequently, the hero and the opera are spelled differently—Wozzeck— while the other names remain. Berg did not become involved in the aria-recitative-chorus idea that has organized almost every opera. Instead, he placed his emphasis in two ways: the sound of the music should follow the psychological implications of the acts of Wozzeck; then, only those forms should be used which best convey the meaning of the work. Consequently, he used instrumental as well as new forms. Without going into detail in this matter, suffice it to say this has led to a complexity in the musical accompaniment and vocal line that supercedes that of almost any other opera.

The opera may be listened to in more than one way. The person may listen for the mood and the expressive aspects of the music and how they fit with the intent of the text. Others may listen for the forms and glean a new understanding into the unification of the scenes through these forms. All should understand that Berg sought to portray in the music a meaning of the situation found only by an understanding of the subconscious; that the music does not describe the futility and the emotion evidenced by the text as much as it helps the listener to see into the inner self of the characters. Just as psychoanalysis is the science of the unconscious, Berg's score could be termed the music of the unconscious. Although interested in the psychoanalytic, Berg was in no way attempting to describe that medical process musically.

Although time has increased the attention and respect for the work, the critics were in different camps after the first performance, and even today there are those who would disown this work as an opera. Two reports of the first performance emphasize this conflict:

1. Leaving the State Opera House *Unter den Linden* last evening, I had the feeling that I was not leaving a public institute of art but a public madhouse. On the stage, in the orchestra, in the stalls: a lot of madmen. . . Wozzeck by Alban Berg was the battle-cry—the work of a chinaman from Vienna. For these massed attacks and convulsions of instruments had nothing to do with European music and its development. . . . The applause from the stalls is nothing other than a cracking lie. But what attitude does the master criminal of this work strike? There are only two possibilities: either he recognizes laws, forms, skill and submission to higher inspiration in music, or he denies everything that has existed, that has developed and been created in hallowed hours, he scoffs at forms and laws, he despises all the great masters, he scribbles down whatever leaks out of his pen, he is completely unscrupulous, he builds confidently on the stupidity and mercifulness of his fellow men, and for the rest relies on God in Heaven and the Universal Edition. In the whole vocal score of Wozzeck I cannot find a single instance that would indicate honest and genuine inspiration. . .In Berg's music there is not the slightest trace of melody. There are only scraps and shreds, sobs and belches. Harmonically, the work cannot be discussed, for every single thing sounds wrong. . . . The instrumentation is varied. He runs through all the possibilities between the last gasp of violin harmonics and the bass tuba's meanest grunt. A whole zoological garden is opened up . . .I consider Alban Berg a musical impostor, and a treacherously dangerous composer. Yes, one seriously has to consider the question, whether and to what extent activity in music can be criminal. This is a matter of a capital crime in the field of music.

2. It is difficult to do justice to the strange perfection and uniqueness of this work within the limits of a review. There can never before have been chosen for an opera a libretto whose literary value so completely corresponds to the possibilities of musical interpretation as does that of this magnificent fragment by Georg Büchner. Berg has succeeded in writing a music for this libretto that not only does not diminish the value of the literary work but actually enhances it to an unheard of degree. It is a music that brings latent matters to the surface and uncovers the most secret psychological factors without waiving the most important things, namely the dramatic conception and the musical unity. The fact that Berg has done this is evidence of genius, and places him right next to the most important music-dramatists of our time. . . . Not only was the evening the greatest sensation of the season, it was a significant event in the history of music-drama in general.[9]

The Music

For our immediate study, Act III gives an excellent introduction to the style of the music, and at the same time permits one to witness the climax of the plot and the musical method used to assist the mood. As in the first two acts, five scenes are used, and as Berg has arranged them the division of the acts does not detract from the movement and continuity.

---

[9] *Alban Berg*, Willi Reich; trans. by Cornelius Cardew. Harcourt, Brace and World, Inc., New York, 1963, pages 61–62.

Scene 1: The orchestra begins quietly, but almost immediately we hear Marie reading from the Bible in a half-singing, half-reading sound that is typical of much of the opera. The verses are interrupted by her tormented laments and prayers, the high range indicating the extent of her torment. The semisinging expresses a different and more intense kind of emotion which the orchestra echoes not in pitch but in manner.

Scene 2: Tinkling sounds of the celesta indicate a change of mood and scene. The accompaniment gives a clue to the strangeness felt by both, while the more sentimental sounds reminisce of an earlier time. The gradual crescendo of the timpani forbodes the oncoming death struggle, after which the unison note in the orchestra followed by the timpani announces the completion of the deed and its powerful but sudden realization. Unusual quiet ensues.

Scene 3: The piano changes the mood and implies a kind of tavern playing often heard but without tune or obvious form. This soon changes to tormented music as Margret and Wozzeck talk. When she finds blood on his arm, the voices of others in the tavern are heard in the background stabbing at Wozzeck as if with pointing fingers.

Scene 4: The snare drum roll changes the scene to the pond. Again we hear Wozzeck in an emotional kind of song-speech, while the orchestra carries the musical burden with its sounds of terror and mental anguish. His call of remorse leads to an indefinitely pitched ascending line in the orchestra as Wozzeck sinks into the water. The Captain and Doctor speak rather than sing, while the orchestra plays a type of dream march for their walk.

Interlude: The timpani introduces an orchestral interlude which contains the most powerful musical lines of the entire opera. The themes are given enough time to portray the haunting interplay of two lives and the mounting tension between them. The final dissonance is descriptive of the former scene with its descent into a quiet ending.

Scene 5: The harp introduces the children's play song. This scene, although not always included in the play, was found among Büchner's notes and was used by Berg to bring a stronger and more appealing emotional ending to the opera, and yet at the same time offer a gesture of hope. Inconclusive as we know life to be, from the point of view of the children the end has not been reached.

Study Procedures

1. Read the play, which is available in a paperback edition.
2. Compare the play with the libretto of the opera, which is available on records.
3. Which of the scenes of the play do you believe might have been added to assist the opera, and why?
4. Do you believe that the final scene of the opera is necessary, and do you find it effective?

Boris Godounov (Mussorgsky)

Boris Godounov was crowned Czar (Caesar) of Russia in 1598, even though not a member of the royal family; in fact, he claimed a peasant's birth.

Boris had been a member of the court and a favorite of Ivan IV, usually called The Terrible, often taking over the responsibility for affairs of state. When Ivan died in 1584 his weakminded twenty-seven-year-old son, Feodor, ascended the throne and retained Boris, his brother-in-law, as regent. Although an obstetrician was brought from England to help provide an heir, Feodor died in 1598 leaving no family successor. The lower middle class, concerned that they had no ruler, and the boyars, the aristocracy, fearful of an uprising or an invasion, pleaded with Boris to accept the throne. Although he feigned some disinterest, his vanity welcomed their solicitations. He was acclaimed Czar by peasant and aristocracy alike in a magnificent ceremony.

As regent he had been most successful in recolonizing Siberia and regaining lands from Sweden. However, upon gaining the throne serious troubles almost immediately began. Because of successive years of crop failure, poverty swept through the land followed by epidemics (1601–1603). Law and order disappeared, the peasants turned against Boris, and a rumor persisted that the youngest son of Ivan IV, Dimitry, had been found on the Polish border and desired to reclaim the throne.

Dimitry had been the son of Ivan's seventh wife, and since the church permitted only three wives, this son could not legally ascend the throne except by popular acclamation. Boris had been unsure of this ruling as well as the sentiments of the people, and sensing the possibility that Dimitry could claim the throne, Boris, while regent, had had the nine-year-old child put to death (1591).

The young man who claimed to be Dimitry during the reign of Boris was an impostor, but the peasants believed him to be Ivan's son. Faced with the fear that the true Dimitry had been miraculously spared and could claim the throne, or accepting the guilt for the death of the child, gradually drove Boris to deep mental anguish and to the edge of a breakdown. The "False Dimitry" did take over the throne upon Boris's death (poisoning?) in 1605, but reigned less than a year. When the peasants discovered the impostor, the "False Dimitry" was killed, his body dragged through the streets, and Shuisky, a prominent minister in the court of Boris, became Czar.

This series of historical events has proved fascinating not only to historians but likewise to writers, poets, and musicians, because it offers opportunity for interpretation in a number of ways. Mussorgsky, in his opera *Boris Godounov*, has capitalized upon the drama of the events, and yet has been able to show the deterioration of the mind of a man weighed down with guilt, suspicion, and fear. In some ways, then, this opera also is a study in the psychology of the human personality, although the music is more Romantic in nature and contents itself mainly with a descriptive role.

Two scenes are sufficient to capture the brilliance of the writing and the impact of the psychological weight built into the opera.   Other scenes will also afford worthwhile listening for those interested.

   Prologue, Part II: the Coronation of Boris. The scene is the courtyard of the Kremlin.   The audience faces the apartments of the Czar, while on the sides are the cathedrals.   Peasants and boyars fill the stage awaiting the ceremony. After attending services in both churches, the Czar comes into the courtyard for the coronation.   It is a time of jubilation, worship, and thanksgiving.   We hear the prayers of Boris, the acclamations of the people, and the bells of the churches announcing the historic event.   This is a magnificent scene for an opera and Mussorgsky has orchestrated it excitingly.

   The text is as follows:[10]

Scene II

(The Square in the Moscow Kremlin. In the distance, directly in front of the spectators, the Red Staircase leading to the Czar's chambers. To the right, in the foreground, the kneeling populace fills the space between the Cathedrals of the Archangel and the Assumption. The porches of both Cathedrals are visible.)

PRINCE SHÚISKI
(From the porch of the Assumption Cathedral)
Long live Czar Boris Feodorovich!

THE CHORUS
Long live the Czar, our little father!

PRINCE SHÚISKI
Glory to you!

THE CHORUS
Even as glory to the radiant sun in the sky, so glory to Czar Boris in Russia!

(An imperial procession from the Cathedral. Police officers keep the people in line on both sides of the procession)
Long live the Czar! Rejoice and make merry, all ye faithful of the Russian church, and glory to the great Czar Boris.

BOYARS   *(From the porch)*
All hail to Czar Boris Feodorovich!

THE CHORUS
All hail!

(Boris now appears and crosses the stage)
Glory to Czar Boris in all Russia! Glory, glory to the Czar! Glory, glory, glory!

BORIS
My soul is torn with anguish! Involuntary fears and sinister forbodings clutch my heart. Oh, righteous and sovereign Father, look down from heaven and behold the tears of these your faithful servants! Bestow Thy sacred blessings upon me and my dominion! Help me to be kind and just like Thyself, and rule over my people in glory! . . .   And

PRINCE SHÚISKI
Da zdrávstvuyet Tsar Borís Feódorovich!

THE CHORUS
Zhivi i zdrávstvui, Tsar násh bátyushka!

PRINCE SHÚISKI
Slávte!

THE CHORUS
Uzh kák na nébe sólntsu krásnomu, Sláva!
Uzh i sláva na Rusí Tsaryú Borísu! Sláva!

Zhivi i zdrávstvui!
Rádulsya, veselísya pravoslávnyi lyud!
Velichái Tsaryá Borísa i sláv!

THE BOYARS
Da zdrávstvuyet Tsar Borís Feódorovich!

THE CHORUS
Da zdrávstvuyet!

Uzh, kák na Rusí Tsaryú Borísu!
Sláva, sláva Tsaryú!
Sláva, sláva, sláva!

BORIS
Skorbít dushá!
Kakói-to strákh nevólnyi
Zlovéschim predchúvstviyem
Skovál mne sérdtse.
O právednik, o mói otéts derzhávnyi!
Vozzrí s nebés na slyózy vérnykh slug
I nisposhlí ty mné svyaschénnoye na vlást
Blagoslovénye.

---

10 From text of *Boris Godounov*, translated by Louis Biancolli, as found in Victor recording LHMV-6400.

now let us bow in homage to the great departed rulers of Russia. Then let us summon the people, from the Boyar to the blind beggar, to a feast. All are free to come and be my dear and welcome guests.

Da búdu blag i práveden kak tý,
Dá v sláve právlyu svói naród.
Tepér poklónimsya pochíyuschim
Vlastítelyam Rusíyi.
A tám szyvát naród na pir,
Vsekh, ot boyár do níschevo sleptsá,
Vsem vólnyi vkhod, vse gósti dorogíye.

(Bells are rung on stage as the procession continues to the Archangel Cathedral)

THE CHORUS
Long live the Czar, our little father!

THE CHORUS
Zhiví i zdrávstvui Tsár nash bátyushka.

(Police officers try to restore order, but the people break away and dash towards the Archangel Cathedral)

Even as glory to the radiant sun in the sky, so glory to Czar Boris in Russia! Glory, glory and a long life!

Uzh kák na nébe sólntsu krásnomu,
Sláva, sláva!
Uzh, kák na Rusí Tsaryú Borísu,
Sláva, sláva i mnógaya léta!

(Great commotion. The police officers struggle with the people. Boris emerges from the Arch-angel Cathedral and proceeds to his chambers.)

The second act is interesting and powerful but in a different manner. The scene is laid in the sumptuously furnished apartment of the Czar in the Kremlin. The nurse sits with the two children of Boris: the teenage daughter, Xenia, who weeps over the death of her young husband, while the nine-year-old boy, Feodor, reads a book. The nurse consoles Xenia by telling her that she still is young and there will be other men who will come to court her. In order to take her mind from the picture of the young man the nurse decides to sing a humorous song. The following "Song of the Gnat" also interests the young boy, and when the nurse finishes Feodor engages the nurse in a clapping and dancing song. As the song ends Boris enters, consoles his daughter, and sends her to her room where she will associate with some friends. Boris calls his son to him.[11]

And you, my boy, what are you so engrossed in? What's that you have?

A tý, moi sýn, chem zányat?
Éto chto?

FEÓDOR
A map of Muscovy showing our Kingdom from border to border. Look—here's Moscow, there's Novgorod. Here's Kazan and Astrakhan. There's the sea—the Caspian Sea; and here is the densely wooded land of Perm. . . . And that's Siberia.

FEÓDOR
Chertézh, zemlí moskóvskoi,
Náshe tsárstvo iz kráya v krái,
Vot vídish: Vot Moskvá, vot Nóvgorod,
A vot Kazán, Ástrakhan.
Vot móre, Káspii móre,
Vot pérmskiye dremúchiye lesá,
A vot Sibír.

BORIS
Excellent, my boy! You can survey the whole realm, as if from a cloud, in a single glance: Borders, rivers, cities. Study, Feódor! Some day —it might be soon—all that kingdom will be yours. Study, my child! . . .

BORIS
Kak khoroshó, moi sýn!
Kák s oblakóv yedínym vzórom
Ty mózhesh obozrét vsyo tsárstvo:
Granítsy, réki, grády.
Uchís Feódor! Kogdá-nibúd,

(Feódor returns to his map)

Supreme power is mine. Five years and more have I now ruled in peace. Yet my weary soul knows

I skóro mózhet byt,
Tebé vsyo éto tsárstvo dostánetsya.

11 *Ibid.*

not happiness. In vain the soothsayers promise me long years of untroubled rule. Nothing brings me cheer—neither life nor power; neither the blandishments of fame nor the plaudits of the crowd. I fancied I would find happiness amid my own family. I made preparations for a joyous marriage feast for my daughter—for that pure and gentle dove, my Czarevna. Like a storm, death carried off the man she was to marry. . . . The heavy hand of God's wrath is fearful punishment to a soul burdened with crime. . . . Around me all is darkness, and an impenetrable gloom. If only there were one little gleam of joy!

My heart is bursting with woe! Anguish tears at my weary spirit! Something secretly trembles inside of me—waiting fearfully, waiting for what? . . . I've tried to stifle the suffering of my soul with fervent prayers to all the saints in heaven. . . . I prayed—I, ruler of Russia, Czar of boundless power—I prayed for tears to bring me solace. Denunciations are heard everywhere—sedition is stirring among the Boyars. Intrigues in Lithuania and underhand sabotage. Famine threatens, pestilence, faintheartedness, and ruin. The afflicted crowds snarl like savage beasts—all Russia groans in misery and hunger! . . . And for this vast wretchedness sent down by God as punishment for my enormous sin, the people now blame me alone. They curse the name of Boris in the public squares! And even sleep has fled me . . . In the gloom of night that child appears before me—covered with blood, eyes afire, little hands clenched together pleading for mercy. . . . There was no mercy! . . . I still see that frightful gaping wound—I hear that final gasp of death! Oh my God, my God!

Uchís, dityá! . . .
Dostíg ya výsshei vlásti,
Shestói uzh gód ya tsárstvuyu spokóino,
No schástya net moyéi izmúchennoi dushé!
Naprásno mne kudésniki sulyát
Dni dólgiye, dni vlásti bezmyatézhnoi.
Ni zhízn, ni vlást, ni slávy
Obolshchénya, ni klíki tolpý
Menyá ne veselyát!
V semyé svoyéi ya mníl naití otrádu,
Gotóvil dócheri vesyólyi bráchnyi pir,
Moyéi tsarévne, golúbke chístoi.
Kak búrya smért unósit zhenikhá . . .
Tyazhká desnítsa gróznovo sudiyí
Uzhásen prígovor dushé prestúpnoi . . .
Okrést lish tmá i mrák neproglyádnyi;
Khotyá melknúl by luch otrády.
I skórbyu syértse pólno,
Toskúyet, tomítsya dukh ustályi,
Kakói-to trépet táinyi. . . .
Vsyo, zhdyósh chevó-to . . .
Molítvoi tyóploi k ugódnikam
Bózhyim ya mníl zaglushít dushí stradánya . . .
V velíchyi i bléske vlásti bezgraníchnoi,
Rusí vladýka, u nikh ya slyóz prosíl na
    uteshénye . . .
A tam donós, boyár kramóly,
Kózni Litvý i táinyie podkópy,
Glád i mór i trús i razorénye . . .
Slóvno díkii zver rýschet lyud zachúmlennyi,
Golódnaya, bédnaya stónet Rus! . . .
I v lyútom góre nisposlánnom Bógom,
Za tyázhkii moi grekh v ispytánye,
Vinói vsekh zol menyá narekáyut,
Klyanút na ploshchadyákh ímya Borísa!
I dázhe son bezhít i v súmrake nóchi
Dityá okrovávlenoye vstayót.
Óchi, pyláyut, stísnuv ruchónki,
Mólit poshchády . . .
I né bylo poshchády!
Stráshnaya rána ziyáyet,
Slýshitsya krik yevó predsmértnyi . . .
O, Góspodi, Bózhe moi!

At this point there is a tremendous noise, and Boris sends Feodor to ascertain the problem. A servant enters stating that Shuisky is without and seeks an audience. When the Czar grants the audience, the servant comes close to Boris and whispers that a serf had come last night with news that there had been uprisings in outlying areas, and that they will be meeting with Shuisky in secret to plot against the crown. Just as the servant leaves Feodor re-enters and begins to tell a humorous tale of their pet parrot and a maid servant. After he finishes the boy is thanked and complimented for being able to relate the incident so accurately. At this point Shuisky enters.[12]

(Enter Shúiski)

SHÚISKI	SHÚISKI
Mighty lord, your most humble servant.	Velíkii gosudár, chelóm byu.

12 *Ibid.*

BORIS

Ah, it's you, my bold and glorious knight! Worthy leader of a brainless mob! Criminal head of those seditious Boyars! Traitor to the imperial throne! Vilest of liars! Thrice a perjurer! Sly hypocrite! Crafty flatterer! Mallow-maker parading as a prince! Imposter! Scoundrel!

SHÚISKI

Czar! I bring you news—ominous news that concerns your throne!

BORIS

The same news, no doubt, which the secret messenger brought to Pushkin, or to you perhaps, from your Boyar friends who are now in disgrace?

SHÚISKI

The same, my lord! A pretender to the Czar's throne has appeared in Lithuania. The King, the nobles, and the Pope are supporting him!

BORIS

(Rises in alarm)

Under what name does he propose to take up arms against us? What name has this scoundrel appropriated? What name?

SHÚISKI

Of course, my lord, your power is enormous. Your conscientiousness, your liberality, and your gentleness, have won you the hearts of all your serfs. Your throne has their sincerest devotion. Yet, I dare not conceal the truth from you, mighty lord, much as my anguished heart bleeds to tell it. If that impertinent scamp should carry out his plan and cross the Lithuanian border into Russia, the crowds may very well flock after him, lured by the resurrected name of Dimitri.

BORIS

Dimitri!! . . . Czarevich, leave the room!

FEÓDOR

Ah, please let me stay, my lord, and hear of the danger that threatens your throne!

BORIS

That's out of the question, my child! Please do as I say, little Czarevitch!

(Feódor leaves; Boris follows his son to the door, locks it after him, and then quickly returns to Shúiski)

Measures must be taken immediately to close and watch the Lithuanian borders so that not a single soul can slip into Russia. Hurry! . . . No, wait, wait, Shúiski! Tell me, have you ever heard of a dead child rising from his coffin to cross-examine a lawful Czar chosen at large by the people and crowned by the great Patriarch himself! Ha, ha, ha, ha, ha, ha, ha!! . . . What! Don't you find that amusing?

BORIS

A, preslávnyi vítyaz!
Dostóinyi konovód tolpý bezmózgloi,
Prestúpnaya glavá boyár kramólnykh,
Tsárskovo prestóla supostát,
Náglyi lzhets, trízhdy klyátvu prestupívshii,
Khítryi litsemér, lstéts lukávyi,
Prosvírnya pod shápkoyu boyárskoi, obmánschik,
Plut!

SHÚISKI

Tsar! Yest vésti,
I vésti vázhnyie dlya tsárstva tvoyevó.

BORIS

Ne té-l, chto Púshkinu ili tebé tam, chtó-l,
Privyóz gonéts potáinyi
Ot sopriyátelei boyár opálnykh?

SHÚISKI

Dá, gosudár!
V Litvé yavílsya samozvánets,
Koról, paný i pápa za nevó!

BORIS

Chyím zhe ímenem na nás on opolchítsya vzdúmal? . . .
Chyó ímya negodyái ukrál? Chyó ímya?

SHÚISKI

Konéchno, tsar, silná tvoyá derzháva
Ty mílostyu, radényem i schedrótoi
Usynovíl serdtsá svoyíkh rabóv,
Dushóyu prédannykh prestólu tvoyemú.
Khotyá i bólno mne, velíkii gosudár,
Khotyá i króvyu moyó sérdtse obdayótsya,
A ot tebyá skryvát ne sméyu,
Chto yésli dérzosti ispólnennyi brodyága
S Litvý granítsu náshu pereidyót,
K nemú tolpú, byt mózhet, privlechyót
Dimítriya vozkrésnuvsheye ímya.

BORIS

Dimítriya . . . Tsarévich udalís!

FEÓDOR

O! gosudár, dozvól mne pri tebé ostátsya,
Uznát bedú, grozyáschuyu
Prestólu tvoyemú.

BORIS

Nelzyá . . . Nelzyá, dityá!
Tsarévich! Tsarévich, povinuisya!

Vzyat méry séi zhe chás,
Chtób ot Litvý Rus ogradílas zastávami,
Chtób ni odná dushá
Ne pereshlá za étu gran . . .
Stupái! . . .
Nét, postói, postói, Shúiskii!
Slykhál li ty kogdá-nibúd,
Chtob déti myórtvyie iz gróba vykhodíli
Dopráshivat tsaréi . . . tsaréi zakónnykh,
Izbránnykh vsenaródno,
Uvénchannykh velíkim patriárkhom? . . .

Kha kha kha kha kha kha kha kha! . . .
Chtó? . . . Smeshnó? . . .

(Seizes Shúiski *by the collar)*

Well, why don't you laugh? . . . eh? . . .

Chto-zh ne smeyóshsya? . . . A? . . .

SHÚISKI

Forgive me, my lord!

SHÚISKI

Pomílui, velíkii gosudár!

BORIS

Listen to me, prince! The day that awful crime was committed, the day that infant perished . . . Think, think! That dead infant—was it, was it . . . Dimitri?

BORIS

Slúshai, knyáz!
Kogdá, velíkoye svershílos zlodeyánye,
Kogdá bezvrémenno malyútka pogíb,
Malyútka tot . . . pogíbshii . . .   byl Dimítrii?

SHÚISKI

Why, yes!

SHÚISKI

On!

BORIS

Vasili Ivanych! I command you, in all conscience and by the Holy Cross and God, to tell me the whole truth! You know that I have a forgiving nature. But if you trick me, heaven help you! I'll prepare such a horrible death for you that even Czar Ivan will shudder in his coffin from fright! . . . Answer me!

BORIS

Vasílii, Iványch!
Krestóm tebyá i Bógom
Zaklináyu, po sóvesti vsyu
Právdu mne skazhí.
Ty znáyesh, ya mílostiv.
No yésli ty khitrísh, klyanús tebé!
Pridúmayu ya zlúyu kazen, takúyu kázen,
Chto Tsar Iván ot úzhasa vo gróbe
Sodrognyótsya! . . . Otvéta zhdu.

SHÚISKI

It is not death that is hard to bear, but your displeasure, my gracious lord!
Five full days and more, at Uglich, in front of all the people, I stood guard over the boy's body. Around him lay thirty bloody and mutilated bodies, clad in filthy rags and already marked by decay. But the face of the little Czarevitch was clean and radiant with light. The wound upon him gaped terrible and deep. A wondrous smile played on his unblemished lips. He lay there as if peacefully asleep in his cradle, his arms crossed and his little right hand tightly clutching a baby toy.

SHÚISKI

Ne kázen strashná, strashná tvoyá nemílost.
V Úgliche, v sobóre pred vsém naródom,
Pyat slíshkom dnéi ya trúp mladéntsa poseschál
Vokrúg nevó trinádtsat tel lezhálo,
Obezobrázhennykh, v kroví, v lokhmótyakh gryáznykh;
I po ním uzh tléniye zamétno probegálo.
No détskii lik tsarévicha byl svétel,
Chist i yásen.
Glubókaya, stráshnaya ziyála rána,
A na ustákh yevó neporóchnykh
Ulýbka chúdnaya igrála.
Kazálosya, v svoyéi on kolybélke
Spokóino spit, slozhívshi rúchki,
I právoi krépko szhav igrúshku détskuyu.

BORIS

Enough!

BORIS

Dovólno! . . .

(Makes a sign for Shúiski *to go.* Shúiski *leaves.*
Boris *sinks into an armchair)*

God, how stifling it's become! I'm fairly gasping for breath! It's as if all the blood had rushed to my face and suddenly dropped back like a weight. What a savage thing conscience is! How sternly it avenges itself! One single blot on my conscience—a blot put there by evil chance—and I feel my soul aflame and my heart poisoned. Remorse and damnation beat, beat, beat, like a hammer, in my ears. I feel something strangling me, closing its grip. My head reels! My eyes see . . . the blood-stained body of that child! . . . Look there! . . . What is it? . . . There in the corner! It's something rocking! It's growing larger! Now, it's coming nearer . . . threatening . . . groaning . . . Stand back! Don't touch me! No, no, it was not I . . . I'm

Uf tyazheló! Dái dukh perevedú . . .
Ya chúvstvoval, vsya króv mne kínulas
V litsó i tyázhko opuskálas.
O, sóvest lyútaya, kak tyázhko ty karáyesh!
Yézheli v tebé pyatnó yedínoye . . .
Yedínoye slucháino zavelósya.
Dushá gorít,
Nalyótsa sértse yádom,
Tak tyázhko, tyázhko stánet,
Chto mólotom stuchít v ushákh
Ukórom i proklyátyem . . .
I dúshit chtó-to . . . dúshit . . .
I golová kruzhítsa . . .
V glazákh dityá okrovávlenoye!
Vón . . . von tám . . . chto éto? Tam v uglú
Kolýshetsya, rostyót . . .

not the one you want! Back, back, child! It was not I, not I . . . It was the will of the people! Go, go, my boy! Oh, God, God! you have not wished death for my crime! Have mercy on the sinful soul of Czar Boris!

Blízitsya . . . drozhít i stónet . . .
Chúr, chúr! . . . Ne yá . . .
Ne yá tvói likhodéi . . .
Chur! . . . Chur, dityá! . . . Ne yá . . . Ne yá . . .
Vólya naróda . . .
Chur, dityá . . . Góspodi! Ty ne khóchesh smérti gréshnika,
Pomílui dúshu prestúpnovo Tsaryá Borísa!

CURTAIN

Although a few performances of this opera have been given in English or in Italian, it is usually recorded in Russian. You will find it difficult to fit the English translation shown above with the music unless you hear it more than one time, or unless you have a libretto which contains the Russian side by side with the English.

Nonetheless, the second act creates a powerful effect. Some observations will be helpful:

Study Procedures

1. Listen to the record of the Prologue, Part II, and Act II. Observe the following points as you listen:
   a. On record the voice of the young son, Feodor, is usually sung by a girl. Both Xenia and Feodor are sopranos, while the nurse is a mezzo-soprano or lower-voiced woman.
   b. The gaiety of the early part of Act II balances well with the somber and emotionally weighty second part.
   c. Consider how tenderly Boris sings to his own children and how roughly he sings to Shuisky.
   d. Act II permits a bass singer to portray a wide range of emotion. Although he moves little around the stage, often sitting in his large chair, the drama of the music and the intensity of the words keep the mood at a peak.
   e. Each time Boris sings to or about Xenia the same theme is heard. This theme identification device is common in operas of the Romantic period (the nineteenth century).
   f. Along with his actions and words, the groveling tone of Shuisky assists in painting his character.
   g. The orchestra describes well the emotions expressed by Boris in his quick shifts from fear, to bravado, to submissive prayer.

Mussorgsky faced difficulty in having his opera accepted for presentation at the St. Petersburg Opera House. Often he had performed portions of the work at social gatherings in or near the city, playing the piano and singing all the parts, and each presentation had been received with praise. The first version of the work had been for an all-male cast, and the opera house believed that this would not be a feasible production. After revision to include female voices, it was accepted and finally presented. The night of the first performance hundreds of persons in the city, who had heard the music from the score beforehand, sang portions of the opera on the bridges and in the streets of St. Petersburg before and after the performance. The work had the rare distinction of being accepted with open arms by the populace well before the professionals acknowledged its merits.

Study Procedures

1. Read Mérimée's original story of *Carmen* and compare it to the opera.
2. Listen to one act of *Carmen* and work out an outline such as the one for *Wozzeck*.
3. Compare the style of music in *Carmen* to *Butterfly*. Both were written by men who used music from other countries as a basis for their work; both wrote during the Romantic period, when an accent on the common man became more obvious; both used a woman as the central focus. Name other similarities and differences, but especially the style of the music.
4. Both *Wozzeck* and *Boris Godounov* have a man as the leading character. Do these operas have more of a masculine impact than *Butterfly* or *Carmen?*

THE SHORT OPERA

As we stated early in the chapter, not all operas are tragic or long. After the Second World War a number of one-act operas became popular in university presentations, and others were instigated by this interest.

The one-act opera reached a peak with Puccini, when he composed three (a trilogy) which were originally intended to be presented during one performance. Of these, two were tragic, and one humorous. Although all three are still given regularly, the comedy, *Gianni Schicchi,* has had more frequent presentations.

The short opera is not as attractive to a composer as the larger form. It is difficult to find a good script for one act, it is difficult to set the characters in the mind of the viewer and listener, and it is difficult to unify the music so as to create an emotional impact without seeming frivolous on the one hand or overdone on the other. Then, too, the work perhaps will never be performed in a major opera house.

But the increase of interest in opera in communities and on the campus has offered composers an opportunity for performance that did not exist some years ago. Consequently, there exist a number of works which are quite attractive to produce, interesting to sing, and worthwhile for the audience.

Amahl and the Night Visitors (Menotti)

One of the most famous one-act operas is *Amahl and the Night Visitors.* Written by Gian Carlo Menotti for presentation over a television network in 1951, this work immediately attracted the attention of layman and musician alike. We will examine this work in more detail. Menotti for years has been a master of the one-act opera, and a number of his works have become well-known. If *Amahl* appeals to you, you might be interested in *The Old Maid and the Thief, The Medium,* or *The Telephone.* These operas are all in English, and consequently may have an attraction for you that others may not have; in addition, they are contemporary in effect even, as in the case of *Amahl,* if not in actual setting. It might be tempting to study only these short operas in English, but it would be indeed unfortunate if your experience with this form were not to include some of the major compositions discussed earlier in the chapter.

The Music

Amahl is in five sections. Since the recordings are in English, there is no need to study the text. Menotti wrote the texts for all of his operas, and part of his success can be attributed to his natural feeling for the prose line and its primary and secondary accents, which he accommodates with his music.

Scene from television production of Menotti's opera Amahl and the Night Visitors, *performed on April 14, 1952; left to right: Leon Lishner, Andrew McKinley, David Aiken, Chet Allen and Rosemary Kuhlmann (National Broadcasting Company photo).*

The outline of the opera is as follows:

1. Amahl and His Mother—recitatives, arias, and a short duet
   Amahl sings three short arias; the mother, one extended one
2. Entrance and Introduction of Kings—march, trio, three arias, a quartet with mother and the kings, and a humorous scene at the door with kings and Amahl
3. Shepherds' Chorus and Dance
4. Mother's Theft and Fight—mother's aria, Amahl's aria, Melchior's aria
5. The Miracle—trio and finale (shepherds' chorus)

Beyond the attractive story itself, Menotti writes well for the voices. He understands the boy soprano voice, so that the writing is usually in his best range and occasionally moves into the upper notes where the boy can show his ability. The trios and arias for the kings are well suited to the text and to the situation of the moment. Paramount throughout the work, however, is the feeling for the dramatic. The music is attractive though contemporary in its way, but the music never keeps the drama from moving and unfolding toward its high points. If you have not heard this opera on TV or seen it presented at a local school, a study of this work will be most revealing and attractive. If you have heard it before, a rehearing will prove all the more informative and pleasing.

Study Procedure

Compare the styles of the operas studied, considering: a) the impact each opera had upon you, b) the intent of the text, c) the manner in which the music fits the text, and d) how the music gives added dimension to the text.

OTHER FORMS OF MUSICAL THEATER

The musical stage is not limited to opera. While opera developed into an art medium, numerous other forms featured music in different ways. These included vaudeville, extravaganza, minstrel, burlesque, revue, pantomime, ballad opera, comic opera, operetta, light opera, musical comedy, and musical play. Some of these are merely different names for practically the same kind of event; others have shifted their emphasis through the years. All of these forms use the spoken word with song-style music to convey their intent to the audience (the pantomime being the only exception), with the crucial factor being whether the songs are connected or related to the spoken material.

The chart below will assist you in understanding this relationship:

Unrelated Songs and Material	Related Songs and Material
Vaudeville	Operetta
Minstrel ◄———	Burlesque
Extravaganza	Comic opera
Ballad opera ———►	Singspiel

During its time of popularity the ballad opera increased its relation between songs and spoken material, while burlesque has moved in the opposite direction.

Definitions

Some definitions will assist you in understanding the forms of musical theater and their positions on the chart:

Vaudeville: The present meaning is a distortion of an old French phrase which meant that a song used a well-known tune with rearranged or parodied words. Such songs often were sung in jest, or seriously in morality plays. Later, the name came to be used for a short comedy act interspersed with songs, some of the latter being well-known or containing altered words to fit the comedy situation.

Minstrel: This two-act variety show featured different novelty and musical numbers interspersed with jokes or humorous dialogue between an interlocutor and end men. (See Chapter 15 for additional references.)

Extravaganza: Using unrelated musical material, elaborate costumes and settings are featured. Even from the first this form used a chorus line with dance sequences. The music became a vehicle for featuring a singer, dancing girls, or as a background for costume and scenery display.

Ballad opera: Despite the name, the early form used spoken dialogue along with tunes taken from the more popular ballads or folk songs of the day. At first its main intent was to entertain the public, which was different than that of the opera. It later came to parody, imitate, or make fun of serious opera.

Operetta: In the 1700s the word meant a short opera; later it came to mean a stage work consisting of a light plot, usually sentimental in nature, with spoken dialogue. The songs have some relation to the plot and tend to give the audience additional information or feeling for it.

Burlesque: Originally this form was a parody or satire upon a serious drama. Often the parody included not only a reworked script, but travesties upon the actors, singers, and dancers as well. Because many of the serious plays of the nineteenth century included music, burlesque also poked fun at the music and the manner in which it was performed.

Comic opera: This is a light opera with music close to the popular idioms of the day. The superficial plot usually resolves itself as a result of contrived situations just before the end of the work, while spoken dialogue separates the musical numbers. A heavier emphasis is placed upon the music than in some of the preceding forms.

Singspiel: A German term for opera, light and serious, this popular dramatic presentation later came to be restricted to the lighter forms containing spoken dialogue.

Pantomime: In this form action is directed toward some kind of plot; music is frequently used as a background, but there is no singing. Sometimes the music is related to the action in minor ways. There are no spoken words.

A Little History

Most histories of musical theater in America point to a first dramatic presentation in the courthouse of Charleston, South Carolina in 1735, where without scenery, costumes, or a stage, music was interspersed between lines of the play *Flora*. Some considered this a ballad opera, and it well could have been. The first musical-dramatic presentation composed by Americans was given in New York City at the John Street Theater in 1796 (April 18). This play, entitled *The Archers or the Mountaineers of Switzerland,* emphasized liberty rather than love, as could be expected considering the date. In the colonies the concert singer was also the dramatic entertainer, and all actors were expected to sing well; thus, the two forms were bound to merge regularly.

Although the first burlesque in our country, in 1828, was a travesty upon *Hamlet,* its present emphasis upon the female body began in 1869, when Lydia Thompson brought her four blondes (at least one was brunette) into New York to present a farce upon the Greek drama *Ixion,* and had the girls dress in skin-colored tights. The most famous burlesque, a parody of *Evangeline* in 1874, featured the first complete musical score created specifically for a light production. It had been customary for some new numbers to be added to older ones, with adaptations and alterations made on familiar tunes or words. With such a step a new emphasis was given to music and its function with the dramatic.

The original Dan Emmett minstrel, introduced at the Chatham Square Theater in February 1843, continued its popularity through its descendants well into the twentieth century. The New Christie Minstrels, although different in emphasis, are an offshoot of the original.

The history of the American musical theater depicts changing forms, shifting of emphases, combining ideas from older presentations to develop a format which would be interesting to a current audience and at the same time more carefully combine dramatic and dance elements with musical ones. Such an amalgamation took place in 1866 with the presentation of *The Black Crook,* which took certain features from ballad operas, burlesque, and the minstrels to offer what came to be the first extravaganza with a female chorus line, elaborate costumes, and fancy settings. This production planted the seed leading to the concept that music and dialogue could successfully work toward one goal. This hit show made over a million dollars through its eight revivals in New York during the nineteenth century. Even at the beginning of the 1900s it played throughout the West and Midwest. One of the later versions became famous for its introduction of serpentine dancing with the high kick and the split, a dance feature which had never been seen on the stage before.

The operetta or light opera in America has derived most of its impetus from Europe. In 1878 *H.M.S. Pinafore* first arrived in our country and became the rage. Other Gilbert and Sullivan presentations appeared almost as soon as they were composed, and inspired American musicians such as Victor Herbert to write operettas with an American emphasis and flavor. Later, between 1907 and

1917, a second surge of popularity for the operetta spread Viennese melodies across the country, with *The Merry Widow, The Chocolate Soldier, The Student Prince,* and numerous others.

The glorification of the American Beauty came into focus in 1893, with the presentation of *A Gaiety Girl.* Billed as a musical comedy, it was part extravaganza, part burlesque, and was the forerunner of the famous "Ziegfeld Follies," shows which glorified feminine form and pulchritude. For some, this was the beginning of the modern musical.

But it was not until 1927 that *Show Boat* introduced the contemporary emphasis into musical presentations. This was a play with musical numbers, each of which emerged from the plot and from the characters naturally and spontaneously so as to give the impression that the plot was being developed and the characterizations aided. This was an excellent production, and its creativity is proved through its popularity even today. In the early 1970s *Show Boat* had a run in London which would equal any recent hit, and in the United States it is regularly presented in theaters and on TV to large audiences. Jerome Kern, the composer, wrote not only musical numbers, but songs which fit the plot, its development, and dramatic focus.

Since that time audiences have demanded a continuation of such unity, and the many musical plays which have been hits on Broadway, on the screen, on TV, and in the high schools and colleges of our country have provided an increasing artistic emphasis. *Oklahoma, Carousel, West Side Story, South Pacific,* and others are well-known examples. Although the musical play has been most attractive, there has also been some emphasis upon the musical comedy, the operetta, and the revue or extravaganza. Each of these productions brings something from past forms into our present.

In summary, plays and stage presentations with music do not exist for the same purpose as operas. Although they contain artistic elements, the main goal is not art but entertainment. Opera employs music in one way, other presentations in quite different ways, with music developed to satisfy each purpose.

Study Procedures

Because recent musical plays are so well-known we will not suggest any particular one for study.

1. Listen to two musical plays from the past two decades and make a comparison of the use of music within them.
2. Listen to *Show Boat* and describe how its music is different from that in one of the later musical plays.
3. Compare *Madama Butterfly* to *My Fair Lady.* Do *not* try to compare the plots; rather, concentrate upon the music and the manner in which it is used in each. Are there similarities as well as differences?

4. *The Marriage of Figaro* is a comic opera. How does the music differ from the musical comedy?
5. *Carmen* was originally written with spoken dialogue. Would this still be considered an opera? Why or why not?

Bibliography—Chapter 12

ADAMI, GIUSEPPE, ed., *Letters of Giacomo Puccini*. Philadelphia: J. B. Lippincott Company, 1931.

BEAUMARCHAIS, CARON DE, *The Barber of Seville* and *The Marriage of Figaro*. Baltimore: Penguin Books, 1964.

BENN, CHRISTOPHER, *Mozart on the Stage*. New York: Coward-McCann, Inc., 1946.

BROPHY, BRIGID, *Mozart the Dramatist*. New York: Harcourt, Brace and World, Inc., 1964.

CALVOCORESSI, M. D., *Modest Mussorgsky, His Life and Works*. Fair Lawn, N.J.: Essential Books, Inc., 1956.

CHARQUES, R. D., *A Short History of Russia*. New York: E. P. Dutton and Company, Inc., 1956.

CLARKSON, JESSE D., *A History of Russia*. New York: Random House, 1966.

CURTISS, MINA, *Bizet and His World*. New York: Alfred A. Knopf, 1958.

DEAN, WINTON, *Bizet*. London: J. M. Dent and Sons, Ltd., 1948.

————, *George Bizet, His Life and Work*. London: J. M. Dent and Sons, Ltd., 1965.

DENT, EDWARD J., *Mozart's Operas*. London: Oxford University Press, 1960.

EWEN, DAVID, *The Story of America's Musical Theater*. Philadelphia: Chilton Company, Publishers, 1961.

GROUT, DONALD JAY, *A Short History of Opera*. New York: Columbia University Press, 1965.

HARHOLINSKY, ABRAHAM, ed., *The Poems, Prose and Plays of Alexander Pushkin*. New York: Modern Library, 1964.

KLUCHEVSKY, V. O., *A History of Russia*. New York: Russell and Russell, 1960.

LAYDA, JAY, and SERGEI BERTENSSON, eds., *The Mussorgsky Reader*. New York: W. W. Norton Company, Inc., 1947.

MARHERBE, HENRY, *Carmen*. Paris: Editions Albin Michel, 1951.

MATES, JULIAN, *The American Musical Stage Before 1800*. New Brunswick, N.J.: Rutgers University Press, 1962.

PARKER, D. C., *Bizet*. London: Routledge and Kegan Paul, Ltd., 1951.

PUSHKIN, A. S., *Boris Godunov*. Chicago: Russian Language Specialties, 1965.

REICH, WILLI, *Alban Berg*. New York: Harcourt, Brace and World, 1963.

RIESEMANN, OSKAR VON, *Moussorgsky*. New York: Tudor Publishing Company, 1935.

SMITH, CECIL, *Musical Comedy in America*. New York: Theatre Arts Books, Robert M. MacGregor, 1950.

WHITE, ERIC WALTER, *The Rise of English Opera*. New York: Philosophical Library, 1951.

Recordings—Chapter 12

Berg: *Wozzeck*   Harrell, Farrell Conducted by Mitropoulos   Columbia   Col SL-118

Menotti: *Amahl and the Night Visitors*	Kuhlman, original TV cast Conducted by Schippers	Victor LM-1701
Mozart: *The Marriage of Figaro*	Schwarzkopf, Moffo Conducted by Giulini	Angel SDL-3608
Mussorgsky: *Boris Godounov*	Christoff, Gedda, Ustino Conducted by Dobrowen	Capitol GDR-7164
Puccini: *Madame Butterfly*	Steber, Tucker, Madeira Conducted by Rudolf	**Columbia Col SL-104**
Puccini: *Madama Butterfly*	Rankin, Tebaldi Conducted by Erede	London RS-63001

Additional Suggestions for Listening

Bizet: *Carmen*	De los Angeles, Gedda Conducted by Beecham	Capitol GCR-7207

PART TWO

Instrumental Music

Section E *Instrumental Music Expresses the Moods of the People*

Chapter 13

The Influence of Vocal Music on Instrumental Forms

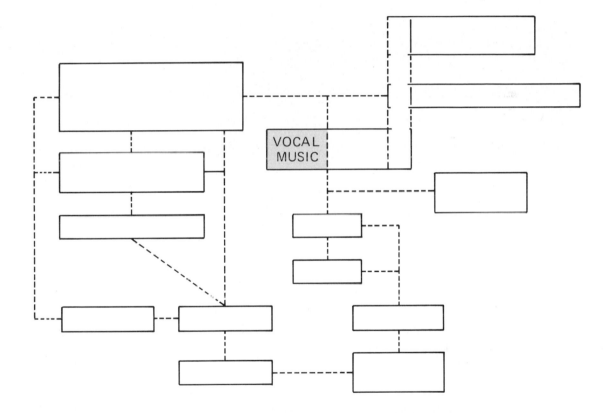

All evidence seems to point to singing as man's earliest attempt at music. In certain geographic areas song gradually became predominately rhythmic, and consequently limited movements of the body to such rhythm soon appeared. This movement of the body led to some type of dancing, and usually it was accompanied by rhythmic singing, and only later by crude instruments. Early instruments were solely rhythmic in nature, and so the rhythm of the song was

Three young musicians (Reproduced by Courtesy of the Trustees of the National Gallery, London; Art Reference Bureau, Inc., Ancram, N.Y.).

underlined and often duplicated by the instrument. In chantlike dances the voice sang the same rhythm played by the instrument; in more progressive communities the voice rose above the rhythm so that the instrument produced only an accompaniment to the wandering voice. African and American Indian tribal music are examples of this growth.

Independent forms in instrumental music were little-known before the thirteenth century, and even much later instruments were assigned an inferior role as compared to the voice. About the middle of the fourteenth century instrumental self-sufficiency began to appear. Prior to this time most of the instrumental music had been either an accompaniment, wherein the players performed the exact music of the vocal line along with the singer, or a variance of the vocal line depending on the technic of the player; the performer could play fewer notes if his technic were modest, but if the vocal line made few demands the performer might add notes to the line giving the instrumental part more interest, color, and texture; or an introduction or interlude might be improvised. Since instruments were not yet fully developed, technical passages in the voice usually meant the performer had to provide a less demanding part. The music of the troubadours exemplifies these characteristics.

In the fifteenth century instrumentalists more often performed without the aid of voices, by transcribing vocal literature from the lines commonly sung, and later by creating new forms from vocal ones. These compositions were designed for a keyboard instrument, the lute, or a group of winds or strings.

The following diagram may be of assistance in noting this evolution. By using established vocal forms as a base, three types of instrumental music developed:

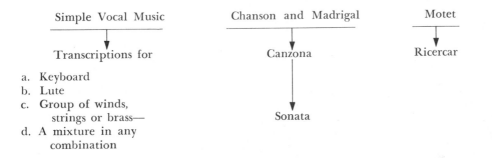

One method of obtaining instrumental music was to transcribe the vocal literature. Vocal music was rearranged for the organ, keyboard, lute, or any mixed group of instruments which might be available. Even today we use keyboard arrangements of orchestral numbers, or choral compositions adapted from musical comedies or motion pictures. When a song from a movie is transcribed for a high school band, although the words are never seen or heard, the hearer immediately appreciates its meaning and remembers it as a song. This was also true in earlier times.

The *chanson* and *madrigal* were polyphonic vocal forms usually coming from an Italian or Franco-Flemish background. These vocal compositions placed considerable emphasis upon interior form, and consequently the newer instrumental *canzone* did the same. In the canzona this alteration of form often meant an alteration of texture as well. This new instrumental form prepared the way for the later *sonata* and the larger instrumental form, the *symphony*. Each of these will receive considerable attention in later chapters.

Usually an unaccompanied choral composition, polyphonic in nature and based upon a Latin text, one of the classical *motet*'s main characteristics was the imitative treatment given within the various sections of the work, many times followed by homophonic sections. Since motets employed from four to eight voices, they could easily be played by a group of instrumentalists, and the style could easily be imitated in an instrumental composition. This gradually led to an independent composition called the *ricercar*. Although more often adapted to the keyboard in later literature, the ricercar was at first an instrumental form.

Let us examine some specific compositions which will assist us in understanding these developments.

CANZONA

Canzona (a 4) (Giovanni Battista Grillo) (Pro Musica; Decca DL-9419)

This four-voiced example seems to imitate or duplicate vocal lines. It is moderately imitative, and often pairs the instruments so as to create a two-against-two effect. This work, simple in texture and development, has the typical long, short, short rhythmic beginning which for a number of years distinguished the canzona from other musical compositions. Not far removed in style from a direct imitation of voice lines, this example of a canzona indicates a first step toward independence.

Study Procedures

1. Compare the Pro Musica performance of this canzona with that of E. Power Biggs combining organ and brass instruments (Columbia MS-7142).
2. For a contemporary canzona listen to Peter Mennin's *Canzona for Band* (Mercury MG-50084).
3. Listen to Viadana's *Canzone* and Gabrieli's *Canzone,* and compare them to the Grillo *Canzone.*

RICERCAR

This form appears less definite than the canzona, and although it began as an outgrowth of the motet, it became a purely instrumental form independent of its ancestor. In the process, however, it often lost attractiveness and freshness of style.

Ricercare del Duodecimo Tono (a 4) by Andrea Gabrieli (Pro Musica; Decca DL-9419)

This work, similar to the motet, exemplifies the imitative style of ricercar. "Ricercar" means to search and research for a theme, and in works such as this the title is well exemplified. The form assists this searching wherein a theme is given, and found again only at the end of the composition; in the meantime, two new themes alternate, seeming to keep us from locating the original melody. In all, the work has five sections:

A—Long statement in two parts using a submelody; in two pulsations
B—Short; note its pick-up in the reed instrument; in three pulsations
C—Short; a new theme in two pulsations
B—Restatement of the second theme, now given greater emphasis
   Bridge built into the composition using material from the C theme
A—Restatement of first theme and used as an ending for the composition

Some obvious motet characteristics may be noted: the work is sectional; any imitation is complete within its section, beginning anew with each theme; the range of the four parts indicates an affinity to singing. Rather than using the four instruments chosen, it could have been played on a keyboard instrument.

The later ricercar lost some of the characteristics of the classic motet, placing emphasis upon technically brilliant passages possible with any given instrument or group of instruments. This was particularly true of those compositions written for the lute and keyboard instruments. Although imitative near the beginning of the work, the writing became more technically oriented toward the ending. Instead of using several themes as evidenced above, the later type ricercar usually centered upon one theme throughout the imitative portions. Along with the technic it could include augmentation, diminution, or other technical compositional characteristics. This often resulted in dull and uninspired compositions. A good example of this style of ricercar is to be found in the *History of Music in Sound* Series, Vol. IV (*Ricercar Arioso, No. 1* (Andrea Gabrieli), RCA Victor LM-6029).

REVIEW

When instrumental production developed sufficiently, when society could comprehend instrumental compositions independent of voices or dancing, and when performers developed their own expressive skills, then independent instrumental forms began to emerge. This chapter has explored this emergence from vocal forms and vocal music. Chapter 14 will explore it from the background of the dance.

The main point is this: that instrumental forms often appear independent, but are usually rooted in vocal forms, man's earliest and easiest means of musical expression.

Bibliography—Chapter 13

LANG, PAUL HENRY, *Music in Western Civilization*.   New York: W. W. Norton and Company, Inc., 1941.
SACHS, CURT, *The Rise of Music in the Ancient World*.   New York: W. W. Norton and Company, Inc., 1943.

Recordings—Chapter 13

Canzona (Peter Mennin)		Mercury MG-50084
Canzoni (G. Gabrieli)	E. Power Biggs, Tarr Brass Ens.	Columbia MS-7142
Giovanni Gabrieli	New York Brass Ens.	Period Records SPL-734
History of Music in Sound, Vol. IV		Victor LM-6057
Masterpieces of Music Before 1750		Haydn Society HS 7-9039
Music for Organ and Brass	Biggs, New England Brass Ens.	Columbia MS-6117
Renaissance Festival Music	New York Pro Musica	Decca DL-9419

Chapter 14

The Influence of the Dance on Instrumental Forms

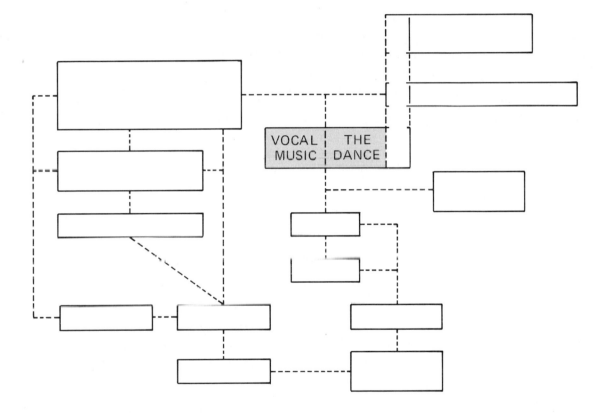

VOCAL MUSIC | THE DANCE

Although the dance was originally sung, instruments were added at an early time. At first they only assisted with the singing by duplicating the sung pitches, or adding to the rhythm while the voices sang the melodic lines. But it is natural to assume that the instruments would move into their own, and as voices were used less and less for the dance, instruments came to be used more and more.   One reason probably was that simultaneous dancing and singing winded the performers, so in order to continue the dance instruments began to be relied upon.   Then too, the development of instruments made it easier to play the tunes used for dancing, so melodies could be entrusted to instruments with more confidence.   When instruments became more reliable, melodic lines became more intricate and voices could no longer keep apace.

Instrumentalists were at some disadvantage, since they could not use words to assist with meanings and suggest emotions.   Consequently, they had to devise technics to bring to the listener a different but equally effective result.   The first method was through the instruments themselves.   There developed many kinds of instruments, each with a particular quality and range producing an individual effect.   The potential of using two or more instruments together, lending presence or absence of tone color for short periods of time throughout the composition, created numerous possible effects.

The second method chosen by instrumentalists was to imitate the form of the dance.   This model, imitated later in some vocal forms, relied upon a certain regularity.   Coming from the people, the dances had symmetrical phrasing so the steps could be easily followed; the music adopted this idea.   This orderliness produced a kind of esthetic satisfaction based partly upon its reoccurrence, and partly because it could be easily remembered.   Usually in these dances the phrases were four, eight, or sixteen measures in length, and the instrumental compositions followed this idea.   In addition, dances often repeated the phrase using a slightly different ending for the repeat.   Such repeats and regularity of phrasing brought a periodicity to the composition that evoked familiarity and pleasure.

Since early instrumental music was simple in construction, a third method was found that could give a simple composition additional meaning and more emotional possibilities.   This was the *variation*.   Variation is not only a musical term, but it means the same in music as elsewhere: a varying, a modification, a repetition wherein the major features remain the same with the lesser features altered.   With early dances being assimilated as instrumental forms, and since these dances were simple in melodic and harmonic content as well as in construction, the variation was a great aid in repeated phrases.   One phrase could be played in a direct manner, while the repeat could be altered, giving the listener a new esthetic impression and meaning plus variety.   After its simple beginning, this idea was to grow in complexity until it became a complete form by itself.   We shall discuss the variation further in Chapters 17, 19, 20, and 23.

These ideas were not restricted to any one type of dance or geographic area.   Early dance forms progressed from the folk song, to the dance, to an independent instrumental form advancing in complexity with each new step of development.   Even though the dance form, the geographic locale, or the time period may differ, such change happens early or late in musical history with obvious similarity.   We shall pursue this idea further in this chapter and also in Chapter 15.

EARLY DANCES

The earliest of the known instrumental forms is a simple dance from the thirteenth and fourteenth centuries.

Estampie

This form usually consists of four to seven repeated sections. One estampie from the thirteenth century easily available on records features a recorder and viola da gamba. Listen to this short composition for two instruments and note the five sections which are equal in length. In two main parts, this little composition includes two periods (a double phrase) in one part, and three periods in the second part. Part one includes two different melodies; all three periods of the second part are based upon the same melody. In the fourth period the viola plays an innocent variation of his own part which he played in the third; in the fifth, the recorder plays a slightly fancier part than in either the third or fourth. This composition could be diagrammed as follows:

$$A \quad B \quad C \quad C' \quad C''$$

Each period contains two phrases of eight pulsations each. This dance is in a fast three, with one obvious pulsation to each three beats. By counting the pulsations, eight equals the phrase, sixteen the period. Note that the first two sixteens contain different melodies, while the last three contain the same melody with variations.

Although simple, this indicates a beginning method of instrumental music, as it captures the flavor of the dance without the dance having to be actually performed.

INFLUENCE OF FOUR EARLY DANCES

Dancing had been a ritual in most early civilizations; then, during the Middle Ages, the church had suppressed it to the extent that it led only a token existence. Later, in the fourteenth century, it bubbled forth, modestly at first, but growing with continual peaks and recessions until the present time. During most periods of cultural history dance seems to be an upswelling from the common man followed by an acceptance into aristocratic society, so that when the creative spirit of rural society became unproductive, artistic efforts waned.

Four dances of the fifteenth and sixteenth centuries have been important to the development of instrumental music, and at the same time interesting from the standpoint of form and style. Within these simple forms dynamic dances of the people evolved into polished dances of the court, and we evidence a shift in cultural emphasis as well as musical characteristics.

The basse dance, the branle, the ronde, and the pavane are well exemplified in an album by the New York Pro Musica (Decca DL-94192).

1. The *basse dance,* a fifteenth century ceremonial court dance in moderate tempo and duple meter, took its name from the word "Bas," meaning to glide or walk, which was in contrast to the leaping or springing dances of most common folk. In the record listed above, two basse dances are played, one in duple meter, the other in triple. Although originally duple, for the sake of variety the musicians often played some of the dances in a different meter after they had memorized them.

2. The *branle,* a group dance of the sixteenth century, was fashioned more closely after the dances of the folk—a follow-the-leader type of dance with singing. Two types existed: the branle simple, a duple-meter dance, and the branle gay, usually in triple meter. In the recorded composition the dance begins in simple style, changes to the branle gay, and returns to the simple. Although fashioned after folk dances, this type of juxtaposition by Susato would indicate that the particular dance heard was composed in the style of those common for the day, rather than being an original folk dance.

3. The *ronde* began as a quick duple dance with short phrases. In the recorded version the ronde has been arranged into two parts, the first more indicative of the early dance, while the latter exhibits more style and probably is typical of the dance after some polish and elevation into society. Even though the middle portion seems different in coloration, the tempo maintains the same quick duple feeling, though not evident at first hearing. The instrumentation and the manner of playing give this section a feeling of slowness and stateliness. This arrangement could be a forerunner of the trio as part of the dance, wherein the main portion of the dance is stated, followed by a section played in a quieter vein by a smaller group. In this composition each section has three parts. The first two repeat, while the third differs. As stated above, the first section contains short phrases of eight measures, while the second section has longer phrases of sixteen. The form would be:

A   B   A

a   a   b   c   c   d   a   a   b

4. Two *pavanes* of contrasting styles are found in this dance collection. The first, more typical of the early, slow, stately dance with solemn dignified movements, patterned itself after the peacock for which the dance seems to have been named. Of Italian origin, this dance usually was a song of the period which had been turned into a dance. This example fits such a description, since it had been a song by a noted composer only a few years earlier. The basse dance had been the most popular dance of the Franco-Flemish courts, but when Spain had become one of the cultural centers of Europe near the beginning of the 1500s, the pavane became the popular dance. Originally of duple nature, yet when it became stylized as a musical composition rather than a dance, it could often be found in triple meter. The first pavane on this record adheres to song style,

while the second describes but does not rely upon a song. In the second, notice the imitative section between the colors of instruments indicating the contrasting forces in battle. The tempo in each part is slow. This form was short-lived as a dance, but has been surprisingly long-lived as an instrumental form. Some pavanes are still being written in the twentieth century, not only describing in a contemporary way the feelings of a past era, but also depicting the emotions of the present in a slow but regularly measured manner.

Study Procedures

1. Since the pavane followed the basse dance as the most popular dance of the period, contrast the two types musically. What type of society would you envision based upon the styles of music heard?
2. Of the four dances heard, which seem to belong more to the folk? Which seem more closely related to royalty or the ruling class?
3. Listen to the Cabezón *Pavane for Harp.* Can you hear the differences in the variations? Can you describe why the variation became a part of the instrumental music of the early period? Why would Cabezón choose the pavane for this type of musical composition?
4. Listen to a twentieth century pavane, *Pavane for a Dead Princess* by Ravel. What musical characteristics does this composition bear from its earliest predecessors? What is the meter, duple or triple? Can you hear the overall form of the work? Compare the colorations to the first pavane by Susato.
5. Compare the musical style of the Susato dances with Praetorius's *Branles* and *Pavane*, and then with Schein's Pavanes from *Banchetto Musicale.* What accounts for the differences in style between the two Schein Pavanes?

THE MINUET

The minuet belongs to the seventeenth and eighteenth centuries, and once introduced it replaced earlier dances almost completely. This was due partly to the changes of fashion and manners which seem inevitable, but it also indicated the greater concern for grace and style, social behavior and refinement. So popular was this dance, so meaningful a social form, and so indicative of the times that some texts speak of the era from 1650 to 1750 as the period or age of the minuet. Left behind were the more rustic movements and steps, and into prominence came the "menu" (small) step of the minuet, placing its emphasis upon regularity, balance, and subtle expression with hidden meanings behind each stereotyped movement, a contrast to outward expression and obvious bodily movements portraying the personal feelings of the individual. As Curt Sachs declares: "To dance the minuet is to pay homage to woman."[1] This phrase alone tells us something beyond the nature of the dance, concerning the fundamental

---

[1] *World History of the Dance,* Curt Sachs. W. W. Norton and Co., Inc., New York, 1937, page 399.

quality of society in which the lady no longer took her place side by side in a circle with men using the same high or low steps, but rather one in which her role became a symbol of graciousness and apparent servility, to be respected and given a position of honor because of her charm and femininity. To give the impression that this was the sole dance of the period would be an error, but it was symbolic of the times and became a most important musical form, so that as an instrumental piece it has lasted until the present day.

Because we shall become involved with the minuet more in later chapters (17 and 25) we will introduce only the more popular independent examples here.

Minuet in G (Beethoven)

Probably the most famous of all minuets is the Beethoven *Minuet in G*. Written when he was a young man in Vienna in 1797, it has taken the grace and form of the dance and woven around these a delicate melodic line reminiscent of the minuet period and its popularity. Originally written only for piano, it has been orchestrated. Either version will prove interesting and of value.

There is no introduction, and the music evenly divides into four-measure phrases and two phrase periods. Each section or period is repeated. As was the custom, a trio is used, and because of the greater speed of the notes the listener gains the impression of a type of variation. The *trio,* originally for three players, was a second minuet designed to offer contrast with the first in style and loudness. The form is typical of the minuet.

Part I		Part II	Part I
A B		Trio	A
x x' y x		g h	x y x

Each period is repeated. Each second melody (B and h) returns to the main theme of that section (x and y), giving the dance its unity. Part I is played again after the trio but without repeats.

Minuet (Bolzoni)

This minuet follows the same form as the Beethoven. Note particularly that you hear a countermelody in the trio, and that there is a coda or ending to complete the work.

Study Procedures

1. Listen to both the Beethoven and the Bolzoni. Can you follow the form of the Bolzoni? Make a form diagram such as the Beethoven one.

2. Listen to Two Minuets by Sor as played by Narciso Yepes on the guitar.   Do these minuets follow the form used by Beethoven and Bolzoni?
3. Listen also to the early minuets of Mozart, K. 315a.   Although simple in makeup and sound, they still convey the grace and movement of the minuet.   Do you believe that the orchestra adds to the colors and general impression of the minuets as compared to the guitar or piano?   Which method of performance do you believe might have been used under certain circumstances for dancing?   Do we still have dances today in which we use one or two instruments?   And dances in which we use a larger orchestra?

THE WALTZ

In the 1800s the waltz became the world's most popular dance, partly because it came from the folk and although society developed it into a stylish event, it could be danced at any level of manners or ability.   Then, too, it was a dance that accommodated various degrees of movement.   Whereas the minuet was stately and discouraged the steps of folk dances, the waltz used small and gracious motions for those who wished them, or large and springing steps for those who were agile and athletic.

Coming from the folk of the Germanic countries, it incorporated the movements of several active dances with the music of Austria, Germany, and Switzerland; in addition the waltz was the first dance in which the couples embraced, and to some this was inviting and to others most daring.   Early it contained the vestiges of a work song, with the motions imitating in some symbolic way the actions of the work which it originally accompanied.   When it became solely a dance the musical portions were emphasized, the motions and steps became more refined, and it often lost some of its obvious imitation; in its place motions and steps were substituted which symbolized a kind of love play.

About 1775, while most of Europe was dancing the more stiffly defined dances of society, the peasants of southern Germany and Austria were dancing the *ländler*.   Stamping and hopping, they held each other in embrace by placing an arm about the waist; occasionally a gliding step was used, but since they usually wore hobnailed boots and danced on the dirt in the village square or in front of the tavern, gliding was almost impossible.   Occasionally they passed under the arm of the partner, or the man would toss the girl over his shoulder.

Gradually, as this dance made its way into the towns to be danced upon polished floors, more gliding steps were added and the tempo of the music increased.   The interest in this dance increased for all strata of society, so that it spread quickly over all of Europe and England.   But the center of the waltz was Vienna, for it was here where the peasants of southern Germany would come, floating down the Danube on freight boats, bringing their music with them and playing for the taverns and restaurants along the waterfront.

As interest increased, so did the complexities of the footwork.   Dancing schools were not uncommon; younger and older ladies alike, not to mention the gentlemen of the day, were not in any sense a part of their generation if they could not dance the waltz with some ability.

It has usually been true that dancers should respond to the music, but with the waltz this became an even more exact requirement. The general form of the dance remained, but the footwork followed the exact notation of the music. For example, if the music used three equal-valued notes to the measure the steps were appropriate; if the music became more intricate, the steps followed.

(Most of the time in these patterns, the left foot is moved upon the accented beat of the measure, just as with marching in an army unit or a high school band. It can be assumed that marching style came from early dancing.)

The third pattern above was used for a very fast waltz in which young people would move as quickly as possible the length of the hall, only to turn and come back as quickly as possible. A Viennese writer of the time, Adolph Bauerle, wrote of this passion:

> The Mondshein-Saal [The moonlight room, a dance hall] made an immortal name for itself by the mortality among the young people who visited it, and there danced nothing but the Langaus [the dance based upon the third pattern above]. At that time it was the fashion to be a dashing dancer, and the man had to waltz his partner from one end of the hall to the other with the greatest possible speed. If one round of the immense hall had been considered sufficient, one might perhaps have allowed this bachantic dance to pass. But the circle had to be made six to eight times at a breathless speed and without pause. Each couple tried to outdo the other and it was no rare thing for an apoplexy of the lungs to put an end to the madness. Such frightful intermezzi finally made the police forbid the Langaus.[2]

So great was the influence of the dance that composers everywhere contributed to the waltz. Not only the dance composers of the day, but also some of the great composers of all time such as Mozart, Haydn, Schubert, and Dittersdorf wrote music in waltz style, along with the hacks of the period as well as the rural folk who created their own tunes, some of which no doubt were borrowed and appropriated by others. Music was everywhere in Vienna. Each park, tavern, restaurant, and public house, whether small or large, had its orchestra. The music of the waltz and its devotees abounded. Peasants came from rural areas with violins, a clarinet, a guitar, and perhaps a string bass, and wandered about the streets playing and seeking employment. Even the musicians had categories such as *Tafelmusikgeiger* (table music fiddler), or *Bierfiedler* (beer fiddler for the tavern), or *Bratgeiger* (roast meat fiddler), depending upon where the person played and at what point during the meal.

2 *The Waltz,* Mosco Carner. Max Parish and Co. Ltd., London, 1948, page 25.

Washing girls dancing the waltz in Vienna at the height of its craze
(Courtesy of the Austrian National Library)

Through all of this music making three names stand out in history as the great musicians of the time and the greatest composers of waltzes: Joseph Lanner, Johann Strauss the elder, and Johann Strauss the younger. The elder Strauss began his career playing violin with Lanner in a five-piece orchestra. When the demand for music became great and his popularity increased, the orchestra was enlarged, then divided, and Strauss was placed in charge of the second group. Soon afterward, he was leading his own orchestra. Some years later, his son was a director of still another orchestra. All three of these gentlemen directed not only one orchestra, but several orchestras, dashing from one garden, dance hall, or restaurant to another, spending twenty minutes here and thirty there. In addition, there was a constant demand for compositions, and all three contributed to the form of the waltz and to its refinement. The waltz advanced from a peasant expression to a highly stylized dance with long introductions and codas or endings between which were several waltzes combined under one descriptive title, which appealed to the Viennese but also gives us some indication of the romance of the times.

But historical events and political pressures conspired to bring the gay, musical period in Vienna to a close, and with it came the end of the waltz emphasis throughout the world. However, the form continued dynamic in musical composition, and the waltz maintained a vital role throughout opera, ballet, and solo literature, as well as influencing larger forms such as the symphony.

Johann Strauss the Younger in 1899 (Courtesy of the Austrian National Library).

Through the mid-nineteenth century, when the waltz was at its peak of influence, a musical style developed wherein graceful rhythms, kaleidoscopic musical feelings, enchanting melodies, and attractive orchestrations all combined to the enhancement of music generally. In addition, instrumental music implanted itself deeply into the hearts of the populace so that it became more meaningful than ever before. It proved that instrumental music could describe the feelings of the composer and that these feelings could be shared by large numbers of people.

The Strauss Waltz

Lanner composed 112 waltzes, 25 Ländlers, 10 quadrilles, 3 polkas, and 28 galops; Johann Strauss the elder composed 152 waltzes, 24 galops, 13 polkas, 32 quadrilles, and 18 marches; Johann Strauss the younger composed 500 pieces of dance music, most of which were waltzes. Although both Strausses were famous, it was the younger whose reputation became worldwide because of his compositions; one of his waltzes, *The Blue Danube,* is probably the most celebrated of all.

In *The Blue Danube* the symphonic sounding introduction hints at the main theme of the waltz. The coda or ending, similar to the introduction, is brief but equally significant, giving a balance to the musical construction.

The number of individual waltzes in this composition becomes obvious with careful listening.

If you hear a number of Strauss waltzes notice the similarity of style, the movement of the melodic lines, the subtle afterbeats of the rhythm, the length of the introductions and codas, and the manner in which the melodies indicate a sway of movement for the dancing. Many persons have favorites among the Strauss waltzes, and you may enjoy one or more of these: *Tales of the Vienna Woods, Roses from the South, Wine, Woman, and Song, Vienna Blood, Voices of Spring,* and *Morning Papers.*

Think of this dance form not only as an accompaniment for the dance itself, but also as an instrumental composition which captures in its orchestration, its melodies, and its rhythm those very characteristics which relate the charm of the era, the musicality of the city, the grace of the ballroom; and underlying all of this the creativity, the love of life, and the expressiveness of the rural people.

Study Procedures

1. Waltzes have been popular not only in Vienna; they have a large audience even at the present time. Why is this true? Why does the Strauss waltz seem the epitome of a gay, likable dance tune?
2. Listen to those waltzes listed above. Which is your favorite? Why? Answer by considering the melodic lines, the rhythm, the introductions, and codas. What is different enough within each to influence you?
3. How would you compare the waltz to the minuet? Do you believe the music is an outgrowth of the dance, or the dance an outgrowth of the music?

The Concert Waltz

With so great an interest in the waltz, it was destined to become a concert form as well as a dance. Carl Maria von Weber gave the original impetus to such a step. He was probably first to place the waltz onto the concert stage, with his piano composition *Invitation to the Dance.* Although later imitated by Strauss and others, it was he who gave it an introduction which was poetical in character, and it was his piece whose coda was reminiscent of the introduction, giving the form greater unity than many of the earlier dances. Likewise, it was he who used the return of the first waltz to aid this unity rather than employ a string of disconnected dances. All of these features were copied by most composers, especially Strauss the younger.

Since that time in Vienna, almost every composer of note has written concert waltzes. Some have been written for orchestra, others for small groups of

*The waltz craze comes to America: Johann Strauss the Younger
conducting a waltz concert in Boston (Courtesy of Austrian
National Library).*

instruments or a solo instrument. Tchaikovsky has written several waltzes, all
of which make delightful listening. One universal favorite with listeners is
from the *Serenade for Strings* in C, op. 48. This waltz has no introduction or
coda as used by Strauss, probably because it is a movement of a larger work.

La Valse (Ravel)

Ravel wrote one of the great compositions associated with the waltz. As an
impressionist he wished to give a general effect for the feeling of this dance
without writing "just another waltz." Almost as if one were involved with a
vague remembrance, Ravel paints a scene not only for the ear but for the mind
as well. The score contains the following statement by Ravel:

> Whirling clouds give glimpses, through rifts, of couples waltzing. The
> clouds scatter little by little. A huge hall filled with a twirling crowd is
> revealed. The scene gradually is illuminated. At the fortissimo the light of
> the chandeliers bursts forth. An Imperial Court about 1855.

This musical composition in no way relies upon the dance to portray what
it intends. Rather, the music speaks to the senses and feelings through combina-

tions of sounds, so that each of us may define the scene in a manner suitable to our own backgrounds and perceptions.

The work is in three parts, each growing in intensity:

a. *Birth of the Waltz*—Rumblings of melody take shape, following a throbbing, regular rhythm. The melody forms are interspersed with short silences; finally the melody breaks through to—
b. *The Waltz*—Seemingly unrestrained by reality, we hear a greater and more complex sound than Strauss. The music is melodic, yet it gives the impression of swirling and moving with less emphasis upon the form of the melody than upon the overall effect. It returns to the original theme, then moves into the—
c. *Apotheosis* (supreme exaltation of an idea)—Introduced by high woodwinds and harp glissandos, the sounds of the introduction return followed by a fantasy of a waltz. The melodic phrases, in several tonalities, mount in intensity of pitch and tempo. The ending calls for the complete orchestra in a phantasmagoria of sound in which all instruments recall the waltz and the concentration of living around it.

Canticle No. 1 (Harrison)

Lou Harrison, a contemporary composer, used the waltz as the format for this contemporary composition. Written for the dance department of Mills College, this is not an ordinary waltz but has several unique characteristics, the most obvious being that it features only percussion instruments. Listen to this short composition and try to feel the waltz rhythm and the waltz meter. What kind of dance do you imagine would be presented with this music?

Study Procedures

1. Listen to *Invitation to the Dance* by Weber with an understanding that the form of this composition established itself in most later compositions, even on the dance floor.
2. What is different about the Ravel composition as compared to the Strauss waltzes? Describe these differences in your own words.
3. Can you think of any other dance form which has been concertized in the same way as the waltz? Consider the popular field and dance music of the past several years.

ADDITIONAL DANCE FORMS

At the time of the waltz the rise of nationalism in the arts was prominent. Consequently, other national dances became popular also. None ever reached the general acclaim of the waltz, yet from many peoples came their native dances, bringing into the literature of music many interesting and attractive forms.

The Poles contributed the *mazurka;* the Czechs, the *polka;* the French, the *quadrille* and the *galop;* the Spanish brought the *seguidilla,* and the Cubans, the *habanera;* from South America came the *tango,* and from Russia, the *gopak.* This is not a complete list, but these dances have attained particular acceptance in instrumental literature because of the attractiveness of their basic characteristics and their universal appeal.

The Polka

Originally a round dance, the polka lost this link to the past when it came into society. For a short time the favorite dance of Paris, it created such a stir that there were those who thought it would become as popular as the waltz. When it came to the United States Polk was running for the presidency, and you can imagine the play on words that was created. In duple time, it is usually played at about the tempo of a slow march. It has pleasant melodies, most of which are playful and humorous. In recent years the Polish people have taken over this dance but the characteristic rhythms that really separate it from other duple dances still remain.

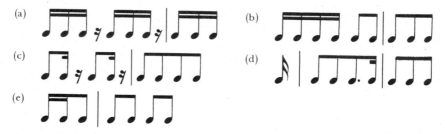

Polka from *The Bartered Bride* by Smetana. This well-known polka is from a comic opera concerned with the folk of Czechoslovakia. In this composition rhythm (e) is followed by rhythm (c).

Pizzicato Polka by Strauss. This is based upon the reverse of (b) rhythm.

Tritsch-Tratsch Polka by Strauss. The rhythms employed are (a) and (d); others are used in the trio. Form: ABA; trio, CDC; return, ABA.

Galop

This is the fastest dance that we will study. Originally a round dance, it is executed with hopping steps.

Geneviève de Brabant by Offenbach. The first part uses this rhythm:

The trio of this famous galop apparently was well-known in the United States at one time because it has become a song for one of the military services. You will enjoy hearing this original version of a well-known tune.

Auf der Jagd by Strauss. Notice the sound effects for this galop, which come from the percussion section. The title means "From the Hunt."

Ohne Sorgen by Strauss. The title means "Without Fear"; hence, the mood is gay with little or no concerns.

Gopak

Gopak by Mussorgsky, from *The Sorochintsy Fair*. This piece comes from an opera left unfinished at his death, which treats of peasant life in the Ukraine. The Gopak ends Act One. The dance, in duple time, is of modest tempo and has an Eastern flavor in the melodic line and rhythm but a Western orchestration.

Tango

A dance of African origin transplanted into South America during the 1800s, it became mixed there with Spanish rhythms and melodies. It arrived in Europe in 1915, soon to become popular all over the world. Originally it was a dance by one couple, full of sex implications in which slow movements conveyed the meanings of their feelings. Part of its success was due, no doubt, to the fact that it was so different from the popular jazz dances of the period. Similar in rhythm to the habanera, except faster, the tempo should increase toward the end.

The most famous tango is one by Albéniz. Strangely, it does not follow the well-known formulas; hence it should be played at about the same tempo as the habanera with no increase in speed to the end. Despite this, it has been accepted as an attractive instrumental piece conveying a type of Spanish flavor.

Habanera

Most authorities believe that this dance originated in Spain, traveled through Africa to Cuba, and thence back to Spain. The name comes from Havana, but its rhythms and style come from the Spanish and the African. Review the "Habanera" from the first Act of Bizet's *Carmen* which we studied in Chapter 12, for there we have a good example of this form in vocal style. The dance is usually in two parts, the first being in the minor and the second in the major. Usually in regular phrases of eight or sixteen measures, this singing dance had become famous as an instrumental form in addition to its use in *Carmen*. Two rhythms will be heard: the first, a syncopation, the second, guitarlike.

Three habaneras are popular as instrumental selections:

Habanera (Chabrier). The short introduction imitative of the guitar is followed by the oboe solo using rhythm (a). The rhythm throughout the entire composition is subtle and the tempo is a moderate duple. The cello plays a countermelody at the repeat of the main theme.

Habanera (Sarasate). This composition is for solo violin, and is more gypsy in flavor than Spanish. This selection uses rhythm (b), and as the composition proceeds the variations in the violin convey a feeling for the skill of the performer rather than a singing dance. The tempo in this instance is faster than usual.

Habanera (Ravel). Most of the composition uses rhythm (b), but the piano uses (a) in its upper register occasionally. Slow, pensive, more Spanish in character than the preceding composition, it places less emphasis upon technic; consequently, it seems more songlike. This habanera has a definite character and portrays it consistently.

Study Procedures

1. Compare three national dances in style, tempo, rhythm, use of melodic line, and general effect. Which would be your first choice for listening? Why?
2. Choose a dance form not discussed in this chapter and trace its history from folk dance to concert piece. Does it follow a route similar to a dance discussed in this chapter? Has it been readily accepted as an instrumental form? If not, why?

Contemporary Influences

The dance has influenced the contemporary composer and Peter Schat, a young Dutch musician, responds with his composition *Dances from "The Labyrinth."* Explosive sounds are pitted against musical rhythms; moments of hesitation prepare for the next irregular outburst. The dance seems not of the body but of organismic matter, as if we were observing the violent movement of part of nature.

Study Procedures

1. Listen to *Dances from "The Labyrinth,"* and describe the dance which the composition would accompany.
2. How does this compare to the peasant dances of the earlier part of the chapter? To the refined dances which grew from peasant dances?
3. Why is this composition entitled Dance? Is it a misnomer?

Bibliography—Chapter 14

CARNER, MOSCO, *The Waltz.* London: Max Parrish and Co. Ltd., 1948.

CRANE, FREDERICK, *Materials for the Study of the 15th Century Basse Dance.* New York: Institute of Medieval Music, Ltd., 1968.

DOLMETSCH, MABEL, *Dances of Spain and Italy, 1400 to 1600.* London: Routledge and Kegan Paul, Ltd., 1954.

HURST, LOUIS, *Pre-Classic Dance Forms.* New York: Kamin Dance Publishers, 1960.

LAWLER, LILLIAN, *The Dance in Ancient Greece.* Middletown, Conn.: Wesleyan University Press, 1965.

NETTL, PAUL, *The Dance in Classical Music.* New York: Philosophical Library, 1963.

———, *The Story of Dance Music.* New York: Philosophical Library, 1947.

REESER, EDUARD, *History of the Waltz.* Stockholm: Continental Book Company, n.d.

SACHS, CURT, *World History of the Dance.* New York: W. W. Norton and Company, Inc., 1937.

WOOD, MELUSINE, *More Historical Dances.* London: Imperial Society of Teachers of Dancing, Inc., 1956.

Recordings—Chapter 14

Albéniz	*Tango*	Berlin Orchestra	MGM E 3910
Beethoven	*Minuet in G*	Carmen Dragon and orchestra	Capitol P-8542
Bolzoni	*Minuet*	Carmen Dragon	Capitol P-8542
Bolzoni	*Minuet*	Boston Pops	Victor LM-2213
Cabezón	*Pavane and Variations*	Marie Claire Jamet, harp	Nonesuch H-71098
Chabrier	*Habanera*	Ansermet	London LL-1404
Estampie	*Masterpieces of Music Before 1750*	Haydn Society	HSE-9038
Harrison	Waltz: *Canticle No. 1*		Mainstream MS-5011
Milan	*Two Pavanes for Guitar*	*Spanish Music for Guitar*	London LL-1042
Mozart	*Eight Minuets and Trios, K. 315a*	Walter Gieseking	Capitol Seraphim ID-6049
Mussorgsky	*Gopak*	Ansermet	London LL-1404
Offenbach	*Geneviève de Brabant:* "Galop"	Boston Pops	Victor LM-1990
Praetorius	Two Branles Pavane	Conrad Instrumental Ensemble	Nonesuch H-71128
Ravel	*Habanera*	Michael Rabin	Capitol P-8506
Ravel	*Pavane for a Dead Princess*	Reiner, Chicago Symphony	Victor LM-2183
Ravel	*La Valse*	Pittsburgh Symphony	Capitol P-8475
Sarasate	*Habanera*	Michael Rabin	Capitol P-8506
Schat	*Dances from "The Labyrinth"*	Boulez, Amsterdam	Radio Nederland L-109517
Schein	Two Pavanes from *Banchetto Musicale*	Conrad Instrumental Ensemble	Nonesuch H-71128

Schubert	*German Dances*	Craft, Columbia Symphony	Columbia MS-6344
Schubert	*Ländler*	William Kapell	Victor LM-1791
Smetana	*Polka*	Berlin Orchestra	MGM E-3910
Sor	Two Minuets	*Spanish Guitar Music*	London LL-1042
J. Strauss	*Auf der Jagd*	Vienna Philharmonic	London CM-9042
J. Strauss	*The Blue Danube*	Vienna Philharmonic	Victor LBC-1008
J. Strauss	*The Blue Danube*	Vienna Philharmonic	London CM-9042
J. Strauss	*Morning Papers*	Vienna Philharmonic	Victor LBC-1008
J. Strauss	*Ohne Sorgen*	Vienna Philharmonic	London CM-9042
J. Strauss	*Pizzicato Polka*	Vienna Philharmonic	Victor LBC-1008
J. Strauss	*Roses from the South*	Vienna Philharmonic	Victor LBC-1008
J. Strauss	*Tritsch-Tratsch Polka*	Vienna Philharmonic	Victor LBC-1008
J. Strauss	*Voices of Spring*	Vienna Philharmonic	Victor LBC-1008
J. Strauss	*Voices of Spring*	Vienna Philharmonic	London CM-9042
Susato	Collection of Dances: Basse Danse Branle Two Rondes Basse Dance Two Pavanes	Pro Musica	Decca DL-9419
Tchaikovsky	Polka and Waltz from *Album for the Young*	Dorfmann	Victor LM-1856
Tchaikovsky	"Waltz of the Flowers" from *The Nutcracker*	Berlin Orchestra	MGM E-3910
Tchaikovsky	Waltz from *Serenade for Strings*	Berlin Orchestra	MGM E-3910
Weber	*Invitation to the Dance*	Brailowsky	Victor LM-1918

Chapter 15

Pop Music Overlay

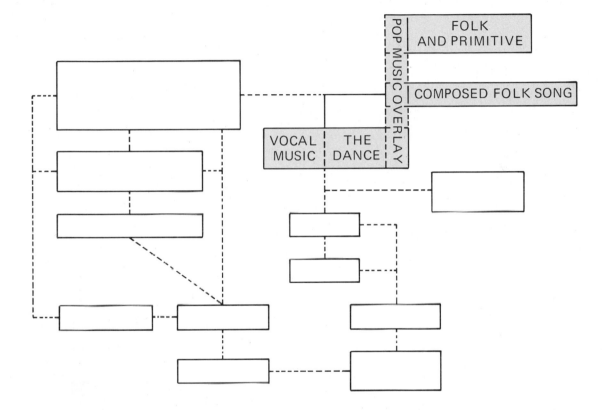

Since the early 1900s popular music has been more often a type of dance music replacing an earlier vocal emphasis. However, it refuses to relinquish its long-time association with folk song and its equally strong tie with composed folk music.

The preceding chapter chart places the area of popular music over and to the left of the foundational blocks of Folk Song and Composed Folk Song. It also overlays the area block Music from the Dance.

Popular music's position on the chart shows it as an independent area, as an associate with instrumental forms, and also indicates it as a bridge between many instrumental ideas and their roots in vocal expression.

The second chart shows in detail the popular music section and subsections which overlay the three areas mentioned above. By looking at the second chart one will ascertain in greater detail those subsections which overlay Folk Song, Composed Folk Song, and Music from the Dance. In the chapter which follows, we will consider the background of several of these subsections. Not all of them will be discussed; nor will they contain the detail some readers may wish. This large area has elicited numerous publications, many of which can be found in almost any library. The main points will be discussed in this chapter but additional readings should be sought, since many young people have a keen interest in certain of these areas. Our discussion will not attempt to place them in a chronology, nor should you evaluate them solely in terms of the amount of material mentioned.

MUSIC IN AFRICAN CULTURE

During the past two centuries Western civilization has been impressed with the backwardness and savagery of African peoples. In contrast, twentieth century anthropologists have discovered information to negate such ideas. Also in contrast, early explorers wrote of their visits to Africa and of its highly civilized peoples with complex cultures. For example, Richard Jobson, explorer for King James I of England in 1623, wrote: "There is without a doubt no people on the earth more naturally affected to the sound of musicke than these people."[1] His detailed description of their living habits proved an entirely different reaction than that of the European exploiters of a later time. Mungo Park, another English explorer about 1800, stated: "With the love of music is naturally connected a taste for poetry, and fortunately for the poets of Africa, they are not neglected."[2]

It is true that great kingdoms existed in Africa until conquered by the white man in the nineteenth century. The people had highly organized religious systems, no written language but a complex oral system of communication, a carefully executed system of law and equity, a continuous census, a pride of history and tradition, organized farming and stock raising, moral and ethical codes, a guild system including one for music, highly developed arts and crafts, and a freedom for and acceptance of women which superceded anything in Europe or America until the twentieth century.

Music played an important part in the life of the African. Indeed, there was music for every activity including marriages, funerals, love, war, festivals, religious occasions, and work. Most of these involved songs, instrumental accompaniments, and dances. In some cases it was difficult to separate them, since the dance, the song, and the accompaniment were closely interwoven. But all were based upon their oral tradition or the inflection and rhythm of the song.

[1] *Readings in Black American Music,* compiled and edited by Eileen Southern. W. W. Norton and Company, Inc., New York, 1971, page 1.
[2] *Ibid.,* page 7.

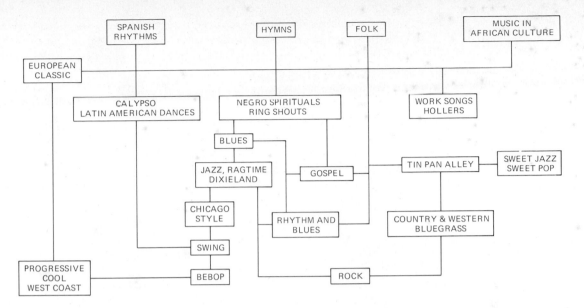

Two musical characteristics were less advanced in African culture than in Western civilization. Harmony was seldom present. Although antiphonal responses were prevalent, there was little counterpoint as such and little use of chordal harmony. The harmony of multiple rhythms can rarely qualify as an example of the term. Secondly, African melody was tied closely to the rising and falling of speech inflections so that a vocal melody had to take the meaning of the word into consideration. If a word was stated or sung at a high pitch it carried one meaning, and if at a low pitch, something entirely different. Consequently, the limitations on melody were rigid.

Four highly developed musical characteristics carried more intricacy than in Western civilization. Improvisation was a standard element of all music. While the melodies and words were known and used consistently, they did not have a specific set form, and the musician or singer was expected to modify the song in some manner appropriate to the feeling of the situation associated with each performance. This was not considered just an embellishment but a creative act. Tied closely to this idea was the characteristic of vocalized tone. In the singing, and later in the playing of instruments, the African treated the melody only as a tune and not as the true expression of its meaning. Consequently, tones were rarely begun at pitch but usually above or below. The amount above or below, or the length of time for this deviation of pitch, depended upon the interpreter and the situation surrounding the singing. In Western music one strives for a highly regulated pitch, a regulated time, a concise timbre, and if used, a controlled vibrato. All of these were left to the discretion of the performer as he worked with a given pitch of the melody.

Thirdly, and perhaps most complex, was the musical characteristic of rhythm. Until recently, in European tradition rhythm had been treated linearly. The African treated rhythm vertically, using two or more rhythms simultaneously and usually of different accents and meters. This complexity, aided by the use of different timbres, demanded that the performer feel and adhere to a strict underlying pulsation to hold the rhythms together. The single patterns were not overly complex, but the combination of these patterns with their cross accents provided an intricate result.

Closely associated with rhythm was the musical characteristic of tension. Western music produces tension through an increase in loudness built upon coincidence of melodic accents with time accents. In African music the melodic accents, usually free of rhythmic pulsation (since the latter may be complex, a regular pulsation might be difficult to follow), sometimes occur with the underlying rhythm, but just as often they fall between the underlying rhythmic pulsations. Tension results by staggering these accents.

The African knew or realized two points which are only recently coming to the attention of musical psychologists. 1) Rhythm is a way of transmitting an experience so that it becomes real to the person hearing and feeling it. Because it affects the breathing, the heart pulse, and the brain patterns, rhythm shares with others the feelings about an experience in such a way that they too feel they have witnessed it firsthand. 2) Since the oral man stores information through a living of the experience as the literate man stores information through writing, then, as McLuen might say, the oral man becomes the information. If he lives the experience, it is a part of him. If rhythm then can produce for man a synthesis of an experience, it appears possible for rhythm to alter the experiential areas of man affecting not only the immediate but possibly later attitudes as well.

As we read through this chapter we will be aware that the African, upon being brought to America, Haiti, South America, and other localities, absorbed the culture dominant in the area where he found himself to the extent necessary for life in a new and changing world, but he retained some aspects of African life where he found psychological stability or no satisfactory substitutes.

Study Procedures

1. Discuss points 1 and 2 above in relation to your own experience. Under what conditions have these been true for you? Do you believe that this is more apt to be true for rock music because of its emphasis upon rhythm?
2. Listen to one or more recordings of African music and ascertain the musical characteristics discussed in this section of the chapter. The American Indian places considerable emphasis upon rhythm and less upon melody and harmony. To what extent do you believe these musics are similar? Can you explain why?

WORK SONGS, HOLLERS, AND RING SHOUTS

Hollers were a simple, sung expression of one person in reaction to his environment. Rarely were they tuneful as a song, but they were often consistent; some were individualized and could be recognized as belonging to one person.

There were hollers of different types. Some communicated to others, such as a type of greeting to a girl in the distance, or the call of one man to his wife in another field or another plantation; some were hollers to call workers from the fields, to a different field, or to begin work; some made one's whereabouts known to others, or were ways of keeping in touch.

Other hollers communicated only to oneself. These were self-expressions or vocalizations of emotion, much as we find some people today talking aloud to themselves when worried, when surprised, when falling down, or stubbing a toe; a worker in the field may sing a holler as an outcry against the hot sun, fatigue, or the length of the working day; it could be a declaration of joy for good feeling; it could be a release of tension; or it could be a bolstering of the spirit when alone.

Although many of the hollers used words, the text was usually not as important as the sound. Many of them were wordless and yet communicated the situation. Most often they were the oral expression of a personality that was fearful of losing completely his inner self. Whereas we today rely upon words for communication, the black man felt the individuality of the person through an expression of vocal pitch and coloration. The tonal qualities of the voice could describe the extent and exuberance of association in a group or the intent of the communication.

This was a rural musical expression, and many city blacks considered it beneath them to participate, but they would be able to recognize another black by his individual holler. The city had its different types of hollers for food vendors, chimney sweeps, fish peddlers, or junk buyers.

Singing as he worked was commonplace with the African native, so it was only natural that he should continue this in the fields of Haiti, Jamaica, the West Indian Islands, or the Southern states of our country. In ordinary work the entire group might sing in unison; if working alone a simple song might be used. However, with certain kinds of work, particularly those requiring group effort or some specialization, a leader sang and the rest of the group responded.

The leader was more than the person who supplied the verse of the song so that the remainder could sing the refrain. He was a person who had to know the rhythm of the work and to determine the speed of the tasks so that the men could work well together. The rhythm would keep the tasks moving at a pace fast enough for efficiency and completion. Many a slave was bought at a higher price when he was advertised as a singer and leader of work rhythms. In addition to his assistance with the work, the leader was also an entertainer. His task was to choose the song, to make up new ones, and to provide humor at the appropriate time by using the men or the boss as the point of a joke.

Many kinds of texts could be used for a work song, but its rhythm must fit the task. Since the song often kept the mind of the worker from the difficulty of the effort, the song often would not mention the kind of work for which it was used. One humorous song was a reworking of the Lord's Prayer:

Our father who is in heaven,
White man owe me eleven and pay me seven.
Thy kingdom come, Thy will be done,
And if I hadn't taken that, I wouldn't have none.[3]

Another work song appealed to the worker through a romantic situation. The spaces in the center and end of each line indicate the moment in rhythm when the worker would be expected to pound, pull, or complete some task:

Well, she asked me . . . . . in de parlor . . . . .
An' she cooled me . . . . . wid her fan . . . . .
An' she whispered . . . . . to her mother . . . . .
"Mamma, I love that . . . . . dark eyed man . . . . ."
Well, I ask her . . . . . mother for her . . . . .
An she said she . . . . . was too young . . . . .
Lord, I wished I . . . . never had seen her . . . . .
An' I wished she . . . . . never been born . . . . .
Well, I led her . . . . . to the altar . . . . .
An' de preacher . . . . . give his comman' . . . . .
An' she sware by . . . . . God that made her . . . . .
That she never . . . . . love nuther man . . . . .[4]

Each line relies upon a bit of suspense before its completion while the worker considers what has already been sung.

The form of the work songs varied, and this aided their ability to fit a number of situations and remain attractive to the workers. Thus, the leader had to know a number of songs to fit the rhythm of a large variety of work.

The following forms exemplify the variety of response in various examples. The leader sings those sections given a capital letter, and the workers respond where lowercase letters are found. The letter R is used for the refrain. A fraction indicates the latter half of A or B.

1. A, R, r, B, r, C, r, etc.
2. A, a, B, b, C, c, etc.
3. A, r, B, r, C, r, etc.
4. A, r, A, r, B, r, B, r, C, r, C, r, etc.
5. A, $\frac{a,}{2}$ B, $\frac{b,}{2}$ C, $\frac{c,}{2}$ etc.
6. Unison singing of leader and workers together.

Music was not only an activity but it was a way of performing an act. The black participated in the group experience partly through his actions and presence, but just as much through his vocalization of the music. He was not an observer but a participator, and his vocal expression told the community about his participation.

---

[3] *Black Music in America,* John Rublowsky. Basic Books, Inc., New York, 1971, page 66.

[4] *The Negro and His Songs,* Howard Odum and Guy B. Johnson. Folklore Associates, Inc., Hatboro, Penn., 1964, page 258.

In his religion he was not an audience, he was meant to become part of the experience. The work leader was the judge of the activity that could be performed, just as the religious leader was the judge of the religious activity that the group was psychologically ready for at any given time. Both were successful if they could move the group through rhythm from one point to another.

The *ring shout,* like the work song, was a group expression. Whereas the latter involved music, work, and movement, the former involved music, movement, and devotion. After prayers, testimonies, and regular hymns, the benches were shoved back and the persons in attendance at the meeting would move about the floor in a ring, shuffling and stamping as they sang a spiritual. Some congregations used two kinds of spirituals, regular spirituals and runnin' spirituals, the latter belonging strictly to the ring shout. The shout was not particularly loud, but the term indicated the emotional involvement of the entire expression through its singing, the rhythmic sound of the feet and the voices, the feelings associated with worship and movement. Those persons who crossed their feet during the movement were considered to be dancing and would be dismissed from the church. Since African worship included dancing, particularly those portions involving supplication, the black retained the custom of his African background but did not violate the spirit of the rule of no dancing in the church of his new culture.

Study Procedures

1. Many young people use contemporary versions of the holler in their everyday activities. How do these sound and what do they signify?
2. What is the modern version of the work song? Do you believe this to be as effective as the older singing type? Why?
3. Listen to work songs and hollers from some of the original recorded material. Can you hear differences in the style of the form?

SPIRITUALS

The *spiritual* is a religious folk song and differs particularly from, yet contains certain similarities to, the psalm of the Reformed Church and the hymn (see Chapter 5). While the psalms were metrical versions of the Biblical verses, and the hymns were poetic religious expressions, the spirituals were free spirit-motivated songs which grew from the emotionally charged atmosphere of the camp meeting.

Two distinct types of spirituals exist: the white spiritual, and the Negro spiritual. The former came into prominence during the early decades of the nineteenth century as an outgrowth of the frontier and the Second Great Awakening, and has persisted in certain closely-knit areas of our country up to the present. Negro spirituals were first sung between 1830 and 1865, aroused attention on the part of the white population about 1865, and since 1880 have been used for local color and as entertainment.

During the late 1700s the Scotch, Scotch-Irish, and Germans came to our country in conspicuous numbers. Landing at Philadelphia, some of the Germans settled in the farm areas of eastern Pennsylvania; others, along with the Scotch and Scotch-Irish, moved south into the hills and valleys of Virginia, Kentucky, and Tennessee. Here the Germans adopted the Scotch-Irish style of singing.

It was in Kentucky that the first camp meeting was held in 1800, during the peak of the Second Awakening. At first these protracted meetings made use of the usual psalms and hymns. However, because of the more informal atmosphere of the meetings, a type of informal singing evolved. Because of the emotional impact of these meetings, emotional music was a natural outcome. One narrator tells of the camp meeting spiritual:

> Spontaneous song became a marked characteristic of the camp meetings.
> Rough and irregular couplets or stanzas were concocted out of scripture
> phrases and every-day speech, with liberal interspersing of hallelujahs and
> refrains. Such ejaculatory hymns were frequently started by an excited audi-
> tor during the preaching, and taken up by the throng, until the meeting dis-

An early American Camp Meeting (Courtesy of Kenneth M. Newman,
Old Print Shop, New York).

solved into a singing ecstacy culminating in a general hand-shaking (or walk around which led to the ring shout). Sometimes they were given forth by a preacher who had a sense of rhythm, under the excitement of his preaching and the agitation of his audience. Hymns were also composed more deliberately out of meeting, and taught to the people or lined out from the pulpit.

Many of the rude songs perished in the using, some were written down, passing from hand to hand. . . .

A distinctive type is thus established, the Camp-Meeting-Hymn. It is individualistic, and deals with the rescue of a sinner, sometimes through direct appeal, sometimes by reciting the terms of salvation, sometimes as a narrative or personal experience for a warning or encouragement. . . .

The literary form of the Camp-Meeting-Hymn is that of the popular ballad or song, in plainest every-day language and of careless or incapable technic. The refrain or chorus is perhaps the predominant feature, not always connected with the subject matter of the stanza, but rather ejaculatory.[5]

In the Southern Uplands this also was the situation, so that some camp meetings in Virginia in 1810 became bilingual, with sermons in German and English being preached simultaneously in different parts of the camp ground. Others were bilingual and interracial. Sutcliff, the English Quaker traveler, describes a Methodist camp meeting held at Merion, Pennsylvania in 1805, at which a great number of black families were in attendance, many of them in handsome carriages. They participated in the singing of spirituals and often sang with greater fervor and loudness than the whites:

What of the Negro in this white man's environment? He was its beneficiary. Whether slave or free (as many of them were) the Negro found himself among real friends—among those who, by reason of their ethnic, social and economic background, harbored a minimum of racial prejudice; among those whose religious practices came nearest to what he, by nature a religious person, could understand and participate in. He found himself a churchless pioneer among those white people who built meeting houses and invited him not only to attend their services and sing their songs but also to join with them in full membership; white people who were concerned not only with his soul's welfare but also even with his release from slavery.[6]

In the year 1800 there were over 20,000 free blacks in Virginia, 20,000 in Maryland, 15,000 in Pennsylvania, 10,000 in New York, and smaller numbers in other seacoast states. These blacks, as well as slaves, were welcomed regularly into the churches of the singing and shouting Reformed Protestant denomina-

---

5 *The English Hymn,* Louis F. Benson. Presbyterian Board of Publication, Philadelphia, 1915, page 284; reprinted 1962.

6 *White and Negro Spirituals,* George Pullen Jackson. J. J. Augustin, Publisher, Locust Valley, N.Y., 1943, page 285.

tions, since the whites recognized their Christian responsibility to them as persons, but also because they accepted them as immigrants in America seeking a new life. Thus we see that at the time the white man was concerned with the camp meeting and its informal singing, the black was in attendance at the meetings and witnessed the turn from the Watts hymns to the spiritual song.

Despite earnest efforts on the part of the evangelical faiths, they could barely keep pace with the importation of blacks, and so to attempt to service the blacks more adequately the concerned denominations, particularly the Baptists, began erecting all-black churches in predominantly black areas. At the same time, it was during these second and third decades of the nineteenth century that the laws of the Southern states became more restrictive concerning the privileges of the black man. For example, whereas once he was permitted to attend public places of worship, his actions became more restricted.

Thus, when the fires of the Second Awakening were dying in the white man's churches the laws were tightening against black attendance at those services. The spirit of the revival and camp meeting continued to burn in the hearts of the churched blacks throughout the South, and when all-black churches were organized they took the style of service and the style of music with them to their own meetings. This is not to say that they sang only the songs of the white man, and that the Negro spiritual was a white man's creation. The white spiritual was the white man's creation, and the Negro spiritual was a reworking of it. Whereas the rural Southerner was primarily a singer not a poet, the black was as adept at word symbolism as at musical creativity. Consequently, the black made the spiritual into a composition expressive of his own soul and his own feelings within the years between 1820 and the Civil War—years which presented the black with an entirely different style of life than he had witnessed in the Colonial Period or the post-Revolutionary era.

The white religious folk song material was about twenty percent ballads (religious storytelling songs usually sung by individuals), forty-six percent hymns (usually emphasizing praise and sung by the group), and thirty-four percent spirituals (camp meeting songs with exhortations and exultations). The black focused more often upon the spiritual and remade hymns into this style, adapted some songs of the whites, or created his own songs of the spirit. It is this latter group, with their picturesque language and poignantly descriptive phrases, for which the black is best-known and through which his creative genius most clearly shines. It was not until the rise of the black Christian tradition that the musical style of black oral culture began to reassert itself. The spiritual aided the re-emergence of an oral tradition and their former creativity. Once begun, it was to continue into the popular field with an outgrowth into instrumental forms.

As inspiration for their songs the blacks did not rely solely upon a small number remembering the camp meetings of the whites during the early days of the 1800s; nor did they rely only upon the preached word by black ministers. Being servants to the white man, they were constantly in touch with the Bible and the songs of the white church as they sat in the slave galleries of the churches and as they heard the Bible read in the children's quarters of the master.

To believe that the spiritual was merely an escape from his troublesome world to a land of dreams, or that it was purely religious, is to miss part of the picture which outlines the social implications of religion and the songs as being equally important. The spiritual sang of the black's thirst for freedom; it spoke of his desire for justice and judgment upon his malefactors, and it relayed his hope for the future. The "I" in the songs was really the editorial "We," and meant some of his relatives in the future if not himself. The spiritual was a communal expression and the black was sharing with others his hopes for the future, for his children, and for himself, if possible. Some of the spirituals were immediate, such as directions for the underground railway, but others were poetic explanations of his hopes and desires.

In summary, the gospel song of the later 1800s and early 1900s copied the music hall or Tin Pan Alley. The spiritual was a folk effervescence applied to and taken from the symbolism of religion.

Study Procedures

1. Listen to a number of spirituals recorded by the Library of Congress or Folkways. How do these differ from those heard in concert or commercial recordings?
2. Many white churches occasionally use a Negro spiritual during their services but never use a white spiritual. How would you account for this?
3. Listen to at least one recorded black service as recorded by the Library of Congress. What of the spiritual do you hear? What of the ring shout? Can you differentiate between spirituals which would be used in a service and those meant as ring shouts? How would you describe the difference?

BLUES

The blues heard in some forms of popular music today differ in style and intent from the early songs of the black.

Blues belong primarily to that period of history after the Civil War when the slaves, being free, could move about the land. The black had been primarily an agricultural worker, and so most of his job-seeking centered in that direction. Many were migrants. If married he had family responsibilities, and some found it difficult to adjust to the freedom of movement and to accept those realities. Civil responsibilities were new to him, and under some circumstances he found them difficult to assume. When employment was not available, when money was scarce, when a wife was untrue or a girl friend did not respect a promise, when the law was broken and no master paid the fine, the black faced a discouraging situation. Hence, the blues.

As slaves, most of their discouragements were discussed and considered by the group. Group problems were sung about in the work songs, the spirituals, and the ring shouts. These new problems were personal ones, and the person was forced to consider these as an individual. A new type of expression, a personal expression, developed. The blues, like the holler, called community attention to a personal concern or misfortune. A buildup of tension needed release, and extemporizing and singing was one outlet. Here was the black talking to himself about the world, attempting to maintain his inner self in equilibrium.

The shout had been an improvised form wherein the caller had repeated lines until a new one had been thought of or because it expressed his feelings well. Some of these new forms, now known as "field blues" or "rural blues," repeated one line over and over, or two lines in some type of alteration. Four lines were often irregular and crudely constructed, but they carried the verbalization of the problem which the person faced. Almost all early blues were unaccompanied. Although the lines were sung, music was secondary to personal meaning. The black was verbalizing. This was important to his polishing of a language which he recognized as significant to his finding employment and a new life. Secondly, he was articulating a problem which confronted him. Some blues probably were singsong without an exact melody; others used borrowed tunes from the hollers, from the ring shouts, or from religious songs or spirituals.

Often the holler was nonverbal or minimally verbal. The blues were poetically verbal and did not develop until the black had gained an ability with the English language.

Early blues, then, were almost any form of simple poetry with repetitive lines and tunes borrowed or copied from other black forms. Copied tunes could be out of character, or they could match the mood of the words. With use, the tunes became more definitive and more closely aligned to and descriptive of the texts, but two additional changes brought focus to the form.

First, the text became more picturesque by including a type of poetic language which the black had felt and only recently had been able to express. The black discovered that the more descriptive the expression the more catharsis he was able to procure. Then too, it was natural that if a song were to find sympathetic feelings beyond the individual, the language had to reflect the experience of a number of persons. Secondly, the words to the songs became more obviously a reflection of the secular world. Although early blues were not religious, later words dealt with a worldliness which indicated an experience based upon travel. Jail, prison camp, the electric chair, discrimination, homesickness, poverty, contacts with many women, the gambler, the outlaw, the railroad, the steamboat, the chain gang, fire and flood, big labor, or little towns presented problems suitable to the blues. Underlying all texts was an inference that one's life was not controlled by himself nor in the hands of a forgiving God, but tossed about by a bitter and futile fate. But despite any series of reverses, despite the melancholy tunes which aided the overall effect, one hears an occasional humor, a bit of hope, a determination to proceed, a recognition that tomorrow may be no better but that the human personality must continue. In this hope the black ties himself back to the spiritual and the nobleness of the Christian faith or the religion of his ancestors.

Although the early texts of the blues were often crude, they did not emphasize the sexual as they did later. By the time the blues had become an entertainment song, both black and white listeners considered this form a sexual expression, with lyrics often becoming vulgar. Most blacks who remember early blues do not recall any sexual implications.

Although the blues began as unaccompanied songs, instruments were added later. The guitar, most often used, permitted the singer to accompany himself as he sang and adapted well to the requirement of a plaintive sound using only three simple chords (I, IV, and V). The harmonica, also an often used instrument, had a coloration which aided the blues and was easily carried.

By the time the blues had solidified as to style and form they became known as "classic," meaning that they had refined themselves through tradition and had arrived at a standard form which was appealing to both creator and listener. Most of the recorded blues are in this form; very few if any of the field or rural blues (not to be confused with the later "country blues") exist because most listeners would not appreciate them. The form contained the elements of earlier black music and had synthesized with the following characteristics:

1. *A three-line poem and song set to twelve measures of music.* Longer by four measures than the usual rhymed couplet used in many simple songs and shorter than the often used four-line stanza, the three-line song achieves its form from a repeated first line. Often the second line alters one or two words in order to bring a new insight to the meaning, a new dimension, or it may repeat it exactly as before. Here we witness the black's attempt to poetically guide our thought or extend the emotion of the phrase. The third line, often the one which explains the first two lines, is the clincher, the punch line for the preceding two. As with the work song described earlier, it prolongs the suspense and then drives home the point.

2. *The establishment of a definite key.* Early blues avoided a sense of tonality or used a pentatonic scale; often pitch alterations were used which avoided the diatonic sound of Western music. With its accompaniment a definite tonal center was established.

3. *The existence of specific chord changes.* With the classic or instrumental blues a definite chord pattern was established: the I chord (built upon the first note of the scale) for four measures, the IV chord (built upon the fourth note of the scale) for two measures, the I chord for two measures, the V^7 for two measures, and the I chord for two measures.

4. *A lack of rigid bar limitation in the melody.* The rhythm of the melodic line does not follow the specified accents of the underlying accompaniment. Rather, it is a free flowing melody, filled with syncopation, with rhythm accents reminiscent of African music.

5. *An infectious melody.* Although early blues borrowed melodies or considered the tune of secondary importance, the tunes for classic blues are distinctive and individual.

6. *Melody completed in the middle or before the end of the phrase.* The verbal portion of the song almost always is considerably shorter than the overall length of the single line, leaving the accompaniment to supply the remainder. When only a singer is involved he often interpolates a portion of the line into the open area. Where instruments are used for accompaniment, they often supply the line with additional material. This kind of statement and answer is a direct carry-over from the responsive African tradition discussed earlier in the chapter. For the student of blues, both parts are essential for complete performance.

7. *The existence of two melodic lines.* As explained in point 6, the voice does not complete the lines of the form, and so another melody is used to esthetically aid the first. The quality of the first melody and the ability of the instrumentalist determine the extent to which the second melody accommodates the first through extension, blue notes, breaks, alterations of intonation, or other devices. The second melody is almost always improvised, while the first melody or known tune is used with a minimum of alterations.

8. *A series of verses, usually in rhyme.* These develop or repeat the theme put forth in the first stanza.

The blues differs from the spiritual mainly in the following ways:

Spirituals	*Blues*
Communal song	Individual song
Religious-centered	Secular-centered
Everyday concerns translated into religious symbolism	Everyday concerns explained in common terminology
No instrumental accompaniment	Began without accompaniment, later used accompaniment
The world is other-centered	The world is self-centered

As instruments gradually adopted the vocal forms in the early 1900s the blues became an instrumental form as well as a vocal one. The instrument did not imitate the voice, although this was evident in some cases, but rather the instrument became a synthesizer of black song and the blues. Playing with melodic improvisations and breaks, exploring the tonal characteristics of the instruments, and still reminding us of the vocal heritage and the text, instruments brought a new dimension, new colorations, and power to the blues without words, which in themselves began to color and drive home the feeling of the individual. The blues were vocal music. When instruments were first used they were imitative of the voice and only slowly took on their own individuality. As the black mastered the instruments he began to think in terms of new colorations rather than vocal extensions. When the blues lost most of its vocal elements, black music changed, and the era of jazz was at hand.

Study Procedures

1. Listen to a number of blues and decide if they are early or late. Do you hear the style characteristics described in this chapter?
2. Why have the blues such universal appeal? To answer this, consider first the text and then the music.
3. What precise characteristics of the blues do you believe to have come from the spiritual? From the hollers? From early Western folk music?
4. Some of your classmates probably can play the chords for the blues on the guitar. As one person plays, have another create a melody for one or two verses of the blues found in one of the texts listed in the bibliography.

JAZZ, RAGTIME, AND EARLY DIXIELAND

Music styles change with the times. Although we can point to one or two major influences, the numerous minor ones usually go unmentioned. So it was with black music.

Although the blues was originally an unaccompanied vocal style, instruments were gradually added. It was the instruments, accompanied by an increased skill on the part of black performers, which effected the change in the music.

Before the Civil War the black had used almost all homemade instruments which either resembled the African ones he remembered or the ones he saw in the culture of the white man. After the war he found standard instruments which he could purchase. Little by little he taught himself to play the tubas, clarinets, trumpets, and trombones of the marching bands famous throughout the South. At first only a vocal style prevailed, the imitation of the song and song forms which he knew and had grown up with.

His freedom of movement permitted the black to come in contact with legitimate instrumental playing of bands and orchestras. In New Orleans French refinements predominately influenced the culturalization of the black. Musically, there were the street and parade bands of the Creoles of New Orleans, the Napoleonic bands of the French which dressed in finery equal to their regimental history, playing for open-air functions through the day and the dances or quadrilles by night. The black imitated these practices by marching for his functions, by dressing in special kinds of clothing even though often ludicrous, by bringing the daytime band into the halls for dancing at night. Black bands marched for weddings, for political rallies, for holidays such as the Fourth of July or Jackson Day, the Carnival or All Saints' Day, for funerals, picnics, boating trips, and the special events sponsored by the large number of clubs, secret societies, and fraternities in the black community. Since most of the members did not read music or read it only falteringly, they imitated the Creole bands to the best of their ability, playing slow marches or Negro spirituals for the funerals, playing their version of the street marches for other events, and their own version of the quadrilles along with some of their own blues for the dances. It was truly a people's music.

The funerals became famous. The march to the cemetery was played in a slow dirgelike tempo using white man's hymns such as "Nearer, My God, to Thee," "Rock of Ages," or "Onward, Christian Soldiers," or a favorite spiritual—all with a military air to maintain the tradition of the funeral march. Following the band were the family and mourners, some singing or moaning, some tapping in rhythm to the slow music. On the return to the town, the band would play a different tune and style, a fast tempo march or quadrille. "Didn't He Ramble" or "When the Saints Go Marching In" were two famous songs which are still heard.

But this music which did not closely follow the tunes, this music which relied much upon improvisation and memory, was considered music of the lower class even by many blacks, who called it "jass" or "dirty music." Even some blacks, as well as the Creoles (blacks of mixed descent) would have little to do with it. But it still served the black man in many ways. The parades continued, and when people were not parading they were in wagons being pulled around the streets advertising a picnic, a church function, or a political candidate. The trumpet played the melody and improvised around it; the clarinet added a high obbligato built mostly upon technic; the trombone, leaning over the back of the wagon (hence the term "tailgate"), played a type of countermelody underneath the trumpet; and the drummer added an individual rhythm which accented and emphasized the melody or improvisations.

In 1897 New Orleans adopted legalized prostitution. Alderman Story had introduced the bill, so that section of the city open to the white men's vice became known as Storyville. Visitors to Storyville appreciated this uninhibited, lowdown music as an accompaniment to the unconventional activities of the sporting houses, since the black "dirty" music better set the atmosphere than the proper music of the literate musicians be they Creole or black. Although Storyville did not promote jazz, it did offer the black an opportunity to play regularly and earn enough to live from his music. Indirectly the music was advertised along with the famous "maisons."

But to give the impression that jazz developed only in New Orleans would be an error, for it was springing up in other cities all over the South. New Orleans did offer more opportunities for playing, and thus probably more opportunities for musical development.

One reason for the attraction of jazz is that the musical language used is familiar to both performers and audience. The listeners usually know the tunes, and in most cases can follow them while they are played. During an improvisation the listener shares the moments of creativity with the performer and mentally, as well as musically, appreciates the turn of the phrase. This creates an esthetic experience different from most music. The music produces a creative force within a recognizable form. The listener knows the form, anticipates its climax and conclusion, and relishes the manner in which the musicians work within these limitations.   After several hearings a listener is in a position to be a judge of good and poor improvisation.   The true artist works with the melody and creates other melodic lines out of, or as a result of, the original, while the second-rate improviser plays solos time after time which are too similar and whose rhythmic and melodic patterns too closely imitate the melodies for which they are intended, or whose rhythm and melodies contain no ingenuity or drive.

Ragtime was predominantly piano music, although its popularity was such that bands did imitate the style.   Unlike jazz, it was composed and written music.   Although imitative of jazz through its use of syncopation, most rags were written for the white man.   The white consumed most of it all over the country, and in the big cities it superceded the "cakewalk" as the popular dance of the day.

In 1893 the World's Fair in Chicago advertised a popular piano competition as part of its activities.   A syncopated kind of piano playing had been judged the most interesting and most creative, and a Chicago newspaper tagged it a "raggy" style.   The name remained and its popularity spread.   Thousands of rags were written, and thousands of sheets of music were sold.   Blacks playing piano in the houses of prostitution, in halls, dives, or bars, learned and wrote the rags at the request of the whites, but their performances always carried a special flavor—not so square and not so forced.

By listening to rags it becomes evident that the form came from the march.   In fact, early rags were called marches and, among other noticeable similarities, changed key at the trio section.   Most standard rags follow the A A B B A C C D D form, with the C and D themes as the trio.

The rags exerted a strong influence on jazz, since they brought a type of virtuosity that had not been as evident earlier, a more complex musical form, an emphasis upon the sixteen or thirty-two–bar strain or section, a realization of and value to the modulation, and a simple harmony which could permit a standardizing of the larger ensemble.

Blacks were not the only group interested in the innovative improvisations called jazz.   The one-time Creole musicians who had looked down their noses at the "dirty" music of the lower class blacks, were pushed into the black community by stricter color laws during the early years of the twentieth century. This forced them to learn jazz in order to join the other groups and to find employment.   But the popularity of the music spread beyond houses of prostitution, poor bars, and dives, and it was being requested at more and more social gatherings.   Consequently, white musicians were adopting the style.   When played by the whites it was known as Dixieland, and because of certain prejudices, it was Dixieland music which came north to the large cities more quickly and was recorded earlier.

Study Procedures

1. Listen to a street march by a New Orleans black band.   What differences do you hear in their method of performance as compared with the usual street march?   What would lead some blacks to refer to this as "dirty" music?

2. Compare an instrumental blues with a vocal one. How do they differ? How are they alike?

3. During the playing of a ragtime piano recording concentrate upon the sounds created by the left hand of the player. Do you hear their rhythm? Their accompaniment function? Does the left hand involve syncopation? It has been stated that true ragtime places the syncopation of the right hand on the second and fourth beats of the measure. Most rags do not follow this rule. How consistent was your composer in this regard?

4. Listen to a New Orleans style recording and discuss the function of each of the instruments in your own words. Through concentration, can you follow each of the instruments as desired during an ensemble chorus?

TIN PAN ALLEY

During the early days of our country most songwriters were amateurs, writing music for the fun of it or because it expressed their feelings. In the early 1800s songwriters were mostly lyric writers and they borrowed their tunes from varied sources. When the minstrel was popular songwriters were either the entertainers who wrote songs for themselves to sing or amateurs who wished to hear their songs performed.

About 1880 the expanding economy of the nation led us to seek entertainment of all kinds. People wished to be entertained, and it made little difference to most if it were a tear-jerking ballad, the rowdy songs of the variety or burlesque stage, the humorous song of the minstrel, or the semioperatic presentation of the European singer. Vocal music was in demand, and those who could supply the nation with this commodity were beginning to establish it as a business. The amateur simply could not supply or distribute enough material, so professional songwriters and commercial distributors came into existence.

At first the song business was made up mostly of young people confident they could supply the entertainment world with music. They came into New York from the farms, from the hill country, and from the poorer housing districts of the large cities and haunted the entertainment centers, restaurants, and theaters around the 14th Street district. These people were not competent theorists or trained musicians, but rather those with quick talents and quick wits, with the clever word and the singable tune.

They made contacts with the entertainers on the sidewalks around 14th Street, in the green rooms of the theaters, or in their hotel rooms. When the theater district moved to 28th Street and the songwriting business had become better established, the larger companies decided they should have "parlors" for the receiving of their clientele. Consequently, they took over the brownstone houses of the area, those houses that at one time had been the homes of the elite who had wished to live "uptown" away from the commercial center; more recently they had been the music studios of the teachers who taught piano and violin to young students. When the music publishers took them over, they made several small cubicles from each room. These cubicles were approximately eight by ten and usually contained a hat rack, a desk, a spittoon, and most importantly, a secondhand, untuned piano. Into these cubicles would come the singers and entertainers of the day to hear the latest songs, to learn them by rote, and to be trained in how the song could be "sold." The persons who did the training were usually a two-man team, a vocalist and a pianist. Many of the great names of popular music began either as the "plugger" (the vocalist) or the accompanist.

It was also in these same cubicles that the songwriters hammered out their new creations. Many of these writers placed newspaper between the strings of the piano to muffle the sound so that their new songs would not be heard in the hall by a loafing writer from another publisher, or outside the open window when summer heat made the cubicles almost unbearable.

Many are the stories concerning the origin of the name given this small geographic area where music thrived. Some say that the writer O. Henry dubbed the area; others give credit to Rosenfeld, a songwriter and sometime journalist as he conversed with Harry von Tilzer in his cubicle and, hearing the latter pound upon his newspaper-stuffed piano, remarked that it "sounded like a Tin Pan; in fact, the entire area sounds like a lot of tin pans; this is just like a tin pan alley." The name stuck, and has been used ever since to signify the commercial music business.

Tin Pan Alley, West 28th St., New York (Courtesy of Culver Pictures, Inc., New York).

When Tin Pan Alley was at its height of effectiveness in the days just around the turn of the century, one could get off a horse-drawn streetcar at the corner of 28th and Broadway and, walking east toward Fifth Avenue, pass the office of almost every music publisher in the business. By the time you had come to Everard's Cafe, a hangout for the pluggers and songwriters, you would have walked about a block and a half and would have passed the Tin Pan Alley brownstones.

While the products of the songwriters were common throughout the land, it was the song pluggers who lived the romantic life of the Gay Nineties. The music publisher or his plugger had to know his way around the city or go out of business before long. This was a life that put you in touch with the Bowery beer joints, the famous downtown red-light districts, the uptown cafes with their elegance and elegant customers, and the theaters; the plugger had to be at home in them all:

On a typical evening he might start at the Atlantic Gardens on the Bowery where an all-girl orchestra would, for a round of drinks, play several of his tunes. They would, that is, if the plugger got there early enough to treat the ladies before rival publishers' men managed to buy up all the time the evening contained.

The plugger carried with him a set of parts for the orchestra and a quantity of chorus slips on which were printed the lyrics of the tune's refrain. The slips were distributed by his own hand among the guests seated at tables or standing at the long, well-worn bar.

When the orchestra struck up the first notes, the plugger jumped up and beckoned the revelers to join in the chorus. . . .

Leaving the Atlantic Gardens while people were still humming the tune, the plugger would visit in turn several variety houses which lined the Bowery. Variety was the name attached to what in later years, and in somewhat different guise, would be called vaudeville . . . .

After banter with specialty acts at the variety houses and some ribald repartee with the girls in back rooms, the plugger would hustle over to the more dignified and prophylactic Tony Pastor's on 14th Street in time to catch one of the era's great singing stars before she left her dressing room. A plug at Tony's meant a lot, for Pastor toured America and Europe with his respectable entertainment and a song in an act's repertoire could build up nationwide and international popularity.

Across the street from Pastor's was another music hall, Theiss' Alhambra, where a round of drinks for the orchestra might buy a rendition or two. A silver dollar pressed into the hand of a singing waiter would bring an additional plug. The waiters sang as they handed out mugs of beer. At intervals, one stepped onto a clear spot in the middle of the room and, bar rag draped over his arm, lifted his voice above the din.

From the 14th Street theater and night spot district the now defunct Third Avenue El, then steam-driven, would carry the wearying song-plugger to within walking distance of Koster and Bial's on 23rd. Here, as at Tony

Pastor's, a plug could lead rapidly to widespread exposure of a song, for Koster and Bial's was famous for importing European talent of superb quality.

New York was studded from Battery to Harlem with saloons, cafes, restaurants, music halls, hotels, dance halls and sporting arenas where songs would be exposed to large numbers of pleasure seekers. Not every plugger could make all of the stops every night, but every stop had to be covered with every song.[7]

But this was not all. During the day the plugger demonstrated songs for vaudeville acts in the "parlors" and then some nights would visit the picture houses and there, with his piano-playing partner, direct community singing while illustrated word slides were shown on the screen during reel changes.

On Saturday afternoons music had to be plugged at the local department stores. A favorite spot was the great Siegel-Cooper store on the corner of 18th and 6th, where thousands of mothers and daughters met at the fountain and shopped. At the music counter the chorus slips were passed among the crowd and everybody sang the songs of the plugger, and then afterward the salesgirls sold the music by the hundreds.

When there was a parade, the plugger would dash toward the band and pass out a band arrangement of the tune he was pushing, and hope they would give it a try. Also, at political parades or rallies the plugger would make an appearance. Usually candidates would hire a wagon and three musicians—a trumpet, banjo, and drums—to attract crowds to a corner. Without television or even the radio this means of communication was standard. The pluggers would hand out the newest tunes to the musicians, pass the chorus slips to the crowd, and sell the sheet music if anyone wished to buy it after singing it. Lucky was the plugger whose publisher had Irish, Italian, and German songs in his library.

After midnight the pluggers would visit the six-day bicycle races at Madison Square Garden and would lead the crowd in singing as they watched through the early hours of the morning. Baseball games, public parks, picnic grounds, river excursion boats, and of course, Coney Island were common visiting places.

And so the songs were sold, and sheet music by the thousands made its way into the homes of the country as a result of the high-pressure salesmanship of the plugger.

But times changed. The song gave way to a craze for dancing the Cakewalk, the Bunny Hug, the Fox Trot. If it couldn't be danced, it wouldn't be published. The singer was not as important as the dance band and its director. So publishers and song pluggers changed their emphases. No longer was he the singer and extrovert of years past, but an arranger who could talk the language

---

[7] *Gold in Tin Pan Alley*, Hazel Meyer. Copyright © 1958 by Hazel Meyer. J. B. Lippincott Co., Philadelphia, 1958, page 46. Reprinted by permission of J. B. Lippincott Co.

of the instrumentalist, the solo performer, or conductor.   The publishers saw the sheet music business wane and hurried into the gap with stock arrangements for orchestras.

Tin Pan Alley is no longer one single place.   To meet the men who write our songs and publish them one would now have to visit New York, Chicago, Hollywood, Nashville, Springfield, Missouri, Boston, Philadelphia, Dallas, and Houston.   But the spirit of Tin Pan Alley is abroad in the land, a spirit which plugs a song after it has been created upon the hunch that it will meet the musical interests and esthetic needs of the people.

Tin Pan Alley stands for the commercially contrived song, the love song of the past and present, written for consumption by millions and written in such a style as to take advantage of the popular taste of the moment.   It is most often foot-and-heart music, placing most of its emphasis upon rhythm and melody, an emphasis which we can never forget, but whose limitations become obvious.

Study Procedures

1. Can you think of a song that you like which is not a product of Tin Pan Alley?
2. What is the real difference between a composer who writes for commercial consumption and one who writes music as an art form?   How does a composer of art form music make a living?
3. To what extent do you consider the disc jockey a molder of public consumption as the song plugger of another era?
4. What song from a recent movie would you consider most popular?   Was this a Hollywood production or a foreign import?   Most likely some member of the class owns a copy.   Examine it and ascertain its form.   What are the appealing elements of the song?   Is the song outstanding, or did the movie "sell" the song?
5. Considering that movies, books, magazines, TV stations, and other modes of communication are controlled by two or three large corporations, do you consider that your taste is your own?

CHICAGO STYLE

Even before Storyville closed musicians had headed north to the big cities. Some wanted to gain new experiences, some had heard of the wages paid workers in the factories and thought that music too would pay well, others just wanted to join some of the 60,000 blacks who came into Chicago between 1910 and 1920.   During World War I the Army had provided unforgettable experiences away from the South, while others had worked the steamship lines up and down the Mississippi and had climbed off at different northern points to play, live awhile, and move on.

Although jazz musicians played in most cities, and bands did exist throughout the North, Chicago has rightly been noted as the "hub of jazz" during the decade of the 1920s.   Most of the reasons for this were nonmusical:

1. A black community existed in this growing city which had a sympathy for music based on the blues and the spiritual.

2. Chicago had a great demand for heavy and rough labor, and many of the unskilled workers liked the rough and unsophisticated music which the black played.

3. The city accepted this style of music in its various forms without considering it inferior and gave it opportunity to mature.

4. This was a city, probably more than most Northern cities, where the blacks of the South and middle-class white musicians could intermingle and openly exchange musical ideas. Chicago was a center of young musicians who were quick to learn, who had a good technic, were eager to prove themselves, and had little care for some of the social inhibitions that had been a part of an earlier generation.

5. The city was proud of its business and cultural growth. Anything which developed with the city received direct or indirect encouragement. As the people became less rural, their popular music had to keep pace.

6. Probably most important for jazz was the general atmosphere in the city. Because of the high level of prosperity most citizens supported good social times, music, clubs, bars, dance halls, and bootleg liquor. Often the clubs were controlled by the gangsters, which in Chicago usually meant Al Capone. Jazz appealed not only to the gangster and bootlegger but also to other Chicago citizens who protested against an unpopular prohibition law. Jazz was a symbol of this protest because it was emotional, had a history of lowness, and was condemned by the more straightlaced portion of society.

Recordings flourished for both white and black bands during the 1920s, with 151 million records being sold in 1926 alone. Although white bands made more of the recordings, some were cut particularly for the large black population in the North. Often called "race" records, these did give employment to black musicians, enabled them to become better-known, and tended to indicate style shifts or popularity emphases. For the first time large numbers of Americans could live an imaginary dream life as outlined in a gay and wild music, matching in their minds an image which they had created for themselves of the "Roaring Twenties."

The music at the end of the decade sounded some different from that at the beginning. When the blacks and whites had begun their playing in 1920, it was usually the old New Orleans Jazz or an imitation of it. By the end of the decade some changes had been made, and whether authentic jazz or not, most of the listeners liked it, and most of the musicians played it.

Whereas most of the New Orleans music had been consciously or subconsciously controlled by the melody in a vocal style, rhythm began to be the boss of Chicago jazz. From a few standard syncopations it explored many rhythmic differences in the accompaniment as well as the tunes. The accents in New Orleans music had been a strong two beats and weak two beats to the measure, but in Chicago the rhythmic background had evened out with almost an equal emphasis on all four beats.

Bands grew in size. Part of the purpose was to experiment with sounds which more instruments could give, part was due to an increased emphasis upon harmony, part probably was to give a good musician employment, and unconsciously, part of it was to match the growth of the city with its emphasis upon larger buildings, more population, and greater demand for the spectacular.

New Orleans music was a community item. There were solos, although these often were short, but most of the music was played together. In the newer style the emphasis shifted to the individual. Persons and their names became important, and the style of each person meant something to a number of listeners. Most importantly, the musician himself determined the form of his improvisation.

The improvisations of the Chicago group moved a bit further away from the original melody, away from a straight arpeggio or scale figure, and at times the phrasing broke away from the two- or four-bar sections. Although the blues were still a vital part of black music, bands accepted the popular songs of the day with greater willingness and played versions of these in jazz style. The saxophone was added to the ensemble, and before the decade was over more than one saxophone was used in most organizations. The drummer had increased his kit by adding sock cymbals, wire brushes, and high hat cymbals as well as the conventional bass drum and snare drum played with sticks. The piano, when used as soloist, tried to forget the old Storyville or ragtime slide style in favor of a chordal style. Most tunes began with an ensemble, played one or more choruses with solo instruments, and ended with an ensemble.

Chicago style, if anything, came to mean that the white musician had learned black music, had smoothed it, adapted it to popular songs, and was on his way to altering it to suit the needs of another generation.

Study Procedures

1. Listen to recordings of New Orleans jazz and Chicago style jazz. Can you hear a difference? How would you describe this difference in your own words?
2. Listen to a recording of Chicago style jazz played first by a black band and then by a white band. Does a difference exist? How would you describe it?
3. Listen to a recording of Louis Armstrong from the Chicago period and one from a much more recent period. Describe the similarities and differences.
4. Listen to a recording of Benny Goodman from the Chicago period. Are there differences here as compared to other bands of the period?
5. Listen to a number of recordings from the Chicago period and then choose one which you believe best epitomizes the decade. Give your reasons for making the choice over other recordings.

SWING

For young players and listeners, swing broke upon the scene in 1935 as a great, bright, new sound whose rhythm was light, driving, and bouncy in such a way that the feet wanted to move, and the body follow. For older players and followers of the jazz scene, it was nothing more than an obvious extension of the bands which had played around Chicago just ten to fifteen years before.

Both were correct in their opinions, for if today we compared a record of a jazz group playing in 1922 with a great swing band of 1936 the sound would be marvelously different; and unless you were a student of jazz, including its beginnings in New Orleans, you would probably prefer the later sound and would not recognize the similarities immediately. But they existed.

The swing bands had increased tension and drive, replacing the ease and relaxation of the New Orleans and Chicago styles. The tension came from the style of rhythm but reflected the pace of life itself.

In the twenties the ensemble style had smoothed some, and the swing bands went beyond anything earlier bands could have conceived.

Most of the solos in the early bands had been trumpet solos developed along a certain style which was a synthesis of the vocal procedures of the black. In the swing bands this style was extended to all the instruments including the clarinet, tenor saxophone, and piano.

A greater emphasis was placed upon material in AABA form, with the sections being eight measures each and totaling thirty-two in length. The older blues form, although used, was given less emphasis.

A new ensemble style was invented which treated an entire section as one musician, so that entire sections provided a background for a soloist or an entire section became the soloist. Sometimes the section would solo in harmony, other times in unison. A higher degree of technical facility was in demand, particularly in reading skills.

The arranger was one of the most important men in the new style. It was he who set the concept of the type of jazz which would be played, and created the manner in which the tunes were handled.

Even though blacks were involved with the making of some of this swing music, it was more often a white man's music and the black, from whose music it had come, felt little part of it. The white man considered it his music and his style of music, rarely associating it with an outgrowth from social upheaval or as an expression of a race as it grew within a culture. But when the white man could actually play swing and make it wholly his, then, and not until then, could it become a part of a growing art, for it meant that the American could experience the music completely and make it a part of his life; but more than that, he could learn to play in such a way as to take over the main concepts of a style that had at one time been wholly a black art form.

Four specific points concerning swing should be emphasized, as to their major differences from preceding styles:

1. *This was music for the big band.* The New Orleans group had been five or six players; Chicago style had increased this to nine or ten, including two or three cornets and a trombone, three reeds, sometimes two of these being saxophones, and four rhythm usually including the tuba and banjo at first, but

later substituting the bass viol and the guitar. Swing bands usually consisted of four saxophones, including two altos and two tenors, and at times the baritone; at least six brass, including three trumpets and three trombones; and four rhythm, including piano, string bass, guitar, and drums.

2. *This was arranged jazz.* Because of the size of the group, all members were readers of music and the arrangements were written imitations of the jazz improvisatory style. Using harmonies with textures borrowed from the impressionistic music of some thirty years before, swing arrangements used chords of the seventh, ninth, eleventh, and thirteenth, many of these unresolved. There was an increased use of chromatic chords.

3. *This was a music of limited improvisation.* The band itself became the soloist most of the time. When an improvisation did occur, one, two, or three selected players would be involved. The "riff" often created a background for a section or a soloist. When called upon for improvisation, the performer would use less of a hot tone, but the melody would be more highly decorative, with the soloist more concerned with harmonic variation than melodic.

4. *This was a music with emphasis upon rhythm.* All sections were involved with the projection of rhythmic figures some of the time. Rhythmic figures were executed as a background to the melodic line of another section or for a soloist. There was a greater and more subtle variety of syncopation.

Because a large number of commercial tunes were used and few tunes based upon the blues, some believed that this music was only a commercialization of jazz and that it was artificial. Others maintained that it made no difference how many persons were involved or whether it were read, so long as it had a certain swing or drive; if the drive were present, then it became jazz. Fletcher Henderson maintained that swing meant premeditation while jazz meant spontaneity.

But the bands of the swing era did sound spontaneous to many for a number of years, particularly when the arrangements were good and were executed by skillful performers. All the sweet bands of former years jumped on the bandwagon and called their music "swing," and introduced elements to satisfy the listening and dancing public. The result was a wide variety of sounds which ran the gamut of almost every taste in America and Europe.

The beginning of World War II brought a close to the era, with the musicians entering the Armed Forces or vital industry. The spirit and vigor of American popular music would not rejuvenate itself until almost ten years after the end of the war.

Study Procedures

1. Compare an early Chicago style recording of Benny Goodman with a swing recording of him and his band. What similarities exist? How would you describe the differences?

2. The Benny Goodman band of the late thirties usually is considered the epitome of swing. Compare any other band with the Goodman band and describe the differences in your own words.

3. Goodman also played small-group jazz with a select group of his players. What differences do you hear with this group as compared to a small group of New Orleans or Chicago style?

4. When a pop tune ballad was played, what swing characteristics were present which kept the arrangement in the style of the period? What was missing from the ballad as compared to a great swing arrangement?

5. In your own words, define blues, New Orleans style jazz, Chicago style jazz, and swing. Can you place a composition in the proper style by hearing only part of a recording?

BOP AND ROCK

After World War II swing tried for a comeback and failed. Musicians and young people rejected contrived orchestrations, pretty lyrics, overrefinement, and smoothness. The musicians wanted a greater freedom of improvisation along with more variety in rhythms, chords, and melodies. The listening public had appreciated the brilliant, articulate big band, but now its music seemed inconsequential; it had little to say. Some bands tried to revive the old sounds, Tin Pan Alley turned out some songs, but no excitement was generated.

A group of instrumental musicians led a revolt for a resurgence of jazz. These musicians developed a new type of improvisation, mostly a mental concept, rooted in characteristics of earlier jazz. Up to this time, jazz had been almost entirely a dance music. With bebop the music was intended for listening, and one was almost required to have a background in the characteristics of jazz to understand what the musicians were playing and meaning.

1. The small group featured an advanced improvisational technic and a firm understanding of harmony and form.

2. The rhythm became free to add another dimension to the melodic structure. Rather than being limited to a straight four beats to the measure, the pulsation, if provided, was light and delicate and could be supplied by any member of the group.

3. Improvisation was based upon a thematic outline rather than being dependent upon the harmonic progressions of an old melody. Following more closely the conditions of the twelve-tone system, almost any note could become a part of the chord.

4. Phrasing was changed so that it followed the desires of the improviser rather than the dictates of the melody, a four-bar phrase, or the standard eight-measure section. The rhythm of phrasing became part of the art itself.

5. Instrumentation often included a trumpet, saxophone (the clarinet moving from the picture), and four so-called rhythm instruments: the drums, guitar, bass viol, and piano. All were considered solo members which could be-

come a part of the melodic fabric as well as the rhythmic structure. The bass viol often played with a bow and was free to add a counterline to the upper instruments. The piano rarely played in the slide style of former years, but concentrated almost entirely upon a melodic line in the upper pitches, leaving the bass line all but exclusively to the bass viol. The drummer's role changed drastically. If pulsations were given they were supplied by the brushes on the cymbal, the bass drum being used only for special accentuations as an aid to the improvisation; the left hand on the snare drum created a type of counterelement to the melodic lines of the other instruments. Thus the drummer participated as a full-fledged member of the ensemble rather than being kept in the background. The electric guitar played both rhythmic and melodic lines, and its new loudness enabled him to become an active member of the front group rather than being relegated to rhythm.

6. Blues, original compositions, and a few old standards became the basis for improvisations.

7. Exotic new chords were used instead of the same old standard ones. Even when playing standard compositions the chordal background became more complex.

Because the music sounded intricate and emphasized the intellectual, it invited other types of experiments which bordered on symphonic or classical music styles. The so-called "cool jazz" or "West Coast jazz" used string instruments, flutes, bass and alto clarinets, and other symphonic instruments; with larger groups, arrangements were often of symphonic proportions.

But this music had little appeal to the average layman. The performers, having come from the ranks of popular music, insisted on treating it as a mass medium, meaning that it should be supported by and attractive to the general public as was early jazz. They performed in bars and clubs and attempted to find esthetic and financial support for their music in recreational businesses. Since the style was too similar to an art form, it received little support from the public; since it was too much like jazz, it received little support from the regular promoters of art music. During the early fifties a tour of college campuses brought a last spark of life to the music, but it was quickly supplanted by the growing interest in rock.

After the war interest in popular music was divided between pop (sweet and Tin Pan Alley), rhythm and blues (a type of music which mostly serviced the black community and had been called "race" music at an earlier time), and country and western (an alliance between hillbilly and Western cowboy music). Gospel, an amalgam of rhythm and blues, with certain characteristics of pop music, was considered religious and had not yet become a true part of mass-consumed music.

In the fifties the country professed an interest in minority groups and causes, and attempted the unification of splintered factions on a variety of fronts. This could be seen most plainly in the concern for a strong United Nations, and in the numerous church unions throughout the country. Such concerns sub-consciously affected the unity of four musical types into one music known as *rock and roll*.

Rhythm and blues, the old-fashioned black singing blues, contributed the beat and the form. Country and western contributed the guitar and its accompaniment possibilities. Bop had promoted the new electric guitar, which could match the amplification of the voice, and by supplying a complete chordal background by only one performer, made possible the small group with a loud impact. Gospel supplied the big rhythms, the drive which for years had enveloped the people in an emotional experience. These together bubbled forth as rock, and have commanded the popular music scene since 1954.

With this amalgam three commercial music fields pooled their talents as well as their esthetic effects to attract a mass audience. Pop music had a large following and an industry to promote and support a major undertaking; rhythm and blues and country and western possessed a rich assortment of performers, particularly singers who could play the guitar, percussion, and assorted minor instruments. It was this group which benefited most from the merger.

As we have seen in this chapter, popular music, the music of the people, has always come from a small underground, developing their concerns in insignificant bars or dance halls where a particular portion of the public was willing to listen to something different. Then, because of certain characteristics, it disseminated beyond its original confines and swept up large population blocks as it universalized.

But to envelop the masses in a popular music a dance had to be included, one which would appeal primarily to the young, but also to other elements of the population. Early jazz had its black dance; ragtime supported the Cakewalk; Chicago style had coupled with the Charleston; and swing attracted jitterbugs and Lindy Hop dancers. Rock also had to develop a dance. It came subsequently with the "Twist," a version of the Lindy, but with unique differences: the partners did not touch each other, and at times did not even look at each other.

When rock emerged it spoke of values to the young and of a changed way of life. It protested the music of the past and the values of the older generation as expressed in the pop music of the forties and early fifties. Much of early rock contained no direct or formal protest, but the implications were present and these were not lost upon the youth.

Most rock styles encompassed some of eight general characteristics:

1. *The voice became an instrument.* Early rock placed the amplified voice at the same loudness level as the instruments. Often the words were indistinguishable, which did not rob from the overall impression, since the sounds alone made the effect. Some songs contained nonsense syllables, continuing a custom of the blues or finishing a line of text which was out of meter, thus giving the impression that the song was being composed as recorded and thereby strengthening the amateur impression.

2. *A "wall of sound" enveloped the listener.* Everything struck him at the same time: the voice, lyrics, instrumental sound, and a certain amount of extraneous noise. The overall effect was sound plus beat.

3. *The rhythm and blues style predominated.* The blues form prevailed but simple experimentations in form and style added to its modernism.

4. *Subject matter came from the pop field.* The lyrics did not imitate the older blues with earthy descriptions; rather, a type of sentimental or romantic text extracted from earlier pop tunes took precedence.

5. *A hard-driving vocabulary heightened the contemporary effect.* The choice of words implied protest, even though the song professed innocence.

6. *Small groups prevailed.* Similar to early jazz bands and the later bebop ensembles, rock groups contained four to six musicians. Electronic sounds and professional recording technics assisted the overall effect. Everybody sang as well as played an instrument.

7. *Tension and spontaneity formed the true appeal of the music.*

8. *Rock became the first medium to express itself primarily through mechanical and impersonal media.* The record was the prime means of communication between the artists and their audience, while the radio aided the distribution. The radio disc jockey show replaced the old-fashioned folk gathering or revival meeting.

Although rock began in this country, English groups soon took over predominance of the medium. Their success was due to their talent, their refreshing sound, a heritage of the English folk tune, and a return to the big beat of the mid-fifties. For years, by means of records, movies, and personal appearances, the Beatles led the rock field and popular music followed their lead.

Finally, this dominance was challenged by two American developments. Once again two musical styles in American musical life united: Appalachian folk and rock. Throughout the fifties folk music had captivated the American musical scene. Even many of the young people who were rock enthusiasts were also devoted to the folk singer. Much of this devotion was stimulated by the protest songs written and sung by these young performers and with which other young people could empathize. The unification of the two styles came from Bob Dylan, a popular folk song singer who has been called "the first American poet of the electronic age," "the first poet of the jukebox." In bringing folk and rock together, his single most important contribution lies in his textual content and treatment. Discarding the romantic lyrics of Tin Pan Alley and the weak lyrics of early rock, he sang and wrote songs with words which were particularly perceptive of the contemporary scene, setting a new trend in rock itself in which the lyrics became a social commentary. While the early rock lyrics were meant to convey mood, later lyrics placed great emphasis upon meaning.

A second challenge to British dominance came from Detroit and its "soul" music. Very much like a pure rhythm and blues, soul was the black person trying to regain his foothold upon the music which had been his in the first place and which, at least once before, the white man had taken and used to his own devices.

Soul is black music, played and sung by blacks, on black radio stations, and publicized by blacks. This movement parallels the assertion of black rights in economic and political arenas. In cases where it has moved more closely to popular music, the black has considered this a sellout by his friends and has failed to see it as a natural tendency. Soul is the black man trying to achieve cultural definition.

During the past few years there have been indications that rock might produce so many splintering factions as to cause a weakening of its impact. But rock will always be with us, just as other former styles are still with us even though something new has replaced them in majority appeal. More to the point is an attempt on the part of rock musicians to forget their original function of mass music and to become exponents of either social commentary or a fine art. The latter trend had begun with bebop and "cool" segments during the early fifties. Although this is possible, it also means that certain limitations must be placed upon the music in lieu of mass appeal. In the Beatles' last album it would appear that they were asking somewhat the same questions: "Where do we go from here?" "Is it possible to make rock into a fine art?" "Do the changes in rock necessarily make it better?" Some of the changes projected during the past decade were superficial, and yet because of the beat, rock has been able to absorb such changes and still remain popular. Other changes seemed to push it toward a fine art by absorbing, again superficially, some characteristics of art music, such as references to Bach, Mozart, Cage, and others.

Rock music as social commentary has increased in most groups since its amalgamation with folk music. Although some groups are able to remain impersonal with their lyrics, not linking their songs with their personalities, the exact opposite has occurred with most writers of rock. Although this often propels them into the limelight momentarily, it also acts to turn attention away from them sooner. In order to understand a work of art or an artistic movement it is necessary to remove the art from the artist and the audience and examine it independently. Popular music, including most of rock, has not been willing, or in most cases able to do this.

Where does the future of popular music lie? Will rock splinter and find some way of appealing to a large audience as an expression in a future decade? Or will it synthesize with a new idea or remold an old one? Only the times and the emotional currents of the future can bring these items into focus.

Note: This study of popular music indicates two ideas for us. First, we witness, even within our own time and surely within an understandable period of time, the changes which can come to an expression as it is fashioned by the artist and by society's demands upon him. Secondly, and probably more important, we can begin to understand how folk music becomes art music: how it develops in a modest manner with common people, how the masses use it and shape it to make a set and determinable form, and finally, how this form is adapted by an artist and used to create a work of art which could be understandable by comparatively few persons, and whose execution is limited to those practitioners with great skill and interpretative ability.

All the forms we are studying in this book were once at the first stage; some of them have remained there. Others have gained the second stage but as yet have gone no further; this we have found to be true with jazz and certain types of popular music. Many of the forms have reached the third stage, and it is hoped that you will make every attempt to understand such forms and comprehend their artistic expressions.

Study Procedures

1. Discuss Dylan's poems from a standpoint of literature. Compare them with those of other contemporary poets.
2. Choose any selection by the Beatles and define its form, the musical characteristics as you hear them, and the type of rock you believe it to be. To begin, consider if it is more closely aligned to the pop song, to rhythm and blues, to country and western, or to the protest song.
3. Listen to a recording by Dave Brubeck and explain to members of your class why you believe this to be a part of the jazz field, but also why it inclines toward art music.
4. Select two records of Bob Dylan: one of folk song and one of folk-rock. Explain why you chose each for the style it represents.
5. Choose any one single composition from any contemporary group; after playing it for the class, explain in musical terms why you believe it to be a quality composition. *Caution:* do not become involved with personalities.
6. If you could choose only one selection in the entire contemporary rock field to demonstrate to an unknowing person what rock is, which record would you choose and what would you say to explain it?

Bibliography—Chapter 15

BELZ, CARL, *The Story of Rock.* New York: Oxford University Press, 1969.

BRAUN, D. DUANE, *The Sociology and History of American Music and Dance.* Ann Arbor, Mich.: Ann Arbor Publishers, 1969.

COURLANDER, HAROLD, *Negro Folk Music, U.S.A.* New York: Columbia University Press, 1963.

DANKWORTH, AVRIL, *Jazz.* London: Oxford University Press, 1968.

DEXTER, DAVE, JR., *The Jazz Story.* Englewood Cliffs, N.J.: Prentice-Hall, Inc., 1964.

EISEN, JONATHAN, *The Age of Rock.* New York: Random House, 1969.

FEATHER, LEONARD, *The Book of Jazz.* New York: Bonanza Books, 1965.

FINKELSTEIN, SIDNEY, *Jazz, a People's Music.* New York: The Citadel Press, 1948.

GOLDBERG, ISAAC, *Tin Pan Alley.* New York: Frederick Ungar Publishing Co., Inc., 1961.

HEILBUT, TONY, *The Gospel Sound.* New York: Simon and Schuster, 1971.

HEMPHILL, PAUL, *The Nashville Sound.* New York: Simon and Schuster, 1970.

JACKSON, GEORGE PULLEN, *White and Negro Spirituals.* Locust Valley, N.Y.: J. J. Augustin, 1943.

———, *White Spirituals in the Southern Uplands.* Chapel Hill, N.C.: University of North Carolina Press, 1933.

JONES, LEROI, *Black Music*. New York: William Morrow and Company, Inc., 1971.

————, *Blues People*. New York: William Morrow and Company, Inc., 1963.

KATZ, BERNARD, ed., *Social Implications of Early Negro Music in the United States*. New York: Arno Press and the New York Times, 1969.

LONGSTREET, STEPHEN, *Sportin' House*. Los Angeles: Sherbourne Press, Inc., 1965.

MEYER, HAZEL, *Gold in Tin Pan Alley*. Philadelphia: J. B. Lippincott Company, 1958.

MYRUS, DONALD, *Ballads, Blues, and the Big Beat*. London: Macmillan Company, 1966.

ODUM, HOWARD W., and GUY B. JOHNSON, *The Negro and His Songs*. Hatboro, Penn.: Folklore Associates, Inc., 1964.

PATTERSON, LINDSAY, ed., *The Negro in Music and Art*. New York: Publishers Company, Inc., 1969.

RUBLOWSKY, JOHN, *Black Music in America*. New York: Basic Books, Inc., 1971.

————, *Popular Music*. New York: Basic Books, Inc., 1967.

RUSSELL, ROSS, *Jazz Style in Kansas City and the Southwest*. Berkeley, Calif.: University of California Press, 1971.

SCHULLER, GUNTHER, *Early Jazz*. New York: Oxford University Press, 1968.

SHAW, ARNOLD, *The World of Soul*. New York: Cowles Book Company, Inc., 1970.

SIDRAN, BEN, *Black Talk*. New York: Holt, Rinehart and Winston, 1971.

SIMON, GEORGE T., *The Big Bands*. London: The Macmillan Company, Collier-Macmillan Ltd., 1967.

SOUTHERN, EILEEN, ed., *Readings in Black American Music*. New York: W. W. Norton and Company, Inc., 1971.

TOLEDANO, RALPH DE, ed., *Frontiers of Jazz*. New York: Frederick Ungar Publishing Co., Inc., 1962.

ULANOV, BARRY, *A History of Jazz in America*. New York: Viking Press, 1957.

WILLIAMS, MARTIN T., ed., *The Art of Jazz*. London: Cassell and Company Ltd., 1960.

WILSON, JOHN S., *Jazz, the Transition Years*. New York: Appleton-Century-Crofts, 1966.

WORK, JOHN W., *American Negro Songs and Spirituals*. New York: Bonanza Books, 1940.

YODER, DON, *Pennsylvania Spirituals*. Lancaster, Penn.: Pennsylvania Folklife Society, 1961.

Recordings—Chapter 15

Unlike other chapters, no specific items will be suggested. Too many excellent examples may be found in commercial catalogues, libraries, and personal collections. To single out one particular group for each style would tend to eliminate other excellent examples.

Mention should be made of two excellent sources for early examples: Folkways records and Library of Congress albums of early black music.

Section F *Dance Becomes Stylized*

Chapter 16

Music for Ceremony

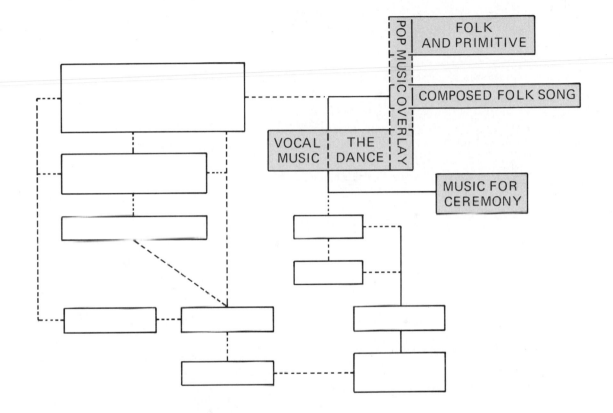

When we see and hear a band move down the street, a choir followed by church officials walk down a church aisle, a public official take an oath of office, a young couple participate in a wedding service, or friends in a receiving line at a social event, we are witnessing a ceremony. All of these ceremonies come to us out of a history of related traditions. Some have been changed by persons or groups wishing more simple or more complex ceremonies; others have been changed because of society's demand to be more modern in dress and action.

Almost all public ceremonies are associated with music in some way because music adds emotion and prestige to the occasion. In learning of the style and background of the music that often is a part of ceremony, we can better appreciate its function and form.

HISTORY

In various ways the last three chapters have considered dance and the music of dance, as evidence of the changes that can be brought about through the geography and backgrounds of people when they superimpose their social customs on music. Similar statements could be made of music for ceremony.

In the early days of civilization, dance was considered a ritual that assisted with the healing of the sick, the calling of the gods to assist in matters of war, food, or tribal relations, or to produce dismay in the observer so that he would be more apt to obey local authorities.

Even in these early beginnings dance seemed to be involved with two styles: those that required actions which were lively, jumping, and gross, contrasted with those which required small movements and slow reactions, wherein the feet moved little or did not leave the ground. The music usually resembled the dances: lively and agitated, with jumping melodic lines, or slow and smooth, with weaving expressions.

Anthropologists have noted that tribes or groups which seemed to be dominated by matriarchal tendencies generally used dances that were slower, involved smaller movements, and were accompanied by music which was often softer, with melodies whose tunes were more compact and moved little or followed scalelike patterns. On the other hand, groups which seemed to be dominated by patriarchal tendencies used more dances that were quick, with large jumps and leaps, the music for which was often loud and shrill with melodic jumps or uneven rhythms. In the former case the drum was usually played by the hand, while in the latter it was beaten by a stick, tending to show the phallic influence. In many groups these tendencies were often mixed, although one or the other usually seemed to predominate.

As dance developed through the ages, both styles of dancing continued, and both styles of music were used to accompany dancers in ceremony. Thus, two kinds of dance promoted two kinds of music.

In the Middle Ages or until the time of the troubadours (c. 1100), one dance with two styles had served gentile folk and country folk alike: the *carole*. Carole is a generic term implying that the dance is sung, usually by the dancers themselves. The two styles of carole that were performed stemmed from the two types of dance discussed earlier. One was the *farandole*, which was a "follow-the-leader" type of dance in which the group moved in a single line with little emphasis upon type of motion or step. The second was the *round*, in which the dancers moved in a circle. The circle could be large or small, but more concern was given to step and type of body motion. Although both of these were impersonal dances with emphasis upon the group, the farandole was to become more closely related to the procession or march, while the round dance was to become more intricate.

This duplicity was carried into the thirteenth and fourteenth centuries, when the basse dance was contrasted with the haute dance. The *basse dance* usually came from lowly or peasant origin, and usually involved keeping the feet on the ground or floor; the *haute dance* usually implied a more courtly design, with the feet and legs more often involved with fancier steps than merely shuffles.

When the courtly troubadours emphasized manners and style they discarded mass activity, choosing instead more subtle dances in which couples were featured. At this point dance lost a style concept that had been prominent for so many years: that large groups of persons could be involved with very simple movements and steps such as in moving along a route, either in festive activities or for fun.

Even after specialized court dances were developed, some simple steps were maintained and incorporated into specific dances. Processionals could be used for beginning sections, to enhance their importance. Sometimes these were known as *demarches,* and later they became part of the pavans (or pavanes). These processionals involved a special kind of music which was less rhythmic but emphasized the beat in such a way as to keep the dancers in step.

Many of these ideas are used today in such familiar forms as the fanfare, processional, march, and polonaise.

THE FANFARE

Many times when a band is about to enter the football field for a halftime presentation, it will play a fanfare to attract the attention of the crowd or to state in musical terms that something important is about to happen. It is usually a short bugle-type call played by trumpets alone or by all the brasses. Other fanfares assist ceremonial music when played during or along with a tune. Thus, ceremonial music may be filled with fanfares or references to them.

By its nature, a fanfare is announcing music, attention-getting, or introductory to a ceremony. Many times it belongs to the military scene, announcing retreat, meals, or "lights out." Some fanfares are light and frivolous, announcing the beginning of a dance or the catching of a fox during a hunt. All of them, however, have a background in dance and illustrate the ceremonial intent.

Study Procedures

Aaron Copland, a famous American composer of the twentieth century, has written a *Fanfare for the Common Man.* This composition, about three minutes in length, encompasses a different kind of sound from the usual fanfare and is attractive enough to warrant several hearings:

1. Note the similarities to medieval music. Can you understand why this is so?
2. What is different about the drum in this composition?
3. What can you state about the form?

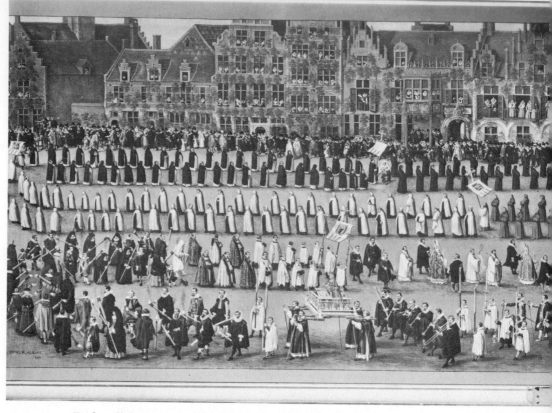

Early religious procession with musicians, in Brussels (Courtesy of Anderson-Art Reference Bureau, Ancram, N.Y.).

THE PROCESSIONAL

We still use the processional on ceremonial occasions when we wish some type of display of personages as they move through the people. Usually this is not a long walk, and it is most often indoors. The most common processionals take place regularly when in certain churches the choir walks down the aisle at the beginning and end of the service often followed by clergy or church officials.

Processional music is usually of a moderate tempo which makes it possible to step with the music without seeming to move too quickly. Too quick a movement would rob from the dignity of the occasion. Even a processional hymn has the feeling of a march. The marchlike hymn was first heard from the Moslems at the time of the Crusades, but was not inserted into the service of the Christian church until the Reformation sought changes from the highly organized, slow, weaving music of plainchant. So, once again, the music and forms of early dance were evident in later activities—even in the church.

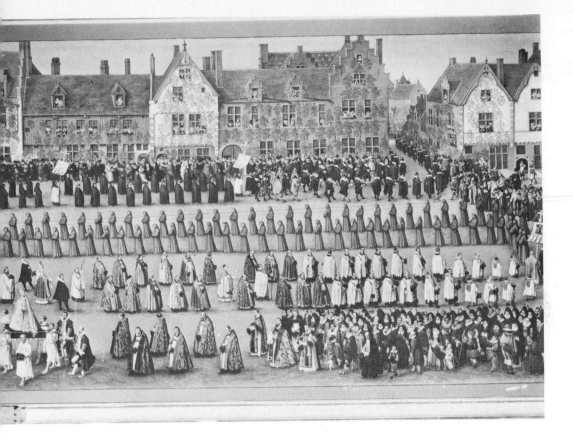

"Pomp and Circumstance" March No. 1 (Elgar)

Probably the most famous processional music in the world is this "Pomp and Circumstance" March by Edward Elgar. Most students know this composition as "commencement music," since it is used so often by high schools for graduating ceremonial marches. This piece has so often been associated with processionals, and processionals are so similar in character to marches, that this composition is known as a march. Note, however, the rather slow character of the music as compared to a street or parade march. Elgar wrote four more "Pomp and Circumstance" processionals after the success of the first, which was written for the coronation of King Edward VII in 1901.

Introduction	1st Theme	Trio	Repeat	D.C.
Fanfare	Agitated	Smooth and Flowing		

The prior diagram shows the form of the work. Part of the appeal of ceremonial music lies in its simplicity of style and form. Much of the attractiveness of this composition is in the trio section, a singable melody that rolls along with considerable smoothness. When first heard, English critics described it as "breezy and beefy" and "distinctively British."

"Crown Imperial" March (Walton)

Another processional march attracted considerable attention some years later at the coronation of Queen Elizabeth II, June 2, 1953. Even though similar in form, with another simple songlike trio, note the difference in the style of the music. Although not dissonant, it definitely speaks for a more recent time and a composer with a more contemporary concept. This is evident in the use of the trumpets, the orchestration, and the style of the melody in the first part. Portions of the composition sound as if they could have been written for a movie; in fact, the composer, William Walton, has written music for several films, although this is not for what he is most noted.

Melody One	Trio (or Melody Two)	Coda or Ending
Gay-modern (jazzy in places) Based on a fanfare-sounding melody	Smooth, songlike Second time, majestic	

Study Procedures

1. Compare the two processionals which have been used for coronations. Describe in your own words how they differ, even though they follow a similar kind of format.

2. You have probably been a part of or heard processionals. What compositions would you prefer for your own graduation if you had the choice? Why? Try to emphasize musical reasons.

3. Some hymns are used regularly for processional purposes in churches. If you belong to such a church, what hymns are used? Have you considered their particular quality on other occasions?

A third example of a processional comes from a composer who wrote music mostly of a nationalistic nature, which means that his compositions describe the flavor or characteristics of his country directly by folk idioms, or indirectly by coloration. Let us examine nationalism briefly before hearing the composition.

Nationalism

During the latter part of the nineteenth century in political circles there developed an intense desire on the part of small states or provinces in Italy and
Germany to become nations by uniting under common leaders and goals. This
was symbolic of the stress on internal matters in almost every European country
or world power.

In the arts this movement spread throughout the world, taking on different
meanings in different geographic areas. In music, the field had been dominated
almost completely by the German mind and the German style. Composers in
other countries, no longer wishing to reflect German art and desiring to call
attention to themselves and their own work, took up the cry of nationalism and
emphasized materials based largely upon folk songs or idiomatic characteristics
from their own country.

Nationalistic tendencies in music developed strongly in most countries of
central or eastern Europe but less so in Germany and France. Even in America,
a few composers attempted to call attention to its native music, requesting its
European-trained native artists to consider indigenous forms.

In Russia the movement was particularly strong and enveloped a group
of five composers (Cui, Borodin, Balakirev, Mussorgsky, and Rimsky-Korsakov)
who attempted to further nationalistic ideals in contrast to Tchaikovsky, then
considered a more international composer. Incidentally, Rimsky-Korsakov was
dismissed from his position at the St. Petersburg Conservatory of Music because
of his agreement with and support of rebellious students during the revolution
of 1905. That revolution involved the working class and peasants, and among
other items found the war with Japan of that year particularly unattractive, since
it was the antithesis of the popular nationalistic spirit.

"Procession of the Nobles" (Rimsky-Korsakov)

Nationalistic music often does not tell us anything about a specific country,
but it does give us a general flavor of a section of the world. In this particular
instance, Eastern colorations seem to be present along with tuneful melodies
reminiscent of folk characteristics. You may or may not be able to ascertain
the Eastern flavors in the music, but there is no mistaking the fact that this
composition is one that implies something important is about to take place (the
piece comes from an opera by this composer). The entire composition is built
around a fanfare. The general form of the music is shown below. A somewhat
different character develops as the music progresses, but there is still great
emphasis upon a military sound and the fanfare.

Fanfare	A B A	Trio	Return to Beginning
Long Military feeling			

THE POLONAISE

In one sense the polonaise is a type of processional. In Europe in the late 1800s and early 1900s, it was played as background music during ceremonial occasions when Polish dignitaries and high society were present, or whenever guests at affairs of state were paying courtesy to or being received by government officials. This music, chosen partially because it has a background of rhythm that tends to sound semimilitary, made it appear official to most people. At the same time, the music is of a light enough character to be considered background or social music.

The polonaise is a dance, and as such could have been confined to Chapter 14. In addition to reviewing its description there, let us examine three of its characteristics:

a. A moderate triple meter with a distinctive rhythm:

b. A melody which often contains a "feminine" ending.
c. A melody tuneful enough to be remembered, which often adds to the military impression. Many of our best dance tunes are easily remembered after one leaves the floor, and even into the next several days.

"Presidential Polonaise" (Sousa)

Sousa was a famous United States composer of ceremonial music. Although most noted for his marches, which we will study in the next section of the chapter, he also wrote waltzes, polkas, and dance tunes including the polonaise. One of his best-known is entitled "Presidential Polonaise." This was written for important social events in Washington where the president would be in attendance. A quote from Sousa describes how it came to be written:

The Arthur administration was drawing to a close. From time immemorial at White House receptions when cabinet members, ambassadors, generals and admirals were assembled in the East Room to greet the President, they were informed of the approach of the executive by the pompous strains of an old

Scotch boating song, "Hail to the Chief." This smacked more of royalty than of the proverbial Jeffersonian simplicity, but neither I nor any bandmaster before me had dared to break the precedent.

President Arthur, however, left his guests in the East Room one evening, and, coming out into the corridor, beckoned to me.

"What piece did you play when we went into dinner?" he asked.

" 'Hail to the Chief,' Mr. President."

"Do you consider it a suitable air?"

"No sir," I answered, "It was selected long ago on account of its name, and not on account of its character. It is a boat song, and lacks modern military character either for reception or a parade."

"Then change it!" said he, and walked away.

I wrote the "Presidential Polonaise" for White House indoor affairs and the "Semper Fidelis" march for review purposes outdoors.[1]

Study Procedures

1. The form of the composition follows:

Introduction	Section A		Trio: Section B
	X	Y	Z

Compare the form of this polonaise to the form of the usual march (the street march is discussed later in the chapter).

2. Can you feel that the polonaise uses 3/4 meter? Do you hear the underlying rhythm of the polonaise?

The Concert Polonaise

Probably the most famous writer of the polonaise was Frederic Chopin. Despite the fact that his are not simple peasant dances, but rather highly refined and polished virtuoso compositions that probably were never used as dances, promenades, or processions, the characteristics of the polonaise should still be obvious. Here is another example of a musical form which began as a common expression of the folk which the artist altered in subtle ways to become a quality product of its type. The artist serves this function regularly. Chopin's polonaises will be discussed in Chapter 19.

---

1 *Marching Along,* John Philip Sousa. Hale, Cushman, and Flint, Boston, 1928, pages 84 and 85.

THE MARCH

Other than a short-lived popular tune, literally millions of people would consider the march the most popular and beloved form in music. This is understandable, considering the march is basically rhythm of the dance with a whistling tune.

At the beginning of the chapter we discussed the history of dance as it led toward the processional. The march is so closely related to regimentation that an association with dance is often not made.

The Grand March

The grand march is closely related to the procession, and yet somewhat different in that the procession could mean indoor activity, a smaller group of people, and possibly less regimentation. Grand marches emphasize pomp, regality, and ostentatious display for some singular festive occasion. Like the procession, the tempo of the music is regal, and not in any way hurried.

Grand March from *Aida* (Verdi)

In music, this grand march stands out above all others. In this opera scene, soldiers are returning from a victorious war bringing with them booty, slaves, and the exuberance and pride of a triumphant army. In the opera, because it is a singing medium, this grand march is sung part of the time. This is not usually the case in real life, but it does make for good drama on the stage and represents the cheering of the crowd.

Intro.	A A B A	A A B A	Intro.	C D	Coda
	Trumpet solo Orch. Trp. Trp. and orch.				

Wedding March

Another slow-type march that warrants consideration is that used for the wedding ceremony. To some this could be considered a procession, but because of the nature of the occasion it warrants special mention. Two wedding marches have been popular for years. One is the famous Wedding March by Richard Wagner, which has been walking music for thousands of brides as they march down the aisle of the church on the arm of their father. The second is the Wedding March by Mendelssohn, which custom has placed at the end of the wedding service.

Wedding March from *Lohengrin* (Wagner)

The form of the march follows:

A B B' A | C | A B B' A

Wedding March (Mendelssohn)

Mendelssohn's Wedding March is usually played a bit faster than Wagner's. This has been the custom of more recent organists, but originally the music was intended to be regal, and fitting for a solemn but happy occasion. For many years Mendelssohn had been interested in the play *A Midsummer Night's Dream* by Shakespeare, and so in 1843 he decided to write incidental music for it. The Wedding March is number nine of twelve pieces designed to be supplemental to the play and not a musical setting of it. (See Chapter 17 for a further discussion of this music.) The wedding music celebrates the reuniting and marriage promises of Theseus and Hippolyta, two human lovers. One of Mendelssohn's letters to his sister discusses the success of the music even when first written:

Felix to Rebecca

Leipzig, October 29, 1843

. . . From early morning till late at night I have sat at my desk and have written orchestral parts until my head was burning, and therefore I had to let several Saturdays go by not being able to take care of my correspondence on these days. I do not have much to tell, except about oboes and trumpets, and they are not much to talk about. The Summer Night's Dream has twelve parts and the music from Thisbe's Death is in the same style as my Preludes, which used to make you laugh; it is played by a clarinet, a bassoon, and a kettle-drum; but as I said, they weren't much to talk about. . . . I assure you that I have especially regretted your absence during each rehearsal and performance. It would have been just right for your taste, and you would have rejoiced from your heart over the success and been saddened over the failures. It is funny, though, how the people in Berlin are surprised and delighted with our old and dear favorite piece by William. Yesterday it was performed in Berlin for the seventh time within the last ten days and there were no seats available anywhere. . . .[2]

Although this composition is often played on the organ during a ceremony, it originally was written for orchestra, and should be heard in this manner to truly appreciate its color and majesty.

---

2 *Die Familie Mendelssohn, 1729–1847,* Sebastian Hensel, Vol. III. B. Behr's Buchhandlung, Berlin, 1879, page 53. Translated by Theodor W. Alexander.

Intro.	A	A	B	A	C	A	D	A	B	A	Coda

Fanfare	aa	Fan.	aa	b	aa	ccc'c	aa	ddd'd'	Fan.	aa	b	aa	Fan.

Note that section D sounds similar to the beginning of a trio, but is short-lived.

Study Procedures

1. If you had to make a choice which of these two wedding marches would you state as a preference? On what do you base your opinion?
2. Each of the wedding marches have been composed for weddings. What in their makeup would seem to make them appropriate for the occasion? What in the music makes them ceremonial? What in the music is reminiscent of dance?

The Quick March (Street March)

If you mention march to the average person he will immediately think of the quick march, since this form is the most common. Many good examples of the quick march have been written since Napoleon decided that 70 steps per minute were entirely too slow for his armies, and requested that his men move at what has come to be the standard: 120 steps per minute. (Some university bands now march at about 150 steps per minute for short periods of time.)

Almost all of the marches commonly played by school bands or professionals have been influenced by or use this form:

Introduction	A :	B :	C (Trio) :

Several points should be made. First, the introduction is often a fanfare, similar to the fanfare in quality, or, if not sounding much like a fanfare, calls attention in some musical way. Most successful marches have this characteristic.

Secondly, the first section of the march is usually in two parts: themes A and B. These are related in one or more ways so that the march carries some unanimity: usually the same key or tonal center, of similar character, and similar in loudness, accent, and/or melodic character.

Thirdly, the second main division of the march is considered the trio. This section is usually in contrast to the first by a change of key or tonal center, and the character of the sound usually changes to something softer and less agitated, and often songlike.

The word "trio" originates from dance whenever the ensemble would give precedence to a select group of dancers, usually three. In later years this custom was transferred to instrumental compositions as well when, in order to give a variety of dynamics when these dynamics were difficult to control, the numbers of performers were reduced to gain that effect. In the march, the number of performers may not be changed, but the loudness level is often greatly and obviously reduced.

In some marches there is an agitated section between the trio and its repeat. This is often reminiscent of the earlier portion of the march in loudness if not in melody. Most people today call this the "break-up" strain, and in reality it breaks up the two parts of the trio.

Most marches carry repeat indications for each portion of the composition, so that A is usually repeated, B is repeated, then the trio (possibly a break-up), and the repeat of the trio. Even with all of the repeats the march may last only from three to five minutes.

It would be an error to leave anyone with the impression that military activity did not influence the march. Even from the days of the Old Testament the trumpet has been referred to and used in connection with the army and wars. All of the information given in the early portion of the chapter is applicable, but in addition we must realize that the movement of armies had its influence upon the march.

In early days the trumpet and drum were mostly used. Later, after the Crusades into the East, the trumpet was replaced by the fife as the main instrument for the accompaniment of soldiers and martial units. Along with the fife the Crusaders brought back the cymbals, triangle, and the concept of the drum major. When modern bands parade down the football field with the colors and the drum section separated from the remainder of the band, they are following a custom which was used by the Turks hundreds of years ago. The Turks always kept the drums and colors together, the drums playing continually during the fighting of a battle. If the drums ceased, the men knew they had to retreat, since the colors were being attacked or had been lost.

Since 1493 most military units in Europe have made accommodations for martial music even if only by eight men, which was standard for years. Even the cavalry had musicians on horseback. Because of the intense pride within the divisions or units of the military, one can readily understand why many marches carry military names. When a particularly rousing or stirring march was written and dedicated to a special unit, this would take on significance—like a theme song—for the group. Today, we have special marches for the Army, Navy, and Marines, as well as special songs for our colleges and high schools. The titles of some famous Sousa marches illustrate this tendency:

"Black Horse Troop"   "Pride of Pittsburgh"
"The Dragoons"   "St. Louis Exposition"
"The Gallant Seventh"   "Boy Scouts"
"Marquette University"   "Liberty Loan"

The town bands of German cities enlivened Renaissance festivals with their brassy playing. A mural ascribed to Hans Holbein (Courtesy of The Bettmann Archive, Inc., New York).

Study Procedures

1. Of all available marches, three warrant our attention as typical of those we hear. Listen to all three of these and compare their style:
   a. Bagley—"National Emblem" (*Note:* Melody A sounds similar to "The Star Spangled Banner")
   b. Sousa—"The Stars and Stripes Forever" (Of all his famous marches, this one contains especially interesting countermelodies)
   c. Hanssen—"Valdres" March (A singable tune)
2. Which of the three is most reminiscent of dance? Of the ceremony? Of the military background of the march? Of the fanfare? Of the personal flavor as compared to the group or unit?
3. Listen to three Sousa marches. Do they each have a particular and singular quality? Can you describe it?

Bibliography—Chapter 16

ALLEN, WARREN DWIGHT, *Our Marching Civilization.* Stanford, Calif.: Stanford University Press, 1943.

CHUJOY, ANATOLE, and P. W. MANCHESTER, *Dance Encyclopedia.* New York: Simon & Schuster, 1967.

DOLMETSCH, MABEL, *Dance of England and France, 1400–1600.* London: Routledge and Kegan Paul Ltd., 1949.

FARMER, HENRY GEORGE, *Handel's Kettledrums.* London: Henrichsen Edition Ltd., 1966.
———, *Rise and Development of Military Music.* Freeport, N.Y.: Books for Libraries, 1912.
HOOPER, KATRINE AMORY, *Dance Pageantry in History and Legend.* New York: Vantage Press, 1964.
KAPPEY, J. A., *Military Music.* London: Boosey and Company, 1894.
KENNEDY, MICHAEL, *Portrait of Elgar.* London: Oxford University Press, 1968.
LAWLER, LILLIAN B., *The Dance in Ancient Greece.* Middletown, Conn.: Wesleyan University Press, 1964.
RAFFE, W. G., *Dictionary of Dance.* New York: A. J. Barnes and Co., 1964.
SELDEN-GOTH, S., editor, *Felix Mendelssohn Letters.* New York: Pantheon Publishers, 1945.
WOOD, MELUSINE, *Historical Dances.* London: Imperial Society of Teachers of Dancing, Inc., 1964.

Recordings—Chapter 16

Bagley	"National Emblem" March	Morton Gould	Victor LM-2080
Chopin	*Polonaise No. 3 in A,* op. 40, no. 1	Rubinstein	Victor LM-1205
Copland	*Fanfare for the Common Man*	Ormandy, Phila. Orch.	Columbia ML-6084
Elgar	"Pomp and Circumstance" March No. 1	Fiedler, Boston Pops	Victor LM-2757
Hanssen	"Valdres" March	Fiedler, Boston Pops	Victor LM-2757
Mendelssohn	Wedding March from *A Midsummer Night's Dream*	Ormandy, Phila. Orch.	Columbia ML-5221
Rimsky-Korsakov	"Procession of the Nobles"	Fiedler, Boston Pops	Victor LM-2757
Sousa	"Presidential Polonaise"	Goldman Band	Capitol SW-1688
	"The Stars and Stripes Forever"	Morton Gould	Victor LM-2080
Verdi	Grand March from *Aida*	Fiedler, Boston Pops	Victor LM-1906
Wagner	Wedding March from *Lohengrin*	Bamberg Sym.	Vox STPL-511550
Walton	"Crown Imperial" March	Fennell, Eastman Wind Ens.	Mercury SR-90197

Chapter 17

The Suite

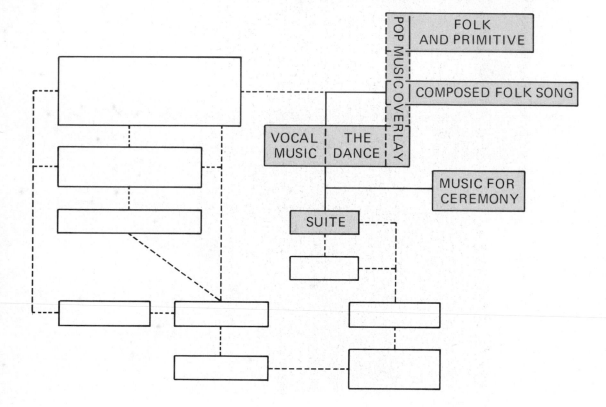

The word "suite" refers to a grouping. Consequently, the word has a number of different usages such as a suite of rooms, a group of pictures, or a grouping of furniture intended for one room. The same word root also includes the suit of clothes which we wear, usually cut from the same cloth but including two or more parts and designed to accentuate those parts. In music the same intent is present: a grouping of moderately short pieces somewhat related; in its early use, it meant specifically a group of dances.

EARLY SUITES

When "suite" denoted a group of dances, usually different types of dances were placed together for the benefit of the dancers, the musicians, or sometimes even the early printers. Many different kinds of arrangements can be found in early manuscripts, and many arrangements probably were used by the peasants as they ordered their dances.

The Two-Dance Suite

When the idea of combining dances began, most folk were attracted to the idea of combining a slower dance with a quicker one. This was true of society dancers as well as rural dancers. Although appearing early, this custom was common throughout all of Europe by the sixteenth century. The most common arrangement at that time placed the pavane with the galliard.

Remember that the pavane is a duple dance, while the quicker galliard is a triple dance producing a slow-fast or moderate-quick alternation. Most of the early dances of Europe were in triple meter and at that time Europeans seemed to prefer triple-meter dances. During the twentieth century, we have almost excluded them from consideration. The pavane, taken from a popular song of the day, often had an attractive and plaintive melody.

In 1945 the mayor of a German city wrote the following account of the two-part dance suite and how the dancers responded to it:

> After the pipers and players have been asked to play the dance, the dancer steps forward in a most elegant, polite, proud and splendid manner, chooses from among the young girls and ladies present a partner for whom he has a special affection and, making his reverences, such as taking off his cap, kissing her hand, bending his knee, invites her with friendly words and other similar ceremonies to have a gay, merry and honest dance with him.
>
> When the person has consented to dance, they both step forward, join hands, embrace and kiss each other, sometimes even on the mouth, and manifest their friendship with suitable words and gestures. Then when the dance itself is about to begin, they perform the preliminary dance. This is rather solemn, with less improper noise and activity than the following dance. During the preliminary dance those couples who are in love have a better opportunity to make conversation than during the next dance when everything is somewhat disorderly—running, scrambling, pressing of hands, secret pushing, jumping, shouting and other improper things.
>
> When the dance is over the dancer takes his partner back to her seat and, with reverences as before, leaves, or he stays, sitting on her lap and talking to her.[1]

---

[1] Johann von Munster, Provost of Pforzheim in 1594. Record notes to *Dance Music of the Renaissance,* RCA Victor record 1328.

These early suites, well-known to all the people, were used in different ways. For example, brass instruments played these suites when they were used as open-air or tower music[2]; when they were danced, they often were played by strings and winds, and when used as music of an intimate nature, they were played upon the lute.

Study Procedures

Two examples of the two-part suite are available for listening:

1. The Attaignant suite, played on the lute, exemplifies this intimacy which seems to negate the change of tempo between the pavane and galliard, leaving most of the differences between the two dances a result of meters. The form of each dance follows the simple ABC formula with each section repeated. On the recording the entire composition is played over again with repeats, probably to accommodate recording purposes, although it originally could have been played in this manner for dancing or listening. After listening to at least one suite played by brass instruments and the Attaignant suite, what generalizations can you make concerning early suites?

2. In the Franck suite, published in 1603, the form is a simple ABC with each of the sections repeated. The galliard also is in the same form, and again the strings predominate. In the repeats of the sections, the winds join with the strings. What differences do you notice between the Attaignant suite and the Franck suite? What similarities?

The Extended Suite

As the concept of grouping dances increased in interest, additional dances were added to the suite. Often this was intended mainly for the listener, and the listener could best be accommodated by grouping three, four, or up to seven or eight dances because they reminded him of the dances, their music, and their intent, without his having to dance them. Suites usually contained four popular rhythms of the day. When suites contained but two dances the courante often was substituted for the galliard, so that when four dances were used both the courante and the galliard were usually included. The newer allemande was a slower dance in duple meter, and during its early history in the suite it usually was followed by a leaping kind of dance known as the *tripla,* which would end the group.

---

2 The American Brass Quintet has published an album which includes three suites of dances for brass reminiscent of outdoor or tower music: Susato, *Five Flemish Dances;* Dowland, *Four Dances;* Pezel, *Six Seventeenth Century Dances.* Unfortunately, the album material does not include the names of the dances, but perhaps you can define the dances from their sound and general characteristics. It is possible that these dances have been organized by the brass quintet rather than the composers. Nonetheless, the arrangement could have been similar at the time of original performance.

Study Procedures

Again, two suites offer excellent study examples:

1. An interesting suite of dances by Johann Hermann Schein was written in 1617 and taken from his *Banchetto Musicale*. This grouping contains a pavane followed by a galliard, a courante, and then the allemande. It will be most obvious when the music moves into the tripla.

2. In some ways Schein's *Suite No. 2 in d minor* is the more interesting of the two. The pavane is slow, almost religious sounding, and in a duple meter; the galliard is a quick triple-meter dance; the courante is again a quick dance, but not so fast as the galliard; the courante and the allemande make use of the same melodic line; the tripla, quick and in duple meter, ends the suite. Since both the courante and the allemande make use of the same melodic line, some authorities consider this a three-section composition with the tripla acting as a coda. The forms of the dances as performed on the recording are as follows:
Pavane: ABC; galliard: AABBCCABC; courante: AABB; allemande: AABBCC; tripla: AABB.

3. Discuss the use of instruments and the interplay between the strings, recorders, and percussion instruments. Do these add to the dance effect? How do they give meaning to the form?

4. Can you hear the form and distinguish the sections? Do you concentrate mainly upon instrumentation or do you rely upon the melodic line? Can you feel the duple and triple meters of the dances? The metrical accents can assist you.

THE CLASSIC SUITE

The word "stylize," often used in connection with the dance suite, means to make conform to a distinctive mode or pattern. By the middle of the seventeenth century the suite became stylized, being known as a classic suite when it contained four particular movements: the allemande, the courante, the sarabande, and the gigue. The pavane disappeared as the introductory dance and the courante replaced the galliard. Two new sections were added: the *sarabande*, a slow Spanish dance usually in triple meter; and the *gigue,* usually accredited to the British Isles, a quick dance in compound duple meter often with a jumping melodic line and/or a fugal texture. Many times this particular classic arrangement has been accredited to Froberger,[3] and although he did use these four movements in his dance suites, most always his order placed the sarabande last. It was almost 1700 before the order of the classical suite became solidified. By this time all of these dances had become idealized types, and the music supplied by the composers of the period were not dance tunes as such, but were highly polished musical compositions which by their nature reminded the listener of the dance of the title.

---

3 Historical record collections usually include at least one suite by Froberger, and it usually follows the prescribed allemande, courante, sarabande, gigue order. In his music, which is not particularly interesting or outstanding, the differences between the movements are not distinct because the tempos are not widely different. The duple form with the repeated strains is obvious. In his *Suite in e minor* the most notable characteristic is the shortness of the sarabande, which later composers, such as Bach, usually extended to become the longest dance of the suite.

Study Procedures

1. Listen to the Froberger *Suite in e minor,* and compare it to the Schein *Suite in d minor* as to melodic inventiveness and esthetic effect.
2. Discuss how other forms have become stylized in music. What vocal forms would you choose for such a discussion? Have other art forms become stylized?

ALTERATIONS OF THE CLASSIC SUITE

Shortly after the turn of the eighteenth century, when Johann Sebastian Bach was writing suites, the custom was to include the four movements of the classic suite, but to place one or more optional dances between the third and fourth movements. Bach chose a number of different dances for the option, depending upon the particular composition. Although best-known as a composer of religious music, Bach composed much secular music, including six French Suites, six English Suites, and six Partitias for the keyboard. The latter resemble the suite in most of their characteristics. Well-known to the pianist, these contain much lovely music, for they help us understand the suite of the period as a stylized musical composition, bringing to the listener an emotional feeling for the dance movements of the preceding decades.

French Suite No. 5 (Bach)

Following the custom of the period, which means that the form had been stylized as well as the order and name of each movement, each of the dances of this suite follows the form AABB. One might conclude that a type of monotony would result, and perhaps this could be true with a lesser composer, but not with Bach. He is capable of giving the suite its unique variety through the type of melodic line chosen, but more importantly through the length of melody he uses and the manner in which he extends the phrases, often giving the listener the impression that a phrase will end, only to weave the line onward so that the phrase cadences at a point other than expected.

The allemande strikes the ear immediately as different from the dance heard in the Schein Suite. Vigorous but with an easy motion, the melodic lines are extended noticeably longer than the short phrases of the dances heard earlier.

The courante is in triple meter, quick but not rough, with a dignity and a haste that still bespeaks the deliberate control which Bach builds into his faster sections.

One would never guess that the sarabande was once an uncouth dance, so much so that the Spanish questioned it on moral grounds. To become refined by an elevation into society produces one type of alteration; to give added depth of meaning to any form is to bring to the dance new insight and meaning. Bach refined most forms in this latter way. In a slow triple meter, with no obvious

Spanish characteristics, the melodic line is clearly presented with a thin accompaniment so that one could imagine this dance being played upon the guitar. Stately, expressive, measured, this is a dance which epitomizes restrained emotion.

Three dances have been added for the optional group. The gavotte, a French dance of moderately fast tempo in duple meter, probably has become the most famous of all the dances of this suite and has been transcribed for a number of different instruments. Using a simple melody, Bach proves his flair for contrapuntal texture by the running bass line which he writes in the B section.

The bourrée is another French dance of the seventeenth century using quick duple meter. Some believe the loure of this suite to be the most beautiful example of this dance available. Slow, but not as slow as the sarabande, it again gives a delicate, refined, and orderly emotional feeling.

The gigue has a character all of its own with its quickly moving lines and imitative parts. In compound duple meter, the running, light, dainty lines seem almost never to phrase, and although the dance is light and fancy-free, the emphasis is clearly upon the technic.

What a contrast between this suite and those from earlier times! Bach was a master at placing the suite in a position of high art, and at the same time, through his form and his melodic lines, reminding us of the dancing character of each movement and the background from which the suite had come.

The suite offers two kinds of variety that have not yet been mentioned. The tempos of the suite follow a definite pattern where the established movements are concerned: the allemande is moderate, the courante is quick, the sarabande is slow, and the gigue is fast. Other dances, when added, usually were both quick and slow so that the same balance would be maintained. In the French Suite just studied, two of the optional dances were quick, and one was slow, matching the original tempos of classic suite format. The older dances more often were in triple meter, while the newer ones tended toward duple meter. In addition, the inclusion of various national dances tended to give variety to the suite; although the French usually were responsible for the bulk of the dances, the gigue is usually accredited to the English and the sarabande to the Spanish. Since the music of the classic suite in no way sounded as if it were taking on the folk characteristics of the countries from which the dances came, the suite was in no way provincial.

Suite for Orchestra No. 3 in D (Bach)

For many, the orchestral suites of Bach reach an even higher and more notable musical peak than his keyboard suites. Writing only four of these works, they are sometimes referred to as "overtures," since each begins with a movement entitled as such. This nomenclature occurred because "overture" was the newest name for a movement at the time, and the entire composition took on this identical name; then too, the overture is the first of several sections, with the remainder of the work dance-oriented, consequently, the relationship to the dance suite becomes obvious.

Suite No. 3 is well-known in musical literature, partly because it contains attractive melodic lines, partly because Bach used three trumpets in this suite and none in the other three, partly because the music contains great energy, but mostly because the second movement (the well-known Air) has been so often played and even sung that it contains a kind of popularity of its own.

Overture

This movement contains a slow introduction, a quick second portion, and then reverts to the slow tempo once again, outlining a three-part form. The slow sections may not sound as such to the listener because of the quantity of running notes which Bach wrote into the parts. The faster section is quite fugal and gives a character to the work which the slower sections do not possess. The slow portion of the overture is composed of a repetitious section followed by a short coda. The overture became such a popular form in following years that we will devote a chapter to it later in the book.

Air

Following the style of the time, Bach reverts to the AABB form for the remainder of the movements. In tempo, one could compare this air to a pavane or a sarabande and the texture to a simple song melody accompanied by a rhythmic bass part. For strings only, this gives a textural change after the full sounding overture. The B section of the movement is noticeably longer than the A section; it contains two long phrases, with the second phrase featuring several sequential patterns which add a typical Baroque color to the movement.

Gavotte I, II

Whenever specific dances were most popular with the people, it had been customary to include more than one of them within a suite. Bach followed this custom by inserting two gavottes as his third movement. Again, within the binary form, the second section is longer than the first. Introduced by a unison theme of the full orchestra followed by a phrase with reduced orchestration, the second gavotte gives us a preview of the trio form which became standard at a later time. These alternating full and reduced phrases are used throughout the second gavotte, with the unison phrase acting as the melodic unit. Following standard procedure, the first gavotte is repeated after the second, giving a three-part form to the movement it would not have had otherwise.

Bourrée

The bourrée is the shortest movement of the suite. The melodic contour of the second section imitates the first but at a higher pitch. During the second section the first melodic line reappears briefly. Both of these standard compositional devices tend to unify the movement.

Gigue

Typical of the gigue, the melodic and harmonic lines are jumpy and running, the form binary, and the meter compound duple.

DANCE SUITES OF LATER PERIODS

The suite has remained an attractive composition to composers because it contained the structure for a number of rather short movements any of which could accommodate flexibility of themes, styles, and tempo, giving balance through variety. Some composers reached beyond the European dances and included those of other civilizations or periods; other composers preferred to drop the dance titles and simply indicate the tempos. Consequently, such terms as *allegro* (fast or quick) or *andante* (moderate) were used to denote the quick and slower sections or movements.

Suite of Old American Dances (Bennett)

Scored for wind band, a most recent composition using different forms is a *Suite of Old American Dances* by Robert Russell Bennett. This suite uses jazz rhythms in the melodic lines and the rhythmic background, along with a semi-show tune character evident in the harmonic lines and orchestration. The suite often makes use of the variation technic in the higher woodwinds as they play over the lower-pitched melodic lines. Again, the composer uses the basic meter and characteristics of the folk dance named in the title of each movement, yet he changes the melodic lines so as to include jazz elements without losing the original dance hall flavor. Similar to a classical suite, these dances belong to different eras in American history. For the listener they contain the flavor and style of the early American scene without referring directly to the early dance tunes, their instrumentation, or their crudities.

Cakewalk

This is a quick dance in duple meter with agitated rhythm set against a broad melodic line; it is light in texture.

Schottische

Although in duple meter, it is not as fast as the cakewalk. This dance contains sudden outbursts of heaviness against a light-textured melodic line.

One-step

This duple-meter dance was the quick step of the early 1900s, with its one step to each measure of music. The movement projects a Western flavor, with a quieter trio. The big ending suddenly fades away.

Waltz

The only triple-meter dance in the suite, it contains the only consistently soft section.

Rag

Although not in the exact character of the old piano rags, this movement with melodic lines filled with offbeat accents contains the flavor of these instrumental pieces.

IMPRESSIONISM

We have heard music by Debussy in other chapters, but the following composition will be our first opportunity to listen to a suite written expressly for the piano. Debussy's piano music has a unique character because it epitomizes the impressionistic school. Before hearing the suite read the following description of this style of composition.

As the Romantic period pushed toward the twentieth century some painters grew restless with tradition which had hardened into an academic formula. They grew tired of painting portraits with exact detail, with the attempt to reproduce lifelike subjects with the brush, with the reworking of detail which brought formality to the picture, with the set structure or form, and with the restraints which were exercised by tradition as to the appearance of any item.

From this restlessness came a new style called Impressionism, which began with the painters, was accepted by the writers and poets, and finally was adopted by musicians. For the artist color and light became an overwhelming concern, helping him realize that a painting did not have to be an exact replica and that subject and detail were really of secondary importance; thus lines and surfaces became indefinite. They realized that a camera could take a picture which would record with exactness, but that the role of the artist was to portray the scene as the individual person sees it: often with differing colors depending upon the particular day or the time of day—with indefiniteness, as if the eye were sweeping across the scene, or with only a momentary impression, since the eye seldom studies what it observes. Visual rhythms were not set by backgrounds. Nature became important—more important than the portrait, so that when man was used in a picture he became the representation of many men rather than one particular face. In some pictures persons were so insignificant as to be represented by mere dabs of paint. Rather than mix paints to produce colors, the impressionist reduced color to small particles and placed many colors in close proximity so that the eye of the viewer could behold all of the colors which go to make up a totality.

The poets also felt this spirit of change and accepted the lead of the painters, turning away from the sentiments of the Romantic period, discarding story elements in their poems, writing no more in moral terms, but using words for the sake of their sound rather than for their meaning, struggling against rhyme, the organization of the verse, and the rhythm of the meter. The flow of the French language, with its freedom and fluidity, aided in developing a kind of expressive but musical poetry typical of the period.

Debussy was the first musician to adapt these ideas so completely to music. He developed a style which placed the color of sound at the heart of his writing, rather than form. Much of his music sounds dreamy, as if we were hearing it with some indefiniteness, so that a kind of attractive ambiguity results. The character of the sound and its length were more important than metric regularity.

In more technical terminology, impressionistic music has the following characteristics:

1. A melody usually made up of fragments, with uncertain direction in melodic contours
2. Unresolved dissonances
3. An emphasis upon whole tone or pentatonic scales and modal sounds
4. Continual shifting between tonal centers
5. No major climaxes in the sense of the Romantic period
6. Weak rhythmic structures; sound which hides the pulsation
7. Emphasis upon color rather than form, although form is usually present
8. Little emphasis upon chordal movement or energy
9. Much parallel motion, with large blocks of consonant or dissonant sound
10. The color of the sound makes even trivial melodies sound important
11. Little stress upon counterpoint or contrapuntal movement and textures

With color one of the main emphases, the orchestra with its tonal variety became the major instrument for the impressionists; the piano best could convey their intent if only one instrument were used. Many composers were attracted to the freedom which this style gave them, but few could find the proper balance within the sound spectrum to convey their thoughts meaningfully and expressively to the listener. Debussy became Impressionism's greatest interpreter.

Suite bergamasque (Debussy)

An outstanding suite for the piano, all four movements are worthy of attention; however, one movement has attracted the attention of millions of people all over the world: the third, entitled "Clair de lune." Other sections are the Prelude, Menuet, and finally the Passepied. Two of these are dance movements, and two titles give us only a feeling for the character of the music. Changes of tempo and meter still are obvious characteristics of this suite. Light, airy, coming to us almost from a dream world, this music is not rhythmic in the same sense that other dance suites might be rhythmic. Rather, just the suggestion of the rhythm exists, just as only a suggestion of dance exists, for Debussy's intent is not to imitate the dance itself, but merely to give us feelings and mental impressions of dance. The prelude sets the mood, and it remains through the entire suite.

Three Japanese Dances (Bernard Rogers)

Offering us not the exact music of dance but the feeling for the dances of Japan, much of this suite is built around the percussion section of the band, and the Oriental effects obtained by the combinations of instruments. Unique in that a soprano sings alone during the second movement, the effect is almost that of an exotic instrument playing for us and capturing our minds along with its melody. The movements are: Dance with Pennons, Dance of Mourning, Dance with Swords.

Other interesting suites and their movement titles are listed below, for additional listening:

Bartók	*Suite,* Op. 14	Allegro, Scherzo, Allegro molto, Sostenuto
Böhm	*Suite No. 8 in f minor*	Allemande, Courante, Sarabande, Ciacona
Dohnányi	*Suite in f# minor for Orchestra*	Andante with variations, Scherzo, Romance, Rondo
Nielsen	*Suite,* Op. 45	Allegretto, Poco moderato, Molto adagio, Allegretto, Allegretto vivo, Allegro
	Symphonic Suite	Intonation, Maestoso, Quasi allegretto, Andante, Allegro
Tchaikovsky	*Suite No. 3 in G Major*	Elegie, Valse mélancholique, Scherzo, Theme and variations

COLLECTION OF DANCES FOR THE PROFESSIONAL

The suite has been used as a basis for ballet, which is a dance for the professional. Since this is such a large area, it demands particular attention. Chapter 18 will be devoted completely to the ballet. However, ballet is one step in the development of the suite, and should be considered as such.

THE SUITE AND DRAMA (INCIDENTAL MUSIC)

As we may conclude, the suite changed because of pressures from two directions.

First, new dances were introduced into the suite and these slowly replaced the so-called classic dances. Secondly, composers, wishing to be relieved of the restrictions inherent in the dances, retained only the fast or slow tempo indications, and the dance name and form all but disappeared.

Still another change may be observed. The Greek dramas, the liturgical dramas of the twelfth and thirteenth centuries, the later mystery plays of the fifteenth and sixteenth centuries, the Spanish autos, the pastorales, the eclogues, the intermezzi and the entr'actes—all of these either used music incidentally or as a diversion with the spoken word. Thus, playwrights come from a tradition which recognized the value of music to heighten the dramatic effect of a staged presentation. But to be ultimately effective, the play had to await music's development until such time when it could become expressive instrumentally.

Since music establishes its emotional effects personally and often quickly, it could be used to give a new and interesting dimension to the impact of the drama, offering an interpretation by the composer which could be placed in juxtaposition with that of the author and the listener. The drama could then take on a new perspective. This becomes true, in part, because incidental music usually is made up of rather short pieces and these small pieces create an immediate and definite impression through an attractive melody, a fascinating rhythm, or a calculated mood. This brevity forces the intent of the music to become obvious quickly and with a minimum of introduction or development.

When music which accompanied drama has been of high quality, the composer often rearranges it in the form of a suite. When this is accomplished the suite takes on a double meaning: a relation to the drama, and an entity of its own. Thus the suite recalls for the listener the highpoints of the drama as understood by the composer. The intent is not to recreate the play in music, but rather to bring to mind a few isolated and yet important moments in the drama so that the listener will find himself recreating the drama in his mind. Paradoxically, incidental music written to certain plays has been well-remembered and well-liked, while the plays themselves have often been forgotten. In some of these instances the music seems not to fit the character of the drama; despite this, the music has such quality as to become a favorite with concert audiences. In these cases, the perception of the composer superceded the exact limitations of the play, thus producing a suite of music which came into being as a result of the play, but whose musical characteristics have moved beyond it.

Like the dance suite, the movements are modestly short and vary in tempo, form, and meter to give a variety to the whole. The titles of the sections relate to the characters of the play, the dramatic events, or the locale.

Some well-known and well-written suites fit this category of incidental music.

Lt. Kijé (Prokofiev)

Written in 1934, this suite originally was background music to a Russian film. Prokofiev was asked to write the music, since his compositional style seemed to fit the general intent of the plot. At this time Prokofiev was still uncertain as to the exact direction he would move in his artistic life, and although he had been living in Paris and was becoming well-known as a contemporary Russian composer, the Russian government wished him to come back to his home country. This film opportunity was part of the inducement for him to return.

Prokofiev believed that most Russian films of the day needed better music, and since a film has such a large audience he agreed to create the score. "Perhaps," he wrote, "because of the early stage of development of this art, we in Russia have not learned to value the other 'member' in the structure of the film, and are apt to regard music as something of a sideline, not deserving much attention." That the world has accepted his music while forgetting the film is proof that Prokofiev approached his assignment with seriousness.

The plot of the movie is a humorous one. The story, set during the days of the Czars, pokes fun at the mistake of either Nicholas I or Paul. It seems more logical that Paul would have been the Czar, since he had a mania for the military, proper discipline, and parades in strict Prussian style. It is reported that after his biweekly parade and review he once remarked that it was a pity that one could still see the men breathe.

The Czar mistakenly reads a report which had been correctly written, "Parootchiki Je," and translated from the Russian means, "The Lieutenants." When read it became "Parootchik Kije," taking the last two letters of one word and joining it to the article. The newly-formed word attracts the attention of the Czar because of the strange spelling for a Russian name. Since the Czar can do no wrong, those surrounding him permit the error to stand, so the Czar believes that a Lt. Kijé really exists in his army. At regular intervals, much to the surprise of the army officials, the Czar requests information concerning the lieutenant. To satisfy him, one of his aides makes up stories about his activities. When pushed by the Czar, Kijé is given a respectable birth, a love life, a marriage, a drinking tavern, and other fascinating data. One day the Czar asks if the lieutenant can come to the palace. The aides are faced with a sudden decision; they have Kijé meet an untimely death, and give him a proper burial.

The music fits the mood of the story well. It is Russian in sound, particularly in the Troika; it appears to be making fun of the events which it describes, and each movement of the work carries its own character so that it is believable in description.

The movements are five: Birth of Kijé, Romance, Wedding of Kijé, Troika, and Death of Kijé. Two of the sections, the second and fourth, are based upon Russian folk songs and would have been familiar in older versions to large numbers of people. Because they were folk songs, Prokofiev wrote one arrangement of the suite so that the folk songs could be sung by a baritone. Another arrangement was made for orchestra alone. The folk song chosen for the second movement is known as "The Little Gray Dove":

> *The little gray dove is cooing*
> *Alone both day and night,*
> *Because her beloved has flown;*
> *No longer does she sing,*
> *Gaily trilling in the arbor.*
>
> *Sadly from branch to branch*
> *She hops and flutters here and there,*
> *Flying, vainly seeking,*
> *Hoping that soon he will return.*
>
> *Dear heart, be calm again,*
> *Not like frail, trembling butterflies.*
> *Other pleasures lie near*
> *And who seeks will surely find them.*

Does this romantic verse carry implications for the love life of an army lieutenant?

The Troika is based upon an old Russian tavern song. Although sung at a rapid rate, the message of the text becomes clear:

> *A woman's heart is like an inn*
> *That charges modest fees;*
> *From early morn through night time din*
> *One comes, another goes.*
>
> *Ah, come to me, come quick to me,*
> *And I'll do you no harm. . . .*
> *Who's married, free, bashful, or brave*
> *Will understand my charm.*

Birth of Kijé

Appropriately announcing a military event, a solo trumpet acts as the prelude and postlude for the movement. The movement proper divides into three sections; the first, being the longest, consists of martial sounds: snare drum, piccolo, and flute, followed by fanfaring horns which is taken up by the entire orchestra. Section two states the smoother, more melodic Kijé theme in the oboe and saxophone. The piccolo, flute, and drum briefly return, followed again by the trumpet call, this time with mute. After the gay fanfare music of the orchestra, the trumpet almost seems to predict more sober things to come. This is not fulfilled, however.

Prelude	A Section I	B Section II	A Section I	Postlude
Trumpet alone	Drum, piccolo Horns, fanfare in the orchestra	Kijé theme, smooth, melodic Oboe, saxophone	Short repeat Piccolo, drum	Trumpet alone

Romance

This slow, sad lovers' song proposes a philosophical bent toward love; perhaps one wonders if Kijé bemoans former loves, or if the ladies pine for a Kijé who loves and moves to another.

A				B				A	
X X Low, soft	X Sax.	X X Celesta	Flute, sax. bridge	Y Y Sax.	Z Broad theme	Y	Z Repeats	X Flute, oboe	X Coda, strings

Wedding

Reminiscent of the wedding day rather than the ceremony itself, the broad introductory theme reminds us of the march beginning the service, while the light, quick theme making up most of the movement reflects upon the dance music after the ceremony and the old-time songs often sung. With this theme Prokofiev uses an orchestration that parallels a village band which in small towns often plays for the ceremony as well as for the dancing afterward.

A	B	A	B	A

Announcing theme	Dance music
	  a a b a a
	saxophone
		Announcing theme	Dance music
			  a a a
				Announcing theme

Troika

After a slow introduction, the troika begins with dash and vigor. Although a dance, the music of the troika depicts a sleigh ride through the snowy woods in an open sled pulled by three horses running abreast. The orchestration portrays the sleigh bells and the percussive sounds in an exciting manner.

Introduction	A B A	C	A (BC) A

Death of Kijé

Typical of one's dying moments, life is reviewed: the Kijé themes from earlier movements are played again, but in a new setting, often with an obbligato of higher instruments, and at times even with two of the themes played simultaneously. The first two sections are kept relatively simple, but in the third section themes alternate quickly from one to the other with counterpoint and obbligato. Once again the trumpet introduces the movement, and completes the suite.

Intro.	1st Mvt. Kijé Theme		2nd Mvt. Romance Theme				Wedding—Kijé—Romance Themes						Ending
Trpt.	A	A	B	B	B	B	B	AA	C	B	C	A	Trumpet
	Clar.,	sax.	Horn, viol. obbli- gato		tuba, strings		Strings, C trpt.	clar. C	stgs.,	trpt., stgs. obbl.	clar., stg. C stg.	fl.	

A Midsummer Night's Dream (Mendelssohn)

In previous chapters we have studied other music by Mendelssohn. In Chapter 16 we heard one movement of the suite which we will now hear in its entirety. The overture to this suite was written when Mendelssohn was only seventeen. Other music for the play came seventeen years later. Although the music was originally made up of thirteen small pieces, Mendelssohn used only four for the suite. Since the story by Shakespeare is so well-known, we will not discuss the play. Consider the quality of the music in relation to the intent and quality of the play. The play has been given thousands of times without the music, but the music has been heard almost as many times independently of the play.

Overture

A few chords—then delicate, swift music which sets the stage in the mood of fantasy and color of summer magic; this overture infers a knowledge of the plot, and an insight into the feelings of blind love.

Scherzo

The music of Puck, his pranks and fun-poking at mortals.

Nocturne

Predominantly a French horn solo, so popular that it often is played independently of the suite and many times with only a piano accompaniment, this piece challenges the best of horn players, and yet fits the instrument well. In the play this music describes the sleep which finally comes to all the characters.

Wedding March

This movement was discussed in detail in Chapter 16, with analysis and comments.

King Lear Suite (Luening and Ussachevsky)

The admirable qualities of electronic music have never been used more descriptively than in this short suite which originally was designed to accompany the presentation of Shakespeare's drama *King Lear*.

The suite purports to center upon two scenes from the play: the storm scene, and Lear's madness. Listen closely, and you will also hear a bridge between the two main sections and a coda section reminiscent of the storm scene. Although short, the descriptive qualities of the suite and its relation to the drama become evident immediately.

L'Arlésienne, Suite 1 (Bizet)

The music of these suites originally accompanied a play of the same name by Alphonse Daudet. The play had been written by Daudet from one of his short stories. The complete short story is given below. Read it, and decide the kind of music you would have written for the play had you been requested to do so.

THE WOMAN OF ARLES

On the way from my mill down to the village you pass a farmhouse built near the road and approached through a broad, open yard, planted with nettle-trees. It is a typical Provençal farmer's house, with its red tiles, its broad front pierced by irregularly placed windows, and, on top of all, the loft with its wind-vane and pulley for hoisting the bundles of hay, detached brown wisps of which are to be seen clinging here and there.

Why had this house made such an impression on me? Why did I feel my heart contract when I looked at the gate that was always shut? I could not have told you, and yet the place cast a gloom upon me. The silence that enwrapped it was unbroken. No dogs barked at the passer-by; the guinea-fowl fled without a sound. Within, no echo of human speech. Nothing, not even a mule-bell. Had it not been for the white window-curtains and the smoke rising from the roof, you would have thought the house uninhabited.

Yesterday, on the stroke of midday, I was returning from the village, and, to avoid the sun, was walking close to the walls of the farm in the shade of the nettle-trees. On the road in front of the house some men were silently loading a cart with hay. The gate had been left open. As I passed I glanced within, and saw a big, white-haired old man, dressed in a too short jacket and ragged breeches. His elbows were resting on a broad stone table and his head was bowed between his hands. I stopped. One of the men whispered to me:

"Hush! It's the master. He has been like that ever since the dreadful thing that happened to his son."

Just then a woman and a little boy, both clothed in black, passed near us, carrying big gilt prayer-books, and entered the farmhouse.   The man added:

"The mistress and the younger son coming home from Mass.   They go every day since the boy killed himself.   Oh, sir, what an affliction!   Ever since it happened his father has worn the dead boy's clothes; nothing can induce him to wear anything else. . . . Gee-up, you!"

The cart began to move.   But, wishing to learn more, I asked the driver if I could get up beside him; and it was there, on the top of the hay, that I heard this sad story. . . .

His name was Jan.   He was a fine peasant lad of just twenty years, as gentle as a girl, well built, and with frank, open manners.   As he was very handsome the women were all eyes for him; but he had room in his thoughts for one only—a little woman from Arles, all velvet and lace, whom he had met one day when visiting the town.   At the farm the liaison was rather frowned upon at first.   It was said that the girl was flighty, and her parents were not local people.   But Jan was determined to have his Arlesian.   He would say:

"I shall die if I cannot have her."

The thing had to be accepted.   The wedding was fixed for after the harvest.

Now, one Sunday evening, the family were seated in the farmyard and dinner was nearly over.   It was almost a wedding banquet.   The fiancée was not with them, but many toasts had been drunk in her honour. . . .   A man comes to the gate and asks to speak to Mr Estève, alone.   Estève rises and goes out on to the roadway.

"Master," says the man, "you are about to wed your son to a jade, who has been my mistress for two years.   I give proof of what I say: look at those letters!   Her parents know all about it and had promised her to me.   But, since your son has been coming after her, neither they nor our fine lady will have anything to do with me.   And yet I would have thought that, after what has happened, she could never be the wife of another."

"Say no more!" says Mr Estève, after looking at the letters.   "Come in and have a glass of wine."

The man answers:

"No, thank you!   I am more grieving than thirsty."

And he goes away.

The father returns, giving no sign.   He resumes his seat at the table, and the merry meal goes on to the end.

That same evening Estève and his son went out into the fields together.   They were away a long time.   When they returned the mother was still waiting for them.

"Wife," said the farmer, presenting his son to her, "be very good to him!   He is unhappy. . . ."

Jan never spoke again to the woman from Arles.   Yet he still loved her, all the more even since they had shown her in the arms of another.   Only he was too proud to speak of it; that was what killed him, poor boy!   He would sit for whole days in a corner, alone.   And again he would work furiously on the land, doing the work of ten labourers. . . .   In the evening he would set out on the road to Arles, walking straight ahead until he saw the slender steeples of the town silhouetted against the sunset sky.   Then he would turn back.   He never went any farther.

Seeing him in this condition, always sorrowful and alone, his people at the farm didn't know what to do.   They were afraid.   Once, during dinner, his mother looked at him with tear-filled eyes, and said:

"Now, listen, Jan!   If you still want her so much we shall agree to let you have her."

His father looked down, flushing with the shame of it.

Jan made a gesture of refusal and went out.

From that day his demeanour changed. Seeking to reassure his parents, he pretended to be always cheerful. He showed himself again at dances in the café, and at bullbrandings. At the feast of the patron saint of Fontvieille it was he who led the farandole.

His father said, "He is cured." His mother still kept her fears, and watched her boy more closely than ever. Jan slept with his younger brother close by the silkworm-rearing house; the poor old soul had her bed moved next to their room. The silkworms might need attention in the night!

And so time passed until the feast of St Eloi, the farmers' patron.

Great rejoicing at the farm. . . . There was Château-Neuf for everybody, and spiced wine flowed in rivers. There were fire-crackers, fires were lit in the yard, and coloured lanterns hung all about on the bushes. Long live St Eloi! They danced the farandole till they dropped. The younger son burned his new blouse. Even Jan looked happy; he asked his mother to dance with him; the poor woman wept for joy.

At midnight they went to bed. Every one was sleepy. But Jan didn't sleep. His young brother told us later that he sobbed all through the night. Oh, I can assure you that he had got it really badly.

Next day, at dawn, his mother heard some one pass through her room at a run. She had a foreboding that something was wrong.

"Is that you, Jan?"

No answer; Jan is already on the stairs. Quickly, quickly, his mother leaves her bed.

"Jan, where are you going?"

He goes up into the loft; she follows.

"My boy! For God's sake!"

He shuts the door and bolts it.

"Jan, my little Jan, answer me. What are you going to do?"

With her trembling old hands she gropes for the latch. . . . A window opening, the sound of a body falling on the flagstones of the yard, and nothing more.

Poor boy, he had said to himself, "I love her too much. . . . I am going. . . ." Oh, our wretched human hearts! Why, tell me, cannot we cease to love what we despise?

The people in the village wondered who could be calling out so, up at Estève's farm, at that early hour.

In the yard, beside the stone table, a mother, wet with dew and blood, and naked from her bed, was bewailing her son who lay dead in her arms.[4]

The play is similar to the short story: few characters, one inevitable tragic situation, with the action slowly moving to its conclusion. As in the story, the woman from Arles never appears on stage, and yet the action revolves about her.

Bizet emphasized the rural character of the play by including folk songs, carols, and since the short story mentioned it, a farandole. From the twenty-seven short descriptive pieces several were placed into four movements by Bizet for Suite No. 1; after his death others were made into Suite No. 2 by Guiraud, a professional musician, teacher of Debussy, and writer of an orchestration text who spent all of his adult life in Paris even though born in New Orleans.

Suite No. 1: Prelude

Here is a French Christmas tune. The theme, stated in unison, precedes four

---

[4] From *The Works of Alphonse Daudet*. Walter J. Black, 1929.

variations: for woodwinds, for strings with a marchlike feeling, for strings with a bassoon running figure, and for full orchestra in a military setting. The second part is probably the first symphonic solo for alto saxophone. The third part is a romantic-tragic theme. The three parts have the form ABC.

Minuetto

This piece is gay but yet it contains a rural character. The trio is a singable tune with violin and woodwind countermelodies. This is a song-and-trio form with the usual return to the main theme.

Adagietto

Using only strings, this love song is full of yearning, tenderness, and subdued passion; it is sweet but short.

Carillon

Every peasant knew the importance of church, village, and farm bells and soon learned the meaning of each. As the title suggests, the movement recalls the rural flavor of bell sounds above a rhythmic and monotonous bass line. As a folk tune, this was originally wedding music. In ABA form, the movement's second section, devoted to a song, sounds almost as if it belongs to an older time.

ADDITIONAL SUITES FROM DRAMAS

Fauré	*Pelléas et Mélisande*
Grieg	*Peer Gynt*
Khachaturian	*Masquerade*
Kodály	*Háry János*
Offenbach	*Gaité Parisienne*
Prokofiev	*Love of Three Oranges*
Sessions	*The Black Maskers*

Study Procedures

1. Read the play *Peer Gynt;* then decide how effectively Grieg's music assists the drama.
2. Compare the *Masquerade* Suite of Khachaturian with *The Black Maskers* of Sessions. Russian authors provided the texts for which both of these works were written. Which work do you like better? Why?
3. Some musical ideas of the *L'Arlésienne* Suites are forerunners of Bizet's *Carmen*. What in particular do you hear that would fit this description?
4. Read the play *Pelléas et Mélisande*. How well has Fauré captured the essence of the drama through his music?
5. Make a detailed form analysis of either the Grieg or the Bizet suites which would be similar to that found in this book for *Lt. Kijé*.

6. Compare the music of the two Prokofiev suites. In what ways are they similar, and in what ways different? Had you not been told of their authorship, would you have suspected they were by the same person? Why?

7. Which suite best assists you in understanding the underlying implications of the drama for which it was written? What in the music makes this insight possible?

THE DESCRIPTIVE SUITE

Once incidental music had become an accepted type of suite, it was a logical step for the composer to create a series of movements held together by any single unifying idea. Some of these compositions are descriptive because the movements depict a series of related events or paint a series of related pictures. Other suites of this type describe the people of a region through their folk literature or song. In each case the unifying idea becomes the takeoff point for the suite. Usually, as with the original dance suites, the tempos and the meters vary. In order to bring the listener an esthetic impact and still maintain connections with historic origins of the suite, most often the music will begin with a moderate to quick tempo and end with a fast tempo in the final movement. Many suites consist of four movements; however, a few contain as many as eight or ten, similar to a few dance suites of the seventeenth century. Many suites exist in this descriptive category; our review of only a few should not deter the student from exploring others on the suggested list. Some which are not well-known might prove to be of major interest.

Three Places in New England (Ives)

Of recent years Charles Ives has become a major force in American music. His stature was only slowly realized because, as with any artist who works considerably ahead of his time, his music contained certain elements which were completely out of tune with the Romantic period and the Romantic mind. Although contemporary sounding dissonances are commonplace within his style, he was a champion of this type of writing when no other American composer thought this type of music valuable or meaningful.

Ives had an intense love for his country—not the flag-waving kind, although he was apt to wave the flag if he thought it important to the occasion, but the kind of patriotism which places his country's past into perspective with the present. Throughout all of his music he was reminding us of our heritage: our heritage of religious songs, patriotic songs, cowboy songs, or scenes where important events took place. His father had been a musician during the Civil War, and events of any war took on importance for him if they bespoke of any man's efforts to hold the line against intolerance, bigotry, or other forms of personal servitude, mental or physical.

The St. Gaudens Shaw Memorial (Courtesy of Dartmouth College Library, Hanover, N.H.).

The suite involves three important geographical locations for Ives. They are part of his past, part of the past of our country, and he wishes to write them into our present. His music does not describe these scenes in any artificial or cheap manner; he attempts to give us a feeling for the emotions of each scene as he saw it as a young New Englander, and as history has given it some perspective. His music is written to give impressions, to conjure up ideas, to assist us in balancing our present with the past as Ives appreciates it.

The "St. Gaudens" in Boston Common
(Col. Shaw and His Colored Regiment)

This unusual name for a movement is typical of Ives. He often gave his compositions titles that would never satisfy the usual musician. And yet, such a title becomes most proper after its meaning is explained. Augustus St. Gaudens was a prominent American artist and sculptor whose work includes a memorial bronze statuary for the famous 54th Regiment from Massachusetts. The memorial is located in Boston Common, once a grazing area for cows for the villagers of Boston, but more recently a city park on the sloping hillside in front of the state capitol building. Colonel Shaw was requested by the governor to lead the 54th Massachusetts Regiment during the Civil War, the first black regiment in the history of the United States and the pride of the people of Massachusetts.

Robert Shaw had accepted the leadership of the regiment after considerable debate with himself, his family, and concern for his reputation. Blacks were thought to be unable to fight, and not intelligent enough to become reputable soldiers. Shaw's family had great faith in the principle of self-determination of the black man, and urged him to accept the governor's offer. He had trained the men in the flatland outside of Boston. When they were ready, they marched through the Boston streets before embarking by ship for the coast of South Carolina, where they assisted in the seige of Charleston and the battle of Fort Sumter:

> At the head of his regiment, with Patrick Gilmore's marching band, rode Robert Gould Shaw, the young colonel of the regiment, his back straight, his bright sword held in his gloved right hand, the muscles of his horse's flanks reflecting the sky like polished silver.[5]

Shaw had trained his men well, better in fact, than many white units. Their deportment and character was a point of pride for Massachusetts. John Greenleaf Whittier, well-known American poet and pacifist, came out to view the departure:

> The only regiment I ever looked upon during the war was the 54th Massachusetts on its departure for the South. I can never forget the scene as Colonel Shaw rode at the head of his men. The very flower of grace and chivalry, he seemed to me beautiful and awful, as an angel of God come down to lead the host of freedom to victory.[6]

When called into battle, they led the attack upon Fort Wagner at the mouth of the Ashley, Cooper, and Wando Rivers, and across the bay from Fort Sumter. Shaw led his men with raised sword as they rushed up the parapet of the fort, meeting almost sure death. Many of the troops and many of the officers, as well as Shaw, died in the attempt to seize the fort. The men had fought gallantly not only at this battle but in one only a few days before. They were heroes to the men of the Union Army as well as the people of Massachusetts.

Ralph Waldo Emerson dedicated a poem to these men which many remember. Four lines state:

> *So nigh is grandeur to our dust,*
> *So near is God to man,*
> *When duty whispers low, Thou must,*
> *The youth replies, I can.*[7]

> Now the narrow neck of sand where Shaw was buried with his men is washed by Atlantic storms. . . . To New Englanders of his own time, Shaw, in his youthful Victorian innocence, seemed a kind of saint. In the last few months

---

5 *One Gallant Rush,* Peter Burchard. St. Martin's Press, New York, 1965, page 1.
6 *Ibid.,* page 94.
7 *Ibid.,* page 143.

of his life, in his latter days and final hours, he had drawn on his forefathers' deep convictions and sense of duty and his own devotion to the cause which had rekindled the imaginations of New England's poets and scholars, preachers and teachers and practical men. In his last hours, Shaw had indeed caught fire and to those who had devoted their lives to the breaking of the back of the American shame, his death was an evening and a dawn.[8]

The spirit of the sacrifice of these men did not quickly die. Years later the people of Massachusetts requested Augustus St. Gaudens, prominent sculptor and artist, to create a memorial in bronze to this brave regiment and the man who led it. Commemorated on Memorial Day, May 31, 1897, St. Gaudens himself gave us several impressions of the day in his diary:

> I was assigned to a carriage in the parade with Mr. William James, the orator of the occasion, and we followed slowly at the tail end of a long line of regiments and societies. . . . Yet to see this line of faces on each side of the streets, continuing for miles and miles, and all the windows filled with persons gazing at you, is really a profound experience. . . . I was assigned a seat on the lowest platform, a vantage point from which I watched veterans marching toward me up Beacon Hill. These were the officers and colored men of the Fifty-fourth Massachusetts Regiment, whom Shaw had led. Many of them were bent and crippled, many with white heads, some with bouquets and one with a carpet bag. . . . The impression of those old soldiers passing the very spot where they left for the war so many years before, thrills me even as I write these words. . . . The Negro veterans faced the Shaw Memorial as the flags dropped, and when this part of the ceremonies ended, they saluted the statue of their young leader while the regimental band played "John Brown's Body."

Another observer that day stated:

> The Veterans of the old 54th came in for great applause, especially when the torn but still bright colors went by, held up by a lame old Negro.[9]

Ives was a strong believer in the rights of all men. He was the first American composer to write a commemoration and eulogy for a great colored unit who fought in the Civil War. Hazy, misty, melodic fragments attract our attention only to fade; the drum occasionally produces a martial feeling. "Yankee Doodle," "Old Black Joe," and "Reveille" become a part of the fabric through variation and fantasy. Faint bugle calls and unsure melodies begin but quickly fade. No specific form materializes but the music paints a mood reminiscent of a man pondering the multifaceted aspects of the role of the recruitment, fighting, and struggle of the black unit.

---

[8] *Ibid.,* page 147.
[9] *Saint-Gaudens and the Gilded Era,* Louise Hall Tharp. Little, Brown and Company, Boston, 1969, pages 267, 268, 269.

Putnam's Camp, Redding, Connecticut

Here is another war scene, but one of an entirely different nature, and the music reflects this difference. Putnam was a famous fighter in the French and Indian Wars throughout upper New York in the Fort Edward, Lake George, Ticonderoga area. After earning a reputation as a brave and gallant man, it seemed only natural for him to rise to the need of the colonies when fighting began with the British. Putnam reached the Boston area shortly after the Battle of Lexington and became involved even without orders. Shortly thereafter, the Continental Congress named him a major general under George Washington. He was present at the Battle of Bunker Hill, and has the reputation for voicing the oft-heard cry, "Don't shoot until you see the whites of their eyes." Putnam himself denied having said this, but he did make every effort to hold the inexperienced troops to their commitment of the day as he witnessed them running. Afterward he stated that the colonial forces could have won the day easily had they remained to fight. It was Putnam who requested the cannons from Fort Ticonderoga and for whom they were dragged across the mountains to assist with the Battle of Boston, chasing the British from this key city and port.

During the winter of 1778–1779, while Washington and his troops were wintering at Valley Forge, Putnam and the right wing of the Continental Army wintered at Redding, Connecticut. The men were no better treated than those at Valley Forge because they too had little clothing, few supplies, and equal hardships from the weather:

> Putnam's troops in winter camp of 1778–79 at Redding, were ready to rush to the Hudson if Clinton made a move and to ward off dashes from New York for Connecticut supplies, of which the amount was limited. There being no tentage, rude huts had to be constructed and ovens built from the abundant supply of rocks.[10]

During this winter, Washington visited the encampment at least three times, and records indicate that a banquet was held in a local tavern for Washington, Putnam, and other officers by the local Masonic lodge. The ovens built by the men were uncovered by a farmer in the mid-1930s. Three spies were hanged during the winter for being traitors to the cause.

The music, organized into a three-part form by Ives, does not use repeated melodic lines but rather time periods to demark his form: the present, the past, and again the present. In the composition, the present depicts Ives's youth when he attended the Redding Encampment Park for a picnic.

As the movement begins the noise of the celebration makes the band playing sound unclear. Gaiety pervades: there is the village band, and a square dance tune, the distortion of which reminds us of the thin line between present

---

[10] *Burpee's The Story of Connecticut,* Charles W. Burpee. American Historical Company, Inc., New York, 1939, pages 409–410.

and past.   Suddenly the scene shifts; our mind reminisces of the Revolutionary
War, the drumming of the marching men, and the uncertain dedication of the
forces.   Quickly the present returns.   Two bands approach the campground, one
from the north, the other from the south.   The listener hears each play its own
melodies and rhythm as it comes nearer.   The square dance tune is heard, but
it is quickly replaced by the bands.

This is no stunt with Ives, as it could have become.   Rather, it provides
one with a genuine feeling of a remembered boyhood event, with the past crowd-
ing our consciousness with the present.

The Housatonic at Stockbridge

As a contrast, this movement is not war- or battle-connected.   Ives wished us
to join with him in appreciation of one of the many scenic attractions of New
England, and because of a well-liked poem, chose a river scene at Stockbridge,
Massachusetts in the Berkshire Mountains in the western part of the state.   Today, the summer home of the Boston Symphony is nearby.   When Ives was
younger, it was perhaps only a rustic area where some could summer among the
mountains.   Once Ives and his wife walked along the river and could hear the
strains of a camp meeting hymn in the distance.   The movement brings us an
idyllic picture so frequent in New England, nothing more.   The mind of the
listener confronts a scene which Ives assists in focusing for us: a covered bridge,
a walk along a small river, a stop in a horse and buggy to observe the beauties
of the natural scene.

A poem by Robert Underwood Johnson prompted the movement, and
is worth reading.

The Pines of Rome (Respighi)

Like Ives, Respighi loved his country, but his musical compositions reflected this
in an entirely different manner.   While still young, he left Italy to play viola
and study composition in Russia with Rimsky-Korsakov, the great orchestrator.
This study influenced his compositions so that they exhibit meticulous work-
manship along with brilliant use of instruments.   Although melodic and attractive, they never sound as if derived from folk song.

Pines of the Villa Borghese

For hundreds of years the Borghese family had been prominent in Italy.   In
1605 Camillo Borghese became Pope Paul V, and during his tenure assisted
his family to attain great wealth and power.   A later member of the family became husband to Napoleon's sister.   The Borghese family built a fabulous estate
on one of the seven hills of Rome overlooking the city.   Although now a property

The Villa Borghese, Rome (Courtesy of Italian Government Travel Office, New York).

of the state and an art gallery displaying great works, it originally was the locale of important meetings, sumptuous parties, and family activities. Tall pines surround the Villa and border the driveway as it rises from the city below.

This movement exemplifies the composer's use of orchestral colors through the extreme registers of the instruments. The French horns sparkle and the oboe plays a fanfare melody; all the sounds remind us of an entrance or a beginning for some important, gay event. Again we hear the oboe, but with a different theme, and again the fanfares. This time a dissonant note interrupts the sounds and the gaiety. Since the composer wishes this suite to concentrate on the form of dynamics rather than the form of melody, he uses this movement to introduce the dynamic of continual loudness.

Pines of the Catacombs

In another chapter of this book we discussed the Catacombs of Rome as the locale of the worship of early Christians who wished to avoid persecution. Lining the miles of interlacing walkways are the graves of thousands of Rome's great and poor. The pines in this area are old and often partly dead, as might seem appropriate to the area. Only a few trees exist, but these offer solace to the grieving and bring to mind the worship activity of an earlier time.

Dull, heavy, somber sounds contrast with the preceding movement. The muted trumpet plays a melodic line with the strings, but few songlike qualities exist. The low brass begins a chant that repeats over and over; a countermelody in the trombone contrasts with the same chant played in the strings, much as a solo singer of old would have sung a hymn while the worshiping congregation chanted. The first melody reappears as the sounds become fainter. This movement takes a dynamic form of soft to loud to soft.

Pines of the Janiculum

One of the seven hills of Rome, the pines at the crest overlook another portion of the great city. In this movement the winds from the Mediterranean sweep quietly and the birds are heard as they nest and sing.

   The music begins with the clarinet quietly playing a melodic line, but the exact melody is forgotten in favor of the overall effect from the clarinet, the violins, then all the strings. The music imitates the wind and breezes in the trees but is never imitative to the point of cheapness. The piano is heard followed by shimmering strings, and as the movement ends recorded bird calls are dubbed over the orchestra. The dynamics are soft throughout.

Pines of the Appian Way

The most famous roadway into Rome was paved for Caesar's armies. Along the Appian Way soldiers triumphantly returned from their exploitations in near and far places. Pines that grow near the road have witnessed such exaltation, such triumphant celebrations that only the Romans of old knew.

The old Appian Way, Rome (Courtesy of Italian State Tourist Office, New York).

Heavily rhythmic, a melodic fragment is faintly heard as if coming from a distance. The English horn plays an exotic melody to remind us of Eastern conquests and booty. Trumpets begin faintly, only to become louder as the rhythmic pulse also increases in intensity. We hear no melody as such, but the fanfares and rhythmic drive keep the movement alive, even throbbing, ever closer and closer. The section ends at its loudest peak. Additional trumpets and trombones are sometimes added to the orchestra for this movement to give additional brilliance and realism. The dynamic form of the music proceeds from soft to very loud.

Amores (Cage)

The movement titles of this short suite give little indication to the listener as to what to expect. The four movements differ completely; the most interesting are the first and last, which use "prepared piano," a method of altering the piano sound by placing paper, nuts, bolts, or other objects between or on the strings of the instrument. Although the result is not at all like an electronic modification of piano sound, this adjustment may give similar impressions to the listener. After listening, you may wish to add your own subtitles to the movements.

a. Prepared piano (one player)
b. Nine tom-toms and a pod rattle (three players)
c. Seven wood blocks (three players)
d. Prepared piano (one player)

ADDITIONAL DESCRIPTIVE SUITES

Many of the following compositions which fit this category will prove interesting listening and can offer variety to those discussed:

Debussy	*Children's Corner Suite*	Nursery toys and scenes; written for his daughter
Debussy	*Estampes*	Engravings, or pictures, which one might find in a study or den
Respighi	*The Fountains of Rome*	Four additional scenes of Rome, centered about its fountains
Milhaud	*Suite française*	Musical pictures of five provinces of France
Saint-Saëns	*Carnival of the Animals*	Twelve animals described through music
MacDowell	*Indian Suite*	Five scenes of Indian village life

Holst	*Second Suite in F*	Four movements based on Hampshire folk melodies
Vaughan Williams	*Folk Song Suite*	Three movements based on eight English folk songs
Grainger	*Lincolnshire Posy*	Folk song suite using variations on simple themes, canon, augmentation, and countermelodies

Study Procedures

1. Compare the two Respighi suites as to: a) ability to describe scenes, b) orchestral sounds, c) form of the movements, and d) the dramatic and descriptive effect upon the listener.
2. Compare the Milhaud, Holst, Vaughan Williams, and Bartók works in their use of folk song material. Which of these uses folk material for descriptive purposes such as we find in the Bartók? Which of these merely arranges folk song material in different ways so that the melody is heightened?
3. Do any of the above composers use folk song material in the same manner as Percy Grainger?
4. If you were to compose a suite using folk material from one section of our country, what material would be attractive for you to use? Would it be best rearranged, or merely used as a basis for impressional effects?
5. Had Respighi lived in your area rather than in Rome, what might he have composed rather than his *Pines* or *Fountains?* Would the music have been radically different? How would it have sounded?
6. Review another composition of Ives, and state how he focused his patriotism in that composition.
7. Listen to the Grainger suite, and organize each movement by the number of times the melodic line is given different treatment. Describe in some manner the type of sound you hear for each repeat. For example, the first folk song is heard four times; each version is different from the preceding one. Describe this difference in your own words.

Bibliography—Chapter 17

Battles and Leaders of the Civil War, Vol. IV. New York: Thomas Yoseloff, Inc., 1966.
BURCHARD, PETER, *One Gallant Rush.* New York: St. Martin's Press, 1965.
BURPEE, CHARLES W., *The Story of Connecticut.* New York: The American Historical Company, Inc., 1939.
BURROUGHS, JOHN, ed., *Songs of Nature.* Freeport, N.Y.: Books for Libraries Press, 1969.
BURTON, E. MILBY, *The Siege of Charleston, 1861–65.* Columbia, S.C.: University of South Carolina Press, 1970.
COWELL, HENRY and SIDNEY, *Charles Ives and His Music.* New York: Oxford University Press, 1955.
DAUDET, ALPHONSE, *Works of Alphonse Daudet.* Roslyn, N.Y.: Walter J. Black, Inc., 1929.
DOBIE, G. V., *Alphonse Daudet.* London: Thomas Nelson and Sons Ltd., 1949.

FENYO, THOMAS, "The Piano Music of Bela Bartok." Unpublished dissertation. University of California, Los Angeles, 1956.

GOZZI, COUNT CARLO, *Memoirs.* London: John C. Nimmo, 1890.

HEIBERG, HANS, *Ibsen, A Portrait of the Artist.* Coral Gables, Fla.: University of Miami Press, 1967.

HIGGINSON, THOMAS WENTWORTH, *Army Life in a Black Regiment.* Lansing, Mich.: Michigan State University Press, 1960.

LASSAIGNE, JACQUES, *Impressionism.* New York: Funk and Wagnalls, 1966.

LAVRIN, JANKO, *Ibsen and His Creation.* London: W. Collins and Sons and Company Ltd., 1921.

MACHLIS, JOSEPH, *Introduction to Contemporary Music.* New York: W. W. Norton and Company, Inc., 1961.

MAETERLINCK, MAURICE, *Pelléas et Mélisande.* London: George Allen and Unwin Ltd., 1895.

MONRAD-JOHANSEN, DAVID, *Edvard Grieg.* New York: Tudor Publishing Co., 1945.

NESTYEV, ISRAEL V., *Prokofiev.* Stanford, Calif.: Stanford University Press, 1960.

POOL, PHOEBE, *Impressionism.* New York: Frederick A. Praeger, 1967.

SACHS, MURRAY, *The Career of Alphonse Daudet.* Cambridge, Mass.: Harvard University Press, 1965.

SALZMAN, ERIC, *Twentieth Century Music: An Introduction.* Englewood Cliffs, N.J.: Prentice-Hall, Inc., 1967.

SEROFF, VICTOR, *Sergei Prokofiev, A Soviet Tragedy.* New York: Funk and Wagnalls, 1968.

SHAW, GEORGE BERNARD, *The Quintessence of Ibsenism.* New York: Brentano's, 1931.

THARP, LOUISE HALL, *Saint-Gaudens and the Gilded Era.* Boston: Little, Brown and Company, 1969.

Recordings—Chapter 17

Attaignant, Pierre	Pavane, Galliard		Victor VICS-1328
Bach, J. S.	*French Suite No. 5*	Jorg Demus	Remington RLP-199-25
Bartók	*Out of Doors*	Leonid Hambro	Bartók BRS-002
Bartók	*Suite,* Op. 14	Bartók	Bartók BRS-003
Bennett	*Suite of Old American Dances*	Eastman Ensemble	Mercury MG-50079
Bizet	*L'Arlésienne,* Suites 1 and 2	Ormandy	Columbia ML-5946
Böhm	*Suite for Cembalo No. 8 in f minor*	Leonhardt	Telefunken-Decca SAWT-9463-B
Collection	*Music for Brass: 1500–1970*	American Brass Quintet	Desto DC-64474
Debussy	*Children's Corner Suite*	Firkusny	Capitol P-8350
Debussy	*Estampes*	Firkusny	Capitol P-8350
Debussy	*Suite bergamasque*	Firkusny	Capitol P-8350
Debussy	*Suite bergamasque*	Richter	Columbia M2L-274
Dohnányi	*Suite in f# minor*	Sargent, London	Columbia ML-2172
Franck, Melchior	Pavane, Galliard		Victor VICS-1328
Froberger	*Suite in e minor*		Haydn Society HSE-9039
Grainger	*Lincolnshire Posy*	Eastman Wind	Mercury SR-90173

Grieg	*Peer Gynt,* Suites 1 and 2	Fiedler	Victor LM-2075
Holst	*Suite in E♭*	Eastman Wind	Mercury MG-50088
Holst	*Suite No. 2 in F*	Eastman Wind	Mercury MG-50088
Ives	*Three Places in New England*	Ormandy	Columbia ML-6084
Khachaturian	*Masquerade,* Suite	Kostelanetz	Columbia CL-758
MacDowell	*Indian Suite*	Eastman-Rochester	Mercury MG-50082
Mendelssohn	*A Midsummer Night's Dream*	Monteux	Victor LM-2223
Milhaud	*Suite française*	Eastman Wind	Mercury SR-90173
Nielsen	*Suite, Op. 45*	John Ogdon	Victor LSC-3002
Nielsen	*Symphonic Suite*	John Ogdon	Victor LSC-3002
Poulenc	*Suite française*	Poulenc	Columbia ML-4399
Prokofiev	*Classical Symphony*	Ormandy	Columbia MS-6545
Prokofiev	*Love for Three Oranges*	Ormandy	Columbia MS-6545
Respighi	*The Fountains of Rome*	Reiner	Victor LM-2436
Respighi	*The Pines of Rome*	Reiner	Victor LM-2436
Rogers	*Three Japanese Dances*	Eastman Wind	Mercury SR-90173
Saint-Saëns	*Carnival of the Animals*	Fiedler	Victor LM-2075
Schein, Johann H.	*Suite No. 1 in G Major*	Conrad Ensemble	Nonesuch H-71128
Schein, Johann H.	*Suite No. 2 in d minor*	Conrad Ensemble	Nonesuch H-71128
Stravinsky	*Suite II for Small Orchestra*	Stravinsky	Columbia ML-6048
Tchaikovsky	*Suite No. 3 in G Major*	Boult	London LL-1295
Vaughan Williams	*Folk Song Suite*	Eastman Wind	Mercury MG-50088

Chapter 18

Ballet

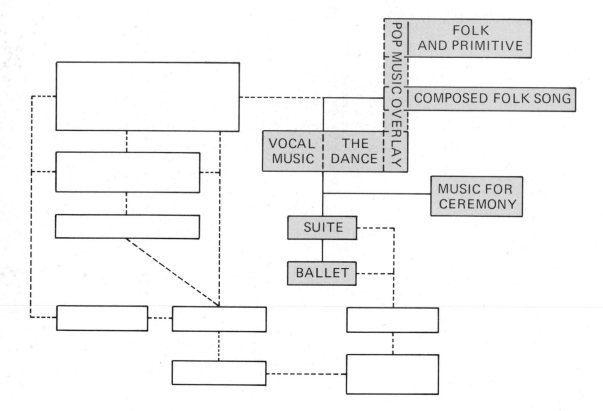

Even before it had a name ballet was destined to develop, since man desires and appreciates skills and artistry of high quality. Those who enjoyed expressing themselves through dance organized it and furthered its possibilities by performing and demonstrating for others.

Early specialized dancing only separated the more skillful performers of stylized folk dances such as the pavane, the saraband, and the gigue. For special occasions these were danced by those who performed them best, often the personages of the court or those in attendance at an event. However, beginning in 1630 these dancers no longer were guests at the social event but appeared suddenly to perform and immediately exited, rarely mingling with the audience, since they were not of the same social stratum. Once this segregation began, an entirely different approach to dance was in the offing.

Since it was customary to offer entertainment at important events such as religious celebrations, marriages, court celebrations, and holidays, special dancing was added to the masquerades and plays which had long been customary on such occasions. Dancing became a part of the play or masquerade, and the dancers also wore costumes and masks in order to aid with character representation. Some of these entertainments were of unusual dimensions, employing hundreds of persons for the entertainment of hundreds more. Dancers were brought into the performing arena in small wagons, each of which stopped before the honored guests, whereupon someone proclaimed a speech, performed a small play, or danced. When dancing was involved, each wagon would be considered an entree or individual entrance, and after several artists had entered and performed, then all would unite for a general closing dance. Thus we see how ballet became sectioned, and how one, two, or more persons were balanced against the group.

Beaumont describes an early dance spectacle in his book:

> An excellent example of the interlude, which for all practical purposes may be regarded as the prototype of ballet, was the splendid entertainment given in 1789 by Bergonzio di Botta, of Tortona, on the occasion of the marriage of Galeazzo, Duke of Milan, with Isabella of Aragon. It took the form of a great feast at which each dish was presented with an appropriate dance. This banquet ballet, most ingeniously contrived and full of graceful allusion, became famous throughout Europe, so that every petty Court aspired to give similar entertainments.[1]

Although beginning in Italy, it was in France where ballet became a discipline and made a beginning toward becoming an art form which expressed the inner feelings of man through movement and visual design. At the court of Louis XIV dancing was considered important both as an entertainment and as an artistic form of expression. The king established a school for dancing, and the dancing master, André Beauchamps, developed five basic steps or formations for the feet which have influenced dancing even until today. With specialized training and personnel, other changes soon followed: young girls were introduced into the dancing group which had heretofore been composed entirely of males wearing masks; the costuming changed, with the skirt being raised between the ankle and the knee so as to enable the observer to see the movement of the feet; and the heelless shoe was developed to enable the dancer to move more easily about the floor.

---

1 *A Short History of Ballet,* Cyril W. Beaumont. C. W. Beaumont, London, 1944, page 7.

Since dancing originally was part mime and part masquerade, it became associated with opera and drama, first being inserted into these forms as a diversion or interlude between sections, but later as a part of the performance itself. Thus began one of history's most intriguing marriages in the arts which was to see a constant shifting of influence between the two, with some periods in which dance was prominent over singing, and others in which singing became more important than dance, with drama almost always present in both.

BALLET CHARACTERISTICS

Our concerns are with the music of the ballet, but to understand this music it is important that we know something of the background of dance as well. Several characteristics of ballet should be discussed:

1. *Ballet is a series of dances.* When specialized dancing first began it was merely a collection of dances which had been performed in the local geographic area. The participants were those most able to perform these stylized dances. When dance was moved into the theater the grouping of dances continued. As it became more original the basic characteristics of the peasant dances or the stylized court dances were supplanted by dancing of a more professional nature. However, the idea of a variety of dances to make up an entire performance still continued, so that it was customary to interchange a soloist, a small group, and the entire group of dancers in order to obtain variety. Length and tempo of the dances also aided in variety. As the ballerina became more the center of focus, she was removed from the dancing group to become a soloist, performing only at specific times. Ballets which feature a ballerina use secondary dancers and chorus (corps de ballet) in alternation, usually keeping the most skillful dancing in abeyance until the ballerina comes onstage. By listening to the music of a ballet, one hears a number of more or less short compositions, all of which are somewhat similar in style. Many times these sections will carry names of well-known dances such as waltz, minuet, or mazurka, depending upon the intent of the ballet and the period from which it comes. In more contemporary ballet, usually that of the twentieth century, the music may not divide so obviously but the dancers onstage still do the dividing so that different groups are onstage for different portions of time. Modern dance may not place an emphasis upon the ballerina as in the past, yet some dancers still take leading roles.

2. *Dance moved from outdoors to indoors.* The earliest folk dances were performed out-of-doors, and when dance became more sophisticated it moved into the dance halls, the rooms of the court, or the larger salons of houses. Even in Vienna at the beginning of the waltz craze, the wheat floor of an old mill was the most popular dance floor, since it was indoors but reminded people of the outdoors. With ballet, even specialty dances began out-of-doors, since many of the spectacles were so large and involved so many persons that an outdoor area

was needed. As skills improved, an even, flat surface was necessary, so the tennis court was often used. When dance moved inside it went to the theater, since that place was associated with mime. Later, when greater musical demands matched the artistry and when opera became so popular as to warrant its own auditoriums, ballet became associated with opera, since the same musicians and facilities could service both types of performance. This union between ballet and opera became a fascinating one and exists even today, since some of the famous ballet companies are supported by and take the name of the opera company; for example, the San Francisco Opera Ballet.

3. *Mime became a vital part of ballet.* During the late 1600s and early 1700s pantomime and mime became a part of ballet and thus enabled the dancers to convey a story to the observer. The early festivities of the court had included dance accompanied by music, song, processions, recitations, and mechanical effects (such as dancers flying through the air). In the court of Louis XIV scenes were danced to words which were spoken or sung. By the turn of the century (1700) the spoken word and the singing were considered unnecessary when the dancers were instructed in the technic of motions similar to those used by actors. Subsequently, dancers were assigned specific roles. Upon becoming definite characters they were expected to act with conviction. Some of the stage business and some of the characterizations did not require dancing or required so little that novices and trainees could be given the parts. The roles demanding more dancing were given to those who were well-trained. Many of the ballets we witness today make this distinction, and the pantomime ballet of the early eighteenth century has its descendants in contemporary ballet. A good example of this can be seen in the roles of the three girls in *Fancy Free*, a ballet by Leonard Bernstein.

4. *Ballet makes use of scenery.* Earliest ballet used little or no scenery. However, when it moved into the theater and mime became a narrative part of ballet, scenery was added. Even in early theaters scenery was considered so important to ballet that extravagant mechanical devices were used to change scenery quickly. Many of the first ballets were influenced by Greek mythology or religious subjects, and scenery aided the plausibility of the locale in heaven, hell, or on earth. Later, peasant stories which had been so popular immediately before the French Revolution required scenery to portray the out-of-doors and pastoral scenes. During the Romantic period scenery became quite realistic, but during the twentieth century modern ballet resorted once again to simple suggestive ideas.

5. *Women have played an important part in the development of ballet.* In folk or social dancing, women participated equally with men. When ballet moved to the theater women were excluded from the stage, and men performed all of the dancing including the roles of women. These women's roles were represented by simulated costumes and masks if necessary. At the court of Louis XIV Beauchamp, the dancing master, and Lully, the musician, created the famous ballet *Le Triomphe de l'Amour*, which was so popular it was decided

to perform it in Paris for the populace. Lully, who had directed the dances as well as composed the music, believed that much would be lost if the ladies did not perform the women's roles as they had at court. He persuaded four women to learn the dances and to perform them in Paris. Women became part of ballet from that time on (1681). During the Romantic period woman's role in ballet increased. The very spirit of the period persuaded men that woman should be idolized, that her charms were greater than previously imagined, that woman was a replica of the good and that man was the seducer. Throughout this period the ballerina was featured while men were given increasingly less important roles. Even today when one witnesses a romantic ballet, this one characteristic stands out even if one does not know the date of composition. Although modern ballet has attempted to rectify this situation, and some ballets have been written in which more men are required than women, yet the preponderance of dancers onstage for most ballets is women. Their agility and grace become evident to the observer, and since these are two important characteristics of ballet, women are preferred by the theatergoer.

6. *The body is an expressive agent in ballet.* The feet have always expressed the rhythm of the dance, and ladies who shared the folk dances often raised their skirts so that the feet could move more easily. Indoors sliding and gliding steps became more popular and the raising of the skirt was not so necessary. Onstage the dance could not be appreciated so well if the feet were not seen, so skirts were raised above the ankle. When jumping and extending the leg became the fashion in ballet, the heel of the shoe was removed to facilitate movement, and the shoe was lightened to assist in these aerial leaps. With such emphasis upon foot and leg movement in the early part of the 1800s ballerinas learned a new type of toe dancing in which they stood on the tips of the toes, or "en pointes." This main emphasis in all the romantic ballets enabled the ballerina to execute a style not possible before. In addition, it gave to dance a different perspective of lightness, grace, and technic. The leg was now a straight line from the waist to the foot, and along with the arm and hand it became an expressor of line and movement in ways never conceived before. Although limited by concepts of grace and beauty prominent in the Romantic period, the increase in the use of the body was evident and did much to further the style of the period and of ballet in general. At the beginning of the twentieth century much emphasis was placed upon greater body freedom and greater expressiveness in dance. Isadora Duncan, followed by numerous others, believed that the body should be used in different ways than those defined by the strict discipline of the Romantic era. The body should be used more completely, and dancing "en pointes" was discarded for a more casual and free movement of torso and limbs. Some expressionist dancers never learned the skills of "en pointes" movement; a minority is skilled in both styles. The latter performers have become the popular ballerinas of the contemporary period, since they are able to express themselves in a greater variety of ways.

7. *Constuming has followed the style of the dance.* When the attention to dance as a visual spectacle became prominent, the skirt rose off the floor to

about midway between the ankle and knee.   Later, when emphasis was placed upon the movement of the leg as well as the foot, the skirt was raised higher. During the Romantic period two innovations became a permanent part of ballet: the maillot, or tights, and the tutu.   Both the male and the female use the maillot, which is a tight-fitting cover for the upper and lower parts of the body.   Many times men wear nothing but tights.   In contemporary ballet this has become acceptable for women too, although they usually wear some type of skirt.

The long tutu became famous in ballets of the Romantic period which wished to portray a misty, or half-real quality to the female dancers.   These skirts, made of light muslin, would seem to float with the slightest movement of the dancer.   Many times they were arranged in tiers or were covered with frills or lace, adding to the feminine quality.   For other roles powder-puff tutus became famous.   These short skirts also were made of several layers of muslin but were cut so as to protrude from the waist rather than hang.   Although brief, they still projected a most feminine appearance.   In more modern ballets, costumes of various styles and colors have been designed.   Some of the early expressionist dancers used only a draping of cloth from the shoulders, as with the early Greeks. Other modern ballets use contemporary dress or stylized dress which often unites the maillot with artistic ideas of color, design, or style.

8. *Music has always been an essential element of ballet.*   Earliest dance music was of a folklike nature.   Even for some of the extravagant displays of the court, the music must have been simple but stylized, as we heard in our study of the suite.   Lully composed music for the ballets of Louis XIV, but as we stated earlier, these were often sung and the dancers either interpreted the singing or interposed the dance between parts of the singing.   In the pre-romantic ballets music was often just a collection of tunes from one composer or another.   The choreographer chose these selections to assist in portraying the mood of the dance, much as music was chosen to accompany silent movies.   Consequently, the music of Mozart or Beethoven might be interspersed between the music of several unknowns.

During the Romantic period the most important ballets, the ones which are still danced today and the ones most highly thought of, had music composed especially for them.   However, most of the choreographers did not use the music as anything but accompaniment, and many times it was rearranged or cut after the composer had submitted it, since the dance master had previously decided that a particular dance would be of a certain length and had not conveyed this to the composer.   In the case of Tchaikovsky, who composed some of the ballets we will hear, he was given specific instructions as to the exact length of each section of the ballet, and it was his genius that gave us the quality of music which overcame such limitations.   In the twentieth century a more complete unanimity of approach existed between composer and choreographer.   Stravinsky and Diaghilev worked together much more than previous composers and choreographers.   Each believed that the greater the unanimity between dance, music, scenery, costume, and mime, the greater the ballet.   This concept has influenced dance of the twentieth century even though it has not been attainable by all.

THE MUSIC OF BALLET

Ballet music, as we have stated earlier, usually contains numerous parts. Each of these parts tends to portray a particular mood or style. Often the tempo and the meter of the music change from part to part, enabling the dancers to vary the type of dancing they will perform. With these various sections following one upon another and with each not extending for any great length of time, it is understandable why such a composition could be called a *ballet suite*.

Yet another use of the term is most appropriate. Since ballet music contains repeats or "fillers" for the dancers, and since these could be of little interest to the listener unless he were witnessing the visual dance, the composer often arranges the music of the ballet for concert and recorded presentation. This condensation also is known as a ballet suite, for it contains several sections and gives one the impression of the ballet without hearing the entire music.

Many ballets were written containing a set of characteristic dances. Although these dances are never the same in any two ballets, yet they are reminiscent of the period when ballet was a suite of nationalistic dances. Many times these characteristic dances have become as popular to the listener as the ballet itself. This is particularly true of *The Nutcracker*. When looking at a recording of a ballet, notice if the jacket states that you will hear a complete ballet or just a suite. Also notice the titles of the sections of the ballet, for these give you some indication of the story and should remind you of the narrative on which the ballet is based. Many of these sections will be characteristic dances which have been placed within the ballet as witness to the past, but also as witness to the skills of the choreographer as he stylizes certain characteristics of the dances of his period and unites these with the skills of his troup.

Much ballet music has a life of its own irrespective of dance. The music may be recorded, played at concert, or heard as background music to drama, the movies, or TV. Many ballets contain excellent music, but the dance is seldom performed. Our concern is with the music, how this music developed and what it means; to understand this, a discussion will be helpful.

NINETEENTH CENTURY BALLET

Many ballets of the nineteenth century have a romantic story, and in some cases were taken from literature of the period. The dancing and choreography were seldom romantic, rarely reflecting the imaginative aspects of this period in their approach to costume, scenery, or dancing. In some ballets the dancing was almost completely classic in routines, steps, and stage design. The music, depending upon the composer, often reflected his imagination or lack of it.

Peter Ilich Tchaikovsky (Photograph by Sarony, New York; Courtesy of Brown Brothers, Sterling, Pa.).

The Nutcracker (Tchaikovsky)

Although this ballet contains less opportunity for skillful dancers, and although Tchaikovsky himself berated the music as being of less quality than his other two compositions for dance, this has become the most famous of all ballets. Children all over the world have taken the music to their hearts, and no Christmas season would seem complete without it. Ballet companies all over the world present it during this season, even if at no other. A ballet suite from this music has become popular, and contains two selections from the first act and a number of characteristic selections from the second.

The first act of this ballet is almost entirely mime. Only three dances exist, and these are not of a technical nature. The first is a dance performed by the parents with their children; the second is a dance of mechanical dolls which an uncle brings for the children; the third is the so-called Grandfather Dance which ends the Christmas party for the children and all of the guests.

In the second act, which provides most of the better-known music, the corps de ballet usually takes part and performs in more obvious ballet style. Many of the characteristic dances have been altered over the years, being given a more contemporary flavor and feeling, and this is one reason this ballet has such a wide appeal.

The first suite from the ballet contains the following sections: Overture and March from the first act; Dance of the Sugar Plum Fairy (the high point of the ballet for the ballerina), Russian Dance, Arabian Dance, Chinese Dance, Dance of the Flutes, and Waltz of the Flowers from the second act.

A second suite contains the following selections: Scene (from the children's party scene), Pas de deux—a dance for two (the children express their appreciation for being permitted to remain up for the party), and the Grandfather Dance (the end of the first act, scene 1), Pas de deux (from act 2, danced by the Sugar Plum Fairy and the Prince), Waltz of the Snowflakes (from scene 2 of act 1), Scene (prelude to act 2 and introduction to the Land of Sweets), Spanish Dance (one of the characteristic dances of the second act), Final Waltz (sometimes called the Beehive Waltz).

The story, similar to many in this period of ballet, is fairyland come to life. It is Christmas Eve, and the parents of Clara are giving a party which includes friends of the family as well as the grandparents. The Christmas tree glows in the living room, where all gather to wish each other the best of the season. A friend brings dancing dolls and a puppetlike nutcracker for Clara. Her brother, jealous of the gift, breaks the nutcracker. After the guests leave the house and the children are supposedly in bed, Clara comes back to the living room to repair her nutcracker. Upon entering, she sees the Christmas tree alight and the nutcracker and the mice having a battle. When the mice appear to be winning, she sides with her nutcracker and kills the mouse king. The nutcracker suddenly turns into a prince and asks Clara to journey with him to the Land of Sweets. Scene 2 of this act represents their journey as they pass through the snowflakes and the cold country.

In act 2, the Sugar Plum Fairy holds court in the Land of Sweets. She welcomes Clara and bades all of the good things to eat to come to court to dance in her honor. A number of characteristic dances are performed by sugar, tea, spices, and various kinds of attractive edibles. The act ends with the Waltz of the Flowers, after which Clara and the prince leave for home.

The music is delightful, particularly those portions in the first suite. Over the years the music and the childlike Christmas story have captured the imagination of children and adults alike, making them unforgettable.

Study Procedures

1. *The Nutcracker* is based upon a short story by the well-known German author of the Romantic period, E. T. A. Hoffman. Read the original as found in the paperback *The Best Tales of Hoffman*, edited by E. F. Bleiler, Dover Publications, Inc., New York, 1967.

2. What differences exist between the original story and the ballet? Are these significant? Do they assist the ballet? Why?

Coppélia (Delibes)

This ballet also has lasted well through the years partly because of the music, which is attractive enough to become well-known, and partly because of the story—a mixture of the jealousy of young love with the toy shop and a mechanical doll—which appeals to children of all ages. This ballet is often given at Christmas even though it does not contain a Christmas theme.

Several musical sections from the ballet have become famous in their own right: the Mazurka, the Czardas, the Waltz of the Doll, and especially the Waltz of the Hours.

ENTERING THE TWENTIETH CENTURY

Near the beginning of the present century two ideas affected ballet greatly. First, in order to make ballet more expressive, the concept arose that music and dance should unite more completely. Russian ballet, having had particular success through its history, had developed a solid base of dancers and choreographers. Wishing to push dance into a more expressive medium than the Romantic period had permitted with its classical footwork and organization, Diaghilev, the Russian producer, emphasized the unity of dance, music, costume, and expressive motion. Most important of these was the unity between the music and the dance itself. He sought out and employed Igor Stravinsky to write the music for three ballets. In some ways these were the most famous three compositions of his life, bringing his music to the attention of the world.

Secondly, a group of dancers pursued the idea that the body should be free to express ideas through dance with no restriction in form. The result was what has been often called "modern dance," with little or no attention given to the famous footwork and gesture that had become known as ballet. We shall examine each type in turn, but particularly the music which has come from each.

THE STRAVINSKY BALLETS

The Firebird

Much as other ballets of the Romantic period, this also deals with a fairy story, with magic, and with maidens who have been wronged by a male ogre. The difference, not so much in the story, came in the unification of the dancing with the music, and in the music itself. Although today the music does not sound particularly startling with its dissonance, it was greeted with amazement because of its modernity, and the demands placed upon the instrumentalists through extreme ranges and special effects.

In the story, a young prince wanders into the forbidden garden of Kashchei. He has been pursuing a firebird. After watching the bird dance, the prince catches it, and promises to release it if he can have one of its magic feathers. Suddenly thirteen maidens appear, playing a game with a golden apple. The prince falls in love with one of them, but learns that they are under the spell of Kashchei and that none can leave the garden or marry. As dawn approaches the maidens must return to the palace, and when the prince follows he is immediately captured by the guards of Kashchei, who threatens to turn him into stone. He waves the magic firebird feather, summoning the bird, which advises him of the secret egg housing the soul of Kashchei. The prince destroys the egg and Kashchei, and the ballet ends with all celebrating their freedom as well as the coming marriage of the prince and his beloved.

The orchestra scintillates throughout the ballet, and although the music is not indicative of the later Stravinsky, it still remains one of his most popular compositions.

Stravinsky arranged three suites for orchestra from this music. Since all of them are recorded, the following list of scenes from the ballet will guide you through the music of any recording and the dramatic sequence of the dances:

a. Introduction
b. SCENE 1: Kashchei's Enchanted Garden
c. Appearance of the Firebird Pursued by the Prince
d. Dance of the Firebird
e. Capture of the Firebird
f. Entreaty of the Firebird
g. Appearance of the Thirteen Princesses
h. The Game with the Golden Apple
i. Sudden Appearance of the Prince
j. The Dance of the Princesses
k. Daybreak
l. Appearance of Kashchei's Guards and Capture of the Prince
m. Arrival of Kashchei—His Dialogue with the Prince—Intercession of the Princesses
n. Appearance of the Firebird
o. Dance of All of Kashchei's Subjects
p. Lullaby (Firebird)
q. Kashchei's Death
r. SCENE 2: End of Kashchei's Magic—General Thanksgiving

Petrouchka

This ballet differs from others in more than one aspect. The music itself firmly establishes us in the twentieth century, where we hear tonalities and rhythms which were to be the trademark of Stravinsky and at the same time set the pace for many composers during the next several decades. The background or narrative of the ballet also is more modern in concept by not adhering to the usual romantic role for the ballerina. In fact, the male is the main character, turning ballet around from its established position of over 200 years.

The music and the story are developed on two planes: the realm of make-believe or the unreal, and the level of day-to-day life or the real. These are exemplified by puppets who might be really alive, who might have a life near to that of humans where they feel and understand and suffer because of their limitations. These planes may be compared to the life of any human who, under some circumstances, may often think of himself as a puppet pulled by exterior forces and in no way the master of his fate; at other times he is led into situations where he believes he is his own master and controller of his own life. The music also adds to this mood of uncertainty. It is full of folk melodies which are danced by everyday persons visiting the fair, but other portions of the music seem unreal, leading the mind into the realm of fantasy or make-believe. This combination of real and unreal, of the nagging question of what is a real life, has led this ballet to become popular beyond the storybook initial impact.

Unlike *Firebird*, the composition consists of only four scenes. The first and last take place on the fairway at the St. Petersburg Fair at Shrovetide, a three-day period similar to our Mardi Gras in that it comes immediately before Lent. The two middle scenes take place in the rather barren rooms of the two male puppets, the clown and the Moor.

Scene 1 is the fair in the afternoon. Attendants are moving before the booths; some begin to dance but are interrupted by the activity. Suddenly, in front of a small marionette theater, an operator comes before the curtain and attracts attention by playing a flute and introducing his three puppets: a ballerina, a clown (Petrouchka), and the Moor (handsomely dressed). At first they dance as if controlled by strings, but as they continue they take on life and even move into the crowd, amazing all with the uncanny ability of the operator.

Scene 2 features the clown in his dingy room behind stage. He laments his dismal plight; the one ray of brightness in his life is his love for the ballerina. She enters his room and he begins to describe his love for her, but she rebukes him and runs out in fright.

Scene 3 immediately follows in the room of the Moor. His quarters are similar but because of his bright attire we receive the impression of higher status. Briefly, he dances alone before the ballerina enters. They dance together, the ballerina dances, and the Moor begins to make love to her when the clown enters. When Petrouchka objects to the intimate scene, the Moor throws him out of the room.

Scene 4 again shows the fair. Night has fallen, and different segments of the crowd participate in numerous dances. Suddenly, from the stage of the little theater the clown is seen chased by the Moor. Before the eyes of the crowd, the Moor overtakes and kills him with his knife. The crowd, aghast, calls the operator of the puppet show. He comes and convinces the crowd that the clown is only made of straw. As he is dragging him back toward the stage, all see the laughing and mocking ghost of the clown over the roof of the theater, leaving us to ponder the humanness of the clown.

The music, appropriately filled with Russian folk tunes, places more emphasis upon complex rhythms and dissonances than *The Firebird*. Although interesting in its own right, this ballet needs dancers more than *Firebird* to complete the effect for the listener.

Rite of Spring (Coronation of Spring[2])

Stravinsky envisioned a pagan rite and wanted his music to portray not only the scene of the ballet and the narrative, but the pagan background of early peoples who lived in the region of Russia. Consequently, he asked Nicolas Roerich, an archeologist, to assist him with ideas for the ballet. Roerich wrote Diaghilev the following description of an original idea for the ballet:

> In the ballet of *The Rite of Spring* as conceived by myself and Stravinsky, my object is to present a number of scenes of earthly joy and celestial triumph as understood by the Slavs. . . . My intention is that the first set should transport us to the foot of a sacred hill, in a lush plain, where Slavonic tribes are gathered together to celebrate the spring rites. In this scene there is an old witch, who predicts the future, a marriage by capture, round dances. Then comes the most solemn moment. The wise elder is brought from the village to imprint his sacred kiss on the new-flowering earth. During this rite the crowd is seized with a mystic terror. . . . After this uprush of terrestrial joy, the second scene sets a celestial mystery before us. Young virgins dance in circles on the sacred hill amid enchanted rocks; then they choose the victim they intend to honor. In a moment she will dance her last dance before the ancients clad in bearskins to show that the bear was man's ancestor. Then the greybeards dedicate the victim to the god Yarilo.[3]

All of these thoughts were not included in the ballet, but the young girl who dances herself to death as a sacrifice to the spring became the central idea. Years later when asked what he loved most in Russia, Stravinsky replied, "The violent Spring that seemed to begin in an hour and was like the whole earth cracking."[4] Not having been to Russia, one can only read and try to appreciate how a country of the north reacts to the violent change from frozen land to one bearing life. Stravinsky's writing of this as part of a pagan rite dramatizes an early reaction to the power of spring.

Much controversy exists over the events of the first performance. Despite the many versions all seem to agree that this ballet caused a near riot. Statements from the musicians of the orchestra indicate that by the end of the composition Pierre Monteux, the conductor, had to run for the stage door to keep from being

---

2 Stravinsky's translation into English from the Russian.
3 *Stravinsky, The Composer and His Works*, Eric Walter White. Faber and Faber, London, 1966, page 171.
4 *Ibid.*, page 172.

assaulted personally, since objects had been thrown in the direction of the orchestra earlier in the evening. Other accounts indicate that an almost constant battle existed between those who thought it was a declaration of war against music, and those who considered it a work of art. The audience apparently became loud, shouting to each other as well as to the musicians and dancers; others became physical and used hands and fists to emphasize their opinions. But the dancers and musicians continued to the end. Nijinsky, the famous male dancer who had choreographed the work, apparently stood on a chair just offstage and counted loudly to assist the dancers in keeping their place with the music.

The ballet in its several versions has never been received as well as the music. The orchestral score, on the other hand, has been a constant concert attraction since its inception.

The scenes for the ballet will assist you in listening to the music, since no suite version exists and only the complete score is recorded:

PART I.   *Adoration of the Earth*
   a.   Introduction
   b.   Foretelling of Spring (Dance of Young Girls)
   c.   Mock Abduction
   d.   Spring Dance (Round Dance)
   e.   Games of Rival Clans
   f.   Procession of the Wise Elder
   g.   Adoration of the Earth (Wise Elder)
   h.   Dance of the Earth

PART II.   *The Sacrifice*
   a.   Introduction
   b.   Mystical Circle of Young Girls
   c.   Glorification of the Chosen Victim
   d.   Summoning of the Ancients
   e.   Ritual of the Ancients
   f.   Sacrificial Dance

The music is outstandingly modern, considering its origin date of 1911. The melodic lines are limited, but the emphasis throughout is upon rhythm and the impact of the irregularity of this rhythm upon our emotions and feelings. A second emphasis in the work comes from the orchestration. Not only is a large orchestra required, but the use of dissonance within the instruments of each group produces interesting but telling results. In addition, this is the first composition to employ the impact of a large percussion section. Many works, even those written in more recent years, often sound dated before a decade has passed. Not one of these three ballets sounds dated, proving their artistic value.

Of interest to the student of music is the progression and widening of the horizon of the musical scene as evidenced by these three ballets. Rarely do we find three works so chronologically close in time with such impact for the entire compositional scene. *Firebird* looks toward the twentieth century through the eyes of the Romantic era; *Petrouchka* is the bridge, using folk material with introductions to dissonance and rhythmic complexities; while *Rite of Spring* shows us the raw material for music of the next sixty years or more. Other composers refined these elements and used them in interesting and complex ways; however, Stravinsky offers these elements to us in a challenging but understandable manner.

LATER CONTEMPORARY BALLET

Through the past forty years expressionism, classical ballet, and free dance combined in different ways offering a wide selection of styles. The influence of the American scene made itself felt, not only in the interpretation of works or through the development of dancers of quality, but also in the themes of some of the compositions, and the manner in which American folk and jazz dance was assimilated into the ballet form. *Rodeo*, based upon folk music, and *Fancy Free*, using jazz, have individual characteristics which are genuinely American in flavor and realization.

Rodeo (Aaron Copland)

Even though American dancers had presented ballet, not often before 1942 had American dancers presented a ballet so typically American. *Rodeo* witnessed to this because the locale was a ranch in west-central America; also, because it made use of dances that were folk-oriented even though country dance itself was not used; most importantly, because the ballet portrayed a common rural American situation: the willingness of the American woman to participate in the rough, tough world of pioneering, but at the same time by maintaining her femininity and control of the situation, attracting the man of her choice.

The first scene depicts the Saturday afternoon rodeo, the week's entertainment for the local cowboys and ranch hands, with the dances imitating the riding in various events. Even the cowgirl, who works regularly with the men and fancies herself as their woman, participates. When the rancher's daughter and her girlfriends arrive from Kansas City the entire scene becomes centered around the girls and the cowboys' attempt to show off for them. When the cowgirl realizes she is no longer the center of attention she spends a large part of the late afternoon and early evening trying to reclaim her position with the various cowboys and the head wrangler.

The second scene is the dance held on Saturday night for the cowboys, the local girls, and the visitors. The cowgirl attracts no attention and no partner. Finally, she decides to change her clothes from jeans to a more feminine dress and hair bows. When she makes her entrance, she is immediately the center of attention, since none of the cowboys had ever seen her so attractive or even considered her as a girl. As a result she has her pick of the men.

The complete ballet is not recorded, although a suite arranged by the composer contains most of the music. Its four parts are: Buckaroo Holiday, Corral Nocturne, Honky-Tonk Interlude, and Saturday Night Waltz and Hoedown. Dance titles and dance implications are evident.

Stravinsky reawakened our interest in the use of rhythm and dissonance as musical forces which can be equally interesting and attractive as melody and form. Copland molded these characteristics into a particularly American composition. The tempos for some of the dances are faster than might have been found at ranches in earlier times, the rhythms are obviously distorted from the straight, heavy foot-pounding by rural clappers or dancers, but the color is present and one sees with his ears the scenes the music intends. Gay, bright, and rural, this ballet speaks of country America with full force.

ADDITIONAL LISTENING

Two additional American ballets deserve mention as concert suites: *The Incredible Flutist* by Piston, and *Appalachian Spring* by Copland. *The Flutist* shows the craftsmanship of a great American composer, even though it is not particularly representative of his style or his compositional tendencies. *Appalachian Spring* seems to be much more in the mainstream of Copland's works. Although we still feel the America of the great frontier, in no way does it repeat what was expressed in *Rodeo*. This music, based upon tunes from the Shaker community, presents a more severe, more austere feeling for settler life where fun was possible, but the business of living, in no way frivolous and often full of sorrow, showed concern for the matters which bring one to an understanding of the religious.

Study Procedures

1. Compare the two Copland ballets as to mood, feeling, musical technics, and dance technics. What kind of dancing would best fit each?
2. Read *Dr. Zhivago* by Boris Pasternak, then relisten to the Stravinsky ballets. Which of the three could best be used to describe certain scenes from the book? Do you believe that Pasternak and Stravinsky have similar artistic expressions to relay to the reader and listener? How would you describe these?
3. Describe in your own words the changes in musical style you hear in the three Stravinsky ballets.
4. Popular music often follows trends set by serious composers. What of Stravinsky's music do you hear in today's popular music?
5. *Rodeo* preceded the ballet sequences in the musical comedies *Oklahoma, Annie Get Your Gun, Carousel,* and others. If you have seen these in movie versions or on TV, what is similar in the ballet work of all of them?
6. Leonard Bernstein wrote the music for *West Side Story* and *Fancy Free*. Listen to both and decide how they are similar in style.
7. *West Side Story* is based upon *Romeo and Juliet,* as is a ballet by Prokofiev. Do you hear similarities between these two? Consider the music of one particular scene in detail.

8. If you were asked to compose a ballet concerning events past or present of your community, what would be its subject matter and what would be the titles of the dances in the suite?

Bibliography—Chapter 18

ABRAHAM, GERALD, *The Music of Tchaikovsky*. Port Washington, N.Y.: Kennikat Press, Inc., 1969.

BEAUMONT, CYRIL W., *A Short History of Ballet*. London: C. W. Beaumont, 1944.

BRINSON, PETER, *Background to European Ballet*. Leyden: A. W. Sijthoff, 1966.

CONYN, CORNELIUS, *Three Centuries of Ballet*. Houston, Texas: Elsevier Press, Inc., 1953.

DEAKIN, IRVING, *At the Ballet*. Toronto: Thomas Nelson and Sons, 1956.

EVANS, EDWIN, *Music and the Dance*. London: Herbert Jenkins Ltd., n.d.

HALL, FERNAU, *World Dance*. New York: A. A. Wyn, Inc., n.d.

NETTL, PAUL, *The Dance in Classical Music*. New York: Philosophical Library, 1963.

————, *The Story of Dance Music*. New York: Philosophical Library, 1947.

NEWMARCH, ROSA, *Tchaikovsky*. New York: Haskell House Publishers, Ltd., 1969.

TANSMAN, ALEXANDRE, *Igor Stravinsky*. New York: G. P. Putnam's Sons, 1949.

TERRY, WALTER, *The Ballet Companion*. New York: Dodd, Mead and Company, 1968.

VERWER, HANS, *Guide to the Ballet*. New York: Barnes and Noble, Inc., 1963.

WHITE, ERIC WALTER, *Stravinsky, The Composer and His Works*. London: Faber and Faber, 1966.

Recordings—Chapter 18

Copland	*Rodeo*	Bernstein	Columbia ML-5575
Stravinsky	*Firebird* Suite (1910)	Boulez	Columbia MS-7206
Stravinsky	*Firebird* Suite	Monteux	Victor LM-2113
Stravinsky	*Petrouchka*	Ansermet	London LL-3018
Stravinsky	*Petrouchka*	Mitropoulos	Columbia ML-4438
Stravinsky	*Petrouchka*	Monteux	Victor LM-2113
Stravinsky	*Petrouchka* Suite	Ormandy	Columbia ML-6146
Stravinsky	*Rite of Spring*	Boulez	Nonesuch H-71093
Stravinsky	*Rite of Spring*	Monteux	Victor LM-2085
Tchaikovsky	*Nutcracker* Suites I and II	Ansermet	London CM-9026
Tchaikovsky	*Nutcracker* Suite	Ormandy	Columbia ML-5257

Additional Suggestions for Listening

Adam	*Giselle*	London Symphony	Capital P-8306
Bernstein	*Fancy Free*	Bernstein	Columbia CL-920
Chopin	*Les Sylphides*	Fiedler	Victor LM-1919
Copland	*Appalachian Spring*	Koussevitzky	Victor LCT-1134
Copland	*Appalachian Spring*	Ormandy	Columbia ML-5157
Delibes	*Coppélia* highlights	Ansermet	London CM-9027

Delibes	*Sylvia*	Monteux	Victor LM-1913
Piston	*Incredible Flutist*	Fiedler	Victor LM-2084
Prokofiev	*Romeo and Juliet*	Mitropoulos	Columbia MS-6023
Tchaikovsky	*Sleeping Beauty*	Covent Garden	Victor LM-6034
Tchaikovsky	*Swan Lake*	Ansermet	London CM-9025

Section G   *Emphasis on Color and Virtuosity*

Chapter 19

The Keyboard Character Piece

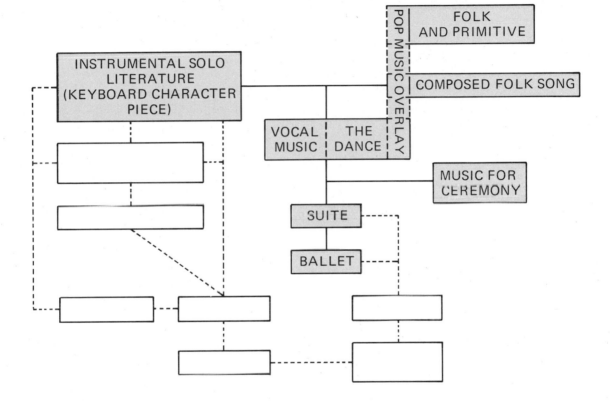

Of all instruments, the piano is probably the best-known, most often used, and most universally recognized as to outward appearance and tonal color. The instrument not only plays the melodic line, but can supply its own harmony as well; no other instrument so easily equals its harmonic possibilities.

At some time during their lives, hundreds of thousands of young people have practiced and attempted to play the instrument, its attraction being that, upon touching the keys the amateur may produce a satisfactory tone immediately, but a controlled and expressive tone quality requires at least as much study and discipline as other instruments.

THE PIANO

Since the strings of the instrument are struck by hammers, the piano combines the tone production technics of two kinds of instruments, strings and percussion. Although there are times when it joins the percussion section as a legitimate member, usually it stands alone as a unique solo instrument.

The most common instrument immediately preceding the piano was the harpsichord, which plucked or pulled the string when one depressed the key. It was for this instrument that most early keyboard music was written. Of the same shape as the modern grand piano, this instrument increased the range of pitch over its predecessors, and offered some dynamic possibilities. By control knobs, one could add the octave above or below a given pitch without actually playing those keys. Some of the larger harpsichords had more than one keyboard, placed under each other, enabling the performer not only to obtain a slightly different tone color, but more important, to couple the two keyboards together to obtain an octave higher in pitch and/or to increase the loudness of the tone. Since this instrument had few dynamic possibilities, this became an important feature.

The piano, originally called the *pianoforte,* which in Italian means "soft to loud," was invented by an Italian harpsichord maker by the name of Cristofori about 1720. The Italians cared little for the instrument, which produced the sound by striking the string with a felted hammer, and so it did not catch the fancy of builders or musicians until the latter part of the century. The modern piano is different in several ways from its predecessors. It has a range of dynamics which responds to the intensity of the finger upon the key; it is a larger instrument producing a very low sound to a high one, quite a bit larger in range than most of the harpsichords or clavichords; because of the key mechanism, the string is struck harder than the key itself, producing a loudness and a tone quality not possible before. The key mechanism, more complicated than any of its predecessors, moves away from the string quickly to avoid dampening it, lying ready to be returned to the string if directed, while the string continues to sound as long as the key is depressed. These features, with the exception of the repetition device, were incorporated in the first piano by Cristofori and the action was changed little for over one hundred years. Modern pianos, like some of the clavichords and harpsichords before them, use three strings per pitch in the upper register, two strings per pitch in the middle range, and one string per pitch for the lowest notes.

Since its invention, three pedals have become common. The one to the right raises the dampers and permits the tone to sound even after the key has been released, thus permitting a legato style from note to note. The center pedal, working primarily in the lower section of the instrument, catches the damper once the key has been depressed, permitting the bass pitches to sound continually while the upper notes are crisp and disconnected. The pedal to the left moves the action of the piano to one side so that the hammer will touch two

Piano Forte, 1720; designed in Florence by Bartolommeo Cristofori.
Compass, four octaves and a quarter: C-F (Courtesy of The
Metropolitan Museum of Art, The Crosby Brown
Collection of Musical Instruments, 1889).

of the three strings in the treble or one of the two in the center of the range. This produces a somewhat softer sound, and also a different coloration.

Most of the modern concert pianos are wing-shaped and horizontal. Home instruments or practice instruments, called "uprights," mount the strings perpendicularly. Since each string mounted in the instrument is pulled tightly to reach a certain pitch, the invention of the iron frame in 1825 enabled the instrument to use larger and longer strings. This placed almost thirty tons of pressure on the pin block, the piece of thick wood holding the tuning pins. When longer and heavier strings were possible, the tone of the instrument could be improved and the loudness increased.

Today's grands vary from about five feet, usually called the "baby grand" and often used in the home, to the nine-foot grand, most often referred to as the "concert grand," usually used on the concert stage. Some pianists, however, believe that the seven-foot instrument contains the best tonal balance and produces the best tone, and some have used this size for piano concerts even in large halls. When playing as soloist with an orchestra the larger size is usually needed.

THE CHARACTER PIECE

The piano was developed during the Romantic period and aided the composer in his attempt toward expressing emotions and moods. When surveying the literature for the instrument, one must focus almost entirely upon the Romantic period. Beginning with Beethoven and his Bagatelles, other composers added short pieces to the literature under a large variety of names. Some of the pieces carry names of forms, while others are entirely descriptive. Literally thousands of such piano pieces were written, many by great composers (in some cases, the compositions made them great), and many more by hacks. Much second-rate piano music is played by students, mostly from the Romantic period, who find it modestly attractive or technically playable.

Almost every composer of merit has written well for a keyboard instrument. Much of their material is of more advanced form and style than the character piece, and will be studied in detail in later chapters. But because the short composition is so expressive and attractive to large portions of the listening public, it has played an important role in musical history. These short forms usually follow the ABA format wherein the composer can write a somewhat different type of music in the center section.

When studying the character piece for the piano, one composer stands out above all others. Part of the reason for this is the beauty and completeness of the romantic style in his works; another is that he wrote almost entirely for the piano and most of his works are character pieces. This one composer is Chopin, a striking personality of the early 1800s. A study of his life through several of his letters and some of the items written about him will not only give us an insight into the composer himself, but in addition it will help us understand the Romantic period and the characteristic piece for the piano.

Frédéric Chopin

When Frédéric Chopin was born in Poland in 1809, the times were full of the talk and action of the restoration of Polish nationalism and a Polish country which had been taken over only a few years before by Russia in the east, Prussia in the west, and Austria in the south. These proud people, who had defended their country many times before, had fought brilliantly with only scythes and farm tools under the famous General Kosciusko, the same general who had assisted the colonies so well in their fight for independence in 1776 that he had been given a pension for life by Congress. But, hearing the cry of the invader in his own country, he returned. Though the fighting was brutal and the defenses well-manned, the much heavier force of the Russians and the Prussians conquered the country, and Poland ceased to exist except in the hearts of men. An intense patriotic feeling was instilled early and deeply into the mind and heart of Frédéric Chopin and constantly came to the fore in his discussions and letters, but most obviously in his compositions.   His mazurkas and polonaises are not dances in the usual sense, but rather give a feeling for the emotions of a patriot who longs for the sovereignty of his native land.

Like many Poles of his time, Chopin went to Paris.   Most went for an escape from the poverty brought by the Russian invader, but Chopin went to Paris to study, concertize, and make a name in the musical world.

The following letters by Chopin will assist us in understanding his personality perhaps better than any biography.   He apparently possessed a good sense of humor as well as a brilliant talent in music.   His letters show us the mind of a high-strung, rather flighty person who had a keen interest in many items, some of which are as superficial as the society which demanded his attention.

The first letter is written from Vienna, where Chopin had gone first on his way to Paris.   Here he would play concerts, compose, and make a name before trying his fortune in the musical capital of the world.

This letter is addressed to "My Beloved Parents and Sisters":

Vienna, Saturday, July, 1831

.   .   .

Louise writes that Mons. Elsner is very pleased with the article; I am anxious to hear what he will say about the others, as he was my teacher of composition. I want nothing but more life and energy.   I often feel low-spirited, but sometimes as cheerful as at home.   When I feel melancholy I go to Madame Schaschek's, where I generally meet several amiable Polish ladies who always cheer me up with their kind and hopeful words, so that I begin to mimic the generals here.   This is my last new trick; those who have seen it are ready to die with laughter.   But there are days, alas! when people do not get two words out of me; then I generally spend thirty kreuzers in going to Hitzing, or somewhere else in the neighbourhood of Vienna to divert my mind. Zacharkiewicz, of Warsaw, was with me, and when his wife saw me at Schaschek's their astonishment knew no bounds at my looking such a proper fellow.   I have only left my whiskers on the right cheek, and they grow very well; there is no occasion to have them on the left, as you always sit with your right to the public.

.   .   .

I dine today with Schaschek; I shall wear the studs with the Polish eagles, and use the pocket-handkerchief with the "Kosynier."

I have written a Polonaise, which I must leave here with Würfel. I received the portrait of our commander-in-chief, General Skrzynecki, but frightfully spoilt, on account of the cholera.   Your letters have also been cut, and each bears a large sanitary stamp; so great is the anxiety here.

Your FRÉDÉRIC.[1]

Chopin was 21 when he wrote the next letter to Titus Woyciechowski, an old friend in Poland, of about Chopin's age.   Dated December 16, 1831, it was

---

[1] *Frédéric Chopin, His Life and Letters,* Moritz Karasowski; translated by Emily Hill.   William Reeves, London, 1879 (third edition, 1938), page 217.

sent from Paris.   Many of his letters were quite long, and this one is no exception, so we shall read only the postscript.

P.S.—In this house, on the floor above mine, there lodges a lady whose husband is never at home from early morning till late evening.   The lady is good-looking, and she often asks me in to be company for her.   She has a stove at which I can warm myself, and she has invited me to fix a day and hour to visit her, and so on.   But I have no taste for adventures which might end in coming to blows with the husband.

I cannot keep this to myself, and must tell you of another adventure with Pixis.   Just imagine: he has with him a very pretty girl of sixteen, whom, he says, he is going to marry.   I met her at his house when I visited him in Stuttgart.   When he arrived here he invited me to go and see him; but did not say that the young lady—whom I had already forgotten—was with him. Probably because he knew that if he had I should have gone to see him sooner. A week after the second invitation, I went, and on the staircase accidentally met the apple of his eye.   She begged me to go in, saying that Mons. Pixis was out for the moment; if I would take a seat he would be sure to come, etc., etc.   A strange embarrassment came over us both.   I begged to be excused— knowing that the old fellow was very jealous—and said I would rather come another time.

While we were innocently talking, Pixis clattered up the stairs, peering over his glasses to see who was speaking to his Bella.   He did not seem to see who it was at once, and, hurrying up, stood before us, and addressing the girl in an angry tone said: "Qu'est-ce que vous faites ici?" and preached her a sermon as to how she dared receive young men in his absence.   I smiled at Pixis as I spoke to him, and remarked to the girl that it was rather unwise to go outside the room in such a thin silk dress.

At last the old chap was pacified, took me by the arm, and led me into the room.   In his excitement he did not know where to place me; for he was afraid that if I were offended, I should make better use of his absence another time.   Finally he accompanied me downstairs, and seeing the smile which I could not suppress at the idea of anyone thinking me capable of such a thing, he asked the porter how long I had been there?   That functionary must have satisfied him, for ever since Pixis has not been able to say enough to his friends about my talents.   What do you think of it?   I a dangerous séducteur![2]

The artistry of Chopin placed him in demand by the favored of society. At one time he reported that a coach waited each day at his door to take him to one estate or another.   When no appropriate instrument was available in the salon where he had been invited, he requested that his own be transported as well as himself, to which they always agreed.

Another letter to still another friend of his youth, by the name of Doma-szewski, describes his reaction to Paris after one year:

I mix in the first circles, with ambassadors, princes, ministers, etc., and I do not myself know how I got there, for I have never pushed myself forward. But this kind of society is very necessary for me: it teaches one good taste.

---

[2] *Ibid.*, page 255.

You possess more talent the moment you have been heard at a soiree given by the English or Austrian Ambassador. Your playing is more refined when Princess Vaudemont "protects you. . . ."[3]

Joseph Nowakowski, a fellow Pole and musician who also had come to Paris, writes of visiting with Chopin. Chopin had heard a symphony by the young composer on a program given about ten years before, but had not met him at that time.

When I visited Chopin in Paris, I asked him to introduce me to Kalkbrenner, Liszt and Pixis. "That is unnecessary," answered Chopin, "wait a moment, and I will present them to you, but each separately." Then he sat down to the piano after the fashion of Liszt, played in his style and imitated all his movements to the life; after which he impersonated Pixis. . . .

Liszt frequently met Chopin in society and had many opportunities of observing his imitative talent. He looked quietly on while Chopin mimicked him, and, far from being offended, he laughed and seemed really amused by it. There was not the slightest jealousy between these two artists, and their friendship remained unbroken.

One day Chopin was asked at a party to play some of his latest works, and Liszt joined in the request. On sitting down to the piano, Chopin noticed that there were no pedals, and the hostess then remembered that they had been sent away for repair and had not been brought back. Liszt laughingly declared that he would furnish them himself, and crawling under the piano, he knelt there while Chopin played, and completely supplied the place of the pedals.[4]

The last quotation is not a letter, but rather a review by the well-known musician Franz Liszt of one of Chopin's few concerts in Paris. He gave only a limited number because he favoured the intimacy of the salon where the listener could become more personally involved with his music. His favorite Pleyel piano did not produce a large tone, but rather a sweet sound from keys which depressed more easily than most. The review gives us a feeling for the times as well as a professional view of Chopin.

PARIS REVIEW AND MUSICAL GAZETTE
May 2, 1841
"Chopin's Concert"

Last Monday, at eight o'clock in the evening, the salons of Mr. Pleyel were splendidly lighted; and numerous carriages carried to the foot of a flight of stairs covered by a tapestry and perfumed with flowers, the most elegant ladies, the most fashionable young people, the most famous artists, the richest financiers, the most illustrious lords, all the élite of society, an authentic aristocracy of birth, fortune, talent, and of beauty.

---

[3] *Ibid.*, page 263.
[4] *Ibid.*, page 306.

A grand piano was opened and placed upon a platform, people crowded around trying to find the nearest places. When the artist arrived, the crowd strained to listen; voices warned one another that they must not miss a chord, a note, an intention, an idea of the man who was going to sit at the piano. The voices were correct to be so avid and attentive, so religiously moved, because the one whom they were waiting for, the one whom they had come to see, to listen to, to admire, to applaud, was not merely a skilled virtuoso, a pianist trained in the art of effecting notes, he wasn't only a well-known artist; he was all of this and more—He was Chopin.

When he arrived in France about six years ago, Chopin did not take his place among the many pianists that one sees everywhere during our time. He wasn't concerned with obtaining a second-rate or even a first-rate fame. He was rarely heard in public; the nature of his talent did not lead him in that direction. He was like a flower that opens its fragrant recesses only in the evening; he needed an atmosphere of peace and retirement to freely expose his melodic treasures that lay within. Music was his language, a divine tongue through which he expressed that full range of sentiments that only a small number of people can understand. . .

We will not undertake here a detailed analysis of Chopin's compositions. Without striving to be original, he has been so both in style and in conception. He has been able to express new thought within new forms. That certain savagery and abruptness that are characteristic of his homeland have found expression in daring dissonance, in strange harmonies; while that delicacy and grace that he possesses are revealed in a thousand turns, in a thousand ornaments of an inimitable fantasy.

For Monday's concert, Chopin expressly chose those of his works which are most different from the classical forms. He played neither concerto, sonata, fantasy, nor variations; but préludes, études, nocturnes, and mazurkas. Addressing himself to society rather than to the public, he dared to show himself as he really is with impunity; an elegiac poet, profound, chaste, a dreamer. He had no need to astonish or to seize the listeners, he brought forth delicate sympathies rather than noisy enthusiasm. Let us say straightaway that there was no lack of sympathy. From the beginning he established between himself and his listeners a sure communication. They begged him to play two études and a ballade for a second time, and without fearing to add to the great fatigue that could be seen on his pale face, they asked him to play again one by one, all the numbers on the program.

The préludes of Chopin are compositions of a completely different type. They are not merely, as the title might make one think, pieces destined to be played as an introduction to another piece, they are poetic préludes, analogous to those of a great contemporary poet, which cradle the soul in golden dreams, and carry it to the regions of the ideal. . . They have the freedom and the high intensity which characterize works of genius.

What can one say of the mazurkas, those tiny masterpieces so capricious and so perfectly accomplished?

"A faultless sonnet has the same worth as a long poem"—words that were once said by a man who was a great authority during the most brilliant century of French letters. We would be tempted to apply to the mazurkas the same exaggeration of this axiom, and to say that for us at least, many of them are worth very long operas. . .

One more word before finishing these few lines which lack of time forces us to abridge. . .

Chopin's genius has not been aided by these particular circumstances. His success, although great, has remained beneath that which he should expect. However, we say it with conviction, Chopin has no reason to envy anyone. Is it not the most noble, the most legitimate satisfaction that an artist can have to be more worthy than his fame, to be superior to his success and even greater than his reputation?[5]

The Music

As Liszt stated in the review, Chopin did not lean strongly to the classical forms, but rather to the characteristic piece which he himself could develop in the manner best suited to his feelings. We shall examine five of his most famous forms.

Impromptu, Op. 66

Four measures act as an introduction to a fast but melodic section built much in the manner of a variation. After two hearings its final descending scale leads us into and makes way for the slower melody of the piece. This is heard several times, with two of the repeats being modifications of the original melody. Immediately the first section returns, is heard twice again, followed by an extension which leads into the coda where the slower melody reenters at a lower pitch.

The first melody sparkles through its minor tonality; the second yearns even though in major, so that one hears a continuity of feeling though the means of expressing it differs. Herein lies the artistry of the composer. This is a compositional form of contrasts:

minor	major	minor
fast	slow	fast
florid	simple	florid

The form may be expressed in detail as follows:

A A′	B B :	B′ → B :	A A′ →	B
				Coda

Berceuse in D♭, Op. 57

A berceuse is a lullaby usually in 6/8 time, with the rhythm of the piece simulating the rocking of a cradle. One of the most famous examples is this Chopin composition. A seemingly simple piece, it contains the same bass notes and

---

5 "Concert de Chopin," Franz Liszt. *Revue et Gazette Musicale de Paris,* May 2, 1841. Translated by Rodney McIntosh.

almost the same left-hand chords from beginning to end. Yet because of the variety of the upper part this does not become wearisome. As the right hand weaves its melodic and technical magic of sixteen variations the bass notes become members of various chords, producing a study in shading and a handling of technic at variance with the melodic line.

Nocturne in E♭, Op. 9, No. 2

Originally related to the serenade, which also was evening or night music, this is a short musical selection reminiscent of pieces played under the balcony of a loved one as an offering of affection. During the Romantic period, and particularly for Chopin, the nocturne became a descriptive piece usually of modest tempo which would describe the falling of night, but more often impressions which one feels at nightfall. Similar to most of his nocturnes, this particular one contains a beautiful but simple melody which is played in the right hand, while the left plays the bass notes and chords. The coda gives some additional weight and substance to the work and offers a bit of technic for the performer. The melody, the chordal choice, the arrangement of the accompaniment, and the balance given by the coda keep this from becoming trite and just another simple piano composition. The form:

A A	: B A′ :	Coda

Waltz, Op. 34, No. 1

Typical of the waltz, Chopin's compositions contain many themes and parts. They capture the romance of the waltz rather than the impressions of a dance. The balances between the second part or trio and the first section are skillfully maintained. The coda contains dazzling technic, only to return to a remnant of the theme.

			bridge			
Introduction A B A B	C C′	D D ⟍ D C C′	A B	C C′	Coda
		Trio Key of trio			

Waltz, Op. 34, No. 2

A rarity since it uses mostly minor sounds, this waltz contains the beauty of sadness, of yearning, of hoping the end of a beautiful night will not come, or that parting will not occur. When the end is imminent the theme must be heard once again as a final remembrance.

A A B B'→C C	D D	D D	B B'→C C	D D	D D
	M	m		M	m

	bridge	
(cont.)	A A⌒A A	

Waltz, Op. 64, No. 1

Probably the shortest waltz by a major composer, this is often referred to as the "minute waltz" because it takes only a few seconds beyond the minute to play it. Some show pianists have played it within the minute, but it loses its charm when it becomes such a stunt. An encore or showpiece, full of technic yet melodic, a favorite for years, it unites beauty and technic in an amazingly short composition. The mood of the waltz is captured even though in an unusually brief span of time.

A B B	C C	A B B

Polonaise in A, Op. 40, No. 1

The history of the polonaise has been discussed in Chapter 16. Although used by other composers, it would never have reached its popularity with the musical public had it not been for Chopin and his ability to make of the musical form a symbol of the power and spirit of a people who had recently lost their native country. Chopin's father had served in the army under General Kosciusko, and even after the Poles had lost their land to the Russians and Prussians, the Chopin home was an intellectual center for those wishing to discuss freedom and to recall the time when the Poles ruled the second largest country in all of Europe. Chopin carried this feeling of patriotism with him to Paris, and shared it not only with many Poles living in Paris as refugees but with all who heard his music as well. Chopin's championing the cause of Poland through his music caused Schumann to remark that in his music the guns spoke loudest of all.

This is a simple composition made up of two main themes with key changes to add variety. The pomp and glory are present, but also the militaristic sounds of battle. Although the themes are similar the piece has brought response from the musical public, while the rhythm has proved exciting.

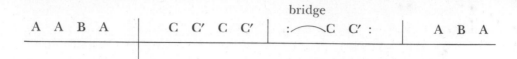

											bridge					
A	A	B	A		C	C′	C	C′	:	⌒	C	C′ :		A	B	A

Polonaise in A♭, Op. 53

The polonaise raised nationalistic feeling to a notable height wherein millions recognized the plight of Poland and felt her past glory and her dedication to freedom.   The descending bass line in the second main section produces an exciting effect; a similar line was used at a later time by Tchaikovsky, also for nationalistic purposes.   The second part of the trio (D) contains a lighter mood and gives us a feeling for the nostalgia and beauty of Poland, while also serving as a compositional relief giving contrast to the composition before the return of the main theme.

								bridge		
Introduction	A	A	B	A		C	C	D ⌒		A Coda
						Trio				

Study Procedures

1. Listen to the compositions by Chopin described in the text.   Based upon these compositions, which form would be your preference for further listening to Chopin?   Why?
2. Chopin wrote a number of compositions using these same forms.   Choose another composition using one of these forms and introduce it to your class.   Do not become involved with biographical material; rather, tell your class about the musical characteristics of the composition.   Why did you choose this particular work?   Can you make a form chart similar to those shown in the text?
3. Chopin also used other small forms for his compositions.   Which ones do you find on the recordings in your school library?   Do you like any of the new forms as well or better than the forms discussed in the text?

Claude Debussy

Debussy, probably the best-known composer of characteristic piano pieces during the late nineteenth century and early twentieth, wrote numerous selections for the piano, none of which are for beginners or the near-beginner.   A favorite with the concert public, many piano recitals feature his works even to the point of all or large portions of the program.   Those who enjoy this impressionistic style believe him to represent the epitome of the short piano selection.

Two Arabesques

The *arabesque,* coming from the Moors or Arabs, is a design of interlacing scroll-work or fanciful artwork. In music it refers to a fancy overlay of technic upon a simple form. The first of the two, marked Andantino con moto, contains a clear-sounding melody despite the floridness of the writing. A certain sheen hangs over the music typical of all Debussy. The form of the piece is almost hidden by the subtleties of the writing.

$$A \ B \ A \ \big| \ Coda$$

The second arabesque is marked Allegretto scherzando. Light, gay, dancelike, and playful, the variance of the first section compared to its repeat later adds to the quality of this short selection.

					bridge
Short introduction	a b a a	c c	a b ⌒ a
	A	B	A

Masques

Originally *masques* were elaborate dramatic productions consisting only of movement, many times including Scaramouche, a boastful, cowardly clown. This music represents the essence of such a presentation in the coloration and style of a more modern period. One hears constant reminders of great technic, yet the intervals suggest the plucking of an ancient string instrument. The form, almost lost in the florid lines and the subtle themes, appears completely of one fabric.

$$A \ \ B \ \ A \ \ C \ \ \rightarrow A \ \ A \ \ \ Coda$$

L'Isle joyeuse

In many ways this composition typifies more completely the style of Debussy and his impressionism. Suggestive of a gay dance tune or happy times, the syncopated melody and the polyrhythms provide interesting effects. Complex in technic, the piece ends with a broadening of chords and theme.

A	B	A	Coda
Technical, gay-polyrhythmic	More subtle, more melodic		Repeated chords, broader in effect

Study Procedures

1. Chopin's style of technic, plus melody, plus emotion, could be said to continue with Debussy. Do you agree or disagree? What differences do you notice?
2. For whom or under what circumstances could these arabesques have been written?
3. Which of the three Debussy compositions do you prefer? Why?

Klavierstück VIII (Stockhausen)

Some contemporary composers use the character piece even though they have altered the form considerably. Karlheinz Stockhausen, a German composer, has titled one such composition *Klavierstück VIII* (Piano Piece 8). Instead of the usual interplay of melodies and themes, he chose to show a contrast between repose and activity. This became all the more difficult, in that he chose to limit himself to about a minute and a half. Consider the following ideas as you listen:

Repose: In quiet (no sound)
In sound (nonrhythmic sound;
  tones which do not generate musical activity)

Activity: In quiet (anticipatory silence)
In sound (highly rhythmic sound;
  tonal energy from the manner in which pitches follow each other;
  tonal energy from the type of pitches which follow each other)

Study Procedures

1. Listen to this composition, defining for yourself which sounds are representative of repose and which represent activity. From the above diagram, choose ideas which determine the source of each.
2. Compare this style of writing to Chopin. In your own words, describe how each composer was able to use musical materials to accomplish his desired ends. What statement could you make concerning the music of Debussy?

Johannes Brahms

Although a brilliant pianist, Brahms never became a concert soloist. He composed numerous works for the piano but his interests in music were so broad that he is known for compositions in many mediums. When young he was taken to play for Liszt, and when the latter seemed to take little interest in him, he became friendly with Robert and Clara Schumann, both of whom championed his cause and his talent. Rarely an innovator, he took the well-known forms and extended their expressive qualities. Living through the height and latter days of the Romantic period, it was only natural that his compositional talents should turn toward the characteristic piece for piano.

Brahms had a style of writing based uniquely upon craftsmanship and coloration. Although his music fits into the Romantic period its tone carries a dark coloration without being thick or heavy, plus a weight of substance from careful construction. The main emphasis has moved from the technical, with no obvious nationalism, no dance reminders, and one confronts music that seems to have its emotions hidden below the surface where they become meaningful only upon seeking.

Intermezzo in b minor, Op. 119, No. 1

Originally a name given to musical compositions placed between the acts of more serious works, the *intermezzo* led to the development of several interesting forms. One such was the ballet, which at one time was placed between the acts of musical dramas. The character piece took this name, since it was meant to indicate that the work was of short duration and not particularly weighty.

Melodic, but in no manner trite; delicate, but not wanting in substance, this composition typifies Brahms's style.

The form: A B A

Intermezzo in a minor, Op. 118, No. 1

Sweeping at the beginning, this piece moves toward a more sedate ending to prepare for the next intermezzo. Short in duration, it apparently was meant to stand alone only in rare instances.

The form: A B A   Coda

Intermezzo in A Major, Op. 118, No. 2

Simple and direct, this is a love song of quiet but deep proportions. This composition is a hidden treasure of themes, fragments of themes, and inverted fragments of themes. The diagram will assist you in hearing the form of the work, but by studying it in detail you will hear these melodic fragments more acutely. Notice the inversion as well as the contrapuntal technics.

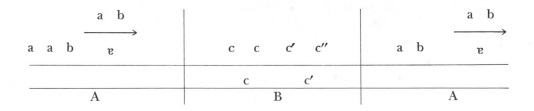

Study Procedures

1. Chopin, Liszt, and Brahms were all composers of the Romantic period. Which of the three seems best to epitomize the period with his music? How would you describe this alignment in your own words?
2. You have heard piano compositions by Debussy, who wrote at a much later time than the three composers discussed in question 1. Which of the three sounds more closely aligned to Debussy and could have been his predecessor? What leads you to this conclusion?

Luciano Berio

An Italian who has come to the United States to teach at one of our music schools, Berio is a contemporary composer who uses all mediums. His *Sequenza IV* explores a different kind of piano characteristic, meaning that the composer is trying to use the piano to meet the demands of twentieth century music.

The piece uses two musical idioms: staccato chords, and fast technical sounds which fill around the chords. The work begins in an advanced jazz manner with some highly interesting chords. A technical section is soon introduced but does not continue. In fact, the chords and technical material alternate in an erratic pattern. The chords contrast to the technical section, controlling the expressive aspect and emotional impact of the composition by their positioning, style, and balance.

Vladimir Ussachevsky

The characteristic sound of the piano is now being challenged by the tape recorder and other electronic devices.

Using the piano as the producer of sound, *Sonic Contours* alters the pitches by electronic means; the listener may not even recognize the piano as the performing instrument.   Throughout, the emphasis is upon changes possible using electronic means with a stable, conventional source.   The composition contains three unseparated sections with no obvious thematic or sectional repetitions.

Study Procedures

1. Compare the Ussachevsky and Berio compositions.   Which do you prefer?   For what musical reasons?
2. Which of the two styles do you believe to be more characteristic of the trends of the future?   Do you believe that original or altered piano sounds will become more meaningful in the future?   Why?

Johann Sebastian Bach

Living before the Romantic period and before the widespread use of the piano, Bach wrote no characteristic pieces for it.   In fact, his keyboard writing was solely for the organ or the harpsichord.   However, some of his compositions are so well-suited to the keyboard (harpsichord or piano) and have been played by so many amateur and professional pianists as they develop their skill, it would be an error not to include them in this chapter.

Inventions in C Major and d minor

The *invention* is almost completely a title devised by Bach.   Although music history contains a few other examples of the term, it was used so seldom that it created no set pattern in style or form.   For Bach, it meant a short contrapuntal composition based on two or three simple themes or fragments.

On the next two pages you will find the *Invention in C Major* with comments within the music.   Even though you may not read music, you will be able to follow the movement of the symbols and the comments.   Afterward, follow a second two-part invention by Bach, one in d minor.   Study the score as you listen to the recording, and write comments of your own through the music indicating which of the musical phrases you hear as themes and fragments. If you are successful with these two, examine the three-part *Invention in d minor*. Listen to the recording, noticing how the voice parts intertwine, and also how the themes move from lower to higher voices.   The themes are used over and over again, which is typical of contrapuntal writing and particularly of the *Inventions*.

INVENTIO 1

Schmieder-Verz. 772

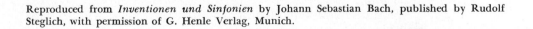

Reproduced from *Inventionen und Sinfonien* by Johann Sebastian Bach, published by Rudolf Steglich, with permission of G. Henle Verlag, Munich.

Study Procedures

1. The Bach two- and three-part inventions are recorded on the piano and on the harpsichord. Listen to both versions of the same compositions. Then, compare the tone of the piano with that of the harpsichord. In comparing the two playings of the Bach inventions, are all the differences those of the instrument? Since the harpsichord was the prevalent instrument during the writing of early keyboard works, some believe that these compositions should be played only upon that instrument. Do you agree, or do you believe that the piano adds a dimension which goes beyond the period?
2. Do you hear certain similarities of style between Brahms and other composers we have studied? Which composer would you choose as similar, based upon our brief survey? How does he differ?
3. Chopin wrote about fifty mazurkas. Listen to one or two of these, and describe the form and general characteristics as compared to other compositions which we have studied. Do they more nearly resemble the polonaise? Or the waltz? Or another form?
4. Make a list of the different forms which we have studied in this chapter. What characteristics do you find common to all? What characteristics are individual for each form?
5. Based upon the music of this chapter, what would you state concerning the times during which these composers lived?
6. A number of interesting biographies have been written about Chopin. Read one of these and make a report on the following topic: "Music as a Means of Understanding the Life of Chopin."
7. Listen to several selections by Liszt. How does his music differ from that of Chopin even though the two men were often together during Chopin's lifetime?
8. The characteristic piece for piano has not been a major compositional type during the twentieth century. Why would you suppose this to be true?
9. Invite a college student pianist to your class, asking him to play a characteristic piece for the instrument.

THE ORGAN

Although one of the oldest of instruments, the organ still remains one of the least understood by most laymen and many times even by the musician as well. Its ancestors date from two centuries before Christ, but in principle the modern organ employs the same means of producing sound, wherein air, supplied to a wooden or metal tube containing an opening, causes the tube to respond with a pitch.

If you are interested in the instrument, read a history of the organ and you will find it fascinating: in early times it was a noisy novelty at fairs and celebrations; it has been carried into battle and on crusades; it has accompanied songs of the lover; but most often it has been used by the church to assist in the worship service, stimulating the singer of songs and soothing the meditator. Until about the sixteenth century most of the instruments had limited keyboards, some with no pedal work. When mechanical developments assisted the musician, the

A modern pipe organ, with shutter manual, exposed ranks and expression pipes (Courtesy of Reuter Organ Co., Lawrence, Kansas).

organ became a marvelous instrument, and certain geographic sections of Europe concentrated upon different styles of tonal design, thus furthering different compositional technics. These even permeate our thinking today.

The contemporary organ consists of two or three keyboards for the hands as well as a pedal keyboard for the feet. Each key on the keyboard activates the air for one or more pipes in the pipe chest. The controls for the player are located on the organ manual in the form of stop tabs or drawbars. These enable a player to control the color of the sound and the number of pipes he wishes to play at any one time. One set of pipes for each key on the keyboard is known as a *rank*. Some organs have as few as three or four ranks, while larger instruments might contain almost 100 ranks. The organist can play each of these ranks one at a time, or all at one time. He can also control the loudness by means of shutters on the swell box where some or all of the pipes are located. Some organs have no shutters, and the only loudness control then is the number of ranks sounding at any one time.

The organ is a magnificent instrument. It contains the largest pitch range, the largest loudness range, and the greatest tonal possibilities of all the instruments.

The Music

The organ supercedes the piano in one regard, that of tonal diversity. The piano strives for differences in tone through touch and speed, but the organ has different ranks at its disposal. In addition, each organ is custom-built, so that the same composition played by the same person on two organs will sound differently. Although technic cannot be the same asset in organ playing as on the piano, technic is a characteristic of organ literature along with melodic lines or themes and the manner in which the themes are handled.

Johann Sebastian Bach

As a composer of organ literature, J. S. Bach's reputation surpasses all others. Living and writing during the early decades of the eighteenth century, he was a master of the musical forms which he used. Not an innovator, but rather one who polished the art of his period to a high luster, his compositions are considered the epitome of Baroque style all over the world. Most often considered a great contrapuntalist, his music, as we noticed in our study of the simple two-part inventions, is rich with the overlay of small themes as they move from one voice to another. A prolific writer, he seemed never to want for thematic material.

Most of his life he was musical director for a prince or organist at a church. The type of composition he wrote seemed to be determined almost entirely by the need of the moment but his scope was immense, including not only organ works, but works for the clavier, for the voice, for choirs, for solo instruments, and for the orchestra. All of his music uses forms common at that time, but his writing contains little that was popular or common. Many of his compositions, particularly those for organ, were based upon well-known chorale or hymn tunes of the time, but through his writing he lifted them above their commonness to an unprecedented level.

Bach's Organ Music

For the organ Bach wrote many chorale fantasias, preludes, fugues, toccatas, a collection of chorale settings, and six trios. We will examine a toccata, a chorale prelude, and one prelude and fugue.

Wachet auf, Chorale Prelude

"Sleepers, Awake," an Advent hymn, admonishes the Christian to prepare for the coming of the Lord. Bach has divided his composition into two main parts. The first is a harmonization of the chorale melody as it was sung in the churches, with an emphasis upon Bach's contrapuntal bass line which frames the character of the entire harmonization. The first half of the chorale is played full organ, while the second half begins with a quieter registration and builds to the end. The second section of the composition features the intertwining of the beautiful countermelody which Bach created with the straightforward melody of the chorale. The countermelody enters and the two vie for our attention. The countermelody is heard in part or in its entirety four times, while the chorale melody is heard only occasionally as Bach works through the chorale. The beauty of the countermelody has endeared this chorale prelude to many.

Full organ X X	Softer but growing to end Y Z		X	Y	Z
		Countermelody repeated 4 times but with alterations			
Contrapuntal bass line for chorale		New bass part serving both melodies			

Toccata in d minor

This florid form for the keyboard was a favorite of Bach's to precede other forms, most often the fugue. Usually employing running passages and large chords, this type of composition showed off the technic of the performer and the tonal resources of the instrument, particularly those which involved loudness. The thematic elements are of less significance in this composition as compared to technic. This form has been a favorite of organists from the sixteenth century to the present.

The *Toccata in d minor* precedes a fugue in the same key. As a type of introduction, it begins with three fanfares and a large chord which Bach took to be the main subject for the following fugue. Then follow some scale figurations upward and downward, although we soon hear that most of the composition centers around the downward movement of the tones. The third portion of the toccata is semimelodic, and for some measures features four bass notes all built on a downward scale. Some phrases sound recitative-like and certain phrases do repeat, but no form exists. This is a favorite composition with young and mature organists alike, with some performers using the large chords to show the expansive qualities of the instrument. Although arranged for orchestra, it should be heard on the organ to capture its original impact.

Prelude and Fugue in e minor, No. 3

The prelude contains a large sound, a slow tempo, and straightforward movement, almost choralelike, with a few moving inner voices to avoid block chords.

As to the fugue: no matter who the composer, all fugues have four or five characteristics which should be kept in mind while listening. Fugues are *contrapuntal,* which means that each voice exists independently and is not a simultaneous rhythmic copy of the melodic line. The theme in fugues is known as the *subject,* and usually is short in duration compared to melodies of other forms. These subjects are heard in one voice after another, much as in a round. By the time the second or third voice is ready for the subject, the earlier entrants have moved into freely-designed counterpoint involving recurring motives or figures which center about particular intervals or inversions of these intervals. At times in the composition a composer moves away from one statement of a theme and prepares for the next entrance. Counterpoint will be heard but the theme will be absent. Such a section is known as an *episode.* Depending upon the subject and the composer, the subjects may enter rather closely upon one another or at some distance. The longer the composition usually the longer the subject, and usually the greater distance between points of entry.

This e-minor fugue is short, and consequently a good example for study by a beginning player or listener. Notice several points. The subject is stated in four voices, from high to low in succession; after stating the subject the upper voices become involved with counterpoint but never restate the subject; the subject is stated in the pedals or lower voice four times; the episodes in this short fugue are also short. The diagram below will assist in listening.

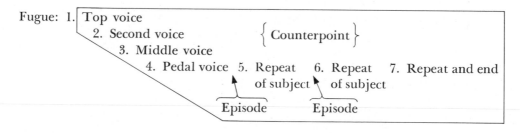

Johannes Brahms

Although Brahms wrote only three major compositions for organ, he still represents the Romantic period well and his chorale preludes are often played in churches and at concerts. Other compositions are heard less often.

Three Chorale Preludes, Op. 122

Numbers 8, 9, and 10 from a set of eleven chorale preludes are more often heard than others in the set. These are less clear-cut than the Bach chorale preludes, with more interplay between the contrapuntal countermelodies and the original chorale melody. A more romantic registration is required to give the correct feeling for these compositions. Number 8 is simple, direct, and melodic, and features a composed countermelody to the well-known Christmas hymn "Lo, How a Rose E'er Blooming." Both 9 and 10 are based upon the same chorale tune: "Herzlich tut mich verlangen." Number 10 is quieter, while Number 9 is bold.

César Franck

The greatest influence in the field of organ during the Romantic period was a Belgian who studied and taught in Paris. Although not the most prolific composer, César Franck wrote a number of famous organ pieces as well as compositions for orchestra, chorus, chamber music, and smaller works. Not only an influence in organ, through his teaching he was a major influence in the entire field of French music, and many well-known composers were his students.

Pièce héroïque

Probably the best-known of Franck's organ compositions is a short bravura piece. Typical of the Romantic period and the instruments which were built during those years, this composition features the hugeness of the organ and the technic which is possible upon it. In the usual **ABA** form with a coda, this work makes use of two main themes, a and c.

The form:

A	B bridge	A	Coda
a b a	c ⌒ a ⌒	a	c
Bold, questioning	quiet, bass interjections		Bold, chorale from quiet theme

> a—Bold but questioning. This main theme is heard four times, and between the second and third time fragments are presented as a type of bridge
> b—Fanfarelike, in block chords followed by more florid arpeggios
> a—Main theme is heard one more time
> c—Somewhat more quiet but tubalike bass notes are interjected between phrases of the theme, growing in regularity until continuous
> ⌒ theme—Fragments are used in higher voices as a bridge
> a—Main theme is heard two times plus some fragments
> Coda—A chorale is developed from the second main theme or c, but a new harmonization is heard. Near the end the same pedal notes assist in the conclusion

Louis Vierne

A pupil of César Franck, Vierne became probably the best-known of the impressionistic organists. Blind, talented in performance and composition, and organist at the Cathedral of Notre Dame in Paris, he added a more modern dimension to the repertoire of the instrument.

Water Nymphs

Not all organ literature is built upon chorale tunes and fugues. As the piano had been used by the romantics, an occasional composer would use the organ to describe and the title of the composition would indicate the general direction of his interest. Probably taking a cue from Debussy, who had always had an interest in water, and trying to describe it with musical sounds, Vierne wrote this delicate but interesting short piece for his major instrument.

Facile, not heavy, the work has a striking sound and appeal from the first few notes. Built upon two main ideas, a continuous running technical display makes up a most fascinating part of the entire composition. The melody of the first theme is played by staccato chords in the left hand, while the right plays the technical variations. In the second section the scale passages continue but a smoother melodic line is heard. An interesting coda completes the work.

A   B   A   B⌒A   Coda

John Weaver

Many excellent young organists are now teaching and playing in our country. They have been well-schooled and their interest has raised the standards of playing and of organ building to an all-time high. In addition to concertizing and teaching, many of these young performers also compose. John Weaver, who has been trained at Peabody Conservatory and the Curtis Institute, is one prime example.

Toccata

Using an older form to express modern ideas, this work exploits the modern organ in a technical manner. Much of the technic has been written into the pedal keyboard for the feet. A scalelike melody makes up most of the main theme and also assists with the rhythmic and technical passages which are part of the harmonic background. This work is united in an interesting manner, since the fanfarelike introduction also is used in fragmented form as bridge material for both the first and second sections. Near the end the first theme is heard in augmentation, or in rhythms which are twice as long as in the earlier portion of the work.

```
                        bridge  |         bridge  |
                                |                 |
Introduction    A ⌒ A ⟶ |    B ⌒       | A  A
                                |                 |   Augmented
```

Study Procedures

1. Visit a local church or auditorium and examine the organ from inside the pipe chamber. Have the organist play the same pitch on each of the ranks in the organ. Can you hear the differences in coloration, or are they too similar?
2. Much organ music is recorded. Choose a composition from a recognized composer which you believe the class would enjoy hearing. Why would you choose this composition?
3. The Bach compositions belong to the Baroque period, while other compositions in the chapter are from the Romantic period or the twentieth century. Which compositions belong to each period? Try to answer this question by listening and defining styles rather than through reading material in the text.
4. Listen to a composition played on an electronic organ. How would you compare this to a pipe organ?

Bibliography—Chapter 19

GLINSKI, MATTEO, *Chopin the Unknown.* Windsor, Canada: Assumption University of Windsor Press, 1963.

HEDLEY, ARTHUR, *Chopin.* London: J. M. Dent and Sons Ltd., 1957.

HUNEKER, JAMES, *Chopin.* New York: Charles Scribner's Sons, 1900.

JAMES, PHILIP, *Early Keyboard Instruments.* London: Holland Press, 1960.

KARASOWSKI, MORITZ, *Frederic Chopin, His Life and Letters.* London: William Reeves, 1938.

LISZT, FRANZ, *Frederic Chopin.* New York: Free Press of Glencoe, 1963.

NIECKS, FREDERICK, *Frederick Chopin.* London: Novello Ewer and Co., 1888.

NORMAN, HERBERT, and JOHN, *The Organ Today.* London: Barrie and Rockliff, 1967.

WALKER, ALAN, *et al., Frederic Chopin.* London: Barrie and Rockliff, 1966.

WEINSTOCK, HERBERT, *Chopin.* New York: Alfred A. Knopf, 1959.

Recordings—Chapter 19

| Bach | *Invention in Two Parts in C Major* | Glenn Gould | Columbia MS-6622 |

	Invention in Two Parts in d minor		
	Invention in Three Parts in d minor	George Malcolm	Nonesuch H-71144
Bach	*Prelude and Fugue in e minor, No. 3*	E. Power Biggs	Columbia M2S-697
	Toccata in d minor		
Bach	*Wachet auf,* Chorale Prelude	E. Power Biggs	Columbia ML-4284-I
Berio	*Sequenza IV*		Candide CE-31015
Brahms	*Chorale Preludes:*	Richter	DGG-138906
	8. "Es ist ein Ros' entsprungen"		
	9. "Herzlich tut mich verlangen"		
	10. "Herzlich tut mich verlangen"		
Brahms	*Intermezzo,* Op. 118, No. 1	Glenn Gould	Columbia ML-5637
	Intermezzo, Op. 118, No. 2		
	Intermezzo, Op. 119, No. 1		
Chopin	*Berceuse in D♭,* Op. 57	Rubinstein	Victor LM-2277
Chopin	*Impromptu,* Op. 66	Rubinstein	Victor LM-2277
Chopin	*Nocturne in E♭,* Op. 9, No. 2	Brailowsky	Victor LM-2160
Chopin	*Polonaise in A,* Op. 40, No. 1	Rubinstein	Victor LM-1205
Chopin	*Polonaise in A♭,* Op. 53	Rubinstein	Victor LM-1205
Chopin	*Waltz,* Op. 34, No. 1	Rubinstein	Victor LM-1892
Chopin	*Waltz,* Op. 34, No. 2	Rubinstein	Victor LM-1892
Chopin	*Waltz,* Op. 64, No. 1	Rubinstein	Victor LM-1892
Debussy	*L'Isle joyeuse*	Casadesus	Columbia ML-4979
Debussy	*Masques*	Casadesus	Columbia ML-4979
Debussy	*Two Arabesques*	Casadesus	Columbia ML-4978
Franck	*Pièce héroïque*	E. Power Biggs	Columbia ML-4329
Liszt	*Three Grand Études* (After Paganini)	Merzhanov	Monitor MC-2012
Stockhausen	*Klavierstücke VIII*		Candide CE-31015
Ussachevsky	*Sonic Contours*		Desto DC-6466
Vierne	*Water Nymphs*	Schreiner	Columbia ML-5425
Weaver	*Toccata*	Weaver	Wicks 832W-4267

Chapter 20

Instrumental Solo Literature

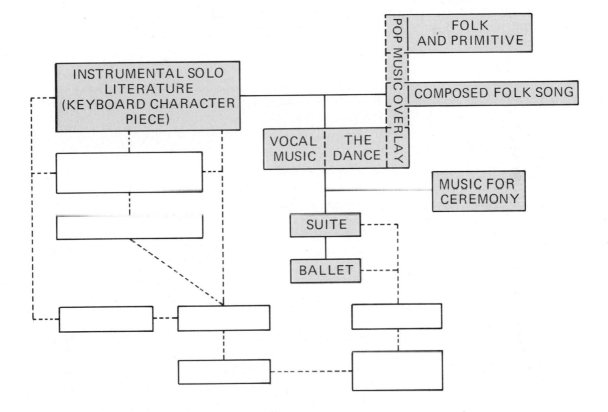

Solo literature for strings, winds, and percussion has attracted the attention of composer and performer since the time when manufacturers succeeded in producing instruments which were technically reliable and whose tone was almost uniform throughout a wide range. The strings were developed into solo instruments during the seventeenth century, but the brass and woodwinds, although used in ensembles, did not become true solo instruments until the nineteenth century. The brass instruments were particularly late in developing, and did not reach this proficiency until the valve became a workable part of the instrument.

When the tone color, intonation, and technical aspects of the instruments became reliable, the players sought musical literature that would permit the performer to show his instrument to a good advantage. Thousands of small solo pieces for all instruments have been composed over the past 100 years. When the literature was not adequate, arrangements of literature from other areas have sufficed. In some cases these arrangements have been part of larger works, or works for other instruments, and some have even been taken from song literature or arranged from vocal selections of operas.

Instrumental music has engaged the attention of leading composers as well as hacks, with an emphasis upon the writing of small pieces as well as occasional large compositions. In this chapter we will examine mainly the smaller forms; in later chapters the larger forms will be studied.

Characteristic solos have been written for enjoyment in the home, as encore pieces for the concert hall, and for the aspiring student of the instrument. Most recently, school contests and festivals have reawakened interest in much solo literature that had long been forgotten or cast aside. Contemporary composers and musicologists have served the student well in this regard, supplying much material of all styles.

The listener is confronted regularly with the characteristic solo at home, at recitals, concerts, or contests; in fact, so numerous are the possibilities that it warrants our study. In addition, such a study introduces the instruments to us in a much more interesting and practical manner than hearing them only as a part of orchestral selections, where they may be featured in solo roles for a short phrase or two. The characteristic solo literature enables the listener to obtain an understanding of the coloration of the tone and the technical possibilities of the instrument under a variety of musical circumstances.

Considering these two facets as most outstanding, composers have written compositions which feature them specifically. Some solo literature emphasizes mainly the technical aspects of an instrument; other compositions feature a specific mood through an instrument's unique tone colorations. As a rule, it takes a good composer to exploit the instrument successfully throughout its tonal spectrum. Less of a problem faces the composer who wishes to feature the technic of the instrument. In fact, some of the well-known technical solos exhibit modest musical value although they have become favorites over the years because of the pyrotechnical aspects of the writing and the challenge they offer to the performer. A few compositions are able to combine both aspects successfully in one solo piece. These are usually in two sections: often a slow section for the tone or mood, and a second section featuring the technic. Many solos use this formula, but only a few unite it with notable musical qualities.

The many and varied titles of these compositions assist us in appreciating their intent, and may be classified under three general headings: musical terms, musical forms, and descriptive phrases.

MUSICAL TERMS

Most often these solos carry the title of the tempo marking of the music. Much instrumental music written by well-known composers is not titled, and musicians and laymen alike refer to the sections only by their tempo markings. The composers of characteristic pieces have adopted this idea and upon occasion have used these terms as the official titles of compositions. Such terms include Allegretto, Introduction and Allegro, Andante and Allegro, Cantabile and Presto, and Allegro Moderato. Understanding the meaning of some of these Italian terms which indicate the tempos of music will assist greatly in understanding the intent of the composer in his solo piece.

MUSICAL FORMS

Most characteristic solos are comparatively short, meeting the requirements of the dances and other short forms discussed throughout our text. The names of these forms are sometimes appropriately used as titles of compositions, so understanding these forms will assist the listener in comprehending the intent of the composer.

Some representative titles taken from compositions in this category include Minuet, Recitative, Sicilienne and Rondo, Aria with Variations, Introduction and Dance, Valse Miniature, Gavotte, Rondo, Cavatina, Piece in Form of Habanera, Rondino, Toccata, and Madrigal.

DESCRIPTIVE PHRASES

By far the largest number of compositions which can be called characteristic solos use descriptive titles. Popularized by Beethoven with a set of Bagatelles, this practice was continued by other romantic composers, most notably Schubert and Schumann. The general meaning of the title may give some indication as to the intent of the composition; at other times, the title gives no indication whether the purpose be mainly technical or to present a mood. By way of generalization, one might conclude that descriptive titles are least likely to be true indicators of the content of a composition.

ACCOMPANIMENT

Most characteristic solos are accompanied by the piano. Occasionally the quality of the solo or the interest of the composer in the composition will stimulate him to write an ensemble accompaniment. Even in this case, usually the composition had only a piano accompaniment originally. Some technical solos have been arranged with band accompaniment. A few solos exist with no accompaniment of any kind; since the instrument plays completely alone in such solos, it takes a good composer and an excellent player to sustain the interest and the musical qualities.

REPRESENTATIVE LITERATURE

Musical Terms

Introduction and Allegro (Ravel; harp)

The accompaniment for this solo consists of a string quartet plus flute and clarinet. The obvious harp quality easily distinguishes it from other instruments. Having the most complex form of all the solos we will study, this piece becomes comparatively easy to follow with the outline shown below. As the title implies, the work is in two sections. The introduction sets the stage from the standpoint of mood, color, and themes. The body of the composition is the Allegro section.

Ravel wrote this solo in about eight days because he wished to accept an invitation for a cruise on a yacht and still meet the deadline for its completion to the Erard Piano Company. It remains one of the outstanding solos for harp.

Introduction

Theme X   (x′)—Woodwinds
          (x″)—Strings   This theme later becomes A
          Reversed
          (x′)—Strings
          (x″)—Woodwinds   Harp glissandos and accompaniment figures are used throughout and as a bridge between sections

Theme Y   —Cello

Allegro

Part I   Theme A—Harp (theme moves downward by step)
        A—Flute
        A—Woodwinds, strings, and harp as accompaniment
    Theme B—Flute and strings (also moves downward but limited in descent)

The next portion of the allegro uses both A and B in a mix.

Part II   Theme A—Harp with accompaniment playing x′ (slower tempo); Bridge from theme B
    Theme B—Harp (this is quickly stated, and then a bridge into:)
    Theme B—Clarinet (harp plays A theme in augmentation)
      Cadenza—Harp (Theme A, x′, Y)

The next portion is similar to the beginning of the Allegro.

Part III   Theme A—Harp
             Theme B—Harp, woodwinds
             Theme B—This time the theme changes accent
             Theme A—Harp and strings (tempo is increased to create an end-
                    ing)

Musical Forms

Simple Minuet (Goldenberg; snare drum)

This piece is a snare drum solo for the student percussionist.

Recitative, Sicilienne, and Rondo (Bozza; bassoon)

Bozza, a well-known French composer of characteristic solos, has written numbers of these for almost all instruments. In this piece, mainly a technical solo,
a simple melody stands between two technical sections. The formless Recitative,
another name for cadenza, although slow, places technical demands and emphasis
upon the range. The Sicilienne is reminiscent of the pastorale, and almost
always in compound meter. The simple AA form of the Sicilienne enables the
other two sections of the solo to dominate. The Rondo, although abbreviated,
carries the form ABACA.

Introduction and Dance (Barat; tuba)

Since the musical materials are not outstanding, the tuba and its particular tonal
qualities become the center of focus in this solo. The Introduction has two
sections: the first is declamatory in nature, while the second is more cadenzalike.
The Dance, a three-part form (ABA), contains a piano interlude between each
section. The contrasting section adopts a pseudo-Spanish rhythm, while the
melodic line itself is reminiscent of the Introduction.

Valse Miniature (Serge Koussevitzky; string bass)

The composer of this composition was a bassist for many years before becoming
conductor of the Boston Symphony Orchestra. Although not available on the
commercial market, some records exist of Koussevitzky himself playing this composition. Gary Karr, winner of several contests, is a young American bassist
who has won renown for his playing. The sound of the instrument should be

of special interest, since seldom is the string bass heard in a solo, and even more rare is a composition written especially for that instrument. This solo, written by a bassist for the string bass, follows the form of a waltz: ABA, contrasting waltz, return to the original waltz.

Aria con Variazioni (Handel; arranged for trumpet by Fitzgerald)

This is a simple tune with a set of variations. Much like other technical solos, the variations place increasing technical demands upon the performer as more and more notes are added to the tune. As you listen to the solo, keep the aria well in mind, since the performer plays the tune over and over again, but each time additional notes are added around the notes of the tune. The first variation doubles the notes of the melody; the second variation triples the notes; in the third, the piano plays the variation but the trumpet adds an obbligato to the piano; variation four demands four notes to every one of the original, while variation five requests the performer to play six notes to each original note. You will hear the trumpet performer playing exceedingly fast, and yet over and beyond the technic, the style of the composition and the aria itself have not been altered.

Descriptive Titles

"The Swan" (Saint-Saëns; cello)

This mood solo for cello is in simple three-part form. Notice the smooth connections between the sections. From the suite entitled *Carnival of the Animals,* the original piece featured the solo cello also. The tone of the cello and the mental image of swans seem compatible to most persons.

Romance (Scriabin; French horn)

This composition is a mood solo for a brass instrument, in simple three-part form.

Caprice Viennois (Kreisler; violin)

For years Fritz Kreisler, one of the most famous violinists in the world, played in large metropolis and small town alike. Many of his encores were pieces he composed himself. Often played by him, this little solo became well-known and has been a favorite for years. After an introduction the first theme, in modest tempo, is played in double stops. A quick section follows, whereupon the first theme returns.

Claude Debussy and his first wife, Rosalie, around 1902 (Courtesy of French Cultural Services, New York).

Première rapsodie (Debussy; clarinet)

Typical for its form, this solo combines contrasts in mood, tempo, and technical demands, and in so doing, places the instrument and the performer on display. One of the major works for clarinet, the original accompaniment was written for piano. The composer wrote an orchestral accompaniment a year later. Being of free form, it follows no standard pattern. Based upon two main themes, a third acts as a bridge of rhapsodic material between the main themes.

Introduction   A B c A   c   B   c   B   A c A   Coda

Poem (Griffes; flute)

This three-part solo begins and ends with a pensive section which, although technical in places, establishes mood as its main function. Even when technical it may not appear so. Throughout the solo, particularly in the first part of the dance, the tonality is unusual, and the entire composition suggests a dream sequence or an otherworldliness.

425

Part I   XX   Rambling section   X
Part II (dance)   Horn introduction, cadenza, AABA
Part III (return to Part I)   X   ending.

Gargoyles (Luening)

The contemporary composer may use electronic synthesized sound as the accompaniment for a solo instrument. Such a composition is *Gargoyles,* by Otto Luening, one of America's leading composers with electronic sound.

Using violin solo and tape, *Gargoyles* is a theme and variations. The following outline will assist in your understanding of this composition:

Theme: Part I of the theme; electronic sound
              Violin and electronic sound
              Electronic sound
              Part II of the theme; violin

Variations: I—Electronic sound based on Part I
                   II—Violin alone; based on Theme II; slow and plaintive
                  III—Electronic sound
                   IV—Violin and electronic sound
                    V—Violin alone; longer than the previous four variations
                   VI—Electronic sound
                  VII—Violin; Theme I
                 VIII—Electronic sound
                   IX—Electronic sound and violin

Coda: Theme II; violin alone

Study Procedures

1. Talk with your friends who are studying an instrument, and inquire of them of the solos they have been or are playing. In which category do they belong? Can you calculate the nature of each solo by the title?
2. Ask a friend of yours to play a solo for you or your class. Can you follow the form of the composition played?
3. Debussy wrote a Rhapsody for saxophone as well as clarinet. Listen to the solo for saxophone and compare it to the one for clarinet. What similarities do you hear? Would you agree that there are more differences than similarities?
4. Most characteristic solos are composed by men who are little-known in the musical world. Why do you believe this to be true?
5. Obtain a glossary of musical terms, and choose those which you believe could be titles for characteristic solos. After making such a list prepare a quiz of these terms for your classmates.
6. Listen to solos of instruments not included in this chapter: viola, oboe, trombone, and mallet percussion.

Bibliography—Chapter 20

BAINES, ANTHONY, *European and American Musical Instruments.* New York: Viking Press, 1966.

HOSIER, JOHN, *Instruments of the Orchestra.* London: Oxford University Press, 1961.

MASON, DANIEL GREGORY, *The Orchestral Instruments and What They Do.* New York: H. W. Gray, 1909.

WINTERNITZ, EMANUEL, *Musical Instruments of the Western World.* New York: McGraw-Hill, 1966.

Recordings—Chapter 20

Barat	*Introduction and Dance*	Tuba, Roger Bobo	Crystal S-125
Bozza	*Recitative, Sicilienne and Rondo*	Bassoon, Robert Quayle Mark	MRS-32286
Debussy	*Première rapsodie*	Reginald Kell	Decca DL-9744
Gaubert	*Allegretto*	Clarinet, Donald McGinnis	Marbeck XCTV-63138
Goldenberg, M.	*Simple Minuet*	Snare drum, Joel Leach	Stockdale TTP-1
Griffes	*Poem*	Camille Wanausek	Desto D-424
Handel (Fitzgerald)	*Aria con Variazioni*	Trumpet, Haynie	Golden Crest RE-7008
Jeanjean	*Arabesques*	McGinnis	Marbeck XCTV-63138
Koussevitzky	*Valse Miniature*	String bass, Gary Karr	Golden Crest RE-7012
Kreisler	*Caprice Viennois*	Leonid Kogan	Victor LM-2250
Krieger (Fitzgerald)	*Allegro*	Trumpet, John Haynie	Golden Crest GCRE-7008
Luening	*Gargoyles*		Columbia MS-6566
Ravel	*Introduction and Allegro*	Harp, Grandjany	Capitol P-8492
Ropartz	*Andante and Allegro*	Trumpet, Haney	Austin Custom, SAM-33-6502
Saint-Saëns	"The Swan"	Carmen Dragon	Capitol PAO-8413
Sarasate	*Capriccio Basque*	Leonid Kogan	Victor LM-2250
Scriabin	*Romance*	John Barrows	Golden Crest RE-7018
Weber	*Fantasia and Rondo*	Clarinet, Donald McGinnis	Marbeck XCTV-63138

Additional Suggestions for Listening

Rapsody for Saxophone (Debussy)	Jules De Vries	Lyrichord LL-38
Eight Solos for Baritone Horn	Leonard Falcone	Golden Crest RE-7001
Seven Solos for Flute	James Pellerite	Golden Crest RE-7010
Numerous Solos for Trumpet	George Reynolds	Golden Crest RE-7004

Chapter 21

Small Ensembles

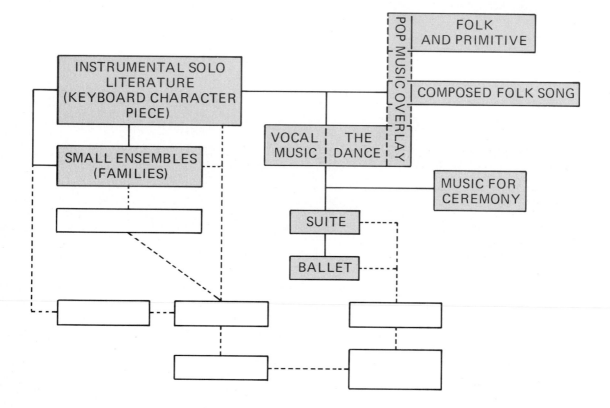

Almost everyone knows the instrument families. A favorite theme of concerts for young people or discussions in classrooms, even some records focus on this subject. As you probably know, the manner in which the musical tone is produced determines the family to which an instrument belongs. Strings are set into vibration by a bow or plucking of the hand; the brasses are long metal tubes with special mouthpieces. The woodwinds (only sometimes wood) usually have vibrating wooden reeds producing the sound, while percussion instruments respond when struck in some manner.

But the composer and listener may unite on a more interesting and more artistic ground: the composition itself which has been written for these groups of instruments. Since the strings were developed into concert instruments earlier than other families, music for strings became prominent soon after the beginning of the seventeenth century. The last family to achieve full concert status was the percussion group. Composers for years passed this family by, because the instruments appeared so nonmelodic, and because the artistic temper of the times negated an association of percussion sounds and expression. Particularly since the Second World War has the percussion ensemble become prominent.

Many excellent compositions exist for these families. We shall study representative examples partly because this will assist us in hearing the families in artistic settings, also because the interest of professionals and laymen alike has become renewed in the smaller ensemble whether it be a homogeneous or heterogeneous grouping. All the compositions we study will be of the former type. Fewer of the latter category exist, but the future will see more important works of this classification.

THE WOODWIND QUINTET

Although the clarinet choir recently has developed in many secondary schools and colleges, the woodwind quintet is the elite woodwind ensemble which has attracted the attention of composers and artists alike. The quintet consists of flute, oboe, clarinet, French horn, and bassoon. These instruments, unique in coloration and with strong individual characteristics, present a musical challenge to the composer in balance and unity. Woodwind quintets exist in most of our schools and a few professional groups play and record regularly.

Kleine Kammermusik, No. 2 (Hindemith)

Written in 1922, this group of short movements for woodwind quintet has become a favorite with woodwind players because Hindemith wrote well for those instruments. In addition, within his style, he employs the instruments expressively. Each movement makes interesting use of the instruments, and although many times the music is difficult for the performer, it still is playable for the amateur and gives him a sense of accomplishment.

The composition has a dry, modern texture which belies its years. Even today it sounds as if it were written recently because of its striking manner of treating dissonances and their resolution into consonances. At the beginning of the fourth movement each of the instruments has a brief cadenza which permits the listener to hear the instrument almost alone, and to be aware of its particular color and range.

Hindemith was one of a school of contemporary composers who used musical terms from his native language. Consequently, the movements of the quintet are listed in German:

Lustig (Jolly)
Walzer
Ruhig und einfach (peaceful and simple)
Schnell (quick)

Trois pièces brèves (Ibert)

Ibert's three short pieces have probably been performed by professionals and amateurs alike more than any one single work for woodwind quintet. It is gay, difficult enough to sound challenging and professional, and yet even the amateur can sound well performing it. Ibert also understands the instruments for which he writes and the manner in which their colorations can fit together and aid each other. In a lighter vein than the Hindemith, the movements proceed in an absorbing manner even in the slow second movement, which is a songlike section using mostly flute and clarinet.

The sections are:

Allegro
Andante
Allegro Scherzando

Study Procedures

1. Compare the styles of writing between the Hindemith and the Ibert. Based upon the information given for the Hindemith, can you determine when the Ibert quintet was written?
2. Another fascinating quintet is Milhaud's *La Cheminée du Roi René*. Typical of Milhaud, this suite is a collection of French folk songs. Listen to this quintet, and then decide how the composer uses the instruments to attain the coloration he wishes for each movement.
3. Almost every high school or college has a student or faculty woodwind quintet. Ask them to perform for your class so that you can watch as well as hear the performance. Do the sounds, when heard in person, seem more united and blended or more individual?

THE PERCUSSION ENSEMBLE

When percussion ensembles first became independent entities, it was customary to use the piano as one of the members. The piano is sometimes considered a percussion instrument, since the tone is produced by striking the strings. Some composers, such as Stravinsky, often used the piano as a pitched rhythmic instrument much as the timpani or tunable bongos, or even disregarded its pitch completely and accepted its percussive qualities only.   Other composers, however, were much more concerned with its melodic than its rhythmic features and used the piano because it could supply a melodic line.   In more recent percussion ensembles melodic lines are not considered a necessity, but if one is required usually it is produced by a true member of the percussion family such as the marimba, the xylophone, or even a set of brake drums from old automobiles.

More and more, the focus in the ensemble has turned from the melodic to the rhythmic aspect, with the texture and compositional emphasis upon the combinations of rhythmic instruments either played together or one after the other.   There seems to be no end to the combinations of percussion instruments which can be used.   Some compositions call for unusual items such as those found in the everyday world, while other compositions are devoted strictly to instruments of the orchestral percussion section.   Between these two poles one finds compositions which call for percussion instruments of rare countries or regions of the world, such as African drums or South American Indian gourds or Arctic skins dried and stretched in some different manner.   Each of these exotic instruments has a unique sound and adds considerably to the composition employing it.   In addition, there is an historical and anthropological movement under way to restore and at the same time share the use of such native instruments.

October Mountain (Hovhaness)

In order to understand the qualities of the sounds in any percussion ensemble composition it is almost necessary to see the instruments which are playing or to have a list of the instruments so that sound and instrument may be matched.

This composition by Hovhaness uses marimba, glockenspiel, timpani, tenor drum, bass drum, gong, and tam-tam.

Although in five movements or sections, none carry a descriptive title or tempo marking.

1. Beginning with the marimba, all the instruments to be heard in the composition participate.   In some ways like an overture or introduction to the piece, this section permits you to hear the instruments which will play in the following sections.   The style of writing, however, does not give one the impression of a passing-in-review of instruments.   Rather, this is a musical section of the work.

2. The marimba plays a chantlike melody over and over.   Because of its tonal limitations, it seems almost nonmelodic.   The tempo is fast and other instruments are heard only as a background.

3. This movement again features the marimba but the glockenspiel interrupts regularly, sometimes with one note, and a few times with a number of notes.   The emphasis centers upon the contrast of the two instruments.

4. The rhythm of the timpani becomes the focal point of this section. Other instruments enter quietly, build to a climax, and then recede.

5. Another repetitious semimelodic line gives the listener the impression that the material is Oriental or native.

Delicate, precise, carefully put together, each note has a purpose. Far from the pounding often associated with percussion, the emphasis of *October Mountain* centers upon the meticulous playing of instruments which, despite an almost repetitious sound, generate interest through the careful handling of the background.

Song of Quetzalcoatl (Harrison)

The following instruments are played throughout the work by four players: five wood blocks, five dragon-mouths, five bells, sistrums, maracas, five suspended brake drums, five muted brake drums, five cowbells, rattle, snare drum, guiro, windglass, triangle, gong, tam-tam, five tom-toms, and contrabass drum.

This one-movement work is in three parts. A loud second section separates two quiet sections. Based upon Aztec melodies, we hear the muted brake drums play the themes quietly in the first and last sections; the nonmuted brake drums play the same melody in the loud section. Both present a persistent antique bell-like sound. Other rhythms and colors join the melodies. Near the end of the loud section, rests or silences create a striking effect immediately before the gong climax. The quiet ending, with imitative bell sounds, is most effective.

Refrain (Stockhausen)

This trio for three percussion players places emphasis upon the effect of colors, timbres, combinations of instruments, and the placement of sound in relation to the previous sound. Time is an important element in this composition, as in all of Stockhausen's works. Silence also is a part of the effect, for one's anticipation of the next sound becomes part of the emotional preparation for it.

Because of the comparative newness and fascination of percussion ensembles, many selections have been composed during the past twenty-five years. The following are suggested for additional listening:

Ballet mécanique (Antheil) (Of particular historical value, it still sounds fresh in many parts)
Ionisation (Varèse)
Percussion Music (Colgrass)
Percussion Music (Strang)
Prelude for Percussion (Miller)

Sketch for Percussion (Lo Presti) (Like the Antheil, this composition makes interesting use of the piano)

Toccata for Percussion (Chávez) (Written by the dean of Mexican composers, this is a standard work for percussion ensemble)

Trio for Percussion (Benson)

Study Procedures

1. Visit the music department of your university and see the percussion equipment. You might be permitted to play some of the instruments. Do they sound as they did on the recordings? Remember that performing skill on any instrument determines the quality of the sound heard.
2. Listen to several of the compositions listed above, and choose one which you prefer. Ascertain if this is the choice of others in your class.
3. Percussion ensembles are popular with laymen and musicians alike. Can you decide why this is true?

THE BRASS CHOIR

The brass ensemble was popular during the sixteenth century in small towns of Europe, playing from the tower of the town for special events, for dancing on the green, and, in some regions, in the churches. During the nineteenth and part of the twentieth century brass music was not as popular as it had been earlier. Recently, composers have turned to the brass ensemble as a legitimate musical expression and hundreds of compositions have been written for professional and school groups. Like percussion and woodwind ensembles, the brasses have strong characteristics; their full sound and exciting technic are two of their best assets. For some the tone quickly becomes tiring, but others prefer the constant vigor and vitality.

Suite for Brass Quartet (Bergsma)

This group of three movements is a showpiece for the trumpets. In fact, that term happens to be the title of the third section. The gay and rhythmic Scherzo demands more of the trumpets than the trombones. Dissonant but not repelling, this short movement, though not particularly tuneful, is a modern impression of a song. The third section, Showpiece, again places emphasis on the two trumpets and demonstrates the seldom-heard technical skill possible in an ensemble. Here is a delightful light composition for brass.

Five Miniatures (Starer)

Written for brass quintet, the French horn having been added to trumpets and trombones, the five sections display the brass instruments in an entirely different manner than the Bergsma. There the focus of attention was upon technic and gaiety; in *Five Miniatures* the composer wishes us to hear a more serious composition, being cognizant of the various tonal colors of the ensemble, but also noting the different way the instruments combine for various effects.

Fanfare: Not a real fanfare, but a reminder of one, we never hear a true trumpet call, although several begin. Although the effect adds up to brilliance, it is not a bugle-type effect.

Air: In this movement all of the instruments are muted. The ever-present dissonance seems to prolong itself throughout the entire movement.

Canon: Fugal entrances are easily heard until all instruments are playing. Then the fugal entrances are heard again in rapid succession. The ending is unexpected.

Chaconne: The lower brass begin in a quiet, smooth manner. The dissonances in this movement always resolve so that the overall effect leads toward a greater smoothness than in the Air. When the trumpets enter their muting creates a striking contrast to the lower brass.

March: Here is a circus-style march, but in a contemporary concept.

Study Procedures

1. The album *Music for Brass: 1500–1970* contains brass music from a large expanse of years. In the chapter on the suite we heard a set of dances by Susato from this album. Compare the brass writing in this early suite (1551) with that of the two suites discussed immediately above. Describe the difference in the writing and the effect which you believe it to have upon the listener.
2. Listen to another contemporary brass ensemble composition and describe it in your own words.
3. Almost all high schools and colleges have brass ensembles. Why would this type of group be popular with a large following?

THE STRING CHOIR

Of all instrumental ensembles, the string choir is the oldest. For centuries violins, violas, cellos, and string basses in combination have appealed to audiences and performers. For years the orchestra has been composed of more than half strings. Many of the "easy-to-listen-to" records playing semipopular music usually are almost entirely strings. The pop singer as well as the concert artist requests a string accompaniment, since it enhances the voice. The universal appeal of string sound comes from the brilliance and flash of the technic, but even more from the smoothness and warmth of tone. Consistent tone quality throughout a large range can be endured for long periods of time without ear fatigue; this is not true in the case of other ensembles.

Composers have recognized the merits of the string ensemble, and some of the great music of the world has been written for it. We shall study several examples. Because of their length only sections of each piece will be discussed.

A violin concerto in the hall of the Paris Conservatory, in 1843 (from a drawing by P. S. Germain, in L'illustration, Journal Universel, *Vol. 1, No. 5, April 15, 1845).*

Eine kleine Nachtmusik (Serenade No. 13) (Mozart)

Famous throughout the world is this four-movement string serenade by Mozart. For the past 200 years it has been played by amateur and professional alike and appreciated by both.   Clean, crisp, precise in structure, it is typical of Mozart, whose compositions always sound fresh even after many hearings and even though composed long ago.   His themes are almost always gay and bright even when in a slow tempo.

Allegro
Romance
Menuetto ⎫
Rondo ⎭ (These two movements will be discussed)

Typical of the minuet, the third movement contains two main sections and each section contains two themes.   Reminiscent of the dance itself, when popularity required that two minuets be played one after the other, custom requested a contrast so that the second minuet was often smoother or quieter than the introductory one. When this dance became a part of serious compositions, the two parts were combined into one movement, but the contrast was retained.

A A B A	X X Y X	A B A
Vigorous	Short; both repeated	Contrasting, smooth	Short; both repeated	

This rondo is typical of its form, since it constantly returns to the first melody. Later rondos often had long contrasting sections between the main theme which offered a change of style, mood, and melody to the composition, often making it quite long. In this Mozart composition the rondo is brief and to the point. Many times the contrasts which come between the sections of the main melody seem more like bridge material, quickly moving us from one hearing of the melody to another. This entire movement is bright, gay, and fast.

A   A   B   A ‿ A ‿ B   A ‿ A   [Ending]
New
key

Serenade for Strings (Tchaikovsky)

Interestingly, Tchaikovsky wrote his serenade because of his attraction to and admiration for the music of Mozart, but no direct imitation exists here. Both compositions consider the serenade form in the broadest interpretation, that is, as a musical composition midway in seriousness between the suite and the symphony, but differing from both, since the serenade usually is written for a select group of instruments. In such a composition, then, one can find formal movements as well as those which indicate a connection to the suite.

Tchaikovsky tried to write in a style that had the same directness and same purity for the strings which Mozart portrayed in his serenade. Tchaikovsky, however, writing in the Romantic period, did not alter his style even though attempting to write in a simple and direct manner.

The Serenade contains four movements. We shall examine in detail the second and the fourth.

Pezzo in forma di Sonatina (Piece in the form of a Sonatina)
Walzer
Elegie (not a sad movement, but slow, melodic, and meditative)
Finale—Tema Russo (Finale on a Russian Theme)

By listening to the Tchaikovsky ballets we know that his writing often contained waltzes of great merit. The waltz movement of the Serenade, often considered one of his best, is written in an extended three-part form but contains no trio, refuting the custom of the time. It does contain a contrasting middle section, but the tonal fabric of the selection does not vary enough to label it a trio. Many times this movement is played as an encore by chamber orchestras without the other movements, and its popularity has caused it to be arranged for solo instruments including the piano.

A B A	C C	A B A	Ending—slower tempo
Low strings with melodic line–high strings with obbligato		Same treatment as near the beginning	

The fourth movement is considerably more complex in design than the second or the third. Not only does it interweave the two main themes, which causes the form to become more complex, but it also uses a Russian folk song as an introduction to the movement, which also acts as a bridge from the third or slower Elegie. Near the end of the composition Tchaikovsky inserts the introduction to the first movement (the introduction to the entire suite), and this unites the whole composition; at the same time it acts as an ending or coda. This will be more meaningful and clearer as you study the diagram of the movement:

Introduction	A	B	B	A
Folk song, bridge from third mvt.	Based on end of folk song and Intro. to Mvt. I	Melodic; violas and cellos play theme	Counter-melody in high strings, with melody in low strings	(Con't on next line)

	A	B A	B	Intro. of Mvt. I	A Ending
Fragments of themes A and B	These sections are almost an exact repeat of the earlier A B A but high strings sweep into this section with a variation				

This entire composition is as appealing and fascinating as the two movements studied. It is hoped you will also listen to the first and third movements.

Adagio for Strings (Barber)

Written in 1938, this contemporary composition surprises the listener with its simplicity and directness. The title indicates the tempo—slow—but it does not indicate the nature of its appeal. This American work brought immediate acclaim to its composer from around the world because its monothematic form attracts and keeps our interest despite its slowness. In its use of only one theme it proves one point only: attractive through its understatement of emotion, it rises to a peak of intensity through the two simple devices of pitch and loudness. As the pitch becomes higher and higher, the loudness increases. This well-known and often used expressional device in music, here treated with reserve and polish, is extended so that the listener has an opportunity to realize its effect and dimension. After the peak is reached, there is a sudden pause, a few chords, then the theme is heard again quietly as it fades into an ending.

A   A ⟶ A   A ⌒ A   Ending

Low strings; melody in
cellos, then
violins, then
cellos again

Study Procedures

1. Compare the Mozart and the Tchaikovsky Serenades as to style. State the characteristics of each work in relation to the period in which it was written.
2. Review the Copland ballet *Rodeo,* and compare the style of writing to David Diamond's *Rounds,* a three-section work for strings.
3. You have heard compositions from the four families. Which family of instruments and their compositions do you prefer? Why? Could you defend your statements against those by one of your classmates who might choose a different family?

Bibliography—Chapter 21

BLADES, JAMES, *Percussion Instruments and Their History.* New York: F. A. Praeger, 1970.

BRINDLE, REGINALD SMITH, *Contemporary Percussion.* London: Oxford University Press, 1970.

EVENSON, PATTEE, "A History of Brass Instruments, Their Usage, Music and Performance." Unpublished Dissertation, University of Southern California, 1960.

FIRTH, VIC, *Percussion Symposium.* New York: Carl Fischer, 1966.

HAYES, GERALD RAVENSCOURT, *The Viols and Other Bowed Instruments.* New York: Broude Bros., 1969.

KETTELKAMP, LARRY, *Singing Strings.* New York: Morrow, 1958.

NELSON, SHEILA M., *The Violin Family.* London: Dobson, 1964.

PLENCKERS, LES J., *Hoorn en Trompetachtige Blaas Instrumenten.* Amsterdam: Knuf, 1970.

TOLBECQUE, AUGUSTE, *L'Art du Luthier.* New York: Broude Bros., 1969.

WEERTS, RICHARD K., *How to Develop and Maintain a Successful Woodwind Section.* West Nyack, N.Y.: Parker Publishing Co., 1972.

WILDMAN, LOUIS, *Practical Understanding of the Percussion Section.* Boston: Humphries, 1964.

Recordings—Chapter 21

Barber	*Adagio for Strings*	Boston Sym., Munch	Victor LM-2105
Bergsma	*Suite for Brass Quartet*	American Brass Quintet	Desto DC-6474-77
Diamond	*Rounds*	Concert Arts Orch., Golschmann	Capitol P-8245
Harrison	*Song of Quetzalcoatl*	Manhattan Percussion	Period SPL-743

ALSO ON THIS RECORD

Benson	*Trio for Percussion*
Colgrass	*Percussion Music*
Miller	*Prelude for Percussion*
Strang	*Percussion Music*

Hindemith	*Kleine Kammermusik*	Fairfield Wind Ensemble	Stradivari STR-606
Hovhaness	*October Mountain*	Manhattan Percussion	Urania US-5134

ALSO ON THIS RECORD

Antheil	*Ballet mécanique*
Chávez	*Toccata for Percussion*
Lo Presti	*Sketch for Percussion*

Ibert	*Trois pièces brèves*	Fairfield Wind Ensemble	Stradivari STR-606
Mozart	*Eine kleine Nachtmusik*	Pittsburgh Sym., Steinberg	Capitol PAO-8432
Starer	*Five Miniatures*	American Brass Quintet	Desto DC-6474-77
Stockhausen	*Refrain*		Time S-8001
Tchaikovsky	*Serenade for Strings*	Boston Sym., Munch	Victor LM-2105
Varèse	*Ionisation*	Ensemble "Die Reihe"	Candide CE-31028

ALSO OF INTEREST

Bartók	*Divertimento for Strings*	Zimbler Sinf., Foss	Siena S-100-2
Berkeley	*Serenade for Strings*	Stuttgart Chamber Orch.	London LL-1395
Hindemith	*Five Pieces for Strings*	Stuttgart Chamber Orch.	London LL-1395
Martin	*Passacaille for Strings*	Stuttgart Chamber Orch.	London LL-1395
Skalkottas	*Little Suite for Strings*	Zimbler Sinf., Foss	Siena S-100-2

Section H *Emphasis Upon Form in Addition to Color and Virtuosity*

Chapter 22

The Sonata

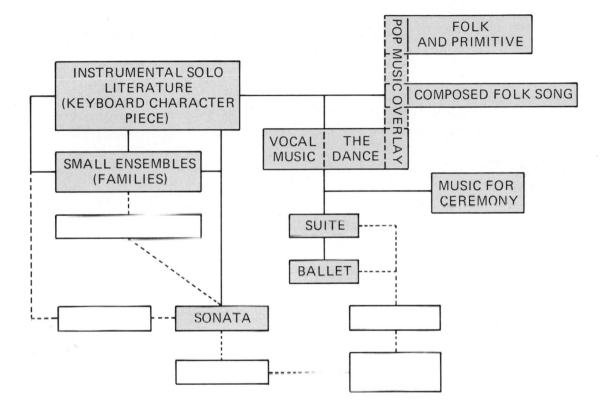

New forms evolve as the unique means of expression for most major musical periods. The Baroque brought changes not only in the style and texture of the music, but also developed the opera, the cantata, and the oratorio which had such strength and such meaning that with modifications they are still in existence today. So also with the music era of classicism or the classic school of composition. The main forms and the focus of the musical attainments of this period, synthesizing from a long progression of vocal and instrumental performance, perfected the sonata (a longer composition), the sonata-allegro form (a manner of organizing a movement), the concerto, the string quartet, and the symphony. This chapter will focus upon the first two, while following chapters will discuss the remaining forms, all of which have dominated instrumental musical expression so noticeably since the late eighteenth century. Some background on the period will assist in understanding this musical development.

THE CLASSIC PERIOD

Those decades which musicians term the Classic period most often are said to include the years from 1750 to 1830. The historian considers this period a part of the larger era known as the Age of Reason, which began circa 1600 and culminated about 1800. During these 200 years the mind was given a high priority and reason was to predominate over faith, revelation, and superstition of earlier centuries. Although not possible at the end of the eighteenth century, given time, men would be able to completely control their environments and their actions. The prominence of secularism furthered the belief that the institution of the church was not infallible but subject to natural law; consequently, it had every reason to expect investigation and criticism. Furthermore, there was no supernatural force above the natural; the mind of man, through scientific discovery and formula, would bring men to a better life. Central to this entire philosophy was freedom of thought, expression, and action. Science would emancipate the mind of man, but man must work and fight, if necessary, to free his body from any enslavement or servitude. To aid these goals, education should be brought to the masses and through education men would find unlimited mental application toward the life of reason.

Practically speaking, optimism was prevalent throughout the period. Merchants and trade achieved new heights and economic power. Cities grew and became industrial centers as well as centers of culture and education.

In addition to a comfortable life, the members of the middle class sought a respectable art which would match the characteristics of the times, an art which would be understandable in form with the content controlled by common sense.

Newton's laws of light and gravity proved that nature was definable and understandable in scientific terms; accompanied by his development of calculus, which dealt with the rate of change in anything moving through time and space, the mysteries of the universe became predictable. All segments of life felt the impact of these revelations and in art an emphasis turned toward precision, methodical and proper arrangement, and established procedures in which the outline was emphasized so that its value could be comprehended.

Thus music, in reaction to the Baroque era with its high ornateness, sought to formulate itself into means which were dignified, emotionally symmetrical, and which emphasized a greater clarity. In place of the intricate texture of polyphonic compositions, music displayed a balance between 1) the homophonic and polyphonic treatment, and 2) the ordered contrast and development of thematic material. This homophonic emphasis, first displayed in the opera, was one trait which stimulated the new instrumental form, the sonata. Instead of the interweaving of one theme with itself often to unintelligible excess, the second characteristic emphasized that themes be stated clearly and restated to assist recognition.

Although the sonata was an Italian word and product initially, this new form with new emphases found its most sympathetic reception within the mind of the German composer, so that a Germanic terminology was enlisted to express its newness and its intent. Taking its name from a literary movement popular in Germany at about the same time, the "classic" in music came to mean a period in which form would be clearly defined, aiding the listener in aural perception; in which the clarity of themes would bring to the common man an understanding of the form and, consequently, the meaning of the work; and where intricacies, if any, were obviously related to other facets of the composition but resolved themselves clearly. Through such a form order would be evident, but individual expression would not be limited. Composers using this form expressed not only personal feelings, but also those ideas which embodied the underlying principles of the Age of Reason.

SONATA: THE SINGLE MOVEMENT FORM

Through previous chapters we have witnessed three characteristics, which when brought together, aided in the organization of the sonata form. The word itself had meant to sound in contrast to singing; consequently, it had been used for compositions of all types when instruments were used either with voices or alone. The dance suite with its binary forms, so prevalent throughout the Baroque and so strongly attached to the aristocracy, was questioned by "reasoning" men during the Classical period, and a new form was sought less obviously related to utilitarian or dance music—one more indication of the emphasis on rationality and order. Baroque compositions often featured thematic fragments moving from tonality to tonality; the classic sonata usually presented at least two themes with two principal changes of tonal center.

The particulars of the sonata as a movement settled into a definite form during the Classical period and became known as the sonata-allegro form. The following diagram gives the basic outline.

Name of Section	Statement		Development	Recapitulation		Coda
Form analysis	A		B	A		
Arrangement of themes	Theme I	Theme II	Composer's choice	Theme I	Theme II	Composer's choice
Tonality	Key 1	Key 2	?	Key 1	Key 1	Usually 1

Overall, it is a three-part construction with the possibility in some cases of a short introduction, bridges between themes or between sections, a closing theme after Theme II, and usually a coda. These additions received emphasis as the esthetic sense of the composer guided him in determining the balance between the length of the themes, the balance within the form between sections, and the balance between the character of the two main themes.

Another important balance was in the key relationship or the tonality of the main themes. Tradition had placed an emphasis upon the variety possible through changes of tonality, and the Classical period accepted this tradition in part, enough so that it was not an all-consuming gesture, but an important one. The tonality of the first theme usually gave the name to the composition. A composer writing in the tonality of G Major for the first theme would almost without fail write the entire recapitulation in that key, the coda in that key, and give that name to the composition. The second main theme, perhaps part of the development, and, if the composer were truly experimental (such as Beethoven in his later years), part of the coda might be in tonality 2. Usually this was in a tonal center five scale steps higher than tonality 1. These tonal relationships aided the listener in understanding the form, but tonality 2 also gave that theme a secondary position in the tonal fabric.

The second section in the sonata is known as the *development*. Here the composer has free reign as directed by his talent and his esthetic sense. Various compositional devices used in this section include sequence (see Chapter 3), modulations, fugal treatment of the themes or of one theme, use of inversion (which places the theme upside down), diminution (which shrinks the theme into quicker time values), or augmentation (which extends the theme in longer time values); there might also be a contrapuntal treatment of motives of the theme or a fragment of the theme, or occasionally a new theme might be introduced. Most popular of all was a reiteration of thematic fragments in which a theme might be begun numerous times only to spin off in different directions than heard in the original statement. In the development the composer was free to use one or both of the main themes and to emphasize either to the extent he wished, but the first or principal theme was regularly developed more fully. The artistic value of a sonata was often determined by the development section and the manner in which the thematic fragments were balanced with the main themes. For example, if the first theme is strong and carries a dominant rhythm as well as a prominent melodic line, a composer might use such a theme only sparingly in the development as he stresses the secondary or lesser theme. This kind of balance enables the listener to receive as strong an esthetic experience as possible.

The third section, the *recapitulation,* reiterates the two main themes of the first section called the *statement*. A major difference exists in this repetition: to maintain the established tonality into the second theme, the composer usually must rearrange his material in the recapitulation to provide for this change.

Sonata in C Major, K. 545: First Movement (Mozart)

Statement A				Development B	Recapitulation A				
Theme I		Theme II		Development	Theme I		Theme II		
1	2	1	2		1	2	1	2	
Delicate theme based upon 1-3-5 of scale	Semimelodic running scales with descending pivot points	Reverse of first theme in direction and interval: based upon 5-3-1 of scale	Descending 7th interval by skip; arpeggios end the section in major	Arpeggios in minor begin section; Number 2 of Theme I is used; running scales tossed back and forth between upper and lower parts	1	2 →	Extended to assist in keeping tonality 1		
This Section Repeated									

Sonata No. 1 in f minor, Op. 2, No. 1 (Beethoven)

Statement A				Development B	Recapitulation A				Coda
Theme I		Theme II		Development	Theme I		Theme II		
1	2	1	2		1	2	1	2	
a) Arpeggio theme followed by b) ornate resolution (8 meas.)	Fragment of 1 in diminuted rhythm and extended, leading to ⟶ (12 meas.)	Descending theme (8 meas.)	Rearranged theme in bass extended with 1-b for end	Theme I, new key (7 meas.) Theme II—two hearings in upper voice, one hearing in lower voice and extended and fragmented. Transition to Recap. from 1-b	Similar to original statement				Part of 1-b (12 meas.)
This Section Repeated									

As we have noted in other forms, if the composer uses a coda he may use either one of the main themes or both, depending upon his desire to add balance to the composition. Occasionally, a composer would add new material in the coda, but when this occurred often the sonata was large and imposing. These forms will be more easily understood through examples. Listen to the music and follow the charts for the two sonata movements shown on page 445.

Sonata in c minor, Op. 10, No. 1 (Beethoven)

Although the preceding movement by Beethoven fits the standard sonata-allegro form well, the first movement of Opus 10, Number 1 in c minor deviates to some extent. As Beethoven became more mature, and as the approaching Romantic period made itself felt with its call for attention to feeling over reason, changes may be noticed within his work. In some cases these are subtle, in others more obvious. The most glaring difference in the form of this movement, although it fits the definition supplied earlier in the chapter, is the introduction of a new theme in the development section. In its way this tends to accentuate the development and make of it a three-part form of a somewhat different character.

Statement A						
Theme I				Theme II		
1	2	1	bridge	1	2	3
Arpeggio theme with smooth resolution (8 meas.)	Falling 5-note theme (8 meas.) plus 6 as transition	Return to give symmetry (10 meas.)	Smooth, syncopated melody heard 3 times (17 meas.) plus 7 of intro. to Theme II (acts as Codetta)	Arpeggiated melody with suspensions (16 meas.)	Chromatic ending for II-1 (14 meas.)	Theme I-1 (8 meas.) Ending of section similar to bridge
This Section Intended to Repeat						

(Con't.)	Development B		Recapitulation A		
	Development		Theme I Theme II		Coda
	1	2	1 2 1	1 2 3	
	Theme I in major (12 meas.)	New material (40 meas.) Ending of section (10 meas.)	Similar to statement except	Theme II is doubled in length	(13 meas.)

Study Procedures

Listen to the following sonata movements by Beethoven and Mozart, ascertain the exact form, and the means of handling the form. Draw a diagram similar to the preceding ones. Review the description of the methods of handling the development material in the earlier portion of the chapter if questions arise.

Sonata in f minor, Op. 2, No. 1: Fourth Movement (Beethoven)
Sonata in c minor, Op. 10, No. 1: Third Movement (Beethoven)
Sonata in C Major, K. 309: First Movement (Mozart)
Sonata in a minor, K. 310: First Movement (Mozart)

SONATA: THE OVERALL FORM

The sonata has given its name to a larger composition as well as the manner of organizing a movement. In order to differentiate between the two, the movement usually is called "sonata-allegro" or "sonata form." The addition of the tempo indication implies that it serves particularly the first movement, being more indicative of its general spirit.

When used to define the complete composition the term "sonata" has come to mean a solo for instrument alone or with piano accompaniment. If written for instruments other than the piano, the instrument's name will be included in the title, such as Sonata for Trumpet. Three-movement sonatas predominate, although exceptions are prevalent. When used, the fourth movement most often will be a minuet or scherzo placed between the second and final movements.

Following the custom of the suite, sonata movements change tempo usually following a fast-slow-fast pattern. Tempo patterns have become flexible, so that some sonatas end with a slow movement. Sonatas differ from suites in the complexity of the form, the length of the movements, the depth of musical expression, and the use of the sonata-allegro form for at least one of the movements.

The original instrumental associations of the word which began as early as the twelfth century have continued until the present day. Up to the time of the Classical period a multifaceted origin and history existed which included among other developments the ricercare and canzone (see Chapter 13), the sonata da camera and sonata da chiesa (chamber and court sonatas), and the Baroque trio sonata. The latter was usually played by four instruments: two treble instruments of similar color, an accompaniment instrument such as the harpsichord or organ, and a cello or bass viol which doubled the bass line along with the keyboard. During the Classical period changes of style as well as form evolved: a greater emphasis was placed upon homophonic texture, the three-movement organization became more generally accepted, and the single movement sonata-allegro form was used in almost every instance.

SECOND (AND THIRD) MOVEMENTS OF THE SONATA

In preceding sections of the chapter we examined carefully the reasons for the change in style and form which came to sonata first movements during the Classical period. In examining second (and third) movements we shall hear a similar style, but note that the forms, less dance-oriented, resort to organizational patterns which bring a balance and a variety to the entire composition.

Song and Trio

This form, often used as a second movement, is similar to other three-part forms we have studied throughout our text. The term "trio" added to the description implies a difference in texture between the first and second sections. Originally, the trio was a section of dance music written for only three instruments as compared to a full instrumentation on the first and third sections. When only a solo instrument is used it becomes difficult and sometimes seemingly unimportant to distinguish between a three-part form and a song and trio. The form was used regularly in minuets, and even when no minuet is present the term still seems applicable if the texture of the middle section differs markedly.

Because most of these forms are simple and easily heard, little detail will be given.

Sonata in F Major, Op. 10, No. 2: Second Movement (Beethoven)

SONG	TRIO	SONG
A	B	A
:a :|: b a———>:	x x y z y z⌒	a a′ b a′

Another song and trio form, similar in design, will be found in the *Sonata in E Major*, Op. 14, No. 1: Second Movement (Beethoven).

Minuet and Trio

When Beethoven was writing in Vienna, the minuet had all but passed away as a dance form and the waltz had not yet caught the fancy of the people. Since he was not writing dance music, and not writing reminiscences of the minuet as some composers had done, he used this form to bring a lighter texture and a 3/4 movement to the sonata. The form of the movement is so similar to the song and trio that no additional information need be given. Listen to the following minuets with trio:

Sonata in f minor, Op. 2, No. 1: Third Movement (Beethoven)
Sonata in D Major, Op. 10, No. 3: Third Movement (Beethoven)

Scherzo and Trio

As the minuet waned in emphasis, the scherzo seemed to take on more importance. Especially is this true with Beethoven, who is credited with introducing it in his sonatas. The minuet, usually a stately dance with dignity, did not meet the requirements of composers, who, seeking a quick and light diversion from the heavier first and the slower second movements, pushed the tempo and quality of the minuet out of character until the scherzo became standard. The fact that a similar form was used speaks for its utility.

The scherzo, also in 3/4 meter, usually a fast, rather whimsical movement, often incorporates elements of surprise or musical humor. It is meant to be gay and robust.

The form of the movement, again, is so similar to the song and trio that no further comments need be added.

Sonata in A Major, Op. 2, No. 2: Third Movement (Beethoven)
Sonata in C Major, Op. 2, No. 3: Third Movement (Beethoven)

Three-Part Form (ABA Form)

Thinking back through the forms of vocal and instrumental music studied previously, the three-part form is the one most often used. This form may be simple and short or longer and more complex. The most complex of the three-part forms is the sonata-allegro. When used as a second movement in the sonata, the three-part form is neither the most simple nor complex. The contrast of the middle section is less marked than in the movements using trios, while the main sections are often divided into two or three subparts giving length and unity as needed.

Sonata in E♭ Major, Op. 7: Second Movement (Beethoven)

A	B	bridge	A	Coda
a b a⟶	x x′	a	a b a′⟶	x a

Other examples may be found as follows:

Sonata in A Major, Op. 2, No. 2: Second Movement (Beethoven)
Sonata in E♭ Major, Op. 27, No. 1: Second Movement (Beethoven)

Sonatina

The diminutive form of the word "sonata" indicates that a smaller sonata-allegro form would be used. The sonatina uses two main themes, and sometimes even employs bridge material; the major difference comes in the development section. In the following example, no development exists and only one chord takes its place. The manner in which the second main theme dissolves into an extended series of phrases tends to give balance to the form and in some ways takes the place of the development.

Sonata in c minor, Op. 10, No. 1: Second Movement (Beethoven)

A		B		A		B	
THEME I		THEME II		THEME I		THEME II	CODA
a a	Episode	B ⟶	(chord)	a a	Episode	B ⟶	a

Rondo

This form, usually used with fast movements and often a favorite of composers for the final movement of a sonata, makes interesting use of the main theme and subordinate themes: after each subordinate theme the main theme returns (ABACA). The continuous appearance of the first theme gives the movement its character, and demands that the main theme be attractive enough to hear again and again. Beethoven, although using the form more often for fast, final movements, also used it occasionally for a slow second movement. A good example is detailed below:

Sonata in c minor, Op. 13: Second Movement (Beethoven)

$$A \quad A' \quad B \quad \overset{\frown}{\quad} A \quad C \longrightarrow A \quad A' \quad \text{Coda}$$

In this work Theme A, the main theme, is heard twice at the beginning of the composition, the second time an octave higher. The second theme, of modest length, requires a bridge or transition for balance before the return of the main theme. The second deviation, or Theme C, begins three times before being completed; its modulatory phrase leads back to the main theme, which is heard twice again before introducing a short coda. The use of this form for a slow movement typifies the unorthodox approach Beethoven used as he worked with his forms. The main theme, songlike in quality, pleases through its several returns. It would lose its simplicity and some of its character if treated to a development.

FINAL MOVEMENTS OF THE SONATA

The forms used for final movements have all been studied in the preceding pages. That is to say, final movements do not differ from earlier ones in form but always in tempo. The rondo and the sonata-allegro are most often used. Rarely, the final movement will consist of a set of variations. Now it only remains to listen and understand their application.

THE COMPLETE SONATA

The solo sonata is a three- or four-movement composition making use of the forms studied earlier in the chapter. You should now listen to several solo sonatas to assist in understanding the style, the manners in which composers appropriate these forms, and to gain an appreciation for the serious solo literature. Students in high schools, as well as music students all over the world, perform sonatas or movements of sonatas for practice, to learn the literature of the instrument, to play at contests, and for enjoyment.   The following list will make an interesting beginning, but hundreds of others exist and can be heard with benefit.

Study Procedures

Begin your sonata listening with a complete piano solo sonata.   One of the following will prove interesting, since you have already studied parts of it, and it will have a familiar sound.   In your listening aim for two goals; first, listen to ascertain the form. A pencil and paper might be good assistance as you note the themes and their repeats. Second, listen for the esthetic effect created by the composer as the themes contrast and balance with each other.   Both kinds of listening are valuable.

Sonata in f minor, Op. 2, No. 1 (Beethoven)
   Allegro   (Sonata-Allegro form)
   Adagio   (ABA form)
   Menuetto   (Menuet and Trio form)
   Prestissimo   (Sonata-Allegro form)

Sonata in c minor, Op. 10, No. 1 (Beethoven)
   Allegro Molto   (Sonata-Allegro form)
   Adagio Molto   (Sonatina form)
   Prestissimo   (Sonata-Allegro form)

Sonata in F Major, K. 280 (Mozart)
   Allegro Assai   (Sonata-Allegro form)
   Adagio   (Sonatina form)
   Presto   (Sonata-Allegro form)

Sonata in C Major, K. 545 (Mozart)
   Allegro   (Sonata-Allegro form)
   Andante   (Rondo form)
   Allegretto   (Rondo form)

BEETHOVEN

Others had developed the sonata as an expression of their time, but Beethoven appropriated it so well to his musical concepts that the composition and the form reached an apex with his works.   Thus, like a giant, Beethoven stands upon the musical scene and commands our attention.   It was appropriate, therefore, that most of the examples in the descriptive material on the sonata were taken from his works.

His life represents an enigma to many.   It is difficult to imagine the roughness and the overreactive, defensive personality of the man on the one hand with the music which we have heard on the other.   In one of his letters, Goethe, the well-known German poet and writer, wrote about Beethoven, saying that, "His talent amazed me; unfortunately, he is an utterly untamed personality, who is

The young Beethoven, engraving by Höfel, after Letronne (Courtesy of Beethovenhaus, Bonn).

not altogether in the wrong in holding the world to be detestable, but surely does not make it any the more enjoyable either for himself or others by his attitude."[1]

He came to Vienna when all of its society was concerned with social changes, particularly those dealing with the freedoms of man. Beethoven strongly championed the freedom of the body and the mind, particularly man's freedom from political sovereignty. He verbally struck out against royalty and society which in any way represented the reverse of these goals, despite the fact that many of his adversaries were his protectors, benefactors, and social friends.

Beethoven spoke differently through his music, and he spoke so well for the period in which he lived that he was acclaimed by musician, commoner, and royalty alike. His invitations to many important occasions introduced him to high officers of governments and lands. Yet these social situations meant little to him personally or had little effect on his music, which spoke to all men of their inner feelings—the best combination of emotions and reasoning.

Using the forms so common in his day, he infused them with an intensity that other composers did not have. This intensity spoke of his own mental

---

[1] *The Beethoven Reader,* edited by Arnold and Fortune. W. W. Norton and Company, Inc., New York, page 29.

qualities and discipline, of his ability to rework his material until it spoke of his personal artistic goals, of his ability to work with forms and yet never be enslaved by them, and above all, of his supreme ability to image within his mind the form which best suited his themes and material. Few composers probe this last point so well.

For the past several years, the "Peanuts" gang has brought the name of Beethoven to the attention of millions through the comic strip. When asked why he had chosen Beethoven as the great hero for Schroeder, Schulz, the creator of the cartoon, stated that it was because the name had a strange sound and contrasted well with the others. But Schulz could not have chosen a more feasible musical personage for Schroeder's devotion, since it bespeaks his sophistication and his understanding of the adult world rather than the more superficial things about him. Beethoven's music, made up of attractive themes, contains subjective emotion and adherence to form yet the freedom to change which all of us seek no matter what the endeavor.

Beethoven stands at the culmination of the Classic era and the introduction to another which musicians know as the Romantic period. Some of both are heard in his works, but the Classic ideas predominate.

LATER SONATAS

Although there are some notable exceptions, the sonata and the sonata form has not been the dominant force during later years that it had been in the Classic period. If understood as a form growing from the times, then one realizes that the disciplined mind sympathetic to the rigor of ideas creates well in this form. The Romantic spirit and the twentieth century have for the most part not been conducive to sonata writing.

One of the exceptions is the Russian composer Prokofiev, who wrote nine sonatas for piano, each maturing as he better understood his musical and emotional capacities in relation to this form. His ninth sonata excellently exemplifies the combination of several elements: form, simplicity in writing, beauty of melodic line, contrasts in rhythm, the infusion of jazz elements which bespeak the times in which he wrote, and a uniting of compositional technics common to the twentieth century, such as octave displacement, rhythmic distortion, and sudden cadences. The forms are similar enough to those studied earlier in the chapter that a detailed explanation is not necessary.

Study Procedures

1. Listen to the Ninth Sonata by Prokofiev, noting the simplicity in writing, the attractiveness of the melodic line, and the overall expressiveness of the composition. When finished, discuss why you believe this to be an extension of Beethoven's concepts on sonata writing.

Piano Sonata No. 9, Op. 103 (Prokofiev)

Movement I: Sonata-allegro form

Statement		Development	Recapitulation		Coda
x x' ⌢ y y		x x y x x	x⌢y	y	
Simple, beautiful melody	Rhythmic bridge		Theme in lower part	Theme in higher voices	
	Repeated note used to begin theme				

Movement II: Scherzolike in quality; simple three-part form

Intro.	A	B	A	Coda
	x	y y	x	
Long, primitive sounding	Short, chromatic theme	Slower theme, with quick notes interjected with melodic line		Chordal measures interspersed with scale passages

Piano Sonata No. 9, Op. 103 (continued)

Movement III: A series of variations on the first theme placed in simple three-part form

A		B	A				Coda
x	x″	y	x‴	x⁗	y	x⁗′	x
Slow tempo, chromatic sounds with obvious dissonances		Quick tempo, many notes with Oriental color — Arpeggios					

Movement IV: Light, gay, almost childlike in thematic material, the themes have the quality to be used in rondo, but their brevity make this difficult; three-part form

Intro.	A			B			Bridge		A		Coda
	x	y	x	z	z	z	x	y	x	y	
	Childlike or music for a puppet			Slower							Main theme from first movement

2. Listen to another piano sonata by Prokofiev, and make a design chart for each movement similar to those shown earlier in the chapter. Compare your chart with others in your class. How did you describe certain sections of the work within the form?

Sonata for Piano No. 1 (Boulez)

Composers are constantly seeking artistic forms which will express contemporary feelings in a work of art. This often means a change in the approach to a well-established form, or the creation of a new form. Pierre Boulez, presently conductor of the New York Philharmonic Orchestra, wrote a sonata for piano when he was twenty-two years of age. This work is based upon rhythm and interval motives rather than upon melodic ones. Consequently, such a composition would not contain a theme in the usual sense, but it would contain contrasts in rhythm, sound, and range.

Notice that this work uses more of the sound range than most piano sonatas heard earlier in the chapter. You will not notice it by listening, but you may appreciate the fact that Boulez uses a new kind of counterpoint in the two movements; the usual counterpoint is based upon melodic sounds repeated at various pitch levels; Boulez uses a counterpoint based upon time and the movement with time of each voice.

The movements are marked with French phrases to indicate the tempo, and become even more meaningful to the listener because of the importance of the internal rhythm. Unlike the usual composition, the terms or phrases do not mark the sections in order, but rather are a guide for the listener as he moves through the composition, since the tempos are used repeatedly and not always in the order given.

Movement I: Slow—obviously more movement
Movement II: Rather broad–rapid–moderate without slowness

INSTRUMENTAL SONATAS

The solo instrumental sonata has many notable examples. Since the sonata was always intended as an instrumental form, all instruments have used it, although the amount of literature for the piano far exceeds that for any other instrument. The violin well represents the wind and string instruments, since its lyric qualities are so well-suited to the expressive aspects of the form. Haydn wrote one violin sonata, Mozart forty-two, Beethoven ten; any of these make valuable listening if you wish to survey the Classic period again. In order to offer a change of style, and because the work is notable within the field, we will examine the Franck *Sonata in A Major for Violin.* (You will recall that his organ works were studied in an earlier chapter.)

Sonata in A Major for Violin (Franck)

This famous work for solo instrument is well-suited to listening because it makes interesting use of the sonata-allegro form, it is a good representation of the Romantic period, and the composition carries the nuances of musical emotion to an interesting point without losing those melodic qualities which enable the amateur to find his way through the work while appreciating its beauty.

One other musical characteristic warrants our attention. This sonata represents well the musical term *cyclic* as applied to form, which indicates that related themes from one movement are employed later in the movement or in a subsequent movement, thus unifying the composition. By reviewing the Prokofiev *Piano Sonata No. 9* you will notice that the final movement returned to the first theme of the first movement. Franck became well-known for the cyclic quality in many of his works.

By reading through the following outlines you will notice that themes often are used out of the usual sonata order and borrowed from other sections of the same movement or other movements. The forms detailed for your study will enable you to follow the work easily.

(See examples on pages 459 and 460.)

Typical of many works during the Romantic period, this is not a short composition, but each movement seems to carry itself well and the overall energy of the work never lags.

Study Procedures

1. Many instrumental sonatas have been written for wind and percussion instruments. Choose an instrument which you enjoy hearing, and listen to sonatas written for it. If possible, try to find compositions of different periods; the older instruments will offer wider choices. Be sure to include at least one example of a composition from the twentieth century.
2. Most instrumentalists study sonatas regularly. Request a student from your college to perform a sonata or a movement from a sonata for your class.

Electronic Study I (Davidovsky)

An electronic composer of the twentieth century is just as careful with the manner in which he handles his materials as a composer of the Classic period. Instead of the usual melodic idea or melodic germ, the electronic composer may present sound from square wave generators along with white noise. These sound mixtures are altered through inversion, transposition (both of which have a traditional as well as a special electronic meaning), and even further through changes in density and intensity. Using filters and reverberation chambers, the sound may be altered even again.

Movement I: Calm, restrained emotion, quiet, chromatic, and tuneful; sonata-allegro form with short development

	Statement		Development	Recapitulation		Coda
	Theme I	Theme II	Development	Theme I	Theme II	
	x y x	z z →	x →	x y′—→x	z x	z x
Intro.						Piano Violin
Few chords	Smooth movement between parts; arpeggiated theme; strong cadence	Similar to second part of x; piano only	Short Extension short; chordal piano	Strong cadence at end of theme	Short; piano only	

Movement II: Agitated and emotional with variations in tempo, nuance, and mood; sonata-allegro form with some minor variations

	Statement		Development	Recapitulation		Coda
	Theme I	Theme II	Development	Theme I	Theme II	
	x x y x→	s t s′→	x s	x s	s t s′→	x
Intro.	Piano Vln.			Piano Violin	Violin Violin s′	
Piano arpeggios	Piano Vln.	More melodic and a little slower; s′ slowing into development	Two sections; good balance between violin and piano	Vln. and piano answer		Accelerating into slowing variations of x

Movement III: Recitativo-Fantasia. Slow, deliberate; recitative character gives way to melodic qualities; no themes in the sense of other movements; a melodic cadenza with little form.

Intro.	A	B →
Piano and violin answer back and forth	Cadenzalike but becoming more melodic	Long swinging line with big skips, in contrast to other movements where melody is usually by step. Quiet ending.

Movement IV: Smooth, not slow, singing in style but increasing in power toward the C section, and again during the last statement; rondo form

A			B	A	bridge	C		A	Coda
x	y	x	z	x z x	s x x	v	z v z	x y x	
Canonic statements between piano and violin	Same quality, little contrast with x		Short running figures in violin. Piano plays Theme z, which is second theme of third movement	Violin plays z theme instead of the usual y	Agitated	Running bass figures in piano	Violin; forceful and strong section	Quiet beginning, quickly gaining in power for ending	Powerful running figures in piano with ending figures in violin

Mario Davidovsky, a contemporary Argentine composer, has combined all of these ideas within a composition entitled *Electronic Study I.* Although not a sonata in the historic sense, the five-minute, 30-second composition contains four sections and uses the synthesizer and generator as the solo instrument.

Study Procedures

1. Listen to the composition and ascertain the division points for the four sections. Since this is not the usual type of sound, you will probably wish to hear the composition more than one time before you decide. Electronic composers often divide their compositions into sections using a precise measurement such as the second or part of a second. The first section of the work runs 49:15 seconds. You may wish to time other sections to be sure of the divisions.
2. Discuss why you believe this composition could be a descendant from the sonata or why you believe it has little or no relation to the sonata form.

Bibliography—Chapter 22

ARNOLD, DENIS, and NIGEL FORTUNE, *The Beethoven Reader.* New York: W. W. Norton and Company, Inc., 1971.

LANG, HENRY, *Music in Western Civilization.* New York: W. W. Norton and Company, Inc., 1941.

MELLERS, WILFRID, *Man and His Music: Part III, The Sonata Principle.* New York: Schocken Books, 1969.

NEWMAN, WILLIAM S., *The Beethoven Sonata.* Chapel Hill, N.C.: University of North Carolina Press, 1959.

————, *The Sonata in the Baroque Era.* Chapel Hill, N.C.: University of North Carolina Press, 1959.

————, *The Sonata Since Beethoven.* Chapel Hill, N.C.: University of North Carolina Press, 1969.

SNYDER, LOUIS, *The Age of Reason.* Princeton, N.J.: D. Van Nostrand Company, Inc., 1955.

Recordings—Chapter 22

Beethoven	*Sonata in f minor, Op. 2, No. 1*	Gulda	Mace S-9060
	Sonata in A Major, Op. 2, No. 2	Hungerford	Vanguard 10084
	Sonata in C Major, Op. 2, No. 3	Rubinstein	Victor LSC-2812
	Sonata in E Major, Op. 7	Hungerford	Vanguard 10085
	Sonata in c minor, Op. 10, No. 1	Gould	Columbia MS-6686
	Sonata in F Major, Op. 10, No. 2	Gould	Columbia MS-6686

	Sonata in D Major, Op. 10, No. 3	Gould	Columbia MS-6686
	Sonata in c minor, Op. 13	Gould	Columbia MS-6945
	Sonata in E♭ Major, Op. 27, No. 1	Hungerford	Vanguard C-10055
Boulez	*Sonata for Piano No. 1*	Burge	Candide 31015
Davidovsky	*Electronic Study*		Columbia MS-6566
Franck	*Sonata in A Major for Violin*	Stern	Columbia MS-6139
Mozart	*Sonata in F Major,* K. 280	Gould	Columbia MS-7097
	Sonata in C Major, K. 545	Gulda	Mace S-9060
Prokofiev	*Sonata No. 9,* Op. 103	Kalichstein	Vanguard C-10048

Additional Suggestions for Listening

Bartók	*Sonata No. 2 for Violin*	Druian, Simms	Mercury MG-50089
Beethoven	*Complete Sonatas for Piano*	Schnabel	Angel GRM-4005
Bloch	*Sonata for Violin*	Heifetz	Victor LM-1861
Franck	*Sonata in A Major for Violin*	Francescatti, Casadesus	Columbia ML-4178
Handel	*Sonata No. 6 in E for Violin*	Heifetz	Victor LM-1861
Mozart	*Complete Sonatas for Piano*	Klein	Vox SVBX-5428
Prokofiev	*Piano Sonatas 1–9*	Gyorgy Sandor	Vox SVBX-5408-09
Schubert	*Sonatine in g minor,* Op. 137, No. 3	Heifetz	Victor LM-1861

Chapter 23

The String Quartet

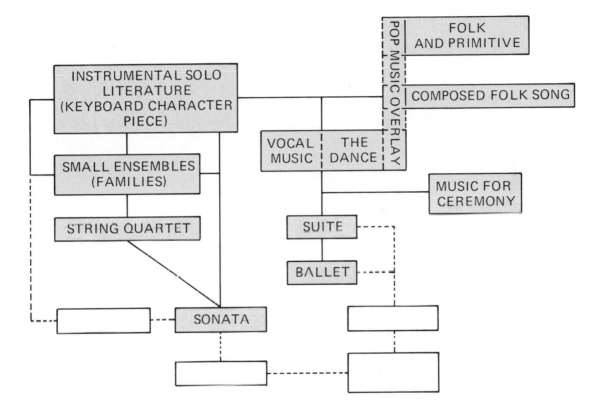

The string quartet is a sonata for four strings: two violins, one viola, and one cello. Except for its being a sonata, it could have been included in the chapter with other small ensembles; except for its being such an individualistic composition, it could have been included with the previous chapter on the sonata. But the coloration of the instruments, the compositional approach and intent differ enough to warrant a chapter of its own. Moreover, there has been considerable literature of quality written for this group, so that to place it within other chapters would be to slight it; to consider it esthetically with other mediums would be to give the impression of too little significance.

Beethoven conducting the Rasumowsky Quartette (Courtesy of
The Bettmann Archive, Inc., New York).

UNIQUE QUALITIES

The string quartet makes use of instruments so similar in design and tonal coloration as to give a quality to the group not found with other small ensembles such as the woodwind quintet or the brass quartet. The clarinet quartet attempts a similar tonal concept, but the expressive qualities of the strings so far surpass the clarinet, particularly the lower instruments, that little similarity exists. In addition, the range of the strings all but equals that of the five woodwinds and far exceeds the brass groups. Thus, the string quartet offers the listener unusually satisfying range and tonal opportunities in chamber music.

This ensemble dates only from the Classic period. Composition and the concepts of composers had to mature enough to discard the keyboard as part of the group (the trio-sonata still contained a keyboard instrument) and thus enable the parts to take on an independence they would not have otherwise. The independence of musical line for each voice becomes a noticeable attribute.

Considering the ensemble of only four strings, those composers are successful who can think and write music which is subtle, sensitive, and yet meaningful. Some composers have adapted orchestral writing concepts to four strings, but have produced works which do not exhibit the textures and tonal combinations to provide the player and listener with those attributes so well-regarded in small ensembles.

Unlike the orchestra, the string quartet relies not at all upon the colorations of brass, woodwinds, or percussion or the large volume of sound these combinations produce. For many, this means a purity of tone that depends little upon effect. Rather, the detail of construction, the method and skill of handling themes, the compatibility of themes, and the overall form become important. Consequently, for those who enjoy string quartets—and the numbers are ever increasing—no finer music can be found.

The music is an intimate expression of the composer, and those who have studied the quartets of famous composers believe they have come to know better their inner feelings and true artistic qualities.

Since such a work depends almost entirely upon four players for its effect, no one performer can become a virtuoso beyond the others. To some, all four are soloists, while to others they seem to be a team that executes the requirements in artistic fashion. Enjoying this teamwork, even as one would in sports, brings greater musical insight than can be obtained from observing one spectacular player.

With these points in mind, to many the string quartet becomes the highest form of musical art. This is particularly true for those who have played in quartets, even though they be amateurs practicing only rarely and performing the music with little grace and charm. Yet, because of the experience of playing a part and hearing it unfold with your playing, while the remaining parts begin to bloom through the efforts of friends, players realize the artistic demands of the music, while disclosing the skill of the craftsmanship; but above all, they sense the responsiveness of the composer through music for the deepest feelings and emotions of man.

OUR GOALS

In this chapter several goals present themselves. First, the literature for the string quartet justifies some consideration. Many excellent quartets have been written but only a few can possibly be discussed in this chapter. Next, the quartet being a sonata (see diagrams on pages 466 and 467), every opportunity to expand our understanding of this form should be taken, since it is the basis of much fine music. Thirdly, several musical ideas need our attention so that we may hear the music with more insight and depth of understanding, but also so that we may better perceive the means of communication between the composer and his listener. Lastly, it always assists a listener to become sensitive to the styles or periods of writing as a means not only of comparing various styles and periods but also to understand the works as means of expression for their times.

Quartet in F Major, Op. 59, No. I: First Movement (Beethoven)
Long themes: smooth, singing, moving mostly by step; rhythm is secondary to melodic content of themes

STATEMENT		
A		Closing Theme
Theme I	Theme II	
More important than Theme II by weight and length. Made up of parts a) and b) Part a) breaks into two parts: 1) and 2)	Also scalelike but reverse of Theme I in that it falls and then rises.	Looks like Theme I but sounds different, since:
a. Introduced by cello; violin succeeds. Theme rises and falls, mostly by step. 1) suspended in feeling because: a) no cadence for 19 meas. b) held notes on weak measures: number 2, 4, etc. c) no final note for theme b. Short note ending-section of 10 meas. Little used. Bridge: 1) running figures in 3rds and 6ths inverted in viola and cello. 2) uses part 1 of theme and inverts figure. 3) cello solo introduces triplets which will be used later in devel.	8 measures theme but extends itself to 13 measures. b. Lapses into triplet figures. c. Answering chords between high and low instruments lead to closing theme.	1) long notes on odd-numbered measures, such as 1, 3, etc. 2) theme rests on tonic. 8 measures extended to 12 by answering figures.

DEVELOPMENT

	B	
Part I	Part II	Part III
1) Cello restates Theme I but ends on modulating note. Answered by violin, viola, second violin but in different keys. 20 meas. 2) Part 2 of Theme I used as a basis for fragments and extensions. 19 meas. 3) Answering chords heard again but in different order. 8 meas. 4) Low voices hold long chords, gradually rising in pitch while violin plays obbligato. 17 meas. 5) Return of Theme I in all voices briefly under violin obbligato. 14 meas.	New Theme in Fugal Style – Entrances in: 1) Second violin 2) Viola 3) First violin 4) Cello Other entrances follow. Fugal idea comes to quick close with long note values and syncopation. 	Return of part of Theme I with answering triplet figures. Return of part b of Theme I leads to Recapitulation.

RECAPITULATION

	C	
Theme I	Theme II	Closing Theme
a. Cello begins, violin repeats and modulates. b. Omits b part of Theme I. Bridge: 1) Running figures. 2) Cello triplet solo with viola.	a. Longer than original. b. Triplet figure heard again. c. Answering chords.	Heard for 10 meas. with increasing loudness.

CODA

a. Theme I in full harmony.
b. Triplet figures precede long statement of closing theme in viola and then violins.
c. Ending figures.

THE THEME

In the previous chapter we concerned ourselves almost entirely with the overall form for a movement. We shall not disregard that element as we look at the movements of string quartets; however, we shall place some of our attention on the themes which make up the form and the manner in which the composer uses the themes he chooses.

First, we shall examine the longer melodic line. Extending over a number of measures, it may become even longer by avoiding a cadence while the composer extends it or attaches it to bridge material. The manner in which the theme is constructed, the manner in which it moves away from its beginning note, the approach to and point of climax, and its rhythm are all aspects which assist us in comparing one with another.

We have become familiar with the music of Ravel on other occasions. His string quartet, first movement, will offer an interesting look at the type of themes he employs and how he uses them.

Quartet in F Major: First Movement (Ravel)

Long melodic lines, the main themes running for eight measures; smooth sounds that make use of the wide range of available pitches. Little emphasis upon development in the Beethoven sense, but he does fragment his themes and work with them even before the development officially arrives, so that **one has the feeling**

STATEMENT		
Theme I	Bridge or Episode	Theme II
a. Theme seems to want to go on for a long time. Actually 8 measures long. Rising effect produced mainly through lower instruments since theme rises and falls. b. A four-note segment of the theme is used to separate the main theme sections. a. Four measures heard before bridge	Taken from a part of Ia. Contains part of Ia.	Another long theme of 8 measures leading almost immediately to the Development.

DEVELOPMENT			
a. Begins with Part A of II which combines with Ia	b. Stretching of Theme Ia	c. IIa is heard	d. Ia returns

RECAPITULATION		
a. Ia b. Ib	Bridge Taken from a part of Ia Part of Ia included	Second theme used and lengthened to move into the Coda

CODA

COMBINED I a and II a

Episode

Ia.

Ib.   II

IIa

that he cannot be detained that long before his work begins.   Similar effects in the recapitulation.

Quartet No. 4 in C: Third Movement (Bartók)

Bartók is Hungary's most famous musician of contemporary times.   A strong nationalist in his personal life, he spent considerable time researching the folk tunes of his native land.   He became aware of the influence of the upper classes and their music upon the folk, and diligently attempted to ascertain the extent to which this influence had been adopted into their music.   His compositions often demonstrate his concern for Hungarian folk tunes, for primitiveness, and exhibit his interest in contemporary composition.   *Quartet No. 4* interestingly combines these elements.   Not only does he use the string quartet in a different manner, but he often has the instruments speak a different type of musical language.   On first hearing the quartet sounds incomprehensible, but after only a few additional playings, the lines appeal because of their musicalness but also because of their primitiveness.

The third movement of this quartet contains the key to the entire work, for here we are introduced to the simplicity of the folk sounds and their chromatic elements in a more original structure.   These chromatic lines and the themes which evolve from them are the main elements of the other movements.

This movement is in three parts, but deviates some from the usual ABA form.

PART A

1. Long tones as a background to a primitive sounding theme.
    a. Long tones make up the harmony.
    b. Harmony is close, dissonant, and alternates between sounds with and without vibrato.

2. Theme: based upon a Hungarian peasant melody played by a primitive instrument.
   a. Extended with many short notes interspersed.
   b. Chromatic in nature.
   c. Most intervals close together but an occasional wide skip.

PART B

1. Held notes move to lower three instruments and increase in intensity.
2. Background becomes rhythmic, irregular, but powerful.
3. High notes of first violin remain in the same style as the original melody.

PART A′

1. Melodic line:
   a. Returns to cello.
   b. Rhythmically more even; longer note values give a smoother impression.
   c. Less primitive with changed rhythm.
   d. Not an exact repetition of the theme, but a repetition of mood, intent, and use of instruments.
2. Background:
   a. First violin inverts the cello theme.
   b. Other two instruments play straight rhythmic lines.

CODA

1. Similar to Part B in effect.
2. Short.

Béla Bartók (Courtesy of Austrian National Library).

470

THE FRAGMENT

Some movements are not built upon themes as such, but upon fragments, which are small melodic sections. Some fragments seem complete within themselves; others are purposely open-ended so that the composer may work with them in different ways. In order to be used for entire movements the fragments must be built so that they contain rhythmic energy and melodic expansion possibilities. Not all fragments fit this purpose, and composers often work many months or years to arrive at one which they believe contains the proper balance. Fragments contrast to the longer themes and offer different compositional possibilities. This means that the movements themselves will unfold differently, depending on whether the themes are long and continuous, or whether they stem from fragments. It is important to be able to hear the fragment and then to recognize it in its various alterations if you are to fully comprehend the sonata as a form.

Quartet in F Major, Op. 18, No. 1: First Movement (Beethoven)

Beethoven worked through several versions of this fragment before he was satisfied that it could become the main element of the movement. On paper it appears too innocent, for in fact it involves only two pitches with a couple of embellishments. When heard it seems to contain energy and life, but most would not consider it a subject for a movement, let alone a main theme at that.

Theme I   Theme II

On the first page of the score we find thirteen different uses of this theme, and when played it requires about thirty-five seconds. It might appear that we would become tired of this little fragment, and undoubtedly with lesser composers this would be true. However, Beethoven continually varies the pitch of the theme, and the method of approaching it, so that rather than becoming tired of it, we wish to hear the movement again to try to understand its drive and the source of its interest. It appears too simple, too obvious, too much in front of us for belief.

The second theme, almost too insignificant, only just holds its place in the form. Beethoven probably considered this an asset, and planned a negligible second theme so that the first could assume greater impact. Such planning becomes meaningful when almost the entire development is devoted to the fragment. The second theme seems fragmentary in its own way also, since it is nothing more than a chord with each note member played twice before moving to the next.

Listen to the movement, perceiving the sonata-allegro form, but also hearing the theme fragments we have just discussed. In addition, at times you will hear the fragment played by one instrument while another plays a variation against the theme. However, in this movement, these variations against the theme are rarely longer than the theme itself, giving a kind of balance to the structure.

On more than one occasion Beethoven holds back the rhythm flow by inserting notes of longer duration, rests, or breaking the theme with a solitary instrument playing only one or two notes. Assess the effect that he creates with these devices.

In the development the fragments may involve a type of canon, so that before one instrument has completed it another has begun. No great complexity results, but enough for this movement and for the theme.

Quartet in g minor, Op. 10: First Movement (Debussy)

The string quartet by Debussy makes use of two fragments as the basis for its first movement. The first, not too unlike his famous *Golliwog's Cakewalk* theme, extends over most of two measures and uses three pitches. In order to assist with this limitation, Debussy adds a small figuration, just as Beethoven does in his Op. 18. There Beethoven uses a turn, a figuration built around a single note, but the notes above and below are played in a special order along with the main pitch so that totally there are four notes. Debussy uses a triplet to enhance his three-note fragment, while Beethoven uses a turn to complement his two-note fragment. Differences result on two points, however; Debussy uses a syncopated rhythm typical of the twentieth century and its concern for jazzy off-beat accents with full, thick harmonies. Because of the speed of performance, this device is hardly recognizable.

Theme I seldom moves beyond the fragment. Though heard many times over in new keys and with different rhythms, the fragment does not expand itself; nor does it become a part of the development in the same manner as in Beethoven. Debussy's develops mostly by restatement of the fragment with the emphasis upon dynamics, shading, and modulation rather than inversion, augmentation, or extension.

The second theme of the sonata-allegro form comes late in the statement. In fact, two bridge themes are heard before the second theme finally appears, so the listener may be misled momentarily. The second theme occurs first in rather slow tempo immediately after the cello has stated a chromatic version of Theme I.   The second theme makes use of four actual pitches, again uses a triplet, but also uses eighth notes to emphasize the second and third principal notes.   Both of these themes are used in the development, but as with the first, neither one is used in the traditional sense.

Theme II

Theme members

Listen to this movement.   During the first hearing, capture only the mood and the style of writing.   Upon subsequent hearings, listen for the fragments and their use within the form.   Being alert to the delay of the entrance of the second theme will assist in recognizing both theme and form.   The recapitulation, obvious since it enters after an appropriate buildup, makes its presentation forceful through added harmonic elements.

Study Procedures

1. Discuss the use of the fragments in each example.   Compare the energy within each, the rhythm, the point of greatest melodic accent, the point of greatest rhythmic accent, and the psychological effect upon you.
2. Listen to each of the examples several times.   It has been reported that Beethoven used his first fragment over 100 times in the development.   Does this detract from the overall effect of the composition?   Does it create an effect?   How would you describe this effect in nonmusical terms?
3. Listen to each of the examples several times.   In your opinion, which of the movements offers you the greatest esthetic satisfaction?   Can you describe why this might be true?   Is it the theme, or could it be the construction of the material?

ARTISTIC EFFECTS

A composition is more than merely form and themes.   A composer must also be alert to the artistic effects which are possible using the material he has chosen.   Some effects would be suitable for some forms, but not the themes.   The reverse would also be true.   A composer knows and can use many effects, but they may not suit his overall artistic goal.   When listening to his work in performance we should be aware of the effects which he has requested, and considering the total composition, evaluate them.   We may not verbalize this evaluation, but we evaluate it by our response to the work, in whole or in part, or by our complete disregard of the effect.   If we disregard it, it could be that the effect was conceived on too small a scale, or that other items overshadowed it.   Let us examine four of these artistic effects so that we may be confident that we hear what others hear in the composition.

Dynamics

One of the special effects used by all composers is the difference in loudness levels as the theme and various portions of the composition progress. Many of these dynamics are indicated within the score by the composer. Some of the early scores and some of the more obvious dynamic effects even in modern scores are not marked; these are left for the performer to indicate by his interpretation.

Some themes and phrases become more meaningful when they are played beginning at one dynamic, increasing in loudness, and then falling downward to about the beginning level. This archlike flow satisfies thousands of musical phrases. Exceptions can be found in almost any composition, phrases which are more meaningful when they increase in dynamic and remain so, or the reverse.

Over and beyond the expected dynamics, some composers employ special effects to assist the composition. Beethoven was such a composer. His music is full of the musical marking **SF,** which means that a special accent should be given a particular note or chord. In the first movement of Op. 18, No. 1, these are found rather near the beginning, after the first theme statement, and again several times immediately before the development (longer chords). These give the music a special character usually not found in the works of other composers. In the works of more contemporary composers dynamics are used in more subtle ways, particularly in those of Debussy or Ravel.

Study Procedure

Listen to the movements of these quartets again, paying particular attention to the dynamic level. Notice how dynamics become a part of the statement and development of themes. Much of the artistic effect of the music comes from dynamics as well as structure.

Pizzicato

Almost always the violin string produces tones through bowing. At times the finger might pluck the string, producing a special kind of effect called *pizzicato*. Usually pizzicato is associated with lighter, more playful, musical feelings, and consequently, it is used more often in the scherzo or a fast, light movement.

Quartet No. 4 in C: Fourth Movement (Bartók)

When discussing the third movement of the Bartók, primitivism was mentioned as well as its supplying the mood and basis for themes for the remainder of the piece. Hence in this movement, which is in ABA form, the first theme adopts the chromatic and scale passages which were part of the third movement melodic line. The repetitive middle section concerns itself with small scale movements or repeated notes.

All of this movement is played pizzicato. Some of the instruments play only one pitch at a time; later they may play more than one pitch simultaneously, producing a different pizzicato effect. A few times the string is pulled particularly hard so that it buzzes on the fingerboard, producing a sound almost similar to a country style ukulele. Bartók also asks the players to play certain chords in the fashion of a harp, meaning back and forth, in order to give more volume and more constancy to the tone.

Study Procedure

Listen to this movement, noting the interesting effects as well as the form.

Quartet in g minor, Op. 10: Second Movement (Debussy)
Quartet in F Major: Second Movement (Ravel)

Both of these quartets use pizzicato in the second movements, but both use this effect differently. Because of the similarity in overall style, they make an interesting contrasting study. The main themes of the Debussy follow.

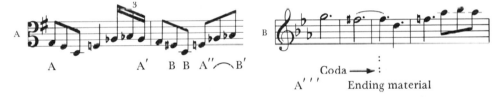

This is an excellent example of the cyclic principle, and of the manner of using material for different purposes.

Study Procedures

1. Listen to the second movement of Debussy's quartet, and note the form. Pay particular attention to the use of pizzicato. Can you determine when all the instruments are playing with this method, and when some are bowing and some using pizzicato? Can you imagine in your mind how the movement would sound if all of it were bowed? Would the effect be changed noticeably, or would it make only a little difference? Would it destroy the esthetic effect which the composer desired?
2. Review the main theme of the first movement, and perceive how it was changed for the second movement.
3. The Ravel quartet uses the following form:

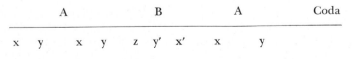

A		B			A		Coda
x	y	x	y	z	y' x'	x	y

The variance of form in the second section is based upon the rhapsodic use given the themes. Although earlier material is present, the sound differs because of the treatment. This could be termed a Song and Trio.

Here again, the pizzicato effect balances interestingly with the bowed material. All instruments begin with the pizzicato. When the y theme enters (a sweet melody bowed by the first violin), the second violin and viola also add a bowed accompaniment, but the cello continues with pizzicato figures. This unites the first section. The cello bows its slow melody in the Trio, and here the coloration of the entire movement changes noticeably.

Portamento and Mute

It is rare to find this effect in string quartets. Only a composer such as Bartók would consider this a vital and artistic complement to his music. In *portamento* the performer moves his hand on the string upward or downward so that all of the pitches are sounded with a sliding effect. This would include sounds which are not normally used in the pitches required by notation, or to say it another way, all of the sounds between the pitches. In addition, Bartók asked that the performers place mutes on their instruments. This makes the tone a bit softer, but with strings the lack of overtones becomes more important, resulting in a unique, somewhat nasal tone quality.

Quartet No. 4 in C: Second Movement (Bartók)

The previous paragraphs on the Bartók quartet pointed out that the third movement contained thematic implications for the others. The chromatic, recitative-like, undulating solo line has been appropriated into other movements and combined with primitive effects and contemporary harmonies. In the second movement these characteristics are accentuated by the use of portamento and the mute.

The themes for this movement are different from any which we have studied. They resemble effects more than themes or fragments. The first is a chromatic scale executed with special articulation, the second a series of repeated notes, the third a couple of pitch changes around a single note; all these bespeak the main characteristics.

---

1 From *String Quartet No. 4,* by Béla Bartók. Copyright 1929 by Universal Edition; Renewed 1956. Copyright and renewal assigned to Boosey & Hawkes, Inc., for the U.S.A. Reprinted by permission.

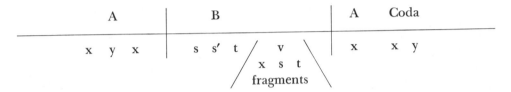

These have been combined into a three-part form, ABA, with each section containing subdivisions. Again, upon first hearing this music seems unapproachable; however, after only a few hearings the form becomes evident, but in addition, the primitive effects become artistic and the special effects assist with the mood and esthetic qualities. There are times in this movement when the listener forgets that a string quartet is playing and hears it as if only one performer were involved, so closely knit are the lines and the musical effects.

A	B	A	Coda
x y x	s s' t / v \ / x s t \ fragments	x	x y

Study Procedures

1. In the Beethoven quartets sudden dynamic change was used for particular effect. Bartók uses this also. Are the overall effects similar or quite different? Do these add to the Bartók as much or less than to the Beethoven? Which composer could more quickly have omitted them?
2. Primitivism has been heard before in the Stravinsky *Rite of Spring*. Describe the similarities and differences you hear between the ballet and the quartet movement. In your opinion, which composer is the more primitive sounding? Can you define why?
3. Review all of the movements of the quartets, and try to describe how they differ in effect and overall sound; how are they similar?
4. Choose two of the quartets which you particularly liked and listen to additional movements. Are these equally appealing and interesting? Can you perceive the form and style?

Bibliography—Chapter 23

ANDERSON, EMILY, ed., *The Letters of Beethoven*. New York: St. Martin's Press, Inc., 1961.

DEMUTH, NORMAN, *Ravel*. London: J. M. Dent and Sons Ltd., 1956.

FERGUSON, DONALD, *Chamber Music*. Minneapolis: University of Minnesota Press, 1964.

HUGHES, ROSEMARY, *Haydn String Quartets*. Seattle: University of Washington Press, 1966.

KERMAN, JOSEPH, *The Beethoven Quartets*. New York: Alfred A. Knopf, 1967.

LACKSPEISER, EDWARD, *Debussy*. New York: E. P. Dutton and Company, Inc., 1936.

MARLIAVE, JOSEPH DE, *Beethoven's Quartets*. New York: Dover Publications, Inc., 1961.

MASON, DANIEL GREGORY, *The Quartets of Beethoven*. New York: Oxford University Press, 1947.

RADCLIFFE, PHILIP, *Beethoven's String Quartets*. London: Hutchinson University Library, 1965.

ROBERTSON, ALEX, ed., *Chamber Music*. Baltimore: Penguin Books, 1967.

STEVENS, HALSEY, *Life and Music of Bartók*. New York: Oxford University Press, 1953.

STUCKENSCHMIDT, J. J., *Maurice Ravel*. Philadelphia: Chilton Book Co., 1968.

Recordings—Chapter 23

Bartók	*Quartet No. 4 in C*	Juilliard	Columbia ML-54279
Beethoven	Op. 18, No. 1	Fine Arts	Murray Hill S-3455
Beethoven	Op. 59, No. 1	Fine Arts	Murray Hill S-3455
Debussy	Op. 10	Juilliard	Victor LSC-2413
Ravel	*Quartet in F*	Juilliard	Victor LSC-2413

Additional Suggestions for Listening

Haydn	Op. 76, No. 3	Budapest	Columbia ML-4923
Haydn	Op. 77, No. 1	Juilliard	Victor LM-2168

Chapter 24

The Concerto

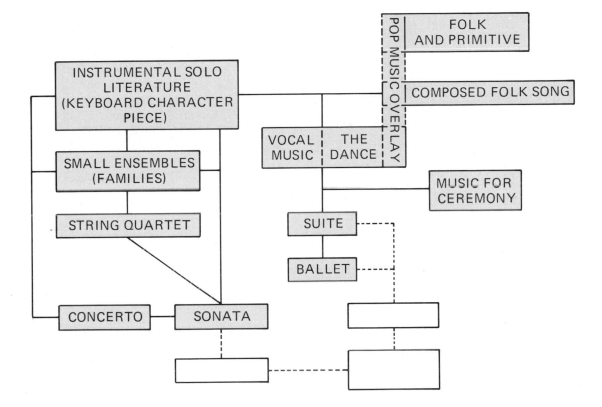

Such a powerful concept as the sonata form could not resist additional use through alteration, application, and expansion by creative musicians. Adapting an older idea, the concerto became a sonata for orchestra and soloist, and like the sonatas previously studied, the sonata-allegro form was used. When compared to other forms several differences exist:

1. The concerto almost always consists of three movements: the sonata-allegro first; the more lyrical second, usually with simpler form; and the quick ending.

2. The final movement usually is a rondo. Although introduced earlier, this form will be explored further in this chapter since the concerto used it so advantageously.

3. Featuring a solo instrument, the composition pairs the one against the many. Although at times used as an accompaniment, the orchestra balances with the soloist in presenting themes, bridges, developments, statements, and coloration. With the emphasis upon equality despite differences, the listener finds variety through contrast, and unity through form.

4. Much of the solo work, particularly during the Romantic period, places considerable emphasis upon virtuosity. The skill of the soloist through his technic and interpretive powers is pitted against the coloration and interpretive possibilities of the orchestra. A good concerto will give the listener a great satisfaction: the soloist interprets and dazzles with technic, and the orchestra satisfies through power, coloration, and dynamic drive.

5. Many concertos contain cadenzas for the soloist. A *cadenza*, a technical passage inserted within the composition and often built around themes of the work, usually occurs near the end of the first movement. Those composers wishing to deviate from the traditional pattern have eliminated the cadenza in some cases, or placed it in different locations.

Keeping these characteristics in mind, listen to the music to hear how the composer expresses his musical ideas using this form. Let us begin by examining third movements and the often-used rondo form.

RONDO: THIRD MOVEMENTS

As we noticed in earlier chapters, occasionally the rondo was used for final movements of the sonata. In the concerto, the rondo assists third movements in offering a fast, brilliant, bouncy ending where technical display could be further exploited. Since the sonata-allegro form had been used for the usually longer first movement, and the slower second movement had captured the subtleties of melodic possibilities, a change of pace was needed to complete the composition. The rondo provided such an opportunity. Secondly, a form was needed which would not be as involved or complex as the first movement, but one which would support brightness of tempo and melody. The rondo, with its constant return, satisfied both of these qualifications. The composer could use the ABACA idea to suit his wishes by emphasizing the B and C sections, or he could stress the often-heard main theme and lessen the importance of the deviations. This form also offered the composer an opportunity to alter the tempo and/or mood of the third movement during the diversions; such divergence is almost impossible with the main themes of the sonata-allegro. Since most concertos of merit have been written for the piano or the violin, our study will concentrate upon these solo instruments.

Violin Concerto in e minor, Op. 64 (Mendelssohn)

One of the great masterpieces in concerto form for violin was composed by Mendelssohn. During the period of its composition, his letters indicate a correspondence with Ferdinand David, a famous violinist of his day. This procedure has been typical of many composers, even those who played the violin rather well. The composer wished not only to write an attractive composition, but in order to be assured that the difficult technical passages were idiomatic for the instrument and playable for the artist, it became standard practice to seek the advice of a stellar violinist of the day. Many times such advice preceded dedication and a first performance. These latter events were matters of politeness, while the seeking of advice assured that the piece would be feasible and meaningful to future artists.

David played the first performance of the concerto in 1845, and wrote a letter to Mendelssohn thanking him for "one of the most beautiful pieces in this form. It fulfills to the highest degree all that could be expected from a concert piece; the violinists cannot thank you enough for this gift." I suppose if one were to count performances, this concerto would surpass all others. It has become not only well-known, but beloved by listeners, orchestra members, and artists alike.

Most composers who write well alter the form to suit the composition and the melodic and rhythmic structure of the work. Using the extended rondo form, Mendelssohn omitted the final return. Although the coda used a portion of the main theme, the second theme predominates. The form is ABACAB Coda.

Again the main theme is bouncy, full of life, and gay. The soloist literally bounces the bow along to keep up with the notes as they roll out. The orchestra introduces the second theme, B, as a tutti, extending it considerably before the return of the first theme. This time the main theme is heard for only a few measures before the solo dashes into the second deviation, C. While the solo violin introduces this new theme, the orchestra plays the main theme, or A. This interesting effect has a tendency to tighten the form. When the violin relinquishes the C theme to the orchestra, the solo turns to variations on theme A, and thus the balance again is maintained. The orchestra repeats the C theme, and again the violin plays the A theme in variation and with extension. The orchestra, after fast scale passages in the solo, plays the B theme again in tutti, but the violin, not ready to move in that direction, intersperses the A theme between the phrases. With the orchestra playing the phrases of the B theme, the violin interrupts with ascending trills to introduce the coda. Although a bit of the first theme is present, most of the coda centers about the second theme. The movement and the concerto end in a blaze of pyrotechnics, which often brings the audience to its feet with applause for both the orchestra and the soloist.

Although the form is a bit more difficult to perceive due to overlapping themes, the above diagram should enable you to hear the structure with little difficulty. Listen to the work to understand its structure, but also to capture the true rondo flavor and artistic qualities built into it by the composer.

Piano Concerto No. 1 in C Major, Op. 15 (Beethoven)

This rondo is a masterpiece of color and movement. Consequently, it epitomizes the main characteristics of the form. This is not a timid movement, but begins with the piano in a dancelike melody which drives its brilliance toward the listener. This twenty-measure theme in no way seems out of balance with the shorter second theme. The piano introduces the first theme, the orchestra answers; a bridge leads into the second main theme, which is played first by the orchestra and then by the piano. To give added color and interest to this theme, in the repeat Beethoven places the melody in the lower sounds of the piano and extends the latter measures. The typical Beethoven accents occur frequently and off the beat, aiding in the general character. Before the return of the main theme another transition follows, which is stated clearly by the piano and then the orchestra.   The C theme heard immediately in the piano is one of Beethoven's jauntiest, and almost displays a kind of jazziness.   Its two parts alternate.

Unlike most rondos, this movement contains a cadenza.   Custom has decreed that the first movement contain a cadenza, and if the artist wished it could become quite long.   The score rarely contained the cadenza, so that it often was interpolated by the soloist—at least, this was the custom in Beethoven's day.   Since it is unusual for a third movement to contain a cadenza, a short one is used.   In this movement the short cadenza appears before the final statement of the main theme.   Beethoven indicated that a cadenza should be begun, then wrote a false start for the main theme, after which the cadenza was completed.   Some recordings do not use the second portion of the cadenza but move immediately into the main theme by the orchestra, which leads to the coda.   Note the style of the cadenza, the manner in which it is played, and the effect it has upon the form.

A			B			A		C			A	
Piano	Orch.	Bridge	Orch.	Piano	Tr.	Piano	Orch.	P P P P P	Tr.	P O		
a	a		b	b		a	a	x y x y x		a	a	con't.

B					A	Coda			
Orch.	Piano	⟶	Cadenza	False start	Orch				
b	b			a	a	a	a	y	a

Study Procedures

1. Review the differences in rondo form exemplified in the two movements which we have studied.

2. Although each movement follows the format and general characteristics of a rondo, each has its individual effect. In your own words, describe these differences by considering the style of writing, the type of thematic material, the use of the soloist, and other musical characteristics.

3. Compare the two movements. Which of the two would seem to indicate a more mature feeling and sensitivity?

SLOW: SECOND MOVEMENTS

Placed between two faster movements, the slow or second movement of a concerto bears a tremendous responsibility. Its character must be such that the interest of the listener does not lag after the technical and brilliant first movement; it must give some relief to the quick tempo which has been driving through what usually is the longest movement of the work; many composers do not wish to sacrifice the technical display even in a slow section; it must be simple in form so as to contrast with the more intricate forms of the other movements; it must relay a sense of beauty, and still give some depth to the work by not being superficial; it must extend to the listener the composer's feelings and his sensitivity to emotion which the other movements may not give; and, it should have some relation to the other movements so that the listener and the performer will sense the unity of the whole. These artistic demands have eliminated many compositions from those best liked by performers and listeners. Yet, the concertos which are most often performed contain jewels as second movements. Some are long, some short; a simple three-part form usually is adhered to, while each projects the intent of the composer in a unique way.

Piano Concerto in a minor, Op. 54 (Schumann)

This second movement, one of the shortest in the major concertos, contains a simple, easily followed form, and the themes are contrasting enough to be obvious. Although the orchestra is present, the piano is at center stage almost throughout.

$$
\begin{array}{ccc}
A & B & A \\
a \quad b \quad a & x \quad y \quad x & a \quad b \quad a \qquad \text{extended}
\end{array}
$$

The extension leads into and prepares us for the third movement. The sweeping lines of the middle section typify the romantic character of the work.

Piano Concerto No. 2 in c minor (Rachmaninoff)

Although a composer of the twentieth century (having died in 1943), the music of Rachmaninoff contains a decided romantic flavor. A certain melancholy per-

Sergei Rachmaninoff (Courtesy of Brown Brothers, Sterling, Pa.).

vades his music, but throughout, the beauty and the technic never falter. He was a concert pianist and a fabulous technician, proved by the fact that it was not uncommon for him to play octaves with his thumb and first finger.

The *Second Concerto* has been a favorite all over the world, with a renown so widespread that popular songs have been developed from its themes. In some ways it could be called the last of the romantic concertos. Young people of this generation find it difficult to consider a Russian as a romantic figure, but the music of Rachmaninoff should dispel this opinion.

Successful as a student of music in college, his *First Concerto* was only a student work, and Rachmaninoff destroyed the score because it was not of the quality his later maturity desired. When his *First Symphony* was not a success he developed a mental block against composing, and it was a Dr. Dahl who aided him through hypnosis. Appropriately, the *Second Concerto* is dedicated to him, for it was written while he was under the doctor's care. Interestingly, the second movement was written first, then the third, and finally the first. In fact, the second and third movements were performed publicly before the first was even written. Once acclaimed, the first movement was added.

The three-part simple form of the second movement deviates from the norm to give it an individual character. The orchestra plays a brief chordal introduction, while the piano follows with a short arpeggiated one. The flute and clarinet state the main theme, the piano repeats it, and the strings pick it up for a few measures only to introduce the second theme.   Although similar in format to the first, it carries a different feeling and melody.   Rachmaninoff creates a bridge between parts of the second theme so that it is interrupted momentarily before it concludes.   A long cadenzalike section appears before the return of the main theme.

Intro		A			B							
		a	a	a″	b	bridge	b	conc.	b	bridge	b	conc. con't
orch	piano	orch	piano	strings	piano		piano			piano		

Cadenza	Intro	A	Coda
		a	
accompanied and solo	piano	strings	large chords accompanied by sustained strings

Study Procedures

1. Why would a second movement seem to demand a simple form? Of the movements studied, which one seems to be simple yet expressive enough to be effective?
2. Examine a second movement from a concerto for an instrument we have not studied in this chapter. Your teacher or music librarian will be able to recommend a composer and composition to you. For the time being, limit your choice to solo concertos.

SONATA-ALLEGRO FORM: FIRST MOVEMENTS

In considering the sonata-allegro form earlier, we observed some of the outward characteristics, its appeal to the mind of the nineteenth century, and the reasons for its existence. To truly know the numerous details of the form one would need to review its treatment by numerous composers. Although possible in a small way, this survey does not permit the depth of study which this form could entail. Consider it as a dramatic form wherein we come to know two characters. Occasionally a third enters the scene, but only briefly, and then only to assist us in knowing or understanding something about the other two. As in a play, it is possible that one character outperforms the other to some of the audience while the second seems more attractive to the remainder. The two, although not alike in outward appearance, often present some items in common. When placed side by side these common elements appear more attractive or interesting; at other times they point up differences which only appeared to be similar at first glance. As the dramatic presentation unfolds, we learn more and more about each, their personality becomes clearer, and we learn how well the author understands the inner workings of the personality.

So it is with the composer and his two themes in a sonata-allegro form. In the statement we come to know them in one way, but in the development, much of their subtle characteristics and energies begin to appear. Beethoven was a master at development, where he used segments of the themes to reveal their potential and subtle meanings. He shows them to us from many sides, and this is one of the greatnesses of his music.

The sonata-allegro in the concerto varies the original form we studied in the sonata. In the latter the two themes were presented and then the development began. In the early concerto it was customary for the themes first to be presented by the orchestra, and then they were presented by the soloist. This double presentation, creating a double statement or exposition, gives an added length to the concerto which other forms do not have. During the Romantic period composers changed this approach, and often introduced the themes with the soloist while the orchestra never played them in entirety. Other changes also were evident. We shall hear examples of these, but first, let us examine in some detail the use Beethoven made of this form in the first movement of his *First Piano Concerto*.

Piano Concerto No. 1 in C Major, Op. 15 (Beethoven)

When you hear this movement, remember that Beethoven was a young man at the time of its writing. He had been asked to play for a special social occasion and decided to write the concerto for this event. Because of illness he had postponed the writing of the work until almost the last minute. Copyists were about his room madly writing out the orchestral parts as he completed each page. In addition, remember that Beethoven was known for his technical skill on the piano. He had entered several improvisation contests when he had first come to Vienna and had won. To please the public, which was enamored with technic, he would have to write a composition which would display his ability at the keyboard as well as present his themes and musical ideas in an appropriate form. Although the movement is not overly long for Beethoven, yet there are places in the form where he displays technical aspects for measure after measure. The fact that he could do this and not dissipate the strength of the form was evidence of his ability.

In this movement we have another evidence of the motive versus the melodic line. The first theme, based upon a motive, is heard throughout the movement and particularly in the development, where Beethoven uses this musical idea to build a background for the soloist. Notice that upward scale lines are heard at the very beginning; he uses upward scale movement as a basis for the technical passages in the piano. Conversely, the second theme contains a downward scale passage, which offers contrast but equal opportunities for technical display. When the little-used third theme enters, it seems in many ways related to the first.

Here are some additional points to listen for as the movement progresses:

1. The first theme comes to a definite cadential point before the second begins.
2. Two measures of undulating strings in a new tonal center precede the second theme.
3. The second theme cadences before the piano enters to begin the second statement.
4. The piano does not begin immediately with the first theme; instead, using a variation of the second theme for a few measures, it creates an introduction to the first theme.
5. The orchestra presents the second theme a second time before the piano picks it up; we hear the completion of the theme for the first time in this section.
6. There is a long extension of the second theme before the cadence concludes the end of the statement section. Typical of Beethoven, he warns us several times of the approaching cadence.
7. The orchestra begins the development; although not long, it mixes both themes, never using either one in its entirety, but rather, fragments of each. The first theme will be more easily recognized because of its distinctive rhythm.
8. The recapitulation begins in the orchestra, and the piano never plays the theme but ornaments its extension.
9. The second theme of the recapitulation is begun by the orchestra but the piano also plays it in its entirety. It too is extended until the cadenza.
10. The cadenza begins with a fragment of the first theme, but quickly turns to the second, and then to technical passages.
11. The coda, long enough to balance the movement, is built around the little-used third theme.

	Double Statement						Development
	A	B	c	A	B	c ➔ Extension	Development on A and B
	orch.	orch.	orch.	piano	o & p	o & p	piano	orch. and piano
measures	1-46	47-86	86-106	107-154	155-181	182-191	192-256	257-345

Recapitulation				
A	B	Extension	Cadenza	Coda
o & p	o & p	piano	piano	orchestra
347-369	370-389	390-465	a & b	466-478

Piano Concerto No. 2 in c minor (Rachmaninoff)

The first movement of this concerto has a wide appeal because of the melodic nature of its themes. Unlike Beethoven, the movement is simply organized and constructed. It carries a different kind of weight, with emotional drive always present. It is an emotion based upon the long and sentimental theme rather than the compact motive.

The form is simple and avoids the repeated statement, which was the standard procedure during the time of Beethoven and before.

The coda is comparatively long in this movement and acts as a summary, building in intensity to the end.

	Statement		Development	Recapitulation		Coda
Intro.	A	B ──▶ Bridge	A B	A	B	
Piano	a b orch with themes piano figurations	x y x piano	Increase in intensity	a b		

A.a.

A.b.

B

Violin Concerto in e minor, Op. 64 (Mendelssohn)

This exciting movement follows the allegro-sonata form, making use of an obvious bridge passage throughout.   The contrast between theme A and theme B offers the composer opportunity to show the violin at its melodic and technical best.

STATEMENT				DEVELOPMENT				CADENZA	RECAPITULATION			CODA
A vl	A orch	bridge o & v	B o & v	A v & o	B vl short	bridge v & o	A orch	violin	A orch Arpeggios in violin from cad.	bridge o & v	B o,v,o,v	A bridge orch

A

Bridge

B

THE TWENTIETH CENTURY CONCERTO

Music of the twentieth century features two main approaches: the first, descending from the Romantic period, absorbed many composers who wrote with good technic but in the style and forms of the earlier era. Little of this music is heard today. A second style developed during the early part of the century but as yet has not reached a culmination. Examples of this have been heard in compositions by Bartók, Stravinsky, and Berg. Although difficult for many to accept, this music persists because it describes the feelings of its period in significant forms. Quality music, particularly when it comes from the feelings of its era, has a way of persisting until such time as it becomes meaningful to a large group of people as they perceive that era in retrospect.

One division of composition of the twentieth century has become known as the *twelve-tone school*. During the latter part of the Romantic period chromaticism had pushed at tonal centers until music less and less located around a specific note or series of chords. Composers made a specific effort to eliminate regular tendencies for tonal and chordal centers, and tonal and chordal movement. From such ideas a system of organization developed which became known as twelve-tone. Its premise states that every tone of the scale equals every other tone in aural importance.

Alban Berg, a pupil of Schoenberg (the founder of the system), made use of the twelve-tone system in many of his works. His *Violin Concerto* is such a work.

Concerto for Violin (1934) (Berg)

Through our study you have probably become aware of music's attempts to gain diversion and expression through a variety of forms. Each chapter has included a new form, a different way of expressing feeling. Diversion has been evident even within a form, for each composer has used the form in slightly or more obviously different ways to express his artistic ideas. On the other hand, there is a tendency in music, seldom realized, for unification and integration. Beethoven sensed this and built some of his greatest compositions around the motive, or the integration of feeling into a small group of notes carefully placed and with an appropriate rhythm.

Composers of the twentieth century also attempt to solve these problems by altering standard forms or seeking new motives. The concerto by Berg does not follow the classic definition of its form, but one which seemed to him to be more expressive of his style and the emotional meanings of the twentieth century. His themes were also small units, often taken from parts of the twelve-tone series which he chose for a work. As you will see, this concerto uses both of these ideas.

To assist you with understanding this concerto, several characteristics may be pointed out:

1. Themes are not apt to be repeated as you have learned to expect in the forms of the Romantic or Classical period. When used again each theme probably will be altered by inversion, abbreviation, or other compositional devices.
2. A preconceived tonal scheme will be used in order to eliminate the tendency to group sounds around a chordal or tonal center.
3. Brevity of material leads to short motivistic themes which often move from one instrument to another, frequently producing a type of contrapuntal texture.
4. Accepted forms are altered.
5. Simple, well-known musical themes are placed within the work, but wrapped in contemporary surroundings or hidden with contemporary accompanying figures and tonalities.

Berg considered the first section of this composition as comprising two movements, but since there is not the slightest evidence to the listener that a new movement has begun, we shall consider it as one movement in two parts.

I.	Intro		A		bridge	B		Bridge inverted			A	
II.		A			B ·	C	B		A			
	x	y	x		Trio 1	Trio 2	abbreviated		x	y	x	
	Sch-V-Sen		V-Sch						Sch-Sen		Sch con't.	

	Folk Tune	Coda	

It will be difficult to hear this form unless you listen to the movement a number of times. The themes are not easily heard or quickly recognized as such. The above diagram will assist and the themes below will also aid, but this is difficult music to absorb in one or two hearings.

Built upon the 1, 3, 5, 7 tones of the twelve tone row, but also the first four are the open strings of the violin; the second four are the 2, 4, 6, 8 notes of his series. This is an example of the compositional technic used by twelve tone composers.

This theme, although quite extended in range, becomes closely aligned when octave displacement is not used. This device is common in contemporary works.

This twelve tone row is played by the solo violin near the beginning of section A, immediately after the first theme is heard in the low winds.

Bridge   Bridge Inverted

- - - - - - - - - - - -

- - - - - - - - - - - -

II A x-Sch

x-v

The first theme of the second section divides
itself into three parts: The x theme itself
is made up of three small sections which
Berg intended to remind us of three moods
by marking them scherzo (Sch), Viennese
(V), and Sentimental (Sen).

x-Sen   y

- - - - - - - - - - - -

B   C

Folk Song

A letter from Alma Mahler to the famous violinist Joseph Szigeti, gives us
some background for the concerto:

Alban Berg cared for my daughter as if she were his own child from her birth.
My daughter became more beautiful as she approached womanhood. When
Max Reinhardt saw her, he asked if I would allow her to play the part of
the first angel in the Grosses Welttheater in Salzburg. But before everything
could be arranged she was stricken with polio. So she lay one year and died
on Easter day, 1935. She did not play the angel, but in reality she became one.
After her death Berg lay aside his opera, *Lulu*, and composed the *Violin Concerto*, dedicating it to the memory of Manon.[2]

The score carries the dedication: "To an angel, Manon."

---

2 By permission of Joseph Szigeti.

Alban Berg in 1935 (Courtesy of Austrian National Library).

Upon first hearing, this concerto may seem strange music to dedicate to a young girl whom one considered as a daughter. Yet each of us, in assessing sorrow, happiness, or other emotions, must express ourselves in ways which are meaningful to ourselves, our background, and the style in which we live. So with Berg; his composition synthesizes deep-felt emotions but in a style which he believed to be expressive of the twentieth century artist as he lived in a changing world looking toward the future.

Berg often traveled to a city where his opera *Wozzeck* was to be performed. He gave lectures about his style and the form of the work. Often he concluded his remarks with a statement such as the following:

> Before we begin with the performance, I would like to express a request, addressed to the audience. Ladies and gentlemen—I beg you to forget all theory and musical explanations which have served my explanations, before the performance begins.[3]

We should follow his advice: listen first with an attempt to understand the themes and the form; then, listen to acquire only his expression of feelings for our time.

---

[3] *Alban Berg, the Man and His Music,* H. F. Redlich. Abelard-Schuman Ltd., New York, 1957, page 285.

Nocturnes (Andriessen)

Composed in 1959 when he was twenty years of age, Louis Andriessen, a Dutch composer of the contemporary period, wrote *Nocturnes* as a concerto using the voice as the solo instrument. No text is heard, although there are times when the voice seems to be enunciating correct syllables. The effect is meant to be psychological rather than literary. The music intends to project four psychological states of mind: hope, desire, fear, and liberation.

Listen to this work as an intermediate step between music of the early portion of the twentieth century and the more recent electronic compositions.

Study Procedures

1. We have listened to parts of several concertos. Choose one which you particularly enjoy and listen to the complete composition. After hearing it two or three times, choose one of the movements not discussed in this chapter for analysis and diagramming.
2. Choose another contemporary concerto, and listen to its various movements. Choose one of the movements for presentation and discussion before your class.
3. Listen to the second movement of the Berg concerto. Part of it is built around a chorale by Bach. Discuss the use of this chorale with your classmates.
4. Beethoven wrote five concertos for piano. Choose one of the later ones for listening. Can you perceive how he developed as a musician through comparison with the two we studied?
5. Many of your friends who play the clarinet are familiar with the Mozart *Clarinet Concerto*. Ask one of your friends to perform a movement of this composition for your class. Other friends who play instruments probably have studied and are playing concertos by other composers. Ask them to play a movement of a work not studied in this chapter.

THE CONCERTO GROSSO

Originally the word "concerto" meant a choral number using an instrumental accompaniment as compared to unaccompanied choral music. In the Baroque period, the word "concerto" was used in three different ways: 1) an orchestral composition which used contrasting technics of loud and soft, or block chords as compared to more florid passages; 2) a solo concerto, which was the forerunner of the compositions studied earlier in the chapter, and 3) the *concerto grosso,* a composition which again used contrasting technics, but relied upon a small group of players (*concertino*) compared to a larger group of players (*ripieno*). The concerto grosso was the most important of the three during the Baroque period.

To be specific, the concerto grosso featured a solo violin, a solo second violin, a solo cello, and a harpsichord or keyboard instrument. This group of four performers alternated against a larger group of string players with continuo.

Since the orchestra was then only beginning, most often a dozen or so performers made up the entire group.

The concerto grosso was so popular during the early decades of the eighteenth century that this was the chief musical form heard at the newly established public concerts. Almost sure to be heard was some piece by Corelli. His compositions were considered the model from which all others stem. So well-organized, so clear was the style and technic that these works are still heard in concerts today.

Concerto grosso No. 8 in g minor ("Christmas Concerto") (Corelli)

Each year at Christmastime this Corelli concerto is heard throughout the world. Not only is it delightful music, but the final section contains a pastorale in honor of the newborn child. This tells us something of the background of the concerto grosso: a heritage from music of the church, the theater, and the chamber. Corelli's *Concerto grosso No. 8* is most appropriate for study, since it exemplifies concerto grosso style and may be heard regularly.

A historian living at the time of Corelli wrote of his music: "Amidst all the innovations which the love of change had introduced, it continued to be performed and was heard with delight in churches, in theaters, at public solemnities and festivities in all the cities of Europe for forty years." Those "forty years" have extended themselves even into the twentieth century.

The composition contains nine short sections, and these may be grouped into threes, so that in part we may consider this a forerunner of the three-movement idea. Not placing any emphasis upon development, the sections offer contrast through tempo; variety is obtained through varying the tonal color and dynamics.

During the playing be aware of the short movements, the color of three solo instruments against the full string ensemble, the repetitions which many times are emphasized by the concertino versus the ripieno, the echo effects, and the sequences. The *sequence* was a musical device used by almost all composers of the Baroque period, and consisted of a phrase or motive heard again at a different pitch, usually one step higher or lower. (See Chapter 3.) The movements of the Corelli concerto are:

Vivace—An introduction of only six measures
Grave—A slow section beginning with the cello and bass in simple contrapuntal
    style
Allegro—A fast section with running bass figures and continual contrast with the
    performing groups

Adagio—A short, slow section
Allegro—A sequential, fast section, with the melodic line in the second violin
Adagio—A repeat of the first adagio, with four measures added as an ending

Vivace—A short, quick section somewhat reminiscent of dance

Allegro—The longest section of the concerto, full of motives and answers

Pastorale—The famous stable adoration music which sets this concerto apart from almost all others; most such works end with a quick section

The pleasure in hearing a concerto of this period comes from an understanding of it as a predecessor of the solo concerto, a feeling for the contrast between the concertino and the ripieno groups, an understanding of sequence, an appreciation of this form as an early orchestral composition, and the simple beauty of the string writing by this master of the Baroque period.

Study Procedures

1. Listen to the concerto grosso discussed above; enumerate items of similarity and difference to the concerto of the Romantic period.
2. Listen to concertos by Handel and Corelli. Do you find similar characteristics in style and form? What differences exist?
3. Listen to the Poulenc *Concerto in g minor for Organ, Strings, and Timpani*. What characteristics of this work remind one of a concerto grosso? What characteristics remind one of twentieth century music? What characteristics are present from the Romantic period? Is this a technical concerto, or does it represent a closer alignment with twentieth century goals?

Bibliography—Chapter 24

ARNOLD, DENIS, and NIGEL FORTUNE, *The Beethoven Reader*. New York: W. W. Norton and Company, Inc., 1971.

BERTENSSON, SERGEI, and JAY LAYDA, *Sergei Rachmaninoff*. New York: New York University Press, 1956.

CULSHAW, JOHN, *Rachmaninov*. New York: Oxford University Press, 1950.

EVANS, EDWIN, *The Pianoforte Works of Johannes Brahms*. New York: Burt Franklin, 1970.

HUTCHINGS, A. J. B., *The Baroque Concerto*. London: Faber and Faber, 1963.

MURDOCH, WILLIAM, *Brahms*. London: Rich and Cowan, 1933.

REDLICH, H. F., *Alban Berg*. New York: Abelard Schuman Ltd., 1957.

REICH, WILLI, *Alban Berg*. New York: Harcourt, Brace and World, 1963.

SCHAUFFLER, ROBERT HAVEN, *Beethoven*. Garden City, N.Y.: Doubleday, Doran and Company, Inc., 1929.

SWALIN, BENJAMIN F., *The Violin Concerto*. Chapel Hill, N.C.: University of North Carolina Press, 1941.

ULRICH, HOMER, *Symphonic Music*. New York: Columbia University Press, 1952.

VEINUS, ABRAHAM, *The Concerto*. London: Cassell and Company Ltd., 1948.

Recordings—Chapter 24

| Andriessen | *Nocturnes* | Amsterdam Concertg. | Radio Netherlands L-109517 |

Beethoven	*Piano Concerto No. 1 in C Major*	Gilels, Vander root	Angel 35672 Angel S-36130
Berg	*Concerto for Violin*	Stern, Bernstein	
Corelli	*Concerto grosso No. 8 in g minor*	Virtuosi di Roma	Columbia MS-6373
Mendelssohn	*Violin Concerto in e minor*	Francescatti, Szell	Columbia ML-5751
Poulenc	*Concerto in g minor for Organ, Strings, and Timpani*	Duruflé, Prêtre	Angel 35953
Rachmaninoff	*Piano Concerto No. 2 in c minor*	Reiner, Rubinstein	Victor LM-2068
Schumann	*Piano Concerto in a minor*	Serkin, Ormandy	Columbia ML-6088

Additional Suggestions for Listening

Beethoven	*Piano Concerto No. 2 in B flat Major*	Gilels, Vander root	Angel 35672
Beethoven	*Concerto in D Major for Violin*	Heifetz, Munch	Victor LM-1992
Brahms	*Piano Concerto No. 2 in B flat Major*	Richter, Leinsdorf	Victor LM-2466
Bruch	*Violin Concerto No. 1 in g minor*	Francescatti, Schippers	Columbia ML-5751
Handel	*Concerto grosso in a minor, Op. 6, No. 4*	Menuhin	Angel SD-3647

Section I *Form and the Large Ensemble*

Chapter 25 *The Symphony*

Chapter 25

The Symphony

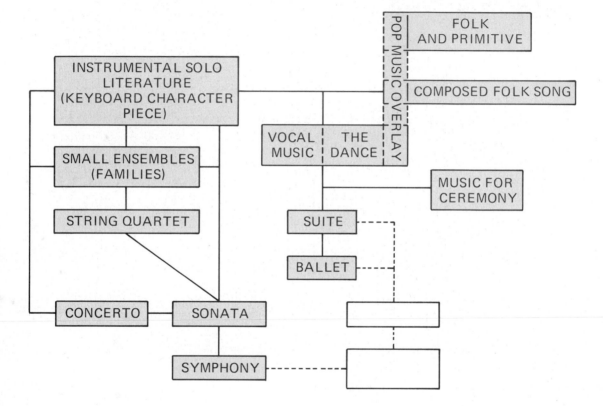

The symphony, the most imposing structure devoted completely to instrumental music, is, in reality, a sonata for orchestra. Because it uses the entire orchestra as its instrument with varied tonal colors and dynamics, the composition contains the possibilities of added length, extra musical depth, and impressionable weight.

For the past several chapters we have studied the sonata form and have come to understand how it could be used in various ways. The symphony, yet another means of using this form, developed during the eighteenth century to express expansive musical ideas and has served composers well until the past two or three decades. Only recently has the form been less attractive to serious composers.

HISTORY OF THE FORM

In order to bring some importance to the presentation of certain musical productions such as the ballet, masque, opera, or even the plays of the period, it was customary during the late sixteenth and throughout the seventeenth centuries to introduce them with a piece of music which might set the mood or at least call attention to what was to follow. In France these came to be known as Overtures, and in Italy as Sinfonias. Both had a similar purpose despite the difference in name.

As the overture developed, it took on a specific three-part character, while in Italy the sinfonia also expanded to become a three-part composition. The difference came through the order of the parts and their tempos. The overture usually began with a slow section, contained a fast section, and ended slowly. The sinfonia reversed the order.

As time elapsed, the sinfonia separated from the dramatic presentations and became an independent musical form. Such independence developed further as the concert evolved into a social event of its own, with instrumental music containing enough content and self-determination to offer the listener a reason for listening without being dependent on song texts or dramatic events.

In its beginnings the concert declared the rights of the common man. For centuries music had either been the property of the church or its performance held almost exclusively within the courts of the nobility. Although the commoner had his instruments, folk songs, and dances, rarely was the gentile art music heard except in churches or halls of the court. When in the eighteenth century certain courtly centers disintegrated upon the death of the ruler, often a patron of the arts, the musician looked outside the court for an audience and sustenance and the middle class welcomed his creativity by attending his concerts.

As the concert became a more popular social event, the need for repertoire for the orchestra became a reality. Rather than borrow the overtures or sinfonias which preceded the plays or ballets, music was composed especially for the concert. A composer of this period wrote a sinfonia in order to attract and please the listener as well as express himself musically. He realized this would have to be accomplished during the first hearing, and although not interested in writing only folk or song material, he was challenged by the necessity to meet personal standards and yet produce a composition which would be tuneful enough to be attractive to the listener. The Italians had a flair for the melodic, while the Germans tended to focus upon the organization of the composition or its form. A subtle and skillful combination of the two brought the most satisfactory results. In the town of Mannheim, Germany, in the orchestra for the Elector of the region, these two ideas were most ably united so that the form became logical and focused without losing any attractiveness of melodic content.

For about forty years during the eighteenth century the sinfonia was hammered into an explicit structure as it lost its indefiniteness, focused more upon the idea of movements which were independent of each other in form, dismissed its connection with dramatic events, and finally accepted the sonata-allegro form particularly for the first movement.   As Adam Carse has stated in his book on the symphony, "It would be difficult or impossible to find a movement in Sonata Form that was written much before 1740, and it would be very unusual to find a first movement of a symphony composed after 1775 that was not in Sonata Form."[1] Thousands of compositions were written under the title of symphony, sinfonia, or overture for the newly developing orchestra.   But while the overture retained its connection with dramatic productions, the sinfonia became the main composition for the orchestra.   As it developed, the form changed until it became a composition of weight equal to its task.   Hundreds of lesser composers added to the small changes within this development, and upon such a base there finally came a number of composers who understood the form and the role of the orchestra well enough to give us music which demands our attention and respect decades or centuries after completion.

Study Procedures

By reviewing what you know of the sonata, the sonata-allegro form, the concerto, the concerto grosso, and the string quartet, you should have a means for building anticipations concerning the symphony.   Historically, some of the orchestral characteristics developed prior to their use in the simpler forms, yet our study should have led you to understand the development of the symphony.   As a review, answer the following questions, thus bridging other forms to the symphony:

1. Considering the acceptance of alternation of tempos in the dance suite, what would you expect in the movements of the symphony?

2. The concerto grosso had developed changes in loudness through what means?   As instruments became more adept at producing musical sounds in an artistic fashion how did this aid the composer in the area of dynamics?

3. Rather than repeat a theme verbatim, how did the sonata-allegro form assist in repetition with a certain variety?   What would this mean considering an orchestra?   How could an orchestra affect tonality and form?

4. In a sonata for one instrument a limitation of tone color exists although range and style of playing assist in giving character to the composition.   If an entire orchestra were the player of the sonata, what would you expect in the handling of themes?   Of tone colors?   What instruments might have been first added to the strings?

5. The orchestra developed after the emphasis in music had turned toward homophony. What problems would you foresee for the early composer who wished to write for the orchestra using this style?   (Consider the length of phrases and the kind of writing necessary for the middle and lower voices.)

6. In the discussion of the concerto grosso we learned about the continuo.   The continuo was used with the orchestra for a number of years before it was realized to be of little value in that new context.   Can you suggest why it was used, and why composers gradually eliminated it?

---

1 *18th Century Symphonies,* Adam Carse.   Augener Ltd., London, 1951, page 17.

THE NEW MEANS OF EXPRESSIVENESS

For decades we have accepted the orchestra as an excellent medium of musical expression; in fact, it becomes difficult to imagine any time when this was not the case. Even with the early orchestra the listener and the composer looked upon its growth as an opportunity for additional expressiveness, and the form which developed for the orchestra had to assure this idea. Consequently, there evolved a multimovement form which was expressive, understandable, yet forceful. At the same time it enhanced the content of the composition by displaying it most attractively.

THE MUSIC OF THE SYMPHONY

The remainder of this chapter deals with the music of the symphony. For study purposes we will examine a number of different movements, then, later, a complete symphony. In this way you will come to understand the manner in which different composers approached the movements, their esthetic effect, possibilities, and responsibilities, and you will hear different periods and styles of writing for a particular movement. After the study sessions, the hearing of a complete symphony will be in order and will not seem the insurmountable obstacle it could have been earlier.

The music will be approached in a particular manner. Some introductory material will be given for most of the movements. These comments will assist you in knowing something of the composer, his feelings about his work, or some incidental material about the composition that may prove of interest before you study the music.

Following the introductory material, you will find outline charts for each movement. Since the movements of a symphony are somewhat more intricate than the previous material studied, these charts will be of greater detail to assist your hearing. You will benefit by following some of the movements in score. Even if you do not read music well, the scores often may be followed easily. Your teacher can assist you by calling page numbers from time to time. You will find that after some practice the score can be followed without much difficulty. Following the score and reading it are two distinct items. Reading requires much practice and musical skill; following gives you a visual idea of the character of the composition as you hear it. The score is another assist to understanding and increasing the expressiveness which you can obtain from the music.

FIRST MOVEMENTS

Symphony No. 5 in c minor (Beethoven)

The Beethoven *Fifth Symphony* probably has been heard and discussed more than any other. During the Second World War the theme of the first movement became the "Victory" music for the Allied Armies. Coincidentally, its rhythm is the same used in International Morse Code for the letter "V," so that the rhythm and pitches of this fragment became the "V" for "Victory."

More importantly, however, this symphony contains a movement which is built around one of Beethoven's best fragments. Its compact, energetic rhythm becomes a driving force and its varied use defies boredom despite constant repetition. This, if you think back over the piano sonatas and their themes, was one of Beethoven's great talents.

The *Fifth Symphony* was first performed January 7, 1809, with Beethoven assisting with the conducting. Because of the length of the program and the number of new compositions requiring rehearsal, much of the music did not go well. However, the second performance, January 23, 1809, produced a better reception.

Study Procedures

The following score pages from the first movement bracket the varied uses of the first theme, the famous melodic fragment.

1. Study the score, noting the various uses of the main theme.
2. Listen to the music with the score so as to hear the theme and its use.
3. Review the printed material given in the outline chart.
4. Listen to the music with the outline chart so as to follow the themes, the divisions of the form, and the form itself.
5. Finally, listen to the composition without referring to the score or the outline chart, sensing the impact and expressiveness of the work. Reexamine this composition in relation to the descriptive material in the earlier part of the chapter.

Symphony No. 5 in c minor: First Movement (Beethoven) (Allegro con brio; sonata-allegro form)

Intro.	Statement				Development	Recapitulation				Coda
	Theme I	Bridge	Theme II	Ending phrases		Theme I	Bridge	Theme II	Ending phrases	
	A A	C	B →	X A		A A	C	B →	X	C → Y A
Famous 4-note theme played twice slowly	Same theme as intro. First portion ends with held note in violin before proceeding	Elongation of theme A played only once by horn	Played 3 times by violins, clarinets, and flute before being extended	After ending theme, theme A is heard to unify section	Introduced by horn Fragments of A in various sections and in descending and ascending directions Bridge is heard twice completely and then in fragments as a lead into →	Used with obbligato in woodwinds, ending with oboe cadenza	Same as state-ment	Violins and flutes only; heard 4 times	Same as statement; concludes differently to lead to Coda Hesitates before moving to ↑	Strong sounds; full of accents in timpani and in the rhythm
	This section repeated on some recordings									

Vᴱ SYMPHONIE

I

L. van BEETHOVEN op. 67
1770 - 1827

Heugel & Cie., Publishers, Paris.   Pocket score PH-11.   Used by permission.

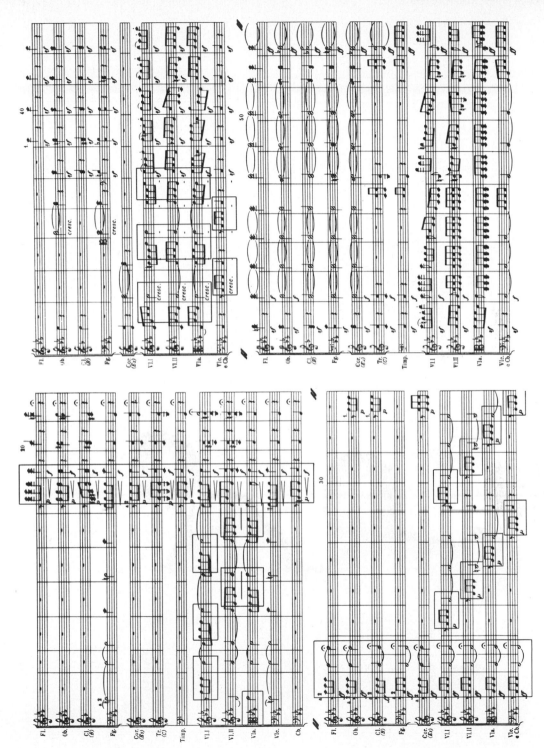

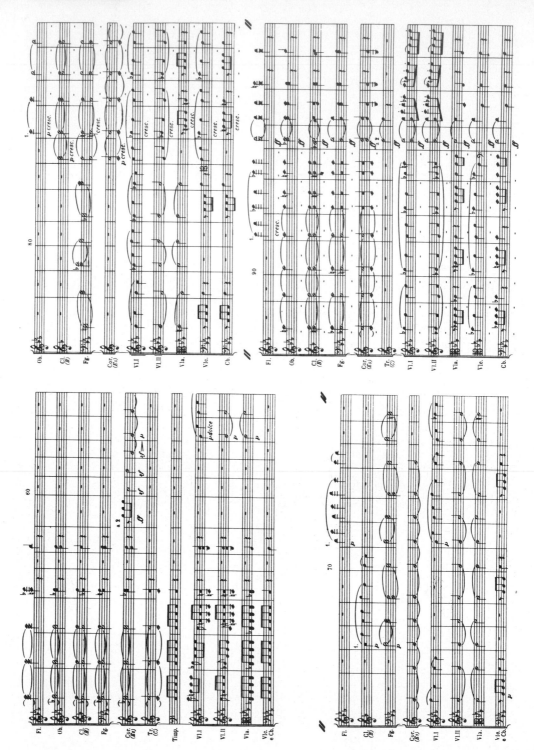

Symphony No. 1 in F Major (Shostakovich)

Shostakovich was but nineteen years of age, in fact, a student in college, when he wrote his first symphony. Because of this it might have special interest for other students. But the interest goes beyond the mere fact of prodigy, for the work exemplifies well a symphony of the twentieth century, relating contemporary idioms to the sonata-allegro form.

To many observers of the musical scene Shostakovich's talent never developed to its fullest because of necessity he directed his work to fit the Politburo's attitude toward creative works. Since communist official dictum has varied over the years, his work has not followed a direct course. In some ways this symphony seems to be the most forthright statement of his talent and feelings.

Study Procedures

1. Listen to the work following the outline chart.
2. What in the music gives you the clue that this is a product of the twentieth century?
3. What predominant feelings do you sense in the composition? How could you describe these in relation to the Beethoven? The reviewer in 1809 wrote that Beethoven's first movement was a "serious, somewhat gloomy yet fiery allegro, noble in feeling." If you agree with this statement concerning Beethoven, how would you describe the Shostakovich?
4. Had you not been told that the music you have just heard was by a Russian, would you have been able to detect this in the music? Some people believe that music betrays its geography since it is too universal; others believe that the expressions of the composer are universal but are expressed in terms of idioms typical of certain regions or nationalities. Can you defend either statement using the Shostakovich as an example?

Symphony No. 40 in g minor (Mozart)

In the early part of this chapter the point was made that thousands of symphonies had been written during the growth process of the form and style. During the latter days of the eighteenth century two composers wrote symphonies of such high quality that we still hear them regularly in concert halls today. Although the style of each composer differs and should never be confused, they both achieved a peak in the expressiveness of this form. Mozart and Haydn epitomize the heights of symphonic form during the Classic period.

Mozart, well-known to us as a composer through compositions studied earlier, was able to fuse symphonic form with the melodic writing for which he has become famous.

At the time of writing this symphony Mozart faced more problems than most men. In the summer of 1788, three years before his death and at only thirty-two years of age, Mozart was woefully in debt. His wife had given birth to their fifth child the preceding December but the sickly child had died in June.

Symphony No. 1 in F Major: First Movement (Shostakovich) (Allegretto; sonata-allegro form)

Introduction						Statement										Development		
Tri	sectional					Theme I				Theme II								
$\frac{X}{Y}$	$\frac{X}{Y}$	Z1	X1	Z	$\frac{X}{Y}$	A	A	A	A	B	B	B	B	B	B	Z/X	Z/B	A →
Trumpet on X, Bassoon on Y	Clarinet on X, pizz. cello on Y	Basses, horn trp.	Strings play fragments on X, ending with piccolo note	Violins	Strings and cellos	Clarinet	Flute and bassoon	Strings play and extend; other instruments join in for elaboration	X used as bridge to B	Flute	Clarinet with flute trill	Cellos and basses ascending into upper strings	Clarinet	Many instruments play fragments of theme; definite ending but basses hold through		Violin, bassoon	Violins; cellos, basses lead to →	Trumpet call becomes bridge which leads to Recap.; march-like fragments of A / Usual development technic used with theme A

Recapitulation						Coda			
Theme I	Theme II								
A	B	B	B	B	B	A	A	$\frac{X}{Y}$	$\frac{X}{Y}$
Violins loud but quiet immediately for →	Flute	Clarinet	Low strings	Horn and trumpet, then strings		Quietly in low instruments; loudness grows, and marchlike atmosphere returns briefly	Bassoon	Clarinet and bassoon	Clarinet, cellos; pizz. note ends mvt.

The continued ill health of his wife had caused mounting doctor bills, his own commissions had fallen off, and the subscription concerts of the summer which were to provide living expenses had failed to attract any audience and had had to be cancelled.   He and his wife had moved out of Vienna to a small suburb in order to save money.   With these problems facing him, he composed his last three symphonies, completing one every three weeks.   Unfortunately, Mozart never heard them.   One may suppose his greater attention was spent in writing letters to borrow money, caring for his wife, and trying to make arrangements for performances.

Mozart needed money so desperately that he finally wrote to a fellow member of the Masonic order.   He could not write to a nobleman, his friends were also without means, but a businessman might assist him.   His first letter to Michael Puchberg asked for 2,000 gulden, and he received 200.   Within ten days all 200 had been used, and he was writing again for a loan from the same person:

Vienna, June 27th, 1788

Most Honourable Brother of the Order
Dearest, Most Beloved Friend!

I have been expecting to go to town myself one of these days and to be able to thank you in person for the kindness you have shown me.   But now I should not even have the courage to appear before you, as I am obliged to tell you frankly that it is impossible for me to pay back so soon the money you have lent me and that I must beg you to be patient with me.   I am very much distressed that your circumstances at the moment prevent you from assisting me as much as I could wish, for my position is so serious that I am unavoidably obliged to raise money somehow.   But, good God, in whom can I confide?   In no one but you, my best friend!   If you would only be so kind as to get the money for me through some other channel.   I shall willingly pay the interest and whoever lends it to me will, I believe, have sufficient security in my character and my income.   I am only too grieved to be in such an extremity; but that is the very reason why I should like a fairly substantial sum for a somewhat longer period, I mean, in order to be able to prevent a recurrence of this state of affairs.   If you, my most worthy brother, do not help me in this predicament, I shall lose my honor and my credit, which of all things I wish to preserve.   I rely entirely on your genuine friendship and brotherly love and confidently expect that you will stand by me in word and deed.
If my wish is fulfilled, I can breathe freely again, because I shall then be able to put my affairs in order and keep them so.   Do come and see me.   I am always at home.   During the ten days since I came to live here I have done more work than in two months in my former quarters, and if such black thoughts did not come to me so often, thoughts which I banish by a tremendous effort, things would be even better, for my rooms are pleasant, comfortable, and *cheap*.   I shall not detain you any longer with my drivel but shall stop talking—and hope.
Ever your grateful servant, true friend, and Brother of the Order.

W. A. Mozart[2]

---

2 *The Letters of Mozart and His Family,* edited by Emily Anderson.   Macmillan and Co. Ltd., London, 1938, page 1363.

Although Puchberg again sent a small sum, Mozart was unable to manage his affairs well enough to repay the wine merchant.   Being an amateur musician, Puchberg had a certain sympathy for Mozart and did not press him for the money, although he had a reputation of being unsympathetic with others in money matters.   Again, in July, Mozart wrote him:

Vienna, early July, 1788

Dearest Friend and Brother of the Order!

Owing to great difficulties and complications my affairs have become so involved that it is of the utmost importance to raise some money on these two pawn broker's tickets.   In the name of our friendship I implore you to do me this favor; but you must do it immediately.   Forgive my importunity, but you know my situation.   Ah!   If only you had done what I asked you!   Do it even now—then everything will be as I desire.

Ever your
Mozart[3]

Symphony No. 40 in g minor: First Movement (Mozart) (Molto allegro; sonata-allegro form)

Statement					Development	Recapitulation					Coda
Theme I		Bridge	Theme II	Ending phrases	Theme I only	Theme I		Bridge	Theme II	Ending phrases	C
A	A	C	B B scales	A		A	A	C	B	A	A
Delicate theme	Shortened	Bolder than theme I or II	Descending theme, as is I		After 3 chords of introduction; at times theme is modulatory and fragmentary		Modulation	In high voices, then lower; longer than statement		Modulates to scales	

3 *Ibid.*, page 1364.

It was on July 25, 1788, that Mozart completed his *Symphony No. 40.* He seemed to understand the potential of the symphonic form and wrote creatively; his personal problems and concerns seem never to have influenced his creative self. For this we are in his debt.

Study Procedures

1. Listen to the work with the outline chart.
2. What in the music gives you the clue that it is of the Classical period?
3. What differences do you hear in the style of Mozart as compared to that of Beethoven? To that of Shostakovich? How do the thematic materials differ? What is different in the orchestration? Review some music from the Mozart opera *The Marriage of Figaro,* and then write a statement indicating wherein these two compositions sound similar; be sure to discuss musical characteristics.
4. Many consider Mozart the master of form, that his compositions bespeak an all but perfect proportion, and that the melodies and feelings never suffer because the form is so carefully adhered to. Listen again to the first movement, attending to the balance in the form. Would you agree with the above statements?

SECOND MOVEMENTS (SLOW)

It was customary for the second movement of the symphony to offer a contrast in tempo and become the lyric section. Some later composers have altered this order so that the second movement is the scherzo. We will discuss slow movements whether they be placed second or third.

Symphony No. 5 in e minor (Tchaikovsky)

One hundred years after Mozart wrote his fortieth, Peter Tchaikovsky wrote his *Fifth Symphony.* Tchaikovsky, a well-known composer throughout all Europe and America, had not been received as well as Wagner in his homeland. Requests for him to conduct his own music had caused him to travel throughout Europe. His letters are filled with regrets that he had to be away from his native land, his home, and friends. Not having married, Tchaikovsky wrote often to his sister and her children. Another recipient of many letters was Nadezhda von Meck, wealthy widow of a railway enterpriser, whose commissions led to a voluminous correspondence throughout the last seventeen years of Tchaikovsky's life as she came to the financial support of his creative efforts. Shortly after he completed the *Fifth Symphony* he wrote to her:

December 1888

After two performances of my new Symphony in Petersburg, and one in Prague, I have come to the conclusion that it is a failure. There is something repellent, something superfluous, patchy and insincere which the public instinctively recognizes. It was obvious to me that the ovations I received were prompted more by my earlier work, and that the Symphony itself did not really please the audience. The consciousness of this brings me a sharp twinge of self-dissatisfaction. Am I really played out, as they say? Can I merely repeat and ring the changes on my earlier idiom? Last night I looked through *our* Symphony (No. 4). What a difference! How immeasurably superior it is! It is very, very sad![4]

After the new year Tchaikovsky started on a new tour, most of which was through Germany. His music was received well there despite the musical feud between the camps of Brahms and Wagner. Despite his earlier feelings, Tchaikovsky conducted the *Fifth Symphony* on the tour and it went well. To his favorite nephew, Bob Davidov, he wrote the following letter:

Hanover, March 5th, 1889

The concert at Hamburg has taken place, and I may congratulate myself on a great success. The Fifth Symphony was magnificently played, and I like it far better now, after having held a bad opinion of it for some time. Unfortunately, the Russian Press continues to ignore me. With the exception of my nearest and dearest, no one will ever hear of my success. In the daily papers here one reads long telegrams about the Wagner performances in Russia. Certainly I am not a second Wagner, but it would be desirable for Russia to learn how I have been received in Germany.[5]

History has a way of making amends, and Tchaikovsky's lack of stature in Russia was offset by his reception in other parts of the world. Thus, he was invited to conduct at the opening of Carnegie Hall in New York in the summer of 1891. He accepted because the excellent fee promised would permit him to own a house and a small piece of land for the first time in his life. His diaries of the trip to the United States are too detailed and long to include in this book; however, they make excellent reading because of his ability to describe the American with objectivity and some humor.

Study Procedures

1. Listen to the second movement of this symphony, observing the outline chart.
2. Tchaikovsky's music has often been considered an excellent example of the Romantic period. Describe in your own words the romantic characteristics you hear in the music. What are the musical idioms you hear which designate to you that the work comes from the Romantic period?
3. Discuss the use of instruments in this movement; the use of melodic line; the use of rhythm both in the melodic line and in the accompaniment.

---

[4] *The Life and Letters of Peter Ilich Tchaikovsky*, edited by Rosa Newmarch. Dodd, Mead and Company, New York, 1904, page 575.
[5] *Ibid.*, page 581.

Symphony No. 5 in e minor: Second Movement (Tchaikovsky) (Andante cantabile; three-part form)

Intro.	Part I					Part II				Part I			Coda	
	M		O	M	O	X	Y	XY	Trans.	M		O		
	A A	B B	C	A A	C' C'	X	Y	XY	Trans.	A' A' B' B'	A' A	C C	Trans.	C'
Slow, smooth chords in low strings	Horn solo one of the most poignant in the literature of the instrument	Horn con't. to spin theme and increase intensity	Oboe changes mood but horn maintains a secondary roll; clarinet bassoon, and basses prepare for →	Cellos play theme, other instruments add counter-melodies to increase emotion	Violins sing this theme and extend it as it climbs higher in pitch to fall to its cadence	Clarinet, then bassoon play new theme which maintains mood and effect	Strings introduce A theme, similar to X but with minor contrast	Bassoon returns to original theme of this section but strings persist in Y; intensity mounts	Theme from first mvt. is heard in trp.; pizz. chords prepare for return to theme A	Same theme as Part I in strings; many counter-melodies assist in providing contrast to Part I and adding new emotions	Wood Winds begin but full orch. takes over with bridge material for →	Strings sing and extend this theme to increase intensity, then taper to an impending cadence which fails to arrive	Theme of first mvt. again interrupts; theme C returns to remind us of the general nature of the mvt.; clarinet offers final phrases	

4. As a special project, read the diary of Tchaikovsky's visit to America.[6] What does this diary tell you about the man? About his music? Considering his diary, would you have expected him to write music such as this? Why or why not?

Symphony No. 9 in e minor (Dvořák)

For years this symphony was known as No. 5. Recently a more accurate numbering has been assigned, although the older numbering may still be found on some recordings. Most of the reference materials of the past ten years make use of the correct numbering.

Dvořák was a Bohemian, and remained true to this national spirit all of his life. When he was twenty-five, he had published but one song. By the time he was fifty, he had been invited to become director of a new National Conservatory of Music recently established by Mrs. Jeanette Thurber in New York City. Some forward-looking persons in the United States recognized that although talent existed in our country, almost all of it went wanting, since most young persons could not follow the customary procedure of traveling to Europe for study. Mrs. Thurber, the wife of a wealthy grocer, not only accepted the idea of developing music talent locally but used her money to establish and operate a conservatory of music to further the aim of American music.

She was determined to acquire a well-known composer as director of her school. When she first contacted Dvořák he was reluctant to accept, since he had just that year signed a contract to teach composition at the Prague Conservatory. Mrs. Thurber's persistence prevailed, and he came to New York in 1892, just a year after Tchaikovsky's visit.

Because of the popularity of this work, particularly in our country, much has been written and said concerning the *Symphony No. 9* and its relation to our indigenous music. Dvořák himself seemed to foster such statements by placing the phrase "From the New World" on the title page, by inviting one of his students at the National Conservatory, Harry Burleigh, a black, to sing for him on several occasions, by claiming that his visit to Buffalo Bill's Wild West show had had some affect upon the music, and by claiming that the American soil had influenced his thought beneficially. Those who are prone to make associations in music, quickly hear repeated references to black and Indian music. However, scholars who know well the musical characteristics of both cultures, recognize almost no similarities between the music of Dvořák and native American music.

When writing of this matter, Dvořák seemed to take a more reserved and cautious approach:

> It is this spirit which I have tried to reproduce in my new symphony. I have not actually used any of the melodies. I have simply written original themes

---

[6] The diary of his trip to the United States may be found in *The Diaries of Tchaikovsky*, Wladimir Lakond, translator. W. W. Norton and Company, Inc., New York, 1945, pages 299–336.

embodying the peculiarities of the Indian music, and using these themes as subjects, have developed them with all the resources of modern rhythms, harmony, counterpoint, and orchestral colour.[7]

But Dvořák could have had a greater influence than he realized, had he pursued with greater intensity an idea which he mentioned in an article appearing in Harper's Magazine, February 1895:

> The music of the people is like a rare and lovely flower growing amidst encroaching weeds. Thousands pass it, while others trample it under foot and thus the chances are that it will perish before it is seen by the one discriminating spirit who will prize it above all else. The fact that no one has as yet arisen to make the most of it does not prove that nothing is there.[8]

Dvořák began work on his symphony during December 1892, and completed it May 24, 1893. It was premiered at Carnegie Hall in New York, December 16, 1893, and Dvořák was present, bowing to the enthusiastic audience from his box. Other performances followed soon after, until it became well-known throughout our country. It was also received well in Europe.

Dvořák remained in New York as director of the school until April 1895, when he returned to his native land, whereupon he repudiated his earlier statements that the symphony had been based upon black and Indian music. Although his symphony may not contain influences from America, at least it is not as Bohemian as some of his other music. But the journey to America was not unproductive. Here he composed his most famous and well-known symphony as well as numerous other compositions, three of which have become well-known as quality items: the *String Quartet in F Major,* the *Biblical Songs,* and the *Cello Concerto in b minor.*

Study Procedures

1. Listen to the second movement of this symphony with the outline chart.
2. Both the Dvořák and the Tchaikovsky make use of solo instruments during the early portions of the movements. What is the difference in the use of the instruments? How does the melodic content of the themes differ?
3. Both of these movements are built to appeal to the emotions of the listener. Which one seems more expressive to you? Why?
4. Considering the discussion of influences given above, do you believe that the Dvořák movement is more suggestive of nationalistic influences than the Tchaikovsky? Why do you agree or disagree?

---

[7] *Antonin Dvořák,* John Clapham. St. Martin's Press, New York, 1966, page 87.
[8] *Ibid.,* page 86.

Symphony No. 9 in e minor: Second Movement (Dvořák) (Largo; three-part form)

Intro.	Part I						Part II				Episode (bridge and contrast)		Part I			Coda
	A b	A' →	Bridge	B	A'	Ending phrases	X X	Y	X X'	Y	Z	F	A	B	A	
Slow brass chords crescendo to a climax	Eng. horn solo well-known theme, songlike in character	Clarinet extends to five, a balance and more complete finish	Chords of intro. in woodwind and horn	Violins and cellos extend theme	Eng. horn returns; bssn. is added for color; clar. and vlns. extend	From A, muted horns	Flute and oboe play this more florid melody	Clarinet plays a slow theme as a contrast to X; basses pizz.	Counter-melody in oboe gives a new coloration; vlns. extend this to lead to	Violins, with cellos in tremelo underneath.	Oboe, in gay dance tune, offers bridge and contrast; this is interrupted by →	Fanfare theme from first mvt. in brass	Eng. horn returns to theme A	Violins; hesitation brings a greater weight to this folklike melody	Solo violin and solo cello begin, leading to full string section; single line completes section	Return of introductory material; quiet ending in strings

Symphony No. 40 in g minor (Mozart)

A different approach to the second movement may be heard in the Mozart *Symphony No. 40*. This famous movement employs the sonata-allegro design rather than the song and trio design used by Romantic composers.

Study Procedures

1. Listen to the Mozart second movement, following the chart outline.
2. Compare the style of music of Mozart with that of Tchaikovsky and Dvořák. What is the difference in orchestration? In the type of theme? In the handling of the themes? In the effect upon the listener? Why might a person prefer to listen to the Mozart rather than the other movements? Why might a person prefer to listen to the Romantic composers rather than Mozart?
3. Consider the difference in the type of musical ideas which each composer expresses. Romantic composers more quickly indicate their emotional concerns in an obvious manner. Mozart becomes expressive in his own way. What is the difference in the feelings which you have after listening to each movement? If these are difficult to verbalize, can you relate your feelings to art? To color? To movement?

THIRD MOVEMENTS (DANCE-TYPE)

The third movement of symphonies originally was a minuet. Beethoven retained the dance form but broadened the mode of expression by substituting a scherzo. Later composers placed the scherzo as a second movement in some compositions. For our study the type of movement is more important than its location.

Symphony No. 5 in B flat Major: Second Movement (Prokofiev)

The first performance of this symphony in Moscow, on January 13, 1945, came near the ending of the Second World War. Prior to the concert word was received that the Russian army had been successful in a battle on the Vistula. While the orchestra began the first movement a cannon salute was still being heard from the army barracks on the outskirts of the city. Although not necessarily linked, the two events created an emotional impact upon those present.

On November 9 and 10, 1945, the Boston Symphony introduced this work to our country. One critic wrote that it burst more like a bonbon than a bombshell over New York. (Was he being influenced in his choice of words by the ending of the war, or by the events under which the first performance took place in Moscow?) He continued that he did not wish to disparage the work because it was beautifully orchestrated, cleverly linked together, and packed with wit and invention.

Symphony No. 40 in g minor: Second Movement (Mozart) (Andante; sonata-allegro form)

Statement				Development	Recapitulation			
Theme I		Bridge	Theme II →		Theme I		Bridge	Theme II →
A	A	C A	B		A A'		C' A	B
	With Woodwind obbligato; ending melody in lower voices	Strings alternate with winds	Strings, then winds	Ending figures	Built from part of theme I and inverse figures of bridge	Modulation; shorter than in statement		With Woodwind obbligato	Ending figure

With such a review it is possible that the writer missed the intent of the composer. Prokofiev had written in a magazine article: "Work on this symphony was very important to me, since it marked my return to the symphonic form after a long interval. I regard the Fifth Symphony as the culmination of a long period of my creative life. I conceived it as a symphony of the grandeur of the human spirit."[9]

Prokofiev was pointing out that his earlier symphonies had been allied with stage works, but the fifth was in no way programmatic. His earlier symphonies had even contained themes from his ballets or music for the theater. Nor had he written a symphony for sixteen years. His skills in orchestration gleaned over that period, his emotional maturity brought about partly by age and partly by the events of the Second World War, led him to realize that this music was the "culmination of a long period of my creative life."

Study Procedures

1. Listen to this movement with the outline chart.
2. Considering Prokofiev's statement of a "symphony of the grandeur of the human spirit," how would you describe this second movement? Which characteristics make themselves evident to you?
3. We have heard movements by two Russian composers of the twentieth century. Compare the style of writing, the musical meanings, musical depths, and expressiveness which you witness in the Shostakovich and the Prokofiev.

Symphony No. 9 in e minor (Dvořák)

The third movement of the Dvořák symphony is a fascinating scherzo, and is partially responsible for the initial impact of the work as well as its popularity with listeners and performers alike.

Study Procedures

1. Listen to the third movement of the Dvořák with the outline chart.
2. Having heard two movements which are scherzos, how would you describe the general characteristics of the scherzo, and its role in the symphony? Why would a scherzo be found in the symphony? Would the work have the same meaning and impact if the scherzo were omitted? Could a different kind of movement be substituted?

Symphony No. 40 in g minor (Mozart)

In order to understand the development of the symphony one should hear at least one symphonic minuet. The third movement from the Mozart *Symphony No. 40*

---

[9] *Prokofiev*, Israel V. Nestyev. Stanford University Press, Stanford, Calif., 1960, page 365.

Symphony No. 5 in B flat Major: Second Movement (Prokofiev) (Allegro marcato; song and trio form)

Song						Trio					Song				
A	A'	A''	A'''	B	A'''' Coda	X	Y	X'	Y	X	Bridge	A	A''''	B Violins	A' →
Violins	Violins	Oboe		Violins, with trumpet in background	Violins	Oboe and clarinet;	Violas and clarinet;	Trumpet and violins	Full orch.;	Repeat of first X;	Chords in pizz. strings, with trp. moving in background	Fragments in various instru.,	Violins	Violins	Oboe, clar., foll- owed by strings
Background rhythm; clarinet answered by violins	Variations of A theme; makes use of octave displacement, a favorite device of twentieth century composers			background		rhythm ceases, only to begin again with Y	singing melody of a semi-jazz nature, becomes louder and more complex		rhythm has a semi- Oriental sound	ending seems imminent, only to begin again		tempo regained			Ext. to driv- ing end- ing
This section acts as a theme and a set of variations.					other variations added										
Rhythm and syncopation evident throughout															

Symphony No. 9 in e minor: Third Movement (Dvořák) (Scherzo, Molto vivace; song and trio form)

Intro.	Song								Bridge	Trio			Trans.	Intro.	Song	Coda
	A (minor)		B (major)				A (minor)			X X	Y	Y' X				
‖:	A	A':‖	B	B	B'	B	A	A'				‖: :‖				
Loud rhythmic and melodic fragments set mood for mvt.	Oboe and clar. state theme in dialogue	Violins, with counter-rhythm and line in horns; repeats from beginning	Tempo slows; flute sings new, smooth melody		Flute and oboe	Cellos, bassoons	Violins	Climax of this section	Cellos, then violas sweep up and down on arpeggiated theme	Dance theme in woodwind	Strings in a trilly theme; extended to return to X	Last part of Y and X repeated		As beginning	Same as first part but without repeats	Bridge theme in horns	Theme of first mvt. quickly stated to end mvt.

X

Y

A

B

B'

is an excellent example of the classic minuet as part of a symphony.   Remember that this was not the dance minuet, but a synthesis of the dance form used in a concert manner.   The greatness of Mozart lies in his ability to make a concert piece using the form and still not lose its melodic quality which originally appealed to the dancers, nor lose its rhythmic intent which to many epitomized a large hall with gracefully moving couples.

Study Procedures

1. Listen to the third movement of the Mozart, following the outline chart.
2. Considering the difference of time and the period in which each work was written, compare the impact of the minuet with that of the scherzo.   What reasons can you give for changing the symphony in this manner?

Symphony No. 40 in g minor: Third Movement (Mozart)
(Menuetto, Allegro; song and trio form)

Song						Trio				Song		
A A	B	A' ending	B	A' ending		X X	Y Y	A	B	A' ending		
Minor sound; although titled menuet, it has a more robust sound, sometimes considered Germanic	Major sound	Ending, mostly in woodwind				Thin orchestration featuring various instruments	Begins with low strings	Minor	Major			

FOURTH MOVEMENTS

You will recall that in many examples the final movement of the concerto used the rondo form.   Because of the musical weight needed, and because of the overall length of the work, the symphony more often uses the sonata-allegro form for its last movement.   For many composers this means that three of the four movements have been based upon that one form.

Symphony No. 1 in C Major: Fourth Movement (Beethoven) (Adagio, Allegro molto e vivace; sonata-allegro form)

Intro.	Statement				Development	Recapitulation			Coda	
	Theme I ($\frac{A}{an.}$ $\frac{A}{con.}$)	Bridge (C)	Theme II (B →)	Ending Phrases (→ X)		Theme I ($\frac{A}{an.}$ $\frac{A}{con.}$)	Theme II (B →)	Ending phrases (X)	Theme I ($\frac{A}{an.}$ $\frac{A}{con.}$)	Ending phrases (Y)
Long chord; slow scale fragments	Strings pre-dominate Woodwind	Longer chords with descending scales; lower pitched instruments on ascending scales	Lilting theme in violins	Punctuated chords followed by ascending scale passages	Fragments of theme A; scale passages used in ascending and descending directions in various sections; ending rhythm X used for emphasis	Similar to statement; changes tonal center to move to theme II		Ends with scales and long chords		Woodwinds, then full orch.

This section repeats on some recordings

$\frac{A}{an.}$ = Antecedant or first portion of theme I

$\frac{A}{con.}$ = Consequent or latter portion of theme I

Symphony No. 40 in g minor: Fourth Movement (Mozart) (Allegro assai; sonata-allegro form)

Statement				Development	Recapitulation			
Theme I	Bridge	Theme II	Ending phrase	Theme I	Theme I	Bridge	Theme II	Ending phrases
A A	C	B B	Clarinet		A	C	B B	A
Contrast of soft and loud; ascending theme	Long compared to theme I; theme extended to give weight and balance	Less vigorous and more melodic; descending in character	Uses second part of theme I	Dialogue between sections or instruments using phrases or motives of theme I; part 1 of theme predominates	Shorter than in statement	Shorter than statement	Clarinet	Uses part I of theme with scales

Symphony No. 5 in e minor: Fourth Movement (Tchaikovsky) (Andante maestoso, Allegro vivace; sonata-allegro form)

Intro.	Statement				Development	Recapitulation				Coda	
	A	Bridge	B	Ending phrases		A	Bridge	B	Ending phrases		Ending phrases
gg' h gg' h Tr.	a a→	e e f f	b b'	g g→	a' a a/b · b	a" a a"' → e a"'	e e f f	b b'	g	g g' · g→ e b	Mt
Fanfare theme from first mvt. in 2 parts: strings (g); brass (h); repeated by winds, with strings playing triplets	Fast theme built on descending line	Oboe, flute play a lilting theme taken from A; strings play another modification of A	Singing theme in winds repeated with modification in strings	Fanfare theme played with scale passages in strings and winds, leading immediately to →	Increase of tension through a mix of A and B themes; B theme in low voices with countermelody in winds · In winds; leads to a slower tempo; softer sounds of oboe lead to a crashing chord, ending the development	Theme A in bass, with an inversion in the violins; loud again	Almost same as statement	Almost exact repeat of statement	Strings persist in their scale passages while brass introduces fanfare theme	Strings, introduced by winds · Trumpets — Version of bridge material plus a short reworking of theme B	Main theme of 1st mvt. in trumpets and horns

g   Andante maestoso   *mf*   *f*

a   Allegro vivace   *f*   *ff*

b   *mf*   *f*

e   *mf*   *p*   *f*   Derived from

Main Theme   *ffff*   *fff*

528

Study Procedures

1. Listen to each of the above movements, using the outline charts.
2. These three works show a progression in symphonic style as well as in use of musical elements. How would you describe the difference in style of the three movements? What differences in melodic content do you hear? In accompaniment rhythm? In melodic rhythm? In the use of harmony? Is one composer more dissonant than the other two, or are they all similar?
3. Considering the problem of balance within the entire work, generally how would you describe the fourth movement? (The form offers a fast first movement, a slow second, a dancelike third, and a rapid fourth.) What is the esthetic balance involved here, and does it have merit or could it be beneficially altered?

SUMMARY

The symphony is a large form. We have studied its various movements in order to understand the form and its meaning, to appreciate the changes which have taken place over the years, and to make study logically possible. You should now be ready to consider the entire form by listening to a complete symphony. First, choose one which is familiar, at least in part, so that you may hear again movements which are somewhat familiar, and so that you may become better acquainted with them. Later, you will have opportunities to hear new compositions.

Study Procedures

1. Choose one of the compositions we have studied, and listen to the complete symphony in one sitting. The Mozart *Symphony No. 40* would be a good choice, since this work is not long, it moves along easily, and you have already heard most of the movements of the work.
2. We have listened to only one movement of the well known Beethoven *Symphony No. 5.* Listen to this symphony in its entirety. Can you begin to understand why this work is so popular all over the world? What does it express to you?
3. Having heard two symphonies completely, can you describe the merits of the form as compared to other instrumental forms which we have studied? Why is the symphony considered by many to be the epitome of instrumental expressiveness? To many the symphony is an overly long work. After your study, why might you disagree with this statement if you consider one composition which you felt was of high quality?
4. Prokofiev wrote a *Classical Symphony*. This classic form contains contemporary melodic lines, rhythms, and orchestration. Since this is a short work, listen to this composition on your own and write a descriptive and expressive statement about each movement.
5. Another contemporary symphony which might be of interest to some is the Randall Thompson *Symphony No. 2*. This work combines jazz idioms within the symphonic format.
6. Some contemporary composers have experimented with major alterations in the form of the symphony. Sibelius, writing in 1925, composed his *Symphony No. 7* in one movement. Although one may refer to subsections as statement or development, the work

is not sectionalized, and if divided can be so considered only as a study device. In other words, the composer attempted to exemplify the same expressive qualities in one movement that other composers have done in three or four. Listen to the composition, and decide for yourself if this revision of the form has been satisfactory. Why would other composers not wish to use this type of modification? In order to assist with your listening, the following formal outline could serve as a guide:

Statement—89 measures (6 measures after E in the score)
Development—44 measures (6 measures after I in the score)
Transition—8 measures (15 measures after I in the score)
Scherzo—66 measures (14 before L)
Transition—14 measures (to letter L)
Development—30 measures (to 4 measures before N)
Transition—16 measures (to 13 measures after N)
New Statement—57 measures (to 9 before Q)
Subtheme—28 measures (to R)
Restatement—66 measures (to Vivace)
Second Scherzo—40 measures (to Presto)
Transition—27 measures (to Adagio)
Recapitulation—50 measures (to end)

Bibliography—Chapter 25

ABRAHAM, GERALD, *The Music of Sibelius*. New York: W. W. Norton and Company, Inc., 1947.

ANDERSON, EMILY, ed., *The Letters of Mozart and His Family*. London: Macmillan and Company Ltd., 1938.

BERLIOZ, HECTOR, *A Critical Study of Beethoven's Nine Symphonies*. London: William Reeves, 1958.

CARSE, ADAM, *18th Century Symphonies*. London: Augener Ltd., 1951.

CLAPHAM, JOHN, *Antonin Dvořák*. New York: St. Martin's Press, 1966.

FORBES, ELLIOT, ed., *Beethoven's Symphony No. 5 in c minor*. New York: W. W. Norton and Company, Inc., 1971.

HAGGIN, B. H., *A Book of the Symphony*. London: Oxford University Press, 1937.

HOPKINS, ANTONY, *Talking About Symphonies*. Belmont, Calif.: Wadsworth Publishing Company, Inc., 1961.

HUGHES, GERVASE, *Dvořák, His Life and Music*. New York: Dodd, Mead and Co., 1967.

LAKOND, WLADIMIR, trans., *The Diaries of Tchaikovsky*. New York: W. W. Norton and Company, Inc., 1945.

LEVEY, MICHAEL, *The Life and Death of Mozart*. New York: Stein and Day, 1971.

MARTYNOV, IVAN, *Dmitri Shostakovich*. New York: Philosophical Library, 1947.

NESTYEV, ISRAEL V., *Prokofiev*. Stanford, Calif.: Stanford University Press, 1960.

NEWMARCH, ROSA, ed., *The Life and Letters of Peter Ilich Tchaikovsky*. London: Dodd, Mead and Company, 1924.

SAINT-FOIX, GEORGES DE, *The Symphonies of Mozart*. New York: Alfred A. Knopf, 1949.

ULRICH, HOMER, *Symphonic Music*. New York: Columbia University Press, 1961.

Recordings—Chapter 25

Beethoven	*Symphony No. 5 in c minor*	Szell, Cleveland	Epic BC-1282
Dvořák	*Symphony No. 9 in e minor ("New World")*	Toscanini, NBC	Victor LM-1778
Mozart	*Symphony No. 40 in g minor*	Steinberg, Pittsburgh	Capitol PAO-8432
Prokofiev	*Classical Symphony*	Ormandy, Philadelphia	Columbia ML-2035
Prokofiev	*Symphony No. 5 in B flat Major*	Leinsdorf, Boston	Victor LSC-2707
Shostakovich	*Symphony No. 1 in F Major*	Ormandy, Philadelphia	Columbia ML-5452
Sibelius	*Symphony No. 7 in C Major*	Ormandy, Philadelphia	Columbia ML-5675
Tchaikovsky	*Symphony No. 5 in e minor*	Monteux, Boston	Victor LM-2239
Thompson	*Symphony No. 2*	Dixon, Vienna	Desto D-406

Section J   *Links Between Form and Narrative*

Chapter 26

The Overture

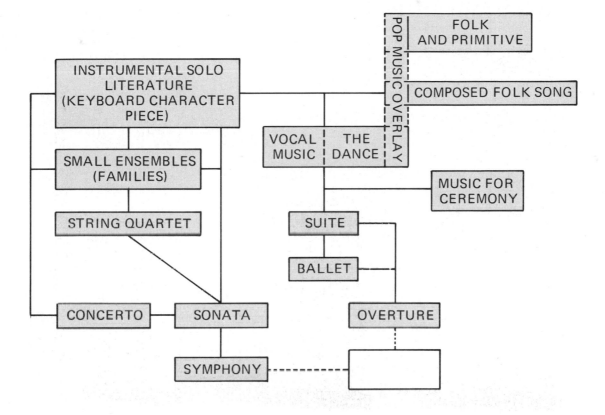

The overture has been a favorite form with listener and composer alike for centuries partly because of its brevity, and partly because of its thematic variety. Historically, it looks back to the opera and the ballet, relates to the symphony, but can be as individualistic as the composer wishes.

Like the symphony, it began as a fanfare announcing the beginning of a drama or a dance presentation. In its early days it was a sung prologue explaining a locale or the background of an event to the observer; other times it was dedicatory in nature. When it grew to an independent instrumental selection preceding a dramatic work, two types evolved: the Italian overture with its fast-slow-fast structure, and the French overture with a slow-fast organization.

The Italian overture expanded into the symphony; this was discussed in Chapter 25.   The French overture remained closely aligned with the dramatic events of the theater and became an introduction to the opera, oratorio, or cantata.   As other types of overtures developed the dramatic element remained closely tied to the form, so that even in cases where it preceded no dramatic event, it could be affected by one or allude to one.

PRELUDE TO DRAMATIC EVENTS

When writing a complete short composition to precede a dramatic event, composers usually attempted to establish a mood for that which was to follow.   Although content became the creative province of the composer, various formal structures aided with this intent.

French Overtures

The original French overture contained two divisions; the first was a slow, melodic section, homophonic in texture with simple organization.   The fast section which followed, often moderately fugal, created its energy from speed as well as from the polyphonic structure and textures.   In all parts of Europe these compositions were most often used as the introduction to a dramatic musical event.   The overture to *Messiah* by Handel exemplifies well this type of overture:

Slow		Fast	Ritarded ending
A	A	B	
Modestly loud	Soft	Loud	Loud
		polyphonic	homophonic

At times the ritarded ending of the fugal second section has been considered a third part of the form; however, it should not be so considered in most cases.

Classical Forms

Even though connected with a dramatic work, some composers wrote overtures in forms usually attributed to the symphony.   Thus, the overture could employ the sonata-allegro form, the three-part song form, or the rondo.   Most often the

Wolfgang Amadeus Mozart, painting by Johann Neidl (Courtesy of Austrian National Library).

sonata-allegro form was chosen. An excellent example of an overture using a classic form was written by Mozart for his opera *The Marriage of Figaro*. We have listened to parts of the opera and have learned of its background. Today, the overture sparkles and attracts as it has for almost 200 years, and is heard just as often alone in concert as it is when performed as a prelude to the opera. It has been transcribed for band and played by many college and high school groups.

Mozart refuted tradition and focused upon only one tempo: fast.

Exposition		Recapitulation
A A bridge theme, bridge theme, B B	4 meas. of violins instead of devel- opment	A A bridge, bridge, B B

As you see by the diagram, Mozart used the sonatina form rather than the more involved and developed sonata-allegro. This kept the overture lighter and shorter, and better fits the mood and character of the opera.

Potpourri

In an attempt to unify the overture with the opera, composers incorporated into the overture themes sung later in the opera. Although the French or the classic form could have been used, it more often became customary for the composer to appropriate a number of his themes diversely. For example, some composers would alternate tempos, some would alternate musical pulsations so that duple sections interchanged with triple meters, while other composers relied upon the character of the music to offer the necessary changes of mood.

When a number of melodies were placed one after the other with little concern for form, it came to be known as "Potpourri," which actually means a mixture of incongruous or disparate elements. When used before an opera or Broadway musical, the listener has an opportunity to hear some of the melodies which will be sung later; consequently, when they appear in the production they are not completely unfamiliar. It also entails the added advantage to the composer of requiring no new creative effort but only a rearrangement.

The overture to *Carmen* fits this description. It consists of three main themes from the opera: first, the parade theme from the fourth act as the toreadors enter the bullring; second, the "Toreador Song" from the second act; lastly, the theme of "fate" associated with Carmen throughout the opera. Although the first two themes are similar in style, all three parts are easily recognizable.

THE CONCERT OVERTURE

If the overture indicated the mood of a dramatic event either through new material in a specified form or by using themes to be heard later, why not a description of mood without attachment to a dramatic event? Thus, the overture came to be a concert piece in its own right. The title, and hence the music, could propose conflict, action, a mood, or general character. In this manner it became a type of music intending to suggest specific ideas to the mind rather than "absolute" music, the latter being free from extramusical implications, while the former usually relates to pictorial or poetic ideas. The concert overture became a favorite with symphony orchestras and later with school and semiprofessional groups. Thousands of these compositions have been written, many by well-known composers, and accepted as quality compositions. We will examine but a few.

French Style

Berlioz wrote a concert overture in this slow-fast style. The two melodies used are a love song and a saltarello, the latter a gay dance of the Italian peasants.

The *Roman Carnival Overture* was composed for one of his Paris concerts in 1844.[1] An entry from his diary explains something about the overture as well as about the man himself:

> When I had written the *Carnaval romain* overture, in which the theme of the allegro is a saltarello, Habeneck (conductor of the Berlioz unsuccessful opera containing the same saltarello) happened to be in the green room of the Herz concert hall the evening that this overture was to be played for the first time. He had heard that we had rehearsed it in the morning without the wind instruments, part of the band having been called off for the National Guard. "Good," said he to himself. "There will certainly be a catastrophe at the concert this evening. I must be there." On my arrival, indeed, I was surrounded on the orchestra by all the wind players, who were in terror at the idea of having to play an overture of which they did not know a note. "Don't be afraid," I said. "The parts are correct; you all know your jobs; watch my baton as often as you can, count your bars correctly, and it will be all right."
>
> Not a single mistake occurred. I launched the allegro in the whirlwind time of the Transteverine dancers. The public cried "Bravo." We played the overture over again; it was even better done the second time. And as I passed back through the green room, where Habeneck stood looking a little disappointed, I just flung these few words at him: "That is how it ought to go!" to which he took care to make no reply.[2]

After a second playing the themes of the overture will be heard more clearly. The speed of the dance makes it difficult to comprehend the form upon only one hearing.

Slow	Fast			Coda
A B A B A	X Y Z	X Y Z	A Z	X A Y Z
			A	

Classical Forms

When intended as a concert selection the overture could employ the sonata-allegro form and still suggest pictorial or poetic ideas. Beethoven's *Egmont Overture* excellently exemplifies such a type. This work, originally written as incidental music for the Goethe play *Egmont,* satisfies classic form. The complete work fits

---

1 Although both of these melodies were used by Berlioz in an earlier opera (*Benvenuto Cellini*), he considered this a different composition, since it employs a different form than originally conceived. The tunes never were used in the overture to his opera.
2 *Memoirs of Hector Berlioz,* translated by Rachel Holmes and Eleanor Holmes, rev. by Ernest Newman. Alfred A. Knopf, Inc., New York, 1932, pages 222–223.

the framework of the French overture, with its slow section at the beginning followed by a fast section, while the latter uses sonata-allegro form.

Beethoven intended his music to portray the feelings and emotions of the freedom-loving Count Egmont as he led the people of the Netherlands in revolt against the suppressions of the ruling Spanish. Although we may not hear these exact conflicts in the music, we do sense a mood and respond to its general character.

Introduction		Exposition	(Con't.)
From Theme B	Theme A	Theme B	Closing
1–24 —→	25–81 —→	82–97 —→	98–115

Development	Recapitulation			Coda
Mostly theme A	A	B	Closing	
116–156 —→	157 224	225 240	241 286	287–end

William Schuman's contemporary *American Festival Overture* follows classical form. Once president of Juilliard School of Music in New York and later director of Lincoln Center, Mr. Schuman writes complex and intricate music. Although this overture begins on a simple three-note theme taken from a street call of his childhood, there is nothing childish about the work, its orchestration, or its content. This is a concert overture based upon a three-part form, but each part carries the complexities of a major concert work for a large orchestra. The flavor is definitely American, but the piece portrays feelings of action and mood of a well-trained American composer with complex musical thoughts which match our times.

A—Based on a three-note theme and scale passages; severe sounds with a fast tempo
bridge—Slowing of tempo
B'—Fast tempo regained but fugal in nature; strings only: middle strings introduce fugue, followed by high strings then low strings, entrances brilliant but brittle
B"—Woodwind with fugue, strings in flowing lines; short section
bridge—Brass enters; tempo slows again
A'—Tempo regained; flavor and coloration of first section. Same three-note theme is heard but different treatment of material; complex sonorities and interesting woodwind colorations

The general flavor of the work as indicated by the title is festive, with the brilliance and dissonance of American life subtly conveyed throughout.

Potpourri

Although the potpourri overture more often contains a collection of dissimilar elements, its various parts can be of a similar character or tempo. Brahms wrote one of the most popular and famous of such overtures in appreciation of his receiving an honorary doctorate from Breslau University. His composition contains a number of student college songs interspersed with independent material to give unity and substance to the whole.

Numerous stories abound concerning the *Academic Festival Overture.* One relates that the faculty of the University expressed dismay and disgruntlement that Brahms would write a work using frivolous material, particularly student drinking songs. Although there seems to be no written record of such feelings, this attitude could easily be understood, since one of the tunes antecedes our child's song "The Farmer in the Dell." We do know from Brahms's letters that he was dissatisfied with the title and asked his publisher to suggest another; Brahms wished to stress the impression that the music was gay, and he referred to it as a "laughing overture."

Johannes Brahms (Courtesy of Austrian National Library).

The four student songs are shown below. The music will assist you in recognizing them. Sixty-three measures elapse before the entrance of the first: "Wir hatten gebauet"; Brahms composed thirty-nine more measures before introducing the second tune, "Der Landesvater"; almost immediately the gay freshman song "Was kommt" separates it from a reentrance of "Der Landesvater"; lastly, the famous "Gaudeamus igitur" builds a strong conclusion.

Study Procedures

1. Following the outline charts, listen to each of the compositions discussed in the text material. Be sure that you understand the differences between a French, a classic, and a potpourri overture.
2. Listen to the Toccata which begins the Monteverdi opera *Orfeo*. This short prelude will help you understand the early overture.

Wir hatten gebauet [3]

August von Binzer, 1819   Folk tune

Freely Translated
A house we have raised, a strong stately house.
Within we trust in God
through lightning, storm, and fear;
Within we trust in God
through lightning, storm, and fear.

[3] From *Erk's Deutscher Liederschatz*, page 188. Used by permission of C. F. Peters Corporation, New York, N.Y.

Der Landesvater[4]

August Niemann (1781)   Well-Known Melody (1770)

Feierlich.

Al - les schweige! je-der nei-ge ern-sten Tö-nen nur sein Ohr!   Hört, ich sing' das

Lied der Lie - der, hört es, mei - ne deut-schen Brü-der, hall' es wie - der, fro-her Chor!

Freely Translated
Everyone, silence:
Hark! All should listen to these earnest tones!
Hark, I sing the song of songs.
Hear it, my good German brothers;
Sing it once again, oh joyful choir.

Fuchslied[5]

Folk tune (Bei Hall' ist eine Mühl')

Was kommt dort von der Höh', was kommt dort von der Höh'? was kommt dort von der

le - der-nen Höh', ca, ca,   le - der-nen Höh', was kommt dort von der   Höh'?

Freely Translated
What's coming from the hills,
What's coming from the hills?
What's coming from the leathery hills,
ca, ca, leathery hills,
What's coming from the hills?

4 *Ibid.,* page 182.
5 *Ibid.,* page 77.

Gaudeamus igitur[6]

Old Melody
Composer Unknown

Writer Unknown

Gau - de - a - mus i - gi - tur, ju - ve - nes dum su - mus;

post ju - cun - dam ju - ven - tu - tem, post mo - les - tam se - nec - tu - tem

nos ha - be - bit hu - mus, nos ha - be - bit hu - mus!

Freely Translated
Let us rejoice, therefore,
Since we are young.
After our carefree, youthful years,
After our troubled aged years,
We shall toast to life again,
We shall toast to life again.

3. Listen to the overture to Haydn's *Creation,* an oratorio. Which style of overture do you hear?

4. A famous opera overture is Wagner's *Tannhäuser.* Listen to it, to appreciate both the music and the overture form.

5. The Schuman overture belongs to the twentieth century. Compare it with other contemporary works in style of orchestration, use of thematic material, and general overall effect on the listener.

6. Only twenty-four years separate the composition of Mozart's *Marriage of Figaro* Overture from Beethoven's *Egmont.* Consequently, they should have some elements in common as to their musical period. Can you mention two or three similarities? Probably more obvious will be their differences. What differences do you hear in the scores? Do you believe this to be the result of the time lapse between the two? The difference in the style of the composers? Or the intent of the overture as described in the text material?

---

6 *Ibid.,* page 227.

7. Many bands have used opera overtures as successful pieces in their programs. Listen to *Zampa* by Herold, *Raymond* by Thomas, or *The Crown Diamonds* by Auber. What type of overture have you heard? Can you understand the popularity of these compositions over the past 100 years or more?
8. Almost every high school or college band plays an overture during each school year. Visit a local band and listen to them rehearse an overture. Can you decide which overture style it is? Why is the overture such a popular form with the amateur performing group and the amateur listener?

Bibliography—Chapter 26

BARZUN, JACQUES, *Berlioz and the Romantic Century*. New York: Columbia University Press, 1969.
CARSE, ADAM, *18th Century Symphonies*. London: Augener Ltd., 1951.
Deutsches Liederbuch für Amerikanische Studenten. Boston: D. C. Heath and Company, 1907.
Erk's Deutscher Liederschatz. Leipzig: C. F. Peters, n.d.
EVANS, EDWIN, *Handbook to the Chamber and Orchestral Music of Johannes Brahms*. New York: Burt Franklin, 1970.
HOLMES, RACHEL, and ELEANOR, trans., *Memoirs of Hector Berlioz*. New York: Alfred A. Knopf, 1932.
SPAETH, SIGMUND, *Great Program Music*. New York: Garden City Publishing Co., 1940.
ULRICH, HOMER, *Symphonic Music*. New York: Columbia University Press, 1961.

Recordings—Chapter 26

OVERTURES AND PRELUDES:

Beethoven	*Egmont*	Walter	Columbia ML-5232
Berlioz	*Roman Carnival*	Munch	Victor LM-2438
Bizet	*Carmen*	Beecham	Capitol GCR-7207
Brahms	*Academic Festival*	Walter	Columbia ML-5232
Handel	*Messiah*	Robert Shaw	Victor LSC-6175
Mozart	*The Marriage of Figaro*	Giulini	Angel SDL-3608
Schuman	*American Festival Overture*	Hendl, Vienna	Desto D-404

Additional Suggestions for Listening

| Copland | *Outdoor Overture* | Boston Pops | Polydor 295006 |
| Van Vlumen | *Gruppi per venti Instrumente* | Boulez | Radio Netherland L-109517 |

Chapter 27

The Symphonic Poem

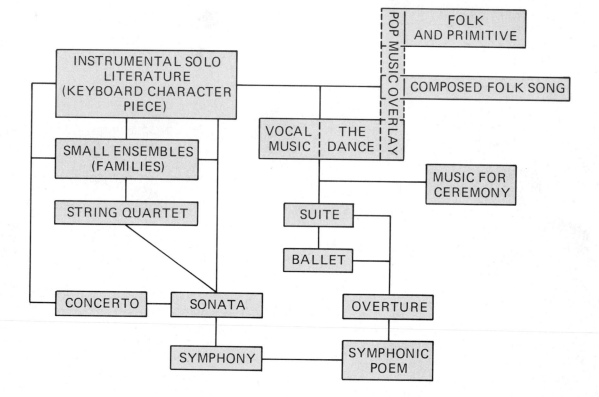

Descriptive sounds are not new to music. Through earlier study of specialized vocal forms it should have been noted how the music appropriated the words in more respects than just the meter. Sympathy to style, mood, and accent is most common. Beyond these, since the fifteenth century a special musical device called "text painting" or "word painting" has gone through periods of wide use and other periods of disdain (see Chapter 8). When instrumental descriptive music became popular with the listener in the nineteenth century, composers accepted it equally enthusiastically since it aided the prevailing musical nationalism with its stories, heroes, scenery, or the spirit of the country all described in musical terms.

For some listeners music constantly describes, and consequently, every musical composition or musical timbre must be accompanied by a concrete image or narrative. Although some music has been composed with narrative ideas in mind, most quality composers write music in order to express feelings which go beyond the visual, beyond the narrative, beyond description by verbal or picturesque means. To most of those who know music well, it speaks where words fail, and is less effective where words speak best.

Coming from the background of the sung text, and from the overture which set the mood for the dramatic event to follow, the symphonic poem—or tone poem—became a musical composition of some length describing ideas in sound which can be translated into visual or verbal descriptions. Two types of symphonic poems exist: those which narrate a story from beginning to end in sequence; and those which give concrete impressions of a narrative but depend upon the listener to know the story, poem, or historical event so as to place the parts together in his own mind when the music reminds him of particular chosen sections. Such compositions usually follow symphonic form; hence the name "symphonic poem." The former imitates the form of the story.

REALISTIC ORGANIZATION

The Sorcerer's Apprentice (Dukas)

Famous for years because of its simplicity and attractiveness to children of all ages, this tone poem relates an old Greek story retold by Goethe in verse wherein the master upon leaving for the day orders his apprentice to do a certain amount of work. The apprentice, not wishing to work any harder than necessary, decides to practice the magic of his master and states the magic words over a broom, ordering it to bring water from the nearby creek. The broom comes to life and brings pail after pail of water. The apprentice realizes that he has forgotten the magic words to stop the broom, and so decides to chop the broom in two, only to find that now he has two servants carrying water. When the place is almost flooded, the sorcerer returns, says the magic words, and the broom and the apprentice limp to separate corners becoming lifeless—one from fear, the other by becoming an inanimate object again.

The music retells the story vividly and is easy to follow. Musically, the composition contains an introduction, three main sections, and a coda. The first and third sections are a modified rondo, while the middle section simulates a development.

Rugby and Pacific 231 (Honegger)

The symphonic poem has described almost everything imaginable, but never more common, everyday items than in the works of the composer Honegger. Two

*Arthur Honegger in 1961 (Courtesy of French Cultural Services,
New York).*

symphonic poems which he wrote early in his career were entitled *Pacific 231*
(after a famous American locomotive), and *Rugby* (after the European game).
A lover of sports, Honegger once remarked that the game could be described in
music. After his statement was quoted in the newspapers he seriously considered
the idea, and wrote the composition which was given its world premiere at an
international rugby match between France and England.

The exact impressions of the music can be distinguished easily by the
listener once he understands that the two themes represent the two teams, with a
kind of mathematical balance between them paralleling the game itself. The
sudden changes in harmony, counterpoint, movement, and rhythm assist in describing the game, the running of the players with the ball, the pursuits, and the
efforts on the part of the teams to oppose the aggressor.

The more famous of the two tone poems, *Pacific 231*, describes a large
steam engine making initial efforts toward movement, gaining speed, moving
rapidly, and applying brakes to come to a stop. Honegger himself preferred a
different description of the work which is less vivid in pictorial imagery. In an
interview with Bernard Gavoty he stated:

So many critics have so minutely described the onrush of my locomotive across the great spaces that it would be inhuman to disabuse them! One of them, confusing *Pacific* with Pacific Ocean, even evoked the smells of the open sea. To tell the truth, in *Pacific* I was on the trail of a very abstract and quite ideal concept, by giving the impression of a mathematical acceleration of rhythm, while the movement itself slowed. Musically, I composed a sort of big, diversified chorale, strewn with counterpoint in the manner of J. S. Bach.[1]

The Moldau (Smetana)

One of Bohemia's great composers, Smetana was best-known professionally as a conductor and composer of opera. Throughout his lifetime he worked diligently to establish a national art for Bohemia, writing operas and instrumental music based upon nationalistic themes. The Moldau, the largest river in Czechoslovakia, became the subject of his second tone poem of a set of six composed near the end of his life in honor of his country (the complete cycle is entitled *My Fatherland*). On the title page of the score Smetana wrote a description of what the music portrayed. His ideas can be interpreted by the following paragraph:

> Two springs surface in the depths of the forests of Bohemia, one warm and bubbly, the other cool and peaceful. As they seek lower ground they join and sparkle in the sun (meas. 1–79). The little stream flows through the woods where hunters pursue their game and whose horn signals of their success (meas. 80–117). A rustic village is encircled by the stream and a wedding ceremony and dance are heard at the nearby church and tavern (meas. 118–180). As the water flows onward, becoming the Vltava (Moldau), night falls and in the moonlight water sprites dance along its bubbly surface (meas. 181–238); near the rocks by the shore old castles, mansions, and ruins remind one of the past glories of knights and heroes (meas. 239–270). The water gushes over the St. John rapids, over the cataracts, around the large rocks and into the large river basin to move toward Prague (meas. 271–358). At the outskirts of the city the river flows beside the old fortress, Vysehrad, moves past the docks, under the bridges, and heads toward its confluence with the Elbe (meas. 359–427).

What a poetic description! And yet this is the program (a prearranged plan), and it enables the listener to follow the music precisely. (Note the measure numbers above.)

Study Procedures

1. Listen to each of the musical selections discussed in the above material. Can you follow the program which the composer intended? How well do you believe the music fits the expectations? Does the music seem to surpass the program or lead you in a different direction than the program? Why might this be true?

---

[1] *I Am a Composer,* Arthur Honegger. St. Martin's Press, New York, 1966, page 101.

2. Compare the two symphonic poems by Honegger. Which do you prefer? Why?
Which seems better to describe and meet its intent? Considering Honegger's dis-
claim for *Pacific 231* as not being descriptive of a steam engine but a study in rhythm,
what might he have said concerning *Rugby?*

3. Dukas used an old fable as the basis for his tone poem. Can you think of another
well-known fable or children's story which could be a basis for a tone poem? Why
would you like to hear this tale told in orchestration? If you were a composer, what
would lead you to use this story as a background for a musical composition? What
form would you use? What instruments of the orchestra would have featured roles?

POETIC ORGANIZATION

The poetic approach to this form, probably easier for most composers, eventually
becomes more attractive for the listener, since the composer can create his own
balance between tempos and moods rather than follow exactly those of the
narrative. In addition, the composer may choose a form which he feels more
precisely suits his themes and the overall intention of his work. As for the
listener, he soon may tire of music which follows a narrative too closely and
prefer those compositions which suggest to him the personality of the main
characters, the mood of the plot, or the intensity of the forces which play
against each other. In other words, those feelings which are merely suggested
to the listener may become more real for him than those which are detailed too
minutely and carefully.

Romeo and Juliet (Tchaikovsky)

Although Tchaikovsky labeled this composition an overture, it so admirably fits
the definition of a symphonic poem that it usually is considered a part of this
literature. The music does not follow the story, but rather creates a study of
the characters and moods of this famous Shakespearean play. Musically, it employs the sonata-allegro form, but here this form adapts to the programmatic
aspects so well one could easily fail to recognize the form while listening to the
representational ideas.

The slow introduction suggests Friar Lawrence. Originally the score had a
different slow theme, but Balakirev, to whom the score is dedicated, then titular
head of the famous "Russian Five," objected to the first theme as "lacking in
beauty and power and not even sketching the character of Friar Lawrence." He
recommended that "you need something there on the lines of a Liszt Chorale with
an ancient Catholic character, something like the Orthodox." Instead, "your
theme bears quite a different character—the character of Haydn's quartet, the
genius of petty bourgeois music [even in 1869 this phrase was popular in Russia],
awakening a strong thirst for beer."[2] At this time Tchaikovsky was willing to

---

[2] *The Music of Tchaikovsky,* edited by Gerald Abraham. W. W. Norton and Company, Inc.,
New York, page 80.

take suggestions from the well-considered Balakirev, and rewrote the introduction. The love theme which represents the character of Romeo in the tone poem has become famous all over the world. Rimsky-Korsakov thought it one of the "best themes in the whole of Russian music," and Tchaikovsky's use of it in the recapitulation is strong yet full of human passion.

Introduction—Devoted to the music representing Friar Lawrence

Exposition—Theme I: Represents the feud between the Montagues and Capulets; agitated, rhythmic, often contrapuntal, which represents the physical combat of the families; the strong, irregular chords of the orchestra at one point indicate the clash of swords

Theme II: The love themes symbolize the two lovers: the masculine first part represents Romeo; the second, which is feminine, Juliet; these are used interchangeably

Development—Theme I fragments remind us of the feud and its consequences; fragments of the slow introduction remind us of the attempt of the Friar to bring understanding between the families; the trumpet proclaims the Friar theme while the battle rages in the orchestra

Recapitulation—The feud theme
                     Juliet's theme
                     Romeo's theme heard with more passion than before

Coda—The love theme is stated in dark moods and minor mode
       The feud theme is heard again
       Tragedy approaches in the ruffle of drums
       Romeo's theme avows his love
       Ending phrases indicate the sweetness of death

Poème électronique (Varèse)

An early electronic composition in the field of music, this symphonic poem was written in 1958 for the Brussels World's Fair. The Philips Radio Corporation had requested the architect Le Corbusier to design an attractive building which would be an embodiment of the artistic efforts of the electronic age. From the outside, the building appeared to be a three-peaked tent. When the spectator entered the interior, which was designed in "the shape of a cow's stomach," he heard electronic music from 400 speakers, while on the walls he saw projected images of various types including photographs, montages, paintings, printed and written script. The contrast between the visual and the aural created a sensation which appealed to some, revolted others, and mystified many. The eight minutes of music, the length of time required for a spectator to walk through the building, was designed so that it mattered little where you began just so all of it was heard.

549

Because of the prerequisites placed on the composer, no form is observable by the listener even if heard from the beginning. Yet, some form seems implied within its mood changes, rhythmic alterations, and tonal organization.

Afternoon of a Faun (Debussy)

Once again literature provided the impetus for another art. A French poem by Mallarmé inspired Debussy to write the music and retain the title. Originally intended to be read by a single actor on stage, the obscure verses would have been difficult to project, considering their use of symbolism and their difficult comprehension even after considerable study. The sensuous implications of the poem are much better and more quickly realized through the Debussy music, but an explanatory statement about the poem will make the music even more meaningful.

A faun awakens at high noon in the heat of a summer's day. As he attempts to regain the present, he realizes that he has either dreamed of loving two nymphs or has held them just before he slept; but he cannot remember whether the two were part of his dream or part of his waking hours. He considers that he has a poor brain.

As he muses upon the sweetness of this dream or this past reality, he cuts a reed flute and plays a tune upon it, trying to recapture his ecstasy through music. Playing this reed, the faun recognizes mastery of himself and his feelings.

Suddenly, his passions rise and he searches through the reeds for the nymphs and finds they have all disappeared. Coming upon two Naiads, he grasps them but they, frightened, struggle away. He decides that if reality cannot lead him to the nymph he desires in a conscious world he will seek her through his visions and imagination; he will pursue his ecstasy in the realm of the mental image. Hence, the title *Afternoon of a Faun*.

This poem commands our attention on two levels. The poet wishes us to understand the half-dream–half-real world of the faun. He also proposes that art can bring a type of reality to life not found in other ways, that it brings reality through what appears to be an unreal world, and yet the person involved with art has difficulty in sorting out the real from the imaginary. Lockspeiser makes an interesting observation: "Hidden in this myth is the theory, restated by Mallarmé, that a function of the dream is to allow love to be sublimated into music."[3]

The poem suggests a question: Can a person always describe reality with accuracy? Or, to say it another way, does reality not sometimes take the appearance of a dream? The faun is only a romantic characterization, an external representation of the self, used by the poet and ourselves when we do not wish the human personality to be involved with problems of the world which appear too fantastic to be believed.

---

[3] *Debussy: His Life and Mind,* Edward Lockspeiser. The Macmillan Company, New York, 1962, page 153.

The music by Debussy changes constantly from the real to the dream world, and the mind of the listener can associate with the poem of Mallarmé or with the thoughts which he himself can bring to this world of half-reality.

Section A—Chromatic theme played by flute, with other instruments joining

Section B—Division 1: Two themes are heard, both rising and falling chromatically; changing moods and colors with the instrumentation

Division 2: One additional new theme is introduced, more diatonic and tuneful in nature, still in the same basic tempo and mood

Division 3: This subsection borrows the theme of Section A but the melodic lines are in a different meter, thus having greater impact

Section A—A repeat of Section A as at the beginning, with a few changes to effect the introduction of the Coda

Coda—Another modification of the main theme in rhythm and instrumentation

Poem in Cycles and Bells (Luening and Ussachevsky)

A sectional composition which employs imaginative treatment of materials and a careful use of language may be considered a tone poem. This definition also is appropriate for a musical composition such as this one by two contemporary American musicians who have focused compositional efforts upon electronic materials. One of the best combinations of music for orchestra and electronic sounds on tape, this composition features the full orchestra with accompaniments and main themes produced by the tape recorder used as an instrument of the ensemble.

The following diagram will assist in your understanding of the composition:

Section I		Transition	(Con't.)
Orchestra	Tape recorder	Orchestra	
A B	A B		
Violin theme	Orch. accomp.	Tape recorder acc. with low sounds	

Section II			Coda
Tape		Orchestra	Tape
W	X $\longrightarrow$	Y Z $\longrightarrow$	
Fast piano figures	Slow, bell-like theme with several acc. figures	Tape accomp. in echoes and distracting rhythms	Quiet sounds

Study Procedures

1. In the chapter on the suite we discussed some compositions of a descriptive or narrative nature. What differences do you perceive between this type of suite and the symphonic poem? What relation does the symphonic poem have to the symphony? What relation does it have to vocal forms? Why is it considered a bridge with vocal forms?

2. In some ways *An American in Paris* describes a large city. How does the composer do this? Do you know of other musical compositions which describe a city? Do they do this as realistically as Gershwin?

3. Sibelius, as well as Debussy, wrote a tone poem concerning an animal: *The Swan of Tuonela,* a well-known solo for English horn. Listen to the composition, and then make a comparison of the orchestral style and the intent of the composers. Which of the two do you prefer to listen to?

4. Although we studied Ravel's *La Valse* in the chapter on dance, yet it might be considered a symphonic poem. Listen again to this composition, and decide if it is. Upon what do you base your opinion?

5. Copland, an American composer whose works we have heard, wrote a symphonic poem entitled *El Salón México* depicting a large dance hall in Mexico City. Listen to this composition, and then ascertain if you like the work as well as other compositions of his which we have studied. What is striking about the work? Is it a strong and appealing tone poem?

6. Tchaikovsky wrote another composition, which he entitled *Overture 1812.* In 1880 Moscow planned an All-Russian Art and Industrial Exhibition. To add to the occasion construction of the new Cathedral of the Redeemer, built as a memorial to those valiant defenders of 1812, was being hurried so that its completion would coincide with the exposition. Tchaikovsky, asked to supply an original composition for the occasion, decided also to commemorate the valiant Russian victory of 1812. The first performance of the work took place in front of the cathedral, using orchestra, band, and extra performers. The composition makes use of a Russian liturgical theme, the "Marseillaise," "God Save the Tsar," a Russian folk tune, and some original material. Listen to the composition, and decide if it is more appropriately a symphonic poem or an overture.

HISTORICAL NOTE

Franz Liszt is credited with having written the first tone poem, *Les Préludes.* The title comes from a poem by Lamartine, but the music is borrowed by Liszt from one of his earlier compositions for chorus upon poems by Joseph Autran. The Autran poems describe the atmosphere of the Mediterranean, but Liszt preferred to have his listeners believe that the music followed Lamartine's poem which regarded life as a prelude to death. The soul, exhausted by its struggle with an earthly life and wounded or defeated time and again, retreats and rests; but later in life rushes back into the fray to test and again attempt to conquer.

Listen to the music, and decide which of the programs you prefer. Then consider this proposition: Music's meaning is not well accommodated in verbal terms, since it speaks its own language; even when listeners or composers ascribe verbal significance to sounds, the sounds escape from those intentions and challenge us with new and more important meanings based upon feelings, sensitivities, and inner understandings.

Bibliography—Chapter 27

ABRAHAM, GERALD, ed., *The Music of Tchaikovsky*. New York: W. W. Norton and Company, Inc., 1946.

CHIARI, JOSEPH, *Symbolism from Poe to Mallarmé*. New York: Macmillan Co., 1956.

DEL MAR, NORMAN, *Richard Strauss*. New York: Free Press of Glencoe, 1962.

EVANS, EDWIN, *Tchaikovsky*. London: J. M. Dent and Sons Ltd., 1957.

HONEGGER, ARTHUR, *I Am a Composer*. New York: St. Martin's Press, 1966.

JABLONSKI, EDWARD, and LAWRENCE D. STEWART, *The Gershwin Years*. Garden City, N.Y.: Doubleday and Company, Inc., 1958.

KRAUSE, ERNEST, *Richard Strauss*. London: Collet's Ltd., 1964.

LAMARTINE, A. DE, *Premières et Nouvelles Méditations Poétiques*. Paris: Pagnerre, Furne, V. Lecou, 1855.

MACINTYRE, C. F., trans., *Selected Poems of Stephane Mallarmé*. Berkeley, Calif.: University of California Press, 1957.

PAYNE, ROBERT, *Gershwin*. London: Robert Hale Ltd., 1960.

WHITEHOUSE, H. REMSEN, *The Life of Lamartine*. Boston: Houghton Mifflin Company, 1918.

Recordings—Chapter 27

Debussy	*Afternoon of a Faun*	Boulez, N.Y. Philh.	Columbia MS-7361
Dukas	*The Sorcerer's Apprentice*	Ormandy, Philadelphia	Columbia ML-2156
Honegger	*Pacific 231*	Scherchen, London	Westminster W-7010
Honegger	*Rugby*	Scherchen, London	Westminster W-7010
Liszt	*Les Préludes*	Monteux, Boston	Victor LM-6129
Luening-Ussachevsky	*Poem in Cycles and Bells*		CRI-112
Smetana	*The Moldau*	Ormandy, Philadelphia	Columbia ML-5261
Tchaikovsky	*Romeo and Juliet*	Munch, Boston	Victor LM-6129
Varèse	*Poème électronique*		Columbia ML-5478

Additional Suggestions for Listening

Copland	*El Salón México*	Fiedler, Boston Pops	Victor LM-6129
Gershwin	*An American in Paris*	Steinberg, Pittsburgh	Everest SDBR-3067
Messiaen	*Oiseaux Éxotiques*		Candide CE-31002
Ravel	*La Valse*	Munch, Boston	Victor LM-6129
Strauss, R.	*Till Eulenspiegel*	Reiner, Vienna	Victor LM-2077
Varèse	*Intégrales*		Candide CE-31028

Name Index

Subject Index

560